EIGHTH EDITION

LEGAL RIGHTS OF SCHOOL LEADERS, TEACHERS, AND STUDENTS

MARTHA M. McCARTHY

Loyola Marymount University, Los Angeles

SUZANNE E. ECKES

Indiana University, Bloomington, Indiana

JANET R. DECKER

Indiana University, Bloomington, Indiana

Pearson

330 Hudson Street, NY NY 10013

Director and Publisher: Kevin M. Davis
Executive Portfolio Manager: Aileen Pogran
Managing Content Producer: Megan Moffo
Content Producer: Faraz Sharique Ali
Portfolio Management Assistant:
 Maria Feliberty and Casey Coriell
Executive Product Marketing Manager:
 Christopher Barry
Executive Field Marketing Manager: Krista Clark
Manufacturing Buyer: Deidra Smith, LSC
 Communications, Inc.

Cover Design: Carie Keller, Cenveo
**Editorial Production and Composition
 Services:** SPi Global
Full-Service Project Manager:
 Kabilan Selvakumar, SPi Global
Editorial Project Manager: Shiela Quisel,
 SPi Global
Cover Printer: Phoenix Color/Hagerstown
Printer/Binder: LSC Communications, Inc./
 Crawfordsville
Text Font: 10/12 Times New Roman

Credits and acknowledgments for material borrowed from other sources and reproduced, with permission, in this textbook appear on the appropriate page within the text.

Every effort has been made to provide accurate and current Internet information in this book. However, the Internet and information posted on it are constantly changing, so it is inevitable that some of the Internet addresses listed in this textbook will change.

Library of Congress Cataloging-in-Publication Data
Names: McCarthy, Martha M., author. | Eckes, Suzanne, author. | Decker, Janet
 R., author.
Title: Legal rights of school leaders, teachers, and students / Martha M.
 McCarthy, Loyola Marymount University, Los Angeles, Suzanne E. Eckes,
 Indiana University, Bloomington, Indiana, Janet R. Decker, Indiana
 University, Bloomington, Indiana.
Description: Boston : Pearson, 2018.
Identifiers: LCCN 2018004584 | ISBN 9780134997537
Subjects: LCSH: Teachers—Legal status, laws, etc.—United States. | School
 principals—Legal status, laws, etc.—United States. | Students—Legal
 status, laws, etc.—United States.
Classification: LCC KF4175 .M34 2018 | DDC 344.73/078—dc23 LC record available at
 https://lccn.loc.gov/2018004584

25 2022

ISBN 10:   0-13-499753-0
ISBN 13: 978-0-13-499753-7

Never has it been more imperative for teachers to understand the law. Since World War II, lawmakers have significantly reshaped educational policy. Most school personnel are aware of the escalating litigation and legislation, and some are familiar with the names of a few landmark U.S. Supreme Court decisions. But many educators do not understand basic legal principles that are being applied to educational questions. As a result, they are uncertain about the legality of daily decisions they must make in schools. Information provided in this book should help alleviate concerns voiced by educators who feel that the scales of justice have been tipped against them.

NEW TO THIS EDITION

This book replaces *Public School Law: Teachers' and Students' Rights* (2014) and *Legal Rights of Teachers and Students* (2014), building on the strengths of these two texts and adding important legal material. This volume is appropriate for undergraduate and graduate school law courses intended for school leaders, teachers, and other school employees. It also can be used in law school courses addressing education law. While designed to be used as a course text, this book is invaluable to school practitioners, lawyers, government employees, and others as a reference book.

All topics have been thoroughly researched to reflect current laws, policies, and judicial decisions, and detailed documentation is provided. Readers can use the footnotes to locate a wealth of additional resources on each topic (e.g., guidance from the U.S. Department of Education). This book's extensive treatment of the current status and evolution of the law governing schools makes it the most comprehensive and well-documented school law text available.

Seasoned school leaders and even legal experts will find the in-depth coverage enlightening, while legal explanations are sufficiently clear for pre-service teachers and others unfamiliar with the law. The book uniquely blends inclusive coverage of landmark cases with a thorough discussion of the legal context, trends, and generalizations to guide all school personnel in their daily activities. Among new features are:

- an expanded introductory chapter that addresses why school leaders, teachers, and others should learn about the law (legal literacy);
- a chapter on alternatives to traditional public schooling to increase educational choice including charter schools and voucher programs;
- more than 300 new cases and at least 50 new or amended federal and state laws;
- an emphasis on emerging and unresolved issues (e.g., rights of LGBTQ employees and students; discipline of students for off-campus Internet speech; legality of fair share requirements; changes in interpreting the First Amendment's Religion Clauses);

- Coverage of the ever-evolving legal issues that arise as technology advances (e.g., searching cell phones and laptop computers; copyright concerns; acceptable use policies; teachers' posts on social media); and
- Reorganization of all chapters with additional visuals and links to websites to make them more readable, user friendly, and engaging for readers.

Legal Rights of School Leaders, Teachers, and Students differs from other texts currently available because it addresses legal principles applicable to practitioners in a succinct but comprehensive manner. For this book, we have selected topics particularly pertinent to educators and students. In analyzing specific school situations, we have explored the tension between government regulations and individual freedoms in the school context. We discuss the implications of legal mandates and provide guidance for educators. Throughout the chapters, we have highlighted in bold type or placed in boxes some of the most important legal concepts. Also, we have included learning objectives at the beginning of chapters and generalizations at the end to make the information presented more meaningful.

We have covered the topics thoroughly but in a nontechnical manner, avoiding the extensive use of legal jargon. Given our combined seventy years of teaching school law, we have been able to identify legal concepts that seem particularly difficult for those new to studying the law and have given special attention to those topics. Unlike some school law textbooks, our book provides readers with current legal guidelines on a range of school issues instead of abridged versions of selected court decisions. However, all topics are documented in footnotes that appear at the bottom of the pages if the reader wants to explore particular cases, statutes, or points of law in greater detail. These notes provide additional information that should assist the reader in understanding specific concepts. Also, a glossary of basic legal terms and a table of selected Supreme Court cases are provided at the end of the book.

NATURE OF THE LAW

A few comments about the nature of the law might assist the reader in using this book. Laws are not created in a vacuum; they reflect the social and philosophical attitudes of society. Moreover, individuals who have personal opinions and biases make laws. Although one may prefer to think that the law is always objective, personal considerations and national political trends do have an impact on the development and interpretation of legal principles.

Also, the law is not static, but rather is continually evolving as courts reinterpret constitutional and statutory provisions and as legislatures enact new laws. In the 1960s and early 1970s, courts and legislative bodies tended to focus on the expansion of personal rights through civil rights laws and constitutional interpretations favoring the individual's right to be free from unwarranted government intrusions. However, since 1975, judicial rulings in the school context have supported government authority to impose restraints on individual freedoms in the interest of the collective welfare. Although the themes of educational equity and individual rights, which dominated litigation earlier, remain important, efforts to attain educational excellence have generated a new genre of legal activity pertaining to teachers' qualifications, performance standards for students, and alternatives to traditional public schools.

In this book, much of the discussion of the law focuses on court cases because the judiciary plays a vital role in interpreting constitutional and legislative provisions. Decisions are highlighted that illustrate points of law or legal trends, with particular emphasis on recent litigation. A few cases are pursued in depth to provide the reader with an understanding of the rationale behind the decisions. Reviewing the factual situations that have generated these controversies should make it easier for educators to identify potential legal problems in their own school situations.

As we completed this book, judicial decisions were being rendered and statutes being proposed that could alter the status of the law vis-à-vis school employees and students. Additionally, some questions confronting school personnel have not yet been addressed by the Supreme Court and have generated conflicting decisions among lower courts. It may be frustrating to a reader who is searching for concrete answers to learn that in some areas, the law is far from clear.

In spite of unresolved issues, certain legal principles have been established and can provide direction in many school situations. It is important for educators to become familiar with these principles and to use them to guide their decisions. Although the issues generating legal concern will change over time, knowledge of the logic underlying the law can make teachers more confident in dealing with questions that have not been clarified by courts or legislatures. With increased legal literacy, school personnel can respond appropriately to legal violations, practice preventive law, and understand better how to navigate the legal system to advocate for school reform.

ORGANIZATION OF THE TEXT

We have attempted to arrange the chapters in logical sequence for those reading the book in its entirety or using it as a text for school law classes. An introductory chapter establishes the legal context for the subsequent examination of students' and educators' rights, and a concluding chapter provides a summary of the major legal principles. Subheadings appear within chapters to facilitate using this book for reference if a specific issue is of immediate interest. The reader is encouraged, however, to read the entire text because some topics are addressed in several chapters from different perspectives, and many of the principles of law transcend chapter divisions. Taken together, the chapters provide an overall picture of the relationship among issues and the applicable legal principles.

The material will assist school personnel in understanding the current application of the law, but it is not intended to serve as a substitute for legal counsel. Instead, readers should be better able to spot legal issues and understand when it is necessary to prevent a legal violation or call an attorney. Also, there is no attempt here to predict the future course of courts and legislatures. Given the dynamic nature of the law, no single text can serve to keep teachers abreast of current legal developments. If we can provide an awareness of rights and responsibilities, motivate educators to translate the basic concepts into actual practice, and generate an interest in further study of the law, our purposes in writing this book will have been achieved.

ACKNOWLEDGMENTS

A number of people contributed to the completion of this text. We are extremely grateful to the following individuals who provided valuable assistance in reviewing drafts of chapters, locating legal materials, and verifying citations: Ilana Linder, Ingrid Barce, and Jessie Lauren from Indiana University, and Heather McManus from Loyola Marymount University. We would also like to extend our sincere gratitude to the reviewers of this edition of our text: Julie Fernandez, Houston Baptist University; Rick Geisel, Grand Valley State University; and Aaron Milner, University of South Alabama.

This text would not have been completed without the support of our families, who offered constant encouragement as they do in all of our professional endeavors. Their contributions simply cannot be measured.

Martha M. McCarthy
Suzanne E. Eckes
Janet R. Decker

BRIEF CONTENTS

CONTENTS

CHAPTER SIX

Student Classifications   134

CHAPTER SEVEN

Rights of Students with Disabilities   164

CHAPTER EIGHT

Student Discipline   197

CHAPTER TWELVE

Termination of Employment   326

INTRODUCTION TO SCHOOL LAW

How do courts influence the law that affects public schools? What are constitutions, statutes, regulations, and case law? Where can educators find state and administrative law? This chapter begins by clarifying why all school employees benefit from legal training. It then establishes the context for subsequent chapters by providing an overview of the legal framework. After outlining the state and federal structure of the U.S. educational system, the chapter identifies which primary and secondary sources of law affect education, describes the structure and function of the judicial system, and offers guidance about how to locate legal resources.

Readers of this chapter should be able to:

- Explain why school employees should study school law.
- Distinguish between the federal, state, and local role in education.
- Define the four primary sources of law affecting education.
- Describe the levels of the federal and state court systems.
- Summarize how to locate primary and secondary legal resources.

LEGAL LITERACY

School employees should increase their legal literacy to improve decision making, prevent lawsuits, increase confidence, and become more empowered to affect change.

Put simply, nearly everything public school educators do is governed by the law. While school leaders and teachers may not be consciously aware of how the law affects their daily lives, they are often the first people who must respond to legal dilemmas. For instance, they must make on-the-spot legal decisions, such as whether to search a student suspected of hiding drugs or whether to discipline a student for offensive speech or inappropriate clothing. They must understand the legal protections owed to all students, as well as specific student populations, such as English Learners, students with disabilities, and homeless students. Understanding how to navigate the legal system also allows educators to advocate for themselves when they believe their constitutional or statutory rights have been violated, their contracts have not been followed, or other employment disputes arise.

1

When school leaders and teachers are legally literate, they are "able to spot legal issues, identify applicable laws or legal standards, and apply the relevant legal rules to solve legal dilemmas."[1] Although research about legal literacy is limited, two large-scale, national studies found that teachers and principals lack legal knowledge. The first study discovered that the vast majority of teachers had never received legal training and often learned about school law from other teachers who were also uninformed.[2] The second study found that a majority of principals were misinformed or uninformed about students' and teachers' legal rights.[3]

School leaders and teachers who lack legal training may unintentionally violate students' rights. Additionally, because educators often fear the law, their anxieties may cause them to "fail to act when they should and overreact when they should not."[4] Increasing the legal literacy of all school employees could alleviate anxiety, improve decision making, prevent lawsuits, and ultimately protect the rights of students and employees.[5] Additionally, once educators learn about the law and the legal system, they become empowered to advocate about changes that they would like to see occur in schools. And with such knowledge, educators can assist their students in understanding the legal environment in our nation and the values upon which it is built.

STATE AND FEDERAL STRUCTURE OF EDUCATION

 State and federal constitutional and statutory provisions provide the framework that governs how schooling is structured and the legal rights of students and school employees.

Law can be defined as a collection of rules created to govern a community. Considering that American public schools served approximately 50.3 million students in the 2014–2015 school year,[6] it is important to understand how the law governing the U.S. education system was established, how it is structured, and who creates the law that educators must follow.

[1]Janet Decker & Kevin Brady, *Increasing School Employees' Special Education Legal Literacy*, 36 J. Sch. Pub. Rels. 231 (2016).

[2]David Schimmel & Matthew Militello, *Legal Literacy for Teachers: A Neglected Responsibility*, 77 Harv. Educ. Rev. 257 (2007).

[3]Matthew Militello, David Schimmel & H. Jake Eberwein, *If They Knew, They Would Change: How Legal Knowledge Impacts Principals' Practice*, 93 Nat'l Ass'n Secondary Sch. Principals Bull. 27 (2009).

[4]Janet Decker, *Legal Literacy in Education: An Ideal Time to Increase Research, Advocacy, and Action*, 304 Educ. L. Rep. 679, 680 (2014); *see also* David Schimmel, Suzanne Eckes & Matthew Militello, Principals Avoiding Lawsuits: How Teachers Can Be Partners Practicing Preventative Law (2017); Martha McCarthy, *The Marginalization of School Law Research: Missed Opportunities for Educators*, 331 Educ. L. Rep. 564 (2016).

[5]Janet Decker, *How to Use* The Principal's Legal Handbook *to Increase Legal Literacy*, in The Principal's Legal Handbook (Janet Decker, Maria Lewis, Elizabeth Shaver, Ann Blankenship-Knox & Mark Paige eds., 6th ed. 2017).

[6]Mark Glander, *Selected Statistics from the Public Elementary and Secondary Education Universe: School Year 2014–2015*, Nat'l Ctr. for Educ. Statistics (Sept. 2016).

State and federal constitutional and statutory provisions provide the framework that governs how schooling is structured and the legal rights of students and school employees. Policies and practices at the local, state, and federal levels must be consistent with legal mandates. School employees cannot claim as a defense that they were unaware or ignorant of the law when the law is violated. At the same time, educators must navigate a complex environment to comply with legal requirements. They must understand the interplay between the federal and state constitutions, Congress and state legislatures, federal and state courts, as well as the policies of various governmental agencies (such as local school boards and state departments of education). In an effort to untangle the various relationships, this section discusses the roles of the state and federal governments in establishing, overseeing, and reforming education.[7]

State Control of Education

The word "education" does not appear in the U.S. Constitution, and nothing in the Constitution requires Congress to enact laws governing education. Additionally, there is no federal right found within the Constitution that entitles students to a public education.[8] Because the Constitution does not authorize Congress to provide for education, the legal control of public education resides with the states. The Tenth Amendment to the U.S. Constitution stipulates that "the powers not delegated to the United States by the Constitution, nor prohibited by it to the states, are reserved to the states respectively, or to the people." **The Supreme Court repeatedly has affirmed the comprehensive authority of the states and school officials to control public schools so long as actions are consistent with federal constitutional safeguards (such as freedom of speech) and civil rights laws**. Although each state's educational system has unique features, many similarities are found across states.

State Authority.   It is a widely held perception that local school boards control public education, but local boards have only those powers conferred by the state. Therefore, school buildings are *state* property, local school board members are *state* officials, and teachers are *state* employees. Public school funds, regardless where collected, are *state* funds.

The state legislature is typically bicameral—comprised of the Senate and the House of Representatives (sometimes called the Assembly). All state constitutions specifically address the legislative responsibility for establishing public schools. Usually the legislature is charged with providing for a uniform, thorough and efficient, or adequate system of public education. In contrast to the federal government, which has only those powers specified in the U.S. Constitution, state legislatures retain all powers not expressly forbidden by state or federal constitutional provisions. **Thus, the state legislature has plenary, or absolute, power to make laws governing education**.

State Administrative Agencies.   It has been neither feasible nor desirable to create state laws—commonly referred to as statutes—that provide every minor detail governing public

---

[7]In addition to operating in states, U.S. public schools are found in other jurisdictions including the Department of Defense, Bureau of Indian Education, District of Columbia, American Samoa, Commonwealth of the Northern Mariana Islands, Guam, Puerto Rico, and U.S. Virgin Islands. *Id.*

[8]San Antonio Indep. Sch. Dist. v. Rodriguez, 411 U.S. 1 (1973).

4

CHAPTER ONE

schools. Thus, state agencies play a role in providing details for state laws by adopting regulations. **The regulations are often referred to as administrative law, and they help provide guidance to the laws passed by the state legislature.** Most states have established a state board of education that is generally considered a policy-making body and often supplies the structural details for implementing broad legislative mandates. Members of the state board of education usually are elected by the citizenry or appointed by the governor, and the board usually functions immediately below the legislature in the hierarchy of educational governance.

Accreditation is an important tool used by state boards to compel local school districts to abide by their directives. School districts often must satisfy state accreditation requirements as a condition of receiving state funds. Though accreditation models vary, it is common for states to assess student outcomes as well as establish minimum standards in areas such as curriculum, teacher qualifications, instructional materials, and facilities. In some states, different grades of school accreditation exist (e.g., A–F letter grades), with financial incentives in place to encourage local schools to increase student achievement. **Since the mid-1980s, there has been a movement toward performance-based accreditation under which a school's performance is assessed against predicted outcomes calculated for the school in areas such as student achievement, absenteeism, and retention.**

Within legislative parameters, the state board of education can issue directives governing school operations. In some states, rules pertaining to such matters as proficiency testing for students and programs for children with disabilities are embodied in state board rules rather than state law. Courts generally have upheld decisions made by state boards of education unless the boards have violated legislative or constitutional mandates. In addition to the state board, all states have designated a chief state school officer (CSSO) to function in an executive capacity. The CSSO, who is often known as the superintendent of public instruction or commissioner of education, works with the state board to create policy and make other decisions affecting the state's education system. Each state also has established a state department of education, consisting of educational specialists who provide consultation to the state board, the CSSO, and local school boards. State department personnel often collect data from school districts to ensure that state law and board policies are properly implemented.

Local School Boards.   Although public education in the United States is state controlled, it is for the most part locally administered. All states except Hawaii have created local school boards in addition to state departments of education and have delegated certain administrative authority over schools to these local boards. Whereas state departments of education are referred to as the state education agency (SEA), the local governing body is typically referred to as a district and is the local education agency (LEA). **Nationwide, there are approximately 13,700 local districts, ranging from a few students to several hundred thousand.**[9] Some states, particularly those with a large number of small school districts, have established regional administrative units that perform service functions for several local districts. For example, regional education service agencies may coordinate special education services or offer professional development for school employees.

[9]Glander, *supra* note 6.

As with the delegation of authority to state agencies, assignment of powers to local school boards is handled differently across states. Some states with a deeply rooted tradition of local control over education (e.g., Vermont) give local boards a great deal of latitude in making operational decisions about schools. In states that tend toward centralized control of education (e.g., Florida), local boards must function within the framework of detailed legislative directives. **State legislatures retain the legal responsibility for education and can restrict the discretion of local boards by enacting legislation to that effect.**

The voters within the school district usually elect local school board members. The U.S. Supreme Court has recognized that the Equal Protection Clause requires each qualified voter to be given an opportunity to participate in the election of board members, with each vote given the same weight as far as practicable. If "at-large" elections result in a dilution of the minority vote, an abridgment of the federal Voting Rights Act may be found.[10]

A local board must act as a body; individual board members are not empowered to make policies or perform official acts on behalf of the board. School boards have some discretion in adopting operational procedures and policies, but they are legally bound to adhere to such procedures once established. **Although courts are reluctant to interfere with decisions made by boards of education, they will invalidate any board action that is arbitrary, capricious, or outside the board's legal authority** (i.e., an ultra vires act).

School board meetings and records must be open to the public.[11] Most states have enacted "sunshine" or open meeting laws, acknowledging that the public has a right to be fully informed regarding the actions of public agencies. Certain exceptions to open meeting requirements are usually specified in the laws. For example, in many states, school boards can meet in executive session to discuss matters that threaten public safety or pertain to pending or current litigation, personnel matters, collective bargaining, or the disposition of real property. Although discussion of these matters may take place in closed meetings, statutes usually stipulate that formal action must occur in open meetings.[12]

Local school boards hold powers specified or implied in state law and other powers considered necessary to achieve the purposes of the express powers. Thus, school boards typically have the authority to determine the specifics of the curriculum offered within the school district (e.g., sex education), raise revenue to build and maintain schools, select personnel, and enact other policies necessary to implement the educational program pursuant to law. Courts have recognized that even without specific enabling legislation, boards have authority to enter into contracts and make decisions necessary to operate the schools. But local school boards cannot delegate their decision-making

[10]42 U.S.C. § 1971 (2018). Section 1973(a) states that "[n]o . . . practice or procedure shall be imposed or applied . . . in a manner which results in a denial or abridgment of the right . . . to vote on account of race." *See, e.g.*, Moore v. Itawamba Cty., 431 F.3d 257 (5th Cir. 2005) (upholding redistricting plan that would alter school board voting districts as not violating one-person, one-vote principle).

[11]However, the New Jersey Supreme Court has explained that not all documents prepared by public employees, such as handwritten notes taken during a school board meeting, are considered government records pursuant to open public records acts. O'Boyle v. Borough of Longport, 218 N.J. 168 (2014) (citing O'Shea v. W. Milford Bd. of Educ., 918 A.2d 735 (N.J. Super. Ct. App. Div. 2007)).

[12]*See, e.g.*, *In re* Kan. City Star Co., 73 F.3d 191 (8th Cir. 1996) (holding that a closed session between the desegregation monitoring committee and school board did not violate the Missouri Sunshine Act).

authority to other agencies or associations unless state law permits this. For example, Kentucky law authorizes school-based decision-making councils.[13]

Additionally, some states allow for other governance structures. For example, some charter schools exist within the traditional structure and might be governed by the locally elected school board. Most charter schools, however, are run by organizations with their own self-appointed boards. Chapter 13 provides an in-depth discussion of charter schools and other alternatives to traditional public schools.

Federal Role in Education

It may be confusing that states are primarily responsible for education considering that Congress has passed many federal education laws, such as the Every Student Succeeds Act (ESSA, which replaced the No Child Left Behind Act) and the Individuals with Disabilities Education Act (IDEA). The federal government influences education through its funding powers and the enforcement of constitutional rights.

Although the U.S. Constitution is silent regarding education, it does confer basic rights on individuals, and school personnel must respect these rights. Furthermore, Congress has authority to provide funding to education and can regulate schools through the enforcement of constitutional provisions. Specifically, the General Welfare, Commerce, and Obligation of Contracts clauses grant Congress authority to influence education policy and practice.

- **General Welfare Clause.** Under Article I, Section 8 of the Constitution, Congress has the power "to lay and collect taxes, duties, imposts and excises, to pay the debts and provide for the common defense and general welfare of the United States." Using the general welfare rationale, Congress has enacted legislation providing substantial federal support for research and instructional programs in areas such as science, mathematics, reading, special education, career and technical education, and bilingual education. Congress also has provided financial assistance for the school lunch program and for services to meet the special needs of various groups of students, such as the low-income students.[14] In addition, the federal government, in passing the Children's Internet Protection Act, attempted to protect the welfare of minors by policing the suitability of materials made available electronically.[15]
- **Commerce Clause.** Congress is empowered to "regulate commerce with foreign nations, among the several states, and with Indian tribes" under Article I, Section 8,

---

[13]Starting in the mid-1980s, there were some efforts to decentralize operational decisions to the school level (i.e., site-based management). Where school-based councils are created with delegated authority in certain domains (e.g., curriculum, personnel), their decisions have the force of law. *See, e.g.*, 105 ILL. COMP. STAT. 5/34-2.2(c) (2018) (authorizing the local school council to appoint a principal without school board approval); KY. REV. STAT. ANN. § 160.345(2)(h) (2018) (requiring superintendent to forward all principal applicants to site-based school council); MASS. GEN. LAWS ch. 71, § 59B (2018) (granting authority for hiring and firing of teachers and other building personnel to principals under the supervision of the superintendent).

[14]National School Lunch Act, 42 U.S.C. §§ 1751–1763 (2018).

[15]20 U.S.C. § 9134(f) (2018). *See* text accompanying note 34, Chapter 4.

Clause 3 of the Constitution. Safety, transportation, and labor regulations enacted pursuant to this clause have affected the operation of public schools. Traditionally, courts have favored a broad interpretation of "commerce" and an expanded federal role in regulating commercial activity to ensure national prosperity. The Supreme Court has provided limitations on the reach of the Commerce Clause as well.[16]

- **Obligation of Contracts Clause.** Article I, Section 10 of the Constitution stipulates that states cannot enact any law impairing the obligation of contracts. School leaders, teachers, and other school personnel are protected from arbitrary dismissals by contractual agreements. Because of this constitutional protection, federal courts often evaluate the validity of a given contract or assess whether a party has breached its contractual obligations.

Similar to state governments, much of the regulatory activity at the federal level is conducted by administrative agencies. Specifically, after Congress passes a law, federal administrative agencies issue regulations, which help to provide more clarity to the federal law that was enacted. Most of the federal regulations that relate to education are drafted by the U.S. Department of Education. For example, when Congress passed ESSA in 2015, the U.S. Department of Education issued regulations for this law in 2016.

The primary functions of the Department of Education are to coordinate federal involvement in education activities, identify educational needs of national significance, propose strategies to address these needs, and provide technical and financial assistance to state and local education agencies. Regulations promulgated by the Department of Education to implement funding laws have had a significant impact on many schools. The department solicits public comments on proposed regulations, and Congress reviews the regulations to ensure their consistency with legislative intent. **The Department of Education administers more than 100 different programs, ranging from services for Native American students to awarding grants to improve teacher quality.**[17] It also oversees the enforcement of civil rights in public schools through its Office for Civil Rights (OCR). Because federal agencies are part of the executive branch of government, the Secretary of the Department of Education is a member of the President's Cabinet.

Other Cabinet-level departments also administer educational programs and include the Departments of Agriculture, Labor, Defense, Justice, and Health and Human Services. For example, the Department of Agriculture facilitates the National School Lunch Program, which provides free or reduced price meals to children in schools. Outside of these departments, there are numerous federal agencies that influence state and local education policies through their regulatory activities. The Equal Employment Opportunity Commission (EEOC) reviews claims of discrimination in public schools and initiates lawsuits against school districts that are not in compliance with civil rights laws. The Environmental

---

[16]*See* U.S. v. Lopez, 514 U.S. 549 (1995) (invalidating the federal Gun Free School Zones Act of 1990, finding that a law to regulate guns in a school zone was not "economic activity" and had no substantial effect on interstate commerce). The Act was subsequently amended to clarify that that the Commerce Clause only applies only to guns that had been transported via interstate commerce. Thus, the Gun Free School Zones Act remains in effect. *See* text accompanying note 21, Chapter 8.

[17]*See* U.S. Dep't of Educ., *Programs* (n.d.), https://www.ed.gov/programs/landing.

Protection Agency (EPA) also places obligations on schools in connection with the maintenance of safe school environments. School districts can face the termination of federal assistance if they do not comply with such federal regulations.

PRIMARY SOURCES OF LAW

 Constitutions, statutes, regulations, and case law are the primary sources of law affecting schools.

State and federal governments are responsible for the creation and interpretation of the law affecting schools. A hierarchy of the sources of law exists (see Figure 1.1). State laws cannot contradict federal laws, but state statutes can supplement the federal provisions. Primary sources of law have been defined as "the law itself."[18] Federal and state law includes the following four primary sources: constitutions, statutes, regulations, and case or common law.[19] All three branches of the U.S. government—the executive, legislative, and judicial branches—create primary sources of law.

Federal and State Constitutions

A constitution is a body of precepts providing the system of fundamental laws of a nation, state, or society. **As the supreme law in the United States, the U.S. Constitution provides**

FIGURE 1.1   Sources of Law Affecting Public Schools

Federal	• U.S. Constitution • Federal Statutes • Federal Regulations • Federal Case Law
State	• State Constitution • State Statutes • State Regulations • State Case Law
District/School	• School Board Policies • Collective Bargaining Agreements • District/School Rules • Classroom Rules

[18]Steven Barkan, Roy Mersky & Donald Dunn, Fundamentals of Legal Research xxxix (9th ed. 2009).

[19]Charles Russo, *Legal Research: The "Traditional" Method*, in Research Methods for Studying Legal Issues in Education (Steve Permuth, Ralph Mawdsley & Susan Silver eds., 2d ed. 2015).

the framework for the American legal system. State and federal governments must follow the U.S. Constitution, but state constitutions and statutes are supreme in their state jurisdictions so long as they do not contradict federal constitutional provisions.

Every state constitution includes language mandating the creation of a public education system. Thus, the right to a public education is a constitutional right, but pursuant to each state's constitution as opposed to the federal constitution. The judiciary often reviews state constitutions, statutes, and regulations to determine whether they align with the U.S. Constitution.

The U.S. Constitution establishes a separation of powers among the executive, judicial, and legislative branches of government. These three branches form a system of checks and balances to ensure that the intent of the Constitution is respected. The Constitution also provides a systematic process for altering the document if deemed necessary. Article V stipulates that amendments may be proposed by a two-thirds vote of each house of Congress or by a special convention called by Congress on the request of two-thirds of the state legislatures. Proposed amendments then must be ratified by three-fourths of the states to become part of the Constitution. All federal constitutional mandates affect public education to some degree; however, the following amendments have had the greatest impact on public school policies and practices (see Figure 1.2).

FIGURE 1.2   Most Influential Constitutional Amendments in School Law

> **First Amendment**   **(Religion, Speech, Press, Assembly, Petition)**
>
> • *Congress shall make no law respecting an establishment of religion* **(the Establishment Clause)**, *or prohibiting the free exercise thereof* **(the Free Exercise Clause)**; *or abridging the freedom of speech, or of the press* **(the Free Speech Clause)**; *or the right of the people peaceably to assemble, and to petition the government for a redress of grievances.*

> **Fourth Amendment**   **(Search and Seizure)**
>
> • *The right of the people to be secure in their persons, houses, papers, and effects, against unreasonable searches and seizures, shall not be violated, and no warrants shall issue, but upon probable cause, supported by oath or affirmation, and particularly describing the place to be searched, and the persons or things to be seized.*

> **Fourteenth Amendment**   **(Due Process, Equal Protection)**
>
> • *Section 1. All persons born or naturalized in the United States, and subject to the jurisdiction thereof, are citizens of the United States and of the state wherein they reside. No state shall make or enforce any law which shall abridge the privileges or immunities of citizens of the United States* **(the Immunities Clause)**; *nor shall any state deprive any person of life, liberty, or property, without due process of law* **(the Due Process Clause)**; *nor deny to any person within its jurisdiction the equal protection of the laws* **(the Equal Protection Clause)**.

First Amendment.   The Bill of Rights, comprising the first ten amendments to the U.S. Constitution, safeguards individual liberties against governmental encroachment.[20] The most preciously guarded of these liberties are contained in the First Amendment's protection of speech, press, assembly, and religious liberties. Multiple lawsuits filed against schools have claimed violations of the religion clauses (the Establishment and Free Exercise Clauses). Some have challenged providing government aid, such as special education services, to nonpublic schools; others have alleged that public schools have advanced religion or impaired free exercise rights. For example, prayer at school events has been a hotly litigated area. Cases involving students' rights to express themselves have been initiated under First Amendment guarantees of freedom of speech and press. In recent years, students have claimed their free speech rights were violated after schools disciplined them for their online speech. Moreover, teachers' rights to academic freedom and to speak out on matters of public concern have precipitated numerous lawsuits. The right of assembly has been the focus of litigation involving student clubs and employees' rights to engage in collective bargaining activities with teachers' unions.

Fourth Amendment.   This amendment guarantees the right of citizens to be free from unreasonable searches and seizures. It safeguards individuals against arbitrary governmental intrusions and has frequently appeared in educational cases involving drug-testing programs and searches of students' lockers, cars, backpacks, cell phones, and persons. Some cases also have involved alleged violations by school officials of school employees' Fourth Amendment rights.

Fifth Amendment.   In part, the Fifth Amendment provides that no person shall be "compelled in any criminal case to be a witness against himself, nor be deprived of life, liberty, or property without due process of law; nor shall private property be taken for public use, without just compensation." Several cases have addressed the application of the self-incrimination clause in instances where teachers have been questioned by superiors about their activities outside the school.

Eighth Amendment.   The Eighth Amendment prohibits cruel and unusual punishment and has been at issue in some corporal punishment cases.[21]

Ninth Amendment.   The Ninth Amendment stipulates that "the enumeration in the Constitution, of certain rights, shall not be construed to deny or disparage others retained by the people." This amendment has appeared in educational litigation in which teachers have asserted that their right to personal privacy outside the classroom is protected as an unenumerated right. Furthermore, grooming regulations applied to teachers and students have been challenged as infringing on personal rights retained by the people under this amendment.

---

[20]The Bill of Rights applies to the states through the Due Process Clause of the Fourteenth Amendment. When the Bill of Rights was ratified, it applied to only the federal government. Through the Doctrine of Incorporation, the first ten amendments are now applicable to the states. *See infra* text accompanying note 24.

[21]*But see* Ingraham v. Wright, 430 U.S. 651 (1977) (finding that Eighth Amendment's prohibition of cruel and unusual punishment did not apply to school personnel who used force when disciplining students).

Thirteenth Amendment.   The Thirteenth Amendment prohibits involuntary servitude and has been invoked by parents contesting public schools' community service requirements.

Fourteenth Amendment.   The Fourteenth Amendment, adopted in 1868, is the most widely invoked constitutional provision in school litigation. It contains two important clauses: the Equal Protection Clause and the Due Process Clause. The Equal Protection Clause provides that no state shall "deny to any person within its jurisdiction, the equal protection of the laws." It has been interpreted to mean that similarly situated individuals must be treated the same. For example, in *Brown v. Board of Education*, Black students were not being treated similarly to White students.[22] This clause has been significant in school cases involving alleged discrimination based on race, national origin, ethnicity, disability, sex, sexual orientation, and gender identity. Also, school finance litigation often has been based on the Equal Protection Clause, although with very little success.[23]

In addition, the Due Process Clause has played an important role in school litigation. The federal judiciary has identified both procedural and substantive components of due process guarantees. *Procedural due process* ensures fundamental fairness if the government threatens an individual's life, liberty, or property interests. Minimum procedures required by the U.S. Constitution are a notice of the charges, an opportunity to refute the charges, and a hearing that is conducted fairly. To illustrate, before a tenured teacher is dismissed, the teacher must be afforded certain procedural rights. *Substantive due process* requires that state action be based on a valid objective with means reasonably related to attaining the objective. In essence, substantive due process shields the individual against arbitrary governmental action that impairs life, liberty, or property interests. Property rights are legitimate expectations of entitlement created through state laws, regulations, and contracts. Compulsory school attendance laws confer on students a legitimate property right to attend school, and the granting of tenure gives teachers a property entitlement to continued employment. Liberty rights include interests in one's reputation and fundamental rights related to marriage, family matters, and personal privacy.

Also, the U.S. Supreme Court has interpreted Fourteenth Amendment liberties as incorporating the personal freedoms contained in the Bill of Rights.[24] Thus, the first ten amendments, originally directed toward the federal government, have been applied to state actions as well. Although the principle of "incorporation" has been criticized, Supreme Court precedent supports the notion that the Fourteenth Amendment restricts state interference with fundamental constitutional liberties. **The incorporation principle is particularly important in school litigation since education is a state function; claims that public school policies or practices impair personal freedoms (e.g., First Amendment free speech guarantees) are usually initiated through the Fourteenth Amendment**.

Because the Fourteenth Amendment protects personal liberties against unwarranted state interference, private institutions, including nonpublic schools, are not subject to these restrictions. For private school policies and practices to be challenged successfully under the Fourteenth Amendment, there must be sufficient governmental involvement in the

---

[22]347 U.S. 483 (1954).

[23]*See, e.g.*, San Antonio Indep. Sch. Dist. v. Rodriguez, 411 U.S. 1 (1973).

[24]*See, e.g.*, Cantwell v. Connecticut, 310 U.S. 296 (1940); Gitlow v. New York, 268 U.S. 652 (1925).

private school to constitute "state action."[25] To date, this has rarely occurred, although the Supreme Court may have opened the window for possible future inclusion when it determined that state athletic associations (typically nonprofit corporations) are entwined with state government and therefore are involved in state action.[26]

Federal Legislation

Congress is empowered to enact laws to translate the intent of the U.S. Constitution into actual practices. **These federal statutes reflect the will of the legislative branch of government, which, theoretically, in a democracy represents the citizenry**. Because the states have sovereign power regarding education, the federal government's involvement in schools has been one of indirect support, not direct control. Congress has enabled the federal role in education by enacting funding and civil rights laws.

Funding Laws. The most comprehensive law offering financial assistance to schools, the Elementary and Secondary Education Act of 1965 (ESEA), in part supplied funds for compensatory education programs for low-income students attending public and nonprofit nonpublic schools. With the passage of ESEA, federal aid to education doubled, and the federal government's contribution increased steadily until reaching almost 10 percent of total public education revenue in 1980. In 2017, the federal share to elementary and secondary education was 8 percent with the remaining 92 percent of funding coming from state and local sources.[27]

In 2001, Congress reauthorized ESEA as the No Child Left Behind Act (NCLB), which marked the most comprehensive reform of ESEA since it was enacted.[28] This law, directed at improving the performance of public schools, pledged that no child would be left in a failing school. Specifically, the law required states to implement accountability systems with higher performance standards in reading, mathematics, and science along with annual testing of all students in grades three through eight. Furthermore, assessment data was categorized by socioeconomic status, ethnicity, race, disability, and limited English proficiency and schools faced consequences if they did not make adequate yearly progress. The law also greatly expanded choices for parents of children attending schools that did not meet state standards.

In 2015, Congress again reauthorized ESEA replacing NCLB with the Every Student Succeeds Act (ESSA). Although provisions of NCLB remain, ESSA is designed to provide more leeway to states to determine accountability standards. The emphasis of ESSA is on "narrowing the achievement gaps between groups of students" instead of NCLB's previous

[25]*See, e.g.*, Rendell-Baker v. Kohn, 457 U.S. 830 (1982).

[26]*See* Brentwood Acad. v. Tenn. Secondary Sch. Athletic Ass'n, 531 U.S. 288 (2001); *see also* Tenn. Secondary Sch. Athletic Ass'n v. Brentwood Acad., 551 U.S. 291 (2007) (finding no due process violation as appropriate procedures were followed, notwithstanding minor procedural irregularities).

[27]U.S. Dep't of Educ., *The Federal Role in Education*, https://www2.ed.gov/about/overview/fed/role.html (May 25, 2017).

[28]20 U.S.C. § 6301 (2018).

focus on "attaining minimum proficiency levels on state assessments."[29] To receive funding, states are still required to administer statewide testing of students; however, teachers no longer must be designated as "highly qualified."[30]

Through legislation like ESSA, Congress and federal administrative agencies have exerted considerable influence in shaping public school policies and practices with categorical funding laws and their accompanying administrative regulations. Individual states or school districts have the option of accepting or rejecting such federal assistance, but if categorical aid is accepted, the federal government has the authority to prescribe guidelines for its use and to monitor state and local education agencies to ensure fiscal accountability.

Much of the federal categorical legislation enacted during the 1960s and 1970s provided funds to assist school districts in attaining equity goals and addressing other national priorities. For example, the Bilingual Education Act of 1968 and the Education for All Handicapped Children Act of 1975 (which became IDEA in 1990) have provided federal funds to assist education agencies in offering services for students with special needs. Although in the 1980s, Congress shifted away from its heavy reliance on categorical federal aid by consolidating some categorical programs into block grants with reduced funding and regulations, aid for students from low-income families, English Learners, and children with disabilities has remained categorical in nature. For example, two more recent examples of funding laws include the Healthy, Hunger-Free Kids Act of 2010, which requires improved nutritional standards for school lunches,[31] and the McKinney-Vento Homeless Assistance Act of 1987, which was reauthorized as a part of ESSA in 2015 and ensures schools provide services to students experiencing homelessness.[32]

Civil Rights Laws.   In addition to laws providing financial assistance to public schools, Congress has enacted legislation designed to clarify the scope of individuals' civil rights. **Unlike the discretion enjoyed by state and local education agencies in deciding whether to participate in federal funding programs, educational institutions must comply with these civil rights laws.** Some federal antidiscrimination laws are enacted to enforce constitutional rights and have general application. Others apply only to recipients of federal financial assistance. Various federal agencies are charged with monitoring compliance with these laws and can bring suit against noncomplying institutions. Under many

---

[29]Paige Perez & Mario Torres, Jr., *The Evolution of NCLB to ESSA* D3, *in* Decker et al. eds., *supra* note 5.

[30]Under ESSA, state education agencies must develop plans with challenging state academic standards for math, reading or language arts, and science. States must carefully monitor student achievement and provide evidence-based support for consistently underperforming schools and students. For accountability purposes, data must be disaggregated based on race/ethnicity, gender, socioeconomic status, disability, and English language proficiency. ESSA also added subgroups for reporting purposes including homeless children and those in foster care or with a parent in the military.

[31]Pub. L. No. 111-296, 124 Stat. 3183 (2018). Some of the regulations were altered in 2017. *See, e.g.,* Jessica Taylor, *Trump Administration Rolls Back Michelle Obama's Healthy School Lunch Push*, NPR (May 1, 2017), http://www.npr.org/2017/05/01/526451207/trump-administration-rolls-back-2-of-michelle-obamas-signature-initiatives.

[32]42 U.S.C. §§ 11431–11435 (2018).

civil rights laws, individuals also can initiate private suits to compel compliance and, in some instances, to obtain personal remedies. Some of the key federal civil rights statutes that students and school employees use when their federally protected rights have been violated include the following laws.

- **Section 1983 of the Civil Rights Act of 1871 (Section 1983)** provides a private right to bring suit for damages against any person who, acting under the authority of state law (e.g., a public school employee) impairs rights secured by the U.S. Constitution and federal laws.[33] Although Section 1983 does not confer specific substantive rights (i.e., it must attach to another federal law and cannot be the basis for suit standing alone), it has been significant in school cases because it allows individuals to obtain damages from school officials and school districts for abridgments of federally protected rights.[34] However, Section 1983 cannot be used to enforce federal laws where congressional intent to create private rights is not clearly stated.[35]
- **Section 1981 of the Civil Rights Act of 1866, as amended in 1991 (Section 1981)** prohibits race or ethnicity discrimination in making and enforcing contracts and in the terms and conditions of contractual relationships and allows for both compensatory and punitive damages.[36] It applies to all public and private schools, regardless of whether they receive federal aid.
- **Title VI of the Civil Rights Act of 1964 (Title VI)** prohibits discrimination on the basis of race, color, or national origin in programs and activities receiving federal financial assistance.
- **Title VII of the Civil Rights Act of 1964 (Title VII)** prohibits employment discrimination on the basis of race, color, national origin, sex (including pregnancy), and religion.
- **Age Discrimination in Employment Act of 1967 (ADEA)** prohibits age-based discrimination on the basis of (1) hiring, promotion, discharge, and compensation, or (2) terms, conditions, and privileges of employment for employees over age forty in programs and activities receiving federal financial assistance.[37]
- **Title IX of the Education Amendments of 1972 (Title IX)** prohibits sex discrimination against participants in education programs and activities receiving federal financial assistance.

---

[33]School boards as well as school officials are considered "persons" under 42 U.S.C. § 1983 (2018). Monell v. Dep't of Soc. Servs., 436 U.S. 658 (1978) (holding that a governmental unit is a person for purposes of § 1983).

[34]*See, e.g.*, Barrett v. Steubenville City Schs., 388 F.3d 967 (6th Cir. 2004) (finding that the superintendent violated the substitute teacher's right to direct the education of his child as protected by the Constitution and § 1983 when the superintendent refused to consider him for a full-time position because his son was enrolled in a parochial school).

[35]*See, e.g.*, Gonzaga Univ. v. Doe, 536 U.S. 273 (2002) (noting that Congress did not intend to create privately enforceable rights under the Family Educational Rights and Privacy Act); text accompanying note 82, Chapter 4.

[36]42 U.S.C. § 1981 (2018). The Civil Rights Act of 1991, 42 U.S.C. § 2000e (2018), expanded § 1981's protections and strengthened several other civil rights mandates.

[37]*See also* Age Discrimination Act of 1975, 42 U.S.C. §§ 6101–6107 (2018) (prohibiting age discrimination in programs and activities receiving federal funding and applying to *all* ages).

- **Section 504 of the Rehabilitation Act of 1973 (Section 504)** prohibits discrimination of individuals with disabilities in programs and activities receiving federal financial assistance.[38]
- **Americans with Disabilities Act of 1990 (ADA)** prohibits discrimination of individuals with disabilities in both private and public entities by ensuring equal opportunity for persons with disabilities in employment, state and local government services, public accommodations, commercial facilities, and transportation.

Other Federal Laws.   Additional federal laws offer protections to individuals in educational settings and place responsibilities on school officials. For example, the Family Educational Rights and Privacy Act (FERPA) guarantees parents access to their children's school records and safeguards the confidentiality of such records. This federal law also applies to both public and private educational recipients of federal financial assistance.[39] Federal laws also protect human subjects in research projects and require parental consent before students participate in federally supported psychiatric or psychological examination, testing, or treatment designed to reveal information in specified sensitive areas.[40] Courts have played an important role in interpreting the protections included in these laws and ensuring compliance with the federal mandates.

State Legislation

State legislatures also pass statutory law on a variety of issues affecting schools. For example, all fifty states require that students between specified ages (usually six to sixteen) attend a public or nonpublic school or receive equivalent instruction such as homeschooling. Parents can face criminal prosecution for violating compulsory education laws, and students can be judicially ordered to return to school. Some states have encouraged students to stay in school by conditioning a driver's license on school attendance for students under age eighteen.

Legislatures can authorize other school governance arrangements, such as state-funded charter schools or voucher programs. In some instances, when state laws are subject to several interpretations, courts are called on to clarify legislative intent or to assess whether the law is constitutional. If the judiciary misinterprets the law's purpose, the legislature can amend the law in question to clarify its meaning. However, if a law is invalidated as abridging state or federal constitutional provisions or civil rights laws, the legislature must abide by the judicial directives. A state's attorney general may be asked to interpret a law or to advise school boards on the legality of their actions, and such opinions are binding unless overruled by the judiciary.

---

[38]The Civil Rights Restoration Act of 1987, 20 U.S.C. § 1681 (2018), amended Title VI, ADEA, Title IX, and § 504 to make them applicable to entire institutions if any of their programs receive federal funds. This law was enacted in response to the Supreme Court's ruling in *Grove City College v. Bell*, 465 U.S. 555 (1984) (holding that federal grants received by some of the college's students did not trigger *institution-wide* coverage but only coverage for its financial aid program).

[39]20 U.S.C. § 1232g (2018), text accompanying note 76, Chapter 4.

[40]*See* 20 U.S.C. § 1232h (2018), text accompanying note 111, Chapter 4.

Federal and State Regulations

Whereas statutes are the actual law, regulations are supplements to the law that are legally binding. They help explain how the law should be interpreted and implemented. Administrative agencies—such as state departments of education or the U.S. Department of Education—draft regulations. Collectively, the regulations made by administrative agencies are referred to as administrative law. In most states, this collection of administrative law is referred to as administrative code (e.g., Indiana Administrative Code). Whereas regulations are binding law, they should not be confused with nonregulatory guidance that is not legally binding, but is also issued by federal and state administrative agencies.[41]

Case or Common Law

As early as 1835, Alexis de Tocqueville noted that "scarcely any political question arises in the United States that is not resolved, sooner or later, into a judicial question."[42] A case is a written opinion from a judge (or judges). When individuals or other entities (e.g., school districts) are unable to resolve a legal dispute, they initiate a lawsuit by filing a complaint in a court. The party who files the suit is called the plaintiff, and the party against whom the complaint is filed is the defendant. Case law describes the collective body of law that is derived from court opinions. These judicial decisions usually interpret how a primary source of educational law applies to a set of facts (e.g., whether a statutory or constitutional provision has been violated). Courts, however, do not initiate laws as legislative bodies do; courts apply appropriate principles of law to settle disputes. The terms *common law* and *case law* refer to judicially created legal principles that are relied on as precedent when similar factual situations arise. Some have made the distinction that judges make common law or case law; whereas statutes are the law enacted by Congress and state legislative bodies. Yet, others are quick to clarify that judges cannot "make law" because they are not part of the legislative branch; instead, the role of the judiciary is to interpret the existing law.

THE JUDICIAL SYSTEM

A hierarchy of federal and state court systems exists where judges interpret how the law applies in school settings.

The function of the judiciary is to answer legal questions, which often means courts must interpret statutes and constitutional principles. Although most constitutional provisions and statutory enactments never become the subject of litigation, some provisions require judicial clarification. **Because federal and state constitutions set forth broad policy statements rather than specific guides to action, courts serve an important function in interpreting such mandates and in determining the legality of various school policies and practices.**

[41]*See infra* text under section on Locating Legal Resources, Secondary Sources, describing Dear Colleague Letters.
[42]ALEXIS DE TOCQUEVILLE, DEMOCRACY IN AMERICA 280 (1960).

Judicial Review

The Supreme Court has articulated specific guidelines for exercising the power of judicial review. The Court will not decide hypothetical cases and will not render an opinion on issues in nonadversarial proceedings. A genuine controversy must be initiated by a party with standing and a private right of action to sue (e.g., the right to sue for damages). To achieve such standing, the party must have a "real interest" in the outcome of the case, such as having been adversely affected by the challenged practice (e.g., taxpayers may not have standing to sue public schools unless they have a child who has been directly aggrieved). **In applying appropriate principles of law to specific cases, the Court generally relies on precedents established in previous decisions.**

Lower courts also apply precedent when deciding new cases. The legal principle requiring courts to use precedent when deciding similar cases is known as *stare decisis.* In Latin *"stare decisis et quieta non movere"* translates as "those things which have been so often adjudged ought to rest in peace."[43] The purpose for this legal principle is to ensure fairness so that similar cases are decided similarly. *Stare decisis* also promotes stability and predictability in court decisions. The only time courts may decide not to follow *stare decisis* is when it is "absolutely necessary to avoid an injustice or to reflect current policy concerns."[44] For example, prior to *Brown v. Board of Education,* courts followed the precedent allowing government-sponsored racial segregation to exist.[45] However, *Brown* is a rare example of precedent being overturned; the U.S. Supreme Court reversed an earlier decision and held that racial segregation was in violation of the Fourteenth Amendment.[46]

In interpreting constitutional and statutory provisions, courts have developed various criteria to evaluate whether the law has been violated. These judicially created standards or "tests" are extremely important and in some instances appear to go beyond the original intent of the constitutional or statutory provision in question. For example, the U.S. Supreme Court has developed a test to determine whether school districts are liable for student-to-student harassment.[47] Judicial standards are continually evolving and being refined by courts. The judiciary thus occupies a powerful position in shaping the law through its interpretive powers.

Court Procedures

Procedures vary somewhat by type of suit and jurisdiction, but a plaintiff typically initiates a suit by filing a complaint with the appropriate court clerk. After a period of *discovery*, that is, when both parties gather, review, and analyze the evidence, if warranted, the defendant may submit two types of pretrial motions. First, a *motion to dismiss*—sometimes

---

[43]DAVID ROMANTZ & KATHLEEN ELLIOTT VINSON, LEGAL ANALYSIS: THE FUNDAMENTAL SKILL 8 (1998).

[44]*Id.*

[45]Plessy v. Ferguson, 163 U.S. 537 (1896).

[46]347 U.S. 483 (1954).

[47] *See* text accompanying note 124, Chapter 6.

filed shortly after receipt of the complaint, before conducting discovery—argues that the plaintiff has failed to state a legal claim or that the claim is barred by the applicable statute of limitations. Second, either party may file a motion requesting *summary judgment*, noting that the facts of the case are not in dispute and that the party is entitled to judgment based on applicable law. If summary judgment is not granted, the plaintiff's case then is presented.

Presenting Evidence.   Success in court is determined by plaintiffs' ability to persuade a judge or jury that they have been wronged and deserve a remedy or by defendants' ability to show that their action was either allowed or required by law. The parties' persuasive abilities are limited by the availability of creditable, admissible evidence.

Remedies.   Various remedies are available through court action. In some suits, a court-ordered injunction is sought to compel school officials to cease a particular action or to command performance of a particular action. Specifically, in offering *injunctive relief*, a court might issue a preliminary injunction, a temporary restraining order, or a permanent injunction. Courts may also provide *declaratory relief*, which simply states that specific rights must be respected. Courts can order personal remedies, such as reinstatement of fired teachers to their previous positions or removal of a student's disciplinary charges from school records. Courts also may award monetary damages and reimbursement for attorneys' fees to compensate individuals for the deprivation of their rights. Under certain circumstances, courts may order defendants to pay punitive damages if their conduct represents a willful or reckless disregard of protected rights.

Appeals Process.   Following a trial court decision or a jury verdict, each party then must make the decision whether it is in its best interest to appeal, given the allocation of time and resources. If the original ruling is appealed, the appellate court must accept the trial court's findings of fact unless they are clearly erroneous. The appeals court reviews the written record of the evidence but does not hold a hearing for witnesses to be questioned. The appellate court may accept the trial court's *findings of fact* but disagree with the *conclusions of law*. In such instances, the case is usually *remanded* to the trial court for reconsideration in light of the appropriate legal principles enunciated by the appeals court.

Class Action Lawsuits.   In addition to individual suits,[48] education cases often involve class-action suits brought on behalf of all similarly situated individuals. To be certified as a class action, the suit must satisfy four rules of civil procedure that specify prerequisites to establish class members' commonality of injury and circumstances. If a suit is not properly certified as a class action, and the circumstances of the original plaintiff change (e.g., a student graduates from school before a judgment is rendered), the court may dismiss the suit as *moot* because the plaintiff is no longer being injured by the contested practice.

---

[48]Most educational litigation involves civil suits, initiated by individuals alleging injury by another private party. Civil suits often involve claims for damages or requests for specific conduct to cease because it impairs the individual's protected rights. In contrast, criminal suits are brought on behalf of society to punish an individual for committing a crime, such as violating compulsory school attendance laws or selling drugs on school grounds.

Court Structure

In the United States, there are two main court systems: the federal court system and the state court system. However, some school controversies never reach the federal or state court systems because they are settled outside of court. A case may settle because the parties were able to reach a compromise before a judge/jury reached a decision or because the parties went through an administrative process aimed at resolving the dispute. **Courts will not intervene in a school-related controversy if the dispute can be settled in an administrative forum** (e.g., administrative courts may resolve special education disputes, or labor relations boards or arbitrators may resolve collective bargaining disagreements). All state educational systems provide some type of administrative appeals procedure for disputes involving internal school operations. For example, teachers who believe they were unjustly dismissed may appeal the decision through the state's administrative appeals procedure. Where relevant, courts require such administrative appeals to be exhausted before plaintiffs are permitted to file a case in state or federal court. To illustrate, before filing a case under IDEA in state or federal court, plaintiffs must first go through an administrative appeals process—which is commonly referred to as exhaustion of administrative remedies. However, other education disputes are permitted to proceed directly to state or federal courts (e.g., free speech claims).

There are two main types of jurisdiction: subject matter jurisdiction and geographic jurisdiction. Although courts have to follow precedent, they do not have to follow *all* precedent. Instead, they only must follow the precedent within their jurisdiction. *Subject matter jurisdiction* limits the type of cases that a court can consider. Any type of case can be heard in state courts because state courts are courts of general jurisdiction. **On the other hand, federal courts only accept cases if there is a federal question involved (e.g., a dispute about a constitutional amendment or federal law) or when parties are from different states or countries.**[49] Thus, if students were injured on the playground and were filing negligence lawsuits, they would file their complaint in state court (there is no federal question involved). If students were suing under the First Amendment because their right to free speech was denied, they could file in federal court (because of the First Amendment) or in state court (because it is a court of general jurisdiction). Additionally, a federal bankruptcy court could not hear a criminal case because it must decide cases based on a specific subject matter.

Geographic jurisdiction restricts a court from deciding cases outside of the physical boundaries assigned to that court. An example of a geographic boundary is the U.S. Seventh Circuit Court of Appeals having geographic jurisdiction over the federal courts in Indiana, Illinois, and Wisconsin, and thus, a court in California would not be bound by a Seventh Circuit ruling. It is possible for two state supreme courts or two federal courts to render conflicting decisions on an issue; nonetheless, such decisions are binding in their respective jurisdictions. Only decisions of the U.S. Supreme Court have national application.

---

[49]The claim must also involve more than $75,000 in damages. 28 U.S.C. § 1332 (1996).

State Courts

State courts are established pursuant to state constitutional provisions, and the structure of judicial systems varies among states. In contrast to federal courts, which have only those powers granted by the U.S. Constitution, state courts can review most types of controversies unless restricted by state law. State judicial systems usually include trial courts of general jurisdiction, courts of special jurisdiction, and appellate courts. All states have a court of last resort, and decisions rendered by state high courts can be appealed to the U.S. Supreme Court (see Figure 1.3).

In most states, the highest court or the court of last resort is called the supreme court or supreme judicial court. However, in New York and Maryland, the highest court is the Court of Appeals, and in West Virginia it is the Supreme Court of Appeals. Courts occupying the next level in the state judicial system below the highest courts usually are referred to as appeals courts or superior courts. State trial courts of general jurisdiction often are called district or circuit courts (but New York trial courts are referred to as supreme courts of their respective counties). The most common special jurisdiction courts are juvenile, probate, domestic relations, and small claims. The majority of state judges are either elected by the voters or appointed by the governor.[50]

Federal Courts

Article III, Section I, of the U.S. Constitution establishes the Supreme Court and authorizes Congress to create other federal courts as necessary. As mentioned, to file a case in federal court, the issue must involve either a federal constitutional or statutory question, or the parties must be from different states or countries. Because suits involving federal issues also may be heard by state courts, individuals may choose whether to file in state or federal court, but they cannot relitigate an issue in federal court if they have been denied relief in state court. There are three levels of federal courts of general jurisdiction: district courts, circuit courts of appeal, and the Supreme Court.[51] A total of ninety-four federal district

FIGURE 1.3   Federal and State Court System

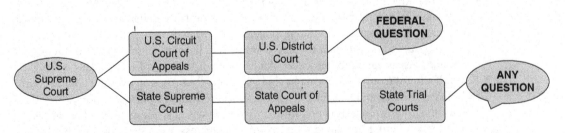

---

[50]*See* Alicia Bannon, *Rethinking Judicial Selection in State Courts*, Brennan Ctr. for Just. (2016), https://www .brennancenter.org/sites/default/files/publications/Rethinking_Judicial_Selection_State_Courts.pdf (describing four primary methods for state judicial selection including: contested elections, merit selection, gubernatorial appointment, and legislative appointment).

[51]The federal court system also includes courts of special jurisdiction, such as the claims court, tax court, and court of international trade.

courts exist in the United States. The number of federal district courts in a state is based on population. Each state has at least one federal district court; many states have two or three; and California, New York, and Texas each have four. Judgments at the district court level are usually presided over by one judge.

On the federal appeals level, the nation is divided into twelve geographic circuits, each with its own federal circuit court of appeals. A thirteenth federal circuit court has national jurisdiction to hear appeals regarding specific claims (e.g., customs; copyrights, patents, and trademarks; international trade). Federal circuit courts have from six to twenty-nine judges, depending on the workload of the circuit. A panel of the court (three judges) renders most circuit decisions, but in some instances, the majority of the court's judges (en banc) will rehear a case. Although a federal circuit court decision is binding only in the states within that circuit, such decisions often influence other appellate courts when dealing with similar questions. For example, if the Second Circuit ruled that students have a constitutional right to wear campaign T-shirts to school, this decision would apply only to Connecticut, New York, and Vermont; however, the decision may be considered a "persuasive authority" because it could be used to influence other appellate courts. The jurisdiction of the federal circuits is as follows:

- **First Circuit:** Maine, Massachusetts, New Hampshire, Rhode Island, and Puerto Rico
- **Second Circuit:** Connecticut, New York, and Vermont
- **Third Circuit:** Delaware, New Jersey, Pennsylvania, and the Virgin Islands
- **Fourth Circuit:** Maryland, North Carolina, South Carolina, Virginia, and West Virginia
- **Fifth Circuit:** Louisiana, Mississippi, Texas, and the Canal Zone
- **Sixth Circuit:** Kentucky, Michigan, Ohio, and Tennessee
- **Seventh Circuit:** Illinois, Indiana, and Wisconsin
- **Eighth Circuit:** Arkansas, Iowa, Minnesota, Missouri, Nebraska, North Dakota, and South Dakota
- **Ninth Circuit:** Alaska, Arizona, California, Idaho, Hawaii, Montana, Nevada, Oregon, Washington, and Guam
- **Tenth Circuit:** Colorado, Kansas, New Mexico, Oklahoma, Utah, and Wyoming
- **Eleventh Circuit:** Alabama, Florida, and Georgia
- **D.C. Circuit:** Washington, D.C.[52]
- **Federal Circuit:** National jurisdiction on specific claims

The U.S. Supreme Court is, of course, the highest court in the nation. The Supreme Court has the ultimate authority in interpreting federal constitutional guarantees.[53] When the Supreme Court finds a specific practice unconstitutional (e.g., intentional school segregation), this judicial mandate applies nationwide. If the Court, however, concludes that a given

---

[52]Washington, D.C., has its own federal district court and circuit court of appeals; only federal laws apply in this jurisdiction.

[53]*See* Marbury v. Madison, 5 U.S. (1 Cranch) 137 (1803).

activity does not impair federal constitutional guarantees (e.g., corporal punishment in public schools), states and local school boards retain discretion in placing restrictions on the activity. In the latter instances, legal requirements will vary across jurisdictions. Supreme Court Justices are appointed for life. The President nominates someone for the Court, and the Senate must confirm the choice. There are currently nine Justices on the Court.

As noted previously, if the judiciary interprets a statutory enactment contrary to legislative intent, the law can be amended to clarify its purpose. Congress has done so with a number of civil rights laws in response to Supreme Court rulings. However, the legislative branch does not have this discretion in connection with constitutional interpretations. When the Supreme Court rules that a federal law conflicts with its interpretation of the U.S. Constitution, the law is invalidated. Assuming that Congress persists in its desire for change, a constitutional amendment is required.

Each term, approximately 7,000 to 8,000 cases are filed in the Supreme Court. Although the Court disposes of approximately 180 cases, it only hears oral arguments in 80 cases (approximately 1 percent of cases filed). The Court often concludes that the topic of a case is not appropriate or of sufficient significance to warrant Supreme Court review. **At least four Justices must concur for a case to be accepted, and denial of review (certiorari) does not imply agreement with the lower court's decision**. Because the Supreme Court has authority to determine which cases it will hear, lower courts are left to resolve many issues. Accordingly, precedents regarding some school controversies must be gleaned from federal circuit courts or state supreme courts and may differ from one jurisdiction to another. When this occurs at the federal level, it is referred to as a *circuit split*. A circuit split is one factor the Supreme Court considers when deciding whether to review a case.

Judicial Trends

There has been a notable shift in the posture of the federal judiciary since the mid-twentieth century. Traditionally, federal courts did not address educational concerns; fewer than 300 cases involving education were initiated in federal courts prior to 1954.[54] However, starting with the landmark *Brown* desegregation decision in 1954,[55] federal courts assumed a significant role in resolving educational controversies and have addressed nearly every facet of education. Much of this judicial intervention has involved the protection of individual rights and the attainment of equity for marginalized groups.

In the 1960s and early 1970s, federal courts expanded constitutional protections afforded to individuals in school settings, but since the 1980s, the federal judiciary has exhibited more deference to the decisions of the legislative and executive branches and greater reluctance to extend the scope of civil rights. As a result, diverse standards exist across states and local school districts. Of course, the Supreme Court has the authority to create more uniform national standards and has resolved circuit splits affecting certain aspects of education (e.g., the Court has resolved multiple special education issues since

---

[54]JOHN HOGAN, THE SCHOOLS, THE COURTS, AND THE PUBLIC INTEREST 11 (1985).

[55]Brown v. Bd. of Educ., 347 U.S. 483 (1954).

the 1980s). Thus, the composition of the Supreme Court does have a profound influence on education. The Justices can determine whether to remain silent on an issue and allow variation to exist across the country or to establish a national standard. Although the debate will likely continue over whether courts should play a key role in shaping educational policies, courts do influence what occurs in schools today.

LOCATING LEGAL RESOURCES

Reviewing primary and secondary sources of law is an ideal strategy to increase legal literacy, as well as to identify solutions for legal dilemmas faced in schools.

The Internet has greatly increased school employees' abilities to access legal resources. The law is constantly evolving, and thus, educators must obtain the most recent legal information and understand how to distinguish primary from secondary sources.

Primary Sources

Although secondary sources may *describe* cases, statutes, and regulations, it is important to review the actual sources. The following list provides guidance as to how to conduct legal research based on the primary source.

- **Federal Statutes and Regulations.** The primary federal statutes and regulations relating to schools are available online. For example, the Department of Education provides links to many of them at https://www2.ed.gov/policy/landing.jhtml. The Government Publishing Office also houses federal statutes and regulations at www .gpo.gov/fdsys/. To locate pending federal legislation, the following websites can be utilized: www.congress.gov/; www.regulations.gov/; and www.govtrack.us/.
- **State Statutes and Regulations.** An easy strategy for locating state-specific statutes is to conduct an Internet search that includes the state and "code" (e.g., "North Dakota code"). To find regulations, add "administrative" to your search terms (e.g., "North Dakota administrative code"). Pending legislation (known as a bill) typically is also available on the state's website that provides the state code.
- **Case Law.** A case can be found in an official reporter or can be accessed by using an online database such as LexisNexis or Westlaw. When locating a case, the first page will include the case name and the case citation. To view a Supreme Court case, go to www.findlaw.com/casecode, click on U.S. Supreme Court, and put the case citation or case name into the search box. See Figure 1.4 for an example of what you will find if you search for *Brown v. Board of Education*, 347 U.S. 483 (1954). Note that the plaintiff's and defendant's names will not be in parentheses or brackets in the heading as it will appear on your screen. These have been added here to distinguish between the two. To listen to this case and other Supreme Court cases (and to view the transcribed proceedings), go to www.oyez.org.

FIGURE 1.4   Finding a Case

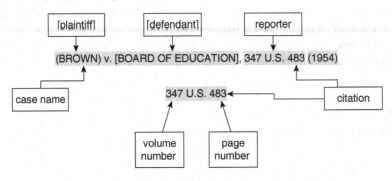

(BROWN ET AL.) v. [BOARD OF EDUCATION OF TOPEKA ET AL.]
APPEAL FROM THE UNITED STATES DISTRICT COURT FOR THE DISTRICT
OF KANSAS. * No. 1.
Argued December 9, 1952. Reargued December 8, 1953.
Decided May 17, 1954.

Secondary Sources

A good strategy when conducting legal research is to begin by reviewing secondary sources. Secondary sources of law provide legal guidance but are not the actual law and thus do not have the legal authority of primary sources. Instead, secondary sources provide commentary about the law to explain, analyze, and offer recommendations for changes to be made to the primary sources of law. In general terms, secondary sources include legal encyclopedias, law review and other scholarly journal articles, legal treatises, and restatements of the law. The following list includes secondary sources that relate directly to legal issues arising in elementary and secondary schools.

- **Law review articles** are scholarly articles written by legal scholars and located in legal periodicals called law journals that are published primarily by law schools. Primary sources of the law often appear in the footnotes of law review articles. Many law review articles are behind a paywall, making it difficult for education practitioners to access; however, an increasing number of law review articles are available online. Some examples of law journals devoted to education law include West's *Education Law Reporter, Brigham Young University Education and Law Journal, Journal of Law and Education,* and *Education Law and Policy Review;* however, education-related articles may be found in a variety of other law journals.

- **Dear Colleague Letters** are issued by the U.S. Department of Education and are intended to provide information, guidance, and clarification about the implementation of education law into practice. They provide nonregulatory guidance and may be persuasive in court cases, but they do not have the legal authority that primary sources of law do. In recent years, offices within the Department, including the Office for Civil Rights (OCR) and the Office of Special Education and Rehabilitative Services (OSEP), have drafted Dear Colleague Letters on a wide variety of topics including the rights of students with disabilities in charter schools, gender equity in career and technical education, and transgender student rights. The letters and other guidance are located on the following pages of the U.S. Department of Education website:

- OCR web page: https://www2.ed.gov/about/offices/list/ocr/newsroom.html
- OSEP web page: https://www2.ed.gov/policy/speced/guid/idea/memosdcltrs/index.html

- **Education law websites** provide clarification and commentary on general legal topics as well as resources for specific populations such as students with disabilities. A sample of potential websites include:
  - Education Law Association: https://educationlaw.org/
  - National School Boards Association Legal Clips: https://www.nsba.org/legalclips
  - *Education Week*, The School Law Blog: http://blogs.edweek.org/edweek/school_law/
  - Cornell Legal Information Institute: https://www.law.cornell.edu/
  - Education Law Prof blog: http://lawprofessors.typepad.com/education_law/
  - The EdJurist: http://www.edjurist.com/
  - SCOTUSblog: http://www.scotusblog.com/

CONCLUSION

Public schools in the United States are governed by a complex body of rules that are grounded in constitutional provisions, statutory enactments, agency regulations, and court decisions. Since the mid-twentieth century, legislation relating to schools has increased significantly in both volume and complexity, and courts have played an important role in interpreting statutory and constitutional provisions. Although rules made at any level must be consistent with higher authority, administrators and teachers retain considerable latitude in establishing rules and procedures within their specific jurisdictions. So long as educators act reasonably and do not impair the protected rights of others, their actions will be upheld if challenged in court.

School personnel, however, cannot plead "ignorance of the law" as a valid defense for illegal actions.[56] Thus, educators should be aware of the constraints placed on their rule-making prerogatives by school board policies and federal and state constitutional and statutory provisions. Subsequent chapters of this book clarify the major legal principles affecting teachers and students in their daily school activities. The following generalizations pertain to material covered in this chapter.

1. School employees should be legally literate in order to spot legal issues, apply the law, and solve legal dilemmas.

2. Learning about the law can alleviate fear, improve decision making, prevent lawsuits, and ultimately protect the rights of students and employees.

[56]*See* Wood v. Strickland, 420 U.S. 308 (1975).

3. The U.S. legal framework has a unique system of checks and balances and includes the executive, legislative, and judicial branches.

4. Because education is a state function, federal involvement is indirect, but influential in the daily operations of schools.

5. Constitutions, statutes, regulations, and case law are the main sources of education law.

6. All schools must follow federal civil rights laws that implement constitutional guarantees, but only schools that receive federal funds must follow funding laws.

7. Although state legislative bodies have plenary or complete control over education, they delegate some decisions to local school boards.

8. Courts do not make law like legislative bodies, but they play an important role in interpreting the law.

9. State courts accept cases involving any question, whereas federal courts accept only cases involving a federal constitutional or statutory question or when parties are from different states or countries.

10. When conducting legal research, it is important to locate and review both primary and secondary sources.

CHAPTER TWO

TORT LIABILITY

Can a teacher or school leader be held liable when a student is injured in the classroom, on a field trip, or during recess? Can a school official be found liable for breaking up a fight that results in injury to a student? Would an educator be liable for defamation after making negative comments about students to colleagues? Such questions often evoke anxiety and self-doubt among teachers and administrators. When a parent sues the school district or its employees after a student has been injured, courts are asked to determine whether school officials could have prevented the injury. This chapter explores the circumstances under which school districts and their employees might be responsible for student injuries that occur at school-related events. It also examines intentional torts and defamation.

Readers of this chapter should be able to:

- Identify what an injured student must prove in order for teachers, school districts, and other employees to be held liable for negligence.
- Apply the various negligence defenses to scenarios that arise in schools.
- Explain the legal issues related to intentional torts.
- Analyze what damages might be awarded in tort cases.

Tort law offers civil rather than criminal remedies to individuals for harm caused by the unreasonable conduct of others. A tort is a civil wrong, and individuals who believe they have been injured can sue alleged wrongdoers in civil court for damages. Tort cases primarily involve state law and are grounded in the fundamental premise that individuals are liable for the consequences of their conduct that result in injury to others.[1] Most school tort actions can be grouped into three primary categories: negligence, intentional torts, and defamation (see Figure 2.1).

---

[1]Similar claims also have been brought under 42 U.S.C. § 1983 (2018), which entitles individuals to sue persons acting under color of state law for damages in connection with the impairment of federally protected rights. *See* text accompanying note 122, Chapter 12.

FIGURE 2.1   Tort Liability

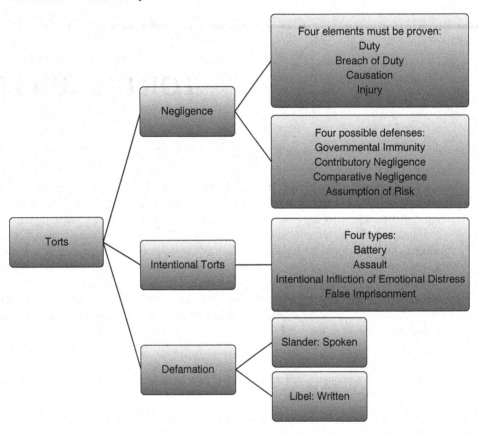

- - - - - ▬▬

NEGLIGENCE

> To determine whether an educator is negligent in a given situation, courts assess if a reasonably prudent educator (with the special skills and training associated with the role) would have acted in a similar manner under like conditions.

Negligence is a breach of one's legal duty to protect others from unreasonable risks of harm. The failure to act or an improper act that results in injury or loss to another person can constitute negligence. To establish negligence, an injury must be avoidable by the exercise of reasonable care. Four elements must be present to support a successful negligence claim:

- The defendant had a *duty* to protect the plaintiff.
- The *duty was breached* by the failure to exercise an appropriate standard of care.
- The negligent conduct was the *proximate or legal cause* of the injury.
- An actual *injury* occurred.

Duty

School officials have a common law duty (or responsibility) to anticipate foreseeable dangers and to take necessary precautions to protect students entrusted in their care. Among the specific duties school personnel owe students are the following:

- to give proper instruction;
- to provide adequate supervision;
- to maintain equipment, facilities, and grounds; and
- to warn students of known dangers.

Instruction. **Teachers have a duty to provide students with adequate and appropriate instruction prior to commencing an activity that may pose a risk of harm**—the greater the risk, the greater the need for proper instruction.[2] Following such instruction, effort should be made to determine whether the material was heard and understood. Proper instruction was not given to a Nebraska freshman, who was severely burned in a welding course when his flannel shirt ignited.[3] The school failed to make protective leather aprons available to the students, as was recommended for such activities, and the instructor had informed the students simply to wear old shirts. Perhaps most damaging to the district's case was the testimony of the instructor, who stated on four separate occasions that it was not his responsibility to ensure that students wore protective clothing.

Supervision. **Although state statutes require educators to provide proper supervision, school personnel are not expected to have every student under surveillance at all times during the school day or to anticipate every possible accident or incident that might occur.** Moreover, there is no set level of supervision required under common law for each activity or population. The level of supervision required in any given situation is determined by the aggregate circumstances, including the age, maturity, and prior experience of the students; the specific activity in progress; and the presence of external threats. Accordingly, there may be situations in which no direct supervision is needed, for example, when a nondisruptive student is permitted to leave the classroom to use adjacent restroom facilities in a building with no known dangers.[4] Other times, close supervision is prudent (e.g., when students with a history of disruptive behavior are assigned to the same activity),

---

[2]Some instructional negligence cases have focused on educational malpractice, with students claiming that they are entitled to monetary damages because public schools did not provide them with appropriate instruction. These claims have not been successful in court, and several states do not recognize a cause of action for "educational malpractice." *See* Miller v. Loyola Univ. of New Orleans, 829 So. 2d 1057 (4th Cir. 2002) (observing Louisiana state law as well as other jurisdictions do not recognize educational malpractice as a cause of action); Donohue v. Copiague Union Free Sch. Dist., 407 N.Y.S.2d 874 (App. Div. 1978) (noting that New York has not recognized a cause of action for educational malpractice), *aff'd*, 391 N.E.2d 1352 (N.Y. 1979).

[3]Norman v. Ogallala Pub. Sch. Dist., 609 N.W.2d 338 (Neb. 2000).

[4]*See, e.g.*, Patel v. Kent Sch. Dist., 648 F.3d 965 (9th Cir. 2011) (finding no teacher liability after unsupervised student was injured while using a bathroom immediately adjacent to the classroom). *But see* Miami-Dade Cty. Sch. Bd. v. A.N., 905 So. 2d 203 (Fla. Dist. Ct. App. 2005) (affirming jury verdict when the school board failed to warn a substitute teacher of the sexually aggressive history of a student; the student was permitted to go to the restroom unsupervised and while in the restroom attacked another student).

and yet other situations require one-on-one supervision (e.g., aquatic exercise class involving students with significant physical disabilities).

In assessing the adequacy of supervision, courts will determine if the events leading up to the injury foreseeably placed the student at risk and whether the injury could have been prevented with proper supervision. For example, a New York court found the school district liable for negligence because the evidence suggested that the teacher was aware of previous problematic behavior, which had occurred in the classroom and involved the same students. Four special education elementary school students had been playing in the bathroom during which time one of the students was injured after another student picked him up, spun him, and dropped him on the floor.[5] In another case, the Supreme Court of Washington found that a school district breached its duty when a student was lured off campus during track practice and raped. The eighteen-year-old male student who assaulted the fourteen-year-old female student was a registered sex offender. The court observed that the principal knew the male student had previously sexually assaulted a younger girl and that school officials had a duty to supervise students during track practice.[6]

Proper supervision is particularly important in settings that pose significant risks to students, such as vocational shops, gymnasiums, science laboratories, and other school grounds where known dangers exist. In these settings, it is critical that school personnel provide both proper instruction and adequate supervision to reduce the likelihood of injury to students and staff. Even when such care is provided, courts acknowledge that accidents will occur. In a New York case, a high school student injured his leg while playing floor hockey in gym class. In ruling for the school district, the court observed that no level of supervision could have prevented the injury.[7]

The school district's duty to supervise also includes the responsibility to protect pupils and employees from foreseeable risks posed by other students or school personnel as well as persons not associated with the school district. Depending on the circumstances of a particular case, school districts can meet this duty by warning potential victims, increasing the number of supervisory personnel, or providing increased security where assaults, batteries, and other violent acts are reasonably foreseeable. **Courts do not expect schools to ensure the safety of students in the event of unforeseeable risks,[8] but they do require that officials respond promptly and professionally when confronted with potentially dangerous circumstances**.[9]

[5]Johnson v. Ken-Ton Union Free Sch. Dist. 850 N.Y.S.2d 813 (App. Div. 2008). *But see* Shannea M. v. City of N.Y., 886 N.Y.S.2d 483 (App. Div. 2008) (finding no school district liability because there was no notice of prior assaults in the restroom).

[6]N.L. v. Bethel Sch. Dist., 378 P.3d 162 (Wash. 2016).

[7]Odekirk v. Bellmore-Merrick Cent. Sch. Dist., 895 N.Y.S.2d 184 (App. Div. 2009); *see also* Tanenbaum v. Minnesauke Elem. Sch., 901 N.Y.S.2d 102 (App. Div. 2010) (observing no district liability because accident involving a student pushed in a lunch line could not have been prevented even with intense supervision).

[8]Jorge C. v. City of N.Y., 8 N.Y.S.3d 307 (App. Div. 2015) (finding it was unforeseeable when a student injured himself by walking backward into a pole; school officials could not have anticipated this injury).

[9]*Compare* Coleman v. St. Tammany Par. Sch. Bd., 13 So. 3d 644 (La. Ct. App. 2009) (denying school board's motion for summary judgment because it may have been foreseeable that a student would be attacked on the playground at lunchtime; school officials had been on notice that an attack was likely to occur), *with* Brandy B. v. Eden Cent. Sch. Dist., 907 N.Y.S.2d 735 (App. Div. 2010) (finding that a school district had no notice that a student would attack another student and that school personnel did not have specific knowledge to guard against the attack).

When the alleged violator is a school employee, a school district may be held liable under the doctrine of *respondeat superior* if the school employee committed a tort while performing a job duty.[10] Some courts have rejected claims of school district liability, finding conduct such as battery and sexual assault to represent independent acts outside an individual's scope of employment.[11] Generally, the conduct of the individual violator and not the negligent supervision by the school district is the proximate cause of injury. For example, an Oklahoma court rejected the parents' claim for *respondeat superior*, finding that the teacher who assaulted a student at school was working outside the scope of his employment.[12] Likewise, in an Indiana case, the Seventh Circuit found no school district liability for negligent hiring, supervision, or retention because the parents failed to demonstrate that school officials knew that a teacher who had a sexual relationship with their daughter had engaged in such conduct previously.[13]

Notwithstanding the general requirement to provide supervision, there may be times when students pass out of the "orbit of school authority," even though they may remain on school property. This often occurs today, given the wide range of uses of school buildings and the variety of activities. In one such case, an Indiana appeals court found that a district had no duty to supervise male students who secretly videotaped female lifeguards in their locker room in various stages of undress.[14] A Red Cross lifeguard class, although held in school facilities after school hours, was not part of the public school curriculum, and school employees neither taught nor supervised the course.

Supervision of students en route to and from school also has generated considerable litigation. Over the years, parents have argued that school officials are responsible for their children from the time they leave home until the time they return. The Louisiana Supreme Court found that a school district provided reasonable supervision after a twelve-year-old student was raped on her two-and-a-half-mile walk home from school. State law required the district to provide transportation to students who lived more than one mile from the school. The student in this case had been kept after school for a behavior clinic. The school district offered to arrange transportation for her, but the student chose to walk home.[15]

There is no bright-line test to assist courts in rendering uniform decisions in cases involving students en route to and from school because such a test would place an unrealistic demand on school resources and an unfair burden on personnel. Thus, courts instead focus on whether:

- the events that caused the injury were foreseeable;
- the school district had an express or implied duty to provide supervision on and off school grounds both before and after school hours; and
- the student was injured due to a breach of that duty.

---

[10]Schafer v. Hicksville Union Free Sch. Dist., 2011 U.S. Dist. LEXIS 35435 (E.D.N.Y. Mar. 31, 2011).

[11]*See, e.g.*, Acosta-Rodriguez v. City of N.Y., 909 N.Y.S.2d 712 (App. Div. 2010).

[12]Jackson v. Okla. City Pub. Schs., 333 P.3d 975 (Okla. App. 2014).

[13]Hansen v. Bd. of Trs., 551 F.3d 599 (7th Cir. 2008). *But see* C.A. v. William S. Hart Union High Sch. Dist., 270 P.3d 699 (Cal. 2012) (reasoning school district was negligent because supervisory personnel knew or should have known about a counselor's propensity toward sexual harassment).

[14]Roe v. N. Adams Cmty. Sch. Corp., 647 N.E.2d 655 (Ind. Ct. App. 1995).

[15]S.J. v. LaFayette Par. Sch. Bd., 41 So. 3d 1119 (La. 2010).

Where the district is responsible for providing transportation, officials should ensure that involved staff are properly trained and district procedures are communicated and practiced. Personnel should strictly adhere to transportation requirements, including those related to special licensure; background checks of drivers; vehicle maintenance; driving, loading, and unloading practices; conduct during transport; and criteria for the assignment of aides.[16]

In addition, school officials have a duty to provide supervision during school-sponsored, off-campus activities. As with other supervisory roles, school officials accompanying the students need to assess foreseeable risks associated with each activity and be aware of the abilities of participating students.[17] However, when the activity is neither curricular nor school sponsored, liability is less likely, given the difficulty of identifying a continuing duty on the part of school officials to provide supervision. To illustrate, no school district liability was found when a student died in a car accident after attending an off-campus event where alcohol was consumed.[18] The court reasoned that the party was not school related, and the school year had ended prior to the party. In those instances in which districts are not responsible for transporting children to and from school, proper supervision still should be provided at the pick-up and drop-off area. Crossing guards should be stationed at nearby intersections for walkers, and assistance should be provided to parents and children to help identify safe routes to and from school.

Moreover, parents need to be informed about the earliest time supervision will be provided before school so that students do not arrive before school personnel. Parents also should be aware of when supervision ends after the school day. Where a student was assaulted by other youths while walking from school, no school district liability was found because the assault occurred thirty minutes after the student had left school grounds. The court held that the student was no longer in the custody or control of the school.[19] **As a general rule, school districts are not expected to protect truant and non-attending students** or students who are injured in their homes.[20] This is true for those who never arrive at school as well as for those who leave school grounds during the school day without permission, notwithstanding an appropriate level of surveillance of the school building and grounds as determined by the age and ability of the students. For example, no duty to supervise existed where a high school student was hit by a car after she left school property before the school day to smoke.[21]

Maintenance of Buildings, Grounds, and Equipment.   By law, some states protect frequenters of public buildings from danger to life, health, safety, and welfare. Individuals may use these *safe place statutes* to obtain damages from school districts for injuries resulting

---

[16]*See, e.g.,* Miloscia v. N.Y.C. Bd. of Educ. 896 N.Y.S.2d 109 (App. Div. 2010) (finding bus driver did not create a dangerous situation when he stopped quickly to avoid an accident, and a student on the bus was injured).

[17]*See* Hansen v. Bath & Tennis Marina Corp., 900 N.Y.S.2d 365 (App. Div. 2010) (determining that it was not foreseeable or preventable when a student burned herself at a school-sponsored event).

[18]Archbishop Coleman F. Carroll High Sch. v. Maynoldi, 30 So. 3d 533 (Fla. Dist. Ct. App. 2010).

[19]Pistolese v. William Floyd Union Free Sch. Dist., 895 N.Y.S.2d 125 (App. Div. 2010). *But see* Nash v. Port Wash. Union Free Sch. Dist., 922 N.Y.S.2d 408 (App. Div. 2011) (affirming summary judgment in favor of student who was severely burned while working on science experiment after school). *See* text accompanying note 127, Chapter 8.

[20]*See, e.g.,* Maldonado v. Tuckahoe, 817 N.Y.S.2d 376 (App. Div. 2006).

[21]Dalton v. Memminger, 889 N.Y.S.2d 785 (App. Div. 2009).

from defective conditions of school buildings and grounds. Furthermore, school officials have a common law duty to maintain facilities and equipment in a reasonably safe condition. Districts can be held liable when they are aware of, or should have been aware of, hazardous conditions and do not take the necessary steps to repair or correct those conditions.

The duty to provide reasonable maintenance of facilities does not place an obligation on school personnel to anticipate every possible danger or to be aware of and correct every minor defect as soon as the condition occurs. For example, a Louisiana student was unsuccessful in establishing a breach of duty in connection with an injury she sustained when she slipped and fell in a puddle of liquid on a school hallway floor.[22] The state appeals court explained that the presence of liquid on the hallway floor did not automatically create liability; the plaintiff, in failing to demonstrate how long the liquid had been on the floor, had not shown that the school had knowledge of any hazardous condition.

If dangers are known, damages may be awarded when injuries result from unsafe conditions of buildings or grounds. A Michigan student was successful in obtaining damages for the loss of sight in one eye; the injury was sustained while playing in a pile of dirt and sand on the playground after school hours.[23] The area was not fenced, and prior to the incident, parents had complained to school officials about "dirt fights" among children. The state appeals court concluded that the school district breached its duty to maintain the school grounds in a safe condition. In contrast, when a student was injured after her thigh hit the net winder on the school district's tennis courts, the court did not find the district negligent in the maintenance of the courts and found no creation of any specific safety hazard.[24]

In addition to maintaining buildings and grounds, school personnel are required to maintain equipment—such as that used in woodshop, science labs, athletics, or transportation—and to use it safely. A Texas appeals court determined that the school district was partially liable where a five-year-old child fell asleep on her way to school and was locked in the bus for the remainder of the school day. The court reasoned that although the district was immune for its alleged failure to supervise the unloading of the children, the district could be sued for the negligent locking of the door, given that such an act did not qualify as the "operation or use of a motor vehicle" for which immunity is granted.[25]

Warn of Known Dangers.   In nearly all states, courts have recognized either a statutory or common law duty to warn students, parents, and at times educators and staff of known risks they may encounter. This duty has been identified in areas such as physical education and interscholastic sports, vocational education, laboratory science, and other occasions when a student uses potentially dangerous machinery or equipment. Informing, if not warning, students and parents of known dangers is necessary so that they then may assume the usual risk associated with the activity. For example, no school district liability was found after a seven-year-old student injured herself on a slide at recess. The teachers had repeatedly warned her not to slide on her knees.[26]

[22]DeGruy v. Orleans Par. Sch. Bd., 573 So. 2d 1188 (La. Ct. App. 1991).

[23]Monfils v. City of Sterling Heights, 269 N.W.2d 588 (Mich. Ct. App. 1978).

[24]Bendig v. Bethpage Union Free Sch. Dist., 904 N.Y.S.2d 731 (App. Div. 2010).

[25]Elgin Indep. Sch. Dist. v. R.N., 191 S.W.3d 263, 268 (Tex. App. 2006).

[26]Simonides v. Eastchester Union Free Sch. Dist., 31 N.Y.S.3d 210 (App. Div. 2016).

In addition to the somewhat traditional warnings connected with sports or the use of equipment, educators, school psychologists, and counselors have a duty to warn when they learn through advising, counseling, or therapy that students intend to harm themselves or others.[27] Those in receipt of such information are required to inform potential victims or to notify parents if the student threatens to self-injure. This requirement supersedes claims of professional ethics, discretion, therapist/client privilege, or confidentiality.

However, school officials will not typically be found liable when the harmful act is unforeseeable (e.g., the threat of suicide was neither explicitly stated nor apparent), even if they knew that a particular student was under stress or seemed depressed or preoccupied. The Ninth Circuit found no school district liability when a student committed suicide at home.[28] The student left school without permission to attend a civil rights rally. When he returned, the vice principal called him dumb and threatened to notify the police. The student was especially worried about being found truant because he was already on probation for bringing a knife to school. Later that night at home, he shot himself. The court observed that the student had the opportunity to appreciate the nature of his actions after he returned to class and that school officials could not be held liable for his decision to take his own life.[29]

School officials also have a duty to warn employees of known dangers, whether structural, environmental, or human. Accordingly, a Florida court reversed a lower court's grant of summary judgment in a case where district officials failed to warn a teacher about a student's propensity for violence.[30] In a later proceeding, the court stressed that in order to overcome the general rule of workers' compensation immunity, the battered teacher will have to show that the employer engaged in conduct that was substantially certain to result in injury.[31]

Breach of Duty/Standard of Care

Once a duty has been established, the injured individual must show that the duty was breached by the failure of another to exercise an appropriate standard of care.[32] The degree of care teachers owe students is determined by:

- the age, experience, and maturity level of the students;
- the environment within which the incident occurs; and
- the type of instructional or recreational activity.

---

[27]*See* Tarasoff v. Regents, 551 P.2d 334 (Cal. 1976) (discussing the duty to warn if students pose a known danger to themselves or others).

[28]Corales v. Bennett, 567 F.3d 554 (9th Cir. 2009).

[29]*Id*. at 572; *see also* Mikell v. Sch. Admin. Unit, 972 A.2d 1050 (N.H. 2009) (finding no school district liability when student suicide is considered a deliberate, intentional, and intervening act).

[30]Patrick v. Palm Beach Cty. Sch. Bd., 927 So. 2d 973 (Fla. Dist. Ct. App. 2006), *aff'd mem.*, 50 So. 3d 1161 (Fla. Dist. Ct. App. 2010).

[31]For a discussion on workers' compensation, *see, e.g.*, Wyble v. Acadiana Preparatory Sch., 956 So. 2d 722 (La. Ct. App. 2007) (determining that a school employee was eligible for workers' compensation when injured at work while moving a desk; it did not matter that the task was routine rather than an accident).

[32]*See, e.g.*, S.J. v. LaFayette Par. Sch. Bd., 41 So. 3d 1119 (La. 2010).

For example, primary grade students will generally require closer supervision and more detailed and repetitive instructions than high school students, and a class in woodwork will require closer supervision than a class in English literature. Variability in the level of care deemed reasonable is illustrated in a Louisiana case in which a student with intellectual disabilities was fatally injured when he darted into a busy thoroughfare while being escorted with nine other classmates to a park three blocks from the school.[33] The state appellate court noted that the general level of care required for all students becomes greater when children with disabilities are involved, particularly when they are taken away from the school campus. The court found the supervision to be inadequate and the selected route to be less safe than alternate routes.

The reasonableness of any given action will be pivotal in determining whether there is liability. A duty of care might also arise with school busing. To illustrate, the school district was found to have breached its duty when it required a student to cross a four-lane highway to get to her bus stop.[34] The court held that the school district owed a duty of care to have bus stops on *both* sides of the highway.

In assessing whether appropriate care has been taken, **courts consider whether the defendant acted as a "reasonable person" would have acted under the circumstances**. The reasonable person is a hypothetical individual who has:

- the physical attributes of the defendant;
- normal intelligence, problem-solving ability, and temperament;
- normal perception and memory with a minimum level of information and experience common to the community; and
- such superior skill and knowledge as the defendant has or purports to have.

Courts will not assume that a defendant possesses any predetermined physical attributes (e.g., size, strength, agility) but rather will consider each defendant's actual physical abilities and disabilities in determining whether the defendant was responsible in whole or in part for an individual's injury. Accordingly, if a child requires physical assistance to avoid being attacked by another student, a different expectation will exist for a large, physically fit teacher as compared to a small, frail teacher.

Although a defendant's actual physical characteristics and capabilities are used in determining whether his or her conduct was reasonable, that is not the case when considering mental capacity. Courts will assume all adult individuals have normal intelligence, problem-solving ability, and temperament, even when the evidence indicates that they do not possess such attributes.[35] This may initially appear unfair, but any other approach is likely to result in defense claims that are judicially unmanageable. For example, if defendants' own intellect were used, they could argue that consideration should be given to factors such as their inability to make good or quick decisions, lack of perception or concentration, poor attention to detail, confrontational personality, or inability to deal with stress. Trying to determine each person's mental abilities and capabilities would be

---

[33]Foster v. Houston Gen. Ins. Co., 407 So. 2d 759 (La. Ct. App. 1981).

[34]Davis v. Bd. of Educ. for Prince Georges Cty., 112 A.3d 1034 (Md. App. 2015).

[35]Dan Dobbs, The Law of Torts 284–85 (2000).

impractical, if not impossible, given the dearth of valid and reliable assessment instruments or techniques and the ease of those being assessed to misrepresent their abilities.

In an effort to determine whether the defendant acted as a reasonable person, courts also consider whether the defendant had or claimed to have had any superior knowledge or skill. Teachers, who are college graduates and state licensed, are expected to act like reasonable persons with similar education. In addition, any special training an individual has received may affect whether a given act is considered reasonable. To illustrate, a physical education instructor who is a certified lifeguard or a teacher who has an advanced degree in chemistry may be held to higher standards of care than others with lesser skills and knowledge when, respectively, a student is drowning or chemicals in a school laboratory are mixed improperly and ignite. In reaching a decision on whether an appropriate standard of care has been used, courts also determine whether an injured individual was an invitee, licensee, or trespasser, with invitees receiving the greatest level of care and trespassers receiving the least.[36]

Causation

The plaintiff must demonstrate a causal link between the negligent act and the harm before the defendant can be found liable for negligence.[37] **In order to prevail, the plaintiff must show that the defendant's breach of duty caused the harm.**

There are two types of causation: cause-in-fact and proximate cause. In determining whether a school official's conduct was the cause-in-fact of a student's injury, sometimes courts employ the "but for" test. Under this test, the plaintiff must show that "but for" the defendant's act or failure to act there would not have been an injury. With proximate cause, courts decide whether the defendant's action is close enough to the chain of events that caused the harm. For example, there must be a causal connection between the alleged negligent conduct and the resulting injury. The courts might ask whether the incident was foreseeable when making a determination regarding proximate cause.[38]

To illustrate, while playing tag in gym class, a fourth-grade student was unintentionally knocked down by a classmate. He lost two front teeth when a different student tripped over him and caused his face to hit the floor.[39] Affirming the lower court's decision to grant summary judgment in favor of the school district, the appellate court found that the student failed to establish a lack of the school employees' supervision as the proximate cause of the injury. Similarly, a New York court ruled that a school district's lack of supervision was not the proximate cause of a student's injuries where a fight, in which the student was injured, occurred in such a short period of time that not even the most intense supervision could have prevented it.[40]

---

[36] *See* Codisco & Saile, *Trespassers v. Licensees v. Invitees in Premises Liability Cases* (May 24, 2016), https://www.cordiscosaile.com/blog/trespassers-v-licensees-v-invitees-in-premises-liability-cases/.

[37] David Owen, *The Five Elements of Negligence*, 35 HOFSTRA L. REV. 1680 (2007).

[38] *Id.*

[39] Doyle v. Binghamton City Sch. Dist., 874 N.Y.S.2d 607 (App. Div. 2009); *see also* Santos v. City of N.Y., 30 N.Y.S.3d 258 (App. Div. 2016) (finding lack of supervision was not the proximate cause when student tripped and injured himself during obstacle course).

[40] Keaveny v. Mahopac Cent. Sch. Dist., 897 N.Y.S.2d 222 (App. Div. 2010).

Injury

Legal negligence does not exist unless actual injury is incurred directly by the individual or by the individual's property. An injury could be physical or psychological (e.g., post-traumatic stress disorder). Most often, an individual will know of the injury as soon as it occurs. In some instances, however, the individual may not be aware of the injury for many months or even years (e.g., development of asbestosis due to exposure to asbestos twenty years previously). Most states have a statute of limitations of one to three years within which plaintiffs must file tort claims, but the actual time can be greater if the limitations period does not begin until the plaintiff reaches the age of majority or becomes aware of the injury.

Defenses against Negligence

Although tort law is generally addressed in state courts, teachers might find protection against claims of negligence under a federal law. The Paul D. Coverdell Teacher Protection Act provides protection to teachers who are "acting within the scope of the teacher's employment or responsibilities to a school" or when the teacher is attempting "to control, discipline, expel, or suspend a student or maintain order or control in the classroom or school."[41] Similarly, in some states, laws provide that public employees cannot be held personally liable for injuries they cause due to their negligence if the injury occurs in the scope of their employment. For example, in Colorado, teachers are generally immune from lawsuits when supervising students unless the action is committed willfully and wantonly.[42]

In addition, there are several state law defenses available to school districts when employees have been charged with negligence. At times, in an effort to thwart liability claims, districts have identified procedural defects (e.g., the failure to adhere to statutory requirements regarding notice of claim) or have proposed that an individual's injury was caused by uncontrollable events of nature. More commonly, defenses such as immunity, contributory negligence, comparative negligence, and assumption of risk have been asserted.

Governmental Immunity.　　The doctrine of sovereign or governmental immunity means that states cannot commit a legal wrong and are therefore immune from lawsuits. Only states or arms of the state have immunity, and when school districts claim governmental immunity, they will be scrutinized for their links to the state.[43] One of the reasons for

---

[41]20 U.S.C. § 6736(a) (2018). *But see* Sanchez v. Unified Sch. Dist., 339 P.3d 399 (Kan. Ct. App. 2014) (finding that the trial court erred in granting school district's motion for summary judgment because the Coverdell Act does not cover the school district as an entity).

[42]COL. REV. STAT. ANN. § 22-12-104 (2018).

[43]*See, e.g.*, M.S.D. v. Jackson, 9 N.E.3d 230 (Ind. Ct. App. 2014) (holding that the school district was not entitled to discretionary function immunity because principal's creation of a safety plan was not an exercise of political power under state's immunity statute).

immunity is to help the government avoid a lawsuit that might significantly impact its ability to operate. Immunity, however, has been criticized as violating modern concepts of justice. Thus, it is important to note that a state can choose to waive its immunity (through constitutional or legislative provisions), and lawsuits can then proceed against a governmental entity (e.g., a school district). In fact, to some extent, nearly all states have limited the use of the immunity defense by considering factors such as whether (1) the claim was related to the maintenance of the school building or property,[44] (2) acts were proprietary or governmental,[45] (3) decisions qualified as discretionary or ministerial,[46] (4) school property was being used for recreational purposes, (5) the injury was compensable under the state's workers' compensation laws (employees only), or (6) school officials' actions were wanton and reckless.[47]

Contributory Negligence.   In states that recognize contributory negligence as a defense, plaintiffs are denied recovery if their actions are shown to have been substantially responsible for the injury; it makes no difference that the defendant was negligent and also partially at fault. In most jurisdictions today, a slight degree of fault will not prevent a plaintiff from prevailing; typically, the contributory negligence must be significant, although it need not be dominant.

In assessing whether contributory negligence exists, children are not necessarily held to the same standard of care as adults. Rather, their actions must be reasonable for persons of similar age, maturity, intelligence, and experience. Many courts make individualized determinations as to whether a minor plaintiff appreciated the risks involved and acted as a reasonable person of like characteristics and abilities. Other courts have established age ranges in an effort to more objectively and uniformly determine whether

[44]*See, e.g.*, Kinderdine v. Mahoning Cty. Bd. of Dev. Disabilities, 69 N.E.3d 49 (Ohio Ct. App. 2016) (finding immunity for county board and other agency in a case where a child had entered a pool and drowned; the faulty latch at the pool's entrance was not a defect that contributed to the child's death).

[45]In states that distinguish between governmental and proprietary functions, *governmental functions* are those that are performed in discharging the agency's official duties (e.g., hiring faculty), and *proprietary functions* are those that are only tangentially related to the curriculum, can as easily be performed by the private sector, and often require the payment of a fee (e.g., community use of school pool). Typically, school districts will be liable for negligence involving proprietary functions but will be immune for negligence associated with those that are governmental functions. It may be difficult, however, to identify activities that are proprietary because most school endeavors in some way can be linked to the mission of the district.

[46]In states that distinguish between discretionary and ministerial functions, *discretionary functions* are those that require consideration of alternatives, deliberation, judgment, and the making of a decision (e.g., the discretion used in the selection of a new teacher), and *ministerial functions* are those that are performed in a prescribed manner, in obedience to legal authority, and without discretion (e.g., procedures used for stopping a school bus at a railroad crossing). Typically, school districts will be liable for negligence involving ministerial duties but will be immune for negligence associated with those that are discretionary. As with governmental and propriety functions, differentiation between functions that qualify as discretionary and ministerial will be obvious only when assessing extreme examples.

[47]*See, e.g.*, Coonse v. Boise Sch. Dist., 979 P.2d 1161 (Idaho 1999) (ruling that absent malice or criminal intent and without reckless, willful, and wanton conduct, a governmental entity was not liable for any claim arising from an injury caused by a person under the supervision, custody, or care of a governmental entity).

children have the capacity to contribute to or cause their own injuries.[48] Although courts vary greatly and designated ages may seem arbitrary, the most commonly used ranges are:

- children below the age of seven are considered incapable of negligence;[49]
- children between the ages of seven and fourteen are considered incapable of negligence, but this presumption can be rebutted;[50] and
- students age fourteen and over are generally presumed capable of negligence, although this presumption too can be rebutted.

When adults are injured on school grounds or at school functions, courts will assess the nature of the risk involved and whether such a risk was known to the injured party or reasonably should have been known. An Indiana court upheld a grant of summary judgment where a father fell from backless bleachers while watching his son's basketball game. The court found the plaintiff to be contributorily negligent in that he failed to exercise the degree of care that an ordinary, reasonable, and prudent person in a similar situation would exercise.[51]

Comparative Negligence. Forty-six states have adopted some form of comparative negligence statute.[52] With the comparative model, the plaintiff and/or one or more defendants bear responsibility in proportion to fault. For example, a school district in Wisconsin was found 80 percent liable for an injury an eighth-grade student sustained while dissecting a plant with a scalpel. The court observed that the teacher had been aware that others had been injured in the past and that she could have done more to avoid this injury.[53] Similarly, an Arizona appeals court upheld a jury verdict where a student was hit by a car when he ran into the street trying to flee another student after he safely exited a school bus on his way home. Liability was apportioned to the injured boy (45 percent), his parents (40 percent), and the district (15 percent) in a $6 million award. Although the school district was not responsible for escorting the child home, school officials were aware of the conduct of the students at the bus stop, a nearby busy street with fast-moving traffic, and the availability of an alternative and safer bus stop.[54]

[48]*See, e.g.*, Berman v. Phila. Bd. of Educ., 456 A.2d 545 (Pa. 1983) (finding that an eleven-year-old student who was injured by a hockey stick after the school failed to provide gear could not be found contributorily negligent).

[49]This is sometimes referred to as the "rule of sevens." *See, e.g.*, Crockett v. Sumner Cty. Bd. of Educ., 2016 Tenn. App. LEXIS 905 (Tenn. App. Nov. 30, 2016) (noting there is a rebuttable presumption of no capacity for a child between ages seven and fourteen).

[50]*See, e.g.*, Clay City Consol. Sch. Corp. v. Timberman, 918 N.E.2d 292 (Ind. 2009) (finding no contributory negligence in a case involving a thirteen-year-old student who died at basketball practice).

[51]Funston v. Sch. Town of Munster, 849 N.E.2d 595 (Ind. 2006).

[52]*See* Matthiesen, Wickert & Lehrer, *Contributory Negligence/Comparative Fault Laws in All 50 States* (Apr. 11, 2017), https://www.mwl-law.com/wp-content/uploads/2013/03/contributory-negligence-comparative-fault-laws-in-all-50-states.pdf. This source also provides an overview of the differences between various definitions of comparative fault.

[53]Heuser v. Cmty. Ins. Corp., 774 N.W.2d 653 (Wis. Ct. App. 2009).

[54]Warrington v. Tempe Elementary Sch. Dist., 3 P.3d 988 (Ariz. Ct. App. 1999).

Assumption of Risk.   This defense can be either express or implied. **Express assumption occurs when plaintiffs consent in advance to take their chances of injury, given a known danger. Implied assumption of the risk occurs without an express written or oral agreement, yet it is logically assumed, given the plaintiff's conduct**. For example, implied assumption would exist where spectators at a baseball game elect to sit in unscreened seats; such persons assume the risk of possible injury even if they failed to sign an agreement.

Although inherent risks are associated with athletics and recreation, all participants will not necessarily understand those risks. Understanding risks often is associated with age, maturity, and experience. As a result, school personnel must exercise reasonable care to protect students from unassumed, concealed, or unreasonably high risks.[55] This duty can be met when participation is voluntary, and the student is knowledgeable of and assumes the risks associated with the activity. For instance, an Indiana football player died following extensive conditioning in hot, humid weather. His mother had signed a release form providing permission for him to participate in organized athletics and acknowledging that injuries and even death could result.[56] The appeals court concluded that the lower court was correct in permitting the admission of the form as part of the district's defense. The athlete had several years of general football experience and in prior years had participated in the conditioning program of the current coach. In another case involving the death of a football player, the school district's motion for summary judgment was denied because the coach continued to let the student play despite observable signs that he had a concussion.[57]

Student athletes assume only those risks that occur during normal participation. To illustrate, an injured cheerleader had assumed the risk that she might injure herself during practice,[58] and a baseball player assumed the risk that he might be hit by a baseball at practice.[59] But students do not assume unknown risks associated with a coach's negligence, such as being given faulty equipment. Moreover, they do not assume that they will be exposed to intentional torts or conduct that represents reckless disregard for the safety of others. Likewise, students do not assume a risk when they are compelled to participate in athletic events.

INTENTIONAL TORTS

School personnel can be liable for intentionally harming others in schools.

An intentional tort occurs when someone intends to perform an action that causes harm to another. Among the more common types of intentional torts are assault, battery, false imprisonment, and intentional infliction of emotional distress. Although these are civil

[55]Jimenez v. Roseville City Sch. Dist., 202 Cal. Rptr.3d 536 (Ct. App. 2016) (finding assumption of the risk did not bar a negligent supervision claim that arose from a break dancing injury in an unsupervised classroom; the teacher had a duty to supervise).

[56]Stowers v. Clinton Cent. Sch. Corp., 855 N.E.2d 739 (Ind. Ct. App. 2006).

[57]Swank v. Valley Christian Sch., 374 P.3d 245 (Wash. Ct. App. 2016).

[58]Jurgensen v. Webster Cent. Sch. Dist. 5 N.Y.S.3d 663 (App. Div. 2015).

[59]Woo v. United Nations Int'l Sch., 27 N.Y.S.3d 18 (App. Div. 2016).

claims in which individuals sue other individuals, there are similar criminal offenses in which the government charges individuals with a crime. An individual found liable for an intentional tort may have to pay monetary damages, but a person found guilty of a crime may have to pay monetary fines and/or face imprisonment. Each of these torts, within the civil context, is discussed briefly below.

Assault and Battery

Assault consists of an overt attempt to place another in fear of bodily harm; no actual physical contact need take place. Examples include threatening with words, pointing a gun, waving a knife, or shaking a fist. For there to be an assault, the plaintiff needs to be aware of the threat, and the person committing the assault needs to be perceived as having the ability to carry out the threat. In contrast, **battery is committed when an assault is consummated. Examples include being shot, stabbed, beaten, or struck**. Actual injury need not result for a battery claim to succeed (e.g., the person could have been punched but not injured due to a comparatively weak blow). For the plaintiff to prevail in either an assault or a battery case, the act must be *intentional*; there is no such thing as a negligent assault or battery.

Some school-based assault and battery cases have involved students fighting at school. For example, in Ohio, a student struck another student in the face with a cell phone causing injury.[60] Other assault and battery cases have included the administration of corporal punishment and other forms of discipline that require physical touching.[61] Generally, courts have been reluctant to interfere with a teacher's authority to discipline students and have sanctioned the use of reasonable force to control pupil behavior. A Pennsylvania appeals court ruled that a teacher was not liable for assault and battery; as the teacher was attempting to discipline another student, the plaintiff student tried to hold the teacher's arm. In doing so, that student bumped into a heavy metal bar on a door. The court concluded that the teacher did not push the student and that her response was clearly warranted under the circumstances.[62] In contrast, a Louisiana appeals court did not find the teacher's use of force to be reasonable.[63] The pupil had sustained a broken arm when a teacher shook him, lifted him against the bleachers in the gymnasium, and then let him fall to the floor. The court reasoned that the teacher's action was unnecessary either to discipline the student or to protect himself. Although comparatively uncommon, school personnel may initiate battery suits against students who injure them.[64]

Self-defense often has been used to shield an individual from liability for alleged battery. **An individual need not wait to be struck to engage in defensive acts, although reasonable grounds must exist to substantiate that harm is imminent**. The "test" in

[60]Watkins v. New Albany Plain Local Sch., 2011 U.S. Dist. LEXIS 55322 (S.D. Ohio May 23, 2011).

[61]Corporal punishment is forbidden by the majority of states. *See* text accompanying note 55, Chapter 8.

[62]Betz v. Satteson, 259 F. Supp. 3d 132 (M.D. Pa. 2017); *see also* Frame v. Comeaux, 735 So. 2d 753 (La. Ct. App. 1999) (finding no battery when a substitute teacher grabbed a confrontational eighth-grade student by the arm and escorted him out of the room—the student had been talking during a test).

[63]Frank v. Orleans Par. Sch. Bd., 195 So. 2d 451 (La. Ct. App. 1967).

[64]In most cases, however, courts have found that the incidents were unforeseen and that no special duty existed on the part of the school district to prevent the battery. *See, e.g.*, Genao v. Bd. of Educ., 888 F. Supp. 501 (S.D.N.Y. 1995) (holding that the school district had not established a special duty to protect the teacher in several incidents involving battery).

such cases is to determine whether a reasonable person would have engaged in conduct like the defendant's given the circumstances. Consideration should be given to the magnitude of the existing threat, possible alternatives to physical contact, and the time frame available to make a decision (i.e., whether the defendant acted instantaneously or had time for contemplation and deliberation). Even where contact is justified, the defendant must use only force that is reasonably necessary for self-protection. Furthermore, if the alleged aggressor is disarmed, rendered helpless, or no longer capable of aggressive behavior, the defendant may not take the opportunity to engage in revenge or to punish.

In addition to self-defense, individuals accused of battery also may claim that they were acting in the defense of others. This type of tort defense is of particular importance in a school setting where educators often are called on to separate students who are fighting or to come to the aid of someone being attacked. Most jurisdictions not only permit such action on behalf of others but also consider it to be a responsibility or duty of educators, assuming good faith and the use of reasonable and necessary force.

False Imprisonment

False imprisonment results when physical action, verbal command, or intimidation is used to restrain or detain persons against their will. Not all restrictions on the freedom of movement or the effort to enter or exit will qualify as false imprisonment. For example, the court found no false imprisonment where a student was placed for seven minutes in a holding cell in a county detention facility for continually disrupting a tour of the building—the student's behavior jeopardized the safety of the children and disrupted an otherwise orderly environment.[65] Also, a student who was taken out of class to be questioned by the principal and a magistrate judge regarding sexual activities on the Internet could not claim false imprisonment.[66]

To be falsely imprisoned, one need not be incarcerated, and walls, locks, or physical force are not required. Rather, imprisonment can result from being placed in a closet, room, corner, automobile, or even a circle in the middle of a football field; it can occur when confined to an entire building or when forced to accompany another person on a walk or a trip. The taking of a purse, car keys, or other property with the intent to detain the person also may qualify as imprisonment. Tone of voice, body language, and what was reasonably understood or even implied from the defendant's conduct will be considered.

In false imprisonment cases, the plaintiff must be aware of the restraint but does not have to show damages beyond the confinement itself. Accordingly, any time children are unjustifiably restrained against their will, tied or taped to chairs, or bound and gagged, the tort of false imprisonment (as well as other possible violations) may be claimed. For example, a school district's motion for summary judgment was denied when a student with special needs was confined to a very small time-out room. In examining his false imprisonment claim against the district, the record reflected that the student's confinement violated New York law.[67] The plaintiff successfully demonstrated that school personnel intended to

---

[65]Harris *ex rel.* Tucker v. Cty. of Forsyth, 921 F. Supp. 325 (M.D.N.C. 1996).

[66]Howard v. Yakovac, 2006 U.S. Dist. LEXIS 27253 (D. Idaho May 2, 2006).

[67]Schafer v. Hicksville Free Sch. Dist., 2011 U.S. Dist. LEXIS 35435 (E.D.N.Y. Mar. 31, 2011).

confine him, that the student was aware of the confinement, and that the confinement was not otherwise privileged. Similarly, in another false imprisonment case involving a student with disabilities, the court denied a school district's motion for summary judgment where the student claimed that school officials had physically restrained her during a disciplinary matter. According to the student's IEP (Individualized Education Program), she was only to be restrained if she was a danger to herself or others. There were issues of fact raised about whether such a danger was present.[68]

Although there are rare instances when the use of physical restraints may be necessary, educators need to document the circumstances requiring such actions and provide a narrative explaining why restraint is an appropriate and reasoned response to the behavior. Where explanations are insufficient, liability will be possible, if not probable. Additionally, it is imperative that school districts provide training to all personnel who may need to physically restrain a student.

Intentional Infliction of Mental or Emotional Distress

A tort claim of intentional infliction of mental distress is available to individuals who have experienced severe mental or emotional anguish. This claim, however, does not provide a remedy for every trivial indignity, insult, incidence of bad manners, annoyance, or sexist or racist comment, even if disturbing to the plaintiff.

Some forms of communication can result in an assault claim (e.g., a threat to strike another) or defamation suit (e.g., an unfounded claim that a teacher has been sexually involved with students). Other communications might provide a basis for discrimination suits under federal laws (e.g., sexual or racial harassment). **For the conduct to result in intentional infliction of mental or emotional distress under tort law, it must be flagrant, extreme, or outrageous; it must go beyond all possible bounds of decency and be regarded as atrocious and utterly intolerable in civilized society.**[69] No reasonable person should be expected to endure such conduct (e.g., severe and extreme acts of stalking, harassment, and assault). Moreover, in most instances, the conduct must be prolonged and recurring because single acts seldom meet the necessary threshold.

Given the difficulty of meeting this stringent standard, it is not surprising that few school-based intentional infliction of emotional distress claims succeed. Unsuccessful claims include a school supervisor who was callous and offensive when he ridiculed a subordinate's speech impediment;[70] a teacher making a false report against a student for misconduct;[71] teachers refusing to use a student's nickname, Boo, that also has drug connotations;[72]

---

[68]A.G. v. Paradise Valley Unified Sch. Dist., 815 F.3d 1195 (9th Cir. 2016). *See* Chapter 7 for a discussion about restraint and seclusion.

[69]*See* Ott v. Edinburgh Cmty. Sch. Corp., 189 F. App'x 507 (7th Cir. 2006) (concluding that a former coach was not defamed, nor did statements made about him rise to the level of outrageousness that would cause mental or emotional distress, when a school board member disclosed to the superintendent that the coach had a criminal record).

[70]Shipman v. Glenn, 443 S.E.2d 921 (S.C. Ct. App. 1994).

[71]Mikell v. Sch. Admin. Unit, 972 A.2d 1050 (N.H. 2009).

[72]Phillips v. Lincoln Cty. Sch. Dist., 984 P.2d 947 (Or. Ct. App. 1999); *see also* Green v. San Diego Unified Sch. Dist., 226 F. App'x 677 (9th Cir. 2007) (determining that defendant's conduct was neither extreme nor outrageous, and plaintiff failed to meet the standard for emotional distress).

a police officer restraining a student with a disability;[73] and a school administrator explaining that a teacher who had made racially offensive remarks was returning to work following a ten-day suspension.[74] None of these cases were found to have met the necessary threshold to qualify as outrageous or extreme.

In contrast, an Illinois federal district court supported parents' claim of intentional infliction of mental distress against a teacher who had sexually abused their first-grade children.[75] The court noted that the teacher's conduct toward the students was extreme and outrageous. Parents may also file such claims against the district if they themselves suffered mental anguish as a result of their child's injury. For example, a parent alleged an intentional infliction of emotional distress claim when the school released the student to an unauthorized person, and the student was kidnapped.[76] There was no liability found, however, because it was not established that school officials were reckless at the time of the misconduct.

DEFAMATION

Individuals can be awarded damages for written or spoken injury to their reputations, presuming, of course, that the statements are false.

Most tort actions involve claims for damages that are due to physical or mental injuries, but plaintiffs also claim injury to their reputations in the form of defamation.[77] School districts may be liable for the defamatory acts of their employees,[78] but only when they are engaged in school district work and their conduct is within the scope of their employer's authority.[79] Otherwise, claims may be filed only against the individual responsible for the alleged defamation. *Slander* **is the term generally associated with spoken defamation (but also includes sign language), whereas** *libel* **often is used to refer to written defamation (but also includes pictures, statues, motion pictures, and conduct carrying a defamatory**

---

[73]*A.G.*, 815 F.3d 1195.

[74]Elstrom v. Indep. Sch. Dist., 533 N.W.2d 51 (Minn. Ct. App. 1995).

[75]Doe v. White, 627 F. Supp. 2d 905 (C.D. Ill. 2009); *see also* M.S. v. Seminole Cty. Sch. Bd., 636 F. Supp. 2d 1317 (M.D. Fla. 2009) (denying defendant's motion for summary judgment, the court found that a teacher who had physically abused a student with autism could be held liable for her outrageous behavior).

[76]Ramirez v. Escondido Unified Sch. Dist., 648 F. App'x 669 (9th Cir. 2016).

[77]*See, e.g.*, Draker v. Schreiber, 271 S.W.3d 318 (Tex. App. 2008) (dismissing vice principal's causes of action against two students who had created mock Myspace profiles that included personal information and sexual references about her).

[78]*See, e.g.*, Dobias v. Oak Park & River Forest High Sch. Dist., 57 N.E.3d 511 (Ill. App. Ct. 2016) (finding defamation per se when female assistant coach sued school district after head coach told others that she had rolled in bed with a student athlete in a hotel room).

[79]*See, e.g.*, Henderson v. Walled Lake Consol. Schs., 469 F.3d 479 (6th Cir. 2006) (ruling that a coach's slanderous comments were not made within the scope of his authority as a soccer coach).

imputation—e.g., hanging a person in effigy).[80] In determining whether defamation has occurred, courts will consider whether:

- the targeted individual was a private or public person;
- the communication was false;
- the expression qualified as opinion or fact; and
- the comment was privileged.[81]

Private and Public Persons

To prevail in a defamation case, private individuals need prove only that a false publication by the defendant was received and understood by a third party and that injury resulted.[82] Receipt of potentially defamatory information that is not understood (e.g., receiving an unintelligible encrypted message on a computer, receiving a phone call in an unknown language) cannot adversely affect the plaintiff's reputation, dignity, or community standing and does not qualify as defamation. Individuals who are considered public figures or officials additionally must show that the publication was made with either malice or a reckless disregard for the truth. Definitions vary considerably by state, but public figures generally are those who are known or recognized by the public (e.g., professional athletes, actors), whereas public officials are those who have substantial control over governmental affairs (e.g., politicians, school board members).

The trend in recent years has been to broaden the class of public officials and figures, but it is fortunate for teachers that the vast majority of courts have not found them to be "public," in large part because their authority typically is limited to students.[83] Some courts, however, have found school administrators and coaches to be either public officials or figures.[84] This does not mean that all administrators and coaches, even within the same jurisdiction, will qualify as public persons; such a determination is made on an individual basis and is dependent on the role, responsibility, degree of notoriety, and authority of the specific individual.

Veracity of Statements

In assessing defamation claims, courts also consider whether a statement is true or false. If the statement is found to be true, or at least substantially true, judgment will generally be for the defendant, assuming that critical facts have not been omitted, taken out of context,

[80]Dobbs, *supra* note 35.

[81]*See* Charles Russo, Allan Osbourne & David Dolph, *Honesty Is the Best Policy in Writing Letters of Recommendation*, 346 Educ. L. Rep. 21 (2017) (discussing issues related to defamation when writing a letter of recommendation).

[82]*See, e.g.*, Harris v. Pontotoc Cty. Sch. Dist., 635 F.3d 685 (5th Cir. 2011) (finding no defamation because a teacher who accused a student of being a computer hacker did not communicate the information to a third party).

[83]McCutcheon v. Moran, 425 N.E.2d 1130 (Ill. App. Ct. 1981). *But see* Elstrom v. Indep. Sch. Dist., 533 N.W.2d 51 (Minn. Ct. App. 1995) (concluding that a teacher was a public official).

[84]*See, e.g.*, Jordan v. World Publ'g, 872 P.2d 946 (Okla. Ct. App. 1994) (principal). *But see* O'Connor v. Burningham, 165 P.3d 1214 (Utah 2007) (determining that a coach was not a public official as school athletics did not affect in any material way the civic affairs of a community).

or otherwise artificially juxtaposed to misrepresent.[85] Educators must be particularly careful, however, when discussing students and must avoid making comments in bad faith that will result in liability. For example, if a teacher were to comment in class that a particular female student was a "slut," the comment would qualify, even if true, as defamation per se.[86] In such cases, no proof of actual harm to reputation is required.

In addition to proving a communication to be false, the individual must show that he or she was the subject addressed. Interestingly, the individual's identity need not be clear to all third parties (i.e., readers, viewers, or hearers of the defamation); so long as at least one third party can identify the individual, the claim is actionable, even though the individual is not mentioned by name. Furthermore, the defamatory content need not be explicit; it may be implied or may be understood only by third parties with additional information.

Fact versus Opinion

Most opinions receive constitutional protection, particularly when public figures or officials are involved or the issue is one of public concern. **To qualify as opinion, the communication must not lend itself to being realistically proven as true or false and must be communicated in such a way as to be considered a personal perspective on the matter.**[87] For example, when a school psychologist made a professional recommendation that parents needed parent instruction to help their child with disabilities, the court did not find it to be defamation. The statements were opinions and not facts or false statements.[88] Parents may express critical opinions about a teacher (verbally or in writing) and may submit such opinions to a principal or school board.[89] Moreover, parents may even express negative views directly to the teacher, assuming that the expression does not amount to "fighting words"[90] or qualify as an assault. Notwithstanding these examples, allegations that "the teacher sold drugs to a student" or that "the superintendent stole school funds" are factual statements capable of being substantiated and therefore may qualify as defamation unless proven true.

In a few instances, school officials have been accused of defamation for what they have posted on social media[91] or in email.[92] These developments suggest that it is wise for

---

[85]Determining whether something is true can be difficult, as perspectives and standards will vary.

[86]*See, e.g.*, Smith v. Atkins, 622 So. 2d 795 (La. Ct. App. 1993).

[87]*Compare* Milkovich v. Lorain Journal Co., 497 U.S. 1 (1990) (observing that a newspaper's statements about a high school wrestling coach implied that the coach committed perjury in a judicial proceeding and therefore did not qualify as opinion because the statements could be proven true or false), *with* Maynard v. Daily Gazette Co., 447 S.E.2d 293 (W. Va. 1994) (holding that a former athletic director was not defamed by an editorial identifying him as one of several parties responsible for the poor graduation rates of athletes; statements expressed in the newspaper were constitutionally protected opinions regarding topics of public interest).

[88]Luo v. Baldwin Union Free Sch. Dist., 2011 U.S. Dist. LEXIS 26835 (E.D.N.Y. Mar. 15, 2011), *aff'd*, 2017 U.S. App. LEXIS 1470 (2d Cir. 2017).

[89]Ansorian v. Zimmerman, 627 N.Y.S.2d 706 (App. Div. 1995).

[90]"Fighting words" are, by their nature, likely to result in an immediate breach of the peace and do not qualify as First Amendment protected speech. *See* text accompanying note 7, Chapter 5.

[91]Lamberth v. Clark Cty. Sch. Dist., 2015 WL 4760696 (D. Nev. July 1, 2015) (remanding case to state court to resolve whether a guidance counselor's post on Facebook that criticized a parent was defamatory); *see also* Marino v. Westfield Bd. of Educ., 2016 WL 2901706 (D.N.J. May 18, 2016) (dismissing a coach's defamation suit against district for alleged defamatory posts about him on social media; his claims were barred by the statute of limitations) (unpublished).

[92]Samsel v. DeSoto Cty. Sch. Dist., 242 F. Supp. 3d 496 (D. Miss. 2016) (denying a school district's motion for summary judgment because a jury should decide whether a statement in e-mail was defamatory).

everyone in the school community to be educated about what constitutes defamation in order to avoid litigation in this area.

Privilege

Whether a communication qualifies as "privileged" also may affect whether defamation is supported. Statements that are considered *absolutely privileged* cannot serve as a basis for defamation under any circumstance, even if they are false and result in injury.[93] Absolutely privileged communication occurs when school officials' statements are made during a formal judicial or administrative proceeding. This defense has been selectively applied in cases involving superintendents and school board members, although it is less common in education than is qualified privilege. For example, the North Dakota Supreme Court held that a board member's statements about a superintendent at a school board meeting were absolutely privileged.[94] Similarly, a New York court ruled that a superintendent's written reprimand to a coach for failure to follow regulations in the operation of the athletic program was protected by absolute privilege.[95]

Communication between parties with qualified or conditional privilege also may be immune from liability if made in good faith. But, conditional privilege may be lost if actual malice exists (i.e., a person made a defamatory statement that was known to be false, acted with a high degree of awareness of probable falsity, or entertained serious doubts as to whether the statement was true). Qualified privilege has been supported in administrators' rating of school personnel,[96] a board member commenting on the suspension of a student for marijuana possession,[97] and a teacher informing school officials about the inappropriate conduct of another teacher during a school trip.[98]

DAMAGES

Tort suits for damages may be filed against school districts and the individuals responsible for the injury.

Damages are typically monetary awards paid to the victim to provide compensation for an injury. For example, damages were awarded to a plaintiff student when a teacher had been warned about a potentially hazardous situation and did not appropriately respond. During recess, the student specifically told his teacher that other boys were harassing him. The boys eventually pushed him down and broke his arm. The court observed that the teacher should have at least questioned the student when he originally reported that he felt unsafe.[99]

[93]*See, e.g.*, Gallegos v. Escalon, 993 S.W.2d 422 (Tex. App. 1999).

[94]Rykowsky v. Dickinson Pub. Sch. Dist., 508 N.W.2d 348 (N.D. 1993).

[95]Santavicca v. City of Yonkers, 518 N.Y.S.2d 29 (App. Div. 1987).

[96]*See, e.g.*, Malia v. Monchak, 543 A.2d 184 (Pa. Commw. 1988).

[97]Morrison v. Mobile Cty. Bd. of Educ., 495 So. 2d 1086 (Ala. 1986).

[98]Rocci v. Ecole Secondaire MacDonald-Cartier, 755 A.2d 583 (N.J. 2000).

[99]Brammer v. Bossier Par. Sch. Bd., 183 So. 3d 606 (La. App. 2015); *see also* Munn v. Hotchkiss Sch., 165 A.3d 1167 (Conn. 2017) (ordering a private boarding school to pay $41.45 million in damages for failing to warn a student about the potential to contract tick-borne encephalitis on a school-sponsored trip; the boy became paralyzed after being bitten).

Damages in tort suits can be either compensatory or punitive, and many include attorneys' fees that are typically calculated as a percentage of the total award (often one-third if the case settles prior to trial and 40 percent if the case is tried). **Compensatory damages include past and future economic loss, medical expenses, and pain and suffering.** These awards are intended to make the plaintiff whole, at least to the degree that money is capable of doing so. If a plaintiff's previous injury has been aggravated, the defendant is generally liable only for the additional loss.

Although damages vary by state, it is common to cap awards for intangibles (e.g., pain, suffering, loss of consortium, mental anguish) but not to cap damages for actual loss. When plaintiffs prevail, it is important to note that school district assets are not subject to execution, sale, garnishment, or attachment to satisfy the judgment. Instead, judgments are paid from funds appropriated specifically for that purpose, acquired through revenue bonds, or available because of insurance. If sufficient funds are not forthcoming, it is common for states to require fiscal officers to certify the amount of unpaid judgment to the taxing authority for inclusion in the next budget. When the amounts are significant, many states permit districts to pay installments (at times up to ten years) for payment of damages that do not represent actual loss.

Furthermore, in most states, educators can be sued individually unless they are "save harmlessed" by their school district. Under save harmless (also called "hold harmless") provisions, the school district agrees to provide legal representation for their employees and to pay any resulting liability. When educators are not "save harmlessed" and do not have personal or union-provided insurance coverage, their personal assets (e.g., cars, boats, bank accounts) may be attached, their wages may be garnished, and a lien may be placed on their property. Where a lien is filed, the property may not be sold until the debt is satisfied.

Finally, punitive damages are awarded to punish particularly wanton or reckless acts and are in addition to actual damages.[100] The amount is discretionary with the jury and is based on the circumstances, behaviors, and acts. Unlike the calculation of actual damages, the debtor's financial worth may be a factor in determining punitive amounts. When jury verdicts are seemingly out of line, the court may reduce (*remittitur*) or increase (*additur*) the amount where either passion or prejudice is a factor.

CONCLUSION

All individuals, including educators, are responsible for their actions and can be liable for damages if they intentionally or negligently cause injury to others. Educators have a responsibility to act reasonably, but some negligent conduct is likely to occur. Consequently, educators should be knowledgeable about their potential liability under applicable state laws and should ensure that they are either protected by their school districts or have adequate insurance coverage for any damages that might be assessed against them.

[100]*See, e.g.*, Doe Parents v. Dep't of Educ., 58 P.3d 545 (Haw. 2002) (finding Hawaii Department of Education was liable to plaintiff for the full extent of damages awarded, at least $400,000, in a case involving a teacher who molested a student).

Moreover, school personnel should refrain from intentionally injuring others, engaging in assaultive behaviors, detaining students for inappropriate reasons, or participating in conduct that ultimately might result in the emotional distress of another. Educators also should be cautious when sharing information about colleagues or students as the dissemination of incorrect or confidential information may result in a defamation lawsuit. To guard against liability, teachers and administrators should be cognizant of the following principles of tort law.

1. The educator's conduct in a given situation is gauged by whether a reasonably prudent educator (with the special skills and training associated with that role) would have acted in a similar fashion under like conditions.

2. Educators owe students a duty to provide proper instruction and adequate supervision; to maintain equipment, buildings, and grounds in proper condition; and to provide warnings regarding any known dangers.

3. Educators are expected to exercise a standard of care commensurate with the duty owed.

4. Foreseeability of harm is a crucial element in determining whether an educator's actions are negligent.

5. If an educator has information that a student poses a danger to self or others, parents and identifiable victims must be notified.

6. An intervening act can relieve an educator of liability for negligence if the act caused the injury and the teacher had no reason to anticipate that it would occur.

7. The common law doctrine of governmental immunity has been waived in most states (e.g., "safe place" statutes), but school districts may still successfully assert immunity if the claim does not fall under the scope of the waiver.

8. Where recognized, contributory negligence can be used to relieve school personnel of liability if it is established that the injured party's own actions were significant in producing the injury.

9. Under comparative negligence statutes, damages may be apportioned among negligent defendants and plaintiffs.

10. If an individual knowingly and voluntarily assumes a risk of harm, recovery for an injury may be barred.

11. School personnel can be held liable for battery if it is determined that they used excessive force with students.

12. Unnecessary restraint and excessive detainment of students can result in false imprisonment charges.

13. In severe cases in which conduct qualifies as "extreme" or "outrageous," educators or students can be found liable for the intentional infliction of mental distress.

14. Public officials can recover damages for defamation from the media for statements pertaining to public issues only if malice or an intentional disregard for the truth is shown.

15. Educators generally are protected from defamation charges by "qualified privilege" when their statements about students are made to appropriate persons and are motivated by proper intentions.

CHAPTER THREE

CHURCH/STATE RELATIONS

Efforts to identify the appropriate relationship between government and religion have generated substantial controversy in our nation, and since the mid-twentieth century, schools have provided the battleground for some of the most volatile disputes. Can prayers be said in public schools, extracurricular activities, or school board meetings? Can students select religious themes in completing school assignments? Can states provide funds for religious schools? These and other questions guide this chapter's discussion of the evolution and current status of church/state relations involving education.

Readers of this chapter should be able to:

- Describe the judicial tests used to assess Establishment Clause and Free Exercise Clause claims and the different remedies for violations of the two clauses.

- Discuss legal protection of private religious expression and legal prohibitions on government-sponsored religious expression.

- Identify the different legal standards applied to public school access for student religious meetings under the Equal Access Act and community religious meetings under the First Amendment.

- Analyze the circumstances under which students can be excused from public school assignments or requirements for religious reasons.

- Examine the legal issues involved with religious challenges to the public school instructional program.

- Explain how courts apply the Establishment and Free Exercise Clauses to state efforts to fund religious schools.

CONSTITUTIONAL FRAMEWORK

The First Amendment's Establishment Clause is used primarily to challenge governmental *advancement* of religion, whereas Free Exercise Clause claims usually challenge secular government regulations that impair the practice of religious beliefs.

The First Amendment to the United States Constitution stipulates in part that "Congress shall make no law respecting an establishment of religion or prohibiting the free exercise thereof." Although this amendment was directed toward the *federal* government, the Fourteenth Amendment, adopted in 1868, specifically placed restrictions on *state* actions impairing personal rights. In the twentieth century, the Supreme Court recognized that the Fourteenth Amendment's fundamental concept of "liberty" incorporates First Amendment guarantees and safeguards these rights against state interference.[1] **Because education is primarily a state function, most church/state controversies involving schools have been initiated through the Fourteenth Amendment to reach First Amendment protections**.

In the first major Establishment Clause decision, *Everson v. Board of Education*, the Supreme Court in 1947 reviewed the history of the First Amendment and concluded that the Establishment Clause (and its Fourteenth Amendment application to states) means:

> Neither a state nor the Federal Government can set up a church. Neither can pass laws which aid one religion, aid all religions, or prefer one religion over another. . . . In the words of Jefferson, the clause against establishment of religion by law was intended to erect a wall of separation between church and state.[2]

Thomas Jefferson's wall was used widely by the federal judiciary for more than thirty years following *Everson*, even though this phrase does not appear in the First Amendment.

In a 1971 case, *Lemon v. Kurtzman*, the Supreme Court articulated a three-part test to determine whether government acts violate the Establishment Clause.[3] **To withstand scrutiny under the *Lemon* test, government action must (1) have a secular (nonreligious) purpose, (2) have a primary effect that neither advances nor impedes religion, and (3) avoid excessive governmental entanglement with religion**. This test was used consistently in Establishment Clause cases involving school issues until 1992. However, Supreme Court Justices increasingly have voiced dissatisfaction with this test,[4] and few recent Supreme Court Establishment Clause rulings have relied solely on *Lemon*. Support for church/state separation may be waning, even in school cases where the separationist doctrine has been the strongest.

The current Supreme Court seems to favor an *endorsement* standard under which governmental action will be struck down if an objective observer would view it as having the purpose or effect of endorsing or disapproving religion. And on occasion, the Supreme Court has applied a *coercion* test, which bases an Establishment Clause violation on whether there is direct or indirect governmental coercion on individuals to profess a faith.[5] Some lower courts are attempting to cover all bases by reviewing government action under the *Lemon* test, the endorsement standard, and the coercion test (see Figure 3.1).

---

[1] *See* Cantwell v. Connecticut, 310 U.S. 296, 303 (1940).

[2] 330 U.S. 1, 15–16 (1947) (quoting Reynolds v. United States, 98 U.S. 145, 164 (1878)).

[3] 403 U.S. 602 (1971).

[4] *See* Lamb's Chapel v. Ctr. Moriches Union Free Sch. Dist., 508 U.S. 384, 398 (1993) (Scalia, J., concurring) (comparing the *Lemon* standard to a "ghoul" that rises from the dead "after being repeatedly killed and buried").

[5] *See* Lee v. Weisman, 505 U.S. 577 (1992).

FIGURE 3.1   Judicial Standards to Evaluate Challenged Government Action under the Establishment Clause

Government action violates the Establishment Clause if it:	
■ Has a religious purpose ■ Advances or impedes religion ■ Creates excessive government entanglement with religion	*Lemon* Test
■ Has a purpose or effect of endorsing or disapproving religion	Endorsement Test
■ Imposes direct or indirect government coercion on individuals to profess a faith	Coercion Test

While the Establishment Clause is used in public schools to challenge policies that allegedly promote religion, lawsuits brought under the Free Exercise Clause usually focus on secular school policies that allegedly interfere with religious practices. To evaluate free exercise claims, the judiciary traditionally has applied a balancing test including an assessment of whether practices dictated by a sincere and legitimate religious belief were impeded by the government action and, if so, to what extent. Finding such an impairment, the judiciary has evaluated whether the government action served a compelling interest justifying the burden imposed on the exercise of religious beliefs. Even with such a compelling interest, the judiciary still has required the government to attain its objectives through the means least burdensome on free exercise rights.

In a significant school case involving a free exercise claim, *Wisconsin v. Yoder*, the Supreme Court exempted Amish children from compulsory school attendance upon successful completion of eighth grade.[6] Although noting that the assurance of an educated citizenry ranks at the pinnacle of state functions, the Court nonetheless concluded that parents' rights to practice their legitimate religious beliefs outweighed the state's interest in mandating two additional years of formal schooling for Amish youth. The Court cautioned that its ruling was limited to the Amish who offer a structured vocational program to prepare their youth for a cloistered agrarian community rather than mainstream American society.

More recently, the Supreme Court ruled in *Trinity Lutheran Church v. Comer* that the Free Exercise Clause precludes denying a sectarian daycare program the opportunity to compete for a generally available government benefit solely on religious grounds.[7] The Court emphasized that the highest level of judicial scrutiny, *strict scrutiny*, must be applied

[6]406 U.S. 205 (1972). In 1990, the Supreme Court modified this balancing test, ruling that the government does not have to demonstrate a compelling interest to defend a criminal law that burdens the free exercise of religious beliefs. Distinguishing this case from *Yoder*'s combination of free exercise rights and parental rights, the Court majority concluded that without such a "hybrid" situation, individuals cannot rely on the Free Exercise Clause to be excused from complying with a valid criminal law prohibiting specific conduct, Emp't Div. v. Smith, 494 U.S. 872 (1990). Congress responded to this decision by enacting a law to reinstate the compelling interest requirement; *see infra* text accompanying note 116.

[7]137 S. Ct. 2012 (2017), *infra* text accompanying note 159.

FIGURE 3.2 Evaluating Challenged Governmental Action under the Free Exercise Clause

---

If an individual or religious institution alleges that government action:
- Interferes with the practice of religious beliefs or
- Discriminates on the basis of religion

Courts then assess:
- Is the individual/institution acting on a sincere religious belief?
- If yes, does the government action place a burden on the exercise of this belief?

If the above conditions are met, courts apply strict judicial scrutiny. There is a Free Exercise Clause violation, unless:
- The government has a compelling interest to justify the burden, and
- The government action is narrowly tailored to reach its goal (i.e., least restrictive on the practice of religious beliefs)

---

in assessing government discrimination based on an individual's or institution's religious affiliation. In essence, the Free Exercise Clause prohibits the government from disadvantaging persons or entities on the basis of religion without a compelling justification (see Figure 3.2). The full implications of this decision for state restrictions on the use of public funds for religious purposes are not yet known.[8]

Courts not only apply different criteria to assess claims under the Free Exercise and Establishment Clauses; they also impose different remedies for violations of the two clauses. **If government activity abridges the Establishment Clause (e.g., teacher-led prayer in public schools), the unconstitutional activity must cease. Where government action is found to impair the Free Exercise Clause (e.g., requiring student participation in sex education), accommodations to enable individuals or institutions to practice their religious beliefs may be required, but the secular government policy or program would not be eliminated.**

Troublesome church/state controversies involve competing claims under the Free Exercise and Establishment Clauses because there is an inherent tension between the two provisions. The controversies become even more complex when Free Speech Clause protections are implicated. For example, all three clauses are involved in students' assertions that they have a First Amendment right to voice their religious views in graduation speeches. This tension among First Amendment guarantees has complicated the judiciary's task in assessing claims regarding the role of religion in public schools and government relations with religious schools.

RELIGIOUS INFLUENCES IN PUBLIC SCHOOLS

Public schools cannot sponsor devotionals, whereas they must allow *private* religious expression under some circumstances.

---

[8]*See* William Thro & Charles Russo, *Odious to the Constitution: The Educational Implications of* Trinity Lutheran Church v. Comer, 346 EDUC. L. REP. 1 (2017) (arguing that this decision may significantly redefine the relationship between education and religion).

In two precedent-setting decisions in the early 1960s, the Supreme Court prohibited public schools from sponsoring daily prayer and Bible reading, concluding that such activities advance religion in violation of the Establishment Clause, and students' voluntary participation was irrelevant.[9] The fact that daily devotional activities were conducted under the auspices of the public school was sufficient to abridge the First Amendment. Yet, these rulings have not resolved some issues pertaining to religious influences in public education. Is the Establishment Clause violation lessened if students rather than teachers initiate the devotional activities or if religious observances are occasional rather than daily? Can religious speech be distinguished from other types of speech in applying restrictions? These and other issues are addressed below in connection with silent prayer statutes; school-sponsored versus private devotionals; religious displays, music, and holiday observances; proselytization in the classroom; and equal access for religious expression and groups.

Silent Prayer Statutes

Students have a free exercise right to engage in *private* devotional activities in public schools so long as they do not interfere with regular school activities. Indeed, it would be difficult to monitor whether students were engaging in silent prayer. Controversies have focused on state laws or school board policies that condone silent devotionals, thus placing the stamp of public school approval on such activities.

In 1985, the Supreme Court rendered its first and only opinion to date on this issue in *Wallace v. Jaffree*, invalidating an Alabama silent prayer law under the Establishment Clause.[10] The Court majority concluded that the only logical reason for adding the phrase "or voluntary prayer" to Alabama's silent meditation law was to encourage students to pray. But the Court indicated that laws calling for silent meditation or prayer in public schools without a legislative intent to impose prayer might withstand scrutiny under the Establishment Clause. **Therefore, the constitutionality of laws authorizing a moment of silence for prayer or meditation in public schools, which currently are on the books in a majority of the states, must be resolved on a case-by-case basis, and courts have rejected most recent challenges to such laws.**

For example, the Eleventh Circuit supported the termination of a high school teacher for refusing to comply with Georgia's law that requires each public school teacher to conduct a minute of quiet reflection at the opening of the school day.[11] Several other federal appellate courts similarly have upheld silent prayer statutes, reasoning that a time for quiet reflection is a good management strategy to prepare students for a day of learning.[12] Given these rulings, it appears that silent prayer provisions are not vulnerable to being invalidated under the Establishment Clause unless they represent a clear intent to have children pray in public schools.

[9]Sch. Dist., Abington Twp. v. Schempp, 374 U.S. 203 (1963); Engel v. Vitale, 370 U.S. 421 (1962).

[10]472 U.S. 38 (1985).

[11]Bown v. Gwinnett Cty. Sch. Dist., 112 F.3d 1464 (11th Cir. 1997).

[12]*See* Sherman v. Koch, 623 F.3d 501 (7th Cir. 2010); Croft v. Governor of Tex., 562 F.3d 735 (5th Cir. 2009); Brown v. Gilmore, 258 F.3d 265, 270 (4th Cir. 2001).

School-Sponsored versus Private Devotionals

Among the most controversial issues is what constitutes *private* religious expression in public schools. Such private expression does not trigger Establishment Clause restrictions because it is not sponsored by the public school.

***Weisman* and Its Progeny.**   The Supreme Court's 1992 decision in *Lee v. Weisman* generated a wave of legislative activity pressing the limits of the Establishment Clause. The divided *Weisman* Court struck down a Rhode Island school district's policy that permitted principals to invite clergy members to deliver invocations and benedictions at middle and high school graduation ceremonies.[13] The Court majority reasoned that the policy had a coercive effect; students felt peer pressure to participate in the devotionals at the school-sponsored graduation ceremony and should not have to make a choice between attending the graduation ceremony and respecting their religious convictions.

Negative reactions to this ruling resulted in school authorities and students finding creative strategies to include prayers in graduation ceremonies.[14] Because of the prohibition on *school-sponsored* religious activities, most post-*Weisman* controversies have involved *student-led* devotionals. **In some school districts, the graduation ceremony has been designated as a forum for student expression, so students' messages (including religious references) are not subject to review and do not bear the stamp of school approval**. The Ninth Circuit endorsed an Idaho school district's policy that prohibited school authorities from censoring students' graduation speeches and allowed student speakers (chosen by academic standing) to select a poem, reading, song, prayer, or any other presentation of their choice.[15] Finding the ceremony a forum for student expression, the court reasoned that the student speakers were selected based on secular criteria and were not advised to include devotionals in their remarks.

In two other Ninth Circuit cases, however, the appeals court upheld school districts in barring proselytizing graduation speeches that students had submitted to their principals for review in accordance with school policy. Unlike the first case, school authorities in these districts clearly maintained control of the graduation ceremony. Thus, the court found censorship of the proposed religious speeches appropriate to avoid an Establishment Clause violation.[16] The Second Circuit subsequently upheld school personnel in barring a

---

[13]505 U.S. 577 (1992).

[14]Some districts responded to *Weisman* by reinstating baccalaureate services, which had not been held for many years; students, churches, and other groups can rent space from the public school district to conduct such religious services that are not sponsored by the public school district, and school employees can participate in such private religious services. *See, e.g.,* Allen v. Sch. Bd., 782 F. Supp. 2d 1304 (N.D. Fla. 2011).

[15]Doe v. Madison Sch. Dist., 147 F.3d 832 (9th Cir. 1998), *vacated and remanded*, 177 F.3d 789 (9th Cir. 1999) (en banc) (vacating the panel decision because the plaintiff had graduated, but the contested policy remained in force); *see also* Griffith v. Butte Sch. Dist., 244 P.3d 321, 334 (Mont. 2010) (finding that the school district violated a student's speech rights by not allowing her to make "passing references" to her religious faith in her valedictory speech that did not represent the school).

[16]*See* Lassonde v. Pleasanton Unified Sch. Dist. 320 F.3d 979 (9th Cir. 2003); Cole v. Oroville Union High Sch. Dist., 228 F.3d 1092 (9th Cir. 2000); *see also* Corder v. Lewis Palmer Sch. Dist., 566 F.3d 1219 (10th Cir. 2009) (upholding the school's decision to require a student to publicly apologize for making a religious valedictory speech that had not been approved; her speech represented the school and was subject to the principal's review).

student from including a Bible quotation and a blessing of the audience in her speech at the middle school's "moving up" ceremony, finding prohibited religious speech representing the school.[17] **The central consideration seems to be whether the school has explicitly created a forum for student expression in the graduation ceremony or has retained control over students' graduation speeches.**

Student Elections to Authorize Prayers.   Especially volatile controversies surround having students decide by election to include student-led devotionals in graduation cere-monies and other school activities. Federal appellate courts have differed regarding the constitutionality of such elections.[18]

In a 2000 decision, *Santa Fe Independent School District v. Doe*, the Supreme Court found an Establishment Clause violation in a Texas school district's policy authorizing student-led devotionals before public school football games.[19] The controversial policy, and an identical graduation policy, authorized two elections—one to determine whether to have invocations and the other to select the student to deliver them. The Supreme Court limited its ruling to the football game policy, noting that such events occur more often than graduation ceremonies, involve a more diverse age span of students, and cannot be justified to solemnize sporting events. **The Court majority declared that student-led expression at a school event on school property and representing the student body under the supervision of school personnel could not be considered private speech.[20]** The degree of school involvement gave the impression that the devotionals at issue represented the school, leading the Court to conclude that the practice had a sham secular purpose and entailed both perceived and actual endorsement of religion. **Noting that the purpose of the Bill of Rights is to shield certain subjects from the political process, the Court held that the Establishment Clause infraction cannot be eliminated by delegating decisions to students.** But the Court also emphasized that only state sponsorship of devo-tionals violates the Establishment Clause; nothing in the Constitution prohibits public school students from voluntarily praying at school.

Post–*Santa Fe* Rulings.   The *Santa Fe* decision did not resolve what distinguishes pro-tected, private religious expression from unconstitutional school-sponsored devotionals. Indeed, some post–*Santa Fe* federal appellate rulings reflect an expansive stance regarding the reach of the Free Speech Clause in protecting students' private religious expression in public schools. For example, the Eleventh Circuit reaffirmed two pre–*Santa Fe* opinions

---

[17]A.M. *ex rel.* McKay v. Taconic Hills Cent. Sch. Dist., 510 F. App'x 3 (2d Cir. 2013).

[18]*Compare* ACLU of N.J. v. Black Horse Pike Reg'l Bd. of Educ., 84 F.3d 1471 (3d Cir. 1996), *with* Jones v. Clear Creek Indep. Sch. Dist., 930 F.2d 416 (5th Cir. 1991), *vacated and remanded*, 505 U.S. 1215 (1992), *on remand*, 977 F.2d 963 (5th Cir. 1992).

[19]530 U.S. 290 (2000).

[20]*Id.* at 310. The Court emphasized that it is necessary to carefully review the history and context of the chal-lenged action in determining its facial validity, *id.* at 317; *see also* Doe v. Elmbrook Sch. Dist., 658 F.3d 710 (7th Cir. 2011), *rev'd en banc*, 687 F.3d 840 (7th Cir. 2012) (finding an Establishment Clause violation in a public school holding its graduation ceremony in a church with a large cross over the dais and religious banners and staffed information booths displaying proselytizing literature in the lobby).

in which it upheld a school district's policy authorizing seniors to select graduation speakers who could choose religious content[21] and lifted an injunction that had prohibited students from expressing religious views in most public school settings in an Alabama district.[22] The appeals court declared that the Establishment Clause does not *require* and the Free Speech Clause does not *permit* suppressing student-initiated religious expression in public schools or relegating it to whispers or behind closed doors. The Eleventh Circuit reasoned that school censorship of *private* student religious expression abridges the First Amendment, emphasizing that all student religious speech in public schools should not be equated with expression *representing* the school.[23]

TENSION WITHIN THE FIRST AMENDMENT

PRIVATE religious speech
protected by the Free Exercise and Free Speech Clauses

Versus

GOVERNMENT-SPONSORED religious speech
barred by the Establishment Clause

In light of *Santa Fe* and its progeny, courts will review the legislative history of school district policies to ascertain whether there has been a pattern of efforts to infuse devotionals in the public schools. **Student religious expression may be considered private if it is truly student initiated, but the *Santa Fe* decision casts doubt on the legality of holding student elections to determine whether student-led devotionals will be included in school-sponsored activities**.

Other Devotional Expression. The Eighth Circuit broadly interpreted what constitutes private in contrast to school-sponsored religious expression in ruling that a school board member's unscheduled recitation of the Lord's Prayer at the graduation ceremony did not abridge the Establishment Clause.[24] The school district traditionally allowed board members with graduating children to deliver short messages, and the court reasoned that the board member's decision to include the Lord's Prayer at the end of his remarks was private expression. In a more recent case that attracted national media attention, a school district ultimately changed its policy and allowed cheerleaders to display religious messages on banners at athletic events. Despite the policy change, the Texas Supreme Court ruled that the issue was not moot and allowed the case to proceed as the school district could change

---

[21]Adler v. Duval Cty. Sch. Bd., 206 F.3d 1070 (11th Cir. 2000) (en banc), *vacated and remanded*, 531 U.S. 801 (2000), *reinstated on remand*, 250 F.3d 1330 (11th Cir. 2001).

[22]Chandler v. James, 180 F.3d 1254 (11th Cir. 1999), *vacated and remanded*, 530 U.S. 1256 (2000), *reinstated on remand sub nom.* Chandler v. Siegelman, 230 F.3d 1313 (11th Cir. 2000).

[23]*Chandler*, 230 F.3d at 1315.

[24]Doe v. Sch. Dist., 340 F.3d 605 (8th Cir. 2003).

its policy again. The court recognized that the cheerleaders had previously secured an injunction because the banners were considered private expression, but the Texas high court did not resolve this issue.[25]

It was assumed until 2014 that prayers at school board meetings, where students might be present, would abridge the Establishment Clause, and two federal appellate courts had so ruled.[26] However, the continued vitality of these decisions is unlikely, given the Supreme Court's 2014 opinion in *Town of Greece v. Galloway*.[27] **In this decision, the Court relied heavily on historical practices in upholding the use of sectarian prayers in town meetings, similar to the rationale used to uphold ministers saying prayers in legislative sessions,[28] despite children often being present at the town meetings.** In 2017, the Fifth Circuit decided that allowing students to deliver a message—usually religious—before each monthly school board meeting was more akin to devotionals in a town meeting or legislative session than in a school classroom.[29]

Religious Displays, Music, and Holiday Observances

The display of religious documents, the observance of religious holidays, and the use of religious music in public schools also remain controversial. In 1980, the Supreme Court declined to hear an appeal of a decision allowing religious holiday observances and the temporary display of religious symbols in public schools,[30] but a week later, in *Stone v. Graham*, the divided Court struck down a Kentucky law calling for the posting of the Ten Commandments in public school classrooms.[31] In the first case, the historical and cultural significance of Christmas convinced the Eighth Circuit that the prudent and objective observance of the Christmas holiday in public schools does not serve to advance religion, despite religious songs like *Silent Night* being sung and the nativity scene being displayed.[32]

In contrast, the five-member Supreme Court majority in *Stone* was not persuaded that the Ten Commandments' historical and cultural significance justified posting this religious document in public schools. The majority held that the purpose behind the Kentucky legislation was to advance a particular religious faith in violation of the Establishment Clause; the constitutional impairment was not neutralized because the copies were purchased with private donations.

---

[25]Matthews v. Kountze Indep. Sch. Dist., 484 S.W.3d 416 (Tex. 2016).

[26]*See* Doe v. Indian River Sch. Dist. 653 F.3d 256 (3d Cir. 2011); Joyner v. Forsyth Cty., 653 F.3d 341 (4th Cir. 2011).

[27]134 S. Ct. 1811 (2014).

[28]*See* Marsh v. Chambers, 463 U.S. 783 (1983).

[29]Am. Humanist Ass'n v. McCarty, 851 F.3d 521 (5th Cir. 2017), *cert. denied*, 138 S. Ct. 470 (2017).

[30]Florey v. Sioux Falls Sch. Dist., 619 F.2d 1311 (8th Cir. 1980).

[31]449 U.S. 39 (1980).

[32]*Florey*, 619 F.2d at 1314.

Disputes over religious displays have continued. In addition to cases outside the school domain,[33] the Third Circuit in 2016 held that a parent had standing to seek nominal damages and injunctive relief because of her child's exposure to a Ten Commandments monument among other artifacts beside the high school gymnasium entrance.[34] The year before, a Pennsylvania federal district court ruled that a Ten Commandments monument on a junior high school's grounds did not have a secular purpose and would appear to endorse religion to reasonable observers.[35]

Other religious displays in public schools have been controversial as well. **Courts have supported school authorities in removing religious pictures, murals, and banners from public schools**.[36] An Indiana federal district court struck down a school district's use of a live nativity scene, with faculty reciting the story of Jesus' birth from the Bible, in its Christmas Spectacular. But the court upheld the altered program that includes a brief display of the nativity scene using mannequins.[37] The Tenth Circuit endorsed a school district's use of the city's symbol of three crosses in a sculpture and on district maintenance vehicles, finding no religious motives because the city's name (Las Cruces) means "the crosses."[38] Also, the Fourth Circuit upheld a Virginia law requiring the posting of "in God We Trust" in public schools,[39] and the Second Circuit rejected a challenge to a school's policy that was designed to recognize diverse holiday customs.[40] A New Jersey federal district court found that inclusion of religious holidays, such as Christmas, Kwanzaa, and Hanukkah, on school district calendars broadened students' sensitivity toward religious diversity and their knowledge of the role of religion in the development of civilization.[41]

[33]*Compare* Van Orden v. Perry, 545 U.S. 677 (2005) (upholding the long-standing display of a Ten Commandments monument with other monuments on the Texas state capitol grounds to pay tribute to the state's history), *with* McCreary Cty. v. ACLU, 545 U.S. 844 (2005) (striking down the display of framed copies of the Ten Commandments in two Kentucky county courthouses; finding that attempts to add secular items to the displays did not eliminate their initial religious purpose); *see also* Pleasant Grove City v. Summum, 555 U.S. 460 (2009) (rejecting the Summums' claim of a constitutional right to display their seven principles in a Utah city park because the Ten Commandments were displayed, reasoning that the decision as to which privately donated monuments to display represented government speech that is exempt from First Amendment scrutiny).

[34]Freedom from Religion Found. v. New Kensington Arnold Sch. Dist., 832 F.3d 469 (3d Cir. 2016). Nominal damages of a trivial sum (e.g., $1.00) may be awarded when a court finds a legal wrong but no financial loss.

[35]Freedom from Religion Found. v. Connellsville Area Sch. Dist., 127 F. Supp. 3d 283 (W.D. Pa. 2015).

[36]*See, e.g.*, Bannon v. Sch. Dist., 387 F.3d 1208 (11th Cir. 2004); Gernetzke v. Kenosha Unified Sch. Dist., 274 F.3d 464 (7th Cir. 2001).

[37]Freedom from Religion Found. v. Concord Cmty. Schs., 240 F. Supp. 3d 914 (N.D. Ind. 2017); *see also* Freedom from Religion Found. v. Concord Cmty. Schs., 207 F. Supp. 3d 862 (N.D. Ind. 2016).

[38]Weinbaum v. Las Cruces, 541 F.3d 1017 (10th Cir. 2008).

[39]Myers v. Loudoun Cty. Pub. Schs., 418 F.3d 395 (4th Cir. 2005).

[40]Skoros v. City of N.Y., 437 F.3d 1 (2d Cir. 2006) (finding that inclusion of the Jewish menorah and Muslim star and crescent in the display did not abridge free exercise rights of Christian children); *see also* Sechler v. State Coll. Area Sch. Dist., 121 F. Supp. 2d 439 (M.D. Pa. 2000) (rejecting the claim that a school district's winter program featuring Kwanzaa, Hanukkah, Christmas, and other holiday traditions was not Christian enough).

[41]Clever v. Cherry Hill Twp. Bd. of Educ., 838 F. Supp. 929 (D.N.J. 1993); *see also* Guyer v. Sch. Bd., 634 So. 2d 806 (Fla. Dist. Ct. App. 1994) (holding that the display of witches at Halloween does not promote a nontheistic religion or give an impression that the public school endorses Wicca).

The use of religious music in public school programs also has generated controversy. The Ninth Circuit endorsed a Washington principal's decision to prohibit a school woodwind ensemble's choice of *Ave Maria* as its graduation performance piece, finding that the decision did not inhibit religion or free expression under the First Amendment.[42] The Third Circuit also rejected a challenge to a school board policy that prohibited the performance of celebratory religious music in school concerts and programs as not inhibiting religion or impairing students' rights to receive information and ideas.[43] This represents somewhat of a change in judicial posture, because in several earlier cases, courts had upheld school districts' justifications for allowing choirs to perform religious music.[44] It appears that public schools can, but are not obligated to, include religious songs in performances that do not promote a specific faith.

Religious displays, music, and holiday observances are destined to remain controversial. **Courts seem likely to continue to strike down the display of sectarian documents in public schools and to uphold school boards' restrictions on religious music even though the objective recognition of religious holidays will presumably withstand judicial scrutiny.**

Proselytization in the Classroom

Because teachers and other school personnel are working with a vulnerable captive audience in public schools, their actions have been scrutinized to ensure that classrooms are not used as a forum to indoctrinate sectarian beliefs. Courts have enjoined teacher-initiated devotionals in the classroom and ordered teachers to:

- remove religiously oriented books from a classroom library and refrain from silently reading the Bible during school hours;[45]
- stop using religious references in delivering the instructional program;[46]
- cover a proselytizing shirt ("Jesus 2000, J2K") at school;[47]
- remove a classroom display of news articles promoting Christianity and a poster publicizing the National Day of Prayer;[48] and
- remove religious banners from the classroom.[49]

---

[42]Nurre v. Whitehead, 580 F.3d 1087 (9th Cir. 2009).

[43]Stratechuk v. Bd. of Educ., 587 F.3d 597 (3d Cir. 2009).

[44]*See, e.g.*, Bauchman v. W. High Sch., 132 F.3d 542 (10th Cir. 1997); Florey v. Sioux Falls Sch. Dist., 619 F.2d 1311 (8th Cir. 1980).

[45]Roberts v. Madigan, 921 F.2d 1047 (10th Cir. 1990) (enjoining the school board, however, from removing the Bible from the school library, noting its literary and historical significance); *see also* Freshwater v. Mt. Vernon City Sch. Dist., 1 N.E.3d 335 (Ohio 2013) (upholding teacher's termination for refusing to remove religious materials displayed in his classroom, but recognizing the teacher's free exercise right to display his personal Bible on his desk), *infra* text accompanying note 129.

[46]Marchi v. Bd. of Coop. Educ. Servs., 173 F.3d 469 (2d Cir. 1999).

[47]Downing v. W. Haven Bd. of Educ., 162 F. Supp. 2d 19 (D. Conn. 2001).

[48]Lee v. York Cty. Sch. Div., 484 F.3d 687 (4th Cir. 2007) (holding that the expression was curricular in nature, so it constituted an employment dispute and not protected expression).

[49]Johnson v. Poway Unified Sch. Dist., 658 F.3d 954 (9th Cir. 2011).

In these decisions, courts recognized that educators cannot use their positions of power and prestige in public schools to influence their students' religious beliefs. Courts additionally have not been convinced that asking teachers to remove religious postings in the classroom abridges free speech rights.[50]

The Ninth Circuit also rejected a charter school's challenge to Idaho's ban on the inclusion of sectarian texts in public schools, concluding that the ban was designed to avoid religious inculcation. The court reasoned that the school curriculum represents government speech, not private expression, and the policy does not violate the Establishment or Equal Protection Clauses.[51] The Third Circuit previously backed a school district in prohibiting a parent from reading the Bible to her child's kindergarten class because the parent represented the school.[52] And the Maryland federal district court denied a school district's motion to dismiss claims that a teacher was promoting Islam in classroom assignments and that the district retaliated against a parent by barring him from the school for expressing his concerns.[53] Moreover, courts have upheld the dismissal of teachers who disregarded selected aspects of the curriculum that conflicted with their religious values.[54] **Public school educators enjoy a constitutional right to their religious beliefs, but they do not have a right to freely express those beliefs to their students**.

Several controversies have involved coaches praying in locker rooms or during games. The Third Circuit ruled that a coach kneeling and bowing his head when his team engaged in locker-room prayer abridged the Establishment Clause.[55] More recently, the Ninth Circuit did not actually reach the Establishment Clause issue, reasoning that the coach spoke as a public employee when he knelt and prayed on the fifty-yard line immediately after football games.[56] Because his expression represented the school, his request for a preliminary injunction to require the school district to allow such expression was denied. The court noted that the coach took advantage of his position to voice his religious views in a venue where impressionable students were present.

The words "under God," which were added to the Pledge of Allegiance to the American flag in 1954, also have been challenged as unconstitutionally proselytizing students.

---

[50]*See* Silver v. Cheektowaga Cent. Sch. Dist., 670 F. App'x 21 (2d Cir. 2016), *cert. denied*, 137 S. Ct. 2292 (2017).

[51]Nampa Classical Acad. v. Goesling, 447 F. App'x 776 (9th Cir. 2011).

[52]Busch v. Marple Newton Sch. Dist., 567 F.3d 89 (3d Cir. 2009).

[53]Wood v. Bd. of Educ., 2016 WL 8669913 (D. Md. Sept. 30, 2016).

[54]*See, e.g.*, Palmer v. Bd. of Educ., 603 F.2d 1271 (7th Cir. 1979) (upholding dismissal of a kindergarten teacher who refused to teach about patriotic holidays and historical figures for religious reasons); *see also* Grossman v. S. Shore Pub. Sch. Dist., 507 F.3d 1097 (7th Cir. 2007) (upholding dismissal of a school counselor for unilaterally deciding, based on her religious beliefs, to provide students with information on abstinence only rather than on other forms of birth control).

[55]Borden v. Sch. Dist. of Twp., 523 F.3d 153 (3d Cir. 2008) (noting that the coach had engaged in many years of prayer activities with the high school football team, so a reasonable observer would conclude that his silent activities endorsed religion). For a discussion of recent incidents of coaches imposing their religious beliefs on student team members, *see* John Dayton & Betul Tarhan, *Over a Half-Century After* Engel v. Vitale, *Coercive State-Sponsored Prayers Continue in U.S. Public Schools: Why Are Violations of Well-Established Law Tolerated and What Remedies Are Available?* 339 EDUC. L. REP. 595 (2017).

[56]Kennedy v. Bremerton Sch. Dist., 869 F.3d 813 (9th Cir. 2017), text accompanying note 47, Chapter 10.

Saying the Pledge in public schools is prescribed in more than four-fifths of the states, and, as discussed later, students have a right to opt out based on their religious or philosophical beliefs.[57] However, the Ninth Circuit attracted national attention in 2002 when it declared that the phrase "under God" could not be said in public schools because it endorses a belief in monotheism in violation of the Establishment Clause.[58] The appellate panel emphasized that the words "under God" had been inserted in the Pledge to promote religion rather than to advance the legitimate secular goal of encouraging patriotism. The Supreme Court reversed the Ninth Circuit's decision in 2004 without addressing the constitutional claim in *Elk Grove Unified School District v. Newdow*. The Court majority reasoned that under California law, the noncustodial parent, Newdow, lacked standing to challenge his daughter's participation in the Pledge of Allegiance.[59] Other courts have not been sympathetic to such challenges,[60] and the Supreme Court is not likely to strike down the inclusion of "under God" in the Pledge recited in public schools. If it were to do so, a strong negative political reaction could be assured.

Although school personnel cannot proselytize students, the Supreme Court has emphasized that it is permissible, even desirable, to teach the Bible and other religious documents from a literary, cultural, or historical perspective.[61] Many public schools across two-thirds of the states use the Bible as a textbook in academic courses, such as "the Bible as Literature."[62] Yet in some courses, the line is not clear between teaching about religion and instilling religious tenets. Numerous Bible study courses, particularly at the elementary school level, have been challenged as ploys to advance sectarian beliefs. Courts have struck down programs in which private groups have controlled the hiring and supervision of personnel or the selection of curricular materials.[63] While most challenges have involved instruction pertaining to the Bible and the Christian faith, the Ninth Circuit upheld a school's use of role-playing to teach seventh-grade world history students about Islam, reasoning that learning about the five pillars of Islam did not entail the practice of a religion.[64]

---

[57]*See* W. Va. State Bd. of Educ. v. Barnette, 319 U.S. 624 (1943), *infra* text accompanying note 102.

[58]Newdow v. U.S. Cong., 292 F.3d 597 (9th Cir. 2002), *opinion amended and superseded by* 328 F.3d 466 (2003), *rev'd sub nom.* Elk Grove Unified Sch. Dist. v. Newdow, 542 U.S. 1 (2004).

[59]*Id.*, 542 U.S. at 17–18.

[60]*See, e.g.*, Newdow v. Rio Linda Union Sch. Dist., 597 F.3d 1997 (9th Cir. 2010); Freedom from Religion Found. v. Hanover Sch. Dist., 626 F.3d 1 (1st Cir. 2010); Croft v. Perry, 624 F.3d 157 (5th Cir. 2010); Sherman v. Cmty. Consol. Sch. Dist. 21, 980 F.2d 437, 446 (7th Cir. 1992); Doe v. Acton-Boxborough Reg'l Sch. Dist., 8 N.E.3d 737 (Mass. 2014); *see also* Myers v. Loudoun Cty. Sch. Bd., 251 F. Supp. 2d 1262, 1268 (E.D. Va. 2003), *aff'd*, 418 F.3d 395 (4th Cir. 2005) (finding the Pledge's reference to God "theologically benign" and further ruling that nonparticipating students were not punished, even though recitation of the Pledge was part of a citizenship reward program).

[61]*See* Sch. Dist., Abington Twp. v. Schempp, 374 U.S. 203, 225 (1963).

[62]*See* The Bible Literacy Project (n.d.), http://www.bibleliteracy.org; Lauren Cooley, *Accommodating Diversity: Teaching about Religion in Public Schools*, 12 RUTGERS J.L. & RELIG. 347 (2011).

[63]*See. e.g.*, Crockett v. Sorenson, 568 F. Supp. 1422 (W.D. Va. 1983).

[64]Eklund v. Byron Union Sch. Dist., 154 F. App'x 648 (9th Cir. 2005).

Some controversies over proselytization in the classroom have not challenged teachers' activities but have entailed requests by students to include sectarian materials in their presentations, artwork, or other school assignments. In most of these cases, the schools have prevailed in denying the students' requests. For example, the Sixth Circuit upheld a school district's prohibition on an elementary school student showing in class a videotape of herself singing a proselytizing religious song, concluding that student projects can be censored to ensure that the school is not viewed as endorsing religious content.[65] The same court backed a junior high school teacher who gave a student a grade of zero on a report because the student had cleared a different topic with the teacher but then wrote her report on the life of Jesus Christ.[66] One judge observed that the student might have raised a legitimate free speech issue if the assignment had been to write an opinion piece on any topic of personal interest, and religious content had been rejected.[67]

Despite these cases, by 2017, a number of states had enacted or were considering laws to protect students' decisions to use religious materials in completing class assignments. To illustrate, in 2007, Texas enacted a law allowing religious beliefs to be expressed in homework, artwork, and other assignments, and stipulating that students should not be rewarded or penalized because of the religious content of their work.[68] Two years later, Arizona enacted legislation that prohibits public schools from discriminating against students or parents on the basis of religious viewpoint or expression; students cannot be penalized or rewarded for including religious content or views in class assignments.[69] Even though students usually have not been successful in challenging school requirements under the First Amendment, state law may protect their use of religious materials in school assignments.[70]

---

[65]DeNooyer v. Merinelli, 12 F.3d 211 (6th Cir. 1993). *See* text accompanying notes 11, 48, Chapter 5, for a discussion of First Amendment protection in connection with viewpoint discrimination; *see also* O.T. *ex rel.* Turton v. Frenchtown Elementary Sch. Dist., 465 F. Supp. 2d 369 (D.N.J. 2006) (upholding student's right to sing a religious song in the school talent show, which was viewed as a limited public forum; the student was not conveying the school's message in her performance).

[66]Settle v. Dickson Cty. Sch. Bd., 53 F.3d 152 (6th Cir. 1995); *see also* C.H. v. Oliva, 226 F.3d 198 (3d Cir. 2000) (finding no constitutional violation in connection with refusal to let a student read a Bible story to classmates or in the removal of the student's religious poster from the school hallway, but remanding the case to allow plaintiffs an opportunity to substantiate a viable complaint regarding the poster).

[67]*Settle*, 53 F.3d. at 159 (Batchelder, J., concurring).

[68]Religious Viewpoints Antidiscrimination Act, TEX. EDUC. CODE ANN. § 25.151 (2018).

[69]Students' Religious Liberties Act, ARIZ. REV. STAT. ANN. § 15-110 (2018). Also, the U.S. Department of Education has provided guidance stipulating that students may express their religious views in their homework, artwork, and other written and oral assignment, despite some contrary judicial rulings. U.S. Dep't of Educ., *Guidance on Constitutionally Protected Prayer in Public Elementary and Secondary Schools* (Feb. 7, 2003), http://www2.ed.gov/policy/gen/guid/religionandschools/prayer_guidance.html.

[70]Florida's law, enacted in 2017, authorizes school employees as well as students to engage in religious activities under specified circumstances in public schools, Florida Student and School Personnel Religious Liberty Act, FLA. STAT. § 1002.206 (2018). Some of these laws may be vulnerable to Establishment Clause challenges, but these student religious liberties laws have not been invalidated to date.

Equal Access for Religious Expression and Groups

In the 1960s and 1970s, it often was assumed that religious speech must be barred from government forums to comply with the Establishment Clause. More recently, however, the Supreme Court has reasoned that singling out religious views for differential treatment compared with other *private* expression would be unconstitutional viewpoint discrimination, which abridges the Free Speech Clause.[71] In essence, the government can be barred from promoting religious views, but private religious and secular speech deserves the same First Amendment protection.

Equal Access Act.   In 1984, Congress enacted the Equal Access Act (EAA), which augmented the existing protections of the Free Speech Clause. **Under this law, federally funded secondary schools that have established a limited open forum for student groups to meet during noninstructional time cannot deny school access to noncurriculum student-led groups based on the religious, philosophical, or political content of their meetings.**[72] In 1990, the Supreme Court in *Board of Education of Westside Community Schools v. Mergens* rejected an Establishment Clause challenge to the EAA, recognizing the law's secular purpose of preventing discrimination against religious and other types of private student expression.[73] The Court distinguished government speech promoting religion that is prohibited by the Establishment Clause from private religious expression protected by the Free Speech and Free Exercise Clauses.[74] In subsequent cases, federal appellate courts have ruled that the EAA:

- prevails over state constitutional provisions requiring greater separation of church and state than demanded by the Establishment Clause;[75]
- authorizes student religious meetings during lunch if that is considered noninstructional time;[76]
- authorizes student religious groups to require certain officers to be Christians to preserve the spiritual content of their meetings;[77] and
- requires student religious groups to be provided equal access to fundraising activities, school bulletin boards, and other resources that are available to other student clubs.[78]

---

[71]*See* Widmar v. Vincent, 454 U.S. 263 (1981) (finding no Establishment Clause violation in providing student religious group's access to a forum created for student expression on state-supported college campuses). *But see* Christian Legal Soc'y v. Martinez, 561 U.S. 661 (2010) (upholding the Hastings Law School's denial of official recognition to a student religious group that did not comply with the university's nondiscrimination policy).

[72]20 U.S.C. §§ 4071–4074 (2018). *See* text accompanying note 10, Chapter 5, for an explanation of the types of government forums for expression.

[73]496 U.S. 226 (1990).

[74]*Id.* at 250. For a discussion of what constitutes a curriculum-related student group, *see* text accompanying note 84, Chapter 5.

[75]Ceniceros v. Bd. of Trs., 106 F.3d 878 (9th Cir. 1997); Garnett v. Renton Sch. Dist., 987 F.2d 641 (9th Cir. 1993).

[76]*Ceniceros*, 106 F.3d 878.

[77]Hsu v. Roslyn Union Free Sch. Dist., 85 F.3d 839 (2d Cir. 1996). *But see* Truth v. Kent Sch. Dist., 524 F.3d 957 (9th Cir. 2008) (upholding a school district's denial of recognition to a student Bible club that denied voting membership to students who did not pledge to abide by the Bible).

[78]Prince v. Jacoby, 303 F.3d 1074 (9th Cir. 2002).

FIGURE 3.3   Religious Meetings in Public Schools

Equal Access Act:
- protects only student-initiated meetings
- applies to secondary schools receiving federal aid
- is triggered if a school creates a forum for student expression during noninstructional time
- applies to meetings of noncurricular student groups
- allows public school staff to be present to maintain order but not to participate

First Amendment:
- applies to all public schools
- protects community religious meetings if at least one secular group meets during noninstructional time
- allows adults and children to participate in community religious meetings held in the school

Although there are limits on the reach of the EAA, this federal law codified for secondary students the concept of equal access and equal treatment of religious expression that currently guides First Amendment litigation as well. **Indeed, given recent broad interpretations of the Free Speech Clause in requiring equal treatment of private religious expression in public schools, there is some sentiment that the EAA may no longer be needed** (see Figure 3.3).

School Access for Community Groups.   The EAA applies *only* to students in secondary schools, so community religious groups desiring public school access during noninstructional time must rely on First Amendment protection. Since the early 1990s, the Supreme Court has made some definitive pronouncements about protecting private religious expression from viewpoint discrimination. In *Lamb's Chapel v. Center Moriches Union Free School District*, the Court held that if secular community groups are allowed to use the public school after school hours to address particular topics (e.g., family life, child rearing), then a sectarian group desiring to show a film series addressing these topics from a religious perspective cannot be denied public school access.[79]

The Supreme Court in a seminal 2001 decision, *Good News Club v. Milford Central School*, allowed a private Christian organization to hold its meetings in a New York public school after school hours.[80] The Milford School District had denied the Good News Club's request under its community-use policy that allows civic and recreational groups to use the school, but not for religious purposes, contending that the club affiliated with the Child Evangelism Fellowship was engaging in prohibited religious worship and instruction. Disagreeing with the school district and the lower courts, the Supreme Court in *Milford* held that the school district's policy discriminated against religious viewpoints in violation of the Free Speech Clause. **Under the *Milford* ruling, if a public school establishes a limited forum for community meetings during noninstructional time, it cannot bar religious groups, even though elementary students attending the school are the central**

[79]508 U.S. 384 (1993).
[80]533 U.S. 98 (2001).

participants in the devotional activities. The Court did not find a danger that the community would perceive the Good News Club's access as school district endorsement of religion.

In subsequent cases, lower courts have allowed community religious groups to display literature during a public school's back-to-school night and to post flyers and send them home with students.[81] The Eighth Circuit enjoined a school district from dropping the Good News Club from its after-school enrichment program.[82] And the same court even ruled that a teacher could participate in meetings of the Good News Club held at the elementary school where she taught.[83] Thus, the Supreme Court's interpretation of First Amendment protections afforded religious meetings held in public schools is far broader than protections under the EAA.[84]

Distribution of Religious Literature and Gifts.   The Supreme Court has not directly addressed the distribution of religious literature in public schools, and lower courts have rendered a range of opinions on this topic. Courts consistently have ruled that school personnel cannot give students Bibles or other religious materials, and most courts have prohibited religious sects, such as the Gideons, from coming to the school to distribute materials to captive public school audiences.[85]

Many recent controversies have focused on student requests to distribute religious publications. Like meetings of student-initiated religious groups, these requests pit Free Speech Clause protections against Establishment Clause restrictions.[86] **Some courts addressing PK–12 controversies have applied the "equal access" concept in concluding that the same legal principles govern students' distribution of religious and nonreligious literature.** For example, the Third Circuit held that a student's distribution of a flyer about a religious event did not pose a school disruption, so it could not be prohibited.[87] Also, an Arkansas federal district court awarded a

---

[81]*See* Child Evangelism Fellowship [CEF] v. Montgomery Cty. Pub. Schs., 457 F.3d 376 (4th Cir. 2006); CEF v. Stafford Twp. Sch. Dist., 386 F.3d 514 (3d Cir. 2004), *on remand*, 2006 U.S. Dist. LEXIS 62966 (D.N.J. Sept. 5, 2006).

[82]CEF v. Minneapolis Special Sch. Dist., 690 F.3d 996 (8th Cir. 2012).

[83]Wigg v. Sioux Falls Sch. Dist. 49-5, 382 F.3d 807 (8th Cir. 2004). *But see* Am. Humanist Ass'n v. Douglas Cty. Sch. Dist., 859 F.3d 1243 (10th Cir. 2017) (reversing the lower court in part and allowing one plaintiff's Establishment Clause challenge to proceed against the school district's participation in a Christian youth organization's collection and distribution of religious materials and fundraising activities for mission trips).

[84]Unlike meetings of community groups, school districts can likely deny requests for sectarian organizations to hold their weekly religious services in public schools. *See* Bronx Household of Faith v. Bd. of Educ., 750 F.3d 184 (2d Cir. 2014) (distinguishing permissible meetings to voice religious views in a forum created for community meetings from impermissible weekly religious services in public schools).

[85]*See, e.g.,* Roark v. S. Iron R-1 Sch. Dist., 573 F.3d 556 (8th Cir. 2009); Doe v. Duncanville Indep. Sch. Dist., 70 F.3d 402 (5th Cir. 1995); Berger v. Rensselaer Cent. Sch. Corp., 982 F.2d 1160 (7th Cir. 1993).

[86]*See* Rosenberger v. Rector & Visitors, 515 U.S. 819 (1995) (ruling that religious material must be treated like other material in student-initiated publications subsidized by the university).

[87]K.A. v. Pocono Mountain Sch. Dist., 710 F.3d 99 (3d Cir. 2013).

preliminary injunction to allow student distribution of flyers advertising a church party because all organizations but churches had been allowed to distribute flyers at the public school.[88] But a Washington federal district court supported the school district in preventing a student from distributing during the school day religious materials he did not create.[89]

Conflicting opinions have been rendered regarding student distribution of gifts with religious messages to classmates. The Third Circuit sided with school officials in prohibiting elementary school students from distributing pencils and candy canes with religious messages during classroom holiday parties because of the difficulty young children would have in distinguishing school sponsorship from the private religious expression.[90] The Sixth Circuit also upheld a principal's refusal to allow a student to "sell" pipe cleaner candy cane ornaments with religious messages at a simulated marketplace; the principal's decision to prevent use of this activity to advance religious beliefs was based on legitimate educational concerns.[91]

Yet in a long-running suit, the Fifth Circuit ruled in 2011 that two principals likely abridged the rights of students who were not allowed to distribute religious-themed candy canes and pencils with religious messages to classmates, finding viewpoint discrimination against private religious speech.[92] However, the court held that the principals were entitled to qualified immunity because decisions pertaining to student religious speech and the "murky waters of the Establishment Clause" are far from clear; the "general state of the law in this area is abstruse, complicated, and subject to great debate among jurists."[93]

Even private expression is subject to reasonable time, place, and manner regulations. For example, school policies requiring students to give the principal advance notice of the distribution of materials are permissible. The Fifth Circuit upheld content-neutral regulations that restricted where students could distribute materials during noninstructional time, reasoning that the school district had a legitimate interest in providing a focused learning environment for students.[94] Whereas reasonable restrictions can be imposed on *how* material is distributed, school districts cannot place a blanket ban on student distribution of religious literature.

[88]Wright v. Pulaski Cty. Special Sch. Dist., 803 F. Supp. 2d 980 (E.D. Ark. 2011).

[89]Leal v. Everett Pub. Schs., 88 F. Supp. 3d 1220 (W.D. Wash. 2015).

[90]Walz v. Egg Harbor Twp. Bd. of Educ., 342 F.3d 271 (3d Cir. 2003) (concluding that reasonable accommodations were made in that religious materials could be distributed before and after school and during recess).

[91]Curry v. Hensinger, 513 F.3d 570 (6th Cir. 2008).

[92]Morgan v. Swanson, 659 F.3d 359 (5th Cir. 2011); *see also* Pounds v. Katy Indep. Sch. Dist., 730 F. Supp. 2d 636 (S.D. Tex. 2010) (holding that religious messages could not be treated differently from other messages on greeting cards with student artwork for a school fundraiser).

[93]*Morgan*, 659 F.3d at 382.

[94]Morgan v. Plano Indep. Sch. Dist., 589 F.3d 740 (5th Cir. 2009); *see also* Victory Through Jesus Sports Ministry Found. v. Lee's Summit R-7 Sch. Dist., 640 F.3d 329 (8th Cir. 2011) (upholding a policy limiting distribution of a religious group's flyers to one time at the beginning of the school year).

ACCOMMODATIONS FOR RELIGIOUS BELIEFS

Religious exemptions from school observances, requirements, and assignments will be upheld so long as they do not interfere with the management of the school or the excused student's progress.

In addition to challenging sectarian influences in public schools, some students have asserted a right to accommodations so they can practice their religious beliefs. Conflicts have arisen over release-time programs for religious education and religious exemptions from secular school requirements and activities.

Release-Time Programs

Although the Supreme Court has struck down the practice of using public school classrooms for clergy to provide religious training to public school students during the instructional day,[95] the Court has recognized that the school can accommodate religion by releasing students to receive such religious training *off* public school grounds.[96] The Second Circuit found that a school district's release-time program did not endorse Christianity over other religions or violate the rights of nonparticipating students by directing religious criticism toward them,[97] and a release-time program was even upheld in a Virginia school district where students received an hour of religious instruction each week in a mobile unit parked at the edge of school property.[98] Courts have not been persuaded that offering a single choice of attending religious classes or remaining in the public school advances religion or that nonparticipating pupils are denied their state-created right to an education because academic instruction ceases during the release-time period.

In a Utah case, the Tenth Circuit held that time spent by public school students in a release-time program at a Mormon seminary could be counted toward satisfying compulsory school attendance and in calculating the school's state aid.[99] However, the court enjoined the school's practice of awarding high school credit for the secular aspects of daily instruction received at the seminary because the monitoring required would unconstitutionally entangle school officials with the church. In contrast, the Fourth Circuit more recently upheld a South Carolina school district's release-time program that awards students academic credit, pursuant to state law, for attending off-campus religious instruction.[100]

[95]McCollum v. Bd. of Educ., 333 U.S. 203 (1948).

[96]Zorach v. Clauson, 343 US. 306 (1952).

[97]Pierce v. Sullivan W. Cent. Sch. Dist., 379 F.3d 56 (2d Cir. 2004).

[98]Smith v. Smith, 523 F.2d 121 (4th Cir. 1975). It appears that programs in which all students are released early from school one day a week would be easier to defend constitutionally because students would not be restricted to either remaining at the public school or attending sectarian classes.

[99]Lanner v. Wimmer, 662 F.2d 1349 (10th Cir. 1981).

[100]Moss v. Spartanburg Cty. Sch. Dist., 683 F.3d 599 (4th Cir. 2012).

Even though the release-time concept has been judicially endorsed, courts have ruled that a few programs have violated the Establishment Clause. For example, an Indiana federal district court enjoined a nondenominational Christian release-time program that was held in a trailer parked in the school's parking lot because such religious instruction on school grounds during school hours conveyed a message of religious support and endorsement.[101]

Religious Exemptions from Secular Activities and Requirements

Courts have required school districts to accommodate reasonable, but not excessive, absences for students to practice their religious beliefs. More prevalent than requests for religious absences are requests for students to be excused from public school activities and requirements that allegedly impair the practice of their religious tenets. In evaluating whether school authorities must honor such requests, courts have attempted to balance parents' interests in directing the religious upbringing of their children against the state's interest in ensuring an educated citizenry.

Observances. **Courts have relied on the First Amendment in striking down required student participation in certain public school observances**. In the landmark case, *West Virginia State Board of Education v. Barnette*, the Supreme Court ruled in 1943 that students could not be required to pledge their allegiance to the American flag in contravention of their religious beliefs,[102] overturning a precedent established by the Court only three years earlier.[103]

Nonetheless, controversy still surrounds the nature of required exemptions from the Pledge. Courts have struck down laws or policies requiring students to stand during the Pledge, reasoning that such a requirement coerces students to participate, but conflicting rulings have been rendered regarding the legality of mandatory parental notification of nonparticipating students.[104] Furthermore, the Eleventh Circuit concluded that paddling a student because he silently raised his fist in protest during the Pledge of Allegiance was an unwarranted infringement on expression rights.[105] Of course, students who opt not to participate can be disciplined if they create a disturbance while others are reciting the Pledge.

---

[101]H.S. v. Huntington Cty. Cmty. Sch. Corp., 616 F. Supp. 2d 863 (N.D. Ind. 2009); *see also* Doe v. Shenandoah Cty. Sch. Bd., 737 F. Supp. 913 (W.D. Va. 1990) (granting a temporary restraining order against weekday religious education classes being held in buses—almost identical to public school buses—parked in front of the school, with instructors going into the school to recruit students).

[102]319 U.S. 624 (1943).

[103]Minersville Sch. Dist. v. Gobitis, 310 U.S. 586 (1940).

[104]*Compare* Frazier v. Winn, 535 F.3d 1279 (11th Cir. 2009) (holding that a student could not be forced to participate or stand during the Pledge, but upholding the state law provision requiring parental notification of nonparticipating students), *with* Circle Sch. v. Pappert, 381 F.3d 172 (3rd Cir. 2004) (ruling that a parental notification provision in state law abridged the First Amendment).

[105]Holloman v. Harland, 370 F.3d 1252 (11th Cir. 2004) (noting that he was protesting the public chastisement of a classmate for not reciting the Pledge); *see also* note 3 and text accompanying note 29, Chapter 5.

The Supreme Court has not directly addressed teachers' free exercise rights in connection with patriotic observances in public schools, but it is generally assumed that teachers, like students, have a First Amendment right to refuse to pledge allegiance as a matter of personal conscience. Teachers, however, cannot use their religious beliefs to deny students the opportunity to engage in this observance. If a school district requires the Pledge to be recited daily, teachers must make provisions for this observance in their classrooms. As discussed previously, whether "under God" can be said in the Pledge at all in public schools has been controversial, but to date, courts have not concluded that the contested phrase turns this patriotic observance into a prayer.[106]

Vaccination Requirements. Requests for exemptions from vaccination requirements periodically have become controversial following outbreaks of communicable diseases, such as the 2015 measles outbreak in Disneyland that spread to seventeen other states. **States clearly have the authority to require vaccination against communicable diseases as a prerequisite to school attendance and to prosecute parents who fail to have their children immunized for violating compulsory education laws.**[107]

Yet, parents have been quite successful in securing legislative exemptions if vaccination of their children interferes with their sincerely held religious beliefs, even though it can be argued that allowing such waivers negates the compelling need for the immunization requirement in the first place.[108] State religious exemptions have generated a range of judicial interpretations, with some courts broadly interpreting the circumstances that would allow parents to use a religious exemption.[109] However, other courts have more narrowly interpreted such exemptions as requiring immunization to conflict with stated beliefs of a recognized religious sect.[110] While controversies will likely continue in interpreting the

---

[106]*See supra* text accompanying note 59.

[107]*See. e.g.*, Phillips v. City of N.Y., 775 F.3d 538 (2d Cir. 2015); Caviezel v. Great Neck Pub. Schs., 500 F. App'x 16 (2d Cir. 2012); Workman v. Mingo Cty. Bd. of Educ., 419 F. App'x 348 (4th Cir. 2011). *But see* Flynn v. Estevez, 221 So. 3d 1241 (Fla. Dist. Ct. App. 2017) (holding that the church autonomy [ecclesiastical abstention] doctrine precluded the court from resolving a theological controversy between the parent and diocese over a Catholic school's vaccination requirement).

[108]*See* Brown v. Stone, 378 So. 2d 218 (Miss. 1979). All states allow medical exemptions for children, and all but three (California, Mississippi, West Virginia) allow religious waivers. Eighteen states allow exemptions if parents are philosophically opposed to immunization, and these waivers are the most controversial because they are the easiest for parents to obtain. Parents have used philosophical or personal belief exemptions to secure waivers for a range of reasons from ethical considerations to fears that vaccination causes autism. *See* Nat'l Conference of State Legislatures, *States with Religious and Philosophical Exemptions from School Immunization Requirements* (Dec. 20, 2017), http://www.ncsl.org/research/health/school-immunization-exemption-state-laws.aspx.

[109]*See, e.g.*, McCarthy v. Boozman, 212 F. Supp. 2d 945 (W.D. Ark. 2002) (holding that religious exemption confined to church members violated parents' free exercise rights); Berg v. Glen Cove City Sch. Dist., 853 F. Supp. 651 (E.D.N.Y. 1994) (holding that parents can qualify for a religious exemption even if official church doctrine does not prohibit vaccination).

[110]*See, e.g.*, Mason v. Gen. Brown Cent. Sch. Dist., 851 F.2d 47, 49 (2d Cir. 1988) (disallowing the use of a religious exemption based on the assertion that immunization is contrary to the "genetic blueprint"); Hanzel v. Arter, 625 F. Supp. 1259 (S.D. Ohio 1985) (rejecting parents' reliance on the religious exemption for the asserted conflict of vaccination with chiropractic ethics); *see also supra* text accompanying note 107.

reach of religious and other exemptions, the legislature's discretion to adopt these exemptions has not been questioned.[111]

Curriculum Components. Religious exemptions also have been sought from components of the curriculum. Whereas teachers cannot assert a free exercise right to disregard aspects of the state-prescribed curriculum, the judiciary has been more receptive to students' requests for exemptions from instructional requirements. Students, unlike teachers, are compelled to attend school, and for many, this means a public school. Accordingly, the judiciary has been sensitive to the fact that certain public school policies may have a coercive effect on religious practices. In balancing the interests involved, courts consider:

- the extent to which the school requirement burdens the exercise of sincere religious beliefs;
- the governmental justification for the requirement; and
- alternative means available to meet the state's objectives.

School authorities must have a compelling justification to deny students an exemption from a requirement that impairs the exercise of sincere religious beliefs.
Most requests for religious exemptions are handled at the classroom or school level and do not evoke legal controversies. When they have generated litigation, students often have been successful in securing religious exemptions from instructional activities, such as drug education, sex education, coeducational physical education, dancing instruction, officers' training programs, and specific course assignments where alternatives can satisfy the instructional objectives. Although individual children have been excused, the secular activities themselves have not been disturbed. For example, public schools often allow students to opt out of sex education instruction or require parental consent for children to participate in such instruction.

Religious exemptions have not been honored if considered unnecessary to accommodate the practice of religious tenets or if the exemptions would substantially disrupt the school or students' academic progress or pose a safety hazard. In an illustrative case, the Second Circuit rejected a parent's request for his son to be exempted from a Connecticut school district's mandatory health curriculum, finding such attendance rationally related to the legitimate governmental goal of providing students important health information.[112] However, the student was allowed to be excused from certain lessons found to be offensive. In a widely publicized 1987 case, the Sixth Circuit overturned the lower court's decision and rejected fundamentalist Christian parents' request that their children be excused from exposure to the reading textbooks used in elementary grades.[113] The appeals court reasoned that the readers did not burden the students' exercise of their religious beliefs, because the students were not required to profess a creed or perform

---

[111]For a discussion of legal challenges to vaccination requirements and judicial interpretations of religious and other exemptions allowed, *see* Martha McCarthy, *Student Vaccination Requirements: Can Nonmedical Exemptions Be Justified?* 320 EDUC. L. REP. 591 (2015).

[112]Leebaert v. Harrington, 332 F.3d 134 (2d Cir. 2003).

[113]Mozert v. Hawkins Cty. Bd. of Educ., 827 F.2d 1058 (6th Cir. 1987).

religious exercises. Courts also have denied religious exemptions for student athletes if an excusal from specific regulations might pose a safety risk or interfere with the management of athletic teams.[114]

States increasingly have adopted Religious Freedom Restoration Acts (RFRAs) that give citizens the right to be excused from various state requirements for religious reasons unless there is a compelling governmental interest in denying the request, and the government has pursued its interest through the least restrictive means.[115] These state provisions are modeled after the federal RFRA of 1993[116] and, like the federal law,[117] go beyond First Amendment guarantees. As of 2017, twenty-one states had adopted such laws, which have been controversial, particularly their potential conflict with anti-bias provisions that protect individuals based on their sexual orientation.[118] While these laws have not generated a body of school litigation to date, they may become more significant as the grounds used by parents to seek religious exemptions for their children from public school activities, observances, and requirements. Thus, parents may be able to use legislation to secure exemptions for their children, even if they cannot substantiate that particular instructional activities impair free exercise rights.

RELIGIOUS CHALLENGES TO THE SECULAR CURRICULUM

Most lawsuits claiming that components of the public school curriculum (e.g., evolution) advance an antitheistic religious belief have not succeeded.

Although courts often have been receptive to requests for individual exemptions from specific public school activities, the judiciary has not been inclined to allow the restriction of the secular curriculum to satisfy parents' religious preferences. The Supreme Court has recognized that "the state has no legitimate interest in protecting any or all religions from views distasteful to them."[119]

---

[114]*See, e.g.*, Menora v. Ill. High Sch. Ass'n, 683 F.2d 1030 (7th Cir. 1982).

[115]*See* Nat'l Conference of State Legislatures, *State Religious Freedom Restoration Acts* (May 4, 2017), http://www.ncsl.org/research/civil-and-criminal-justice/state-rfra-statutes.aspx.

[116]42 U.S.C. § 2000bb-1 (2018) (requiring a compelling government interest pursued through the least restrictive means for the government to substantially burden an individual's exercise of religion, even if the burden results from generally applicable rules). Congress enacted the federal RFRA in response to the Supreme Court's narrow interpretation of the reach of the Free Exercise Clause under certain circumstances. Emp't Div. v. Smith, 494 U.S. 872 (1990) (upholding the denial of unemployment benefits for violating a state drug prohibition applied to the ceremonial use of peyote). The Supreme Court subsequently invalidated application of the federal RFRA to state actions because it proscribed state conduct beyond the reach of the Fourteenth Amendment. *See* City of Boerne v. Flores, 521 U.S. 507 (1997), which stimulated the adoption of state RFRAs.

[117]*See* Burwell v. Hobby Lobby Stores, 134 S. Ct. 2751 (2014) (holding that the mandated employer insurance coverage for contraceptives under the federal Affordable Care Act violated the federal RFRA as applied to for-profit, closely held corporations).

[118]*See* Heidi Beirich, *"Religious Liberty" and the Anti-LGBT Right*, S. Poverty L. Ctr. (Feb. 11, 2016), https://www.splcenter.org/20160211/religious-liberty-and-anti-lgbt-right.

[119]Epperson v. Arkansas, 393 U.S. 97, 107 (1968) (quoting Joseph Burstyn, Inc. v. Wilson, 343 U.S. 495, 505 (1952)).

Challenges to the public school curriculum raise complex questions involving what constitutes religious beliefs and practices that are subject to First Amendment protections and restrictions. **In protecting the free exercise of beliefs, the Supreme Court has adopted an expansive view toward religion, but it has not found an Establishment Clause violation in connection with claims that public school instruction advances a nontheistic creed.** Nonetheless, several courts have suggested that secular religions should be subject to the same Establishment Clause standards applied to theistic religions, and the Third Circuit ruled that public school instructional modules in transcendental meditation unconstitutionally advanced a nontraditional religious belief (the Science of Creative Intelligence).[120] Also, the Ninth Circuit held that a nonprofit group had standing to proceed with an Establishment Clause challenge to magnet and charter schools using Waldorf methods that are guided by the spiritual science of anthroposophy.[121]

The Origin of Humanity

Instruction pertaining to the origin of human life has generated continuing legal disputes. Historically, several states by law barred the teaching of evolution because it conflicted with the biblical account of creation. In the famous *Scopes* "monkey trial" in the 1920s, the Tennessee Supreme Court upheld such a law, prohibiting the teaching of any theory that denies the Genesis version of creation or suggests "that man has descended from a lower order of animals."[122] However, the U.S. Supreme Court in 1968 struck down an Arkansas anti-evolution statute under the Establishment Clause, concluding that evolution is science (not a secular religion), and a state cannot restrict student access to such information simply to satisfy religious preferences.[123]

Almost two decades later, the Supreme Court in 1987 invalidated a Louisiana statute that mandated "equal time" for creation science and evolution and required school boards to make available curriculum guides, teaching aids, and resource materials on creation science.[124] **Reasoning that creationism is not science, the Court concluded that the law was intended to discredit scientific information and advance religious beliefs in violation of the Establishment Clause.** The Court did not accept the argument that the law promoted academic freedom and reasoned that it actually inhibited teachers' discretion to incorporate scientific theories about the origin of humanity into the curriculum. In subsequent cases, federal appellate courts have ruled that school districts:

- can require instruction in evolution;[125]
- can prohibit teaching the biblical account of creation in science classes;[126]

---

[120]Malnak v. Yogi, 592 F.2d 197 (3d Cir. 1979). *But see infra* text accompanying note 139.

[121]PLANS, Inc. v. Sacramento City Unified Sch. Dist., 319 F.3d 504 (9th Cir. 2003). Developed by Rudolf Steiner, anthroposophy is a formal educational or therapeutic system that relies on natural means to promote mental and physical health.

[122]Scopes v. Tennessee, 289 S.W. 363, 364 (Tenn. 1927).

[123]*Epperson*, 393 U.S. 97.

[124]Edwards v. Aguillard, 482 U.S. 578 (1987).

[125]*See* Peloza v. Capistrano Unified Sch. Dist., 37 F.3d 517 (9th Cir. 1994).

[126]*See* Webster v. New Lenox Sch. Dist., 917 F.2d 1004 (7th Cir. 1990).

- cannot make teachers issue a disclaimer that instruction in evolution is not meant to dissuade students from the biblical account;[127]
- cannot put stickers in biology texts warning that evolution is a theory that should be critically assessed;[128] and
- can terminate a teacher for displaying religious materials, showing videos on creationism and intelligent design (ID), and distributing to students a handout criticizing evolution.[129]

Supporters of teaching ID distinguish it from creationism because the ID doctrine contends that human beings are too complex to have evolved randomly by natural selection, but it does not mention God. In 2005, a Pennsylvania federal district court struck down a school board's requirement that administrators must read a statement that evolution is a theory and must refer students to a book explaining ID as an alternative theory. The court reasoned that the policy was a ploy to infuse religious beliefs into the public school science curriculum, finding little difference between ID and creationism.[130]

Nonetheless, disputes over teaching evolution and alternative theories persist in legislative and judicial forums. There has been political activity at the school district or state level pertaining to such instruction in forty states during the past decade.[131] In 2016, the Tenth Circuit rejected the claim that the current Kansas science standards promote atheism by not recognizing alternatives to evolution.[132] However, the Fifth Circuit previously upheld a teacher's termination for violating the Texas Education Agency's policy, which called for school personnel to remain neutral on the topic of creationism, because she had forwarded an email message to fellow teachers and to science organizations advertising a speech of an opponent of the biblical account.[133] Yet, the Ninth Circuit held that a teacher who allegedly made negative remarks in an advanced placement history course about religion generally and creationism specifically was not provided fair warning that the conduct would be subject to disciplinary action.[134]

Other Challenges

Allegations are being made that other components of the public school curriculum violate the Establishment Clause because they advance Eastern religions or secular humanism/ New Age theology, which critics claim disavows God and exalts humans as masters of

---

[127]*See* Freiler v. Tangipahoa Par. Bd. of Educ., 185 F.3d 337 (5th Cir. 1999).

[128]*See* Selman v. Cobb Cty. Sch. Dist., 390 F. Supp. 2d 1286 (N.D. Ga. 2005), *vacated* with instructions to conduct new evidentiary proceedings, 449 F.3d 1320 (11th Cir. 2006).

[129]*See* Freshwater v. Mt. Vernon City Sch. Dist., 1 N.E.3d 335 (Ohio 2013).

[130]*See* Kitzmiller v. Dover Area Sch. Dist., 400 F. Supp. 2d 707 (M.D. Pa. 2005).

[131]For information on recent controversies across states, *see* Nat'l Ctr. for Science Educ., *Evolution News* (n.d.), http://www.evolutionnews.org/tag/national-center-for-science-education.

[132]Citizens for Objective Pub. Educ. v. Kan. State Bd. of Educ., 821 F.3d 1215 (10th Cir. 2016).

[133]Comer v. Scott, 610 F.3d 929 (5th Cir. 2010).

[134]C.F. v. Capistrano Unified Sch. Dist., 654 F.3d 975 (9th Cir. 2011).

their own destinies. In addition to evolution, central targets have been sex education, values clarification, and outcome-based education, but few aspects of the curriculum have remained untouched by such claims. Inclusion of the popular *Harry Potter* series in public school libraries has been challenged because the books deal with wizardry and magic that allegedly advance the occult/satanism.[135]

Even courts that have considered nontheistic creeds to be "religions" for First Amendment purposes have not usually ruled that challenged public school courses and materials advance such creeds. In a 1987 case, the Eleventh Circuit reversed an Alabama federal judge's conclusion that a school district's use of several dozen home economics, history, and social studies books unconstitutionally advanced secular humanism, finding instead that the books instilled in students values such as "independent thought, tolerance of diverse views, self-respect, maturity, self-reliance, and logical decision-making."[136]

The Eighth Circuit also ruled that a Missouri teacher's contract was not renewed for impermissible reasons after she sent a "magic rock" home with each student, with a letter indicating that the rock is "special and unique, just like you!"[137] The court found community complaints that the letter and rock advanced New Ageism to be the basis for the board's action rather than the asserted concerns about the teacher's grading practices. The Second Circuit similarly found no unconstitutional advancement of a nontheistic religion in celebrating Earth Day or in role-playing as part of a drug prevention program using peer facilitators.[138]

More recently, a California appeals court rejected the claim that a yoga physical education class unconstitutionally established the Hindu religion, ruling that the class was a secular experience designed to improve physical flexibility and reduce stress.[139] Mindfulness programs, which include meditation and breathing exercises to improve students' focus and their ability to handle emotions, are becoming popular in a number of locales, and some parents have raised concerns that these programs advance Buddhist religious beliefs.[140] Although not yet generating litigation, it is unlikely that courts will find that mindfulness instruction violates the Establishment Clause.

---

[135]*See* Elizabeth Kennedy, *The Harry Potter Controversy: Book Banishing and Censorship Battles* (Mar. 18, 2017), http://childrensbooks.about.com/cs/censorship/a/banharry.htm; text accompanying note 26, Chapter 4.

[136]Smith v. Bd. of Sch. Comm'rs, 655 F. Supp. 939 (S.D. Ala. 1987), *rev'd*, 827 F.2d 684, 692 (11th Cir. 1987) (also rejecting the contention that the mere omission of Christian religious facts in the curriculum represented unconstitutional hostility toward theistic beliefs).

[137]Cowan v. Strafford R-VI Sch. Dist., 140 F.3d 1153, 1156 (8th Cir. 1998).

[138]Altman v. Bedford Cent. Sch. Dist., 245 F.3d 49 (2d Cir. 2001). The lower court had ruled that one teacher's assignment for students to construct images of a Hindu deity abridged the First Amendment and that making worry dolls amounted to preference of superstition over religion in violation of the Establishment Clause, but the plaintiffs were no longer attending the schools in question and thus lacked standing to pursue those claims.

[139]Sedlock v. Baird, 185 Cal Rptr. 3d 739 (Ct. App. 2015).

[140]*See* Christine Legere, *Calmer Choice: D-Y Challenge Faces Hurdles*, CAPE COD TIMES (Feb. 14, 2016), capecodtimes.com/article/20160214/NEWS/160219710; Stephanie Warsmith, *Plain Township School Stops "Mindfulness" Program After Some in Community Raise Concerns*, AKRON BEACON J. (Apr. 14, 2013), https://www.ohio.com/akron/news/top-stories-news/plain-township-school-stops-mindfulness-program-after-some-in-community-raise-concerns.

Sex education classes have been particularly susceptible to charges that an antitheistic faith is being advanced, but courts consistently have found that the challenged courses do not denounce Christianity and instead present public health information that furthers legitimate educational objectives.[141] The judiciary has ruled that the Establishment Clause precludes the state from barring sex education simply to conform to the religious beliefs of some parents. But courts have acknowledged that students have a free exercise right to be excused from sex education classes if such instruction conflicts with their sectarian beliefs.[142]

Curricular materials designed to promote tolerance for same-sex relationships have been challenged as interfering with parents' rights to direct the upbringing of their children.[143] The Supreme Court's 2015 decision striking down legislative bans on same-sex marriages[144] may deter future challenges to curricular materials that support such unions.

In a somewhat unusual recent case, Orthodox Jewish parents challenged the individualized education program for their child with Down syndrome for not providing instruction to prepare the child for life in the Orthodox Jewish community. The administrative law judge concluded that neither the Individuals with Disabilities Education Act (IDEA) nor Maryland law requires religious instruction for children with disabilities, and thus the judge did not have to address the Establishment Clause issues. The parents then requested reimbursement for their child to attend a religious school as the appropriate placement under IDEA. Concluding that the student was provided an appropriate education in the public school, the federal district court and Fourth Circuit reasoned that the IDEA's purpose is secular, and states may not use IDEA funds to provide religious instruction.[145]

Although courts have not condoned parental attacks on various aspects of the public school curriculum that allegedly conflict with their religious values, more difficult legal questions are raised when policy makers support curriculum restrictions for religious reasons. Because courts show considerable deference to legislatures and school boards in educational matters, conservative parent organizations have pressed for state and federal legislation and school board policies barring certain content from public schools.

---

[141]*See, e.g.*, Fields v. Palmdale Sch. Dist., 447 F.3d 1187 (9th Cir. 2006), text accompanying note 116, Chapter 4. Abstinence programs also have been controversial. *See* ACLU v. Foster, 2002 U.S. Dist. LEXIS 13778 (E.D. La. July 25, 2002) (instructing state officials to ensure that federal funds are not used to promote religious beliefs under the Governor's Program on Abstinence); Coleman v. Caddo Par. Sch. Bd., 635 So. 2d 1238 (La. Ct. App. 1994) (ordering changes in some parts of a school district's abstinence program that included some erroneous information and promoted Christian doctrine).

[142]*See, e.g.*, Brown v. Hot, Sexy & Safer Prods., 68 F.3d 525 (1st Cir. 1995).

[143]*See* Parker v. Hurley, 514 F.3d 87 (1st Cir. 2008); Morrison v. Bd. of Educ., 507 F.3d 494 (6th Cir. 2007); text accompanying note 19, Chapter 4.

[144]*See* Obergefell v. Hodges, 135 S. Ct. 2584 (2015) (recognizing that same-sex couples have the fundamental right to marry guaranteed by the Fourteenth Amendment); text accompanying note 54, Chapter 9.

[145]M.L. by Leiman v. Smith, 867 F.3d 487 (4th Cir. 2017) (noting further that school authorities made appropriate accommodations to the child's practice of his religious beliefs).

STATE AID TO RELIGIOUS SCHOOLS

The Supreme Court is likely to reject Establishment Clause challenges to government aid to religious schools, and it could find a Free Exercise Clause entitlement to such public assistance.

In addition to disputes over the place of religion in public schools, government relations with private—primarily religious—schools have generated a substantial amount of First Amendment litigation. Unquestionably, parents have a legitimate interest in directing the upbringing of their children, including their education. **In 1925, the Supreme Court afforded constitutional protection to private schools' rights to exist and to parents' rights to select private education as an alternative to public schooling.**[146] Yet, the Court also recognized that the state has a general welfare interest in mandating school attendance and regulating private education to ensure an educated citizenry, considered essential in a democracy.

Some litigation has involved conflicts between the state's exercise of its *parens patriae* authority to protect the well-being of children and parental interests in having their children educated in settings that reinforce their religious and philosophical beliefs. **If the government interferes with parents' child-rearing decisions, it must show that the intervention is necessary to protect the child or the state**. Courts have upheld minimum state requirements for private schools (e.g., prescribed courses, personnel requirements), but the recent trend has been toward imposing outcome measures, such as requiring private school students to participate in statewide testing programs.

About 10 percent of all PK–12 students in the United States are enrolled in private schools, but this percentage could change if additional government aid flows to private education. Despite the fact that thirty-eight states specifically prohibit the use of public funds for sectarian purposes,[147] about three-fourths of the states provide some public aid to private school students, including those attending sectarian schools. The primary types of aid are for transportation services, the loan of textbooks, state-required testing programs, special education for children with disabilities, and counseling services. Several of the most significant Supreme Court decisions interpreting the Establishment Clause have pertained to the use of public funds for private, primarily sectarian, education. The remainder of this section focuses on governmental aid for student services in religious schools. Uses of public funds to enhance parental choice through vouchers, tax-credit scholarship programs, and other measures are addressed in Chapter 13.[148]

The Supreme Court's support of religious accommodations in terms of allowing government support for parochial school students has been consistent since 1993, with some evidence of the accommodationist trend much earlier. Indeed, the "child-benefit" doctrine has been used to justify government aid for transportation and secular

---

[146]Pierce v. Soc'y of Sisters, 268 U.S. 510 (1925), text accompanying note 40, Chapter 13.

[147]Five additional states require government funds to be used for public purposes without mentioning "religion."

[148]Private placements for children with disabilities are addressed in Chapter 7.

textbooks for parochial school students since the mid-twentieth century.[149] In 1993, the Supreme Court found no Establishment Clause violation in publicly supporting sign-language interpreters in parochial schools,[150] signaling a paradigm shift toward the use of public school personnel in sectarian schools. The Court in *Zobrest v. Catalina Foothills School District* reasoned that the aid is going to the child as part of a federal government program that distributes funds neutrally to qualifying children with disabilities under federal law. The child is the primary recipient of the aid, and the school receives only incidental benefits.

Subsequently, in *Agostini v. Felton*, the Supreme Court removed the prohibition it had announced twelve years earlier on public school personnel providing remedial instruction in religious schools.[151] In both *Zobrest* and *Agostini*, the Court rejected the notion that the Establishment Clause lays down an "absolute bar to the placing of a public employee in a sectarian school."[152]

The Supreme Court in *Mitchell v. Helms* found no Establishment Clause violation in using federal aid to purchase instructional materials and equipment for student use in sectarian schools.[153] Specifically, under federal law providing support for disadvantaged students, the ruling allows the use of public funds for computers, other instructional equipment, and library books in religious schools. The plurality reasoned that religious indoctrination or subsidization of religion could not be attributed to the government when aid, even direct aid, is:

- distributed based on secular criteria;
- available to religious and secular beneficiaries on a nondiscriminatory basis; and
- allowed to flow to religious schools only because of the private choices of parents.[154]

The plurality emphasized that the constitutional standard is whether the aid itself would be appropriate for a public school to receive and is distributed in an even-handed manner—conditions it concluded were satisfied by the aid in *Helms*. Six Justices agreed that prior Supreme Court opinions barring state aid in the form of providing maps, slide projectors, auxiliary services, and other instructional materials and equipment to sectarian schools were no longer good law.[155]

There are very few rulings left that reflect the Supreme Court's separationist stance regarding state aid to nonpublic schools. In fact, the Supreme Court seems to

---

[149]*See* Bd. of Educ. v. Allen, 392 U.S. 236 (1968) (finding no Establishment Clause violation in a state law requiring public school districts to loan secular textbooks to all secondary students, including those attending parochial schools); Everson v. Bd. of Educ., 330 U.S. 1 (1947) (rejecting an Establishment Clause challenge to the use of public funds to provide transportation services for nonpublic school students).

[150]Zobrest v. Catalina Foothills Sch. Dist., 509 U.S. 1 (1993).

[151]521 U.S. 203 (1997).

[152]*Id.* at 223–24; *Zobrest*, 509 U.S. at 13.

[153]530 U.S. 793 (2000).

[154]*Id.* at 809–14. A plurality opinion means that no single opinion was supported by a majority of the Justices, but the plurality opinion received the most support.

[155]*Id.* at 835–36 (*overturning* Wolman v. Walter, 433 U.S. 229 (1977); Meek v. Pittenger, 421 U.S. 349 (1975)).

have dismantled most of the decisions rendered during the height of applying the stringent *Lemon* test in the 1970s, when it struck down various types of public assistance to private schools.

It must be remembered, however, that simply because courts have interpreted the Establishment Clause as allowing various types of public aid for nonpublic school students does not mean that states *must* use public funds for these purposes if support for transportation, textbooks, and other services in nonpublic schools conflicts with state law. **In 2004, the Supreme Court delivered a significant decision, *Locke v. Davey*, upholding states' discretion to adopt more stringent antiestablishment provisions than demanded by the First Amendment.**[156] The Court endorsed the state of Washington's prohibition on using state scholarships for college students to pursue pastoral degrees. The Court reasoned that simply because such aid is *permitted* by the Establishment Clause[157] does not mean it is *required* by the Free Exercise Clause. The Supreme Court held that the Washington constitutional provision was intended to keep schools free from sectarian control, rejecting the contention that it emanated from religious bigotry as a so-called Blaine Amendment.[158]

Yet, the Supreme Court in 2017 distinguished its holding in *Locke* when it ruled that a church-related daycare program had a free exercise right to be eligible on the same basis as secular organizations to compete for a state grant for playground resurfacing with materials from recycled tires.[159] The state had denied the daycare center's application because the Missouri Constitution bars public support for faith-based institutions. As noted previously, the Court in *Trinity Lutheran Church v. Comer* applied strict judicial scrutiny in ruling that a generally available government benefit cannot be denied solely on the basis of religion. The Court emphasized that the scholarship students in *Locke* still had options for using the state funds for many other degrees, whereas in *Trinity Lutheran*, the daycare center was completely foreclosed from competing for a grant simply because of its religious affiliation. **The Supreme Court in several of the decisions discussed above rejected Establishment Clause challenges to religious schools receiving state aid, but this is the first decision in which the Court found a Free Exercise Clause right for a sectarian institution to participate in a publicly funded program**.

In a New Mexico case, the state high court had barred the state's use of public funds to loan textbooks to private schools under the state constitution's prohibition on appropriating funds to support private and religious schools.[160] The U.S. Supreme Court vacated this decision in 2017 and returned it to the New Mexico Supreme Court for reconsideration in light of *Trinity Lutheran*.[161] Other state courts have denied various types of aid to

[156]540 U.S. 712 (2004).

[157]*See* Witters v. Wash. Dep't of Servs., 474 U.S. 481 (1986).

[158]*Locke*, 540 U.S. at 724 n.7 (finding that Washington's constitutional prohibition on the use of public funds for religious worship, exercise, or instruction was *not* modeled on a failed constitutional amendment proposed by former House Speaker James Blaine in 1875, which allegedly reflected anti-Catholic sentiment).

[159]Trinity Lutheran Church v. Comer, 137 S. Ct. 2012 (2017), *supra* text accompanying note 7.

[160]Moses v. Skandera, 367 P.3d 838 (N.M. 2015).

[161]N. M. Ass'n of Nonpublic Schs. v. Moses, 137 S. Ct. 2325 (2017) (granting *cert.*, vacating judgment, and remanding *mem.* to the Supreme Court of New Mexico for further consideration in light of *Trinity Lutheran*).

religious schools under their respective state constitutional mandates that are more stringent than the First Amendment, but these decisions may now be called into question. **If courts apply *Trinity Lutheran* to conclude that religious schools have a right to such government aid made available to public schools, this will mean that the federal Free Exercise Clause overrides antiestablishment provisions that most states have adopted.** As discussed in Chapter 13, it also remains to be seen if religious K–12 schools will be able to capitalize on *Trinity Lutheran* to assert an entitlement under the Free Exercise Clause to government aid to increase parents' educational choices for their children.[162]

CONCLUSION

Since the early 1960s, church/state controversies have generated a steady stream of education litigation, and there are no signs of diminishing legal activity in this domain. The principle that the First Amendment demands wholesome governmental neutrality toward religion has been easier to assert than to apply. Some lawsuits have involved claims under the Free Exercise Clause, but most school cases have focused on interpretations of Establishment Clause prohibitions.

From the 1960s through the mid-1980s, the federal judiciary seemed more committed to enforcing Establishment Clause restrictions in elementary and secondary school settings than elsewhere. Since the mid-1980s, there seems to be greater acceptance of government accommodation of religion, especially in terms of public funds flowing to religious schools. Also, religious influences and accommodations in public schools have become more common. The Free Speech Clause increasingly seems to prevail over Establishment Clause restrictions in protecting religious expression in public education, and the Free Exercise Clause may become dominant in terms of state aid to religious schools. The metaphor of separation of church and state seems to have been replaced by the concepts of equal access for religious groups and expression.

Despite some inconsistencies across decisions, the following generalizations depict the current status of the law governing church/state relations in schools.

1. Devotional activities sponsored by public schools, regardless of voluntary student participation, violate the Establishment Clause.

2. Students have a free exercise right to engage in silent prayer in public schools, but school personnel cannot encourage students to pray.

3. Prayers delivered by members of the clergy at public school graduation ceremonies violate the Establishment Clause, but student-initiated devotionals during the ceremony may be permissible if a forum for student expression has been established.

4. Holidays with both secular and religious significance can be observed in an objective and prudent manner in public schools.

[162]*See* Douglas Cty. Sch. Dist. v. Taxpayers for Pub. Educ., 351 P.3d 461 (Colo. 2015) (en banc) (striking down a state-funded voucher program), *vacated*, 137 S. Ct. 2325 (2017) (granting *cert.*, vacating judgment, and remanding to the Colorado Supreme Court for reconsideration in light of *Trinity Lutheran*), text accompanying note 100, Chapter 13.

5. Public schools can place restrictions on the use of religious music in school programs, but they are not obligated to do so unless a particular faith is being promoted.

6. The Ten Commandments and other religious documents cannot be permanently posted in public schools.

7. The academic study of religion is legitimate in public schools as long as it is not a ploy to instill religious beliefs.

8. Under the EAA, if a secondary school receives federal funds and creates a limited forum for student groups to meet during noninstructional time, clubs cannot be denied access based on the religious, political, or philosophical content of their meetings.

9. Religious organizations generally cannot distribute their literature in public schools, but sectarian materials prepared and distributed by students are usually treated like other types of private student expression, subject to reasonable time, place, and manner restrictions.

10. Under the First Amendment, if community groups are allowed to use public schools after school hours, groups cannot be discriminated against based on the religious content of their meetings, even groups that target children attending the school.

11. Students can be released from public schools to receive religious instruction if it is provided off public school grounds.

12. Students are entitled to be excused to observe religious holidays if their absences do not interfere with their educational progress or place an undue hardship on the school.

13. Students have a First Amendment right to be excused from reciting the Pledge of Allegiance in public schools, but challenges to saying "under God" in the Pledge have not been successful.

14. Although states can require students to be vaccinated as a prerequisite to school attendance, they also can enact religious and other exemptions from such immunization requirements.

15. Students can be excused from specific public school assignments that impede the practice of their religion so long as the management of the school or the students' academic progress is not disrupted.

16. Parental challenges to teaching about evolution, sex education, and other secular topics in public schools have not been successful.

17. Public aid for secular services in private schools has been upheld if it benefits the child and only incidentally benefits religious institutions.

18. Religious schools may have a free exercise right to participate in generally available state assistance programs; access cannot be denied solely on the basis of religion.

CHAPTER FOUR

INSTRUCTIONAL ISSUES

Can states prescribe a specific curriculum for public schools? Can school boards censor library and instructional materials? What privacy rights of students must be respected in their school records? These and many more questions about instructional issues continue to be controversial. **Although U.S. citizens have no federal constitutional right to a public education, each state constitution places a duty on its legislature to provide for free public schooling, thus creating a state entitlement (property right) for all children to be educated up to a specified age at public expense.**[1] Substantial litigation has resulted from the collision of state interests in providing for the welfare of all citizens and individual interests in exercising constitutional and statutory rights. This chapter focuses on legal mandates pertaining to various requirements and rights associated with the public school instructional program.

Readers of this chapter should be able to:

- Explain the limitations on state control of the public school curriculum.
- Discuss how judicial standards differ in addressing instructional censorship initiated by parents versus school policy makers.
- Identify conditions that must be met under fair use guidelines for educators to use materials without permission from the copyright holders.
- Describe conditions that must be satisfied for schools to require proficiency test passage as a prerequisite to high school graduation.
- Analyze privacy protections afforded to students and their parents under the Family Educational Rights and Privacy Act.

THE SCHOOL CURRICULUM

States and local school boards control the public school curriculum, but they must respect federal constitutional guarantees in making curricular decisions.

---

[1]*See* Goss v. Lopez, 419 U.S. 565 (1975); *see also* text accompanying note 28, Chapter 8.

The federal government influences the curriculum through funds it provides for particular initiatives. For example, under the Every Student Succeeds Act (ESSA), states can apply for federal aid to strengthen reading and writing instruction in the early grades through high school, with priority on districts serving children from low-income families.[2] However, federal influence is quite limited, other than enacting such laws for the general welfare and enforcing constitutional rights. In contrast, state legislatures have plenary or complete power over education and thus broad authority to impose curriculum directives.

Requirements and Restrictions

A few state constitutions include specific curriculum mandates, but more typically, the legislature is given responsibility for curricular determinations. Most states require instruction pertaining to the Federal Constitution; American history; English; mathematics; and health, drug, character, and physical education.[3] Some state statutes specify what subjects will be taught in which grades, and many states have detailed legislation pertaining to vocational education, bilingual education, and special services for students with disabilities. State laws usually stipulate that local school boards must offer the state-mandated minimum curriculum, which they may supplement unless there is a statutory or constitutional prohibition.

In about half of the states, local school boards are empowered to adopt courses of study, but often they must secure approval from the state board of education to do so. A national initiative was launched in 2010 to establish common core state standards, initially in English language arts and mathematics, which are designed to provide consistency across states and a clear understanding of what students are expected to learn at each grade level. These state-developed standards also are intended to reflect the knowledge and skills that individuals need for success in college and careers.[4]

Despite states' latitude in curricular matters, some legislative attempts to impose curriculum restrictions have impaired federal constitutional rights. The first curriculum case to reach the Supreme Court involved a 1923 challenge to a Nebraska law that prohibited instruction in a foreign language to any public or private school student who had not successfully completed the eighth grade.[5] The state high court had upheld the dismissal of a teacher in a private school for teaching the subject of reading in German to elementary school students. In striking down the statute, the Supreme Court reasoned that the teacher's right to teach, the parents' right to hire him to instruct their children, and the children's right to acquire useful knowledge were protected liberties under the Due Process Clause of the Fourteenth Amendment. The Supreme Court on occasion has ruled that other curriculum

---

[2]20 U.S.C. § 6642(a)(2) (2018).

[3]Reflecting the discretion of state legislatures, in 2011, California adopted a law requiring all grade levels to address historical contributions of men, women, Native Americans, African Americans, Mexican Americans, Asian Americans, Pacific Islanders, European Americans, people with disabilities, and lesbian, gay, bisexual, and transgender Americans, CAL. EDUC. CODE § 51204.5 (2018).

[4]Four states did not adopt the common core standards (Alaska, Nebraska, Texas, and Virginia), and three others subsequently withdrew their adoption (Indiana, Oklahoma, and South Carolina). As of 2017, nine other states were considering rewriting their standards. *See Standards in Your State*, Common Core State Standards Initiative (n.d.), http://www.corestandards.org.

[5]Meyer v. Nebraska, 262 U.S. 390 (1923).

decisions violate constitutional rights. The Court held in 1968 that under the First Amendment, states cannot bar public school instruction—teaching about evolution—simply because it conflicts with certain religious views.[6]

Lower courts also have struck down state laws imposing curriculum requirements if protected rights are at stake. For example, Arizona's law banning the teaching of ethnic studies courses that (1) promote the overthrow of the U.S. government, (2) foster resentment toward a race or class of people, (3) advocate ethnic solidarity instead of treatment of students as individuals, or (4) are designed for pupils of a certain ethnicity was challenged in connection with Tucson's Mexican-American Studies (MAS) program. The Ninth Circuit ruled that the section of the law prohibiting courses designed primarily for students of a particular ethnic group was facially overbroad but severable from the remainder of the law, which was left intact.[7] In subsequent proceedings, the federal district court ruled that the law's other provisions were not discriminatory on their face, but they violated the First and Fourteenth Amendments as enacted and enforced by state officials who acted out of racial animus in using these provisions to close Tucson's MAS program.[8]

Yet, courts will not interfere with instructional decisions made by state and local education agencies, unless the decisions are clearly arbitrary or impair constitutional rights. Federal appellate courts have rejected allegations that mandatory community service requirements for students force expression of altruistic values in violation of the First Amendment, entail involuntary servitude prohibited by the Thirteenth Amendment, or impair parents' Fourteenth Amendment rights to direct the upbringing of their children.[9] The Supreme Court in 2011 declined to review a decision in which the First Circuit held that revisions in the state's curriculum guide did not implicate the First Amendment.[10] In this case, Turkish groups unsuccessfully alleged that changes in the guide addressing teaching about genocide and human rights were politically motivated.

School authorities also have discretion in establishing standards for pupil performance, restricting curricular offerings, and imposing other instructional requirements, such as prerequisites and admission criteria for particular courses, so long as such decisions are not arbitrary and do not disadvantage certain groups of students. To illustrate, eight states have some type of laws written for health and sex education that forbid teachers from discussing LGBTQ issues in a positive light if discussed at all.[11] Given the Supreme Court's decision upholding same-sex marriages,[12] these laws may be vulnerable

[6]*See* Epperson v. Arkansas, 393 U.S. 97 (1968), text accompanying note 123, Chapter 3.

[7]Arce v. Douglas, 793 F.3d 968 (9th Cir. 2015).

[8]Gonzalez v. Douglas, 269 F. Supp. 3d 948 (D. Ariz. 2017); *see also infra* note 27.

[9]*See, e.g.*, Herndon v. Chapel Hill-Carrboro City Bd. of Educ., 89 F.3d 174 (4th Cir. 1996); Immediato v. Rye Neck Sch. Dist., 73 F.3d 454 (2d Cir. 1996); Earl v. Decatur Pub. Schs. Bd. of Educ., 39 N.E.3d 1136 (Ill. Ct. App. 2015).

[10]Griswold v. Driscoll, 616 F.3d 53 (1st Cir. 2010).

[11]A few additional states had enacted such laws but subsequently repealed them. *See* Gay, Lesbian, & Straight Educ. Network, *No Promo Homo Laws* (n.d.), https://www.glsen.org/learn/policy/issues/nopromohomo.

[12]Obergefell v. Hodges, 135 S. Ct. 2584 (2015) (finding the right to marry someone of the same sex to be a fundamental liberty under the Due Process Clause and the Equal Protection Clause of the Fourteenth Amendment), *see* text accompanying note 54, Chapter 9.

to legal challenges, even though to date, they have not been judicially invalidated. States have latitude in curricular matters, but they cannot adopt requirements that implicate fundamental rights.

In addition to having authority over the content of the public school curriculum, states also have the power to specify textbooks and to regulate the method by which such books are obtained and distributed. Local school districts play the primary role in textbook adoptions, but textbooks are adopted at the state level in twenty states.[13] Three-fourths of the states provide free textbooks for public school students. Courts will not interfere with textbook decisions unless the established procedures are not followed or overtly biased materials are adopted. Textbook adoptions have been controversial in some states, especially large states whose adoptions have the greatest influence on publishers.[14]

Censorship of Instructional Materials

Attempts to remove books from classrooms and libraries and to tailor curricular offerings and methodologies to particular religious and philosophical values have led to constitutional challenges. Despite general agreement that schools transmit values, little consensus exists regarding *which* values should be transmitted or *who* should make this determination.

Parental Challenges.   Some civil rights and consumer groups have challenged public school materials and programs as allegedly promoting racism, sexism, or bad health habits for students. But most of the challenges come from conservative advocacy groups[15] and parent organizations alleging that the use of instructional activities and materials considered immoral and anti-Christian impairs parents' rights to control their children's course of study in public schools.[16] As discussed in Chapter 3, courts have endorsed requests for specific children to be excused from selected course offerings (e.g., sex education) that offend their religious beliefs, so long as the exemptions do not impede the students' academic progress or the management of the school. Challenges to the courses themselves, however, have not found a receptive judiciary.

To date, courts have not allowed mere parental disapproval of instructional materials to determine the public school curriculum. Federal appellate courts have been unsympathetic to claims that reading series or individual novels used in public schools conflict with Christian doctrine and advance an antitheistic creed, finding the challenged

---

[13]Educ. Comm'n of the States, *Textbook Adoption* (Sept. 25, 2013), ecs.org/clearinghouse/01/09/23/10923.pdf.

[14]For example, a recent controversy in Texas has involved the adoption of texts for MAS programs. *See* Aliyya Swaby, *Officials Consider Another Mexican-American Studies Textbook*, Tex. Tribune (Sept. 12, 2017), https://www.texastribune.org/2017/09/12/texas-state-board-education-mexican-american-studies-text.

[15]Among advocacy groups, the American Legislative Exchange Council (ALEC) disseminates model state legislation pertaining to the conservative policy agenda.

[16]Some of the best-known conservative parent groups are the Traditional Values Coalition, the Christian Coalition, Citizens for Excellence in Education, Concerned Women for America, the Eagle Forum, and Focus on the Family.

materials to be religiously neutral and related to legitimate educational objectives.[17] Although many challenges have religious overtones, some simply assert parents' rights to govern their children's education. The First Circuit rejected parents' claim that the school district was liable for subjecting their children to a mandatory AIDS-awareness assembly that featured a streetwise, comedic approach to the topic. The appeals court observed that "if all parents had a fundamental constitutional right to dictate individually what the schools teach their children, the schools would be forced to cater a curriculum for each student whose parents had genuine moral disagreements with the school's choice of subject matter."[18] The same court more recently rejected a constitutional challenge to a program teaching respect for gay people and same-sex marriages.[19] The Ninth Circuit previously held that an Oregon law restructuring public schools to impose a rigorous academic program and student assessments did not abridge speech rights or "freedom of the mind," because nothing in the law compelled students to adopt state-approved views.[20] And this court also dismissed Black parents' complaint that their daughter suffered psychological injuries due to being required to read two literary works that contained repeated use of the N-word.[21]

Censorship by Policy Makers.   Although courts have not been receptive to challenges to school boards' curricular decisions simply because some materials or courses offend the sensibilities of specific students or parents, the legal issues are more complicated when policy makers themselves (e.g., legislators, school board members) support the censorship activity. Bills calling for instructional censorship have been introduced in Congress and numerous state legislatures, and policies have been proposed at the school board level to eliminate "objectionable" materials from public school classrooms and libraries. **The Supreme Court has recognized the discretion of school boards to make decisions that reflect the "legitimate and substantial community interest in promoting respect for authority and traditional values, be they social, moral, or political."[22]** Thus, the

---

[17]*See, e.g.,* Monteiro v. Tempe Union High Sch. Dist., 158 F.3d 1022 (9th Cir. 1998); Fleischfresser v. Dirs. of Sch. Dist. 200, 15 F.3d 680 (7th Cir. 1994); Smith v. Sch. Bd. of Sch. Comm'rs, 827 F.2d 684 (11th Cir. 1987), *see* text accompanying note 136, Chapter 3. There were 323 challenges recorded by the American Library Association's Office for Intellectual Freedom in 2016, down from 547 challenges in 2004. *See* Am. Library Ass'n, *Top Ten Most Challenged Books Lists* (n.d.), http://www.ala.org/advocacy/bbooks/frequentlychallengedbooks/top10. Over time, the majority of challenges have been due to allegations of occult or Satanic themes, religious viewpoints, or nontraditional family values.

[18]Brown v. Hot, Sexy & Safer Prods., 68 F.3d 525, 534 (1st Cir. 1995).

[19]Parker v. Hurley, 514 F.3d 87 (1st Cir. 2008); *see also* Mooney v. Garcia, 143 Cal. Rptr. 3d 195 (Ct. App. 2012) (rejecting parental request to be on the school board agenda in order to object to a student-sponsored "Rainbow Day" diversity observance at a school).

[20]Tennison v. Paulus, 144 F.3d 1285, 1287 (9th Cir. 1998).

[21]*Monteiro,* 158 F.3d 1022 (but remanding for further proceedings the allegations that school personnel failed to respond to complaints of a racially hostile environment in violation of Title VI of the Civil Rights Act of 1964).

[22]Bd. of Educ. v. Pico, 457 U.S. 853, 864 (1982). In an Ohio school district, concerned parents convinced the school board to drop a mindfulness program because it allegedly advanced the Buddhist religion. *See Plain Township School Stops "Mindfulness" Program after Some in Community Raise Concerns,* AKRON BEACON J. (Apr. 14, 2013), https://www.ohio.com/akron/news/top-stories-news/plain-township-school-stops-mindfulness-program-after-some-in-community-raise-concerns; *see* text accompanying note 140, Chapter 3.

judiciary has been reluctant to interfere with school boards' prerogatives in selecting and eliminating instructional materials, unless a board flagrantly abuses its authority.[23] To illustrate, the Eleventh Circuit allowed the Miami-Dade School Board to remove from elementary school libraries the book *Vamos a Cuba!* along with twenty-three other books in a series about life in other countries. The appellate court concluded that the board's action was constitutionally sound because evidence showed that the books were removed for factual inaccuracies and not because of impermissible viewpoint discrimination.[24]

Courts generally have upheld school boards' authority in determining curricular materials and offerings, but some specific censorship activities have been invalidated. Courts have intervened if the censorship of library selections has clearly been motivated by a desire to suppress particular viewpoints or controversial ideas in violation of the First Amendment. The Fifth Circuit remanded a case for a trial to decide whether a Louisiana school board was unconstitutionally suppressing ideas in removing from school libraries all copies of *Voodoo & Hoodoo*, which traces the development of African tribal religion and its evolution in Black communities in the United States.[25] Also, an Arkansas federal district court found insufficient justification for a school district's policy requiring parental permission for students to check out specific library books, such as the Harry Potter series, that allegedly deal with witchcraft and the occult, concluding that the policy stigmatized the targeted books and abridged students' First Amendment rights to have access to the materials without parental permission.[26]

Despite considerable activity in lower courts, the Supreme Court has rendered only one decision involving censorship in public schools. This case, *Board of Education v. Pico*,[27] unfortunately did not provide significant clarification regarding the scope of school boards' authority to restrict student access to particular materials, with seven of the nine Supreme Court Justices writing separate opinions. In *Pico*, the school board removed certain books from junior high and high school libraries, in spite of the contrary recommendation of a committee appointed to review the books. The Supreme Court narrowly affirmed the appellate court's remand of the case for a trial because of irregularities in the removal procedures and unresolved factual questions regarding the school board's motivation. However, even the three Justices endorsing the notion that students have a protected right to receive information recognized the broad authority of school boards to remove materials that are vulgar or educationally unsuitable so long as they used regular and unbiased procedures. The *Pico* plurality also emphasized that the controversy involved *library* books, which are not required reading for students, noting that school boards "might well defend

---

[23]Curriculum review committees established by school boards may be required to comply with state open meetings laws. *See, e.g.*, Wisconsin v. Appleton Area Sch. Dist. Bd. of Educ., 898 N.W.2d 35 (Wis. 2017).

[24]ACLU v. Miami-Dade Cty. Sch. Bd., 557 F.3d 1177 (11th Cir. 2009).

[25]Campbell v. St. Tammany Par. Sch. Bd., 64 F.3d 184 (5th Cir. 1995).

[26]Counts v. Cedarville Sch. Dist., 295 F. Supp. 2d 996 (W.D. Ark. 2003).

[27]457 U.S. 853 (1982); *see also* Gonzalez v. Douglas, 269 F. Supp. 3d 948 (D. Ariz. 2017) (relying on the *Pico* plurality in ruling that the removal of otherwise available classroom materials implicates students' rights to receive information unless related to legitimate pedagogical concerns; political motivations or racial animus would be impermissible reasons to remove materials), *supra* text accompanying note 8.

their claim of absolute discretion in matters of *curriculum* by reliance upon their duty to inculcate community values."[28]

Further strengthening the broad discretion of school authorities in curriculum-related censorship was the landmark 1988 Supreme Court decision involving students' free speech rights, *Hazelwood School District v. Kuhlmeier*.[29] The Court declared that public school authorities can censor student expression in school-sponsored activities to ensure that the expression is consistent with educational objectives. Relying on *Hazelwood*, the Eleventh Circuit upheld a Florida school board's decision to ban a humanities textbook because it included Aristophanes' *Lysistrata* and Chaucer's *The Miller's Tale*, which board members considered vulgar. Although not addressing the wisdom of the board's decision, the court deferred to the board's discretion in curricular matters.[30]

Specific issues may change, but controversies surrounding the selection of materials for the public school library and curriculum will likely persist, reflecting the basic tension between instilling community values in students and exposing them to new ideas. School boards would be wise to establish procedures for reviewing objections to course content and library materials *before* controversies arise. Criteria used to acquire and eliminate instructional materials should be clearly articulated and educationally defensible. **Once a process is in place to evaluate complaints relating to the instructional program, school boards should follow it carefully, as courts will show little sympathy when a school board ignores its own established procedures**.

Internet Censorship.   Some recent censorship activity has focused on the electronic frontier. Almost all American teenagers use the Internet and own or have access to mobile phones.[31] In addition to issues addressed in Chapter 5 regarding students' postings on the Internet, concerns are being raised about adults electronically transmitting sexually explicit and other harmful material to minors. With schools and parents increasingly making online services accessible to students, children are vulnerable to sexual predators via the Internet. Many states as well as the federal government have enacted measures to restrict minors' access to harmful electronic postings.[32]

The only federal law addressing schools' responsibilities that has survived a First Amendment challenge is the Children's Internet Protection Act (CIPA), which received

---

[28]*Pico*, 457 U.S. at 869 (emphasis added). As noted in Chapter 3, a plurality opinion means that no single opinion was supported by a majority of the Justices, but the plurality opinion received the most support. Following the Supreme Court's decision, the school board voted to return the controversial books to the school libraries, thus averting the need for a trial regarding the board's motivation for the original censorship.

[29]484 U.S. 260 (1988). *See* text accompanying note 18, Chapter 5, for a discussion of this case.

[30]Virgil v. Sch. Bd., 862 F.2d 1517 (11th Cir. 1989).

[31]*See* Amanda Lenhart, *A Majority of American Teens Report Access to a Computer, Game Console, Smartphone and a Tablet*, Pew Research Ctr. (Apr. 9, 2015), http://www.pewinternet.org/2015/04/09/a-majority-of-american-teens-report-access-to-a-computer-game-console-smartphone-and-a-tablet.

[32]For information on state laws pertaining to Internet filtering requirements, *see* Nat'l Conference of State Legislatures, *Laws Relating to Filtering, Blocking and Usage Policies in Schools and Libraries* (Nov. 16, 2016), http://www.ncsl.org/research/telecommunications-and-information-technology/state-internet-filtering-laws.aspx.

Supreme Court endorsement in 2003.[33] This law requires libraries and school districts receiving technology funds to monitor student Internet use and to implement technology protection measures that safeguard students from access to harmful content.[34] The Supreme Court reasoned that CIPA places a condition on the use of federal funds, which poses a small burden for library patrons, and the law does not penalize those posting materials on the Internet.[35] As an additional condition of receiving funding under CIPA, schools and libraries must educate students about appropriate online behavior.[36] Thus, many schools have established technology use policies that students and their parents must sign in order for students to access the Internet at school or to use school-owned equipment.[37] **These policies provide guidance as to what websites students can visit in completing assignments and include protocols for them to follow in interacting with classmates and school personnel via the Internet**.

In implementing the required Internet safety plans, most school districts are relying to some extent on filtering software and thus delegating to private companies some decisions concerning what materials are appropriate for their students, even though school personnel can override the filters.[38] There are fears that measures such as CIPA can have a chilling effect on schools using computer networks to enhance instructional experiences for students. For example, a Missouri federal district court in 2012 enjoined a school district's use of filtering software that blocked websites with resources directed toward LGBTQ youth, reasoning that the publishers of the websites and students would likely prevail in their First Amendment claim.[39] The competing government and individual interests affected by legislative restrictions on information distributed electronically will undoubtedly generate additional litigation.

COPYRIGHT COMPLIANCE

School personnel must comply with the federal copyright law; some copyrighted materials may be used for instructional purposes without the publisher's permission if fair use guidelines are followed.

Educators extensively use published materials and various other media in the classroom, and as a general rule, teachers should assume material is copyrighted unless explicitly

[33]United States v. Am. Library Ass'n, 539 U.S. 194 (2003).

[34]20 U.S.C. § 9134(f) (2018); 47 U.S.C. § 254(h)(5) (2018); *see also* 15 U.S.C. § 6501 (2018) that regulates website operators and providers of other online services in terms of collecting personal information from children under thirteen, *infra* text accompanying note 107.

[35]*Am. Library Ass'n*, 539 U.S. 194.

[36]Fed. Commc'ns Comm'n, *Consumer Guide: Children's Internet Protection Act* (2012).

[37]Recently, such policies have transitioned in many school districts from Acceptable Use Policies to Responsible Use Policies to focus on educating students regarding proper technology use rather than policing their improper use.

[38]Many schools have established technology use committees to make such override decisions.

[39]Parents, Families, & Friends v. Camdenton R-III Sch. Dist., 853 F. Supp. 2d 888 (W.D. Mo. 2012).

stated that it is in the public domain.[40] Although the law grants the owner of a copyright exclusive control over reproduction, adaptation, publication, performance, and display of the protected material,[41] courts have recognized exceptions to this control under the doctrine of *fair use*. The fair use doctrine allows limited use of copyrighted material under certain circumstances without consent of the copyright holder.

Congress incorporated the judicially created fair use concept into the 1976 revisions of the Copyright Act. In identifying the purposes of the fair use exception, Congress specifically noted teaching. **The exception provides needed flexibility for teachers but does *not* exempt them from copyright infringements**. The following factors are used in assessing whether copying specific material constitutes fair use or an infringement:

- the purpose and character of the use, including whether such use is of a commercial nature or is for nonprofit educational purposes;
- the nature of the copyrighted work;
- the amount and substantiality of the portion used in relation to the copyrighted work as a whole; and
- the effect of the use upon the potential market for or value of the copyrighted work.[42]

To clarify fair use pertaining to photocopying from books and periodicals, the House and Senate conferees incorporated in their conference report a set of classroom guidelines developed by a group representing educators, authors, and publishers.[43] These guidelines are only part of the legislative history of the Copyright Act and do not have the force of law, but they have been widely used as persuasive authority in assessing the legality of reproducing printed materials in the educational environment. The guidelines permit making single copies of copyrighted material for teaching or research but are quite restrictive on the use of multiple copies. **To use multiple copies of a work, the tests of brevity, spontaneity, and cumulative effect must be met** (see Figure 4.1). Furthermore, the guidelines do not permit copying to substitute for anthologies or collective works or to replace consumable materials such as workbooks.

Publishers have taken legal action to ensure compliance with these guidelines. The Sixth Circuit held that a commercial copy shop violated the fair use doctrine in the

---

[40]Congress expressed its intent to abrogate states' Eleventh Amendment immunity for copyright claims brought against state agencies, Copyright Remedies Clarification Act, 17 U.S.C. §§ 501, 511 (2018). Individuals have three years from the time they knew or should have known about the copyright violation to initiate a civil lawsuit. *See* Smith v. Houston Indep. Sch. Dist., 229 F. Supp. 3d 571 (S.D. Tex. 2017).

[41]17 U.S.C. § 106 (2018). The federal copyright law has generated two Supreme Court decisions since 2013 with implications for education. *See* Star Athletica v. Varsity Brands, 137 S. Ct. 1002 (2017) (finding that designs on cheerleaders' uniforms enjoy copyright protection if they are perceived as two- or three-dimensional works of art; distinguishing the shape and cut of the uniforms that cannot be copyrighted from the artistic expression of a design that is protected); Kirtsaeng v. John Wiley & Sons, Inc., 568 U.S. 519 (2013) (holding that copyrighted materials legitimately purchased abroad could be resold in the United States for a profit; the Copyright Act was not intended to place a geographic restriction on the resale of lawfully purchased materials).

[42]17 U.S.C. § 107 (2018).

[43]U.S. Copyright Office, *Circular 21: Reproduction of Copyrighted Works by Educators and Librarians* (2009, rev. Aug. 2014), http://www.copyright.gov/circs/circ21.pdf.

FIGURE 4.1   Copyright Guidelines for Not-for-Profit Educational Institutions: Multiple Copies

---

Each copy must include the copyright notice and meet the following criteria:

Brevity

- For poems, not more than 250 words can be copied.
- For prose, a complete article of less than 2,500 words or an excerpt of not more than 1,000 words or 10 percent of the work, whichever is less, can be copied.
- Copies of illustrations can be one chart, graph, diagram, drawing, cartoon, or picture per book or periodical.

Spontaneity

- The copying is initiated by the individual teacher (not an administrator or supervisor).
- The inspiration to use the material occurs in such a manner that does not reasonably permit a timely request for permission.

Cumulative effect

- The copies are for use in one course.
- Not more than one short poem, article, or two excerpts can be copied from a given source or author during one class term.
- Multiple copying in a term is limited to nine instances.

The following practices are prohibited:

- Copying cannot substitute for compilations or collective works.
- Consumable works cannot be copied (e.g., workbooks, standardized tests).
- The same items cannot be copied from term to term.
- Copying cannot replace the purchase of books or periodicals.

---

reproduction of course packets for faculty at the University of Michigan. The copy shop owner argued that such reproduction of multiple copies for classroom use is a recognized statutory exemption. The appellate court disagreed, reasoning that the sale of multiple copies for commercial, not educational, purposes destroyed the publisher's potential licensing revenue, contained creative material, and involved significant portions of the copyrighted publications (as much as 30 percent of one work).[44] This ruling does not prevent faculty from using course packets or anthologies in the classroom, but it requires them to seek permission from publishers and the possible payment of fees prior to photocopying. Similarly, schools would not be allowed to copy or make available an electronic textbook for student use beyond the contractual agreement with the publisher.

     The fair use doctrine and congressional guidelines have been strictly construed in educational settings. Although materials reproduced for the classroom meet the first factor in determining fair use—educational purpose—the remaining factors also must be met. The Ninth Circuit held that fair use was not met in a teacher's use of a copyrighted booklet to make a learning activity packet used for the same purpose as the protected booklet.[45] The absence of personal profit on the part of the teacher did not lessen the violation. Furthermore, half of the packet was a verbatim copy of the copyrighted material, and the copying did not meet the guideline of spontaneity in that it was reproduced several times

---

[44]Princeton Univ. Press v. Mich. Document Servs., 99 F.3d 1381 (6th Cir. 1996).

[45]Marcus v. Rowley, 695 F.2d 1171 (9th Cir. 1983).

over two school years. Subsequently, an Illinois federal district court ruled that a Chicago teacher and editor of a newspaper committed a copyright violation against the Chicago school board by publishing the board's copyrighted tests used to assess educational levels of high school freshmen and sophomores. The tests were clearly marked with the copyright notice and included a warning that the material could not be duplicated. In dismissing the teacher's affirmative defenses, the court ruled that he did not possess a First Amendment right to publish the copyrighted tests because the Copyright Act limits First Amendment freedoms, and publication of the material did not fall within the fair use guidelines.[46]

Yet, in other cases, the copyright holders have not prevailed. The Second Circuit addressed fair use in a case against Google in which authors of copyrighted books sued because Google made digital copies of parts of millions of books available in its online library.[47] The appeals court sided with Google, concluding that only small portions of each book were made available, which constituted fair use. More recently, an Indiana federal district court ruled that a school district's adaptation of a health-care model of cultural competence for use in a public school setting constituted fair use.[48] Also, a California federal district court rejected a copyright claim by a multimedia company against a high school and its music director, finding that the company did not have exclusive rights to most of the selections at issue and that the director enjoyed qualified immunity as he reasonably could have assumed that fair use applied to using the songs in student performances.[49]

With the increasing ease of sharing or selling materials on the Internet, some teachers have shown interest in marketing lesson plans and other items they have developed for their classes. **In general, materials teachers prepare as part of their employment relationship are owned by the school as "work for hire."**[50] The employer is considered the author for copyright purposes unless the employment contract specifies otherwise. Thus, teachers would be violating the law to sell such materials, regardless of where they are developed or when (e.g., during the summer) if they are used in the teacher's classes. Of course, educators can serve as consultants to companies, and in those instances, the respective companies own the materials created.

Rapid developments in instructional technology pose a new set of legal questions regarding the use of video recordings, digital materials, and computer software. Recognizing the need for guidance related to recording material, Congress issued guidelines for educational use in 1981.[51] **These guidelines specify that recording must be made at the**

---

[46]Chi. Sch. Reform Bd. v. Substance, 79 F. Supp. 2d 919 (N.D. Ill. 2000).

[47]Authors Guild v. Google, 804 F.3d 202 (2d Cir. 2015), *cert. denied*, 136 S. Ct. 1658 (2016).

[48]Campinha-Bacote v. Evansville Vanderburgh Sch. Corp., 2015 WL 12559889 (S.D. Ind. Nov. 5, 2015).

[49]However, questions remained regarding whether the company should have known about the school's use of one song before commencement of the three-year statute of limitations to file a copyright lawsuit, so the court denied the school district's motion for summary judgment on this issue. Tresona Multimedia v. Burbank High Sch. Vocal Music Ass'n, 2016 WL 9223889 (C.D. Cal. Dec. 22, 2016); *see also* Tresona Multimedia v. Burbank High Sch. Vocal Music Ass'n Boosters Club, 2017 WL 2728589 (C.D. Cal. Feb. 22, 2017) (granting summary judgment to the Association Boosters Club, finding no direct, contributory, or vicarious liability for copyright violations).

[50]17 U.S.C. § 201(b) (2018).

[51]*Guidelines for Off-Air Recording of Broadcast Programming for Educational Purposes*, Cong. Rec. § E4751 (daily ed. Oct. 14, 1981).

request of the teacher, and the material must be used for relevant classroom activities only once within the first ten days of recording. Additional use is limited to instructional reinforcement or evaluation, and the recording must be erased after forty-five calendar days. A New York federal district court held that a school system violated the fair use standards by extensive off-air taping and replaying of entire television programs.[52] The taping interfered with the producers' ability to market the materials. In a subsequent appeal, the school system sought permission for temporary taping; however, because of the availability of these programs for rental, even temporary recording violated fair use by interfering with the marketability of the films.[53]

Making home recordings of television broadcasts for later classroom use may constitute copyright infringement if the above off-air recording guidelines are not followed. The Supreme Court ruled that personal video recording for the purpose of "time shifting" is a legitimate, unobjectionable purpose, posing minimal harm to marketability.[54] **But home recording for broader viewing by students in the classroom would be beyond the purposes envisioned by the law and would necessitate careful adherence to the guidelines for limited use**.

Under 1980 amendments to the copyright law, software was included as protected intellectual property.[55] It is clear from the amended law that only one duplicate or backup copy can be made of the master computer program to ensure a working copy of the program if the master copy is damaged. Application of the fair use exception does not alter this restriction for educators. Although duplicating multiple copies would be for educational purposes, other factors of fair use would be violated. The software is readily accessible for purchase, programs can only be duplicated in their entirety, and copying substantially reduces the potential market.

In spite of the amendments, publishers continue to be concerned about the illegal copying of computer software in the school environment, and limited school budgets and high costs have challenged school personnel. A question not answered by the copyright law but plaguing schools is the legality of multiple uses of a master program. That is, can a program be loaded on many computers in a laboratory for simultaneous use, or can a program be modified for use in a network of microcomputers? Again, application of the fair use concept would indicate that multiple use is not permissible. The most important factor is that the market for the educational software would be greatly diminished. Several students using the master program one at a time (serial use), however, would not appear to violate the copyright law. **To acquire broad use of particular software, school systems must either purchase multiple copies or negotiate site license agreements with the publishers**.

As schools increasingly are taking advantage of the Internet, copyright law also is evolving. Congress amended the law in 1998 with the Digital Millennium Copyright Act, reinforcing that an individual's copyright is secured when the work is created and "fixed in any tangible

---

[52]Encyclopedia Britannica Educ. Corp. v. Crooks, 542 F. Supp. 1156 (W.D.N.Y. 1982).

[53]Encyclopedia Britannica Educ. Corp. v. Crooks, 558 F. Supp. 1247 (W.D.N.Y. 1983).

[54]Sony Corp. v. Universal City Studios, 464 U.S. 417 (1984). "Time shifting" means that a program is recorded for a single use and will simply be viewed at a later time.

[55]17 U.S.C. § 117 (2018).

medium of expression."[56] In 2002, greater clarity was provided for educators regarding the use of digital media in distance education with the enactment of the Technology, Education, and Copyright Harmonization (TEACH) Act.[57] The Act gives accredited nonprofit educational institutions more flexibility in using the Internet to distribute copyrighted materials in distance education programs. **Basically, the Act allows copyrighted materials to be used in distance education courses in the same way they can be used in regular classrooms**.

Case law clearly indicates that the Internet is not immune from the basic principles of copyright law; material that is created on the Internet or produced in a different format and then converted for use on the Internet is entitled to full legal protections.[58] Extraordinary technological advances have given teachers and their school systems the means to access a wide range of instructional materials and products, but many of them are federally protected from unauthorized reproduction. **Because violation of the law can result in school district and educator liability, school boards should adopt guidelines to prohibit infringement and to educate school personnel and students regarding unlawful practices**.[59]

STUDENT PROFICIENCY TESTING

Courts have recognized that an educated citizenry is an appropriate government goal, and the establishment of minimum performance standards—including passage of standardized tests—to give value to a high school diploma is a rational means to attain that goal.

The concept of performance assessment is not new, but the use of proficiency tests as a condition of grade promotion or the receipt of a high school diploma has a relatively brief history. In 1976, only four states had enacted student proficiency testing legislation. **Now, all states have laws or administrative regulations pertaining to statewide performance testing programs**. Given the state's authority to establish academic standards, including mandatory

[56]17 U.S.C. § 1201 (2018). For a discussion of the duration of copyright holders' protection, *see* Philip T.K. Daniel & Patrick Pauken, *Copyright Laws in K–12 Settings* D55, *in* PRINCIPAL'S LEGAL HANDBOOK (Janet Decker, Maria Lewis, Elizabeth Shaver, Ann Blankenship-Knox & Mark Paige eds., 6th ed. 2017).

[57]17 U.S.C. § 110 (2018).

[58]In several nonschool cases, courts have addressed file sharing and other issues. *See, e.g.*, Metro-Goldwyn-Mayer Studios v. Grokster, Ltd., 545 U.S. 913 (2005) (finding copyright violations by software companies that distributed free software products allowing individuals to share copyrighted files through peer networks); A&M Records v. Napster, 239 F.3d 1004 (9th Cir. 2001) (enjoining Napster Corporation from distributing a file-sharing program that allowed individuals to download music files). *But see* Fox Broad. Co. v. Dish Network, 747 F.3d 1060 (9th Cir. 2014) (supporting Dish Network in allowing remote access of copyrighted works that included a commercial-skipping feature); Fox Broad. Co. v. Dish Network, 160 F. Supp. 3d 1139 (C.D. Cal. 2015) (reaffirming that the remote access and commercial-skipping features do not violate federal copyright provisions, but denying summary judgment on alleged violations of the retransmission consent agreements).

[59]*See* 17 U.S.C. § 511(a) (2018). Somewhat unusual provisions of ESSA stipulate that school districts shall provide training for educators regarding the use of technology effectively and responsibly and urge school personnel to explain to students the importance of copyright compliance and protecting intellectual property; professional development grants under the law can be used for this purpose, 20 U.S.C. § 8101 (2018). *See* Sean Cavanagh, *An Unlikely ESSA Provision: Warning on Copyright Piracy*, EDUC. WK. (Aug. 30, 2017), at 1, 11.

examinations, the judiciary traditionally has been reluctant to interfere with assessments of pupil performance.[60] Yet, student testing always has been controversial, and since 2014, the movement for parents to secure waivers so their children can opt out of specific state and district testing programs has gained momentum.[61] Also, the number of states conditioning high school diplomas on test passage has declined from more than half of the states a few years ago to twelve states in 2017.[62] However, there has been a significant increase in states requiring high school graduates to pass a citizenship test (similar to the test required for immigrants to become U.S. citizens). No state had such a requirement in 2014, but two years later, thirteen states required passage of a citizenship test to receive a high school diploma.[63]

Recently, other forms of performance assessment, such as portfolios, have received attention, but standardized tests continue to be used in most school districts. Annual student testing is strongly supported by the federal government. Under ESSA, all states are required to implement a set of high quality student assessments in mathematics, reading or language arts, and science. States are expected to align the assessments with challenging state academic standards and to use the same assessments to measure the achievement of all public elementary and secondary school students in the state. The assessments must include multiple up-to-date measures of academic skills and understanding in:

- math and reading or language arts in each of grades 3–8 and once in grades 9–12;
- science once in each grade block of 3–5, 6–9, and 10–12.[64]

High-stakes assessments shape the instructional program, and some states are evaluating educators' performance based on their students' test scores. Not surprisingly, claims are being made that teachers are limiting classroom activities to material covered on the tests and/or unfairly coaching students for the exams. For example, substantial publicity surrounded the test-score tampering controversy in Atlanta that in 2013 resulted in the indictments of thirty-five teachers and administrators, including the former superintendent of the Atlanta Public Schools.[65]

---

[60]*See* Hurd v. Hansen, 230 F. App'x 692 (9th Cir. 2007) (holding that a teacher's grading decision did not violate a student's equal protection or substantive due process rights).

[61]Jonathan Schweig, *Who Does the Movement to Opt Out of Standardized Testing Help?* U.S. News & World Report Rep. (May 9, 2016), https://www.usnews.com/topics/author/jonathan-schweig.

[62]Catherine Gewertz, *Which States Require an Exam to Graduate?* Educ. Wk. (Feb. 15, 2017), http://www.edweek.org/ew/section/multimedia/states-require-exam-to-graduate.html.

[63]Jackie Zubrzycki, *Thirteen States Now Require Grads to Pass Citizenship Test*, Educ. Wk. (June 7, 2016), http://blogs.edweek.org/edweek/curriculum/2016/06/fourteen_states_now_require_gr.html.

[64]20 U.S.C. § 6311(b)(2) (2018).

[65]*See* Don Campbell, *Lessons from Atlanta School Cheating Scandal*, USA Today (Apr. 7, 2013), http://www.usatoday.com/story/opinion/2013/04/07/-atlanta-school-cheating-scandal-column/2044107/; *see also* Stead v. Unified Sch. Dist., 92 F. Supp. 3d 1088 (D. Kan. 2015) (finding no deprivation of liberty or substantive due process rights or defamation in placing principal on administrative leave for testing violations); Buck v. Lowndes Cty. Sch. Dist., 761 So. 2d 144 (Miss. 2000) (upholding nonrenewal of teachers' contracts for noncompliance with testing procedures that resulted in a reduction in the district's accreditation level); Caleb v. Carranza, 518 S.W.3d 537 (Tex. App. 2017) (finding no First Amendment or Equal Protection Clause violations in the dismissal and nonrenewal of teachers based on an investigation of their cheating on student standardized tests and misappropriating school property).

Although the state's authority to evaluate student performance has not been questioned, specific high-stakes assessment programs have been legally challenged as impairing students' rights to fair and nondiscriminatory treatment. In a case still widely cited as establishing the legal standards, *Debra P. v. Turlington*, the Fifth Circuit in 1981 recognized that by making schooling mandatory, Florida created a property interest—a valid expectation that students would receive diplomas if they passed specific courses.[66] **This state-created property right to an education requires sufficient notice of conditions attached to high school graduation and a fair opportunity to satisfy them before a diploma can be withheld.** The court found that thirteen months was insufficient notice of the test requirement and further held that the state may have administered a fundamentally unfair test covering material that had not been taught in Florida schools. The appeals court also enjoined the state from using the test as a diploma prerequisite for four years to provide time for the vestiges of prior school segregation to be removed and to ensure that all students of color subjected to the requirement started first grade under desegregated conditions.

On remand, the district court ruled that the injunction should be lifted, and the appeals court affirmed this decision in 1984.[67] By presenting considerable evidence, including curriculum guides and survey data, the state convinced the judiciary that the test was instructionally valid in that it covered material taught to Florida students. Also, data showed that only students who entered school under desegregated conditions would be subjected to the diploma sanction. Furthermore, there had been significant improvement among Black students during the six years the test was administered. Other courts have reiterated the principles established in *Debra P.* and have reasoned that despite evidence of higher failure rates for students of color, such testing and remediation programs are effectively addressing the effects of prior discrimination.[68]

Administering proficiency tests to children with limited mastery of English and to students with disabilities has been controversial. After school districts and others challenged California's failure to make appropriate testing accommodations under federal testing requirements for English Learners, the parties reached a settlement under which the U.S. Department of Education changed its classification of schools needing improvement to allow more accommodations for English Learners.[69]

Courts in general have ruled that the state does not have to alter its academic standards for students with disabilities; such children can be denied grade promotion or a

[66]474 F. Supp. 244 (M.D. Fla. 1979), *aff'd in part, vacated in part*, 644 F.2d 397 (5th Cir. 1981) (upholding, however, the use of test scores to determine remediation needs in the absence of intentional discrimination).

[67]Debra P. v. Turlington, 564 F. Supp. 177 (M.D. Fla. 1983), *aff'd*, 730 F.2d 1405 (11th Cir. 1984). The Fifth Circuit was divided into the Fifth and Eleventh Circuits while this case was in progress.

[68]*See, e.g.*, GI Forum v. Tex. Educ. Agency, 87 F. Supp. 2d 667 (W.D. Tex. 2000). Courts also have upheld the practice of conditioning grade promotion on test scores. *See, e.g.*, Parents Against Testing Before Teaching v. Orleans Par. Sch. Bd., 273 F.3d 1107 (5th Cir. 2001); Bester v. Tuscaloosa City Bd. of Educ., 722 F.2d 1514 (11th Cir. 1984); Sandlin v. Johnson, 643 F.2d 1027 (4th Cir. 1981).

[69]Coachella Valley Unified Sch. Dist. v. California, 98 Cal. Rptr. 3d 9 (Ct. App. 2009) (denying a writ of mandamus and declaratory relief where the State Board of Education did not abuse its discretion in developing a testing system). Under ESSA, state plans must demonstrate that annual assessments of English proficiency of all English Learners in the schools will be conducted, 20 U.S.C. § 6311(b)(2)(G) (2018).

diploma if they do not meet the specified standards.[70] A student with cognitive disabilities may be given the option of not taking a proficiency examination if the team planning the individualized education program (IEP) concludes that there is little likelihood of the child mastering the material covered on the test. Students excused from the test requirement usually are awarded certificates of school attendance instead of diplomas. Yet such children cannot be denied the *opportunity* to satisfy requirements (including tests) for promotion or a diploma.

The Seventh Circuit suggested that children with disabilities may need earlier notice of a proficiency test requirement than other students to ensure an adequate opportunity for the material on the test to be incorporated into their IEPs.[71] Although students with disabilities are entitled to special accommodations in the administration of examinations to ensure that their knowledge, rather than their disability, is being assessed (e.g., braille tests), they are not entitled to accommodations that would jeopardize the validity of the graduation test, such as reading to the student a test measuring reading comprehension.[72] The types of accommodations required for graduation tests remain controversial, especially when accommodations that are part of the student's IEP for classroom instruction are denied for high-stakes tests.[73]

Specific proficiency testing programs will likely continue to be challenged on constitutional and statutory grounds. Educators would be wise to keep in mind the points listed in Figure 4.2.

FIGURE 4.2   High-Stakes Proficiency Testing Programs

Proficiency tests used as a prerequisite to high school graduation will survive legal challenges if:

- students are advised upon beginning high school of test requirements as a prerequisite to graduation;
- students have the opportunity to be adequately prepared for the tests;
- tests are not intentionally discriminatory and do not perpetuate the effects of past school segregation;
- students who fail are provided remedial opportunities and the chance to retake the examinations; and
- children with disabilities and English Learners receive appropriate accommodations.

---

[70]*See, e.g.*, Brookhart v. Ill. St. Bd. of Educ., 697 F.2d 179 (7th Cir. 1983); Anderson v. Banks, 540 F. Supp. 761 (S.D. Ga. 1982); Bd. of Educ. v. Ambach, 457 N.E.2d 775 (N.Y. 1983).

[71]*Brookhart*, 697 F.2d at 187. *But see* Rene v. Reed, 751 N.E.2d 736 (Ind. Ct. App. 2001), *transfer denied*, 774 N.E.2d 506 (Ind. 2002) (reasoning that three years' notice of the test requirement as a prerequisite to a diploma was sufficient for students with disabilities, given ample opportunities to receive remediation and retake the exam). *See* Chapter 7 for a discussion of federal and state protections of students with disabilities.

[72]*See Rene*, 751 N.E.2d 736. The Office for Civil Rights in the U.S. Department of Education has reasoned that states can deny use of reading devices to accommodate students with disabilities on graduation exams, even though their IEPs allow use of such devices. *See* Ala. Dep't of Educ., 29 INDIVIDUALS WITH DISABILITIES EDUC. L. REP. (LRP) 249 (1998).

[73]*See* Smiley v. Cal. Dep't of Educ., 53 F. App'x 474 (9th Cir. 2002) (dissolving the parts of the lower court's injunction pertaining to required test waivers and alternative assessments for children with disabilities as not ripe for adjudication).

INSTRUCTIONAL PRIVACY RIGHTS

Parents are entitled to review their children's records and instructional materials and to have personal information kept confidential.

The protection of students' privacy rights has become an increasingly volatile issue in political forums. The Supreme Court has recognized that the U.S. Constitution protects a zone of personal privacy, requiring a compelling justification for governmental action that impairs privacy rights, including the right to have personal information kept confidential. Constitutional privacy rights extend to minors, but parents also have rights in directing the upbringing of their children. The Fifth Circuit in 2013 held that there is no clearly established law creating a secondary school student's privacy right that "precludes school officials from discussing with a parent the student's private matters," including the student's sexual orientation and sexual activities.[74] However, a parent was unsuccessful in asserting that she had a constitutional right to obtain information about her children from their school where materials were generally available to the parent who shared legal, but not physical, custody of the children; the Eighth Circuit held that the few instances when her requests were denied did not constitute a deprivation of her fundamental liberty interests.[75]

State and federal laws additionally place dual duties on the government—to protect the public's right to be informed about government activities and to protect the personal privacy of individuals. Often there is a tension between these two legitimate government interests. Laws also have been enacted to protect students from mandatory participation in research projects and instructional activities designed to reveal personal information in sensitive areas. This section provides an overview of legal developments pertaining to students' privacy rights in instructional matters.

Student Records

Due to widespread dissatisfaction with educators' efforts to ameliorate abuses associated with student record-keeping practices, Congress enacted the Family Educational Rights and Privacy Act (FERPA) in 1974.[76] **FERPA stipulates that federal funds may be withdrawn from any education agency or institution that (1) fails to provide parents access to their child's education records or (2) disseminates such information (with some exceptions) to third parties without parental permission.** Upon reaching age eighteen or enrolling in a postsecondary institution, students may exercise the rights previously

---

[74]Wyatt v. Fletcher, 718 F.3d 496, 499 (5th Cir. 2013).

[75]Schmidt v. Des Moines Pub. Schs., 655 F.3d 811 (8th Cir. 2011).

[76]20 U.S.C. § 1232g (2018); 34 C.F.R. §§ 99.1–99.67 (2018). Parents have a right to obtain copies of their children's records, for which they may be charged a fee, and they are entitled to have the records interpreted. The term "parents" is used throughout the remainder of this section, but FERPA provisions also apply to students' legal guardians who may not be their parents.

guaranteed to their parents.[77] FERPA was amended in 1992 to allow the release of records for purposes of law enforcement, which includes school districts' security units, and again in 1998 to specify that records related to discipline for crimes of violence or sex crimes were excluded from FERPA protection.[78] In 2009, the Department of Education issued changes in FERPA rules stipulating that FERPA can apply to alumni records as well as those of current students, and in 2011, the definition of education programs was broadened to cover any programs primarily involved in the provision of education, including early childhood, elementary and secondary, postsecondary, adult, career and technical, and special education.[79] FERPA amendments in 2013 (Uninterrupted Scholars Act) allow education institutions to disclose education records of students in foster care to agency caseworkers or other child welfare representatives if the agency is legally responsible for the care of the student.[80]

After reviewing a student's permanent file, the parent or eligible student can request amendments to any information thought to be inaccurate, misleading, or in violation of the student's protected rights. If school authorities decide that an amendment is not warranted, the parent or eligible student must be advised of the right to a hearing and of the right to place in the file a personal statement specifying objections to the hearing officer's decision. Education officials should assume that a parent is entitled to exercise rights under FERPA unless state law or a court order bars a parent's access to his or her child's records under specific circumstances. In the absence of such legal documentation, noncustodial or joint-custody parents must be given equal access to education information about their child. **Parents and adult students must be given annual notice of their FERPA rights**.

Individuals can file a complaint with the Family Policy Compliance Office in the U.S. Department of Education if they believe a school district exhibits a custom or practice of violating FERPA provisions.[81] The remedy for FERPA violations is the withdrawal of federal funds, and the Department of Education has enforcement authority. Some school districts have been advised to remedy their practices to conform to FERPA, but to date, no district has lost federal funds for noncompliance. See Figure 4.3 for a summary of student information that can and cannot be released under FERPA.

The Department of Education functioned without direction from the Supreme Court until 2002 when the Court rendered two FERPA decisions. **In *Gonzaga University v. Doe*, the Court held that individuals cannot bring damages suits for FERPA violations**

[77]The Family Policy Compliance Office was created to investigate alleged FERPA violations, 20 U.S.C. § 1232g(g) (2018). For a discussion of FERPA protections, *see* Justin Bathon, John Gooden & James Plenty, *Student Records, in* Decker et al. eds., *supra* note 56; Student Press Law Ctr., *FERPA and Access to Public Records* (2011), http://www.splc.org/pdf/ferpa_wp.pdf.

[78]*See* 34 C.F.R. § 99.8 (2018); U.S. Dep't of Educ., *Addressing Emergencies on Campus* (June 2011), http://www2.ed.gov/policy/gen/guid/fpco/pdf/emergency-guidance.pdf.

[79]*See* 34 C.F.R. §§ 99.3, 99.35 (2018); *see also* Ohio *ex rel.* Souffrance v. Doe, 968 N.E.2d 477 (Ohio 2012) (holding that FERPA precluded releasing records with the identities of students who had used particular school computer terminals during specific times; although the individuals no longer were students, they were students when the records were created and originally maintained).

[80]20 U.S.C. § 1232g (b)(1)(L) (2018).

[81]*See* U.S. Dep't of Educ., *Protecting Student Privacy, Student Privacy 101* (n.d.), http://familypolicy.ed.gov.

FIGURE 4.3   FERPA Compliance

School personnel can share the following identifiable student information without notice or consent of parents or qualifying students:

- Personal notes in sole possession of the maker and shared only with a substitute teacher
- Information subpoenaed by courts or law enforcement agencies*
- Material needed by child welfare agencies responsible for the care of specific children
- Information sought by the U.S. Attorney General in connection with terrorism investigations
- Data needed to monitor childhood nutrition laws

School personnel can share the following identifiable student information if parents (guardians) or qualifying students are provided notice and the opportunity to object:

- Directory information (e.g., name, address, date of birth, photo, degree)
- Records made available to authorized school personnel, including personnel at schools to which students are transferring

School personnel can share the following student information so long as individual students cannot be identified:

- Composite student discipline and achievement data
- Material needed to audit and evaluate government programs
- Data for organizations and agencies to conduct research to improve instruction and school services

School personnel cannot:

- Post student grades in alphabetical order or in other formats that allow students to be identified
- Use student personal identification numbers to access student education records
- Disseminate personally identifiable student information to news media or other third parties without written parental consent

*Reasonable effort should be made to notify parents unless they are a party in the legal proceedings.

---

because the law does not create privately enforceable rights; Congress must create such rights in unambiguous terms.[82] In addition to finding no private right to bring suit directly under FERPA, the Supreme Court held that individuals cannot use Section 1983 of the Civil Rights Act of 1871 to initiate damages claims for FERPA violations.[83] The Court reiterated that FERPA has an aggregate rather than individual focus, and the remedy for violations is the denial of federal funds to schools that exhibit a policy or practice of non-compliance. School personnel were relieved that the Court did not authorize private suits for damages to enforce FERPA because such a ruling would have provided a significant incentive for parents to challenge student record-keeping practices in court.

---

[82]536 U.S. 273 (2002) (overturning an award of damages to a student for an alleged FERPA violation in connection with a private university's release to the state education department records of an unsubstantiated allegation of sexual misconduct, which resulted in the student being denied an affidavit of good moral character required to become a public school teacher).

[83]*Id.* at 285. For a discussion of damages remedies available under 42 U.S.C. § 1983 (2018), *see* text accompanying note 122, Chapter 12.

In the second 2002 Supreme Court ruling, *Owasso Independent School District v. Falvo*, the Court reversed the Tenth Circuit's conclusion that peer grading practices violate FERPA.[84] The Supreme Court concluded that peer graders are not "maintaining" student records under FERPA, and even though students may call out the scores in class, they are not "acting for" the educational institution.[85] There may be educational reasons for not having students grade each other's work, but given the *Falvo* ruling, there is no FERPA barrier.

FERPA defines education records as files, documents, and other materials that contain information identifying a student and are maintained by the education agency.[86] In 2009, the Department of Education broadened the definition of education records, specifying that schools can deny requests for records even with identifiable information removed if the records could be linked to a particular student by someone in the school community with inside knowledge.[87] Once identifying information is removed (redacted), it ceases to be an education record and may then be subject to disclosure pursuant to state open records or freedom of information laws.[88]

A student's records can be released to school employees authorized to review such information and to officials of a school where the student is transferring if the parents or eligible student are notified or if the sending institution has given prior notice that it routinely releases such records. It would be wise for school districts to include such information in the annual notice of privacy rights provided to parents.

Students' records must be disclosed when subpoenaed by a grand jury or law enforcement agency, and schools may disclose information under other court orders or subpoenas if a reasonable effort is made to notify the parent or eligible student.[89] The Sixth Circuit ruled that records related to substitute teachers' use of corporal punishment must be disclosed in a suit challenging the use of this disciplinary technique because FERPA does not prevent discovery of such records.[90]

---

[84]233 F.3d 1203 (10th Cir. 2000), *rev'd and remanded*, 534 U.S. 426 (2002), *on remand*, 288 F.3d 1236 (10th Cir. 2002) (granting summary judgment in favor of defendant school district and administrators).

[85]*Owasso*, 534 U.S. at 433. Although peers can call out scores, students' grades cannot be posted or disseminated in any manner that allows individual students to be identified (e.g., by name or listed in alphabetical order).

[86]20 U.S.C. § 1232g(a)(4)(A) (2018). According to the Student Press Law Center, *supra* note 77, a document must not simply mention a student, but the information must be *about* the student to be protected by FERPA.

[87]34 C.F.R. § 99.3 (2018).

[88]Student Press Law Ctr., *supra* note 77. Simply because a student is identified does not mean that such information is a record maintained by the school. *See, e.g.*, Jensen v. Reeves, 3 F. App'x 905 (10th Cir. 2001) (finding that disclosures to parents of harassment and assault victims of how the perpetrator was handled did not comprise an education record under FERPA); *see also* Lindeman v. Kelso Sch. Dist., 172 P.3d 329 (Wash. 2007) (holding that a videotape recorded on the school bus for safety reasons was not a record maintained for students, so it did not qualify as exempt from public disclosure under state law).

[89]In 2013, the parental notification requirement was modified in instances of subpoenas or judicial orders in that schools must simply make a "reasonable effort," and in cases of child abuse and neglect, such notice is not required, 20 U.S.C. § 1232g (b)(2)(B) (2018); *see also* Edmonds v. Detroit Pub. Sch. Sys., 2012 WL 5844655 (E.D. Mich. Nov. 19, 2012) (upholding a court order to release material needed in judicial proceedings).

[90]Ellis *ex rel.* Pendergrass v. Cleveland Mun. Sch. Dist., 455 F.3d 690 (6th Cir. 2006); *see also* People v. Owens, 727 N.Y.S.2d 266 (Sup. Ct. 2001) (finding no FERPA violation in prosecution based in part on records subpoenaed from educational institutions).

Identifiable information also can be disclosed to appropriate authorities or to advocacy groups if necessary to protect the health or safety of the student or others.[91] For example, the Seventh Circuit ruled that the Wisconsin Department of Public Instruction must provide names of students in connection with a state-designated advocacy agency's investigation of alleged abuse or neglect without first obtaining parental consent because the need to investigate suspected abuse or neglect can outweigh privacy interests.[92]

Personal notes pertaining to pupil progress that are kept by educators and shared only with substitute teachers are not considered education records that must be made available to parents. To illustrate, a California federal district court ruled that email messages about students stored on individual teachers' computers were not education records because they were not maintained by the school.[93] Private notes, however, become education records and are subject to legal specifications once they are shared, even among educators who have a legitimate need for access to such information.

FERPA allows release without parental consent of certain public directory information, such as students' names, addresses, dates and places of birth, major fields of study, email addresses, pictures, and degrees and awards received.[94] Any educational agency releasing such data must give public notice of the specific categories it has designated as "directory" and must allow a reasonable period of time for parents to inform the agency that any or all of this information on their child should not be released without their prior consent. Directory data about a student cannot be released if accompanied by other personally identifiable information unless it is among the specified exceptions to the general rule against nonconsensual disclosure.[95] Personal identification numbers for students can be used on student badges and to communicate via electronic systems, but such numbers cannot be used alone or in conjunction with other identifiers to access student records.[96]

Students' privacy rights do not preclude federal and state authorities from having access to data needed to audit and evaluate the effectiveness of publicly supported education programs so long as collected in a way that prevents the disclosure of personally identifiable

---

[91]Under the Healthy, Hunger-Free Kids Act of 2010, education institutions can disclose personally identifiable information about students to the Secretary of Agriculture or authorized representations of the Food and Nutrition Service to monitor programs under federal childhood nutrition laws, 20 U.S.C. § 1232g (b)(1)(K) (2018); *see also* Disability Law Ctr. v. Anchorage Sch. Dist., 581 F.3d 936 (9th Cir. 2009) (ruling that an advocacy organization could have access to personally identifiable information about students with disabilities as part of its investigation of alleged violations of the Developmental Disabilities Assistance and Bill of Rights Act); Doe v. Woodford Cty. Bd. of Educ., 213 F.3d 921 (6th Cir. 2000) (upholding disclosure to coach of information that student was a hemophiliac and carrier of hepatitis B); 34 C.F.R. § 99.36 (2018).

[92]Disability Rights Wis. v. Wis. Dep't of Pub. Instruction, 463 F.3d 719 (7th Cir. 2006).

[93]S.A. *ex rel.* L.A v. Tulare Cty. Office of Educ., 2009 WL 31226322 (E.D. Cal. Sept. 24, 2009).

[94]For a complete list of directory items, *see* 34 C.F.R. § 99.3 (2018). However, "address" is not considered a directory item for homeless children. *See* McKinney-Vento Homeless Assistance Act, 42 U.S.C. § 11431 (2018); U.S. Dep't of Educ., *Education for Homeless Children and Youths Program Non-Regulatory Guidance* 8 (Mar. 2017).

[95]*See* Ohio *ex rel.* Sch. Choice Ohio v. Cincinnati Pub. Sch. Dist., 63 N.E.3d 1183 (Ohio 2016) (denying a private choice organization's request for the school to expand its directory information; FERPA does not compel a school district to change its definition to satisfy a request).

[96]*See* Electronic Privacy Info. Ctr. v. U.S. Dep't of Educ., 48 F. Supp. 3d 1 (D.C. 2014) (rejecting standing for the Center to challenge the law's provision allowing use of student personal identifiers).

information. However, FERPA was amended in 2001 to give institutions permission to disclose, without parental or student consent, personally identifiable information to representatives of the U.S. Attorney General based on an order from a court of competent jurisdiction in connection with investigations of terrorism crimes.[97] Under federal law, public secondary schools must provide military recruiters with access to personal contact information for every student, although parents can request that their children's records be withheld.[98]

Composite information on pupil achievement and discipline can be released to the public so long as individual students are not personally identified. Disciplinary information (number of occurrences and when they occurred without identifiable data) *must* be released to the media pursuant to some state open records laws.[99] But personally identifiable achievement or discipline data cannot be released under FERPA, and state law may be even more restrictive. For example, a Florida appeals court ruled that discipline forms and surveillance video tapes about incidents on school buses could not be disclosed to a television station even with personally identifying information redacted because Florida law goes further than FERPA in preventing the release of such information.[100]

FERPA cannot be used by parents to assert a right to review faculty evaluations used to determine which students will be given academic honors, such as membership in the National Honor Society.[101] Also, students cannot rely on FERPA to challenge teachers' grading procedures, other than whether grades were accurately calculated and recorded.[102] The Fourth Circuit ruled that FERPA does not entitle students to see an answer key to exams to check the accuracy of their grades, because the key is not part of students' education records.[103]

Given the movement to digital student records, the Privacy Technical Assistance Center in the U.S. Department of Education updated its guidance on using online education services in 2015.[104] This *Toolkit* addresses the life cycle of data and how to properly destroy sensitive data that is no longer needed. With new technologies emerging and the popularity of using cloud databases, educators and policy makers will continue to struggle with protecting students' privacy in a digitized environment.[105]

---

[97]20 U.S.C. § 1232g(j) (2018). This change was to comply with the USA PATRIOT Act, 18 U.S.C. § 2332b(g)(5)(B) (2018). Schools are required to record such disclosures in students' permanent files.

[98]20 U.S.C. § 1232h(c)(4)(a)(i) (2018).

[99]*See, e.g.*, Hardin Cty. Schs. v. Foster, 40 S.W.3d 865 (Ky. 2001); Bd. of Trs. v. Cut Bank Pioneer Press, 160 P.3d 482 (Mont. 2007).

[100]WFTV v. Sch. Bd., 874 So. 2d 48 (Fla. Dist. Ct. App. 2004); *see also* K.L. v. Evesham Twp. Bd. of Educ., 32 A.3d 1136 (N.J. Super. Ct. App. Div. 2011) (holding that notes prepared by school personnel concerning bullying incidents would not have to be released to the public under the state's open records law; confidentiality concerns were overriding).

[101]*See, e.g.*, Moore v. Hyche, 761 F. Supp. 112 (N.D. Ala. 1991); Price v. Young, 580 F. Supp. 1 (E.D. Ark. 1983); Becky v. Butte-Silver Bow Sch. Dist., 906 P.2d 193 (Mont. 1995).

[102]*See, e.g.*, Tarka v. Cunningham, 917 F.2d 890 (5th Cir. 1990); *see also* Hurd v. Hansen, 230 F. App'x 692 (9th Cir. 2007) (finding no violation of a student's due process and equal protection rights in a teacher's award of a "C" grade to the student).

[103]Lewin v. Cooke, 28 F. App'x 186 (4th Cir. 2002).

[104]U.S. Dep't of Educ., *Privacy Technical Assistance Ctr. Toolkit* (2015), https://nces.ed.gov/programs/ptac/Toolkit.aspx.

[105]*See* Elana Zeide, *Student Privacy Principles for the Age of Big Data: Moving beyond FERPA and FIPPS*, 8 DREXEL L. REV. 339 (2016).

Other federal laws provide additional protections regarding the confidentiality and accessibility of student records.[106] An important provision is the Children's Online Privacy Protection Act (COPPA) of 1998 that requires operators of websites, online services, and mobile apps to obtain parental consent before collecting personal information on children under age thirteen.[107] Although COPPA does not regulate schools, it has implications for educators; school districts under limited circumstances can serve in place of parents in granting permission for website and other online service operators to collect student data that is strictly for educational purposes.[108]

Many states also have enacted legislation addressing the maintenance and disclosure of student records. In fact, more than three-fourths of the states have provisions addressing the privacy of student data, and many of these laws focus on electronic records.[109] Both state and federal privacy laws recognize certain exceptions to "access and disclosure" provisions, such as a teacher's notes discussed previously.

Because Congress, state legislatures, and the judiciary have indicated a continuing interest in safeguarding students' privacy rights in connection with education records, school boards would be wise to reassess their policies to ensure they are adhering to federal and state laws.[110] School personnel should use some restraint, however, before purging information from student files. Pertinent material that is necessary to provide continuity in a student's instructional program *should* be included in a permanent record and should be available for use by authorized personnel. It is unfortunate that school personnel, fearing federal sanctions under FERPA, have deleted useful information—along with material that should be removed—from student records. The mere fact that information in a student's file is negative does not imply that the material is inappropriate. Public school officials have a *duty* to record true, factual information about students and to communicate such information to schools where students are transferring, including institutions of higher learning.

Student Protection and Parental Rights Laws

Congress and state legislatures have enacted laws to protect family privacy in connection with school research activities and treatment programs. Pursuant to federal law, human subjects are protected in research projects supported by federal grants and contracts in any

---

[106]*See, e.g.,* Individuals with Disabilities Education Act, 20 U.S.C. § 1415(b)(1) (2018) (protecting the right of parents to examine all school records maintained on their children with disabilities).

[107]15 U.S.C. § 6501 (2018).

[108]*See* Lorie K. Dakessian, *Schools as Stewards of Student Data* (Nov. 10, 2017), paper presented at the Educ. Law Ass'n Annual Conference, San Diego, CA; Benjamin Herold, *COPPA and Schools: The (Other) Federal Student Privacy Law, Explained*, EDUC. WK. (July 28, 2017), http://www.edweek.org/ew/issues/childrens-online-privacy-protection-act-coppa/index.html. Securing parental permission to share student information with website operators is always a wise policy as schools will never be faulted for obtaining parental consent when not legally required.

[109]*See* Nat'l Conference of State Legislatures, *Student Data Privacy* (Feb. 10, 2017), http://www.ncsl.org/research/education/student-data-privacy.aspx.

[110]*See* L.S. v. Mt. Olive Bd. of Educ., 765 F. Supp. 2d 648 (D.N.J. 2011) (finding a school social worker and special education instructor liable for violating a high school student's federal and state privacy rights by intentionally disclosing to classmates his confidential psychiatric evaluation that was not properly redacted).

private or public institution or agency.[111] **Informed consent must be obtained before placing subjects at risk of being exposed to physical, psychological, or social injury as a result of participating in research, development, or related activities**. All education agencies are required to establish review committees to ensure that the rights and welfare of all subjects are adequately protected.

Several amendments to the General Education Provisions Act, most notably the 1978 Hatch Amendment, require all instructional materials in federally assisted research or experimentation projects to be made available for inspection by parents of participating students. Under the more recent Protection of Pupil Rights Amendment, parents must be allowed to review in advance all instructional materials in programs administered by the Department of Education, and such federally assisted programs cannot require students, without prior written parental consent, to be subjected to surveys or evaluations that reveal information pertaining to personal beliefs, behaviors, and family relationships.[112] The department is charged with reviewing complaints under this law; if an educational institution is found in violation and does not comply within a reasonable period, federal funds can be withheld.

Parents have not been successful in using these provisions to require parental consent for a student to be seen by a school counselor,[113] to challenge use of certain questions in the statewide student assessment program,[114] or to negate surveying elementary students about their attitudes and behaviors so long as the data are reported only in the aggregate.[115] The Ninth Circuit declared that parents do not have a freestanding fundamental right, or a right encompassed by any other fundamental right, to prevent the school from providing elementary school students with important information pertaining to psychological barriers to learning.[116] Proclaiming that "schools cannot be expected to accommodate the personal, moral, or religious concerns of every parent,"[117] the court found the school's psychological survey to be a reasonable way to advance legitimate state interests.

There is concern among educators that the existing and proposed federal and state pupil protection requirements and similar provisions being considered or enacted by many states that allow parents to seek alternative assignments for instruction they find offensive will cause certain instructional activities to be dropped. Although these measures are couched in terms of protecting students' privacy rights by granting them *exemptions* from particular instructional activities, if a significant number of exemptions are requested, the instructional activity may be eliminated from the curriculum.

---

[111]42 U.S.C. § 289 (2018); 45 C.F.R. §§ 46.101–46.124 (2018).

[112]20 U.S.C. § 1232h (2018). The sensitive areas pertain to students' or their parents' political affiliations; mental or psychological problems; sexual behavior or attitudes; illegal, antisocial, or demeaning behavior; critical appraisals of family members; legally recognized privileged relationships; religious practices or beliefs; and income. Parents must be notified at least annually of their rights under this law.

[113]Newkirk v. E. Lansing Pub. Schs., 57 F.3d 1070 (6th Cir. 1995).

[114]Triplett v. Livingston Cty. Bd. of Educ., 967 S.W.2d 25 (Ky. Ct. App. 1997).

[115]C.N. v. Ridgewood Bd. of Educ., 430 F.3d 159 (3d Cir. 2005).

[116]Fields v. Palmdale Sch. Dist., 427 F.3d 1197, 1206 (9th Cir. 2005) (citing Brown v. Hot, Sexy & Safer Prods., 68 F.3d 525, 533–34 (1st Cir. 1995)).

[117]*Fields*, 427 F.3d at 1206.

CONCLUSION

Issues pertaining to the public school instructional program will continue to generate legal activity—both legislative mandates and judicial challenges to such requirements. Student testing practices are likely to remain controversial, especially the instruments designed to assess mastery of the common core standards. The state and its agents enjoy considerable latitude in regulating various aspects of the public school instructional program, but requirements cannot impair students' constitutional rights. School authorities must be able to substantiate that there is an overriding public interest to be served if school policies or practices abridge students' or parents' protected rights. Educators always should ensure that their instructional activities match course objectives and that they respect federal copyright requirements and students' privacy rights. Based on an analysis of legal developments pertaining to requirements and rights associated with instructional issues, the following generalizations seem warranted.

1. The state and its agencies have the authority to determine public school course offerings and instructional materials, and such curricular determinations will be upheld by courts unless clearly arbitrary or in violation of constitutional or statutory rights.

2. School boards can eliminate instructional materials considered educationally unsuitable if objective procedures are followed in making such determinations.

3. Public schools are required by federal law to implement measures to shield students from access to harmful Internet content on school computers.

4. Educators are expected to comply with federal requirements in seeking permission to use most copyrighted works in their classrooms; individuals will never be faulted for seeking permission that is not needed.

5. Copyrighted material may be used for instructional purposes without the publisher's permission if "fair use" guidelines are followed.

6. For copyright purposes, classroom materials developed by teachers are owned by the schools where the teachers are employed; such materials are considered "work for hire" unless specified otherwise in the employment contract.

7. Licensing agreements for electronic textbooks and other digital materials must be strictly followed to avoid copyright infringements.

8. In the absence of evidence of arbitrary or discriminatory academic decisions, courts defer to school authorities in assessing student performance.

9. Proficiency examinations can be used to determine pupil remedial needs and as a prerequisite to high school graduation if students are given sufficient notice prior to implementation of the test requirements and are provided adequate preparation for the examinations.

10. Parents and 18-year-old students must be granted access to the student's school records and an opportunity to contest the contents.

11. Individuals do not have a private right to bring suits for damages under FERPA; the remedy for violations is the withdrawal of federal aid from the noncomplying agency.

12. School personnel must ensure the accuracy of information contained in student records and must maintain the confidentiality of such records.

13. Under FERPA, education records are files, documents, and other materials that contain information identifying a student and are maintained by the education agency; educators' personal notes about students (shared only with substitute teachers) are not considered education records.

14. FERPA allows certain directory information, such as students' names, addresses, photos, and degrees, to be released without parental consent so long as parents have the opportunity to request that specific information be withheld.

15. Parents have the right to inspect materials used in federally funded experimental projects or surveys; students have a right to be excused from participation in such programs or activities involving psychiatric or psychological testing or treatment designed to reveal information in specified sensitive areas pertaining to personal beliefs, behaviors, and family relationships.

CHAPTER FIVE

STUDENT EXPRESSION, ASSOCIATION, AND APPEARANCE

Can students wear Confederate flag insignia to school? Can school officials discipline students for posting something offensive about their teachers on Instagram? Can a male student wear a dress to the prom? Students continue to test the limits of their personal freedoms in public schools, frequently colliding with educators' efforts to maintain an appropriate school environment. This chapter addresses students' substantive rights regarding First Amendment freedoms of expression and press and closely related association rights.

Readers of this chapter should be able to:

- Discuss the four Supreme Court student expression cases and the legal principles they established.
- Describe what constitutes a true threat.
- Analyze the circumstances under which student Internet expression can be curtailed.
- Explain the conditions under which student clubs can meet in public schools.
- Identify the types of student attire that can be barred in public schools and explain why.

FREEDOM OF SPEECH AND PRESS

Students have the right to express nondisruptive ideological views at school, but restrictions can be placed on their expression that represents the school.

The First Amendment, as applied to the states through the Fourteenth Amendment, restricts *governmental* interference with citizens' free expression rights, which are perhaps the most preciously guarded individual liberties. **The government, including public school boards, must have a compelling justification to curtail citizens' expression, even of unpopular viewpoints.**[1] In addition, citizens cannot be required to express particular views

[1]*See, e.g.*, Texas v. Johnson, 491 U.S. 397 (1989) (upholding political protesters' right to burn the American flag). Yet, free expression rights can be restricted. As Justice Holmes noted a century ago, freedom of speech does not allow an individual to yell "fire" in a crowded theater when there is no fire, Schenck v. United States, 249 U.S. 47 (1919).

(i.e., forced speech).[2] The First Amendment also shields the individual's right to remain silent when confronted with an illegitimate government demand for expression, such as mandatory participation in saluting the American flag in public schools.[3]

Free speech guarantees apply only to conduct that constitutes expression. **Where conduct is meant to communicate an idea that is likely to be understood by the intended audience, it is considered expression for First Amendment purposes.**[4] Even if specific conduct qualifies as expression, it is not assured constitutional protection. **The judiciary has recognized that defamatory,[5] obscene,[6] and inflammatory[7] communications are outside the protective arm of the First Amendment**. In addition, as discussed below, lewd and vulgar comments and expression promoting illegal activity for minors are not protected in the public school context. In short, expression that could not be censored among adults in other settings can be curtailed in public schools.[8] Also, commercial expression, although constitutionally protected, has not been afforded the same level of First Amendment protection as has speech intended to convey a particular point of view.[9]

[2]*See* Frudden v. Pilling, 742 F.3d 1199 (9th Cir. 2014), *infra* text accompanying note 116. *But see* Brinsdon v. McAllen Indep. Sch. Dist., 863 F.3d 338 (5th Cir. 2017) (finding no forced speech in a class assignment for students in an advanced Spanish class to recite the Mexican pledge of allegiance to enhance their cultural awareness).

[3]*See* W. Va. State Bd. of Educ. v. Barnette, 319 U.S. 624 (1943); *see also* text accompanying note 102, Chapter 3. In 2017, national anthem protests moved from the NFL into some high schools. While generally agreed that public school students have the right to abstain from patriotic observances, some school districts have continued to ask all students to stand, so controversies persist. *See* Evie Blad, *Students Have a Right to Protest During National Anthem, Pledge of Allegiance*, EDUC. WK. (Sept. 24, 2017).

[4]For a discussion of these requirements, *see* Johnson, 491 U.S. at 404. In the school context, *see, e.g.,* Jarman v. Williams, 753 F.2d 76 (8th Cir. 1985) (holding that social and recreational dancing in public schools is not expression that enjoys First Amendment protection).

[5]For a discussion of spoken and written defamation in the school setting, *see* section entitled "Defamation" in Chapter 2.

[6]The judiciary has held that individuals cannot claim a First Amendment right to voice or publish obscenities, although there is no bright-line rule regarding what expression falls in this category. *See* Miller v. California, 413 U.S. 15, 24 (1973) (identifying the following test to distinguish obscene material from constitutionally protected material: "(a) whether 'the average person, applying contemporary community standards' would find that the work, taken as a whole, appeals to the prurient interests; (b) whether the work depicts or describes, in a patently offensive way, sexual conduct specifically defined by the applicable state law; and (c) whether the work, taken as a whole, lacks serious literary, artistic, political, or scientific value") (citations omitted). The Supreme Court has recognized the government's authority to adjust the definition of obscenity as applied to minors. *See, e.g.,* Ginsberg v. New York, 390 U.S. 629 (1968) (upholding a state law prohibiting the sale to minors of magazines depicting female nudity).

[7]Courts have differentiated fighting words and other expression that agitate, threaten, or incite an immediate breach of peace from speech that conveys ideas and stimulates discussion. *See infra* text accompanying note 35 for a discussion of litigation pertaining to student expression considered inflammatory or threatening.

[8]*See* Bethel Sch. Dist. v. Fraser, 478 U.S. 675, 682 (1986) (recognizing that "the constitutional rights of students in public school are not automatically coextensive with the rights of adults"); Tinker v. Des Moines Indep. Sch. Dist., 393 U.S. 503, 506 (1969) (noting that free expression rights must be "applied in light of the special characteristics of the school environment").

[9]Bd. of Trs. v. Fox, 492 U.S. 469 (1989). Courts generally have also upheld regulations prohibiting sales and fundraising activities in public schools as justified to preserve schools for their educational function and to prevent commercial exploitation of students.

If protected expression is at issue, an assessment of the type of forum the government has created for expressive activities has been important in determining whether the expression can be restricted. The Supreme Court has recognized that public places, such as streets and parks, are traditional public forums for assembly and communication where content-based restrictions cannot be imposed unless justified by a compelling government interest.[10] In contrast, expression can be confined to the governmental purpose of the property in a nonpublic forum, such as a public school. **Content-based restrictions are permissible in a nonpublic forum to ensure that expression is compatible with the intended governmental purpose, provided that regulations are reasonable and do not entail viewpoint discrimination.**[11]

The government can create a *limited public forum* for expression on public property that otherwise would be considered a nonpublic forum and reserved for its governmental function. For example, a student activities program held after school might be established as a limited forum for student expression. A limited forum can be restricted to a certain class of speakers (e.g., students) and/or to specific categories of expression (e.g., noncommercial speech).[12] Otherwise, expression in a limited forum is subject to the same protections that govern a traditional public forum.

Legal Principles

This section reviews the four Supreme Court rulings that have established the legal principles governing student expression rights in public schools (see Figure 5.1). Application of these principles is addressed in subsequent sections.

In 1969, the Supreme Court rendered its landmark decision, *Tinker v. Des Moines Independent School District*, the Magna Carta of students' expression rights.[13] In *Tinker*, three students were suspended from school for wearing black armbands to protest the Vietnam War. Hearing about the planned silent protest, the school principals met and devised a policy forbidding the wearing of armbands at school. Concluding that the students were punished for expression that was not accompanied by any disorder or disturbance, the Supreme Court ruled that "undifferentiated fear or apprehension of disturbance is not enough to overcome the right to freedom of expression."[14]

In *Tinker*, the Supreme Court echoed statements made in an earlier federal appellate ruling: **A student may express opinions on controversial issues in the classroom, cafeteria, playing field, or any other place, so long as the exercise of such rights does not "materially and substantially interfere with the requirements of appropriate**

---

[10]Cornelius v. NAACP Legal Def. & Educ. Fund, 473 U.S. 788 (1985); Perry Educ. Ass'n v. Perry Local Educators' Ass'n, 460 U.S. 37 (1983). Some speech in public schools, such as that related to the curriculum, is considered government speech and is not subject to First Amendment analysis. *See* Nelda Cambron-McCabe, *When Government Speaks: An Examination of the Evolving Government Speech Doctrine*, 274 EDUC. L. REP. 753 (2012).

[11]Cornelius, 473 U.S. 788. Viewpoint discrimination occurs when the government favors one opinion or a particular side of a controversy. *See infra* text accompanying note 48 for a discussion of circumstances when student viewpoints can be censored in public schools.

[12]*See* R.O. *ex rel.* Ochshorn v. Ithaca City Sch. Dist., 645 F.3d 533 (2d Cir. 2011) (noting that in a limited forum, school authorities can restrict speech in a viewpoint-neutral manner that is reasonable in light of the forum's purpose), *infra* text accompanying note 26.

[13]393 U.S. 503 (1969).

[14]*Id.* at 508.

FIGURE 5.1　Supreme Court Student Expression Decisions

> ***Tinker v. Des Moines*** (1969): Students can express ideological views at school unless the expression threatens a substantial disruption of the educational process or interferes with the rights of others.
> ***Bethel Sch. Dist. v. Fraser*** (1986): School authorities can censor lewd, vulgar, or indecent student expression and can decide what falls in the prohibited categories.
> ***Hazelwood Sch. Dist. v. Kuhlmeier*** (1988): School authorities can censor student expression in school-related activities for pedagogical reasons.
> ***Morse v. Frederick*** (2007): Student expression promoting illegal activities can be curtailed.

discipline in the operation of the school" or collide with the rights of others.[15] In other words, student expression of ideological views can be curtailed only if linked to a school disruption or an infringement on others' rights. The Supreme Court emphasized that educators have the authority and duty to maintain discipline in schools, but they must consider students' constitutional rights as they exert control.

The Supreme Court did not decide another student expression case until 1986. In a significant opinion, *Bethel School District v. Fraser*, the Court granted school authorities considerable latitude in censoring lewd, vulgar, and indecent student expression. Overturning the lower courts, the Supreme Court upheld disciplinary action against a student (Fraser) for using a sexual metaphor in a nomination speech during a student government assembly.[16] **Concluding that the sexual innuendos were offensive to both teachers and students, the Court majority held that the school's legitimate interest in protecting the captive student audience from exposure to lewd and vulgar speech justified the disciplinary action.**

The Court in *Bethel* reiterated that speech protected by the First Amendment for adults is not necessarily protected for children, reasoning that in the public school context, the sensibilities of fellow students must be considered. The majority recognized that an important objective of public schools is the inculcation of fundamental values of civility and that the school board has the authority to determine what manner of speech is appropriate in classes or assemblies.[17]

Only two years after *Bethel*, the Court rendered a seminal opinion further limiting, but not overturning, the reach of *Tinker*. **In *Hazelwood School District v. Kuhlmeier*, the**

---

[15]*Id.* at 509 (quoting Burnside v. Byars, 363 F.2d 744, 749 (5th Cir. 1966)). Debate surrounds whether the two prongs of this standard are independent guarantees or linked, in that evidence of a disruption is required for the expression to collide with others' rights. *See* Martha McCarthy, *Cyberbullying Laws and First Amendment Rulings: Can They Be Reconciled?* 83 Miss. L.J. 805 (2014).

[16]478 U.S. 675 (1986). Throughout his speech, Fraser employed a sexual metaphor to refer to the candidate, using such phrases as "he's firm in his pants . . . his character is firm," "a man who takes his point and pounds it in," "he doesn't attack things in spurts—he drives hard, pushing and pushing until finally he succeeds," and "a man who will go to the very end—even the climax, for each and every one of you," *id.* at 687 (Brennan, J., concurring). Fraser was suspended for two days and disqualified as a candidate for commencement speaker. However, he did eventually deliver a commencement speech, so his claim that the disqualification violated due process rights was not reviewed by the appellate court.

[17]*Id.* at 683 (rejecting also the contention that the student had no way of knowing that his expression would evoke disciplinary action; teachers' admonitions that his planned speech was inappropriate and violated a school rule provided adequate warning).

Court held that school authorities can censor student expression in school publications and other school-related activities so long as the censorship decisions are based on legitimate pedagogical concerns.[18] At issue in *Hazelwood* was a high school principal's deletion of two pages from the school newspaper because of the content of articles on divorce and teenage pregnancy and fears that individuals in the articles could be identified.

Rejecting the assertion that the school newspaper had been established as a public forum for student expression, the Court declared that only with school authorities' clear *intent* do school activities become a public forum.[19] The Court drew a distinction between a public school's *toleration* of private student expression, which is constitutionally required under some circumstances, and its *promotion* of student speech that represents the school. Reasoning that student expression appearing to bear the school's endorsement can be censored, the Court acknowledged school authorities' broad discretion to ensure that such expression occurring in school publications and all school-sponsored activities (including extracurricular) is consistent with educational objectives. The Court's expansive interpretation of what constitutes school-sponsored expression has narrowed the circumstances under which students can prevail in First Amendment claims.

Almost two more decades passed before the Supreme Court rendered its fourth decision pertaining to public school student expression rights. **In 2007, the Court in *Morse v. Frederick* held that given the special circumstances in public schools, students can be disciplined for expression reasonably viewed as promoting or celebrating illegal drug use; incitement to lawless conduct is not required.**[20] *Morse* focused on a banner with the phrase, "BONG HITS 4 JESUS," which Joseph Frederick and some friends unfurled across the street from their school as the Olympic torch relay passed by. The Supreme Court reasoned that the students were under the school's control when they were allowed to cross the street and watch the torch relay because it was a school-authorized event supervised by school personnel.

Reversing the Ninth Circuit's decision in favor of Frederick, the Supreme Court majority emphasized the importance of deterring drug use by students and concluded that Frederick's action violated the school board's policy of prohibiting expression advocating the use of illegal substances.[21] The Court declared that its earlier *Bethel* ruling stands for the proposition that considerations beyond the *Tinker* disruption standard are appropriate in assessing student expression in public schools. However, a majority of the Justices declined to extend school authorities' discretion to the point that they can curtail any student expression they find "plainly offensive" or at odds with the school's "educational mission."[22] All Justices agreed that students can be disciplined for promoting the use of illegal drugs, but they differed regarding whether the banner at issue actually did so.

---

[18]484 U.S. 260 (1988), *on remand*, 840 F.2d 596 (8th Cir. 1988).

[19]484 U.S. at 267.

[20]551 U.S. 393 (2007).

[21]*Id.* All of the Justices concurred that the principal should not be held liable for violating clearly established law, and Justice Breyer thought the decision should have focused only on this issue, *id.* at 425–33 (Breyer, J., concurring in part and dissenting in part).

[22]*See* Morse, 551 U.S. at 423. Justices Alito and Kennedy emphasized that this decision is restricted to the promotion of illegal drug use and does not extend to censorship of expression on social or political issues that may be viewed as inconsistent with the school's mission, *id.* at 422 (Alito, J., joined by Kennedy, J., concurring).

Lower courts have rendered a range of decisions in applying these legal principles articulated by the Supreme Court. Some of these rulings are reviewed below in connection with school-sponsored versus private expression; threats and other inflammatory expression; anti-harassment and anti-bullying provisions; electronic expression; and time, place, and manner restrictions. For the questions that must be answered in assessing students' expression rights, see Figure 5.2.

FIGURE 5.2   Assessing Student Expression Rights

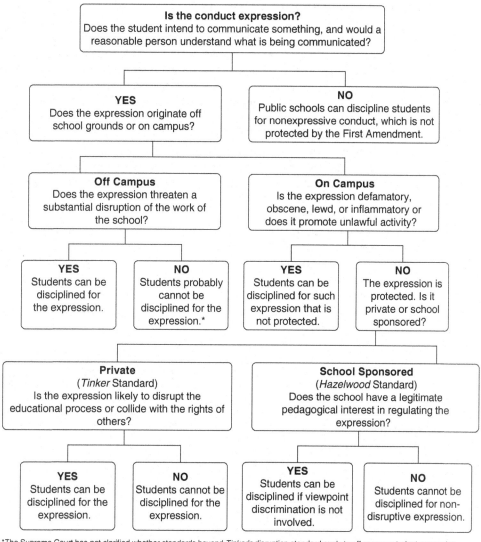

*The Supreme Court has not clarified whether standards beyond *Tinker's* disruption standard apply to off-campus student expression.

School-Sponsored versus Private Expression

During the 1970s and early 1980s, many courts broadly interpreted the circumstances under which limited forums for student expression were created in public schools. School-sponsored newspapers often were considered such a forum, and accordingly, courts held that articles on controversial subjects such as the Vietnam War, abortion, and birth control could not be barred from these publications, placing the burden on school authorities to justify prior administrative review of both school-sponsored and nonsponsored literature.

However, since *Hazelwood*, expression appearing to bear the school's imprimatur can be censored for pedagogical reasons. The *Tinker* standard applies *only* to protected *private* expression, and some lower courts have broadly interpreted student expression that might be perceived as representing the school.[23] Relying on *Hazelwood*, the Ninth Circuit rejected Planned Parenthood's claim that a school district's denial of its request to advertise in school newspapers, yearbooks, and programs for athletic events violated free speech rights, concluding that the school district could bar advertisements inconsistent with its educational mission.[24] The Eighth Circuit similarly relied on *Hazelwood* in upholding a principal's decision to disqualify a student council candidate who handed out condoms with stickers bearing his campaign slogan ("Adam Henerey, the Safe Choice"), noting that *Hazelwood* grants school authorities considerable discretion to control student expression in school-sponsored activities.[25] The Second Circuit also applied *Hazelwood* in ruling that school authorities were justified in prohibiting students from running a lewd, sexually explicit cartoon in the school-sponsored paper as the decision was reasonably related to legitimate pedagogical concerns. Even though students wrote the paper's content, its operation was supervised by the faculty adviser, so the paper was not considered a limited forum for student expression.[26]

Courts have reasoned that the school has the right to disassociate itself from controversial expression that conflicts with its mission and have considered school-sponsored activities to include student newspapers supported by the public school, extracurricular activities sponsored by the school, school assemblies, and classroom activities. **The key consideration is whether the expression is viewed as bearing the school's stamp of approval; only under such circumstances is *Hazelwood*'s broad deference to school authorities triggered.**

[23]In response to Hazelwood, a number of state legislatures considered, and several enacted, laws granting student editors of school-sponsored papers specific rights in determining the content of their publications. Arkansas, California, Colorado, Illinois, Iowa, Kansas, Maryland, Massachusetts, Nevada, North Dakota, Pennsylvania, Rhode Island, and Vermont have enacted laws in this regard, and a number of other states are considering such measures. *See* Demi Vitkute, *A Nationwide Movement Protecting the Student Press from Censorship Gains Momentum*, Reporters Comm. for Freedom of the Press (Sept. 8, 2017), https://www.rcfp.org/browse-media-law-resources/news/nationwide-movement-protecting-student-press-censorship-gains-moment.

[24]Planned Parenthood v. Clark Cty. Sch. Dist., 887 F.2d 935 (9th Cir. 1989), *rehearing en banc*, 941 F.2d 817 (9th Cir. 1991).

[25]Henerey v. City of St. Charles Sch. Dist., 200 F.3d 1128 (8th Cir. 1999).

[26]R.O. *ex rel.* Ochshorn v. Ithaca City Sch. Dist., 645 F.3d 533 (2d Cir. 2011) (holding also that school authorities could bar distribution on campus of an independent student publication with the same cartoon, which was considered lewd and vulgar and thus not protected).

Ironically, since *Hazelwood*, student expression in underground (not school-sponsored) student papers distributed at school enjoys greater constitutional protection than does expression in school-sponsored publications. The former is considered private expression governed by the *Tinker* principle, whereas the latter represents the school and is subject to censorship under *Hazelwood*. As discussed in Chapter 3, most courts have treated the distribution of religious literature by students like the distribution of other material that is not sponsored by the school.

Once it is determined that protected private expression is at issue, courts then are faced with the difficult task of assessing whether restrictions are justified. The imposition of prior restraints on private student speech must bear a substantial relationship to an important government interest, and any regulation must contain narrow, objective, and unambiguous criteria for determining what material is prohibited and procedures that allow a speedy determination of whether materials meet those criteria. **The burden is on school authorities to justify policies requiring administrative approval of unofficial student publications, but such prior review is not unconstitutional per se.**[27] Of course, courts are more inclined to support disciplinary action and confiscation of materials *after* the private expression has occurred, if it is deemed unprotected (i.e., libelous, inflammatory, vulgar, or promotion of illegal activity), threatens a disruption of the educational process, or interferes with the rights of others. To illustrate, students can be disciplined after the fact for expression advocating the destruction of school property in publications they distribute at school, even though the anticipated destruction of school property never materializes.[28]

Courts also have condoned disciplinary action against students who have engaged in walkouts, boycotts, sit-ins, or other protests involving conduct that blocks hallways, damages property, causes students to miss class, or interferes with essential school activities in other ways. The Sixth Circuit held that a petition circulated by four football players denouncing the head coach justified their dismissal from the varsity football team. The court reasoned that the petition disrupted the team, and athletes are subject to greater restrictions than are applied to the general student body.[29] The Ninth Circuit ruled that student athletes could be disciplined for protesting actions of the coach by refusing to board the team bus and to play in a basketball game, which substantially disrupted a school activity.[30] However, this court departed from the Sixth Circuit in finding that the students' petition requesting that the coach resign because of derogatory remarks he made

---

[27]*Compare* Taylor v. Roswell Indep. Sch. Dist., 712 F.3d 25 (10th Cir. 2013) (endorsing policy requiring prior approval of all materials distributed at school and upholding administrators in halting an anti-abortion student group's distribution of rubber doll fetuses), *with* Burch v. Barker, 861 F.2d 1149 (9th Cir. 1988) (holding that school authorities could not subject a student paper produced off campus to prior review under an overbroad policy).

[28]*See, e.g.*, Boucher v. Sch. Bd., 134 F.3d 821 (7th Cir. 1997) (upholding expulsion of a student for distributing at school an article that contained information about how to disable the school's computer system).

[29]Lowery v. Euverard, 497 F.3d 584 (6th Cir. 2007); *see also* Corales v. Bennett, 567 F.3d 554 (9th Cir. 2009) (holding that students could be disciplined for leaving school to engage in a political protest).

[30]Pinard v. Clatskanie Sch. Dist., 467 F.3d 755 (9th Cir. 2006) (remanding the case for a determination of whether the students were impermissibly removed from the basketball team in retaliation for their petition).

toward players was protected speech. Although students can be disciplined for disruptive protests, school authorities have discretion in this regard.[31]

Private student expression enjoys greater constitutional protection than does school-sponsored speech, but there are limits on school authorities' wide latitude to censor student expression that bears the public school's imprimatur. **Blatant viewpoint discrimination in a public school abridges the First Amendment unless the student expression falls within one of the categories where restrictions are allowed (e.g., it can be linked to a disruption).**[32] And even if viewpoint discrimination is not involved, the suppression of expression in a nonpublic forum still must be based on legitimate pedagogical concerns. A Michigan federal district court found no legitimate pedagogical reason to remove from the school newspaper a student's article on a pending lawsuit alleging that school bus diesel fumes constituted a neighborhood nuisance.[33]

Furthermore, a school-sponsored publication might be considered a forum for student expression under certain circumstances. In a Massachusetts case, school authorities had given students editorial control of school publications, so the First Circuit held that independent decisions of the students in terms of which ads to reject could not be attributed to school officials.[34]

Threats and Other Inflammatory Expression

The U.S. Supreme Court has not addressed the application of the First Amendment to alleged threats made by students toward classmates or school personnel, but there is a growing body of lower court litigation on the subject. In determining if a true threat has been made, courts consider a number of factors, such as:

- reactions of the recipient and other listeners;
- whether the maker of the alleged threat had made similar statements to the victim in the past;
- if the utterance was conditional and communicated directly to the victim; and
- whether the victim had reason to believe that the speaker would engage in violence.[35]

In an illustrative case, the Fifth Circuit held that a student's notebook, outlining a pseudo-Nazi group's plan to commit a "Columbine shooting," constituted a "terroristic

---

[31]Students across the nation staged walkouts on Wednesday following the 2016 presidential election, and although some students were given unexcused absences, in many instances, school personnel overlooked student involvement in the demonstrations despite the fact that classes were interrupted at times. *See* Mackenzie Ryan, Linh Ta, & Charly Haley, *Thousands of High-Schoolers Walk Out to Protest Trump*, USA TODAY (Nov. 9, 2016), https:// www.usatoday.com/story/news/politics/elections/2016/11/09/high-school-student-protests/93557834/.

[32]*See, e.g.,* Searcey v. Harris, 888 F.2d 1314 (11th Cir. 1989) (placing the burden on school authorities to justify viewpoint discrimination against a peace activist group that was not allowed to display its literature on school premises or participate in career day when military recruiters were allowed such access).

[33]Dean v. Utica Cmty. Schs., 345 F. Supp. 2d 799 (E.D. Mich. 2004) (ruling that the censorship was based on the superintendent's disagreement with the views expressed about the lawsuit against the school district).

[34]Yeo v. Town of Lexington, 131 F.3d 241 (1st Cir. 1997).

[35]United States v. Dinwiddie, 76 F.3d 913 (8th Cir. 1996).

threat" that was not protected by the First Amendment.[36] The Eleventh Circuit similarly ruled that a student's story about shooting her math teacher was a threat of violence; her suspension was justified because she shared the story with another student.[37] Citing *Morse,* the court reasoned that disciplining students for threats of violence is even more important than curtailing their promotion of illegal drug use.[38]

Also finding a threat, the Eighth Circuit reversed the lower court and upheld the expulsion of a student for writing a letter indicating he was going to rape and murder his former girlfriend. The court was convinced that the writer intended to communicate the threat because he shared the letter with a friend whom he assumed would give it to his former girlfriend.[39] In 2011, the same court found a true threat in a student's online message sent from home to a classmate in which he mentioned getting a gun and shooting other students at school.[40] The serious statements were communicated to a third party, and combined with the speaker's admitted depression and access to weapons, the appeals court held that school authorities did not need to wait until the threat was carried out before taking action.

Utterances can be considered inflammatory, and thus unprotected, even if *not* found to be true threats or fighting words. The Ninth Circuit ruled that a student could be subject to emergency expulsion, with a hearing occurring afterward, for writing a poem about someone who had committed multiple murders in the past and decided to kill himself for fear of murdering others.[41] The poem was not considered a true threat or to contain fighting words. The Wisconsin Supreme Court similarly held that school authorities had more than enough reason to suspend a student for his creative writing assignment, describing a student removed from class for being disruptive (as he had been) who returned the next day to behead his teacher.[42] But the court found no true threat that would justify prosecution of the student for disorderly conduct.

The Second Circuit also ruled in favor of school authorities who detained a middle school student to determine if he posed a danger to himself or others and also reported his parents to Child and Family Services for possible neglect in connection with an essay he wrote that included a discussion of illegal acts, violence, and his own suicide. The court ruled that school authorities did not violate the student's expression rights or his parents' substantive due process rights by taking precautionary actions.[43] The same court ruled that

---

[36]Ponce v. Socorro Indep. Sch. Dist., 508 F.3d 765, 767 (5th Cir. 2007).

[37]Boim v. Fulton Cty. Sch. Dist., 494 F.3d 978 (11th Cir. 2007).

[38]*Id.* at 984 (citing Morse v. Frederick, 551 U.S. 393 (2007)).

[39]Doe v. Pulaski Cty. Special Sch. Dist., 306 F.3d 616 (8th Cir. 2002).

[40]D.J.M. v. Hannibal Pub. Sch. Dist., 647 F.3d 754 (8th Cir. 2011).

[41]LaVine v. Blaine Sch. Dist., 257 F.3d 981 (9th Cir. 2001) (holding, however, that the placement and maintenance of negative documentation in the student's file, after he was readmitted to school and the concern about harm had subsided, went beyond the district's documentation needs).

[42]*In re* Douglas D., 626 N.W.2d 725 (Wis. 2001); *see also* Wynar v. Douglas Cty. Sch. Dist., 728 F.3d. 1062 (9th Cir. 2013), *infra* text accompanying note 75; S.G. v. Sayreville Bd. of Educ., 333 F.3d 417 (3d Cir. 2003) (upholding suspension of a kindergarten student for saying, "I'm going to shoot you," during a game at recess, which violated the school's prohibition on speech threatening violence and the use of firearms).

[43]Cox v. Warwick Valley Cent. Sch. Dist., 654 F.3d 267 (2d Cir. 2011) (noting that the student had a history of misbehavior and was on probation and under a behavior contract when the essay was written).

school authorities reasonably could forecast a disruption from an elementary school student's picture expressing a desire to blow up the school and its teachers.[44] Upholding the student's six-day suspension, the appeals court reasoned that the student's actual intent and capacity to carry out the threat were irrelevant. **Courts generally seem more inclined to uphold school disciplinary action, in contrast to criminal prosecution, for students' alleged threats or other inflammatory expression**.

Anti-Harassment and Anti-Bullying Policies

A number of school districts have adopted policies prohibiting expression that constitutes verbal or physical harassment based on race, religion, color, national origin, sex, sexual orientation, disability, or other personal characteristics. Also, all states and the District of Columbia have anti-bullying provisions, which may reside in the education, criminal, and/ or juvenile justice codes.[45] These laws require local school districts to include an anti-bullying policy in their discipline codes and to specify penalties for engaging in bullying.[46] Anti-bullying laws often share similar language with anti-harassment policies. In some of these provisions, the terms "harassment" and "bullying" are used interchangeably, even though "harassment" is associated with specific legal liability under federal civil rights laws that do not apply to bullying.[47]

Public school policies prohibiting bullying and harassment traditionally have not appeared vulnerable to First Amendment challenges, whereas "hate speech" policies have been struck down in municipalities and public higher education. Public schools have been considered a special environment in terms of government restrictions on private expression because of their purpose in educating America's youth and inculcating basic values, such as civility and respect for others with different backgrounds and beliefs.

A large body of cases interpreting anti-harassment provisions has focused on students displaying Confederate flags, and most courts have upheld restrictions on such displays. In a typical case, the Sixth Circuit upheld a student's suspension for wearing clothing depicting the Confederate flag in violation of the school's dress code.[48] The court held that school officials could forecast a substantial disruption from such displays,

---

[44]Cuff v. Valley Cent. Sch. Dist., 677 F.3d 109 (2d Cir. 2012).

[45]In 2015, Montana became the last state to adopt anti-bullying legislation. *See Laws & Policies* (Sept. 8, 2017), https://www.stopbullying.gov/laws/index.html. All but two of the laws prohibit electronic harassment or cyberbullying, Cyberbullying Research Ctr., *Bullying Laws Across States* (n.d.), http://cyberbullying.org/bullying-laws. North Carolina's law specifies that students can be disciplined for bullying or harassment directed toward classmates *or* school employees, N.C. GEN. STATS. § 115C-4-7.15 (2018).

[46]Most laws broadly define bullying activity and proscribe name-calling, teasing, intimidation, humiliation, and taunts in addition to physical acts. *See, e.g.,* IND. CODE § 20-33-8-0.2 (2018). According to an initiative sponsored by the federal government, peer bullying is a major concern nationally because victims can become depressed or fearful of being at school and can contemplate suicide, *Who Is at Risk?* (Sept. 22, 2017), https://www.stopbullying .gov/at-risk/index.html; *see also infra* note 69 for statutory prohibitions on sexting.

[47]In contrast to federal anti-harassment provisions, many state anti-bullying laws specify that victims cannot sue school districts for liability in connection with violations of the laws. *See* discussion of federal protections against sexual harassment, text accompanying note 77, Chapter 6.

[48]Defoe v. Spiva, 625 F.3d 324 (6th Cir. 2010).

and two of the three judges in a concurrence noted that a link to a disruption is not required to curtail displays that convey racial hostility.[49] The same court previously upheld a school district's ban on students displaying the Confederate flag, again finding racial tension and the potential for a school disturbance.[50] The Tenth Circuit also upheld disciplinary action against a Kansas middle school student for drawing a Confederate flag during math class in violation of the school district's anti-harassment policy.[51] The court was persuaded that the school district had reason to believe that the display of the Confederate flag might cause a disruption and interfere with the rights of others because the school district had already experienced some racial incidents related to the Confederate flag. More recently, the Fourth Circuit ruled that a school's ban on Confederate flag insignia did not abridge a student's First Amendment or equal protection rights.[52]

A few courts, however, have struck down such restrictions on Confederate flag displays. These courts have reasoned that students should prevail in the absence of a link to disruption[53] or if the policies were applied inconsistently. For example, the Sixth Circuit found no evidence that a shirt with a country singer on the front and the Confederate flag on the back, worn to express Southern heritage, would cause a disruption and furthermore questioned whether there may have been viewpoint discrimination in applying the school's prohibition on emblems with racial implications.[54]

Yet, most other anti-harassment or anti-bullying policies have not been struck down, even if the students have prevailed on their free speech claims. To illustrate, the Third Circuit upheld a school district's anti-harassment policy enacted to respond to incidents of race-based conflicts and narrowly designed to reduce racially divisive expression. Although finding that the policy as applied violated the students' expression rights, the court voiced approval of the school's anti-harassment provision.[55] More recently, the Second Circuit upheld school authorities' decision to send a student home for allegedly making a racial slur; the student's request to return to school to explain his version of events to classmates was also denied, given the significant threat of a disruption. In light of the racial tensions created by the situation and concern for the student's safety, his expulsion for the remainder of the school year was considered reasonable.[56]

---

[49]*Id.* at 341 (Rogers, J., concurring, joined by Cook, J.).

[50]Barr v. Lafon, 538 F.3d 554 (6th Cir. 2008); *see also* B.W.A. v. Farmington R-7 Sch. Dist., 554 F.3d 734 (8th Cir. 2009).

[51]West v. Derby Unified Sch. Dist., 206 F.3d 1358 (10th Cir. 2000) (noting that the student had been disciplined numerous times and accused of using racial slurs).

[52]Hardwick v. Heyward, 711 F.3d 426 (4th Cir. 2013), *infra* text accompanying note 112.

[53]*See, e.g.*, Bragg v. Swanson, 371 F. Supp. 2d 814 (S.D. W. Va. 2005) (overturning disciplinary action against a student for wearing a T-shirt displaying the Confederate flag in observance of his Southern heritage; finding overbroad the policy that prohibited displays of the Rebel flag within the category of racist symbols).

[54]Castorina *ex rel.* Rewt v. Madison Cty. Sch. Bd., 246 F.3d 536 (6th Cir. 2001), *infra* text accompanying note 111.

[55]Sypniewski v. Warren Hills Reg'l Bd. of Educ., 307 F.3d 243, 265 (3d Cir. 2002) (upholding the policy but ordering the phrase banning speech that "creates ill will" to be eliminated as reaching some protected expression). See *infra* text accompanying note 100 for a discussion of the application of the policy.

[56]DeFabio v. E. Hampton Union Free Sch. Dist., 623 F.3d 71 (2d Cir. 2010).

Several cases have focused on the conflict between expressing religious views and promoting civil expression; these cases are particularly sensitive because they pit free speech and free exercise guarantees against the school's authority to instill basic values, including respect for others. The Ninth Circuit found the second prong of the *Tinker* standard to be controlling when it ruled that a student wearing a T-shirt degrading homosexuality "'collides with the rights of other students' in the most fundamental way."[57] The court reasoned that the school is allowed to prohibit such expression, regardless of the adoption of a valid anti-harassment policy, so long as it can show that the restriction is necessary to prevent the violation of other students' rights *or* a substantial disruption of school activities. **The court disagreed with the suggestion that injurious slurs interfering with the rights of others cannot be barred unless they *also* are disruptive, reasoning that the two *Tinker* prongs are independent restrictions.**[58]

But other courts have applied the *Tinker* disruption standard in ruling that students have a right to express their religious views that denounce homosexuality.[59] The Seventh Circuit found a T-shirt with "Be Happy, Not Gay" printed on it to be "only tepidly negative" and not linked to a substantial disruption.[60] Thus, the court ruled that school authorities could not bar students from wearing the shirt because "people in our society do not have a legal right to prevent criticism of their beliefs or for that matter their way of life," reasoning that in the absence of fighting words, schools cannot impair students' free expression rights based on their targets' "hurt feelings."[61] **The court recognized that the expression could not be curtailed based on the hecklers' veto, or those opposing the expression could always stifle speakers simply by mounting a riot.**[62] Yet, the court did not enjoin enforcement of the school's rule that prohibited students from making derogatory comments

---

[57]Harper v. Poway Unified Sch. Dist., 445 F.3d 1166, 1178 (9th Cir. 2006) (quoting Tinker v. Des Moines Indep. Sch. Dist., 393 U.S. 503, 508 (1969)), *cert.* granted, judgment vacated, and case remanded to dismiss as moot, 549 U.S. 1262 (2007).

[58]Harper, 445 F.3d at 1180; *see also* Sapp v. Sch. Bd., 2011 WL 5084647 (N.D. Fla. Sept. 30, 2011) (upholding school authorities in prohibiting students from wearing shirts with "Islam Is the Devil" at school and school events; finding the shirts disruptive and in violation of the school's dress code).

[59]*See, e.g.,* Saxe v. State Coll. Area Sch. Dist., 240 F.3d 200 (3d Cir. 2001) (striking down a school district's anti-harassment policy as overbroad in barring expression that could not be curtailed under Tinker; plaintiffs challenged application of the policy to their expression of religious views about homosexuality); Nixon v. N. Local Sch. Dist., 383 F. Supp. 2d 965, 971 (S.D. Ohio 2005) (rejecting school administrators' assertion that a shirt denigrating homosexuality, Islam, and abortion was "plainly offensive" under Bethel; applying Tinker instead and finding no disruption or evidence that the expression interfered with the rights of others).

[60]Zamecnik v. Sch. Dist., 636 F.3d 874, 876 (7th Cir. 2011) (quoting Nuxoll v. Indian Prairie Sch. Dist., 523 F.3d 668, 676 (7th Cir. 2008)).

[61]Zamecnik, 636 F.3d at 876. Might the court's conclusion have been different if LGBTQ students had threatened violence toward those wearing the shirts on the Day of Silence that is intended to recognize LGBTQ rights? Compare this case with the issue and holding in Dariano v. Morgan Hill Unified Sch. Dist., 745 F.3d 354 (9th Cir. 2014), *infra* text accompanying note 91.

[62]Zamecnik, 636 F.3d at 877. The heckler's veto means that one can speak only until someone else objects to the speech and threatens a disruption; courts have ruled that speakers cannot be punished for others' reactions to their expression. *See, e.g.,* Brown v. Louisiana, 383 U.S. 131 (1966) (overturning conviction of African American citizens for breaching the peace for refusing to leave a segregated public library; the disturbance was caused by critics of their passive demonstration).

referring to race, ethnicity, religion, gender, sexual orientation, or disability. Because the Supreme Court has not rendered an opinion in these sensitive cases, the collision of religious views and anti-harassment policies seems destined to remain controversial.

The Supreme Court also declined to review a decision in which the Ninth Circuit in 2016 addressed the application of a school district's sexual harassment policy to off-campus expression.[63] Middle school students were suspended for sexually harassing two students with disabilities in a park adjacent to the public school right after school was dismissed. The court reasoned that the harassing expression abridged *Tinker*'s second prong by interfering with the rights of others and concluded that a link to a school disruption was not necessary.[64] Emphasizing that sexual harassment by definition interferes with others' rights to be secure and left alone, the court showed great deference to the school's harassment policy prohibiting student expression of a sexual nature.[65] Similar to other recent cases involving peer harassment and bullying, the Supreme Court declined to review this decision.

Student Electronic Expression

The most volatile current disputes involve Internet expression, particularly pertaining to social networks. These cases are particularly troublesome because students often prepare and disseminate the materials from their homes, but their expression is immediately available to the entire school population and beyond. **Although the judiciary has not spoken with a single voice on the First Amendment issues raised in these cases, courts usually have applied the *Tinker* disruption standard in assessing Internet expression.**[66] With the increasing use of cellular phones and the amount of material posted or exchanged through Instagram, Snapchat, Twitter, Facebook, and other social media sites, legal activity in this arena is bound to increase. A 2016 survey indicated that almost all teens use social networks.[67] And concerns over students sending sexually explicit or suggestive messages electronically are resulting in legislative responses to curtail such "sexting."[68]

---

[63]C.R. v. Eugene Sch. Dist., 835 F.3d 1142 (9th Cir. 2016), *cert. denied*, 137 S. Ct. 2117 (2017).

[64]835 F.3d at 1152.

[65]*Id*. at 1148 (noting that the harassment does not have to rise to the level that would evoke penalties under Title IX of the Education Amendments of 1972); *see also* text accompanying note 75, Chapter 6.

[66]393 U.S. 503 (1969), *supra* text accompanying note 15.

[67]Associated Press & NORC Ctr. for Pub. Affairs Research, *Instagram and Snapchat Are Most Popular Social Networks for Teens* (Apr. 2017), http://www.apnorc.org/projects/Pages/Instagram-and-Snapchat-are-Most-Popular-Social-Networks-for-Teens.aspx.

[68]Twenty states had adopted sexting legislation by July 2015, with four imposing felony charges and eleven misdemeanor charges for sexting. Many teenagers are unaware that sexting can result in being charged with transmitting child pornography. *See* Sameer Hinduja & Justin W. Patchin, *State Sexting Laws*, Cyberbullying Research Ctr. (Feb. 3, 2015), https://cyberbullying.org/state-sexting-laws; Washington v. Gray, 402 P.3d 254 (Wash. 2017) (upholding conviction of a seventeen-year-old who texted a picture of his private parts to an adult woman; the court concluded that selfies were covered by the state law prohibiting the dissemination of sexually explicit images of minors). *But see* T.V. v. Smith-Green Cmty. Sch. Corp., 807 F. Supp. 2d 767 (N.D. Ind. 2011) (invalidating suspension from extracurricular activities of students who took sexually suggestive pictures of themselves at a slumber party and posted them on the Internet; reasoning that the photos did not constitute child pornography under state law or pose a threat of a school disruption).

Students have prevailed in several challenges to disciplinary actions for the creation of web pages or postings on social media that have originated from their homes. For example, the full Third Circuit in 2011 rendered decisions favoring students' expression rights in two cases that had generated conflicting decisions by different Third Circuit panels.[69] At issue were mock Myspace profiles of the school principals that were vulgar and linked the principals to drugs, alcohol, sexual abuse, and other degrading activities. **Finding no disruption of the educational process, the appeals court required off-campus expression to be linked to a substantial school disruption to justify disciplinary action**. However, the school policies requiring students to express their ideas in a respectful manner and to refrain from verbal abuse were not found to be overbroad.

Not all courts have agreed with the Third Circuit's stringent position on what constitutes the necessary link to a disruption for students' off-campus Internet expression to be curtailed. The Second Circuit ruled in favor of school authorities who prevented a student from running for senior class secretary because of a vulgar blog entry she posted from home that urged others to complain to the school administrators about a change in scheduling an event, Jamfest, an annual battle of the bands concert.[70] The court reasoned that school officials reasonably could conclude that the expression might disrupt student government functions. Also at issue were T-shirts supporting her freedom of speech that students planned to wear to the school assembly where candidates for the class offices were to give their speeches. **Acknowledging that the shirts might be protected under *Tinker* if not linked to a disruption, the court held that the school defendants were entitled to qualified immunity on this claim as well because the rights at issue were not clearly established**. More recently, the Fifth Circuit similarly upheld the school's disciplining of a student for posting a vulgar and profane rap on YouTube and Facebook, finding the rap to be harassing and threatening toward two coaches for their alleged indiscretions.[71] The court concluded that the student intended for his expression to reach a wide audience and to be viewed as intimidating staff members.

The Fourth Circuit also upheld West Virginia school authorities' suspension of a student for creating a website primarily used to ridicule a classmate with accusations that she was a slut with herpes. The disciplined student alleged that the suspension violated her free speech rights because the expression was private speech initiated from her home. But the court sided with the school administrators who reasoned that the student had created a "hate website" in violation of the school's policy forbidding "harassment, bullying, and intimidation."[72] The court found that the contested website's strong connection to the

---

[69]Layshock v. Hermitage Sch. Dist., 650 F.3d 205 (3d Cir. 2011); J.S. *ex. rel.* Snyder v. Blue Mountain Sch. Dist., 650 F.3d 915 (3d Cir. 2011); *see also* R.S. v. Minnewaska Area Sch. Dist., 894 F. Supp. 2d 1128 (D. Minn. 2012) (finding a valid claim that school officials violated a middle school student's free speech rights by disciplining her for Facebook posts critical of a school employee and whoever alerted authorities; her privacy rights were also implicated by school personnel's search of her Facebook posts against her will); J.C. v. Beverly Hills Unified Sch. Dist., 711 F. Supp. 2d 1094 (C.D. Cal. 2010) (finding a violation of a student's free speech rights in disciplinary action imposed for posting a YouTube video that was disparaging toward a classmate because there was not a sufficient link to a school disruption).

[70]Doninger v. Niehoff, 642 F.3d 334 (2d Cir. 2011); *see also* Wisniewski v. Bd. of Educ., 494 F.3d 34 (2d Cir. 2007) (upholding a semester expulsion of a student for displaying in his instant messaging buddy icon a drawing of a pistol firing at a person's head, with the caption "Kill Mr. VenderMolen," his English teacher).

[71]Bell v. Itawamba Cty. Sch. Dist., 799 F.3d 379 (5th Cir. 2015) (*en banc*).

[72]Kowalski v. Berkeley Cty. Schs., 652 F.3d 565, 574 (4th Cir. 2011). The student originally was suspended for ten days, which was reduced to five days, and she received a ninety-day social suspension from school-related activities.

school environment justified school authorities in disciplining speech that "materially and substantially interferes with the requirements of appropriate discipline in the operation of the school and collides with the rights of others."[73] Seeming to rely on both prongs of the *Tinker* standard, the court emphasized that conduct does not have to physically originate in the school building or during the school day to adversely affect the learning environment and the rights of others.

The Eighth Circuit similarly agreed with school authorities in declaring that the lower court should not have enjoined the suspension of twin brothers for creating a racist and sexist website and blog.[74] Finding it reasonably foreseeable that the blog would reach the school community and cause a disruption, the court considered the students' punishment appropriate and did not address whether the website collided with the rights of others. The Ninth Circuit also endorsed disciplinary action against a student who sent instant messages from his home to friends bragging about his weapons and threatening to shoot specific classmates.[75] This court applied both prongs of *Tinker*, finding that the expression posed a risk of disrupting the school and interfered with the rights of others.[76] For a summary of the federal circuit courts that have addressed student electronic expression, see Figure 5.3.

FIGURE 5.3 Federal Circuits Addressing Student Electronic Expression

Circuit	Target of Expression	Prevailing Party	Interpretation of *Tinker* Standard
Second	administrators	school	expression was purposefully designed to reach campus and create a risk of substantial disruption
Third	administrators	students	expression merely reaching school was insufficient without connection to a substantial disruption
Fourth	one student	school	targeted attack connected to school collided with others' rights and interfered with appropriate discipline in operating school
Fifth	coaches	school	substantial disruption could be forecast from harassing, threatening language intended to reach school community
Eighth	classmates	school	substantial disruption was reasonably foreseeable based on racist/sexist blog
Ninth	school community	school	threatening message both interfered with others' rights and allowed reasonable forecast of a substantial disruption

[73]*Id.* at 572 (quoting Tinker v. Des Moines Indep. Sch. Dist., 393 U.S. 503, 513 (1969)). The Fourth Circuit reasoned that expression interfering with another's rights *creates* the necessary disruption to trigger Tinker's exclusion from constitutional protection.

[74]S.J.W. *ex rel.* Wilson v. Lee's Summit R-7 Sch. Dist., 696 F.3d 771 (8th Cir. 2012). Because of the lower court's injunction, the students graduated before their suspensions could be imposed. *See also* D.J.M. v. Hannibal Public Sch. Dist., 647 F.3d 754 (8th Cir. 2011), *supra* text accompanying note 40.

[75]Wynar v. Douglas Cty. Sch. Dist., 728 F.3d 1062 (9th Cir. 2013).

[76]*Id.* at 1071–72; *see also* A.N. by and through Niziolek v. Upper Perkiomen Sch. Dist., 228 F. Supp. 3d 391 (E.D. Pa. 2017) (denying preliminary injunction to halt suspension and possible expulsion of student whose social media post caused a disruption and perceived threat of a school shooting that resulted in closing school for a day).

In these cases, the key determinant of disciplinary action appears to be whether the material created off campus has a direct and detrimental impact on the school. But because the Supreme Court has refused to review appeals of these decisions, and federal appellate courts have rendered a range of opinions, school personnel have conflicting guidance as to the application of the First Amendment to electronic expression that originates off school grounds. Given students' preference to communicate electronically and the growing popularity of social networking sites, texting, and blogs, Supreme Court clarification of the First Amendment standard is sorely needed. There is some sentiment that Internet expression with a negative impact on the school community should be considered the same as in-school speech regardless of where it originates.[77] In the absence of a Supreme Court ruling, the only consolation for school authorities is that they likely can claim immunity for disciplining students for their electronic expression because the law on this topic is far from clearly established.

Time, Place, and Manner Regulations

Although private expression enjoys greater constitutional protection than does school-sponsored expression, the judiciary consistently has upheld reasonable policies regulating the time, place, and manner of private expression. For example, students can be prohibited from voicing political and ideological views and distributing literature during instructional time. Additionally, to ensure that the distribution of student publications does not impinge upon other school activities, school authorities can ban literature distribution near the doors of classrooms while class is in session, near building exits during fire drills, and on stairways when classes are changing. The Fifth Circuit reasoned that student literature distribution could be prohibited in the cafeteria to maintain order and discipline because ample other opportunities were available for students to distribute their materials at school.[78]

Time, place, and manner regulations, however, must be reasonable, content neutral, and uniformly applied to expressive activities. Also, they cannot restrict more speech than necessary to ensure nondisruptive distribution of materials. School officials must provide students with specific guidelines regarding when and where they can express their ideas and distribute materials. Moreover, literature distribution cannot be relegated to remote times or places either inside or outside the school building, and regulations must not inhibit any person's right to accept or reject literature that is distributed in accordance with the rules. Policies governing demonstrations should convey to students that they have the right to assemble, distribute petitions, and express their ideas under nondisruptive circumstances. If regulations do not precisely inform demonstrators of behavior that is prohibited, the judiciary may conclude that punishment cannot be imposed.

---

[77]*See* McCarthy, *supra* note 15. If the Supreme Court would consider student electronic expression to be "in school" as long as it targets the school community, this would resolve the debate over whether *Bethel*'s exclusion of lewd and vulgar expression from constitutional protection applies to Internet expression.

[78]Morgan v. Plano Indep. Sch. Dist., 589 F.3d 740 (5th Cir. 2009).

STUDENT-INITIATED CLUBS

Public schools can deny access to all noncurriculum student clubs during noninstructional time but cannot discriminate against specific groups based on the content of their meetings.

Free expression and related association rights have arisen in connection with the formation and recognition of student clubs. Freedom of association is not specifically included among First Amendment protections, but the Supreme Court has held that associational rights are "implicit in the freedoms of speech, assembly, and petition."[79] The word *association* refers to the medium through which individuals seek to join with others to make the expression of their own views more meaningful.

Public school pupils have not prevailed in asserting that free expression and association rights shield student-initiated social organizations or secret societies with exclusive membership usually determined by a vote of the clubs' members. **In contrast, prohibitions on student-initiated organizations with *open* membership are vulnerable to First Amendment challenge**. It is generally accepted that public school access policies for student meetings must be content neutral and cannot disadvantage selected groups to survive a constitutional challenge.[80] Schools are not required to create a forum for student groups to meet, but once they do so, they must respect students' constitutional rights.

Secondary school students do not have to rely on the First Amendment to assert a right to hold meetings in public schools. **The Equal Access Act (EAA), enacted in 1984, stipulates that if federally assisted secondary schools provide a limited open forum for noncurricular student groups to meet during noninstructional time, access cannot be denied based on the religious, political, philosophical, or other content of the groups' meetings.**[81] The EAA was championed by the Religious Right, but its protection encompasses far more than student-initiated religious expression.

As discussed in Chapter 3, the Supreme Court in 1990 rejected an Establishment Clause challenge to the EAA in *Board of Education of the Westside Community Schools v. Mergens*.[82] The Court held that if a federally assisted secondary school allows even one noncurricular group to use school facilities during noninstructional time, the EAA guarantees equal access for other noncurricular student groups. Of course, meetings that threaten a disruption can be barred. Moreover, school authorities can decline to establish a limited forum for student-initiated meetings and thus confine school access to student organizations that are an extension of the curriculum, such as drama groups, language clubs, and athletic teams.

Controversies have surfaced over what constitutes a curriculum-related group, since the EAA is triggered only if noncurriculum student groups are allowed school access during

[79]Healy v. James, 408 U.S. 169, 181 (1972).

[80]For information on public school access for meetings of community religious groups, including chapters of the Good News Club that target children, *see* text accompanying note 80, Chapter 3.

[81]20 U.S.C. § 4071 (2018). For a discussion of what constitutes a limited forum, *see supra* text accompanying note 10.

[82]496 U.S. 226 (1990) (rejecting the contention that only noncurricular, *advocacy* groups are protected under the EAA); *see* text accompanying note 73, Chapter 3.

noninstructional time. Many of these cases have focused on the Gay-Straight Alliance (GSA) and similar groups.[83] To illustrate, the Eighth Circuit addressed a Minnesota school district's distinction between *curricular* student groups that were allowed to use the public address system and other forms of communication and *noncurricular* groups that could not use such communication avenues or participate in fundraising activities or field trips.[84] Concluding that some groups identified as curricular, such as cheerleading and synchronized swimming, were not related to material regularly taught in the curriculum, the court enjoined the district from treating the club, Straights and Gays for Equality, differently from other student groups. Even if a secondary school has *not* established a limited forum, it still cannot exert viewpoint discrimination against particular curriculum-related groups.

STUDENT APPEARANCE

Restrictions can be placed on student grooming and attire if based on legitimate educational and safety objectives and not intended to suppress expression.

Fads and fashions in hairstyles and clothing have regularly evoked litigation as educators have attempted to exert some control over pupil appearance. Courts have been called upon to weigh students' interests in selecting their hairstyle and attire against school authorities' interests in preventing disruptions and promoting school objectives.

Hairstyle

Considerable judicial activity in the 1970s focused on school regulations governing the length of male students' hair. The Supreme Court, however, refused to hear appeals of these cases, and federal circuit courts reached different conclusions in determining the legality of policies governing student hairstyle. If school officials have offered health or safety reasons for grooming regulations, such as requiring hair restraints intended to protect students from injury or to promote sanitation, the policies typically have been upheld. Furthermore, restrictions on male students' hairstyles at vocational schools have been upheld to create a positive image for potential employers visiting the school for recruitment purposes. Special grooming regulations have been endorsed as conditions of participation in extracurricular activities for legitimate health or safety reasons, and, in some instances, to enhance the school's image. Of course, students can be disciplined for hairstyles that cause a disruption by distracting classmates from instructional activities.

But hairstyle regulations cannot be arbitrary, devoid of an educational rationale, or discriminatory. A Texas federal district court ruled that school officials failed to

---

[83]*See, e.g.,* Carver Middle Sch. GSA v. Sch. Bd., 842 F.3d 1324 (11th Cir. 2016) (finding EAA claim ripe for adjudication regarding middle school's denial of GSA's request to form a student club), *on remand,* 249 F. Supp. 3d 1286 (M.D. Fla. 2017) (holding that EAA rights could be enforced by a private right of action under § 1983); Pratt v. Indian River Cent. Sch. Dist., 803 F. Supp. 2d 135 (N.D.N.Y. 2011) (finding, among claims of differential treatment based on sexual orientation, a sufficient EAA claim that the school district did not give equal access and benefits to the GSA compared to other student groups).

[84]Straights & Gays for Equality (SAGE) v. Osseo Area Schs., 471 F.3d 908 (8th Cir. 2006).

show a valid justification to impair Native American students' protected expression right to wear long hair that posed no disruption.[85] Similarly, the Fifth Circuit relied on a Texas law protecting religious liberties in ruling that a school district violated a Native American student's rights to express his religious beliefs by requiring him to wear one long braid tucked in his shirt or a bun on top of his head instead of wearing his two long braids in plain view.[86] More recently, the Seventh Circuit struck down a requirement that male students playing interscholastic basketball must keep their hair short as abridging equal protection rights and Title IX of the Education Amendments of 1972 by treating male and female athletes differently.[87]

Attire

Although public school students' hair length has subsided as a major subject of litigation, other appearance fads have become controversial as students have asserted a First Amendment right to express themselves through their attire at school. Some courts have distinguished attire restrictions from hair regulations because clothes, unlike hair length, can be changed outside of school. Even in situations where students' rights to govern their appearance have been recognized, the judiciary has upheld restrictions on attire that is immodest, disruptive, unsanitary, or promotes illegal behavior.

If school authorities can link particular attire to gang activities or other school violence, restrictions likely will be upheld. A Nebraska federal district court supported school authorities in suspending students for wearing bracelets and T-shirts with the phrase, "Julius RIP" (rest in peace) in remembrance of their friend who had been shot at his apartment complex allegedly for gang-related reasons.[88] The court agreed with school personnel that the attire could be banned in the interest of safety because it might trigger violence at the school. A West Virginia federal district court upheld a student's suspension for writing a slogan on his hands about freeing a classmate who was accused of shooting a police officer. The court endorsed school officials' prediction that the expression would contribute to gang-related disturbances.[89]

In a case involving the ban of an important national symbol,[90] the Ninth Circuit upheld school authorities in prohibiting students from wearing prominent American flags on their clothing during the observance of Cinco de Mayo, which commemorates Mexican

---

[85]Ala. & Coushatta Tribes v. Trs., 817 F. Supp. 1319 (E.D. Tex. 1993), *remanded per curiam*, 20 F.3d 469 (5th Cir. 1994). Schools likely could not impose hairstyle restrictions that interfere with other cultural or racial traditions. *See* Kay Lazar, *Black Malden Charter Students Punished for Braided Hair Extensions*, BOSTON GLOBE (May 12, 2017), https://www.bostonglobe.com/metro/2017/05/11/black-students-malden-school-who-wear-braids-face-punishment-parents-say/stWDlBSCJhw1zocUWR1QMP/story.html#comments.

[86]A.A. v. Needville Indep. Sch. Dist., 611 F.3d 248 (5th Cir. 2010).

[87]Hayden v. Greensburg Cmty. Sch. Corp., 743 F.3d 569 (7th Cir. 2014).

[88]Kuhr v. Millard Pub. Sch. Dist., 2012 U.S. Dist. LEXIS 56189 (D. Neb. Apr. 23, 2012).

[89]Brown v. Cabell Cty. Bd. of Educ., 714 F. Supp. 2d 587 (S.D. W. Va. 2010).

[90]*See* Brief for Members of Congress et al. as Amici Curiae Supporting Petitioners at 12, Dariano v. Morgan Hill Unified Sch. Dist., 767 F.3d 764 (9th Cir. 2014) (No. 11-17858) (arguing that restrictions should not be placed on displays of the American flag).

heritage and pride.[91] Students were allowed to wear the colors of the Mexican flag to celebrate this holiday, and there were threats of violence directed toward students wearing the American flag. Reasoning that the American flag shirts were intended to provoke Hispanic students, school administrators gave students the option of turning their shirts inside out or going home. The Ninth Circuit held that school personnel had a legitimate fear for student safety posed by the students wearing the American flag, noting that there does not have to be evidence of a disruption, but "the existence of facts which might reasonably lead school officials to forecast substantial disruption."[92] The court did not find that the students reacting to the shirts, rather than those wearing the American flag, posed the threat of disruption (heckler's veto).[93]

Indecent or disrespectful student attire can be curtailed regardless of whether the attire would meet the *Tinker* test of threatening a disruption. For example, an Idaho federal district court held that a school could prevent a student from wearing a T-shirt that depicted three high school administrators drunk on school grounds, noting that the student had no free expression right to portray administrators in a fashion that would undermine their authority and compromise the school's efforts to educate students about the harmful effects of alcohol.[94] A Georgia federal district court also upheld the suspension of a student who wore a T-shirt with the phrases "kids have civil rights too" and "even adults lie."[95] The Seventh Circuit found no First Amendment right for gifted students to wear a T-shirt they had designed that depicted in a satirical manner a child with physical disabilities with the word "gifties." The students wore their shirt to protest the election to select a class shirt, which they alleged was rigged because school authorities did not like their design.[96]

In one of the most expansive interpretations of *Bethel*, the Sixth Circuit upheld a school district's decision to prohibit students from wearing Marilyn Manson T-shirts. The appeals court agreed with school authorities that the shirts were offensive, promoted destructive conduct, and were counter to the school's efforts to denounce drugs and promote human dignity and democratic ideals.[97] The court held that under *Bethel*, schools can prohibit student expression that is inconsistent with its basic educational mission even though such speech might be protected by the First Amendment outside the school environment.[98]

[91]Dariano v. Morgan Hill Unified Sch. Dist., 745 F.3d 354 (9th Cir. 2014) (noting that displays of the American flag on Cinco de Mayo the year before had resulted in student altercations and recognizing there was not a blanket ban in that two students with very small American flags embedded in logos on their clothing were not forced to change their shirts or go home).

[92]745 F.3d at 360 (quoting Karp v. Becken, 477 F.2d 171, 175 (9th Cir. 1973)).

[93]*See* the description of the heckler's veto, *supra* note 62.

[94]Gano v. Sch. Dist., 674 F. Supp. 796 (D. Idaho 1987); *see also* Madrid v. Anthony, 510 F. Supp. 2d 425 (S.D. Tex. 2007) (upholding a ban on students, who were mostly Hispanic, wearing T-shirts with the statement, "We Are Not Criminals," to protest pending immigration legislation; school authorities instituted the ban to curb the escalating racial tension in the school that threatened student safety).

[95]Smith v. Greene Cty. Sch. Dist., 100 F. Supp. 2d 1354 (M.D. Ga. 2000).

[96]Brandt v. Bd. of Educ., 480 F.3d 460 (7th Cir. 2007).

[97]Boroff v. Van Wert City Bd. of Educ., 220 F.3d 465 (6th Cir. 2000).

[98]However, the Supreme Court's opinion in Morse v. Frederick, 551 U.S. 393, 423 (2007), casts doubt on this broad interpretation of Bethel as permitting bans on any expression conflicting with the school's mission, *supra* text accompanying note 22.

In contrast, the Second Circuit relied on *Tinker* in protecting a student's right to wear a shirt expressing political views; the shirt depicted George W. Bush negatively (i.e., calling him "Chicken Hawk in Chief" and linking him to drinking, taking drugs, and being a crook and draft dodger).[99] Reasoning that simply because the expression is in poor taste is not sufficient grounds to curtail students' expression rights, the appeals court narrowly interpreted *Bethel* as requiring student expression to contain sexual innuendos or profanity to be censorable as plainly offensive. Because neither was at issue, the court applied the *Tinker* disruption standard and found that the controversial shirt was not linked to any disruption.

As with hairstyle regulations, school authorities must have an educational rationale for attire restrictions, such as enhancing learning or preventing class disruptions. The Third Circuit struck down a prohibition on wearing T-shirts with the comedian Jeff Foxworthy's "red-neck sayings" as not sufficiently linked to racial harassment or other disruptive activity.[100] A student also prevailed in wearing a T-shirt depicting three black silhouettes holding firearms with "NRA" and "Shooting Sports Camp" superimposed over the silhouettes. School authorities asked the student to change the shirt, contending that it conflicted with the school's mission of deterring violence. Applying *Tinker* instead of *Bethel*, the Fourth Circuit held that the student's free expression rights were overriding because the shirt was not disruptive and did not promote gun use.[101]

The Third Circuit also found no threat of disruption or lewd expression in students wearing breast cancer awareness bracelets with the message, "I love Boobies (Keep a Breast)."[102] Focusing mainly on application of *Bethel*, the court reasoned that if the bracelets were plainly lewd or vulgar, they could be banned, but since the message was ambiguously lewd and pertained to a social issue, the students had a First Amendment right to wear the bracelets at school.[103] But Indiana and Wisconsin federal district courts rejected this rationale in upholding bans on students wearing the bracelets that school authorities considered vulgar.[104]

A few cases have involved attire worn to proms and in yearbook pictures.[105] For example, Mississippi school officials refused the request of a female student to attend the

[99]Guiles v. Marineau, 461 F.3d 320, 322 (2d Cir. 2006).

[100]Sypniewski v. Warren Hills Reg'l Bd. of Educ., 307 F.3d 243 (3d Cir. 2002), *supra* text accompanying note 55.

[101]Newsom v. Albemarle Cty. Sch. Bd., 354 F.3d 249 (4th Cir. 2003).

[102]B.H. *ex rel.* Hawk v. Easton Area Sch. Dist., 725 F.3d 293 (3d Cir. 2013).

[103]*Id.* at 298. The court relied heavily on Justice Alito's concurrence in *Morse v. Frederick*, 551 U.S. 393, 422 (2007) (Alito, J., joined by Kennedy, J., concurring) (arguing that student expression related to social or political issues is protected).

[104]J.A. v. Fort Wayne Cmty. Schs., 2013 WL 4479229 (N.D. Ind. Aug. 20, 2013) (holding that deference to the sensibilities of the school principal is required and that the principal reasonably viewed the phrase on the bracelet as lewd); K.J. v. Sauk Prairie Sch. Dist., 2012 U.S. Dist. LEXIS 187689 (W.D. Wis. Feb. 6, 2012) (rejecting a request for a preliminary injunction to prohibit school authorities from banning the bracelets, reasoning that the bracelets reasonably can be considered vulgar for middle school students).

[105]*See, e.g.*, Logan v. Gary Cmty. Sch. Corp., 2008 WL 4411518 (N.D. Ind. Sept. 25, 2008) (denying the school district's motion to dismiss a suit brought by a transgendered student who was biologically male and was not allowed to attend the prom in a dress under the school district's dress code forbidding clothing that "advertises sexual orientation" among other prohibitions). The district reached a monetary settlement for an undisclosed amount with the student.

prom with her girlfriend and to wear a tuxedo. The federal district court found that school officials impaired the student's First Amendment rights but denied her request for a preliminary injunction because the school district had cancelled the prom, and a private group was hosting the event.[106] Another Mississippi student sued after she was not permitted to wear a tuxedo in her senior picture. When she refused to follow the district's policy requiring female students to wear a drape and male students to wear tuxedos, her picture was excluded from the yearbook. She alleged constitutional and statutory violations, and the federal district court denied the school district's motion to dismiss the case, finding that not allowing her to wear a tuxedo in her picture constituted sex discrimination.[107]

Dress Codes.   Several restrictive dress codes have received judicial endorsement. The Fifth Circuit upheld a dress code prohibiting any clothing with printed words except for school logos as content neutral.[108] Also upholding a restrictive dress code as reasonable to create unity and focus attention on learning, the Sixth Circuit identified no violation of a student's free expression rights, her right to wear clothes of her choice, or her father's right to control his daughter's attire.[109] Previously, the same court upheld a prescriptive student dress code devised by a Kentucky school-based council that limited the colors, materials, and type of clothing allowed and barred logos, shorts, cargo pants, jeans, and other specific items. The court found legitimate safety justifications and no intent to suppress free speech.[110]

Dress codes, however, must not be discriminatorily enforced. In a case mentioned previously, the Sixth Circuit ordered a school district to reconsider suspensions of two students who refused to change or turn inside out T-shirts with a country singer on the front and the Confederate flag on the back.[111] School authorities asserted that the shirts violated the school's dress code prohibiting clothing or emblems that contain slogans or words depicting alcohol or tobacco or have illegal, immoral, or racist implications, but the court found no indication of racial tension in the school or that the shirt would likely lead to a disruption. There also was evidence that the dress code had been selectively enforced in a viewpoint-specific manner; students had been allowed to wear shirts celebrating Malcolm X. Thus, the court remanded the case to determine if the students' First Amendment rights had been violated.

Additionally, students cannot be disciplined for expressing their disagreement with a dress code in a nondisruptive manner. Applying *Tinker*, the Eighth Circuit ruled that

---

[106]McMillen v. Itawamba Cty. Sch. Dist., 702 F. Supp. 2d 699 (N.D. Miss. 2010).

[107]Sturgis v. Copiah Cty. Sch. Dist., 2011 WL 4351355 (S.D. Miss. Sept. 15, 2011).

[108]Palmer *ex rel*. Palmer v. Waxahachie Indep. Sch. Dist., 579 F.3d 502 (5th Cir. 2009).

[109]Blau v. Ft. Thomas Pub. Sch. Dist., 401 F.3d 381 (6th Cir. 2005).

[110]Long v. Bd. of Educ., 121 F. Supp. 2d 621 (W.D. Ky. 2000), *aff'd mem*., 21 F. Appx. 252 (6th Cir. 2001); *see also* Bivens *ex rel*. Green v. Albuquerque Pub. Schs., 899 F. Supp. 556 (D.N.M. 1995), *aff'd mem*., 131 F.3d 151 (10th Cir. 1997) (upholding a student's suspension for violating the school's dress code by wearing "sagging" pants; rejecting the contention that such attire conveyed an African American cultural message).

[111]Castorina *ex rel*. Rewt v. Madison Cty. Sch. Bd., 246 F.3d 536 (6th Cir. 2001). Most courts, however, have upheld restrictions on Confederate flag displays under anti-harassment policies, finding no viewpoint discrimination, *supra* text accompanying note 48.

students had a First Amendment right to wear black armbands to protest the district's student apparel policy.[112]

Student Uniforms.   Many attire controversies might be avoided if public school students were required to wear uniforms as they do in many countries. **Voluntary and mandatory student uniforms have become increasingly popular, being adopted by one-fifth of school districts nationally, disproportionately those in urban settings**.[113] Advocates assert that student uniforms eliminate gang-related attire, reduce violence and socioeconomic distinctions, and improve school climate by placing the emphasis on academics rather than fashion fads. And the line is not always clear between restrictive dress codes and student uniforms.

Courts have upheld uniform policies so long as there are waivers for those opposed to uniforms on religious or philosophical grounds and provisions are made for students who cannot afford the uniforms.[114] Courts have not been persuaded that any rights are violated because a stigma is associated with exercising the First Amendment right to be exempt from uniform requirements.[115]

Departing from the general trend, the Ninth Circuit struck down a Nevada elementary school's uniform policy as abridging free speech rights.[116] The policy required students to wear red or navy polo shirts with tan or khaki pants or skirts, and the front of the shirt had to carry the school's logo, name, and motto ("Tomorrow's Leaders"). The policy allowed students to wear attire of nationally recognized youth organizations (e.g., Boy Scouts) on their regular meeting days but did not authorize other exemptions. Applying strict judicial scrutiny, the appeals court held that the uniform policy compelled speech with which the students and their parents disagreed and found that the exemption provision was not content neutral. But in a subsequent ruling, the Ninth Circuit granted school personnel qualified immunity due to the unsettled nature of the law.[117]

Restrictive dress codes and uniforms without written words do not seem vulnerable to legal challenges as long as the policies allow exemptions. Nonetheless, school officials would be wise to ensure that they have a legitimate educational justification for any grooming or dress restrictions. Policies designed to protect students' health and safety, reduce violence and discipline problems, and enhance learning usually will be endorsed.

[112]Lowry *ex rel.* Crow v. Watson Chapel Sch. Dist., 540 F.3d 752 (8th Cir. 2008). *But see* Hardwick v. Heyward, 711 F.3d 426 (4th Cir. 2013) (holding that a student could not protest the legitimate ban on Confederate flag displays with a shirt depicting the flag, although other nondisruptive "protest" shirts would be allowed).

[113]*See* U.S. Dep't of Educ., Nat'l Ctr. for Educ. Statistics, *Indicators of School Crime and Safety: 2016*, at 112 (Indicator 20) (May 2017), https://nces.ed.gov/pubs2017/2017064.pdf.

[114]*See, e.g.,* Jacobs v. Clark Cty. Sch. Dist., 526 F.3d 419 (9th Cir. 2008); Canady v. Bossier Par. Sch. Bd., 240 F.3d 437 (5th Cir. 2001); Littlefield v. Forney Indep. Sch. Dist., 268 F.3d 275 (5th Cir. 2001).

[115]*See, e.g.,* Wilkins v. Penns Grove-Carneys Point Reg'l Sch. Dist., 123 F. Appx. 493 (3d Cir. 2005).

[116]Frudden v. Pilling, 742 F.3d 1199 (9th Cir. 2014), *on remand,* 2015 WL 540206 (D. Nev. Feb. 10, 2015) (finding the policy narrowly tailored to serve the compelling interests of focusing students on academics and reducing wealth-based bullying), *aff'd in part and rev'd in part,* 877 F.3d 821 (9th Cir. 2017) (criticizing the 2014 panel's reliance on strict scrutiny, but "reluctantly" following its decision to strike down the use of the logo and the exemption provision).

[117]*Id.,* 877 F.3d 821 (granting qualified immunity to school personnel but remanding for a consideration of immunity for the school district and parent-faculty association).

Given the current student interest in tattoos, body piercings, and other fashion fads coupled with school authorities' concerns about attire linked to gangs and violence, controversies over student appearance in public schools seem likely to persist.

CONCLUSION

Student expression and association rights have generated a significant amount of school litigation. In the late 1960s and early 1970s, the federal judiciary expanded First Amendment protections afforded to students following the Supreme Court's landmark *Tinker* decision. Yet, the reach of the *Tinker* standard was narrowed somewhat after the Supreme Court ruled in *Bethel* and *Hazelwood* that lewd or vulgar speech and attire are not protected by the First Amendment and that school authorities can censor student expression that appears to represent the school. The Supreme Court in *Morse* again restricted use of the disruption standard if expression can be viewed as promoting or celebrating illegal activity. *Tinker* has not been overturned, but it governs more limited circumstances than was true in the 1970s.

Students do not need to rely solely on constitutional protections because federal and state laws, most notably the Equal Access Act, also protect students' expression and association rights. And *Tinker* has been revitalized as the primary standard used in First Amendment challenges to anti-harassment and anti-bullying policies and electronic expression. Judicial criteria to weigh the competing interests of students and school authorities under statutory and constitutional provisions continue to be refined, but the following generalizations depict the current status of the law.

1. Students do not have a First Amendment right to engage in expression that is defamatory, obscene, lewd, or inflammatory or that promotes illegal activity in public schools.

2. Private student-initiated expression of ideological views that merely occurs at school cannot be curtailed unless it threatens a disruption or collides with the rights of others.

3. Student expression that represents the school can be censored if the decisions are based on pedagogical concerns.

4. Students can be disciplined for making threats toward classmates or school personnel.

5. School authorities cannot bar controversial or critical content from student literature that is not school sponsored, but the time, place, and manner of distribution at school can be reasonably regulated.

6. School districts' anti-harassment and anti-bullying provisions will likely be upheld unless they are vague or overly broad in restricting protected expression.

7. Student electronic expression can be the basis for disciplinary action if it disrupts the work of the school; whether such expression can be censored because it is vulgar or interferes with the rights of others has not been clarified.

8. Under the EAA, if a federally assisted secondary school establishes a limited open forum for student-initiated clubs to meet during noninstructional time, the access policy must be content neutral; however, public schools are not required to create such a forum for noncurriculum student groups to meet.

9. Beyond the EAA, student and community groups have First Amendment protections against viewpoint discrimination in public school access.

10. School authorities can restrict student hairstyles and attire that are vulgar, jeopardize health and safety, or threaten to disrupt the educational process; any restrictions must be justified for educational reasons.

11. Restrictive student dress codes and uniforms can be imposed in public schools if not designed to suppress expression or discriminate against particular groups of students and if justified by legitimate educational objectives, such as reducing violence and improving achievement.

12. Uniform policies must allow exemptions and cannot entail forced speech.

CHAPTER SIX

STUDENT CLASSIFICATIONS

Is it legally permissible to have female-only math classes, schools for only Black males, or schools that only serve students with autism? Must all students be treated equally in public schools? It might appear from a literal translation of the word *equality* that once a state establishes an educational system, all students must be treated in the same manner.[1] Courts, however, have recognized that individuals are different and that equal treatment of diverse individuals can have negative consequences. Accordingly, valid classification practices, designed to enhance the educational experiences of children by recognizing their unique needs, generally have been accepted as a legitimate prerogative of educators (e.g., Advanced Placement courses). While educators' authority to classify students has not been seriously contested, the bases for certain classifications and the procedures used to make distinctions among students have been the focus of substantial litigation.

Readers of this chapter should be able to:

- Identify what legal grounds can be used to challenge student classifications based on race, ethnicity, national origin, sex, sexual orientation, gender identity, age, and ability.[2]

---

[1] It is important to note the distinction between equality and equity. Whereas equality treats everyone the same, equity gives people what they need to be successful. In other words, to ensure equity, students who may face a disadvantage (e.g., low-income students) might need additional supports (e.g., free and reduced-price meals) to help them do well in school.

[2] It is beyond the scope of this chapter to cover all students who may be marginalized in schools. For additional discussion, *see* U.S. Dep't of Educ., *Education Department Releases Guidance on Homeless Children and Youth* (July 27, 2016), https://www.ed.gov/news/press-releases/education-department-releases-guidance-homeless-children-and-youth (discussing the legal obligations to students who are experiencing homelessness); Nat'l Ass'n of Sch. Psychologists, *Supporting Refugee Children & Youth: Tips for Educators* (2015), https://www.nasponline.org/resources-and-publications/resources/school-safety-and-crisis/war-and-terrorism/supporting-refugee-students (explaining how school officials can better support student refugees); U.S. Dep't of Educ., *Programs: Migrant Education—Basic State Formula Grants* (Oct. 5, 2015), https://www2.ed.gov/programs/mep/index.html (addressing how to better accommodate migrant students in the curriculum); U.S. Dep't of Educ., *Non-Regulatory Guidance: Ensuring Educational Stability for Children in Foster Care* (June 23, 2016), https://www2.ed.gov/policy/elsec/leg/essa/edhhsfostercarenonregulatorguide.pdf (focusing on educational needs of students in foster care); William Galston & Elizabeth McElvein, *Creating Educational Opportunity for Incarcerated Students*, Brookings (Aug. 15, 2016), https://www.brookings.edu/blog/brown-center-chalkboard/2016/08/15/creating-educational-opportunity-for-incarcerated-students-2/ (highlighting how school officials can provide equal opportunities to students who are incarcerated).

- Examine current developments in the law that address race-conscious student assignment plans, transgender students, and native language.
- Analyze the legal entitlements of high-ability students.

■ ■ ■ ■ ■

LEGAL CONTEXT

The Equal Protection Clause of the Fourteenth Amendment to the U.S. Constitution is often at issue when school districts attempt to classify students based on race, national origin, native language, ability and achievement, age, sex, sexual orientation, and gender identity.

The Equal Protection Clause states in part that no state shall deny to any person within its jurisdiction equal protection of the laws. It has been interpreted as prohibiting intentional discrimination and applies to subdivisions of the state, including public school districts. **The Equal Protection Clause requires that similarly situated individuals be treated the same**. (See overview of Fourteenth Amendment's Equal Protection Clause, Figure 6.1.) As a result, equal protection claims often arise if a government's law or policy creates a classification that advantages or disadvantages one group over another. When examining a government policy, courts apply three different levels of review (i.e., strict scrutiny, intermediate scrutiny, and rational basis) for different classes of people and if different interests are at stake.

For example, the government must have a compelling interest for any policy that treats students differently based on race, national origin, or alienage because such classifications are subject to strict scrutiny review. Intermediate scrutiny is applied to challenge classifications

FIGURE 6.1 Judicial Tests to Determine Equal Protection Violation

Strict Scrutiny	Intermediate Scrutiny	Rational Basis
Used with classifications related to race, nat'l origin, alienage	Used with classifications related to gender and illegitimacy	Used with classifications related to sexual orientation, age, disability
This classification must be *necessary* to the achievement of a *compelling* government interest.	This classification must be *substantially related* to the achievement of an *important* government interest.	This classification must have a *rational* relationship to a *legitimate* government interest.

based on sex.[3] This standard requires that the policy have an important governmental interest and that it be substantially related to advancing significant governmental objectives. Where any other classification or form of discrimination is present (e.g., disability, age, sexual orientation), courts apply rational basis review. All that is required under this level of review is that some rational basis was used in the state's decision. This is a very low threshold and is generally met with relative ease. Thus, under the Equal Protection Clause, it would be much more difficult to open a public school that serves only Black students than it would be to open a public school that serves only gay students. The school serving only Black students would need to demonstrate a compelling government interest in segregating students by race and that the classification serves a necessary interest (i.e., strict scrutiny). The school serving only gay students would need to show simply a legitimate governmental objective with a rational relationship between the means and the ends (i.e., rational basis review).

CLASSIFICATIONS BASED ON RACE

The Supreme Court has declared that separate schools based on race are inherently unequal.

The most prevalent reason for classifying students according to race has been to establish or perpetuate racially segregated schools. Widespread racial segregation in educational institutions existed in this country from the colonial period well into the twentieth century. Even after the adoption of the Fourteenth Amendment in 1868, most schools remained segregated either pursuant to state constitution or statute, local ordinance, district policy or practice, or court interpretation, and were seldom equal. When such practices were challenged, courts generally mandated only that children be provided with access to public education. Despite laws and policies to racially integrate student bodies, some school districts remain highly segregated. In addition to traditional public schools, charter schools have also been accused of racially segregating students.[4]

Plessy and *Brown*

Perhaps the most infamous case supporting the "separate but equal" interpretation was *Plessy v. Ferguson* in 1896, in which the Supreme Court upheld racial segregation of passengers in railroad coaches as required by Louisiana law.[5] The doctrine of separate but equal was practiced in U.S. public schools for many years. In the early 1950s, the time

---

[3]Miss. Univ. for Women v. Hogan, 458 U.S. 718 (1982).

[4]Mandy McLaren, *New Charter Schools Debate: Are They Widening Racial Divides in Public Education?* WASH. POST (May 16, 2017), https://www.washingtonpost.com/local/education/new-charter-schools-debate-are-they-widening-racial-divides-in-public-education/2017/05/16/2f324676-0d78-11e7-9d5a-a83e627dc120_story .html?utm_term=.0de8970db216.

[5]163 U.S. 537 (1896); *see also* Bolling v. Sharpe, 347 U.S. 497 (1954) (invalidating school segregation in Washington, D.C., under the Fifth Amendment's Due Process Clause because the Fourteenth Amendment does not apply in that jurisdiction).

appeared ripe to directly attack the separate but equal policy in elementary and secondary schools because of some success in higher education cases.[6] This occurred in 1954 when the Supreme Court combined cases from four states—Kansas, South Carolina, Virginia, and Delaware.[7] **In the landmark decision, collectively called *Brown v. Board of Education*, Chief Justice Warren, writing for a unanimous Court, declared education to be "perhaps the most important function of state and local governments"[8] and repudiated the separate but equal doctrine, stipulating that racially segregated public schools were "inherently unequal."[9]**

Because of the significant impact of this decision and the difficulty in fashioning an immediate remedy, the Supreme Court delayed an implementation decree for one year, soliciting friend-of-the-court briefs[10] regarding strategies to integrate school districts. Then, in 1955, in *Brown II*, the Court concluded that the conversion from dual to unitary districts must occur "with all deliberate speed,"[11] although it gave little guidance as to what specific time frame was required or to what extent integration was mandated. As a result, states varied widely in their efforts to comply.[12]

Early Post-*Brown* Litigation

Despite the *Brown* mandate to end unconstitutional segregation, for more than a decade, little progress was made in integrating schools. The Supreme Court was forced to react to some blatant violations, such as state officials' efforts to physically block the desegregation of schools in Little Rock[13] and an attempt to avoid integration by closing public schools in one Virginia county, while maintaining public schools in other counties in the state.[14] But confusion remained as to whether *Brown* required affirmative action to integrate schools or only the removal of state laws authorizing school segregation.

Then, in a trilogy of cases in 1968, the Supreme Court announced that school officials in systems that were segregated by law in 1954 had an affirmative duty to take whatever steps were necessary to convert to unitary school systems and to eliminate the effects of past

---

[6]*See* McLaurin v. Okla. State Regents, 339 U.S. 637 (1950); Sweatt v. Painter, 339 U.S. 629 (1950); Sipuel v. Bd. of Regents, 332 U.S. 631 (1948) (per curiam); Missouri *ex rel.* Gaines v. Canada, 305 U.S. 337 (1938).

[7]Brown v. Bd. of Educ., 98 F. Supp. 797 (D. Kan. 1951); Briggs v. Elliott, 98 F. Supp. 529 (E.D.S.C. 1951), *vacated and remanded*, 342 U.S. 350 (1952), *on remand*, 103 F. Supp. 920 (E.D.S.C. 1952); Davis v. Cty. Sch. Bd., 103 F. Supp. 337 (E.D. Va. 1952); Belton v. Gebhart, 87 A.2d 862 (Del. Ch. 1952), *aff'd*, 91 A.2d 137 (Del. 1952).

[8]347 U.S. 483, 493 (1954) (Brown I).

[9]*Id.* at 495.

[10]Friend-of-the-court (amicus curiae) briefs are provided by nonparties to inform or perhaps persuade the court.

[11]Brown v. Bd. of Educ., 349 U.S. 294, 301 (1955) (Brown II).

[12]Malcolm Gladwell, *Miss Buchanan's Period of Adjustment*, Revisionist History Podcast (n.d.), http://revisionisthistory.com/episodes/13-miss-buchanans-period-of-adjustment.

[13]Cooper v. Aaron, 358 U.S. 1 (1958).

[14]Griffin v. Cty. Sch. Bd., 377 U.S. 218 (1964).

discrimination.[15] Furthermore, the Court declared that desegregation remedies would be evaluated based on their effectiveness in dismantling dual school systems. **Thus, the notion of state neutrality was transformed into a requirement of affirmative state action to desegregate; the mere removal of barriers to school integration was not sufficient**.

In one of these 1968 cases, *Green v. County School Board*, the Court reviewed a freedom-of-choice plan adopted by a small school district in Virginia. During the three-year period immediately following implementation, no White children enrolled in the historically Black school, while only a few Black children enrolled in the historically White school. The district contended that any resulting segregation was due to the choices of individuals, not to government action, and was therefore permissible; the Supreme Court disagreed. As a result, the district was ordered to come forward with a new plan that promised "realistically to work and to work now."[16] **In addition, the Court ruled that school authorities must eliminate the racial identification of schools in terms of the *composition of the student body, faculty, and staff; transportation; extracurricular activities; and facilities*.** These six elements still are used today and are referred to in the aggregate simply as the *Green* criteria.

In 1971, additional direction was provided when the Supreme Court ruled in *Swann v. Charlotte-Mecklenburg Board of Education* that the elimination of invidious racial distinctions may be sufficient in connection with transportation, support personnel, and extracurricular activities, but that more was necessary in terms of constructing facilities and making faculty and student assignments.[17] The Court endorsed the practice of assigning teachers on the basis of race until faculties were integrated and declared that new schools must be located so that the dual school system would not be perpetuated or reestablished.

Correcting racial imbalance among student populations, however, was more difficult. For the vestiges of segregation to be eliminated, the school district had to achieve racial balance in a sufficient number of schools, although every school did not have to reflect the racial composition of the school district as a whole. The presence of a small number of predominantly one-race schools in the district did not necessarily mean that it continued to practice state-imposed segregation, but the burden of proof was placed on school officials to establish that such schools were not the result of present or past discriminatory action. To achieve the desired racial balance, the Court suggested pairing or consolidating schools, altering attendance zones, and using racial quotas, but rejected the practice of assigning students to the schools nearest their homes if doing so failed to eliminate state-sponsored segregation. The Court also endorsed the use of reasonable busing as a means to integrate schools, yet qualified that endorsement by noting that the soundness of any transportation plan must be evaluated based on the time involved, distance traveled, and age of the students.

By applying the criteria established in *Green* and *Swann*, substantial desegregation was attained in southern states during the 1970s. Where unconstitutional segregation was found, federal courts exercised broad power in ordering remedies affecting student and staff assignments, curriculum, school construction, personnel practices, and budgetary

---

[15]*See* Green v. Cty. Sch. Bd., 391 U.S. 430 (1968); Raney v. Bd. of Educ., 391 U.S. 443 (1968); Monroe v. Bd. of Comm'rs, 391 U.S. 450 (1968).

[16]Green, 391 U.S. at 439.

[17]402 U.S. 1 (1971).

allocations. This judicial activity was augmented also by threats from the former Department of Health, Education, and Welfare to terminate federal funds to school districts not complying with Title VI of the Civil Rights Act of 1964.[18]

Because the Supreme Court carefully limited its early decisions to states and school districts with a long history of school segregation by official policy, questions remained regarding what type of evidence—other than explicit legislation requiring school segregation—was necessary to establish unconstitutional de jure segregation. **De jure segregated schools are those where the separation of the races is required by law or is the result of other action by the state or its agents. De facto segregation occurs by practice (e.g., families choosing to live in a particular neighborhood).**

During this time, there was a debate about what factors would distinguish unlawful de jure segregation from permissible de facto segregation. Answers to this debate began to evolve in *Keyes v. School District, Denver*, in which the Supreme Court in 1973 held **that if "no statutory dual system has ever existed, plaintiffs must prove not only that segregated schooling exists but also that it was brought about or maintained by intentional state action."**[19]

Desegregation Remedies

Courts have considerable discretion in requiring districts and states to take steps to remedy unconstitutional school segregation, and costs often have seemed irrelevant. While some school districts have opened magnet schools[20] to encourage integration, others have attempted to rezone or redistrict[21] or implemented busing[22] plans.

Although sometimes politically unpopular, the rezoning of schools often was the fastest, least expensive, and simplest way to integrate students. Because of a long history of gerrymandering boundary lines with the intent to segregate, many school boundaries during the 1950s and 1960s had little to do with geographic barriers (e.g., rivers, hills); safety issues (e.g., location of busy roads, factories); or the size, location, or dispersion of the student population. As a result, significant integration often has resulted through the simple use of good-faith redistricting and/or, in fairly narrow circumstances, the creation of new or consolidated school districts.[23]

Busing was also used to accomplish integration when other alternatives had not succeeded. The Supreme Court gave federal courts the discretion to use busing to desegregate schools.[24] Even though busing is admittedly effective at achieving student

[18]42 U.S.C. § 2000d–2000d-7 (2018) (prohibiting discrimination based on race).

[19]413 U.S. 189, 198 (1973).

[20]Magnet schools have been used to encourage desegregation by drawing students from across their normal school district boundary lines. Magnet schools sometimes offer a specialized curriculum to attract students from various neighborhoods (e.g., an arts program).

[21]*See* Milliken v. Bradley, 433 U.S. 267, 280–81 (1977) (Milliken II) (finding that an interdistrict remedy may include only those districts that were guilty of de jure segregation).

[22]*See* N.C. State Bd. of Educ. v. Swann, 402 U.S. 43 (1971) (striking down a state law forbidding the busing of students to create racially balanced schools). *But see* Crawford v. Bd. of Educ., 458 U.S. 527 (1982) (upholding a state constitutional amendment in California that permitted busing only when de jure segregation was present).

[23]Newburg Area Council v. Bd. of Educ., 510 F.2d 1358 (6th Cir. 1974).

[24]*See* Swann v. Charlotte-Mecklenburg Bd. of Educ., 402 U.S. 1 (1971).

integration, it also represents a significant expense; is inefficient in the use of student time; and is an unpopular option with many students, parents, taxpayers, and voters of all races. Nevertheless, court-ordered busing was used to desegregate schools—especially in large urban districts. Consequently, several bills to limit the authority of federal courts to order the busing of students have been unsuccessfully introduced in Congress.

Achieving Unitary Status

Federal courts have found numerous school systems guilty of engaging in de jure segregation and have fashioned a variety of remedies. In addressing this problem, courts have ordered school districts to demonstrate that they were complying with desegregation decrees. While most court-ordered desegregation decrees were rendered in the 1960s and 1970s, some court orders still exist today. Critics argue that federal judges generally lack the knowledge and expertise to properly administer schools or to make curricular or instructional decisions. Additionally, lengthy court supervision has been criticized by school districts as usurping the traditional roles of trained and licensed school administrators. School districts that have wanted to end this court supervision have requested that the court declare the school district "unitary." **A school district is considered unitary when it eliminates the effects of past segregation resulting from dual school systems based on race**. Once a district is declared unitary, the court will no longer supervise the school's decisions as they relate to desegregation efforts. In the early 1990s, the Supreme Court began to find districts unitary. While school officials were often satisfied to regain local control, others argued that school districts had not fully eliminated the past effects of segregation.

In *Board of Education v. Dowell*, the Supreme Court concluded that **the federal judiciary should terminate supervision of school districts where school boards have complied with desegregation mandates in good faith and have eliminated vestiges of past discrimination "to the extent practicable."**[25] Then, in *Freeman v. Pitts*, the Supreme Court held that a district court must relinquish its supervision and control over those aspects of a school system in which there has been compliance with a desegregation decree even if other aspects of the decree have not been met. Through this approach, the Court sought to restore to state and local authorities control over public schools at the earliest possible date and noted that "[p]artial relinquishment of judicial control . . . can be an important and significant step in fulfilling the district court's duty to return the operations and control of schools to local authorities."[26] To guide the lower courts in determining whether supervision should be removed, the Court identified three questions:

- Has there been full and satisfactory compliance with the decree in those aspects of the system where supervision is to be withdrawn?
- Is the retention of judicial control necessary or practicable to achieve compliance with the decree in other facets of the school system?
- Has the district demonstrated a good faith commitment to the court's entire decree and relevant provisions of federal law?

[25]498 U.S. 237, 249–50 (1991).

[26]503 U.S. 467, 489 (1992).

Then, in 1995, the Supreme Court ruled in *Missouri v. Jenkins* that the elimination of racial disparities was not required for granting unitary status unless the plaintiffs can demonstrate that the disparity relates directly to prior segregation.[27] With guidance from the *Dowell, Freeman*, and *Jenkins* decisions, numerous districts have been able to show that they have achieved a unitary operation.[28]

Postunitary Transfer and School Assignment

Litigation will not end simply because the school district has achieved unitary status and has initially been relieved of judicial control and supervision. Any decision that may even potentially result in racial imbalance, whether de jure or de facto, is likely to be challenged. **Accordingly, the placement of a new school or the creation of a new school district will foreseeably be scrutinized,[29] as will policies regarding school transfer, initial school assignment, and open enrollment**. However, a transfer policy that results in only an insignificant change in minority-majority enrollment within the district will not typically justify reasserting judicial supervision.[30]

Furthermore, students have challenged school district policies that were designed and administered to maintain the racial balance accomplished through years of court supervision, to integrate de facto segregated communities, or to achieve the goal of a diverse student body. In such instances, students generally were permitted to enroll in schools where their race was a minority or otherwise underrepresented, but not vice versa, which has been challenged. Guidance for lower courts began to emerge in 2003 when the Supreme Court, in *Grutter v. Bollinger*,[31] permitted a law school to consider race as one of several factors in determining the composition of its first-year class. In denying the White plaintiff's race-based Fourteenth Amendment claim, the Court majority identified a compelling interest (i.e., the benefits derived from a diverse student body) and reasoned that the school's admission procedures were sufficiently narrowly tailored not to adversely affect the rights of rejected White applicants.

Additional guidance within the K–12 context was provided in a 2007 Supreme Court decision, *Parents Involved in Community Schools v. Seattle School District* (*PICS*). The plurality opinion identified an Equal Protection Clause violation where the school districts

---

[27]515 U.S. 70 (1995).

[28]Everett v. Pitt Cty. Bd. of Educ., 788 F.3d 132 (4th Cir. 2015) (declaring district unitary because any remaining racial imbalance was related to White students leaving the district); People Who Care v. Rockford Bd. of Educ., 246 F.3d 1073 (7th Cir. 2001) (finding district was desegregated even though minority students were underrepresented in advanced courses); Manning v. Sch. Bd. 244 F.3d 927 (11th Cir. 2001) (holding that the district had achieved unitary status despite the existing demographic imbalance). *But see* Little Rock Sch. Dist. v. Ark., 664 F.3d 738 (8th Cir. 2011) (ruling that one of the school districts involved in this suit had not achieved unitary status because there was noncompliance with assignment reporting, discipline, advanced placement, employment, staff, and special education).

[29]*See, e.g.*, Anderson v. Canton Mun. Separate Sch. Dist., 232 F.3d 450 (5th Cir. 2000).

[30]United States v. Texas, 457 F.3d 472 (5th Cir. 2006).

[31]539 U.S. 306 (2003). Because Grutter, Michigan voters amended the state constitution to prohibit the consideration of race in making admissions decisions, MICH. CONST. art. I, § 26. *See also* Schuette v. Coal. to Defend Affirmative Action, 134 S. Ct. 1623 (2014) (finding the voter-approved amendment prohibiting the consideration of race in admissions to be constitutional).

in both Seattle, Washington, and Jefferson County, Kentucky, considered race in determining school assignment once residence and availability of space were considered.[32] Seattle had never been found guilty of de jure segregation or been subjected to court-ordered desegregation, though Jefferson County had its court order dissolved in 2000 after it had eliminated the vestiges of prior segregation to the greatest extent practicable.

The Court reasoned that each district's diversity plan relied on race in a nonindividualized mechanical way even though other means were available to address integration goals of the de facto segregated communities. The plans were neither race-neutral nor narrowly tailored. Guidelines issued in December 2011 by the U.S. Department of Justice and the U.S. Department of Education provide assistance to both public PK–12 schools and universities when developing student assignment plans that consider race.[33] The guidelines offer examples of what is permissible when school districts are trying to achieve a higher level of student diversity. In 2016, the Supreme Court decided another case involving race-conscious admissions, *Fisher v. University of Texas*, which provided further guidance in this area. In *Fisher*, the U.S. Supreme Court upheld the University of Texas' race-conscious admissions policy, finding no violation of the Equal Protection Clause. The Court observed that the university first attempted using race-neutral measures and then took a holistic review of the student during the admissions process.[34]

As a result of segregated students and the benefits of classroom diversity, some K–12 school districts have attempted to use various approaches to increase the racial diversity of their student bodies that align with the Supreme Court precedent discussed above. These types of plans sometimes take race into account and are controversial, while others create less contentious, race-neutral policies. Not surprisingly, these policies have also been subject to legal challenges and have sometimes been debated as to the applicability of the *PICS* decision.[35]

Race as a Factor in Admission to Private Schools

In a case involving a K–12 private school, the U.S. Supreme Court ruled that racially discriminatory admissions policies in private schools were contrary to public policy.[36] The private, religious K–12 school in this case maintained a racially discriminatory admissions policy stemming from its interpretation of the Bible. This case was combined with another involving a private university that also practiced discrimination in admissions. While the K–12 school only accepted White students, on occasion it accepted children from racially

---

[32]551 U.S. 701 (2007) (aggregating claims from Parents Involved in Cmty. Schs. v. Seattle Sch. Dist., 426 F.3d 1162 (9th Cir. 2005) and McFarland v. Jefferson Cty. Pub. Schs., 416 F.3d 513 (6th Cir. 2005)).

[33]U.S. Dep't of Justice & U.S. Dep't of Educ., *Guidance on the Voluntary Use of Race to Achieve Diversity and Avoid Racial Isolation in Elementary and Secondary Schools* (n.d.), http://www.justice.gov/crt/about/edu/documents/guidanceelem.pdf.

[34]Fisher v. Univ. of Tex. at Austin, 136 S. Ct. 2198 (2016).

[35]*See* Lewis v. Ascension Parish, 806 F.3d 344 (5th Cir. 2015) (upholding the school district's student assignment plan that considered race in rezoning); Spurlock v. Fox, 716 F.3d 383 (6th Cir. 2013) (finding the school district's plan was not adopted or implemented with an intent to segregate students); Doe v. Lower Merion Sch. Dist., 665 F.3d 524 (3d Cir. 2011) (holding that the consideration of race when drawing attendance boundaries does not create a racial classification and therefore does not trigger strict scrutiny).

[36]Bob Jones Univ. v. United States, 461 U.S. 574 (1983).

mixed marriages if one of the parents was White. The Internal Revenue Service (IRS) found these policies to be racist, and it revoked the schools' tax-exempt status. The private K–12 school and the university alleged that that IRS abridged their religious liberty. The IRS argued and the Court agreed that by not having a racially nondiscrimination policy in place with regard to students, they were not "charitable" within the common law concepts reflected in the IRS code.[37] Also, according to the Court, there was no Free Exercise Clause violation because the government's fundamental, overriding interest in eradicating racial discrimination outweighed the schools' sincerely held religious beliefs.[38]

When private schools use race as a factor to determine admission, Title VI of the Civil Rights Act of 1964 and Section 1981 of the Civil Rights Act of 1886 at the federal level have been applied, in addition to any related state laws or local ordinances. Title VI forbids race discrimination but applies only to those schools that receive federal financial assistance. On the other hand, Section 1981 prohibits both race and ethnicity discrimination in entering into and fulfilling contracts and requires compliance of all public and private schools, regardless of whether they qualify as recipients of federal aid. The seminal case applying this law to a private education setting is *Runyon v. McCrary*, in which the Supreme Court held that Section 1981 was violated when private school administrators rejected all applicants to their school who were not White.[39] The Court concluded that the practice violated the right to contract due to race and that its ruling violated neither parents' privacy rights nor their freedom of association.

Notwithstanding the above legal requirements, the Ninth Circuit in 2006 found no Section 1981 violation where a private school in Hawaii founded by the descendants of King Kamehameha I denied admission to an applicant because he was not of Hawaiian ancestry.[40] In rendering its decision permitting continued use of race in making admission decisions and distinguishing the present case from *Runyon*, the court reasoned that the preference was remedial in nature in that it was targeted to assist native Hawaiian students who were performing less well academically than all other classes of students. Additionally, the court held that when Congress reenacted Section 1981 in 1991, it likely intended to allow the operation of Kamehameha schools in Hawaii.

The next decade should continue to provide ample case law dealing with strategies designed to remedy past discrimination and to promote racial diversity in schools. Future cases are likely to be similar to those litigated in the past.[41]

Race Discrimination *Within* Schools

Although there are a number of laws that prohibit race discrimination in educational settings, there is no doubt that discrimination continues, though it is likely to be more subtle and therefore more difficult to prove than in prior years. There are several reasons from an

[37]Bob Jones Univ., 461 U.S. at 598.

[38]*Id.* Some have made the argument that under Bob Jones Univ., it is also contrary to U.S. public policy to permit private K–12 schools to discriminate based on sexual orientation. *See* Suzanne Eckes, Julie Mead & Jessica Ulm, *Dollars to Discriminate: The (Un)intended Consequences of School Vouchers*, 91 PEABODY J. EDUC. 4 (2016).

[39]427 U.S. 160 (1976).

[40]Doe v. Kamehameha Schs., 470 F.3d 827 (9th Cir. 2006).

[41]*See* text accompanying note 8, Chapter 13, for discussion of racial segregation and charter schools.

educational policy perspective about why this issue continues to be worthy of national attention.[42] Many scholars suggest that racially integrated schools help level the playing field and attempt to make up for years of discriminatory practices in schools.[43] Such discrimination has also been alleged in such areas as the assignment to ability-based courses or programs (e.g., gifted, advanced, developmental);[44] athletic eligibility;[45] racial profiling;[46] academic dismissal from special programs;[47] sexual harassment and abuse;[48] the creation of a hostile environment;[49] and the like. More recent controversies have focused on the over-representation of students of color in school disciplinary matters and special education.[50]

Claims of racial discrimination also have been at issue in cases involving school mascots. The Department of Education estimates that there are over 2,400 school districts that have mascots or nicknames that depict Native Americans.[51] While some contend that the mascots honor Native Americans, others find them to be insulting and derogatory. In one case, three Native American students and their mother argued that the school district's use of the Indian logo as a mascot was racially discriminatory. A Wisconsin appellate court found no discrimination because the logo did not depict a negative stereotype.[52] The court further reasoned that the logo did not portray any particular tribe. Given these controversies, it is not

[42]Francisco Negron, *Diversity Is Dead. Long Live Diversity: The Racial Isolation Prong of Kennedy's PICS Concurrence in Fisher and Beyond*, 24 U. Miami Bus. L. Rev. 99 (2015–16); Amy Stuart Wells, Lauren Fox & Diana Cordova-Cobo, Century Found., *How Racially Diverse Schools and Classrooms Benefit All Students* (Feb. 9, 2016), https://tcf.org/content/report/how-racially-diverse-schools-and-classrooms-can-benefit-all-students/; *see also* Gary Orfield & Erica Frankenberg, Civil Rights Project, *Brown at 60: Great Progress, a Long Retreat and an Uncertain Future* (May 15, 2014), https://www.civilrightsproject.ucla.edu/research/k-12-education/integration-and-diversity/brown-at-60-great-progress-a-long-retreat-and-an-uncertain-future.

[43]*Id.*

[44]*See, e.g.*, Hobson v. Hansen, 269 F. Supp. 401 (D.D.C. 1967), *aff'd sub nom.* Smuck v. Hobson, 408 F.2d 175 (D.C. Cir. 1969); T.V. v. Sacramento City Unified Sch. Dist., 2016 U.S. Dist. LEXIS 12451 (E.D. Cal. Feb. 2, 2016) (alleging high-ability program at elementary school divided students by race in violation of Title VI).

[45]*See, e.g.*, Allen-Sherrod v. Henry Cty. Sch. Dist., 248 F. App'x 145 (11th Cir. 2007).

[46]*See, e.g.*, Carthans v. Jenkins, 2005 U.S. Dist. LEXIS 23294 (N.D. Ill. Oct. 6, 2005).

[47]*See, e.g.*, Brewer v. Bd. of Trs., 479 F.3d 908 (7th Cir. 2007) (rejecting the discrimination claim and finding no comparable student of another race who had ever been retained with a grade point average lower than plaintiff's, unless there were extraordinarily compelling circumstances).

[48]Doe v. Smith, 470 F.3d 331 (7th Cir. 2006).

[49]Qualls v. Cunningham, 183 F. App'x 564 (7th Cir. 2006) (finding no support for the claim that school officials had created a racially hostile environment that caused plaintiff to receive poor grades and ultimately resulted in his academic dismissal).

[50]*See* Russ Skiba, Suzanne Eckes & Kevin Brown, *African American Disproportionality in School Discipline: The Divide Between Best Evidence and Legal Remedy*, 54 N.Y.L. Sch. L. Rev. 1071 (2010) (noting that students of color are disproportionately represented in school discipline matters, but few recent cases involve this issue); *see also* J. Weston Phippen, *The Racial Imbalances of Special Education* (July 6, 2015), https://www.theatlantic.com/education/archive/2015/07/the-racial-imbalances-of-special-education/397775/ (discussing the complexities involving special education referrals for minority students).

[51]U.S. Dep't of Educ., *School Environment Listening Sessions Final Report* (Oct. 2015), https://sites.ed.gov/whiaiane/files/2015/10/school-environment-listening-sessions-final-report.pdf.

[52]Munson v. State Superintendent of Pub. Instruction, 1998 WL 61018 (Wis. Ct. App. Feb. 17, 1998) (unpublished).

surprising that the Oregon State Board of Education decided to ban Native American-themed mascots in schools.[53] State legislatures and school districts have also weighed in on this issue. For example, a California law, known as the California Racial Mascots Act, called for public schools to phase out such team names by January 1, 2017.[54] In New York, a school district dropped its "Redskins" mascot after other teams boycotted playing in that district.[55]

Even though there are only a limited number of cases reported with regard to racial discrimination involving students today,[56] it is still prudent for school officials to establish a written policy prohibiting race and other forms of impermissible discrimination, monitor for disproportionality issues, inform educators and staff of their individual responsibilities, promptly and thoroughly investigate claims of impropriety, conduct fair and impartial hearings, and determine an appropriate response (e.g., suspension of a student, termination of an employee) for those who have engaged in discriminatory behavior.

CLASSIFICATIONS BASED ON IMMIGRATION STATUS OR NATIVE LANGUAGE

School districts may not discriminate against students based on their immigrant status, and they have the responsibility to remove English-language barriers that impede equal participation of English Learners.

In 2014, approximately 9.3 percent of the U.S. school-aged population consisted of English Learners (ELs).[57] As the EL population continues to grow, school districts of all sizes are addressing how to equitably and appropriately educate ELs. Allegations have been made that public schools are discriminating against classes of students because of their immigration status or native language. With regard to immigration status, courts have generally ruled that public schools are obligated to educate school-age children who are residents, meaning they live in the district with their parents or legal guardian. In an important 1982 decision, *Plyler v. Doe*, the Supreme Court held that school districts could not deny a free public education to resident children whose parents had entered the country illegally.[58]

---

[53]Kim Murphy, *Home of the Braves No More: Oregon Bans Native American Mascots*, L.A. Times (May 18, 2012), http://articles.latimes.com/2012/may/18/nation/la-na-nn-native-mascots-20120518.

[54]2015 Cal. Assemb. B. No. 30 (ch. 767) (2018).

[55]Associated Press, *Redskins Nickname Is Dropped by School District in Upstate New York*, N.Y. Times (Mar. 16, 2015), https://www.nytimes.com/2015/03/17/sports/upstate-school-district-drops-redskins-nickname.html.

[56]*See, e.g.*, Stout v. Jefferson Cty. Bd. of Educ., 250 F. Supp. 3d 1092 (N.D. Ala. Apr. 24, 2017) (granting in part and denying in part the board's motion to separate four schools from the district; acknowledging that the effort to separate from the existing district was related to race); Cowan v. Bolivar Cty. Bd. of Educ., 2015 U.S. Dist. LEXIS 186583 (D. Miss. May 15, 2015) (ordering racially identifiable public schools in Cleveland, Mississippi, to desegregate).

[57]Nat'l Ctr. for Educ. Statistics, *English Language Learners in Public Schools* (Mar. 2017), http://nces.ed.gov/programs/coe/indicator_cgf.asp.

[58]457 U.S. 202 (1982).

Recognizing the individual's significant interest in receiving an education, the Court ruled that classifications affecting access to education must be substantially related to an important governmental objective to satisfy the Equal Protection Clause. The Court found that Texas's asserted interest in deterring undocumented individuals from entering the country illegally was not important enough to deny students an opportunity to be educated.

Despite this decision, states continue to consider and enact provisions that place obligations on schools to identify and to notify state authorities regarding undocumented students.[59] Although these laws do not specifically bar the education of such students at public expense, which Texas was not allowed to do in *Plyler*, the required identification of undocumented students is viewed as a deterrent to these children enrolling in public schools. In 2012, the Eleventh Circuit blocked implementation of such a provision in an Alabama law as violating the equal protection rights of the affected children.[60] A few months earlier, the Supreme Court struck down several parts of an Arizona immigration law as intruding on the federal government's responsibilities to regulate immigration, but upheld the part allowing police officers to verify the immigration status of those being arrested.[61] The Arizona law has no student identification provision, and whether states can require public schools to identify undocumented students has not yet been addressed by the Supreme Court. However, it is clear that such children cannot be denied a public education.[62]

With regard to native language, among the numerous identifiable "classes" of students in American schools are "linguistic minorities," some of whom have been denied an adequate education due to the failure of the school district to address their language differences through appropriate instruction. Educators may use bilingual education or other appropriate methods that assist ELs in classrooms in which English is the primary language of instruction; school districts have the responsibility to remove English language barriers that impede equal participation of non-English-speaking students.

The rights of linguistic minorities are protected by the Fourteenth Amendment, Title VI of the Civil Rights Act of 1964, and the Equal Educational Opportunities Act of 1974 (EEOA). Title VI stipulates that "[n]o person in the United States shall, on the ground of race, color, or national origin, be excluded from participation in, be denied the benefits of, or be subjected to discrimination under any program or activity receiving [f]ederal financial assistance from the Department of Education."[63] Additionally, this statute requires

---

[59]A few school districts have adopted sanctuary policies where they will not share confidential student information related to immigrant status with immigration agents without parent permission. *See* Howard Blume, *LAUSD Is Making It Harder for Immigration Officials to Enter Schools*, LA TIMES (May 10, 2017), http://www.latimes.com/local/lanow/la-me-edu-lausd-immigrant-resolution-20170509-story.html.

[60]*See* United States v. Alabama, 691 F.3d 1269 (11th Cir. 2012).

[61]Arizona v. United States, 567 U.S. 387 (2012).

[62]*See* Methelus v. Sch. Bd., 243 F. Supp. 3d 1266 (M.D. Fla. 2017) (finding that plaintiffs stated a plausible cause of action under the EEOA when the school district engaged in policies that denied EL students access to a public education); New York v. Utica City Sch. Dist., 177 F. Supp. 3d 739 (N.D.N.Y. 2016) (denying the school district's motion to dismiss; attorney general argued that the school district policy was deliberately barring immigrant students access to the same opportunities as others).

[63]42 U.S.C. § 2000d (2018). Regulations are found at 34 C.F.R. § 100 (2018).

compliance throughout a school district if *any* activity is supported by federal funds (e.g., special education). Discrimination against linguistic minorities is considered a form of national origin discrimination and is therefore prohibited by Title VI.

Moreover, the EEOA requires public school systems to develop appropriate programs for EL students.[64] The Act mandates in part that "[n]o state shall deny equal educational opportunity to an individual on account of his or her race, color, sex, or national origin, by . . . the failure by an educational agency to take appropriate action to overcome language barriers that impede equal participation by its students in its instructional program."[65]

In the first U.S. Supreme Court decision involving the rights of EL students, *Lau v. Nichols*, Chinese children asserted that the San Francisco public schools failed to provide for the needs of non-English-speaking students. The Supreme Court agreed with the students and held that the lack of sufficient remedial English instruction violated Title VI. The Court reasoned that equality of treatment was not realized merely by providing students with the same facilities, textbooks, teachers, and curriculum, and that requiring children to acquire English skills on their own before they could hope to make any progress in school made "a mockery of public education."[66] The Court emphasized that "basic English skills are at the very core of what these public schools teach," and, therefore, "students who do not understand English are effectively foreclosed from any meaningful education."[67]

Lower courts have also addressed important issues involving the rights of EL students. A federal district court, in assessing compliance of the Denver public schools, concluded that **the law does not require a full bilingual education program for every EL student but does place a duty on the district to take action to eliminate barriers that prevent EL children from participating in the educational program**. A good faith effort is inadequate. What is required, according to the court, is an effort that "will be reasonably effective in producing intended results."[68] In the absence of such an effort in the Denver public schools, an EEOA violation was found. Although a transitional bilingual program was selected by district personnel, it was not being implemented effectively, primarily due to poor teacher training, selection, and assignment.

In *Horne v. Flores*, the Supreme Court provided further guidance in this area when it held that states and local educational authorities have wide latitude in determining which programs and techniques they will implement to meet their obligations under the EEOA.[69]

---

[64]20 U.S.C. § 1701 (2018).

[65]20 U.S.C. § 1703(f) (2018).

[66]Lau v. Nichols, 414 U.S. 563, 566 (1974).

[67]*Id.*

[68]Keyes v. Sch. Dist., 576 F. Supp. 1503, 1520 (D. Colo. 1983); *see also* Gomez v. Ill. State Bd. of Educ., 811 F.2d 1030, 1043 (7th Cir. 1987) (finding selection of transitional bilingual education was appropriate, but it had not been effectively implemented). *But see* Teresa P. v. Berkeley Unified Sch. Dist., 724 F. Supp. 698 (N.D. Cal. 1989) (holding school district's bilingual and ESL program was based on sound theory and appropriately implemented).

[69]557 U.S. 433 (2009).

The state of Arizona was ultimately given relief from a decree related to an EL program. The Court looked beyond funding for EL instruction and determined that obligations under the original decree had been satisfied in other ways.

California has generated a significant amount of case law involving the instruction of non- and limited English-speaking students. Many suits had attacked Proposition 227, which required that all children in public schools be taught English through "sheltered English immersion" (SEI).[70] This approach required the use of specially designed materials and procedures where "nearly all" classroom instruction was in English. However, in 2017, a new state law went into effect that repealed Proposition 227; educators now have more leeway to develop their own bilingual and multilingual programs.[71]

Another type of national origin/language discrimination was alleged in Kansas where the principal and several teachers prohibited students from speaking Spanish while on school grounds.[72] A student argued that the school district created a hostile environment based on national origin and race under Title VI. Overruling an earlier decision that granted the school district's motion for summary judgment, the court found that the student had established a prima facie case against the school district. In light of the significant growth of Hispanic and other populations immigrating to the United States, expect more litigation in this area.

Under the Every Student Succeeds Act (ESSA), English Learners must be included in a state's assessment system.[73] In order to assist school districts, the Department of Education and the Department of Justice issued a joint guidance in 2015 that outlines school officials' legal obligations with regard to EL students.[74] The guidance examines several compliance issues that have arisen during Office for Civil Rights (OCR) and Department of Justice investigations under the EEOA and Title VI. Some of these common compliance issues include, but are not limited to, failing to assess EL students who are in need of language assistance in a timely, valid, and reliable manner; providing a language assistance program that is educationally sound; and failing to staff and support language assistance programs for EL students. Other common compliance issues sometimes involve ensuring that EL students are not segregated and that EL students with disabilities receive appropriate services. School districts may also be out of compliance for failing to ensure meaningful communication with EL parents.

---

[70]Other states have passed similar ballot initiatives. For example, Arizona passed Proposition 203 in 2000 (ARIZ. REV. STAT. ANN. § 15-751(5) (2018)), and Massachusetts passed Question 2 in 2002 (MASS. GEN. LAWS ch. 386, § 1 (2018)) (amending ch. 71A). Although the laws have not been repealed, there is momentum in both states to change them.

[71]Cal. Senate B. No. 1174 (ch. 753) (2018).

[72]Rubio v. Turner Unified Sch. Dist., 523 F. Supp. 2d 1242 (D. Kan. 2007). *But see* Mumid v. Abraham Lincoln High Sch., 618 F.3d 789 (8th Cir. 2010) (affirming summary judgment for the school district because school policy did not facially discriminate against EL students based on their national origin).

[73]ESSA, § 1111(b)(2)(B)(vii)(III)(2018).

[74]U.S. Dep't of Justice & U.S. Dep't of Educ., *Dear Colleague Letter: EL Students* (Jan. 7, 2015), http://www2 .ed.gov/about/offices/list/ocr/letters/colleague-el-201501.pdf.

CLASSIFICATIONS BASED ON SEX[75]

Students are protected against discrimination based on sex, including sexual harassment and assault by educators and peers.[76]

Classifications and discriminatory treatment based on sex in public education are as old as public education itself, as the first public schools and colleges primarily served only males. When women eventually were allowed to enroll, programs for them were typically segregated and inferior. Over the years, sex equality in public schools has improved, but at times, classifications based on sex have limited both academic as well as extracurricular activities for females. Aggrieved parties often turn to federal courts to vindicate their rights. In most cases, plaintiffs allege a violation of either the Fourteenth Amendment or Title IX of the Education Amendments of 1972.[77] Under Title IX, educational recipients of federal financial assistance are prohibited from discriminating, excluding, or denying benefits because of sex.[78]

In addition, Title IX has been interpreted to prohibit retaliation against both students and staff who themselves are not the target of intentional discrimination but are adversely treated due to their advocacy roles. The Supreme Court addressed this issue in 2005 in *Jackson v. Birmingham Board of Education*, where a teacher/coach was removed from his coaching position, allegedly due to his complaints about the treatment of the girls' basketball team (i.e., not receiving equal funding, equal access to equipment and facilities, and so forth).[79] The Court reasoned that prohibition of discriminatory treatment against advocates was implied by Title IX and remanded the case for a determination of whether the coach's advocacy was in fact the motivating factor in his removal.

Interscholastic Sports

Sex discrimination litigation involving interscholastic sports has focused on two primary themes: the integration of single-sex teams and the unequal treatment of males and females. Although courts will issue injunctions to correct discriminatory conduct where it is found, they will not award monetary damages unless the school receives actual notice of the violation and then is shown to be deliberately indifferent to the claim.[80]

[75]"Sex" generally refers to having male or female reproductive systems, whereas "gender" generally refers to social identity related to one's sex.

[76]*See* text accompanying note 78, Chapter 9.

[77]20 U.S.C. § 1681 (2018).

[78]If aid is received by any program or activity within the school system, compliance must be demonstrated districtwide, Title IX of the Civil Rights Act of 1972, 20 U.S.C. § 1681 (2018). Also, although Title IX does not include a specific statute of limitations, courts have elected to borrow the relevant limitations period for personal injury. *See, e.g.*, Stanley v. Trs. of Cal. State Univ., 433 F.3d 1129 (9th Cir. 2006) (identifying the appropriate limitations period to be one year).

[79]544 U.S. 167 (2005).

[80]Grandson v. Univ., 272 F.3d 568 (8th Cir. 2001).

Single-Sex Teams.   One of the more controversial issues involving high school athletics is the participation of males and females together in contact sports (e.g., wrestling, rugby, ice hockey, football, basketball, and other sports that involve physical contact). Title IX explicitly permits separation of students by sex within contact sports. However, individual school districts can determine whether to allow coeducational participation in contact sports in their efforts to provide equal athletic opportunities for males and females.[81] Where integration is either permitted or required in a contact sport, each athlete must receive a fair, nondiscriminatory opportunity to participate.

A New York federal district court reviewed a student's claim that she was not allowed to try out for the junior varsity football squad in violation of the Fourteenth Amendment.[82] The school district was unable to show that its policy of prohibiting mixed competition served an important governmental objective, as is required under intermediate scrutiny. In rejecting the district's assertion that its policy was necessary to ensure the health and safety of female students, the court noted that no female student was given the opportunity to show that she was as fit, or more fit, than the weakest male member of the team. A Wisconsin federal district court similarly ruled that female students have the constitutional right to compete for positions on traditionally male contact teams, declaring that once a state provides interscholastic competition, such opportunities must be provided to all students on equal terms.[83]

In addition to the controversies regarding coeducational participation in contact sports, there have been numerous challenges to policies denying integration of males and females in noncontact sports. **Title IX regulations explicitly require recipient districts to allow coeducational participation in those sports that are available only to one sex, presuming that athletic opportunities for that sex have been historically limited.** Thus, females tend to succeed in their claims, whereas males tend to fail.[84]

Fewer Sports Opportunities for Females.   Although athletic opportunities for females have significantly increased since passage of Title IX in 1972, equal opportunity has not been achieved within all school districts. The OCR's Policy Interpretation requires that for schools to be in compliance, they should (1) provide interscholastic sports opportunities for both sexes in terms of numbers of participants that are substantially proportionate to the respective enrollments of male and female students, (2) show a history of expanding sports programs for the underrepresented sex, or (3) provide enough opportunities to match the sports interests and abilities of the underrepresented sex.[85] Given such financial constraints, equality of athletic opportunities for males and females often has been achieved either by reducing the number of sports traditionally available for males[86] or by lowering the number of participants on boys' teams (e.g., football) to provide generally equal opportunities for

---

[81]Elborough v. Evansville Cmty. Sch. Dist., 636 F. Supp. 2d 812 (W.D. Wis. 2009).

[82]Lantz v. Ambach, 620 F. Supp. 663 (S.D.N.Y. 1985); *see also* Adams v. Baker, 919 F. Supp. 1496 (D. Kan. 1996) (upholding female student's right under the Fourteenth Amendment to participate in wrestling).

[83]Leffel v. Wis. Interscholastic Athletic Ass'n, 444 F. Supp. 1117 (E.D. Wis. 1978).

[84]*See, e.g.,* Williams v. Sch. Dist., 998 F.2d 168 (3d Cir. 1993); Croteau v. Fair, 686 F. Supp. 552 (E.D. Va. 1988).

[85]U.S. Dep't of Educ., Office for Civil Rights' 1979 *Policy Interpretation*, 44 Fed. Reg. 71,413 (2018).

[86]*See, e.g.,* Chalenor v. Univ. of N.D., 291 F.3d 1042 (8th Cir. 2002); Boulahanis v. Bd. of Regents, 198 F.3d 633 (7th Cir. 1999); Miami Univ. Wrestling Club v. Miami Univ., 195 F. Supp. 2d 1010 (S.D. Ohio 2001).

males and females.[87] Also, efforts have been made to disguise the existing inequity (e.g., double counting participants in women's indoor and outdoor track, but not double counting men in fall/spring events such as track, golf, and tennis) to avoid taking corrective action.

At times, female athletes have expressed an insufficient interest in a given sport to have it approved by the state athletic association. In a Kentucky case, high school athletes claimed a Title IX violation when the state athletic association refused to approve females' interscholastic fast-pitch softball. The association's decision was based on its policy of not sanctioning a sport unless at least 25 percent of its member institutions demonstrated an interest in participation. Since only 17 percent had indicated an interest, approval was denied. In the original hearing on this controversy, the Sixth Circuit had held that the 25 percent requirement did not violate the Equal Protection Clause because the facially neutral policy was not proven to entail intentional discrimination.[88] The case then was remanded and later appealed. The court again found no Title IX violation and further concluded that grouping sports by sex did not violate federal law.

The U.S. Department of Education issued a Dear Colleague Letter in 2008 to provide further guidance to schools regarding how athletic opportunities are counted for Title IX compliance.[89] The letter outlines factors that may be considered in determining whether an institution has complied with Title IX. It stresses that the OCR will evaluate each institution on a case-by-case basis to allow flexibility in offering sports that align with the specific interests of the student body. Despite attempts to further explain the law, litigation in both PK–12 and higher education will likely continue as schools attempt to achieve greater sex equity.[90] In addition to legal issues related to interest in sports, there has also been a growing number of challenges involving inequities between male and female athletic facilities and sport schedules.[91]

Academic Programs

Allegations of sex bias in public schools have not been confined to athletic programs. Differential treatment of males and females in academic courses and schools also has generated litigation.[92] **Because the "separate but equal" principle has been applied in cases**

[87]Neal v. Bd. of Trs., 198 F.3d 763 (9th Cir. 1999).

[88]Horner v. Ky. High Sch. Athletic Ass'n, 43 F.3d 265 (6th Cir. 1994).

[89]U.S. Dep't of Educ., *Dear Colleague Letter: Athletic Activities Counted for Title IX Compliance* (Sept. 17, 2008), http://www2.ed.gov/about/offices/list/ocr/letters/colleague-20080917.pdf.

[90]*See, e.g.*, Parker v. Franklin Cty. Cmty. Sch. Corp., 667 F.3d 910 (7th Cir. 2012) (remanding the case to determine if scheduling girls' basketball games on weeknights instead of weekend nights like the boys' games amounted to discrimination under Title IX); Equity in Athletics, Inc. v. Dep't of Educ., 639 F.3d 91 (4th Cir. 2011) (finding nonprofit organization failed to show that the three-part test violated the Equal Protection Clause); Pederson v. La. State Univ., 213 F.3d 858 (5th Cir. 2000) (concluding that university had violated Title IX by failing to accommodate the interests and abilities of female athletes); Cohen v. Brown Univ., 101 F.3d 155 (1st Cir. 1996) (rejecting the university's claim that female students were less interested in sports).

[91]*See* Parker, 667 F.3d at 910 (holding that the Title IX claim survived summary judgment because a jury could determine that the present disparity between male and female basketball teams was substantial enough to deny equal athletic opportunity); Ollier v. Sweetwater Union High Sch. Dist., 2014 U.S. Dist. LEXIS 35259 (S.D. Cal. Mar. 17, 2014) (affirming declaratory and injunctive relief that ordered school officials to comply with Title IX in all aspects of their athletic programs and activities at the high school).

[92]Gossett v. Oklahoma, 245 F.3d 1172 (10th Cir. 2001).

alleging a Fourteenth Amendment violation, public school officials are required to show an exceedingly persuasive justification for classifications based on sex that are used to segregate the sexes or exclude either males or females from academic programs.

The Third Circuit held that the operation of two historically sex-segregated public high schools (one for males, the other for females) in which enrollment is voluntary and educational offerings are essentially equal, is permissible under the Equal Protection Clause, Title IX, and the EEOA.[93] Noting that Philadelphia's sex-segregated college preparatory schools offered functionally equivalent programs, the court concluded that the separation of the sexes was justified because youth might study more effectively in sex-segregated high schools. The court emphasized that the female plaintiff was not compelled to attend the sex-segregated academic school; she had the option of enrolling in a coeducational school within her attendance zone. Furthermore, the court stated that her petition to attend the male academic high school was based on personal preference rather than on an objective evaluation of the offerings available in the two schools. Subsequently, an equally divided U.S. Supreme Court affirmed this decision without delivering an opinion. Interestingly, in a later state case, which involved the same Philadelphia school, three female students were denied admission at the all-male Philadelphia high school.[94] In this case, a common pleas court in Pennsylvania did not find the public school for the girls and the public school for the boys to be substantially similar. Some of the alleged inequities between the two schools included a "Bachelor of Arts" degree instead of a typical high school diploma, smaller class sizes, a larger building, and more books and computers at the boys' school. As a result of some of the inequities, the court held that the female students must be admitted to the all-male school.

Detroit school officials did not prevail in their attempt to segregate inner-city, Black male students to address more effectively these students' unique educational needs. Three Black male academies (preschool to fifth grade, sixth to eighth grade, and high school) were proposed. The three-year experimental academies were designed to offer an Afrocentric curriculum, emphasize male responsibility, provide mentors, offer Saturday classes and extended classroom hours, and provide individual counseling. No comparable program existed for females, although school authorities indicated that one would be forthcoming. The district court issued a preliminary injunction prohibiting the board from opening the academies, given the likelihood that the practice violated the Equal Protection Clause.

In a higher education case with PK–12 implications, the Supreme Court in 1982 struck down a nursing school's admission policy that restricted admission in degree programs to females without providing comparable opportunities for males.[95] The Court found no evidence that women had ever been denied opportunities in the field of nursing that would justify remedial action by the state. In applying intermediate scrutiny, the Court concluded that the university failed to meet its burden of showing that the facially

---

[93]Vorchheimer v. Sch. Dist., 532 F.2d 880 (3d Cir. 1976), *aff'd mem. by an equally divided court*, 430 U.S. 703 (1977).

[94]Newberg v. Bd. of Pub. Educ., 26 Pa. D. & C.3d 682 (C.P. Phila. Cty. 1983).

[95]Miss. Univ. for Women v. Hogan, 458 U.S. 718 (1982).

discriminatory sex classification served an important governmental objective or that its discriminatory means were substantially related to the achievement of those objectives.

Similarly, the U.S. Supreme Court addressed male-only admissions policies in *United States v. Virginia*. The Court held that the state had violated the Fourteenth Amendment in failing to provide equal opportunities for women in the area of military training when they were denied admission to the Virginia Military Institute (VMI).[96] A new program at a private, women-only institution would never be able to approach the success, quality, and prestige associated with that provided at VMI.

In 2006, the Department of Education issued regulations permitting school districts to offer voluntary public single-sex classrooms and schools.[97] Under Title IX regulations, coeducational schools must offer equal educational opportunities to both sexes, and enrollment in a single-sex class should be completely voluntary. Specifically, nonvocational public single-sex schools are permitted, but a substantially similar coeducational school or single-sex school for students of the other sex must be available. Also, one of two objectives must be satisfied before implementing a single-sex educational program. The program must (1) improve the educational achievement of a recipient's students through an established policy to provide diverse educational opportunities or (2) meet the particular identified educational needs of a recipient's students.[98] As a result of these amendments, many school districts have begun to experiment with single-sex educational programs. For example, by 2016, there were over eighty single-sex public schools in the United States.[99]

Recent litigation involves the amended Title IX regulations as well as the Equal Protection Clause in combination with other claims arising out of state law. In these legal challenges, the female students generally argue that school officials have failed to demonstrate an "exceedingly persuasive" justification for creating single-sex educational programs. The outcomes of these cases have been mixed. [100]

Sexual Harassment of Students

Title IX and the Equal Protection Clause of the Fourteenth Amendment also have been applied in sex-based claims of sexual harassment and abuse of students. Under the Equal Protection Clause, students have the right to be free from harassment on an equal basis with

[96]518 U.S. 515 (1996).

[97]34 C.F.R. § 106.34 (2018).

[98]34 C.F.R. §106.34(b)(1)(i)(A) & (B) (2018).

[99]Juliet Williams, *What's Wrong with Single-Sex Schools? A Lot*, L.A. Times (Jan. 25, 2016), http://www.latimes.com/opinion/op-ed/la-oe-0125-williams-single-sex-schools-20160125-story.html.

[100]*See, e.g.*, Doe v. Vermilion Parish Sch. Bd., 421 F. App'x 366 (5th Cir. 2011) (denying the school district's motion to dismiss because students provided sufficient evidence that a single-sex program may be harmful); Doe v. Wood Cty. Bd. of Educ., 888 F. Supp. 2d 771 (S.D. W. Va. 2012) (granting the students' request for preliminary injunction prohibiting school district from operating single-sex classes). *But see* A.N.A. v. Breckinridge Cty. Bd. of Educ., 833 F. Supp. 2d 673 (W.D. Ky. 2011) (determining that female students did not suffer an injury when the school district offered optional single-sex classes); S.M. v. Del. Dep't of Educ., 2015 U.S. Dist. LEXIS 49911 (D. Del. Apr. 16, 2015) (finding plaintiffs failed to state a claim under Title IX because implementing regulations do not require that same-gender charter schools exist in equal numbers for males and females).

all other students,[101] while Title IX prohibits discrimination on the basis of sex. Historically, charges of sexual harassment against school districts generally were dismissed. But in 1992, the Supreme Court rendered its decision in *Franklin v. Gwinnett County Public Schools*, a case involving a female student's allegations that a coach initiated sexual conversations, engaged in inappropriate touching, and had coercive intercourse with her on school grounds on several occasions. The Court held that Title IX prohibited the sexual harassment of students and that damages could be awarded where appropriate.[102] Since *Gwinnett*, numerous other cases have been filed—with mixed results—by current and former students alleging hostile environment,[103] student-to-student harassment,[104] sexual involvement and abuse of students by school staff,[105] sex stereotyping,[106] and same-sex harassment.[107] With *Gwinnett* as a starting point, two similar but slightly different standards have evolved: one for employee-to-student harassment and the other for student-to-student harassment.

Employee-to-Student Harassment.   In *Gebser v. Lago Vista Independent School District*, the Supreme Court provided further guidance in 1998 regarding the liability of school districts when students are harassed by school employees.[108] In this case, a high school student and a teacher were involved in a relationship that had not been reported to the administration until the couple was discovered having sex and the teacher was arrested. The district then terminated the teacher's employment, and the parents sued under Title IX. On appeal, the Supreme Court held that to be liable, the district had to have *actual notice* of the harassment. The Court reasoned that allowing recovery of damages based on either respondeat superior or constructive notice (i.e., notice that is inferred or implied) would be inconsistent with the objective of the Act, as liability would attach even though the district had no actual knowledge of the conduct or an opportunity to take action to end the harassment.[109] **Accordingly, for there to be an award of damages, an official who has the authority to address the alleged discrimination must have *actual knowledge* of the inappropriate conduct and then fail to ameliorate the problem. Moreover, the failure to respond must amount to *deliberate indifference* to the discrimination.** In the instant case, the plaintiff did not argue that actual notice had been provided, and the district's

---

[101]*See, e.g.*, Nabozny v. Podlesny, 92 F.3d 446 (7th Cir. 1996) (holding jury could conclude that the school district violated the student's rights to equal protection when it failed to address harassment related to his sexual orientation).

[102]503 U.S. 60 (1992).

[103]*See, e.g.*, Jennings v. Univ. of N.C., 444 F.3d 255 (4th Cir. 2006).

[104]*See, e.g.*, Price v. Scranton, 2012 U.S. Dist. LEXIS 1651 (M.D. Pa. Jan. 6, 2012).

[105]*See, e.g.*, King v. Curtis, 2016 U.S. Dist. LEXIS 184737 (W.D. Mich. Nov. 1, 2016).

[106]*See, e.g.*, Wolfe v. Fayetteville Ark. Sch. Dist., 648 F.3d 860 (8th Cir. 2011).

[107]*See, e.g.*, Shrum v. Kluck, 249 F.3d 773 (8th Cir. 2001); Martin v. Swartz Cmty. Schs., 419 F. Supp. 2d 967 (E.D. Mich. 2006).

[108]524 U.S. 274 (1998).

[109]*See* Henderson v. Walled Lake Consol. Schs., 469 F.3d 479 (6th Cir. 2006) (observing that even if the administrators had notice that a female soccer player was involved in a relationship with her coach, such awareness did not establish notice that the plaintiff, another member of the team, had been exposed to a hostile environment).

failure to promulgate a related policy and grievance procedure failed to qualify as deliberate indifference.

Establishing School District Liability for Employee-to-Student Harassment under Title IX
Did school officials know about the harassment?
Did school officials reflect deliberate indifference toward the victim?

In subsequent litigation, courts have assessed who is an "appropriate official" with authority to act, what constitutes "actual knowledge," and what substantiates "deliberate indifference." *Gebser* did not identify which individuals in the school district must have knowledge.[110] Without deciding whether a principal possesses this authority, several courts have assumed, for the purpose of analyzing claims, that principals have the power to remedy abuse.[111] To illustrate, the Eleventh Circuit concluded that a principal's knowledge of the harassment was sufficient and that he was an appropriate person because of his authority to take corrective measures.[112]

Questions also have arisen concerning notice of sexual harassment or abuse. Evidence indicating a potential or theoretical risk has not been equated with actual knowledge. The Third Circuit warned that "a 'possibility' cannot be equated with a 'known act.'"[113] The Eighth Circuit noted that the principal was unaware of the high school basketball coach having a sexual relationship with a student. Although the coach had sent inappropriate text messages to several female players, the court did not find the messages to have provided the principal with actual notice of the specific relationship. Further, the court observed that the victim's mother's question to the principal about whether something was going on between her daughter and the coach did not constitute actual notice.[114] The Eleventh Circuit, however, reasoned that another principal's knowledge of a teacher's alleged touching and propositions to students provided sufficient notice.[115] A few courts have addressed whether other school officials, in addition to school principals, have the power to respond to abuse. For example, the Eighth Circuit stated that "we do not hold that guidance counselors and

---

[110]*See* Warren v. Reading Sch. Dist., 278 F.3d 163 (3d Cir. 2002) (remanding for a determination of who may qualify as an "appropriate person" to receive actual notice under the Gebser standard; a criminally prosecuted male teacher was fired because of his sexual involvement with male students).

[111]*See, e.g.,* Davis v. Dekalb Cty. Sch. Dist., 233 F.3d 1367 (11th Cir. 2000); Doe v. Dallas Indep. Sch. Dist., 220 F.3d 380 (5th Cir. 2000); Flores v. Saulpaugh, 115 F. Supp. 2d 319 (N.D.N.Y. 2000).

[112]Doe v. Sch. Bd., 604 F.3d 1248 (11th Cir. 2010).

[113]Bostic v. Smyrna Sch. Dist., 418 F.3d 355, 361 (3d Cir. 2005); *see also* N.R. Doe v. St. Francis Sch. Dist., 694 F.3d 869 (7th Cir. 2012) (finding that staff suspicions of inappropriate relationship between a teacher and a student did not qualify as actual knowledge).

[114]Doe v. Flaherty, 623 F.3d 577 (8th Cir. 2010); *see also* Blue v. Dist. of Columbia, 850 F. Supp. 2d 16 (D.D.C. 2012) (finding that appropriate person lacked knowledge of student's sexual relationship with teacher).

[115]Doe v. Sch. Bd. of Broward Cty., 604 F.3d 1248 (11th Cir. 2010); *see also* Lindemulder v. Davis Cty. Cmty. Sch. Dist., 884 N.W.2d 222 (Iowa Ct. App. 2016) (ruling school district did not have actual notice of student's sexual relations with a teacher).

school teachers are never 'appropriate persons' for the purposes of finding a school district liable for discrimination under Title IX," but in this particular case, they had not been vested with sufficient authority to address the harassment.[116]

To counter claims of deliberate indifference, school officials must show that they took action on complaints. For example, a principal was not found to be deliberately indifferent because he contacted his superior and took corrective measures by asking the counselor to interview the student, the accused teacher, and other possible witnesses.[117] Although these actions may have appeared insufficient and did not prevent the teacher from sexually abusing students, the court found the relevant fact to be that the principal did not act with deliberate indifference. It should be noted, however, that school districts might generate legal challenges if they "shuffle" abusive teachers to other districts.[118]

Also of relevance in hostile environment cases where school personnel are allegedly involved is the fact that, at least for younger children, the behavior does not have to be "unwelcome," as it does in Title VII of the Civil Rights Act of 1964 employment cases.[119] The Seventh Circuit reviewed a case where a twenty-one-year-old male kitchen worker had a consensual sexual relationship with a thirteen-year-old middle school female student.[120] The court noted that under Indiana criminal law, a person under the age of sixteen cannot consent to sexual intercourse and that children may not even understand that they are being harassed. To rule that only behavior that is not unwelcome is actionable would permit violators to take advantage of impressionable youth who voluntarily participate in requested conduct. Moreover, if welcomeness were an issue properly before the court, the child bringing the suits would be subject to intense scrutiny regarding their degree of fault.

Student-to-Student Harassment.   Educators must be in control of the school environment, including student conduct, and eliminate known dangers and harassment. Not all harassment will be known, however, and not all behavior that is offensive will be so severe as to violate Title IX.[121] Also, for student-to-student harassment to be actionable, the behavior must be unwelcome. Further clarification regarding liability associated with student-to-student harassment was provided in 1999 when the Supreme Court in *Davis v. Monroe County Board of Education*[122] proposed the following test: **(1) whether the school board acted with deliberate indifference to known acts of harassment and (2) whether**

---

[116]Plamp v. Mitchell Sch. Dist., 565 F.3d 450, 459 (8th Cir. 2009).

[117]Davis v. Dekalb Cty. Sch. Dist., 233 F.3d 1367 (11th Cir. 2000); *see also* R.F. v. S. Country Cent. Sch. Dist., 2016 U.S. Dist. LEXIS 130671 (E.D.N.Y. Sept. 23, 2016) (ruling that school district adequately responded when it had knowledge of sexual relationship between a teacher and a student).

[118]*See, e.g.,* Doe-2 v. McLean Cty. Unit Dist., 593 F.3d 507, 517 (7th Cir. 2010); Shrum v. Kluck, 249 F.3d 773 (8th Cir. 2001).

[119]J.F.K. v. Troup Cty. Sch. Dist., 678 F.3d 1254 (11th Cir. 2012).

[120]Mary M. v. N. Lawrence Cmty. Sch. Corp., 131 F.3d 1220 (7th Cir. 1997).

[121]Because Title IX prohibits discrimination based on sex, these harassment cases involve harassment claims related to sex.

[122]526 U.S. 629 (1999).

the harassment was so severe, pervasive, and objectively offensive that it effectively barred the victim's access to an educational opportunity or benefit.[123]

The *Davis* Court remanded the case to determine whether these standards were met. The plaintiff's fifth-grade daughter had allegedly been subjected to unwelcome sexual touching and rubbing as well as sexual talk. On one occasion, the violating student put a doorstop in his pants and acted in a sexually suggestive manner toward the plaintiff. Ultimately, the youth was charged with and pled guilty to sexual battery for his misconduct. The victim and her mother notified several teachers, the coach, and the principal of these incidences. No disciplinary action was ever taken other than to threaten the violating student with possible sanctions.

Since the *Davis* decision, courts have addressed several cases involving peer harassment under Title IX. In these cases, plaintiffs sometimes have difficulty proving that school officials had actual knowledge of the harassment or that they acted with deliberate indifference. **When making this determination, courts will often consider if someone with authority to act has knowledge of the harassment.**[124] For example, when a cheerleader claimed that she had been harassed by another cheerleader, the school official was not found to have acted with deliberate indifference because he took the action that was required under the school's harassment policy.[125] Specifically, the principal created a formal report outlining the investigation and actions taken to prevent further harassment. He removed the alleged perpetrator from the plaintiff's sixth period class and took other efforts to keep the two students apart. In several cases, school officials prevailed if they took steps that were not clearly unreasonable to address the harassment.[126]

As noted, plaintiffs also need to demonstrate that they were denied educational benefits as a result of the harassment. In a Sixth Circuit case, although a mother outlined that the harassment her daughter experienced at school was pervasive, she failed to explain how the incidents deprived her daughter of access to educational opportunities and benefits.[127] Some plaintiffs have struggled to demonstrate that the harassment is sufficiently severe or

---

[123]*See* Bruneau v. S. Kortright Cent. Sch. Dist., 163 F.3d 749 (2d Cir. 1998) (affirming lower court's determination that offensive behavior of male students toward a female student did not qualify as harassment or adversely affect her education).

[124]*See, e.g.,* Doe v. Columbia-Brazoria Indep. Sch. Dist., 855 F.3d 681 (5th Cir. 2017) (holding school officials had no actual knowledge of the assault that took place in the school restroom; no teacher was present in the restroom, and the student did not inform school officials of the assault for several days); Doe v. Galster, 768 F.3d 611 (7th Cir. 2014) (finding that school officials were not fully aware of harassment that took place in the school until the last day of school).

[125]Sanches v. Carrolton-Farmers Branch Indep. Sch. Dist., 647 F.3d 156 (5th Cir. 2011); *see also* Davis v. Carmel Clay Schs., 570 F. App'x 602 (7th Cir. 2014) (ruling that school officials did not have actual knowledge of harassment against a student athlete); Long v. Murray Cty. Sch. Dist., 522 F. App'x 576 (11th Cir. 2013) (concluding that administrators were not deliberately indifferent toward harassment because they disciplined the harassers, and they took steps to prevent harm).

[126]*See, e.g.,* K.S. v. Nw. Indep. Sch. Dist., 689 F. App'x 780 (5th Cir. 2017) (holding that the district's responses to the harassment were not so ineffective as to be clearly unreasonable; school officials had disciplined students and responded to every instance of harassment specifically identified in the record); Doe v. Bd. of Educ., 605 F. App'x 159 (4th Cir. 2015) (finding that the steps the principal took to address the harassment were not clearly unreasonable).

[127]Pahssen v. Merrill Cmty. Sch. Dist., 668 F.3d 356 (6th Cir. 2012).

pervasive.[128] Interestingly, courts have found that "pervasiveness" may be established under Title IX by a one-time sexual assault.[129] Thus, if the conduct is quite egregious, it does not have to be repeated to abridge Title IX.

Establishing School District Liability for Student-to-Student Sexual Harassment under Title IX
Did school officials know about the harassment?
Did school officials reflect deliberate indifference toward the victim?
Was the harassment so severe, pervasive, and objectively offensive that it interfered with the victim receiving educational benefits?

Neither Eleventh Amendment immunity[130] nor the claim that the violator was engaged in First Amendment protected free speech may be used as defenses to Title IX actions.[131] As a result, damage awards[132] are available from educational institutions receiving federal funds, although not from those persons who were directly responsible for the harassment.[133] Also, plaintiffs can allege that they are entitled to damages under Section 1983 for a violation of their federal constitutional or statutory rights.[134] **Of course, violators can be sued directly under state tort law for sexual battery or intentional infliction of emotional distress,[135] and criminal charges may be filed against perpetrators where force is used or minors are involved.** In 2011, the Department of Education issued further guidance related to the harassment of students.[136] The Department explained that, in addition to prohibiting harassment based on sex, Title IX also prohibits gender-based

---

[128]Wolfe v. Fayetteville, 648 F.3d 860 (8th Cir. 2011) (finding that name-calling does not amount to sex-based harassment under Title IX unless motivated by hostility toward a person's sex); *see also* McSweeney v. Bayport Bluepoint Cent. Sch. Dist., 864 F. Supp. 2d 240 (E.D.N.Y. 2012) (holding that incidents involving a book being dropped on a finger and other threats were not severe or pervasive, nor were they based on sex or gender).

[129]Doe T.Z. v. City of N.Y., 634 F. Supp. 2d 263 (E.D.N.Y. 2009); S.S. v. Alexander, 177 P.3d 724 (Wash. Ct. App. 2008).

[130]*See, e.g.*, Franks v. Ky. Sch. for the Deaf, 142 F.3d 360 (6th Cir. 1998).

[131]*See, e.g.*, Cohen v. San Bernardino Valley Coll., 883 F. Supp. 1407 (C.D. Cal. 1995), *aff'd in part, rev'd in part, remanded*, 92 F.3d 968 (9th Cir. 1996).

[132]*See, e.g.*, Doe v. E. Haven Bd. of Educ., 200 F. App'x 46 (2d Cir. 2006) (affirming award of $100,000 to a victim of student-to-student harassment; finding officials deliberately indifferent to the harassment, taunting, and name-calling following plaintiff's rape). However, it is unlikely that punitive awards are available under Title IX. *See, e.g.*, Schultzen v. Woodbury Cent. Cmty. Sch. Dist., 187 F. Supp. 2d 1099 (N.D. Iowa 2002).

[133]*See, e.g.*, Hartley v. Parnell, 193 F.3d 1263 (11th Cir. 1999).

[134]*See, e.g.*, Fitzgerald v. Barnstable Sch. Comm., 555 U.S. 246 (2009).

[135]*See, e.g.*, Johnson v. Elk Lake Sch. Dist., 283 F.3d 138 (3d Cir. 2002).

[136]U.S. Dep't of Educ., *Dear Colleague Letter* (April 4, 2011), http://www2.ed.gov/about/offices/list/ocr/letters/colleague-201104.html (supplementing the OCR's *Revised Sexual Harassment Guidance* issued in 2001); *see also* U.S. Dep't of Educ., *Dear Colleague Letter* on bullying (Oct. 26, 2010), http://www2.ed.gov/about/offices/list/ocr/letters/colleague-201010.html (updated Oct. 16, 2015); U.S. Dep't of Educ., *Dear Colleague Letter* on special education and bullying (Aug. 20, 2013), http://www2.ed.gov/policy/speced/guid/idea/memosdcltrs/bullyingdcl-8-20-13.pdf.

harassment, including hostility based on sex or sex stereotyping and harassing conduct that is not sexual in nature.

Also, the Department of Education's Revised Sexual Harassment Guidance states that "sexual harassment directed at gay or lesbian students that is sufficiently serious to limit or deny a student's ability to participate in or benefit from the school's program constitutes sexual harassment prohibited by Title IX under the circumstances of this guidance."[137] In recent years, several cases have been filed under Title IX that address same-sex or gender-based harassment or harassment based on perceived sexual orientation.[138] Students have generally been successful in demonstrating that these claims are covered by Title IX.

The high volume of sexual harassment litigation in the education setting will likely continue. Even when administrators deal with claims of sexual harassment in timely and effective ways, parents still may file suit. They will be understandably angry that their child has been subjected to inappropriate behavior and will be looking for someone to blame, if not pay.

Transgender Students

As society's views of sexual orientation and gender identity have advanced in recent years, school officials have attempted to balance requests for equal treatment from transgender students with other requests regarding privacy concerns as they relate to accessing facilities. With a limited number of legal opinions on the topic, school officials might be unclear about which approach to take when confronting this issue.[139]

Most of the legal controversies involving transgender students in public schools include Title IX and/or equal protection claims. The Fourth Circuit Court observed that Title IX's implementing regulations clearly permit restrooms and locker rooms to be segregated by sex but at the same time found that the regulations do not address how school officials should determine whether a transgender individual is male or female for the purposes of facility access.[140] The appeals court held that the U.S. Department of Education's own interpretation of its Title IX regulation, which would permit a transgender student to use the restroom that aligns with his or her gender identity, should be given appropriate deference. The Supreme Court had agreed to hear the case, but it later vacated the decision and sent it back to the district court. The decision was vacated because the Department of

---

[137]Office for Civil Rights, U.S. Dep't of Educ., *Revised Sexual Harassment Guidance: Harassment of Students by School Employees, Other Students, or Third Parties* (Jan. 2001), http://www2.ed.gov/about/offices/list/ocr/docs/shguide.pdf.

[138]*See* Patterson v. Hudson Area Schs., 551 F.3d 438 (6th Cir. 2009) (holding that issues of fact remained regarding whether a school district was deliberately indifferent in responding to harassment of a student who was perceived to be gay); Dawn L. v. Greater Johnstown Sch. Dist., 586 F. Supp. 2d 332 (W.D. Pa. 2008) (finding same-sex sexual harassment had occurred in violation of Title IX); Martin v. Swartz Cmty. Schs., 419 F. Supp. 2d 967 (E.D. Mich. 2006) (denying the school district's motion for summary judgment involving a gay student's Title IX claim of peer harassment). *But see* Tyrrell v. Seaford Union Free Sch. Dist., 792 F. Supp. 2d 601 (E.D.N.Y. 2011) (holding that student failed to demonstrate that alleged harassment based on website postings of her engaged in sexual activity with another female student were related to sexual harassment).

[139]*See infra* text accompanying notes 137–142 discussing transgender access cases.

[140]G.G. v. Gloucester Cty. Sch. Bd., 822 F.3d 709 (4th Cir. 2016).

Education's Guidance allowing transgender students to use the restroom that aligned with their gender identity was rescinded by the new administration in 2017. The case will likely return to the Supreme Court within the next few years.

Similar controversies have involved state anti-discrimination laws. Currently, at least seventeen states and the District of Columbia prohibit discrimination against transgender people.[141] In a Maine case, a transgender student who was born biologically male began from a very young age to identify as female. As a fifth-grader, she was permitted to use the girls' restroom, but school officials changed the policy after receiving a complaint from another student's grandparent. Relying on the state's law that prohibits discrimination based on sexual orientation, the parents filed a lawsuit against the district. The state's high court found that the school district had violated Maine's Human Rights Act, ruling that transgender people are entitled to use the restrooms appropriate to their gender identity instead of their biological sex.[142] The court held that "where . . . it has been clearly established that a student's psychological well-being and educational success depend upon being permitted to use the communal restroom consistent with her gender identity, denying access to the appropriate restroom constitutes sexual orientation discrimination. . . ."[143] The district was ordered to pay the family $75,000.[144]

Due to the current lack of legal certainty, this topic remains in a state of flux. In the meantime, other courts will continue to address this issue.[145] Although the law is unclear, schools in most states are still permitted to bar discrimination based on sex and to allow transgender students to use facilities that align with their gender identity.

CLASSIFICATIONS BASED ON ABILITY

Courts have generally upheld use of ability in decisions related to grade placement, denial of promotion, and assignment to instructional groups.

Ability grouping purportedly permits more effective and efficient teaching by allowing teachers to concentrate their efforts on students with similar needs. Grouping according to ability or achievement is permissible, although there have been challenges concerning the

[141]Am. Civil Liberties Union, *Know Your Rights: Transgender People and the Law* (n.d.), https://www.aclu.org/lgbt-rights/know-your-rights-transgender-people-and-law.

[142]Doe v. Reg'l Sch. Unit 26, 86 A.3d 600 (Me. 2014).

[143]*Id.* at 607.

[144]David Stout, *Transgender Teen Awarded $75,000 in School Restroom Lawsuit*, TIME (Dec. 3, 2014), http://time.com/3615599/transgender-student-restroom-lawsuit-maine/.

[145]*See* Whitaker v. Kenosha Unified Sch. Dist., 858 F.3d 1034 (7th Cir. 2017) (granting the transgender student's motion for injunctive relief; he challenged a school policy that would not allow him to use the restroom that aligned with his gender identity); Evancho v. Pine-Richland Sch. Dist., 237 F. Supp. 3d 267 (W.D. Pa. 2017) (granting preliminary injunction to transgender students in equal protection case involving restrooms); Doe v. Boyertown Area Sch. Dist., 2017 U.S. Dist. LEXIS 137317 (E.D. Pa. Aug. 25, 2017) (denying the plaintiffs' motion for a preliminary injunction; plaintiffs sought to cease school district's practice of allowing transgender students to use the restroom that aligned with their gender identity); Bd. of Educ. v. U.S. Dep't of Educ., 208 F. Supp. 3d 850 (S.D. Ohio 2016) (granting a transgender student's motion for a preliminary injunction; the federal district court found that she was likely to succeed on her Title IX and equal protection claims related to restroom access).

use of standardized intelligence and achievement tests for determining student placements in regular classes and special education programs.[146] These suits have alleged that such tests are racially and culturally biased and that their use to classify or track pupils results in erroneous placements that stigmatize children. Other challenges have arisen regarding the rights of gifted and talented students to an appropriate education.

Tracking Schemes

In the most widely publicized case pertaining to ability grouping, *Hobson v. Hansen*, the use of standardized intelligence test scores to place elementary and secondary students in various ability tracks in Washington, D.C., was attacked as unconstitutional.[147] Plaintiffs contended that some children were incorrectly assigned to lower tracks and had very little chance of advancing to higher ones because of the limited curriculum and lack of remedial instruction. The federal district court examined the test scores used to track students, analyzed the accuracy of the test measurements, and concluded that mistakes often resulted from placing pupils on this basis. For the first time, a federal court evaluated testing methods and held that they discriminated against minority children. In prohibiting the continued use of such test scores, the court emphasized that it was not abolishing the use of tracking systems per se and reasoned that "[w]hat is at issue here is not whether defendants are entitled to provide different kinds of students with different kinds of education."[148] The court noted that classifications reasonably related to educational purposes are constitutionally permissible unless they result in discrimination against identifiable groups of children.

The Fifth Circuit agreed with this latter point in its evaluation of a tracking scheme in Jackson, Mississippi.[149] Although the court had previously struck down the plan given its impact on integration efforts, it later noted that "as a general rule, school systems are free to employ ability grouping, even when such a policy has a segregative effect, so long . . . as such a practice is genuinely motivated by educational concerns and not discriminatory motives."[150]

Based on evidence indicating that ability grouping provided better educational opportunities for Black students, the Eleventh Circuit upheld grouping practices in several Georgia school districts even though they had not achieved desegregated status.[151] Ability grouping allowed resources to be targeted toward low-achieving students and resulted in both gains on statewide tests and the reassignment of many students to higher-level achievement groups. When children are evaluated and provided with appropriate programs or grouped by ability, it is essential that all testing instruments be reliable, valid, and unbiased to the extent practical and possible.

---

[146]*See* text accompanying note 60, Chapter 4, for a discussion of proficiency testing.

[147]269 F. Supp. 401 (D.D.C. 1967), *aff'd sub nom.* Smuck v. Hobson, 408 F.2d 175 (D.C. Cir. 1969).

[148]Hobson, 269 F. Supp. at 511.

[149]Singleton v. Jackson Mun. Separate Sch. Dist., 419 F.2d 1211 (5th Cir. 1969).

[150]Castaneda v. Pickard, 648 F.2d 989, 996 (5th Cir. 1981).

[151]Ga. State Conference of Branches of NAACP v. Georgia, 775 F.2d 1403 (11th Cir. 1985).

High-Ability Students

Often overlooked when identifying unique needs and providing appropriate programs are those students labeled as "high ability," "gifted," or "talented." Included within these populations are students who demonstrate evidence of high-performance in areas such as intellectual, creative, artistic, or leadership capacity, or in specific academic fields. **Over the years, the federal government has provided only limited aid for gifted education, and there is no federal statute specifying substantive rights for the gifted as there is for students with disabilities**.

Given a limited federal role, rights for gifted and talented students are based overwhelmingly on state law or local school board policy. These laws vary greatly by state. Pennsylvania, one of the leading states in mandating programs for the gifted, includes gifted and talented students under its designation of "exceptional children" who "deviate from the average in physical, mental, emotional or social characteristics to such an extent that they require special educational facilities or services."[152] The Pennsylvania Supreme Court interpreted this law as placing a mandatory obligation on school districts to establish individualized programs for gifted students beyond the general enrichment program.[153] However, the court qualified its interpretation of state statute by observing that the law does not require "exclusive individual programs outside or beyond the district's existing, regular, and special education curricular offerings"[154] and does not impose a duty to maximize a student's potential.

The procedures used to select students who are to participate in gifted programs continue to be challenged. Criteria such as intelligence, test scores, grade point average, and teacher evaluations are used in the selection process. Although under certain circumstances age may be a permissible criterion for admission, race will seldom be permitted unless court ordered.[155]

CONCLUSION

A basic purpose of public education is to prepare students for citizenship and work, regardless of their innate characteristics. Accordingly, courts and legislatures have become increasingly assertive in guaranteeing that students have the chance to realize their capabilities while in school. Arbitrary classification practices that disadvantage certain groups are not tolerated. Conversely, valid classifications, applied in the best interests of students, are generally supported. Indeed, some legal mandates require the classification of certain

---

[152]Pa. Stat. Ann. tit. 24 § 13-1371(1) (2018). *See* U.S. Dep't of Educ., *Jacob K. Javits Gifted and Talented Students Education Program* (n.d.), https://www2.ed.gov/programs/javits/legislation.html.

[153]Centennial Sch. Dist. v. Commonwealth Dep't of Educ., 539 A.2d 785 (Pa. 1988); *see also* K.K. v. Pittsburgh Pub. Schs., 590 F. App'x 148 (3d Cir. 2014) (finding no § 504 violation because school district did not demonstrate deliberate indifference in providing instruction to gifted student who was receiving homebound instruction).

[154]*Id.* at 791; *see also* Saucon Valley Sch. Dist. v. Robert O., 785 A.2d 1069 (Pa. Commw. Ct. 2001) (determining that a hearing panel exceeded its authority when it ordered that a gifted student should be placed in the graduating class before his own, given that the district had failed to provide him with accelerated and enriched programming).

[155]Rosenfeld v. Montgomery Cty. Pub. Schs., 25 F. App'x 123 (4th Cir. 2001) (affirming dismissal of case as the plaintiff eventually was admitted to the gifted program; the court acknowledged, however, that if different, less stringent selection criteria had been used for students of color, the plaintiff would have had a basis for seeking damages).

students to ensure that they receive instruction appropriate to their needs. In exercising professional judgment pertaining to the classification of students, educators should be cognizant of the following generalizations drawn from judicial and legislative mandates.

1. School segregation resulting from state laws or other intentional state action (e.g., gerrymandering school attendance zones) violates the Equal Protection Clause of the Fourteenth Amendment.

2. Where a school district has not achieved unitary status, school officials have an affirmative duty to eliminate the vestiges of past intentional discrimination; under such a duty, official action (or inaction) is assessed in terms of its effect on reducing segregation.

3. Segregatory effect alone does not establish unconstitutional intent; however, the consequences of official actions can be considered in substantiating discriminatory motive.

4. Interdistrict desegregation remedies cannot be judicially imposed unless there is evidence of intentional discrimination with substantial effect across district lines.

5. Judicial supervision can be terminated, in whole or in part, where school districts have complied with desegregation mandates in good faith and have eliminated the vestiges of past discrimination as far as practicable.

6. In determining whether a school district has eliminated the vestiges of school segregation, courts assess racial equality in student, faculty, and staff assignments; transportation; extracurricular activities; and facilities.

7. Once a school district has eliminated the vestiges of its prior discriminatory conduct to the court's satisfaction, future acts must represent purposeful discrimination to violate the Fourteenth Amendment; school districts are not obligated to continue remedies after unitary status is attained and resegregation occurs through no fault of school officials.

8. The use of race in determining school or program assignment to achieve diversity in student bodies will not be permitted unless shown to be narrowly tailored.

9. Students who are English Learners are entitled to compensatory instruction designed to overcome English language barriers.

10. Although school districts may operate sex-segregated schools and classes, they must provide a substantially similar coeducational experiences.

11. If a school district establishes an interscholastic athletic program, opportunities must be made available to male and female athletes on an equal basis (i.e., mixed-sex teams or comparable sex-segregated teams).

12. Sexual harassment of students, by either employees or other students, can result in liability against the school district when an official with the authority to correct the situation has received actual notice of the harassment and has failed to correct it or has shown deliberate indifference toward the action.

13. The law remains unsettled with regard to whether transgender students are protected from discriminatory practices under Title IX.

14. Over the years, the federal government has provided only limited aid for gifted education, and there is no federal statute specifying substantive rights for the gifted as there is for students with disabilities.

CHAPTER SEVEN

RIGHTS OF STUDENTS
WITH DISABILITIES

When must students with disabilities be taught in general education classrooms? Does a student with a severe peanut allergy fit within the legal definition of an individual with a disability? What should schools do before disciplining students with disabilities? Questions like these lead to contentious litigation between parents and school districts. In fact, special education is the most litigated area in school law.[1] Although students with disabilities are afforded numerous legal entitlements and protections today, this was not always the case. For many years, individuals with disabilities were segregated in highly restrictive settings and institutionalized where they were often treated inhumanely.[2] In the 1970s, strategic advocacy efforts, paired with two landmark court decisions, compelled Congress to ensure students with disabilities had a legal right to access a public education.[3]

This chapter addresses three federal disability laws: the Individuals with Disabilities Education Act (IDEA), Section 504 of the Rehabilitation Act of 1973 (Section 504), and the Americans with Disabilities Act (ADA).[4] The majority of this chapter provides an overview of IDEA because of its focus on education, but the chapter concludes with a discussion of Section 504 and the ADA, which prohibit disability-based discrimination. Additional mandates required by state legislation are not detailed.[5]

[1]Perry Zirkel & Brent Johnson, *The "Explosion" in Education Litigation: An Updated Analysis*, 265 EDUC. L. REP. 1 (2011); *see also* Zorka Karanxha & Perry Zirkel, *Longitudinal Trends in Special Education Case Law: Frequencies and Outcomes of Published Court Decisions*, 27 J. SPECIAL EDUC. LEADERSHIP 55 (2014).

[2]*See* Eric Neudel, *Lives Worth Living*, INDEP. LENS (Oct. 27, 2011), http://www.pbs.org/independentlens/films/lives-worth-living/.

[3]*See* Mills v. D.C. Bd. of Educ., 348 F. Supp. 869 (D.D.C. 1972); PARC v. Pennsylvania, 343 F. Supp. 279 (E.D. Pa., 1972).

[4]The Fourteenth Amendment and 42 U.S.C. § 1983 also apply to students with disabilities in public schools and to private state athletic associations, but do not apply to most private schools. Private schools that receive federal financial assistance (e.g., National School Lunch Program funding) must comply with § 504; whereas all private schools are subject to the ADA; *see also* the federal regulations that are paired with § 504, the ADA, and IDEA and *infra* text discussing § 504 and the ADA.

[5]*See, e.g.*, 511 IND. ADMIN. CODE 7-32 to -49 (2018) (outlining special education regulations for Indiana).

Readers of this chapter should be able to:

- Explain how students with disabilities are eligible for services under IDEA versus Section 504/ADA.

- Describe each of the six key principles of IDEA.

- Discuss the U.S. Supreme Court's standard to determine whether a district has provided a student educational benefit as required by IDEA.

- Define commonly used special education acronyms (e.g., FAPE, IEP, LRE).

- Detail the Manifestation Determination Review procedures including the ten-day rule.

- Compare IDEA's requirements for school districts with those mandated by Section 504/ADA.

INDIVIDUALS WITH DISABILITIES EDUCATION ACT

Students ages three through twenty-one who qualify under IDEA are eligible to receive a free appropriate public education (FAPE).

In 1975, Congress enacted the Education for All Handicapped Children Act (also called P.L. 94-142) which later became IDEA.[6] Because IDEA is a funding law, the many requirements of this statute must be followed only if a state receives federal IDEA funding—which all states currently do. The U.S. Department of Education's Office of Special Education and Rehabilitative Services (OSERS) supports IDEA's programs that serve over 7 million individuals from birth to age twenty-one.[7] Approximately 6 million students (ages six through twenty-one) are eligible for special education and related services, which amounts to approximately 14 percent of the total number of students enrolled in public schools. Of those school-age children receiving special education, approximately 63 percent spend 80 percent or more of the day inside a general education classroom.[8] Therefore, despite the distinction of teaching credentials between general education and special education teachers, *all* teachers must understand special education law. Special education law uses many acronyms; the most commonly used are defined in Figure 7.1.

---

[6]20 U.S.C. §§ 1400–1482 (2018). Congress has reauthorized and amended IDEA three times, causing it to be referred to differently according to these reauthorizations (e.g., "IDEA Amendments of 1997" or "Individuals with Disabilities Education Improvement Act—IDEIA"). The statutory title of the law, however, has not changed and will be referred to as IDEA throughout this chapter.

[7]U.S. Dep't of Educ. Office of Special Educ. & Rehab. Servs., *38th Annual Report to Congress on the Implementation of the Individuals with Disabilities Education Act, 2016* (Oct. 2016), https://www2.ed.gov/about/reports/annual/osep/2016/parts-b-c/38th-arc-for-idea.pdf.

[8]*Id.*

FIGURE 7.1   Commonly Used Acronyms in Special Education

ADA	Americans with Disabilities Act
BIP	Behavior Intervention Plan
ESY	Extended School Year
FAPE	Free Appropriate Public Education
FBA	Functional Behavioral Assessment
IAES	Interim Alternative Education Setting
IDEA	Individuals with Disabilities Education Act
IEE	Independent Educational Evaluation
IEP	Individualized Education Program
LRE	Least Restrictive Environment
MDR	Manifestation Determination Review
OSERS	Office of Special Education and Rehabilitative Services
PBIS	Positive Behavioral Interventions and Supports
RtI	Response to Intervention

Students with disabilities must be provided related services and supplemental aids as needed to provide a FAPE. School districts are responsible for overseeing special education services, but unlike many other areas of education, parents of students with disabilities have a legal right to participate in the development of their child's education.[9] This collaborative process between the parents and school district begins when a student is deemed eligible and evaluated for special education.[10] Then, parents and school personnel meet to create a written individualized education program (IEP), which not only outlines goals for the student but also describes the child's placement (e.g., general education classroom). IDEA requires that eligible students be taught in the least restrictive environment (LRE), which means that they must be educated alongside their peers without disabilities to the maximum extent appropriate. Finally, IDEA outlines multiple procedural safeguards to protect the rights of parents and students, as well as to allow parents and students to seek legal recourse if they believe IDEA has been violated (e.g., due process hearing). These six key principles of IDEA

[9]*See* Winkelman v. Parma Cty. Sch. Dist., 550 U.S. 516 (2007) (holding that IDEA grants parents independent, enforceable rights related to the formulation of their child's education program).

[10]IDEA defines "parent" broadly as a natural, adoptive, or foster parent; a guardian; an individual acting in place of a natural or adoptive parent (e.g., grandparent, stepparent, or other relative) who is responsible for the child or with whom the child lives; or a surrogate, 20 U.S.C. § 1401(23) (2018).

(i.e., FAPE, eligibility and evaluation, IEP, LRE, related services and supplemental services, and parental rights and procedural safeguards) are detailed in the following sections.[11]

Free Appropriate Public Education

All students ages three through twenty-one with qualifying disabilities must be provided a FAPE that is made available in the LRE.[12] A school district's obligation to provide a FAPE begins when a child with a disability is identified and concludes only when the student withdraws or graduates from school, fails to qualify for services, reaches the age of twenty-one (or older if state law permits), or parents revoke services. IDEA defines a FAPE as special education and related services that:

- have been provided at public expense and under public supervision and direction (even if the school district selects a private school placement);
- meet the standards of the state educational agency;
- include an appropriate preschool, elementary school, or secondary school education; and
- are delivered in conformity with the IEP.[13]

As needed, students with disabilities also must be provided supplementary aids and services including transition services to assist in transitioning from school to postgraduation activities such as postsecondary education, vocational training, integrated employment, continuing and adult education, adult services, independent living, or community participation. Services must be provided as close to the child's home as possible, but all programs are not required to be available in every school.[14]

The "free public education" aspect of a FAPE is fairly straightforward; however, determining what is "appropriate" is more challenging. **Courts have clarified that an "appropriate" education need not be "the best" available or represent "optimum" programs that will maximize learning potential.**[15] For decades, the standard to measure whether a school provided an "appropriate" education was from a 1982 U.S. Supreme

[11]*See* RUD TURNBULL, NANCY HUERTO & MATTHEW STOWE, WHAT EVERY TEACHER SHOULD KNOW ABOUT: THE INDIVIDUALS WITH DISABILITIES EDUCATION ACT AS AMENDED IN 2004 (2d ed. 2008); MITCHELL YELL, THE LAW AND SPECIAL EDUCATION (4th ed. 2016).

[12]20 U.S.C. § 1412(a)(1)(A), (a)(1)(5) (2018). However, IDEA also lists an exception such that states are not obligated to provide a FAPE for children ages three to five and eighteen through twenty-one if state law or practice or any court order specifies that these children are not entitled to a FAPE, 20 U.S.C. § 1412(a)(1)(B). Additionally, parents must have consented to the provision of special education and related services.

[13]20 U.S.C. § 1401(9) (2018).

[14]*See, e.g.*, Lebron v. N. Penn Sch. Dist., 769 F. Supp. 2d 788 (E.D. Pa. 2011).

[15]*See, e.g.*, Endrew F. *ex rel.* Joseph F. v. Douglas Cty. Sch. Dist., 137 S. Ct. 988, 999 (2017) (stating that "any review of an IEP must appreciate that the question is whether the IEP is *reasonable*, not whether the court regards it as ideal"); Doe v. Bd. of Educ. of Tullahoma Schs., 9 F.3d 455, 459 (9th Cir. 1993) (describing the education required under IDEA as one that is comparable to a "serviceable Chevrolet" and not a "Cadillac").

Court decision, *Board of Education v. Rowley*.[16] The *Rowley* Court applied the following two-part test to determine that a district had provided a FAPE even though it did not provide a sign-language interpreter to a girl with a hearing impairment:

- Have IDEA's procedural requirements been followed?
- Was the IEP reasonably calculated to enable the child to receive educational benefit?[17]

For decades following *Rowley*, lower courts applied the educational benefit standard to varying degrees. The courts were predominately split into two standards: "just-above-trivial" (also called "*de minimus*") and "meaningful" educational benefit.[18] **However, in 2017, the U.S. Supreme Court clarified in *Endrew v. Douglas County School District* that schools "must offer an IEP reasonably calculated to enable a child to make progress appropriate in light of the child's circumstances."**[19] Although ruling that the "just-above-trivial" educational benefit standard was unacceptable, the Court did not adopt the "meaningful" standard.

Endrew involved a fifth-grade boy with autism who was not making progress after several years in public school, causing his parents to unilaterally enroll him in a private school designed for children with autism. Within months, "Endrew's behavior improved significantly, permitting him to make a degree of academic progress that had eluded him in public school."[20] Endrew's parents filed a lawsuit claiming that the public school had violated its FAPE obligation, but the Tenth Circuit ruled for the district, explaining that an IEP needed to confer an "educational benefit [that is] merely . . . more than *de minimis*."[21] However, the unanimous Supreme Court disagreed and explained that applying the minimal standard "would be tantamount to sitting idly . . . awaiting the time when [students with disabilities] were old enough to drop out."[22] Accordingly, the Supreme Court vacated the Tenth Circuit's decision and remanded the issue of tuition reimbursement to the lower court for reconsideration.

[16]458 U.S. 176, 191 (1982) (reasoning that IDEA's purpose was to "open the door" to provide access to education instead of "guarantee any particular level of education once inside").

[17]458 U.S. at 207. As noted, *Endrew* alters the second question. The *Rowley* Court held that the girl was receiving an appropriate education as evidenced by her better-than-average performance in class and promotion from grade to grade.

[18]Petition for Writ of Certiorari at 9, *Endrew F.*, 137 S. Ct. 988 (2017). The circuits using the "just above trivial" standard included the First, Second, Fourth, Fifth, Seventh, Eighth, Tenth, and Eleventh Circuits. Those applying the "meaningful" standard included the Third and Sixth Circuits. *Endrew* clarified that the "just above trivial" or "*de minimus*" standard was not permissible under IDEA.

[19]*Id.* at 1001.

[20]*Id.* at 997.

[21]Endrew F. *ex rel.* Joseph F. v. Douglas Cty. Sch. Dist., 798 F.3d 1329, 1338 (10th Cir. 2015) (internal quotation marks omitted).

[22]137 S. Ct. at 1001 (internal quotation marks omitted) (quoting Bd. of Educ. v. Rowley, 458 U.S. 176, 179 (1982)).

The *Endrew* **Court emphasized that what constitutes a sufficient educational benefit must be decided on a case-by-case basis because IEPs are, by name,** *individualized*. If the student is not integrated in a general education classroom, for example, the IEP need not aim for grade-level advancement but must strive for "appropriately ambitious" goals given the particular child.[23] Similarly, the district must offer an IEP that is reasonably calculated to allow a student to "be involved in and make progress in the general education curriculum."[24] The Court declined to adopt a standard that would require "substantially equal" opportunities for students with and without disabilities.[25] Additionally, the Court noted that "the IDEA cannot and does not promise any particular educational *outcome*."[26]

When determining whether a student has been provided a FAPE, courts often defer to educators and administrative review officials regarding matters of pedagogy, including methodology, but still will reject IEPs that are inappropriate or not supported by the data. For example, a Ninth Circuit three-judge panel held that failing to specify in the IEP that a methodology (Applied Behavior Analysis) would be provided by the district was a denial of a FAPE.[27] In a split decision, the majority reasoned that when a particular intervention or methodology is critical to a student's education it should be written into the IEP and not left up to teachers' discretion. In contrast, the Second Circuit ruled that a student with a learning disability was provided an IEP that was appropriately tailored to her individual needs to "ensure meaningful progress."[28] In this case, the district's IEP offered a variety of services, including a resource room placement and counseling; however, the student's mother sought reimbursement for a private, residential school.

Eligibility and Evaluation

The first step to providing a FAPE is to identify all eligible students and conduct evaluations to determine whether they are in need of special education. The initial evaluation will also inform what type of educational program would benefit the student.

Eligibility. To qualify for services under IDEA, students must meet two criteria: (1) they must be a student with a disability based on specific disability categories, and (2) they must be in need of special education and related services. Stated differently, the students' disabilities

---

[23]*Id.* at 992.

[24]*Id.* at 988 (quoting IDEA §1414(d)(1)(A)(i)(IV) (2018)).

[25]*Id.* (discussing that an equal opportunity standard was similarly rejected in *Rowley*).

[26]*Id.* (emphasis added). In 2018, the Colorado federal district court ordered the school district to reimburse Endrew's parents for private school tuition, attorneys' fees, and litigation costs. Endrew F. *ex rel.* Joseph F. v. Douglas Cty. Sch. Dist., 2018 WL 828019 (D. Colo. Feb. 8, 2018).

[27]R.E.B. v. Haw. Dep't of Educ., 870 F.3d 1025 (9th Cir. 2017). *But see* I.Z.M. v. Rosemont-Apple Valley-Eagan Pub. Schs., 863 F.3d 966 (8th Cir. 2017) (holding that a student with vision impairment was provided a FAPE even though services offered in IEP did not guarantee a specific level of proficiency).

[28]D.B. v. Ithaca Cty. Sch. Dist., 690 F. App'x 778 (2d Cir. 2017); *see also* M.L. *ex rel.* Leiman v. Smith, 867 F.3d 487 (4th Cir. 2017) (holding that the student's IEP did not need to provide instruction on student's religious and cultural needs to meet FAPE requirement); C.G. *ex rel.* Keith G. v. Waller Indep. Sch. Dist., 697 F. App'x 816 (5th Cir. June 22, 2017) (denying parents' request for private school tuition reimbursement because the IEP was appropriate).

must adversely affect their educational performance.[29] **It is possible to have a disability, but not be in need of special education and, therefore, not qualify for services under IDEA.**

To be eligible under IDEA, a student must have one of the following disabilities: intellectual disabilities (ID); hearing impairments (including deafness); speech or language impairments (SLI); visual impairments (including blindness); emotional disturbances (ED); orthopedic impairments (OI); autism (sometimes called autism spectrum disorder, ASD); traumatic brain injury (TBI); other health impairments (OHI); or specific learning disabilities (SLD). Another potential category (for children ages three through nine) may include developmental delay (DD) in at least one area: physical, cognitive, communication, social or emotional, or adaptive development. State and local education agencies have the discretion of including and defining DD as an eligible category. The school district does not need to determine the proper label for the child to provide special education and related services.[30] Some of IDEA's disability categories are identified by medical professionals before a child attends school (e.g., blindness), whereas others may not manifest until a child is in the learning environment and may be more subjective (e.g., specific learning disability).[31] Students of color have been overidentified as qualifying for special education, and they have been disproportionately placed in particular categories (e.g., emotional disturbance), causing the Department of Education to carefully monitor special education data based on race.[32]

Child Find and Zero Reject.   Under IDEA's "child find" mandate, states are required to identify, locate, and evaluate all resident children with disabilities (including those who are homeless, English Learners, or wards of the state), regardless of the severity of their disability or whether they attend public or private schools.[33] The mandate to serve all students with disabilities is commonly referred to as "zero reject."[34] Although federal law requires

[29]The need for special education must be due to the IDEA disability, 20 U.S.C. § 1401(3)(A) (2018); *see also* C.F.R. § 300.8 (2018) (providing additional definitions for each category and using the phrase "adversely affects a child's educational performance"); A.J. v. Bd. of Educ., 679 F. Supp. 2d 299, 311 (E.D.N.Y. 2010) (holding that although the student had Asperger's Syndrome, his special needs did not "adversely affect" his educational performance).

[30]However, a child must qualify as "a child with a disability" for the state to receive federal funding, 20 U.S.C. § 1412 (a)(3)(B) (2018); *see also* Heather v. Wisconsin, 125 F.3d 1045 (7th Cir. 1997) (holding that IDEA does not require schools to determine the proper disability category label).

[31]*See* Elizabeth Shaver, *Qualifying for Special Education and Related Services under IDEA*, in A GUIDE TO SPECIAL EDUCATION LAW (Elizabeth Shaver & Janet Decker eds., 2017). In determining whether a child has a specific learning disability, the district is not required to consider whether a severe discrepancy exists between achievement and ability, 20 U.S.C. § 1414(b)(6)(A) (2018).

[32]20 U.S.C. § 1418(a) (2018). *But see* Christina Samuels, *Minority Students Still Missing Out on Special Education, New Analysis Says*, EDUC. WK. (Aug. 28, 2017), http://blogs.edweek.org/edweek/speced/2017/08/minorities_underenrolled_special_education.html (discussing research that has found that students of color are under-identified in special education).

[33]*See* 20 U.S.C. § 1412(a)(3)(A), (a)(10)(A)(ii) (2018).

[34]20 U.S.C. § 1412(a)(2) (2018). *See* Timothy W. v. Rochester Sch. Dist., 875 F.2d 954, 960 (1st Cir. 1989) (stating that "a 'zero-reject' policy is at the core" of IDEA when discussing a student who had multiple severe disabilities and extensive brain damage).

that children with disabilities be identified, it does not dictate how this is to occur. Nevertheless, courts give deference to districts when their identification efforts are substantial, in good faith, and ultimately effective.[35] Consequently, state procedures vary widely and include census taking; community surveys; public awareness activities; referrals from parents, teachers, and doctors; and preschool and kindergarten screening.

The screening process may necessitate the use of tests that are administered to all children, not just students suspected of having disabilities. Prior to testing, parents must be given notice identifying the tests and providing a general explanation of their intended purpose. In the 2004 Reauthorization of IDEA, Congress added language about the evaluation process for students with specific learning disabilities. Through an approach known as Response to Intervention (RtI), districts may determine if a child "responds to scientific, research-based intervention."[36] Typically, RtI involves three tiers of intervention to determine whether a child who is struggling academically can improve with increasingly intensive instruction or if the child should be referred for a special education evaluation. **RtI has gained momentum as an effective tool to identify and assist students; however, districts must not use RtI to delay or deny a comprehensive evaluation.**[37]

Evaluation. Next, based on the results of screenings or referrals, schools must evaluate students who may qualify for special education.[38] The purpose of the evaluation is twofold: (1) to determine if a student is eligible and (2) to determine a student's educational needs. The Ninth Circuit held that a student with autism was denied a FAPE after his school district failed to formally evaluate him. In that case, despite speculation that the child may have autism, a staff member concluded the child had an expressive language delay based on an informal, unscientific observation that had been conducted.[39] The court reasoned that the lack of a formal assessment made it impossible for the district to meet its obligation under IDEA.

---

[35]*See* P.P. v. W. Chester Area Sch. Dist., 585 F.3d 727, 738 (3d Cir. 2009) (finding that the district had complied with "child-find" obligations because their efforts were "comprehensive," noting that the district posted notices in local newspaper and on the district's website, sent information in property tax bills to residents, and placed targeted posters/pamphlets in private schools). *But see* D.L. v. District of Columbia, 194 F. Supp. 3d 30 (D.D.C. 2016) (determining the district had demonstrated bad faith and gross misjudgment in meeting its IDEA obligations, quoting district's attorney who conceded that the district's child-find procedures had been "broken for a long time"), *aff'd*, 860 F.3d 713 (D.C. Cir. 2017).

[36]20 U.S.C. § 1414(a)(6)(B) (2018). Districts are not required to conduct RtI. *See* Elizabeth Shaver, *Qualifying for Special Education Services under IDEA*, in Shaver & Decker eds. *supra* note 31.

[37]*See* Davis v. District of Columbia, 244 F. Supp. 3d 27 (D.D.C. 2017); Jose Martin, *Legal Implications of Response to Intervention and Special Education Identification*, RTI Action Network (n.d.), http://www.rtinetwork .org/learn/ld/legal-implications-of-response-to-intervention-and-special-education-identification; Memorandum from Melody Musgrove, Dir., Office of Special Educ. Programs, to State Directors of Special Education (Jan. 21, 2011), https://www2.ed.gov/policy/speced/guid/idea/memosdcltrs/osep11-07rtimemo.pdf.

[38]Evaluation referrals may be initiated by parents, school personnel, the state educational agency, or another state agency, 20 U.S.C. § 1414 (2018).

[39]Timothy O. v. Paso Robles Unified Sch. Dist., 822 F.3d 1105 (9th Cir. 2016).

After a student is suspected of having a disability, a multidisciplinary team typically meets to determine whether an evaluation is warranted. If the team members decide the student should be evaluated, the school must obtain informed consent from the student's parents before any personalized testing occurs.[40] **However, if parents refuse consent for the initial evaluation or fail to respond to the request to provide consent, the district may file a formal complaint with the state education agency to resolve the issue and possibly to authorize an evaluation**. Evaluations must be completed in a timely manner, usually within sixty days of receiving parental consent.

IDEA requires the administration of a multifactored evaluation using a variety of valid assessment tools and strategies to gather information related to the child's academic, functional, and developmental abilities. Assessments must be validated for the purposes they are used, administered by qualified personnel, selected and employed in ways that neither racially nor culturally discriminate given in accordance with instructions, and available in the child's native language or other mode of communication.[41]

Once assessments are conducted, a group of educational professionals and the parents are assembled as the child's IEP team. Together, the IEP team is responsible for reviewing existing data on the child, including evaluations and information provided by the parents, current classroom-based assessments, and observations by teachers and related service providers. After all relevant input has been aggregated, the team must ascertain whether the child qualifies as a child with a disability and, if so, whether special education and related services are needed.

If parents are dissatisfied with the original evaluation or resulting placement decision, they have the right to request an independent educational evaluation (IEE). The school pays for the additional evaluation, unless officials contest the need for reassessment or the IEE does not meet district criteria.[42] In situations where the district is not required to pay for the IEE, but the parents acquire one, school personnel still must consider, but not necessarily follow, the IEE results.

The 2004 amendments to IDEA made changes to reduce the number of reevaluations, the frequency of IEP meetings, and the amount of overall paperwork.[43] Generally, reevaluations occur once every three years unless parents and district personnel determine they are unnecessary. Reevaluations *may* occur more often than every three years, but the

---

[40]20 U.S.C. § 1414(a)(1)(D)(i)(I), (c)(3) (2018). Consent is not required for curricular, state, or district-wide assessments, 34 C.F.R. § 300.300(d)(1)(ii) (2018). Students with disabilities are required to participate in *all* state and district-wide assessments, with accommodations and alternate forms of assessment as appropriate, 20 U.S.C. § 1412(a)(16) (2018). States may elect to provide students having significant cognitive disabilities with alternate assessments keyed to alternate achievement standards, 20 U.S.C. § 1412(a)(16)(C) (2018).

[41]20 U.S.C. § 1414(b)(2), (3).

[42]If a hearing officer orders an evaluation, the district bears all costs. If a district challenges payment for a second evaluation, it must demonstrate that all procedures were followed during its evaluation, 34 C.F.R. § 300.502(a)–(e) (2018). *But see* Evanston Cmty. Consol. Sch. Dist. v. Michael M., 356 F.3d 798 (7th Cir. 2004) (denying reimbursement for a second, unnecessary evaluation).

[43]*See* 20 U.S.C. § 1414(d)(5)(A)–(B) (2018).

district has no obligation to provide more than one reevaluation per year.[44] Where a reevaluation supports amendment to the IEP, IDEA permits the district to make the necessary changes without conducting a full IEP team meeting, so long as parental approval has been acquired.[45]

Individualized Education Program

After an initial evaluation or a reevaluation, the IEP team meets to use the evaluation data to develop a written plan outlining the special education and related services that the student needs. IEPs do not guarantee that the student *will* make progress, but they must be developed to enable the "child to make progress appropriate in light of the child's circumstances."[46]

The school district is responsible for organizing the IEP team meeting. The parents must agree to the IEP meeting time and location, and the district must ensure that the parents have the opportunity to participate fully, which may require hiring foreign-language translators or sign-language interpreters.[47] If no parent is available or willing to attend, school officials should document each effort to encourage parental involvement.[48] The district may prepare a tentative draft IEP as a basis for discussion.[49]

IDEA stipulates that the IEP team should include the following individuals:

- parents and child (if appropriate);
- special education teacher(s) and general education teacher(s) (if relevant);
- district representative (authorized to commit resources);
- individual who can interpret evaluation results; and
- other individuals with special knowledge or expertise.[50]

---

[44]20 U.S.C. § 1414(a)(2). The school district need not obtain parental consent for a reevaluation if the district demonstrates that it took reasonable measures to obtain consent and parents failed to respond, 20 U.S.C. § 1414(c)(3) (2018); *see also* Shelby S. *ex rel.* Kathleen T. v. Conroe Indep. Sch. Dist., 454 F.3d 450 (5th Cir. 2006) (determining that the district could compel a medical examination to reevaluate a child, notwithstanding a lack of parental consent, where such reevaluation was critical to the district in preparing an appropriate IEP).

[45]20 U.S.C § 1414(d)(3)(D). A written document amending or modifying the IEP suffices in these circumstances.

[46]Endrew F. *ex rel.* Joseph F. v. Douglas Cty. Sch. Dist., 137 S. Ct. 988, 1001 (2017).

[47]34 C.F.R. § 300.322(a), (c) (2018). Participation may be accomplished through video conferencing and conference calls where necessary, 20 U.S.C. § 1414(f).

[48]34 C.F.R. § 300.332(d). *Compare* A.L. v. Jackson Cty. Sch. Bd., 635 F. App'x 774 (11th Cir. 2015) (holding mother's nonattendance at IEP meeting did not constitute a FAPE violation because mother's actions documented by district were tantamount to a refusal to attend), *with* Doug C. v. Haw. Dep't of Educ., 720 F.3d 1038 (9th Cir. 2013) (finding that district violated FAPE when it held an IEP meeting without a parent who was willing to participate).

[49]Yet school officials should emphasize that the IEP is not in final form and requires the entire IEP team members' input. *See, e.g.,* Berry *ex rel.* Berry v. Las Virgenes Unified Sch. Dist., 370 F. App'x 843 (9th Cir. 2010) (holding that the school district violated IDEA by predetermining student's placement before the IEP meeting).

[50]20 U.S.C. § 1414(d)(1). The person who interprets the evaluation results may be one of the other IEP team members.

Some committees consist of ten or more participants, but not all need to be present at every meeting. Excusal is permitted when the parents consent and the members who are not attending have had the opportunity to submit their input in writing prior to the meeting.

The IEP team should determine the child's present level of academic achievement and functional performance and project whether any modifications to the instruction or services are necessary for the child to meet measurable annual goals and to participate, as appropriate, in the general education curriculum. IDEA requires the team to consider the student's strengths; parents' concerns; evaluation results; and the academic, functional, and developmental needs of the student. **The IEP team must also consider individual circumstances, such as whether the student's behavior impedes that student's learning or the learning of other students**. If so, the IEP team must evaluate whether to implement positive behavior interventions and supports (PBIS) as well as other strategies to address the behavior.[51]

Although PBIS is not defined in IDEA, the statute does reference two behavioral strategies that IEP teams may consider: functional behavioral assessments (FBAs) and behavior intervention plans (BIPs).[52] These strategies derive from the field of Applied Behavior Analysis, which analyzes behavior to understand and improve it. First, someone with training, such as a behavior analyst, conducts an FBA to identify the antecedents and consequences of a targeted behavior.[53] For example, if a student is hitting, a behavior analyst may identify that the behavior occurs when the student is faced with a challenging task, and the student is able to escape the task after hitting. Second, the information gleaned from the FBA can be used to develop a BIP for the student. The IEP may include a BIP, which is a written plan designed to reduce undesired behavior. Therefore, it could identify instructional strategies to teach behaviors that are incompatible with the undesired behavior (e.g., teaching the student to request a break when faced with a challenging task) and that reinforce the desired behavior (e.g., student is given extra computer time for requesting a break).[54]

In addition to discussing special considerations such as behavioral interventions, the IEP team should discuss the multiple aspects of the student's education featured in Figure 7.2.[55] After consensus has been reached on these specific components, they should appear in the final written IEP. Next, the IEP team reviews the written document, and the parents sign it. If the procedures surrounding IEP development are not followed, courts may find IDEA violations. To illustrate, a school district unilaterally decided to amend an IEP after the parents had signed it. The Ninth Circuit held that the district had violated

---

[51]*See* 20 U.S.C. § 1414(c)–(d)(3); Perry Zirkel, *Case Law for Functional Behavior Assessments and Behavior Intervention Plans: An Empirical Analysis*, 35 SEATTLE U. L. REV. 175, 186 (2011) (noting that the IEP team must only "consider"—not necessarily "develop or implement"—PBIS).

[52]IEP teams must consider FBAs and BIPs when discussing behavior that could result in expulsion, 20 U.S.C. § 1415(k)(1)(F). *See infra* text accompanying note 109.

[53]*See* Cynthia Dieterich, Nicole Snyder & Christine Villani, *Functional Behavioral Assessments and Behavior Intervention Plans: Review of the Law and Recent Cases*, 2017 B.Y.U. EDUC. & L.J. 195 (2017).

[54]*See* Elizabeth Shaver & Janet Decker, *Handcuffing a Third Grader with ADHD? Interactions between School Resource Officers and Students with Disabilities*, 2017 UTAH L. REV. 1 (2017).

[55]20 U.S.C. § 1414(d)(1)(A)(i); *see also* 20 U.S.C. § 1415(m)(1) (2018) (describing the transfer of parental rights at the age of majority).

FIGURE 7.2   Elements of a Legally Compliant IEP

IEP Team Should Ensure the IEP Includes:
✔ Student's present level of academic achievement and functional performance
✔ Measurable annual goals
✔ Statement of how performance will be measured and communicated to parents
✔ Description of special education, related services, and supplementary aids and services, "based on peer-reviewed research to the extent practicable"
✔ Explanation of the extent, if any, to which the child will not be included in general education activities
✔ Any accommodations that will be made in performing state or district assessments (or an explanation of why alternate assessments are necessary)
✔ Postsecondary goals, transition services (beginning at age sixteen, or younger if required by state law), and a statement indicating that students were informed that their IDEA rights transfer from their parents to them (beginning no later than one year before student reaches age of majority under state law)
✔ Description of benchmarks or short-term objectives (only for students taking alternate assessments)
✔ Date when services will begin
✔ Frequency, location, and duration of services

IDEA, explaining that parents have a right to be included in every step of the IEP drafting process. The court stated: "An IEP is like a contract, may not be changed unilaterally; it embodies a binding commitment and provides notice to both parties as to what services will be provided to the student."[56]

If a student moves into a school district during an academic year, the district may accept an existing IEP from the former district. The receiving district must (1) take reasonable steps to promptly obtain the student's educational records and (2) provide services comparable to those identified by the former district. The student's placement should be continued until the district has developed a new IEP consistent with IDEA procedures.

Finalizing the IEP marks only the beginning of the district's responsibilities to provide a FAPE. District personnel must ensure that the IEP is implemented; they must coordinate the agreed-upon placement and services that are listed in the IEP; and they must obtain parental consent before providing special education services. If parents refuse to sign the IEP and thus do not consent to special education services, the district is not obligated to provide the student with a FAPE or to convene future IEP meetings. Additionally, the

[56]M.C. v. Antelope Valley Union High Sch. Dist., 858 F.3d 1189, 1197 (9th Cir. 2017).

district cannot challenge parental refusal through due process.[57] In other words, parents have the right to insist that their child not be provided special education and related services even after an evaluation has confirmed that the student is in need of these interventions.

Placement in the Least Restrictive Environment

Students with disabilities must be educated with children without disabilities to the maximum extent appropriate. Special classes, separate schooling, or other removal of a student from general education may occur only if the nature or severity of the disability is such that education cannot be achieved satisfactorily in a general education setting.[58] In making LRE decisions, the IEP team should determine the types of placements for delivery of the IEP along the continuum of alternative placements and then select the option that is least restrictive. Educational and noneducational benefits for each placement should be assessed.[59]

General education with supplemental aids and services represents the LRE for most children (e.g., itinerant teachers, pull-out services, resource rooms). For some students, however, the LRE will be in a setting that is more restrictive (e.g., self-contained special education classrooms).[60] In some instances, it is appropriate to deliver the child's program within a range of LRE settings (e.g., "pull-out" services for speech and language therapy, with the majority of instruction in general education classrooms).[61] Students should not be placed experimentally in the general classroom under the guise of "full inclusion" and then provided appropriate placements only after they fail to acquire an educational benefit.[62] Following an appropriate initial placement, adjustments to a child's IEP may be necessary. Before changing a substantive aspect of a student's program, written notice must be given

---

[57]20 U.S.C. § 1414(a)(1)(D)(ii)(II)–(III) (2018). This differs from the evaluation phase when the district can initiate due process after parental refusal; *see also* K.A. v. Fulton Cty. Sch. Dist., 741 F.3d 1195 (11th Cir. 2013) (holding that IEP team's midyear amendment to IEP did not require parental consent).

[58]20 U.S.C. § 1412(a)(5)(A) (2018). *See, e.g.*, P. v. Newington Bd. of Educ., 546 F.3d 111 (2d Cir. 2008) (upholding district court's ruling that full-time placement in the general education classroom was not appropriate and that spending 74 percent of instructional time in general education classroom was the LRE for this student).

[59]If the parents elect not to have their child medicated while at school, the selection of services and the determination of the LRE may be affected. *See* 20 U.S.C. § 1412(a)(25)(A); *see also* Bd. of Educ. of Twp. High Sch. Dist. v. Ross, 486 F.3d 267 (7th Cir. 2007) (holding that the LRE requirement was met for student whose classroom behavior was disruptive).

[60]LRE could also include even more restrictive placements such as special schools, residential instruction, hospitals, or home instruction. *See, e.g.*, D.S. v. Bayonne Bd. of Educ., 602 F.3d 553 (3d Cir. 2010) (supporting placement of student in more restrictive setting—private school for students with learning disabilities—because student's academic needs were not met in the public school).

[61]*See, e.g.*, J.W. v. Fresno Unified Sch. Dist., 626 F.3d 431 (9th Cir. 2010) (affirming that student's placement in both general education classes and speech-language services was the LRE for that student).

[62]The terms "full inclusion," "mainstreaming," and "LRE" are not synonymous. Full inclusion implies an absolute right to be placed in a general education setting, whereas mainstreaming implies integration of students with and without disabilities. LRE is not a location, but an outcome of a process used to determine placement. Jean Crockett & Mitchell Yell, *IEPs, Least Restrictive Environment, and Placement, in* Shaver & Decker eds., *supra* note 31, at 79.

to the parents of their right to review the proposed alteration, and informed consent generally must be provided.[63]

When parents disagree with a district's placement decision, they may challenge it by filing a due process complaint. Federal courts apply varying frameworks when determining whether challenged placements are in violation of IDEA's LRE requirement because no one national standard exists (see Figure 7.3).[64]

FIGURE 7.3 LRE Tests

Name	Jurisdiction	LRE Test
Daniel R.R. Two-Part Test	Second, Third, Fifth, Tenth, & Eleventh Circuits	Asking: 1) whether education in general education classroom with supplementary aids and services can be achieved satisfactorily, and 2) whether school has integrated the student to the maximum extent appropriate
Rachel H. or *Holland* Four-Pronged Test	Ninth Circuit	Analyzing four factors: 1) educational benefits of the general versus special classroom, 2) nonacademic benefits of interaction of students without disabilities, 3) effect of the student with disability on teacher and other students, and 4) cost of including student with disability in general education setting
Roncker Portability Test	Sixth Circuit	Balancing whether specialized or segregated services could feasibly be provided in an integrated environment
DeVries Three-Part Test	Fourth Circuit	Inclusion in general education setting is not required if: 1) student with a disability would not receive educational benefit, 2) any marginal benefit is significantly outweighed by the benefits in a segregated setting, and 3) student with a disability is a "disruptive force" in the general education setting

[63]If parents do not respond to efforts to communicate, district personnel should document the date and type of each effort and then may proceed to deliver the program as amended. *See* 20 U.S.C. § 1414(e) (2018); 34 C.F.R. § 300.501(a)–(c) (2018).

[64]Daniel R.R. v. State Bd. of Educ., 874 F.2d. 1036 (5th Cir. 1989); Sacramento Cty. Unified Sch. Dist. v. Rachel H., 14 F.3d 1398 (9th Cir 1994); Roncker v. Walter, 700 F.2d 1058 (6th Cir. 1983); DeVries v. Fairfax Cty. Sch. Bd., 882 F.2d 876 (4th Cir. 1989).

Public Placement in a Private School.   Students with disabilities are often educated in private settings. They attend private schools either because (1) the public school district has placed them in a private program due to the lack of an appropriate public school program or (2) parents have unilaterally enrolled their children at private schools based on their preference. When a school district cannot effectively address an individual student's needs, where appropriate programs are not available within a child's reasonable commute, or if existing programs are not age appropriate, IDEA does not require districts to create new programs or schools.[65] Therefore, some students are placed in public schools outside of their home district or in private facilities. Although private placements can be extremely expensive, if the school district has identified that the private placement is necessary to provide a FAPE, the district will be held financially responsible for private placements. In such instances, the district must cover all nonmedical costs, including room and board for residential placements.[66] **Importantly, the private school has no legal obligation to implement special programming because private settings are not bound by IDEA.**[67] Moreover, a private school can deny admission to a student with a disability who cannot participate effectively in the private school's curriculum or programming.

Parental Placement in a Private School.   In other instances, parents elect to unilaterally place their children in private schools (e.g., due to dissatisfaction with public placement or based on religious affiliation). **Parents always have the option of selecting an alternative program, but such placements will be at their expense unless the parents can show that (1) the child has not or would not receive a FAPE in the public placement and (2) the child's selected placement in a private setting is appropriate.** This two-part test is commonly used to analyze whether public school districts must reimburse parents for private school tuition and other expenses.[68] The U.S. Supreme Court has clarified that public districts may be responsible for reimbursing parents for private school tuition even in situations where students seeking reimbursement have never received services at the public school.[69]

---

[65]When students are placed at private schools by public school districts, a private school representative should participate in the IEP meetings to determine placement. Subsequent IEP meetings may be initiated and conducted by private school personnel, if approved by district officials. Where this occurs, both the parents and a public school representative must be involved in any decision about the child's IEP, and the district must authorize any change prior to implementation, 34 C.F.R. § 300.325 (2018).

[66]However, if a residential placement is sought by the parents for reasons other than the child's education, the request may be denied. *See, e.g.*, Ashland Sch. Dist. v. Parents of Student E.H., 587 F.3d 1175 (9th Cir. 2009) (denying reimbursement in residential placement because the placement was for medical reasons).

[67]*See* St. Johnsbury Acad. v. D.H., 240 F.3d 163 (2d Cir. 2001) (discussing how IDEA applies only to the state and other public agencies—*not* to private schools); 34 C.F.R. § 300.2(b)(2).

[68]Florence Cty. Sch. Dist. v. Carter, 510 U.S. 7 (1993) (ruling that reimbursement was warranted where IEP placement in public school was inappropriate and parental placement in private school was appropriate); Sch. Comm. of Burlington v. Dep't of Educ. of Mass., 471 U.S. 359 (1985) (reasoning that children should not be educationally disadvantaged by an inappropriate public school placement and that parents should not be economically penalized for unilaterally enrolling their children at appropriate private settings). *See* 20 U.S.C. § 1412(a)(10)(C)(ii)(2018) (codifying the holdings in *Burlington* and *Carter*); *see also* E.M. v. N.Y.C. Dep't of Educ., 758 F.3d 442 n.13 (2d Cir. 2014) (referencing *Burlington* and *Carter* even after Congress had codified their rulings).

[69]Forest Grove Sch. Dist. v. T.A., 557 U.S. 230 (2009).

Courts may determine, however, that the private setting was not required to provide the child with a FAPE. For example, the Eleventh Circuit denied reimbursement for the parents' residential placement for their son because his public school had provided him with an appropriate IEP. Although the parents' expert opined that the family needed someone to help care for their son outside of school, the court failed to see how home care was an educational need.[70] In contrast, the Second Circuit awarded a mother private school tuition reimbursement because the public school district failed to establish that its proposed IEP would provide her son with a FAPE.[71] Despite the public school's provision of special education, the boy could not read until he was placed in a private school in sixth grade. The court ruled for the mother, explaining that the student's progress in the private school demonstrated the appropriateness of the private placement.[72]

Equitable Services in Private Schools. In situations where parents enroll children at private schools without seeking tuition reimbursement from the public school district, the district must, nevertheless, provide *equitable services* to all eligible students with disabilities attending private schools located within its boundaries. Yet, equitable services are not the same as the services students would receive if they attended public schools; **students enrolled in private schools by their parents have no individual right to receive special education and related services that are equal to what the public school would provide.**[73] Instead, the district must initiate meetings with a private school representative to decide who is to receive services; what, where, and how services are to be provided; and how services are to be evaluated.[74] Thus, unlike in public schools, parents and students do not have rights under IDEA such as procedural safeguards and an entitlement to a FAPE. These equitable service plans are not IEPs; they are simply written statements listing the services that the district will provide to a child, including the location of the services and any transportation necessary. The services provided to students at private schools must be

[70]Devine v. Indian River Cty. Sch. Bd., 249 F.3d 1289 (11th Cir. 2001); *see also* T.F. *ex rel.* G.F. v. Special Sch. Dist., 449 F.3d 816 (8th Cir. 2006) (denying out-of-state residential program reimbursement and noting parents risk that they will not receive reimbursement when they unilaterally enroll children in private settings).

[71]J.D. v. N.Y.C. Dep't of Educ., 677 F. App'x 709 (2d Cir. 2017); *see also* Dallas Indep. Sch. Dist. v. Woody, 865 F.3d 303 (5th Cir. 2017) (holding that student was entitled to private school tuition because district failed to provide a FAPE in a reasonable time after student was experiencing mental health issues).

[72]IDEA permits reduction or denial of reimbursement if parents fail to notify school officials of their intent to enroll the child in a private setting or if a court finds the parents' conduct unreasonable, 20 U.S.C. § 1412(a)(10)(C)(iii) (2018); 34 C.F.R. § 300.148(d) (2018).

[73]34 C.F.R. § 300.137(a) (2018); *see also* 34 C.F.R. § 300.37 (2018) (defining equitable services plan). When parents with children in private schools have challenged this disparity, they have generally been unsuccessful. *See* Gary S. *ex rel.* Andrew S. v. Manchester Sch. Dist., 374 F.3d 15, 17 (1st Cir. 2004) (discussing how a private school student "is not entitled by law to the panoply of services available to disabled public school students under the rubric of [FAPE], nor to the due process hearing provided to public school students alone"). *But see* Special Sch. Dist. v. R.M.M. *ex rel.* O.M., 861 F.3d 76 (8th Cir. 2017) (holding that Minnesota law entitled a private school student a FAPE and the right to an impartial due process hearing).

[74]IDEA provides funding for equitable services at a per-pupil prorated amount equal to the federal funds provided for IEP services in the public school district, 20 U.S.C. § 1412(a)(10)(A)(i)(I) (2018).

provided by the public school's employees or contracted to others who can provide special education. For example, the public district may provide speech therapy to a student at a parochial school, but the services must be "secular, neutral, and nonideological."[75]

Related Services and Supplemental Aids

When related services and supplemental aids are found to be essential elements of a FAPE, they must be provided regardless of cost. Related services are defined as transportation and developmental, corrective, and other supportive services necessary for a child with a disability to benefit from special education (e.g., speech pathology and audiology, physical and occupational therapy, behavioral consultation, and parent counseling and training).[76] Supplementary aids and services are tied to placement decisions because removal of students with disabilities from the regular educational environment is to occur only "if the nature or severity of the disability is such that education in regular classes with the use of *supplementary aids and services* cannot be achieved satisfactorily."[77] Thus, aids and services could include paraprofessionals, sign language interpreters, and regularly scheduled collaboration among staff members to ensure a student has access to the general education curriculum. Where appropriate, a school must also provide a student with assistive technology devices and services to enable the child to increase, maintain, or improve functional capabilities.[78] Although many other aids and services are possible, the areas of transportation, psychological services, health services, and extended school year services are reviewed briefly here.

Transportation.   Federal regulations require schools to provide transportation for qualified students to and from school, within school buildings, and on school grounds, even if specialized equipment is needed in making programs and activities accessible.[79] A student qualifies for transportation if it is provided for other students or if it is included as part of an IEP.[80] When districts have failed to provide transportation to qualified students, courts have ordered districts to reimburse parents for transportation costs, time, effort, and babysitting services.[81] Nonetheless, courts also have concluded that where alternative

[75]34 C.F.R. § 300.138(c)(2); *see also* 20 U.S.C. § 1412(a)(10)(A)(i),(iii) (2018).

[76]20 U.S.C. § 1401(26)(A), (33)(A) (2018).

[77]34 C.F.R. § 300.114(a)(2)(ii) (2018) (emphasis added).

[78]20 U.S.C. §§ 1401(34), 1414(d)(1)(A)(i)(VIII).

[79]34 C.F.R. § 300.34(c)(16) (2018). *See, e.g.,* Ruby v. Jefferson Cty. Bd. of Educ., 122 F. Supp. 3d 1288 (N.D. Ala. 2015) (holding that a district that secured transportation with nursing services within sixty-two days of a student's transfer from another state was clearly reasonable).

[80]Transportation can also be included as part of equitable services or § 504 plans. *See* text accompanying note 133 for discussion of § 504 plans.

[81]*See, e.g.,* Taylor *ex rel.* Holbrook v. Bd. of Educ., 649 F. Supp. 1253 (N.D.N.Y. 1986) (requiring district to reimburse for babysitting costs).

transportation was provided, the district was not required to reimburse parents who wanted to transport their own child.[82]

Psychological Services. Psychological services are explicitly identified in federal law as related services to be included within IEPs where appropriate. Such services include:

- administering and interpreting psychological and educational tests as well as other assessment procedures;
- obtaining, integrating, and interpreting information about the child's behavior and conditions related to learning;
- consulting with staff in planning IEPs;
- planning and managing a program of psychological services; and
- assisting in the development of positive behavioral intervention strategies.[83]

When psychological services are needed to help the child to benefit from instruction, the services should be included within the IEP. However, if psychiatric or psychological services are not required to provide a FAPE, such requests may be denied.[84]

Health Services. Courts have differentiated between medical services and health services. Under IDEA, school districts are not required to provide medical services (i.e., those provided by a licensed physician) except for diagnostic and evaluative purposes. But districts must provide health services (i.e., those provided by a nurse or other qualified person) if those services enable the child to attend school and thereby benefit from instruction.[85]

In 1984, the Supreme Court, in *Irving Independent School District v. Tatro*, found a child's need for catheterization to be an essential health service because it would enable the child to attend school and thereby benefit from instruction.[86] Accordingly, the service was not a medical service because a nurse or a trained layperson could perform the procedure, and therefore it belonged in the child's IEP. In post-*Tatro* years, the issue of health care has been volatile given the growing number of medically fragile students in schools, the legal requirement to mainstream them into general education, and the escalating costs of health care. In *Cedar Rapids Community School District v. Garret F.*, a child had a severed spinal

[82]*See also* Roslyn Union Free Sch. Dist. v. Univ. of N.Y., 711 N.Y.S.2d 582 (App. Div. 2000) (holding that transportation was not required at the conclusion of a privately funded after-school program that was not a part of the student's IEP).

[83]34 C.F.R. § 300.34(c)(10) (2018).

[84]*See* Richardson Indep. Sch. Dist. v. Michael Z., 580 F.3d 286 (5th Cir. 2009) (remanding case to determine whether residential psychiatric treatment was necessary for student to receive a FAPE). *But see* Stanton *ex rel.* K.T. v. Dist. of Columbia, 680 F. Supp. 2d 201 (D.D.C. 2010) (holding that student with a mixed anxiety depressive disorder and learning disability was entitled to compensatory education after district failed to provide counseling for five months).

[85]Courts face difficulties determining whether a service is medically versus educationally necessary, but some courts have found that medically necessary services may also be necessary for students to benefit from special education. *See* Douglas v. Cal. Office of Admin. Hearings, 650 F. App'x 312 (9th Cir. 2016).

[86]468 U.S. 883 (1984).

column and was paralyzed from the neck down.[87] To remain in school, he required full-time nursing care. The school district argued that the services collectively should be viewed as medical, even if individually they qualified as health services, and asserted that it would incur an undue financial burden if required to provide the services. The Supreme Court acknowledged the legitimate financial concerns of the district but rejected the undue burden claim.[88] **In applying a bright-line test, the Court ruled that any health service students need to help integrate them into public schools had to be provided, regardless of cost or resulting financial impact on the district.**

Extended School Year Services.   While school districts can prescribe a fixed number of instructional days for students without disabilities, students with disabilities may be entitled to receive extended school year (ESY) services.[89] These services entail special education and related services that are provided beyond the normal school year, typically during the summer. A district must only provide ESY services if they are "essential" for a student to receive a FAPE; they cannot be used to provide a student with greater benefit or be used as childcare services.[90]

IEP teams determine ESY services on a case-by-case basis, and thus, ESY services vary widely based on individual needs. Some students require the full IEP to be provided during school breaks; other students only need a fraction of the services to be provided (e.g., speech therapy). IDEA does not require that IEP teams follow a specific procedure when determining whether a student is eligible for ESY services;[91] however, IEP teams must determine eligibility annually. They should also consult state law to ensure they are following additional state requirements.[92] **School districts must not limit ESY services based on the category of disability and cannot limit the "type, amount, or duration" of ESY services.**[93] Past courts have used a variety of factors when determining whether a student with a disability is entitled to ESY services including regression-recoupment[94] and evi-

[87]526 U.S. 66 (1999).

[88]Although unavailable under IDEA, the undue burden defense is available under both § 504 and the ADA. *See, e.g.*, Greer v. Richardson Indep. Sch. Dist., 472 F. App'x 287 (5th Cir. 2012). *See infra* text accompanying note 118, discussing § 504 and the ADA.

[89]34 C.F.R. § 300.106 (2018).

[90]*See* N.B. v. Hellgate Elementary Sch. Dist. *ex rel.* Bd. of Dirs. 541 F.3d 1202 (9th Cir. 2008) (noting that ESY is required only when the child's gains from the school year would be significantly jeopardized without ESY).

[91]*See id.* (explaining that because IDEA regulations do not list required factors to consider; district court did not apply incorrect regression-recoupment standard).

[92]*See* Meghan Burke & Janet Decker, *Extended School Year: Legal and Practical Considerations for Educators*, 49 TEACHING EXCEPTIONAL CHILDREN 339 (2017) (providing a table that lists every state statute/regulation, eligibility determination, and state guidance).

[93]34 C.F.R. § 300.106(a)(3).

[94]"Regression" refers to the loss of knowledge a student may experience during a break in instruction, and "recoupment" refers to the time it takes to regain the knowledge that was lost. *See, e.g.*, Battle v. Penn., 629 F.2d 269 (3d Cir. 1980) (noting that students with disabilities are more likely to regress over school breaks and to be unable to recoup the skills they lost). *But see* Cordrey v. Euckert, 917 F.2d 1460 (6th Cir. 1990) (finding that proof of regression was unnecessary; instead, a professional can assess a student's need).

dence of progress toward IEP goals.[95] If the IEP team determines the student is entitled to ESY services, it should ensure services will be provided in the LRE and should list the type, amount, and duration of ESY services in the IEP.[96]

Procedural Safeguards and Parent Involvement

In addition to the substantive entitlements to which students with disabilities are entitled, IDEA guarantees numerous procedural protections. Many of these safeguards are tied directly to IDEA's mandate that parents must be included as IEP team members and participate in the educational decision-making process for their child. **If a disagreement arises between the parents and the district about the provision of special education and related services, both parties have the option to file a due process complaint with the state education agency.**[97]

Due Process Generally.   Disagreements may arise with evaluation, program, discipline, or placement decisions. Understandably, many parents seek the best possible education for their children; yet school districts may offer what parents perceive as only a minimally appropriate program. Where disagreement persists, IDEA has provided a variety of dispute resolution processes by which parents or school districts may seek third-party, administrative review.[98]

Figure 7.4 provides a chart of the complaint procedures. At a minimum, schools should provide a copy of the IDEA procedural safeguards to parents at least once a year, but schools must also provide a copy at the initial referral, after a request for an evaluation, upon the filing a complaint, or any time parents request a copy.[99] Moreover, during IDEA appeals, the student remains in the current placement until all dispute resolution processes have been completed (referred to as "stay-put").[100]

---

[95]*See* Johnson v. Indep. Sch. Dist., 921 F.2d 1022 (10th Cir. 1990) (emphasizing the need for IEP teams to analyze multiple criteria, not merely regression-recoupment); Alamo Heights Indep. Sch. Dist. v. State Bd. of Educ., 790 F.2d 1153, 1158 (5th Cir. 1986) (noting that a student's progress would not need to come to a "virtual standstill" to require ESY services; instead, one should analyze "whether the benefits accrued to the child during the regular school year will be significantly jeopardized").

[96]*See* T.M. v. Cornwall Cent. Sch. Dist., 752 F.3d 145 (2d Cir. 2014) (reasoning that district was to provide ESY services in a general education class despite district's argument that general education classes were not part of its existing ESY program).

[97]Disputes may arise prior to the provision of special education. *See, e.g.,* L.J. *ex rel.* Hudson v. Pittsburg Unified Sch. Dist., 850 F.3d 996 (9th Cir. 2017) (holding that district violated procedural protections by failing to provide parents with education records, including assessments, treatment plans, and progress notes).

[98]*See* 20 U.S.C. § 1414(f)(3)(C) (2018) (requiring that a parent or school district must request a due process hearing within two years of when the party knew or should have known about the alleged action that forms the basis of the complaint). If a parent refuses to consent to *portions of an IEP* (e.g., placement only), some states require the district to initiate the due process hearing request. *See, e.g.,* I.R. *ex rel.* E.N. v. L.A. Unified Sch. Dist., 805 F.3d 1164 (9th Cir. 2015) (holding that district's delay of more than eighteen months to initiate a due process hearing following mother's refusal to agree with IEP was unreasonable).

[99]20 U.S.C. § 1415(d)(1)(A); (f)(1)(A) (2018).

[100]20 U.S.C. § 1415(j), (k)(4)(A) (2018).

FIGURE 7.4   IDEA Administrative Complaint Procedure

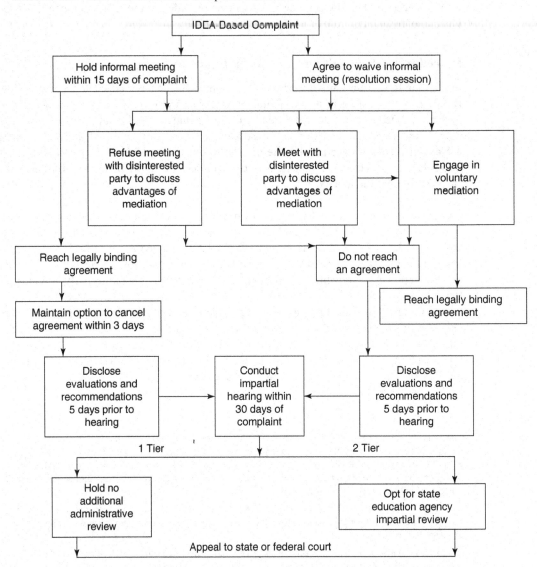

The state education agency must offer mediation at no cost to the parents in an effort to resolve disputes quickly and in a less adversarial manner.[101] Participation is voluntary and is not always selected. When a dispute is not resolved through a legally

---

[101]20 U.S.C. § 1415(f)(1)(B) (2018). State and local education agencies may also establish procedures that offer the opportunity for parties to meet with a disinterested party who is not a mediator, *id.* at § 1415(e)(2)(B). For example, facilitated IEP meetings can be requested by either party and include a neutral third party who facilitates the IEP meeting. *See* Susan Bon, *Procedural Safeguards: Resolving Family-School Disputes, in* Shaver & Decker eds., *supra* note 31.

binding settlement agreement, it proceeds to a due process hearing. This hearing is either conducted by the state or local education agency and must be presided over by an impartial hearing officer. Prior to the hearing, the parties participate in a resolution session, but can agree in writing to waive this meeting. At the due process hearing, the burden of persuasion is on the party seeking relief, and the hearing officer's opinion must be based only on evidence presented by the parties.[102] When the impartial hearing is conducted at the local level, the decision may be appealed to the state. The state-level reviewer must make an independent decision and provide the parties with written findings. **Prior to filing an IDEA lawsuit in state or federal court, parents are required to *exhaust administrative remedies* (i.e., they must have adhered to all of these dispute resolution procedures).**[103]

Due Process in Discipline.   In addition to these methods of dispute resolution, school districts must adhere to special procedures when disciplining students with disabilities. In 1988, the Supreme Court in *Honig v. Doe* held that an indefinite suspension of two students with disabilities was a prohibited change in placement and violated the stay-put provision of IDEA.[104] The teenage boys, both diagnosed with emotional disturbance, were awaiting their expulsion hearings. The district argued that schools needed a "dangerousness" exception to the stay-put provision in order to remove students with disabilities who were violent or disruptive. But the Court disagreed, reasoning that Congress purposely omitted a dangerousness exception in IDEA, and the Court would not infer one considering that one goal of IDEA was to address the long history of past systemic exclusion of students with disabilities in public schools.

Honig clarified that districts must follow heightened due process procedures when removing students with disabilities from their educational placements. It is important to note, however, that students with disabilities are not exempt from reasonable discipline. Instead, they are afforded a layer of due process protections to ensure that they are not removed from schools unfairly.[105] In the years following *Honig*, Congress amended IDEA by providing additional guidelines for schools to help them navigate what they must do when disciplining students with disabilities (and ultimately, added a dangerousness exception).

---

[102]*See* Schaffer v. Weast, 546 U.S. 49 (2005); 20 U.S.C. § 1415(f)(2)(A).

[103]24 U.S.C. § 1415(l) (2018). *See, e.g.,* J.M. v. Francis Howell Sch. Dist., 850 F.3d 944 (8th Cir. 2017) (holding that mother must exhaust IDEA's administrative remedies because exhaustion was not futile; claims about restraint and seclusion pertained to IEP).

[104]484 U.S. 305 (1988).

[105]*See* U.S. Dep't of Educ. Office for Civil Rights, *Civil Rights Data Collection, Data Snapshot: School Discipline* (Mar. 2014), http://www2.ed.gov/about/offices/list/ocr/docs/crdc-discipline-snapshot.pdf (identifying numerous inequities, including suspension rates for students with disabilities that were twice as high (13 percent) as students without disabilities (6 percent) and students with disabilities represented only 12 percent of the student population; however, nearly 60 percent of students placed in seclusion and 75 percent of those who were physically restrained at school were students with disabilities).

Ten-Day Rule. Because the *Honig* Court clarified that a ten-day removal constituted a change in placement, districts must be vigilant in tracking students with disabilities who may be removed from school for more than ten days a principle sometimes referred to as the "ten-day rule." When officials determine that a *suspension* (i.e., removal of a student from the educational setting for ten or fewer days) is justified, no procedures beyond those that apply to general education students are required.

Any time the student has been removed from the IEP, it is considered a change of placement. Thus, when determining what constitutes a suspension, the key question is not necessarily whether the child has received an in-school or out-of-school suspension.[106] If a student is assigned to in-school suspension and instruction and services identified within the IEP do not continue to be delivered by properly credentialed individuals, the time the student is removed from the general education classroom will probably contribute to the ten-day limit.[107] **When students with disabilities are removed from the educational setting (and thus from their special education and related services) for *more than* ten days during the school year, a Manifestation Determination Review (MDR) must occur**. The removal for more than ten days may occur consecutively or when the student has received repetitive brief suspensions that aggregate to more than ten days.[108]

Manifestation Determination Review. The MDR is an informal meeting that must occur within ten days of the student being removed. It is conducted by the district and includes the parents and relevant members of the student's IEP team. **The purpose of the MDR is to evaluate (1) whether the student's conduct was caused by or had a direct and substantial relationship to the student's disability or (2) whether the student's conduct was the direct result of the school district's failure to implement the IEP**.

If the IEP team determines that the misbehavior *was* related to or caused by the student's disability, then the student *cannot* be removed from his or her educational placement for more than ten days. **In these situations where the behavior was a manifestation of the student's disability, the IEP team must ensure that a functional behavioral assessment (FBA) is conducted and a behavior intervention plan (BIP) is implemented**.[109]

---

[106]34 C.F.R. § 300.536(a).

[107]Additionally, legal violations may occur when students are placed in time-out instead of in-school suspension. *See, e.g.,* H.M. v. Bd. of Educ. of the Kings Local Sch. Dist., 2015 WL 4624629 (S.D. Ohio July 27, 2015) (holding school's placement of student in bathroom and janitor's hallway stated a claim for unreasonable seizure); U.S. Dep't of Educ. Office for Civil Rights, *Dear Colleague Letter: Restraint and Seclusion of Students with Disabilities* (Dec. 28, 2016), https://www2.ed.gov/about/offices/list/ocr/letters/colleague-201612-504-restraint-seclusion-ps.pdf.

[108]34 C.F.R. §300.536.

[109]20 U.S.C. § 1415(k)(1)(F)(i) (2018). The PBIS requirements differ during MDRs versus nondisciplinary situations. In these situations when a student's behavior impedes learning, the IEP team *may consider* the use of behavioral interventions. *See* Metro. Bd. of Pub. Educ. v. Bellamy, 116 F. App'x 570 (6th Cir. 2004) (affirming that school's failure to develop a behavior plan contributed to a denial of FAPE). *But see* J.S. v. N.Y.C. Dep't of Educ., 104 F. Supp. 3d 392 (S.D.N.Y. 2015) (holding district's failure to provide FBA and BIP did not constitute a FAPE violation), *aff'd*, 648 F. App'x 96 (2d Cir. 2016). State and district policy regarding MDR timelines may differ (i.e., may require MDR if student will be suspended under ten days).

In situations where the student already has a BIP in place, the IEP team should review and modify it as necessary to address the behavior at issue. If the IEP team decides that the student's conduct *was not* linked to the student's disability, then the student's placement can be changed for more than ten days. In the circumstance where removal justifiably exceeds the ten-day limit, the student's special education and related services must be provided beginning the eleventh day.[110] Stated differently, **educational services cannot be terminated for students with disabilities for longer than ten days**.

When students are removed for more than ten consecutive days, it is considered an *expulsion*. Assuming that the expulsion is supported—meaning that the conduct was *not* a manifestation of the disability and the district did properly implement the student's IEP—the student may be assigned either to a home placement or to an interim alternative educational setting (IAES).[111] An expelled student's services consistent with the IEP must be delivered in the new environment to enable the student to make progress toward achieving identified goals and objectives. These services are required regardless of whether the behavior was disability-related.

In the years after *Honig*, Congress added dangerousness or emergency exceptions to IDEA permitting school personnel to *immediately* remove a student with a disability for up to forty-five days to an IAES. This immediate removal is permitted if the student commits one of the following violations on school grounds or at a school function:

- carries a weapon;
- knowingly possesses, uses, sells, or solicits illegal drugs; or
- inflicts serious bodily injury upon another.[112]

Therefore, when safety is jeopardized, the ten-day rule does not need to be followed; the student with a disability can be removed immediately. Within ten days of that removal, however, the child's IEP team must meet to conduct the MDR and make a decision regarding the IAES. Additionally, school personnel are permitted to consider any "unique circumstances on a case-by-case basis when determining whether to order a change of placement" for a student who has violated a code of student conduct.[113] If the parents disagree with a decision to remove their child from school, they may appeal that decision to a hearing officer.

IDEA also stipulates that nothing in the law prohibits school personnel from contacting law enforcement to report any crime a student with a disability may have committed.[114] Law enforcement officials are not bound by IDEA and may require an unruly or delinquent student to submit to treatment, home detention, or incarceration—in addition to any penalty the district may provide. School officials should, however, consider providing school

[110]34 C.F.R. § 300.530(a)–(e), 300.536.

[111]*See* 20 U.S.C. § 1415(k)(1).

[112]20 U.S.C. § 1415(k)(1)(G).

[113]20 U.S.C. § 1415(k)(1)(a).

[114]20 U.S.C. §1415(k)(6)(A). *But see* text accompanying note 142, Chapter 8 for discussion of police involvement in schools.

resource officers with training about students with disabilities and about special education law in order to prevent potential legal violations.[115]

Unidentified Students with Disabilities.   Interestingly, some students who do not have an IEP in place may, nevertheless, be eligible for IDEA's discipline protections. For example, an Ohio federal court determined that a third grader who had Attention Deficit Hyperactivity Disorder (ADHD) should have received an MDR before her expulsion.[116] The student's teachers were aware of her academic and behavioral needs and were implementing RtI strategies to address them, but the district had not determined that the student should be evaluated for special education. The court reasoned, reasoning that the school officials had sufficient reason to suspect the student was in need of special education when they referred her to an outside mental health agency. This case illustrates that MDRs may be required if school officials had "knowledge" that the students might have a disability. Knowledge exists where parents request an evaluation or express in writing to administrative or supervisory personnel a concern that their child may be in need of special education. Knowledge also may be established where an educator expresses concern about a student's behavior directly to supervisory personnel. Note that the student is not entitled to IDEA protection in a given disciplinary hearing if:

- the child was found not to qualify as disabled given the results of an expedited evaluation;
- the parents did not allow the district to conduct the evaluation; or
- the parents previously refused IDEA services.[117]

When the issue is raised as to whether a student who has been expelled is entitled to an MDR, the district must first establish whether the suspected student does, in fact, have an eligible disability and is in need of special education. If a post-discipline evaluation of a student suspected of having a disability reveals that the student qualifies under IDEA, then special education consistent with the newly developed IEP must be provided no later than practical and feasible, preferably no later than the tenth day of removal.

SECTION 504 AND THE AMERICANS WITH DISABILITIES ACT

Section 504 applies only to public and private schools that *receive federal funding*, whereas the ADA applies to *almost every* public and private school.

In addition to understanding IDEA, educators must also be well versed in how Section 504 and the ADA protect students with disabilities. Together, these two federal statutes prohibit

[115]*See, e.g.*, S.R. v. Kenton Cty. Sheriff's Office, 2017 WL 4545231 (E.D. Ky. Oct. 11, 2017) (holding that a school resource officer who handcuffed two elementary children with disabilities had seized the students and used excessive force in violation of the Fourth Amendment).

[116]Jackson v. Nw. Local Sch. Dist., 2010 WL 3452333 (S.D. Ohio Aug. 3, 2010).

[117]20 U.S.C. § 1415(k)(5).

disability-based discrimination in public and private schools as well as other contexts. Section 504 stipulates that otherwise qualified individuals shall not be excluded from participating in, be denied the benefits of, or be subjected to discrimination by recipient programs or activities if that treatment is due to their disabilities.[118]

Although Section 504 applies more directly to public schools, courts have ruled that the ADA should be interpreted similarly to Section 504.[119] Two titles of the ADA are of particular importance to students with disabilities: Title II applies to public schools, and Title III applies to private schools.[120] Like Section 504, these titles prohibit discrimination against persons (birth to death) who have a disability. Unlike Section 504, the ADA requires compliance of schools that do not receive federal aid and were not heretofore federally regulated.

Eligibility

Students with disabilities who are eligible under IDEA are also protected by Section 504 and the ADA, and students with disabilities who are ineligible under IDEA are protected by Section 504 and the ADA as long as they meet the eligibility requirements for these two laws. **Under Section 504 and the ADA, an individual with a disability is one who has a physical or mental impairment that substantially limits one or more major life activities, has a record of impairment, or is regarded as having an impairment.**[121] These latter two definitions (i.e., "record of" and "regarded as") apply when a person has been subjected to discrimination, such as a student who was excluded from school for being perceived as having cystic fibrosis[122] or a student who was wrongfully placed in special education because she was inaccurately regarded as having a disability.[123] However, only those students who meet the first definition—having an impairment that is substantially limiting—will be eligible for reasonable accommodations and modifications.[124] Accommodations for students under Section 504 may include increased time to complete assignments or reduction of classroom distractions. Thus, students who qualify under Section 504 are entitled to a FAPE that is similar to but not exactly the same as a FAPE under IDEA.[125]

---

[118]*See* 29 U.S.C. § 794(a) (2018).

[119]*See* 28 C.F.R. § 35.103(a) (2018); 29 U.S.C. § 705(20)(B).

[120]42 U.S.C. §§ 12101–12213 (2018).

[121]*See* 29 U.S.C. § 705(20)(B) (2018) (citing 42 U.S.C. § 12102(1) (2018)); 34 C.F.R. § 104.3(j)(2)(i) (2018). Section 504 adopts the ADA's definition of "disability." *See* Adams v. Rice, 531 F.3d 936 (D.C. Cir. 2008).

[122]Chadam v. Palo Alto Unified Sch. Dist., 666 F. App'x 615 (9th Cir. 2016); *see also* Sch. Bd. v. Arline, 480 U.S. 273, 281 (1987) (concluding that a teacher suffering from tuberculosis had a "record . . . of impairment" because she was hospitalized for her illness; thus, she qualified as an individual with a disability).

[123]S.H. v. Lower Merion Sch. Dist., 729 F.3d 248 (3d Cir. 2013); *see also* Ray v. Sch. Dist., 666 F. Supp. 1524 (M.D. Fla. 1987) (holding § 504 was proper authority when parents filed a lawsuit because their sons were excluded from school for being HIV positive).

[124]*See* 28 C.F.R. § 35.130(b)(7)(ii).

[125]*See* Ridley Sch. Dist. v. M.R., 680 F.3d 260 (3d Cir. 2012) (determining that a FAPE was provided under § 504 where district reasonably accommodated the needs of a student).

Students who have serious illnesses such as epilepsy, heart disease, mental health issues, or allergies may not commonly be thought of as having a disability; however, these students may qualify under the broad definition of Section 504 and the ADA. Congress expanded the definition of disability in the ADA Amendments Act of 2008, stipulating that the definition of disability should be "construed broadly."[126] For example, reading and concentration were added to the examples of major life activities that are covered by the Act. Further, the 2008 amendments specified that the "ameliorative effects of mitigating measures," such as medication, prosthetic limbs, hearing aids, and use of technology, should not be considered when determining whether an impairment substantially limits a major life activity. Thus, students who have allergies that substantially limit a major life activity (e.g., concentrating) may be eligible even though they receive allergy shots. However, the 2008 amendments clarified that a student with a temporary impairment (i.e., one that has an actual or expected duration of six months or less) that is also minor cannot qualify as being regarded as having a disability.

To determine whether the disability *substantially limits a major life activity*,[127] courts compare the performance difficulties of the student with those of the theoretical "average person" in the general population. **To qualify, the student will have to be either incapable of performing the designated activity or significantly restricted in such performance; merely functioning below average will be insufficient**. This assessment requires a case-by-case evaluation because impairments will vary in severity, will affect people differently, and may or may not be restricting given the nature of the life activity.[128] As a result, some students with physical or mental impairments will be substantially limited, and others with the same diagnosis will not; only the former qualify as disabled under Section 504/ADA. Failure to recognize the fact that Section 504/ADA provides protection only for persons who are disabled—and not for those who are merely impaired—can lead to the overclassification of students. This could result in increased administrative and instructional costs, greater parental expectations for programming, and the increased likelihood of litigation.

Disability-Based Discrimination

When students' limitations qualify as disabilities under Section 504, it still is necessary to determine whether they were excluded from participating in school programs or activities, denied benefits, or discriminated against "solely by reason of" their disabilities.[129] Discrimination may occur when students with disabilities are segregated or receive inferior or different treatment when compared to their peers without disabilities. For example,

---

[126]42 U.S.C §§ 12101–12102 (2018); *see also* U.S. Dep't of Educ., Office for Civil Rights, *Questions and Answers on the ADA Amendments Act of 2008 for Students with Disabilities Attending Public Elementary and Secondary Schools* (Jan. 19, 2012), http://www2.ed.gov/about/offices/list/ocr/docs/dcl-504faq-201109.html.

[127]"Major life activities" include caring for oneself, performing manual tasks, walking, seeing, hearing, speaking, breathing, learning, and working, 34 C.F.R. § 104.3(j)(2)(ii) (2018).

[128]*See, e.g.*, Smith v. Tangipahoa Par. Sch. Bd., 2006 U.S. Dist. LEXIS 85377 (E.D. La. Nov. 22, 2006) (finding student's severe allergy was not an impairment that substantially limited her ability to learn).

[129]29 U.S.C. § 794(a) (2018).

discrimination claims could be alleged by a student with diabetes who was not provided access to his insulin;[130] a student in a wheelchair who was frequently isolated from his classroom and peers;[131] or a student with autism who was harassed so severely by his class-mates that the hostile environment limited his ability to receive a FAPE.[132]

Students who qualify under Section 504, but not under IDEA (e.g., students with health impairments who are not in need of special education) should be provided with accommodation plans—commonly referred to as Section 504 plans—that will include individualized aids and services that allow participation in the school's educational program, but they are not eligible for IEPs.[133] For example, a Section 504 plan for a student diagnosed with ADHD may not be needed for academic issues but may provide social skill training or behavioral support. The programs must be delivered in accessible facilities,[134] and programming must be designed and selected to meet the needs of students with disabilities to the same extent that their nondisabled peers' needs are met.[135] Furthermore, students with disabilities should not be segregated from other students except for the rare occasion that appropriate services cannot otherwise be provided in the general education classroom. Where such segregation exists, programs must be comparable in materials, facilities, teacher quality, length of school term, and daily hours of instruction.[136]

Complaints and Remedies

The Department of Education's Office for Civil Rights (OCR) and sometimes the Department of Justice (DOJ) are the federal agencies that oversee the enforcement of Section 504 and the ADA in PK–12 schools. When the school district and the parents disagree on whether an appropriate education has been provided, the parents have the right to review records, participate in an impartial hearing, and be represented by counsel. Section 504 is not specific as to the procedures that must be followed, but it does acknowledge that providing notice and hearing rights comparable to those mandated under IDEA will suffice. In addition, parents have the right to file a complaint with the OCR or DOJ within 180 days of the alleged discrimination.[137] Where an investigation determines that the school district is in violation of the law, federal regulations allow for informal negotiations and for the

---

[130]*See* CTL v. Ashland Sch. Dist. 743 F.3d 524 (7th Cir. 2014).

[131]*See* J.S. *ex rel.* J.S. v. Hous. Cty. Bd. of Educ., 877 F.3d 979 (11th Cir. 2017).

[132]*See* Preston v. Hilton Cent. Sch. Dist., 876 F. Supp. 2d 235 (W.D.N.Y. 2012); U.S. Dep't of Educ., *Dear Colleague Letter: Responding to Bullying of Students with Disabilities* (Oct. 21, 2014), https://www2.ed.gov/about/offices/list/ocr/letters/colleague-bullying-201410.pdf.

[133]*See* 34 C.F.R. § 104.33(b)(1) (stating that FAPE shall be provided through individualized "regular or special education and related aids and services"). Furthermore, it is the position of the Office for Civil Rights that a student who qualifies under IDEA is not entitled also to receive a plan formulated consistent with the provisions of § 504. *Letter to McKethan*, 25 IDELR 295 (OCR Dec. 31, 1996).

[134]34 C.F.R. § 104.22(a). To comply, a recipient need not make each existing facility or every part of a facility accessible, but must operate its programs so that they are accessible to individuals with disabilities. *Id.*

[135]*See* 34 C.F.R. § 104.4(b)(2) (describing that supplemental aids and services "are not required to produce the identical result or level of achievement" for students with and without disabilities).

[136]*See* 34 C.F.R. § 104.34(a)(c).

[137]28 C.F.R. § 35.170(b) (2018).

school district to voluntarily become compliant. If the school district fails to correct its discriminatory practices, federal funds may be terminated.[138]

There is a private right of action (e.g., the right to sue) under Section 504 and the ADA, although IDEA exhaustion requirements may need to be met if the relief sought also is available under IDEA.[139] In 2017, the U.S. Supreme Court in *Fry v. Napoleon* held that if a lawsuit is brought under Section 504 or the ADA and the remedy sought is not for the denial of a FAPE, then exhaustion of IDEA's administrative remedies is not required.[140] The substance of the plaintiff's complaint is analyzed to determine whether the plaintiff is seeking relief for a FAPE violation. In lawsuits claiming a 504/ADA violation, immunity defenses under the Eleventh Amendment will not likely be accepted, and attorneys' fees may be awarded to prevailing plaintiffs.[141] In addition, to recover damages, plaintiffs must demonstrate bad faith or gross misjudgment.[142]

Other Issues

Although many topics pertaining to students with disabilities implicate IDEA as well, lawsuits about service animals and participation in sports have commonly been filed under Section 504 or the ADA.

Service Animals.   The Supreme Court case that was previously discussed, *Fry v. Napoleon*, involved an elementary school's refusal to allow a student with severe cerebral palsy to be accompanied by her service dog to help her with activities like opening doors and retrieving dropped items.[143] The Court did not focus on whether exclusion of the dog was disability discrimination, but many lower courts have analyzed this issue.

Parents may request that service animals be incorporated in their child's IEP as a related service under the IDEA, but typically service animal lawsuits involve Section 504/ADA claims. For example, a mother of a kindergarten student requested that the school district allow her child to be accompanied by a service dog who could alert and protect her son when he had seizures.[144] The mother claimed that the district violated Section 504 and the ADA by implementing procedural barriers to limit the access of the boy's dog in the classroom. A Florida federal court denied the district's motion for summary judgment, reasoning that the mother's requested accommodations were reasonable.

Yet courts have also rejected students' service animal requests. A New Hampshire federal district court held that a school's service animal policy did not violate the ADA.[145]

---

[138]*See* 34 C.F.R. § 100.8–100.9 (2018).

[139]*See* Everett H. v. Dry Creek Joint Elementary Sch. Dist., 5 F. Supp. 3d 1184 (E.D. Cal. 2014).

[140]137 S. Ct. 743 (2017); *see also* Martha McCarthy, Fry v. Napoleon Community Schools: *Could This Supreme Court Decision Open a Pandora's Box?* 344 EDUC. L. REP. 18 (2017).

[141]42 U.S.C § 20000d-7 (2018). See, e.g., Bowers v. NCAA, 475 F.3d 524 (3d Cir. 2007).

[142]*See, e.g.,* K.D. v. Starr, 55 F. Supp. 3d 782 (D. Md. 2014).

[143]Fry v. Napoleon Cmty Schs., 137 S. Ct. 743 (2017).

[144]Alboniga v. Sch. Bd. of Broward Cty., 87 F. Supp. 3d 1319 (S.D. Fla. 2015).

[145]Riley v. Sch. Admin. Unit #23, 2015 WL 9806795 (D.N.H. Dec. 21, 2015).

Specifically, a second-grade student sought to be accompanied by her service dog to alert the student of seizures. But unlike the student in the Florida case, the student here could not serve as the dog's handler, which meant the school would have to supervise the dog. The court reasoned that this was in contradiction to the ADA regulations and the student's requests for modifications were not reasonable.

Participation in Sports. Another commonly litigated issue gained national attention after a 2010 governmental report found that students with disabilities were not being afforded an equal opportunity to participate in school-sponsored athletics. In response, the Department of Education released a Dear Colleague Letter instructing schools of their legal obligations under IDEA, Section 504, and the ADA.[146] The guidance stressed that students with disabilities who are otherwise qualified must not be excluded from extracurricular athletics, including club, intermural, or interscholastic athletics. Schools are not required to include students with disabilities in athletics unless they meet the skill or ability required of the sport. Yet the selection or competition criteria must not be discriminatory. For example, athletic programs must not rely on assumptions, generalizations, or stereotypes about students' capabilities.[147]

To adhere to their legal obligations, athletic programs need not lower the hoop, widen the goal, or otherwise alter an essential element of the sport. Instead, they must evaluate any rule that disqualifies an otherwise qualified participant with a disability. If the rules are not essential features of the sport, then they should be altered or eliminated to meet the needs of individuals with disabilities. To illustrate, in a nonschool case, *PGA Tour v. Martin*, the Supreme Court held that a professional golfer should be permitted to ride in a golf cart rather than walk the course, which contradicted what the rules required.[148] Because of the golfer's disability, walking could lead to hemorrhaging and the development of blood clots or fractures. The Court reasoned that "shot making" was the essence of golf and that walking was neither an essential attribute nor an indispensable feature of the sport.

When reviewing athletic rules, school districts and athletic associations should examine whether facially neutral regulations are disproportionately affecting students with disabilities, such as age limitations, grade-point average restrictions, one-year residency and transfer requirements, and eight-semester/four-season limitations.[149] At the same time, rules should not be altered such that they provide preferential treatment for the student athlete with disabilities.[150] Schools also must not compromise student safety.[151]

---

[146]Dear Colleague Letter from Seth M. Galanter, Acting Assistant Sec'y for Civil Rights, U.S. Dep't of Educ. (Jan. 25, 2013), https://www2.ed.gov/about/offices/list/ocr/letters/colleague-201301-504.html.

[147]*Id.*

[148]532 U.S. 661 (2001).

[149]*See, e.g.*, Washington v. Ind. High Sch. Athletic Ass'n, 181 F.3d 840 (7th Cir. 1999).

[150]K.L. v. Mo. State High Sch. Activities Ass'n, 178 F. Supp. 3d 792 (E.D. Mo. 2016) (denying preliminary injunction in part because modification student sought would give her team preferential treatment).

[151]*See* Ripple v. Marble Falls Indep. Sch. Dist., 99 F. Supp. 3d 662 (W.D. Tex. 2015) (granting school district's summary judgment motion because in part, school did not violate its § 504 duty to keep medically fragile football player safe). *But see* K.R.S. v. Bedford Cmty. Sch. Dist., 109 F. Supp. 3d 1060 (S.D. Iowa 2015) (denying summary judgment to school officials who knew that student with ADHD was a victim of disability-based harassment by peers on his football team).

To align with the Section 504/ADA requirement to provide "reasonable modifications," schools must provide aids and services that are needed to afford a student with a disability with an equal opportunity to participate. An example of a reasonable modification may be providing a sign language interpreter at tennis matches.[152] On the other hand, modifications are not required if they are a fundamental alteration to the athletic program and must be made on a case-by-case basis. The U.S. Department of Education has stated that there is no requirement for schools to create separate or different activities designed for students with disabilities, nor must students' IEPs address extracurricular activities.[153] Because sports participation is seldom considered essential to an educational benefit, it typically is not included in IEPs.[154] Furthermore, it may be prudent to avoid including sports, or any other extracurricular activity, in IEPs because doing so could establish an entitlement to team membership and enable sports participation to become a legal entitlement.[155]

Most of the recent athletic litigation has claimed disability-based discrimination under Section 504/ADA. Many lawsuits have also involved athletic associations that monitor interscholastic athletic competitions between schools.[156] For example, a New Jersey federal court did not grant a waiver to play a fifth year to a football player diagnosed with autism and ADHD. The court explained that the athletic association had permitted him to play for eight semesters, and thus, enforcing the semester limit rule did not violate the ADA because it was not based on the student's disability.[157] In contrast, another student athlete was successful in her lawsuit. She was paralyzed from the waist down, and the athletic association permitted her to swim in meets but did not count her points for her team. After an Illinois federal court denied the association's motion to dismiss, the parties entered into a settlement agreement in which the association promised to offer future events for swimmers with disabilities as well as other accommodations.[158]

[152]Settlement Agreement Between the United States of America and the Arizona Interscholastic Association, Inc. Under the Americans with Disabilities Act (Mar. 30, 2012), www.ada.gov/aia_settle.htm.

[153]Letter from John K. DiPaolo, Deputy Assistant Sec'y for Policy, Office for Civil Rights, to Francisco M. Negrón, Jr., Gen. Counsel, Nat'l Sch. Bds. Ass'n (Dec. 16, 2013), https://www.nsba.org/sites/default/files/reports/OCR%20Dec.%2016%20%20Letter%20-%20RE%20-%20NSBA%20May%202013%20Letter.pdf.

[154]*But see* Kling v. Mentor Pub. Sch. Dist., 136 F. Supp. 2d 744 (N.D. Ohio 2001) (requiring the school district and athletic association to allow an overage athlete to participate in sports because he could not receive educational benefits without such participation).

[155]J.M. v. Mont. High Sch. Ass'n, 875 P.2d 1026 (Mont. 1994).

[156]*See* Brentwood Acad. v. Tenn. Secondary Sch. Athletic Ass'n, 531 U.S. 288 (2001) (declaring a state athletic association a state actor).

[157]Starego v. N.J. State Interscholastic Athletic Ass'n, 970 F. Supp. 2d 303 (D.N.J. 2013); *see also* C.S. v. Ohio High Sch. Athletic Ass'n, 2015 WL 4575217 (S.D. Ohio July 29, 2015) (holding student with learning disabilities was not discriminated against based on his disability; thus, athletic association's application of residency requirement was permissible).

[158]Illinois *ex rel.* Madigan v. Ill. High Sch. Ass'n, 2012 WL 3581174 (N.D. Ill. Aug. 17, 2012).

CONCLUSION

The rights of students with disabilities have expanded significantly since 1975 and include rights to accessible facilities, appropriate programs, and least restrictive placements. School districts are responsible for identifying, evaluating, and coordinating the IEPs of all eligible students with disabilities. Also, district leaders must ensure that disability-based discrimination does not occur in their schools. The following generalizations reflect the current status of the law on the topics covered in this chapter.

1. The three primary federal laws impacting students with disabilities are IDEA, Section 504, and the ADA.

2. IDEA is a funding law focused on education; whereas, Section 504 and the ADA are civil rights laws prohibiting disability-based discrimination.

3. Under their child find obligation, school districts must identify all eligible children with disabilities.

4. Students with disabilities are entitled to receive a FAPE in the LRE.

5. To qualify, students are evaluated with valid assessments to determine whether they (1) meet one of IDEA's disability categories and (2) are in need of special education and related services.

6. An IEP is a written document developed by parents and school officials and outlines a student's goals, related services, and placement.

7. The U.S. Supreme Court determined in *Endrew v. Douglas* that a school must offer an IEP reasonably calculated to enable a student to make progress appropriate in light of the student's circumstances; the best program is not necessary.

8. Students with disabilities are placed in private settings by both public districts and parents; however, when parents unilaterally place their children in private schools, they cannot receive tuition reimbursement for the private placement unless (1) the public school did not offer a FAPE and (2) the private placement was appropriate.

9. Related services necessary to support the specially designed instruction for students with disabilities are required regardless of cost; school districts are not obligated to provide medical services, but they must provide other services if they are necessary for the child to attend school and benefit from instruction.

10. Students with disabilities and their parents are entitled to procedural safeguards, including the option to file a due process complaint to resolve disputes.

11. Students are entitled to "stay-put" in their current educational placement during administrative (due process) or judicial proceedings.

12. The ten-day rule states that if students with disabilities are removed from their educational placement for more than ten days, then an MDR must occur to evaluate (1) whether the student's IEP was properly implemented and (2) whether the student's misconduct was caused by or substantially related to his or her disability.

13. Students with disabilities may only be expelled if the MDR determines that the misconduct was not related to the student's disability and that the IEP was properly implemented;

however, emergency exceptions may exist that require removing students for up to forty-five days to an IAES, such as if the student possessed drugs or weapons or inflicted serious bodily injury at school.

14. Any time students with disabilities are removed from school for more than ten days, they must be provided services consistent with their IEP; the IEP team must then consider whether an FBA should be conducted and a BIP should be implemented.

15. Section 504 and the ADA define a person with a disability as one who (1) has a physical or mental impairment that substantially limits one or more major life activities, (2) has a record of impairment, or (3) is regarded as having an impairment; students who meet the first prong are entitled to reasonable accommodations.

16. Students with disabilities who qualify under Section 504 may include students with severe allergies and other medical issues, and they are often provided a written Section 504 plan.

17. If FAPE is not at issue, a plaintiff does not need to exhaust IDEA's administrative remedies prior to filing a lawsuit under Section 504 or the ADA.

CHAPTER EIGHT

STUDENT DISCIPLINE

Is it legal for school employees to strip search students? May teachers reduce grades for student misbehavior? How does due process differ for students who are expelled versus suspended? Student misconduct continues to be one of the most persistent and troublesome problems confronting educators. Public concern has focused on school disciplinary problems, particularly for student behavior involving substance use and violence. In response, schools have directed more efforts toward violence-prevention strategies, including not only stringent security measures, but also modifying the curricula to strengthen students' social skills and training teachers and administrators to monitor the school climate. This chapter focuses on the development of conduct regulations; the imposition of sanctions for noncompliance, such as suspensions, expulsions, and corporal punishment; as well as other school discipline procedures including search and seizure. Some disciplinary strategies have been controversial,[1] but it is not the purpose of this chapter to debate the merits of various practices.

Readers of this chapter should be able to:

- Describe what schools should and should not do when developing student codes of conduct.
- Distinguish the due process procedures for students who are suspended versus expelled.
- Define what constitutes reasonable suspicion to search students.
- Analyze what legal remedies students have if they are wrongfully disciplined.

CONDUCT REGULATIONS

School boards and school authorities are granted considerable latitude in establishing and interpreting their own disciplinary rules and regulations.

For over 150 years, the judiciary has recognized that when parents entrust schools to educate their children, they also bestow some of their parental authority to set and enforce rules

---

[1] *See* Daniel Losen, *Discipline Policies, Successful Schools, and Racial Justice*, Nat'l Educ. Pol'y Ctr. (Oct. 5, 2011), http://nepc.colorado.edu/publication/discipline-policies.

and maintain order.[2] **In fact, the U.S. Supreme Court "has repeatedly emphasized the need for affirming the comprehensive authority of the States and of school officials, consistent with fundamental constitutional safeguards, to prescribe and control conduct in the schools."**[3] Reasonable disciplinary regulations, even those impairing students' protected liberties, have been upheld if justified by a legitimate educational interest.

Regulations in General

The Supreme Court has held that the interpretation of a school regulation resides with the body that adopted it and is charged with its enforcement.[4] Disciplinary policies, however, have been struck down if unconstitutionally vague. Policies prohibiting "improper conduct" and behavior "inimical to the best interests of the school" have been invalidated because they have not specified the exact nature of the impermissible conduct.[5] Although policies should be precise, courts have recognized that disciplinary regulations do not have to satisfy the stringent criteria or level of specificity required in criminal statutes.

The Eighth Circuit noted that the determining factor is whether a regulation's wording is precise enough to notify an individual that specific behavior is clearly unacceptable.[6] The Third Circuit stated that courts should be "hesitant" to apply the overbreadth doctrine to policies in the public school setting.[7] Yet, a Pennsylvania federal district court found a policy overbroad because it prohibited out-of-school conduct that "may cause a disruption in school."[8] The court reasoned that the policy restricted more speech than what was constitutionally permissible.[9] In addition to reviewing the scope of the conduct regulation on which a specific punishment is based, courts evaluate the nature and extent of the penalty imposed in relation to the gravity of the offense. Courts consider the age, sex, mental condition, and past behavior of the student in deciding whether a given punishment is appropriate.

Litigation challenging student discipline typically has focused on the procedures school personnel have followed when administering punishment rather than on the content of the rules or the nature of the sanctions imposed. Implicit in all judicial

---

[2]*Morse v. Frederick*, 551 U.S. 393 (2007) (discussing how the *in loco parentis* principle has applied to schools).

[3]Tinker v. Des Moines Indep. Cmty. Sch. Dist., 393 U.S. 503, 507 (1969).

[4]Bd. of Educ. v. McCluskey, 458 U.S. 966 (1982); Wood v. Strickland, 420 U.S. 308 (1975); *see also* Price v. N.Y.C. Bd. of Educ., 855 N.Y.S.2d 530 (App. Div. 2008) (holding that a board's ban on possession of cell phones had a rational basis).

[5]*See* Monroe Cty. Bd. of Educ. v. K.B., 62 So. 3d 513 (Ala. Civ. App. 2010) (concluding that a school's policy prohibiting use of alcohol at school or a school function did not encompass consumption *prior to* a school function; policy was found to be unconstitutionally vague). *But see* Esfeller v. O'Keefe, 391 F. App'x 337, 340 (5th Cir. 2010) (ruling that student code prohibiting "extreme, outrageous or persistent acts, or communications that are intended or reasonably likely to harass, intimidate, harm, or humiliate another" was not facially overbroad).

[6]Woodis v. Westark Cmty. Coll., 160 F.3d 435 (8th Cir. 1998).

[7]J.S. *ex rel.* Snyder v. Blue Mountain Sch. Dist., 650 F.3d 915 (3rd Cir. 2011) (en banc) (disagreeing that the acceptable use policy was overbroad because it reached out-of-school speech when regulating what students were permitted to do on school-owned computers used in nonschool environments).

[8]R.L. v. Cent. York Sch. Dist., 183 F. Supp. 3d 625, 645 (M.D. Pa. 2016).

[9]*Id. See* Chapter 5 for discussion of the circumstances under which students' off-campus expression can be curtailed.

declarations regarding school discipline is the notion that severe penalties require more formal procedures, whereas minor punishments necessitate only minimal due process. To illustrate, teachers provide adequate due process for minor infractions as long as they: (1) provide students notice of what rules were violated, and (2) offer students an opportunity to refute the charges. **Nonetheless, any disciplinary action should be accompanied by some procedure to ensure the rudiments of fundamental fairness and to prevent mistakes in the disciplinary process**. Courts have emphasized that required procedures vary depending on the seriousness of the punishment to be imposed.

With the advent of the Internet, an increasing number of lawsuits have been filed challenging school discipline of student off-campus conduct. Oftentimes, issues occurring outside of school bleed into the school environment and may require the attention of educators (e.g., a student who cannot concentrate in class because of cyber-bullying). As addressed in Chapter 5, students' use of social networks such as Instagram and Facebook raise difficult First Amendment issues for school officials attempting to discipline students for off-campus conduct. The judiciary has recognized that punishment for student conduct off school grounds must be supported by evidence that the behavior has a detrimental impact on the school environment; however, school personnel may struggle to identify when they should monitor and punish students for off-campus conduct.[10] Educators should be cognizant of their state and local conduct regulations surrounding bullying.[11] State laws often specify that behavior occurring on school property and buses, as well as at school-sponsored events and bus stops, can negatively affect the school community and therefore, be punished.

Developing and Enforcing Student Codes of Conduct

Most schools provide students with a student handbook that outlines the expectations for student behavior and the consequences for violating school rules. When developing student codes of conduct, school personnel should avoid placing unnecessary constraints on student behavior. All possible means of achieving the desired outcomes should be explored, and means that are least restrictive of students' personal freedoms should be selected (see Figure 8.1 for guidelines). It is important to reference state law, because many state codes prescribe discipline policies and procedures that must be followed at the district level (e.g., reporting procedures for bullying incidents).[12] Once it is determined that a specific conduct regulation is necessary, the rule should be clearly written so that it is not open to multiple interpretations. Each regulation should include the rationale for enacting the rule as well as the penalties for infractions. Considerable discretion exists in determining that certain actions deserve harsher penalties (i.e., imposing a more severe punishment for the sale of drugs as opposed to the possession or use of drugs). **To ensure that students are**

---

[10]*See* Catherine Mendola, *Big Brother as Parent: Using Surveillance to Patrol Students' Internet Speech*, 35 B.C. J.L. & Soc. Just. 153 (2015) (discussing schools' use of third-party surveillance companies to monitor students' online behavior).

[11]*See* Chapter 5, for a discussion of bullying, including cyber-bullying.

[12]Educ. Comm'n of the States, *State Legislation, School Safety—Discipline/Code of Conduct* (n.d.), https://b5.caspio.com/dp.asp?AppKey=b7f93000695b3d0d5abb4b68bd14&id=a0y700000009y8ZAAQ.

FIGURE 8.1   Guidelines for the Development of a Student Code of Conduct

School Rules Should:
be publicized to students and their parents/guardians
be appropriate to the offense, taking into consideration student's age, any disability, and past behavior
incorporate references to specific laws and/or court cases
have an explicit purpose and be clearly written to accomplish that purpose
include procedural safeguards that should accompany administration of all punishments; formality of procedures should be in accord with severity of the punishment
be necessary in order to carry out school's educational mission; rules should not be designed merely to satisfy preferences of school board members, administrators, or teachers
be periodically reviewed and revised, and this process should involve students and staff
be specific and clearly stated so students know what behaviors are expected and what behaviors are prohibited
School Rules Should Not:
impair constitutionally protected rights unless there is an overriding public interest, such as a safety threat
be *ex post facto*; they should not be adopted to prevent a specific activity that school officials know is being planned or has already occurred
be applied in a discriminatory manner

knowledgeable of the conduct rules, it is advisable to require them to sign a form indicating that they have read the conduct regulations.

In designing and enforcing student codes of conduct, it is important for school personnel to bear in mind the distinction between students' substantive and procedural rights. *Substantive rights* include those that are stipulated in state or federal law such as the right to be free from excessive force; whereas *procedural rights* ensure that the process is fair, including the right to appeal. If a school rule or punishment violates substantive rights (e.g., restricts protected speech), the regulation cannot be enforced nor the punishment imposed. When only procedural rights are impaired (e.g., failure to follow the district's discipline procedures), however, the punishment generally can be administered if it is determined at an appropriate hearing that the punishment is warranted.[13]

EXPULSIONS AND SUSPENSIONS

Some type of procedural due process should be afforded to students prior to the imposition of expulsions or suspensions.

Expulsions and suspensions are among the most widely used disciplinary measures. Courts uniformly have upheld educators' authority to use such measures as punishments, but the procedural requirements (i.e., notice, hearing, etc.) discussed in this section must

[13]*See* Brown v. Univ. of Kan., 599 F. App'x 833 (10th Cir. 2015) (noting that the failure of an organization to follow its own rules, does not, by itself, mean a Fourteenth Amendment violation has occurred).

be provided to ensure that students are afforded fair and impartial treatment. **States have recognized that students have a property right to an education, but students may be deprived of this right if they violate school rules**.

Expulsions

State laws and school board regulations are usually quite specific regarding the grounds for *expulsions*—that is, the removal of students from school for a lengthy period of time (in excess of ten days).[14] Such grounds are not limited to occurrences during school hours and can include infractions on school property immediately before or after school, at school-sponsored activities on or off school grounds, or en route to or from school. Despite the fact that specific grounds vary from state to state, infractions typically considered legitimate grounds for expulsion include:

- engaging in violence;
- stealing or vandalizing school or private property;
- causing or attempting to cause physical injury to others;
- possessing a weapon;
- possessing or using drugs or alcohol; and
- engaging in criminal activity or other behavior forbidden by state laws.

Procedural Requirements. State statutes specify procedures for expulsion and the limitations on their length. Except for the possession of weapons, a student generally cannot be expelled beyond the end of the current academic year unless the expulsion takes place near the close of the term. A teacher or administrator may initiate expulsion proceedings, but usually only the school board can expel a student. **Prior to expulsion, students must be provided procedural protections guaranteed by the U.S. Constitution; however, school officials can remove students immediately if they pose a danger or threat to themselves or others**. No duty exists to provide an educational alternative for a properly expelled student unless the school board policies or state mandates indicate that alternative programs must be provided or the student is receiving special education services.[15]

Even though the details of required procedures must be gleaned from state statutes and school board regulations, courts have held that students facing expulsion from public school are guaranteed at least minimum due process under the Fourteenth Amendment (see Figure 8.2 for procedural elements). The procedural safeguards required may vary, depending on the circumstances of a particular situation. In a Mississippi case, a student and his parents claimed that prior to an expulsion hearing, they should have been given a list of the witnesses and a summary of their testimonies.[16] Recognizing that such procedural

---

[14]*See* Scott v. Bd. of Tr. of Orange Cty. High Sch. of Arts, 158 Cal. Rptr. 3d 173 (Ct. App. 2013) (distinguishing a dismissal from an expulsion of a charter school student because once dismissed, the student can choose to attend a new school); *infra* text accompanying note 50 for a discussion of involuntary transfers which also do not require heightened due process because students maintain access to education.

[15]*See* Chapter 7 for a discussion of the expulsion of children with disabilities.

[16]Keough v. Tate Cty. Bd. of Educ., 748 F.2d 1077 (5th Cir. 1984).

FIGURE 8.2   Procedural Due Process for Student Expulsions versus Student Suspensions

---

EXPULSION (more than 10 days)

- Written notice of the charges; the intention to expel; the place, time, and circumstances of hearing; and sufficient time for a defense to be prepared
- A full and fair hearing before an impartial adjudicator
- Right to legal counsel or some other adult representation
- Right to be fully apprised of the proof or evidence
- Opportunity to present witnesses or evidence
- Opportunity to cross-examine opposing witnesses
- Some type of written record demonstrating that decision was based on the evidence presented at hearing

SUSPENSION (10 days or less)

- Oral or written notification of nature of violation and intended punishment
- Opportunity to refute charges before an objective decision maker (who could be the teacher or administrator)
- Explanation of evidence on which the disciplinarian is relying

---

protections generally should be afforded prior to a long-term expulsion, the Fifth Circuit nonetheless held that they were not required in this case. The parents had been fully apprised of the charges, the facts supporting the charges, and the nature of the hearing. In a later case involving expulsion for possession of drugs, the same court found no impairment of a student's rights when he was denied an opportunity to confront and rebut witnesses who accused him of selling drugs.[17] The names of student witnesses had been withheld to prevent retaliation against them. Similarly, the Sixth Circuit noted that it is critical to protect the anonymity of students who blow the whistle on classmates involved in serious offenses, such as drug dealing.[18] A student who brought a knife to school and had tweeted threats of violence challenged her expulsion because she had not been able to read the actual witness statements to prepare for her expulsion hearing. The Sixth Circuit held that the school was not required to provide these statements because it had sufficiently communicated their substance and thus, the student could adequately prepare a defense.[19] State laws and school board policies often provide students facing expulsion with more elaborate procedural safeguards than the constitutional protections noted. Once such expulsion procedures are established, courts will require that they be followed.[20]

[17]Brewer v. Austin Indep. Sch. Dist., 779 F.2d 260 (5th Cir. 1985).

[18]Newsome v. Batavia Local Sch. Dist., 842 F.2d 920 (6th Cir. 1988).

[19]C.Y. *ex rel.* Antone v. Lakeview Pub. Schs., 557 F. App'x 426 (6th Cir. 2014).

[20]The failure to enact required rules under state law or to follow them, however, would violate state law rather than the U.S. Constitution; *see, e.g.,* Vann *ex. rel.* Vann v. Stewart, 445 F. Supp. 2d 882 (E.D. Tenn. 2006). State laws vary on expulsion requirements. *Compare* Kresser v. Sandusky Bd. of Educ., 748 N.E.2d 620 (Ohio Ct. App. 2001) (holding that Ohio law had been violated when school board missed the statutory deadline to hold expulsion hearing), *with* Scott v. Bd. of Trs., 158 Cal. Rptr. 3d 173 (Ct. App. 2013) (finding that the student was not entitled to an expulsion hearing because the charter school he attended was exempt from the state law requiring expulsion hearings). *But see* Chapter 13, note 13.

Zero-Tolerance Policies.   Concerns about school safety led to specific federal and state laws directed at the discipline of students who bring weapons onto school campuses. Under the Gun-Free Schools Act of 1994, all states enacted legislation requiring at least a one-year expulsion for students who bring firearms to school.[21] The federal law also requires states to permit the local superintendent to modify the expulsion requirement on a case-by-case basis and allows officials to assign students to alternative instructional programs. In expanding the scope of the federal law beyond guns, state laws have included weapons such as knives, explosive devices, and other offensive weapons, as well as drugs and violent acts.[22]

Zero-tolerance policies were severely criticized in the years following the Gun-Free Schools Act, which resulted in subsequent policies that encourage school officials to exercise discretion and flexibility. The American Bar Association and others have called for an end to such policies that require automatic penalties without assessing the circumstances.[23] A Virginia case underscores the harsh consequences when students encounter inflexible policies. In that case, a thirteen-year-old student, attempting to save a suicidal friend's life, took the friend's binder containing a knife and placed it in his own locker. Despite the fact that the student never posed a threat to anyone, he was expelled from school for four months. The Fourth Circuit, in upholding the expulsion, noted its harshness but found no violation of the student's due process rights.[24] Invoking mandatory expulsion policies may implicate constitutional rights if administrators fail to take into consideration the individual student's history and the circumstances surrounding the conduct. For example, the Sixth Circuit noted that expelling a student for weapons possession when the student did not know the weapon was in his car was unconstitutional.[25] Most courts, however, have been reluctant to impose the *knowing possession* standard that would require the determination of a student's intent.[26]

Suspensions

Suspensions are frequently used to punish students for violating school rules and standards of behavior when the infractions are not of sufficient magnitude to warrant expulsion. Suspensions include short-term removals (ten days or less) from school as well as the denial of

---

[21]20 U.S.C. § 7961(b)(1) (2018). Additionally, most states have enacted gun-free or weapons-free school zone laws restricting possession of firearms in or near schools.

[22]*See* R.H. v. Florida, 56 So. 3d 156 (Fla. Dist. Ct. App. 2011) (holding that a student who brought a common pocketknife to school could not be charged with a crime because Florida law, unlike many other state laws, specifically exempts pocketknives from its ban on weapons); F.R. v. Florida, 81 So. 3d 572 (Fla. Dist. Ct. App. 2012) (determining that a folding knife with a notch grip, a locking blade mechanism, and a hilt guard was not a pocketknife exempt under Florida law).

[23]Stephanie Francis Ward, *Schools Start to Rethink Zero Tolerance Policies*, A.B.A. J. (Aug. 2014), http://www.abajournal.com/magazine/article/schools_start_to_rethink_zero_tolerance_policies.

[24]Ratner v. Loudoun Cty. Pub. Schs., 16 F. App'x 140 (4th Cir. 2001).

[25]Seal v. Morgan, 229 F.3d 567 (6th Cir. 2000).

[26]*See, e.g.*, *In re* B.N.S., 641 S.E.2d 411 (N.C. Ct. App. 2007).

participation in regular courses and activities (in-school suspension).[27] Most legal controversies have focused on out-of-school suspensions, but it is advisable to apply the same legal principles to any disciplinary action that separates the student from the regular instructional program, even briefly.

In 1975, the Supreme Court held in *Goss v. Lopez* that minimum due process must be provided before a student is suspended for even a short period of time.[28] **Recognizing that a student's state-created property right to an education is protected by the Fourteenth Amendment, the Court ruled that such a right cannot be impaired unless the student is afforded notice of the charges and an opportunity to refute them before an impartial decision maker** (see Figure 8.2). The Supreme Court also emphasized that suspensions implicate students' constitutionally protected liberty interests because of the potentially damaging effects that discipline can have on a student's reputation and permanent record. Although the Court recognized students' substantive due process rights, courts have been reluctant to find violations of these rights due to suspensions. To illustrate, the Ninth Circuit ruled that a middle schooler who was suspended for sexually harassing two students with disabilities lacked a substantive due process interest in maintaining a clean, non stigmatizing school disciplinary record.[29]

Procedural Requirements.   Even after the *Goss* Court specifically noted that formal procedures such as securing counsel and cross-examining witnesses are not constitutionally required, students continue to claim that schools violated their procedural rights by not providing more formal procedures.[30] In 1986, the Court reiterated that students are not owed more formal procedures by noting that a two-day suspension "does not rise to the level of a penal sanction calling for the full panoply of procedural due process protections applicable to a criminal prosecution."[31] To emphasize that this is an informal process, the Court explained: "In the great majority of cases the disciplinarian may informally discuss the alleged misconduct with the student minutes after it has occurred."[32]

Lower state and federal courts have also been reluctant to impose additional requirements unless mandated by state law. In a Sixth Circuit case, a student committed suicide after being suspended for stealing a school computer. The parents claimed the school was required to show videotaped evidence to the student. However, the court disagreed, stating that if schools were required to do this, it "would be providing the student with more

[27]*See, e.g.,* Jahn v. Farnsworth, 617 F. App'x 453 (6th Cir. 2015) (discussing that suspensions lasting longer than ten days do not automatically require more extensive procedural due process than those set out in *Goss*).

[28]419 U.S. 565 (1975). Individuals posing a danger or threat may be removed immediately, with notice and a hearing following as soon as possible.

[29]C.R. v. Eugene Sch. Dist., 835 F.3d 1142 (9th Cir. 2016), *cert. denied*, 137 S. Ct. 2117 (2017). *See also* note 63, Chapter 5.

[30]Similarly, courts have not found that students are entitled to special protections during the investigation of the rule infraction. *See, e.g.,* Crawford v. Deer Creek Pub. Sch., 228 F. Supp. 3d 1262 (W.D. Okla. 2017) (ruling that a written confession admitting to sexual assault, obtained in exchange for a more lenient punishment from the student, was not a violation of the student's Fifth Amendment right against self-incrimination).

[31]Bethel Sch. Dist. v. Fraser, 478 U.S. 675, 686 (1986).

[32]Goss v. Lopez, 419 U.S. 565, 582 (1975).

procedural protections than an adult accused of committing a crime."[33] In a Maine case, a student claimed a violation of procedural due process because the school administrator denied him permission to leave during questioning and failed to advise him of his right to remain silent or to have his parents present during the interrogation. The court rejected all claims, noting that there was no legal authority to substantiate any of the asserted rights.[34] The court reasoned that to rule otherwise would, in fact, contradict the informal procedures outlined in *Goss* allowing for immediate questioning and disciplinary action.

The Supreme Court in *Goss* recognized the possibility of "unusual situations" that would require more formal procedures than those outlined, but little guidance was given about what these circumstances might be. The only suggestion offered in *Goss* was that a disciplinarian should adopt more extensive procedures in instances involving factual disputes "and arguments about cause and effect."[35] Courts have declined to expand on this brief listing. The Sixth Circuit rejected a student's contention that drug charges constituted such an "unusual situation" because of the stigmatizing effect on his reputation. The court did not believe that an eighth-grade student suspended for ten days for possessing a substance that resembled an illegal drug was "forever faced with a tarnished reputation and restricted employment opportunities."[36] Similarly, in a Seventh Circuit case, a student originally was given notice only that he was being accused of possessing drugs, but one day before his suspension hearing, he was notified that he was also being suspended for ingesting drugs.[37] Although the student contended that receiving such short notice of the second charge was insufficient to prepare a defense, the court disagreed. More extensive procedures also have been found unnecessary when students have been barred from interscholastic athletics and other activities.[38]

Students have asserted that suspensions involving loss of course credit or occurring during exam periods require greater due process than outlined in *Goss*. The Fifth Circuit, however, did not find that the loss incurred for a ten-day suspension during final examinations required more than a mere give-and-take discussion between the principal and the student. In refusing to require more formal proceedings, the court noted that *Goss* makes no distinction as to when a short-term suspension occurs.[39]

In-School Suspensions and Time-Outs. In-school suspensions or isolation in time-out may entitle students to minimal due process procedures if they are deprived of instruction,

---

[33]Jahn v. Farnsworth, 617 F. App'x 453, 460 (6th Cir. 2015).

[34]Boynton v. Casey, 543 F. Supp. 995 (D. Me. 1982). *But see In re* Andre M., 88 P.3d 552 (Ariz. 2004) (finding that a sixteen-year-old student's rights were violated when police interrogated him at school and refused to permit his parent to be present). *See infra* text accompanying note 157 for further discussion of Miranda rights.

[35]*Goss*, 419 U.S. at 583–84.

[36]Paredes *ex rel.* Koppenhoefer v. Curtis, 864 F.2d 426, 429 (6th Cir. 1988).

[37]Dietchweiler *ex rel.* Dietchweiler v. Lucas, 827 F.3d 622 (7th Cir. 2016).

[38]*See, e.g.*, Donovan v. Ritchie, 68 F.3d 14 (1st Cir. 1995) (finding due process was adequate when a high school student was suspended from extracurricular activities); Mather v. Loveland City Sch. Dist. Bd. of Educ., 908 N.E.2d 1039 (Ohio Ct. App. 2009) (interpreting an Ohio law as providing a student the right to appeal an expulsion or suspension from curricular, but not extracurricular, activities).

[39]Keough v. Tate Cty. Bd. of Educ., 748 F.2d 1077, 1081 (5th Cir. 1984) (noting that a contrary ruling would "significantly undermine, if not nullify" the Court's holding in *Goss*).

but it depends on the extent to which the student is deprived the opportunity to learn. For example, the Sixth Circuit held that a one-day, in-school suspension in which a student completed school work and was considered in attendance did not implicate a property interest in educational benefits or a liberty interest in reputation.[40] Additionally, the Tenth Circuit noted that when multiple, brief time-outs were used, they still allowed for access to education, and "any loss of a property right is de minimis and not subject to procedural protections."[41] In contrast, a Georgia federal district court found sufficient due process claims were alleged by a student with severe disabilities who was isolated in a room so frequently that he developed a fear of dimly lit rooms and muscle atrophy.[42]

Discrimination in Expulsions and Suspensions

Policy makers, researchers, and educators have reconsidered whether the use of zero-tolerance and other harsh discipline measures are warranted, particularly for behavior unrelated to the possession of weapons.[43] In 2014, the U.S. Department of Education released a report identifying that in one academic year over 3.45 million students were suspended. Of particular concern was the data documenting that exclusionary discipline practices such as suspensions and expulsions were disproportionately administered to students with disabilities and students of color.[44] The suspension rates for students with disabilities were twice as high (13 percent) as students without disabilities (6 percent).[45] In comparison with their White peers, Black students were 1.9 times more likely to be expelled and 3.8 times more likely to be suspended.[46]

In 2014, the federal government releasing guidance instructing schools about their legal responsibilities to monitor and reduce disproportionate and discriminatory discipline.[47]

---

[40]Laney v. Farley, 501 F.3d 577 (6th Cir. 2007).

[41]Couture v. Bd. of Educ., 535 F.3d 1243, 1257 (10th Cir. 2008); *see also* Rasmus v. Arizona, 939 F. Supp. 709 (D. Ariz. 1996) (holding that denying a student the ability to work on class assignments during a ten-minute time-out was de minimis and did not violate a property right).

[42]Williams v. Fulton Cty. Sch. Dist., 181 F. Supp. 3d 1089, 1132 (N.D. Ga. 2016) (noting that when time-outs are "so frequent and pervasive as to be fairly characterized as the 'functional equivalent' of a lengthy out-of-school suspension," then they are likely to implicate procedural due process violations); *see also infra* text accompanying note 134 for discussion of courts' analyses of time-outs as seizures under the Fourth Amendment.

[43]Rachel Klein, *Keeping Our Kids in School and Out of Court: Rooting Out School Suspension Hearings and a New Alternative*, 17 CARDOZO J. CONFLICT RESOL. 633 (2016).

[44]Jennifer Sughrue, Maria Lewis & M. David Alexander, *Addressing Discriminatory and Exclusionary Discipline Practices*, in THE PRINCIPAL'S LEGAL HANDBOOK (Janet Decker, Maria Lewis, Elizabeth Shaver, Ann Blankenship-Knox & Mark Paige eds., 6th ed. 2017).

[45]Although students with disabilities comprised only 12 percent of the student population, they represented nearly 60 percent of students placed in seclusion and 75 percent of those who were physically restrained at school.

[46]U.S. Dep't of Educ., Office for Civil Rights, *2013–2014 Civil Rights Data Collection: A First Look* (Oct. 28, 2016), https://www2.ed.gov/about/offices/list/ocr/docs/2013-14-first-look.pdf.

[47]U.S. Dep't of Justice & U.S. Dep't of Educ., *Dear Colleague Letter: Nondiscriminatory Administration of School Discipline* (Jan. 8, 2014), http://www2.ed.gov/about/offices/list/ocr/letters/colleague-201401-title-vi.pdf.

A national movement addressing the school-to-prison pipeline encourages schools to rethink discipline by increasing efforts to create positive school climates and decreasing schools' use of expulsion and suspension.[48] In particular, some have scrutinized the increase of a police presence in school settings. Litigation has also ensued claiming discriminatory discipline policies and practices.[49]

In addition to increasing their awareness about discriminatory discipline, school employees should understand that **students are owed at least minimal due process procedures when they are denied school attendance or removed from the regular instructional program**. Severity of the separation dictates the amount of process due under the U.S. Constitution and state laws. Permanent expulsion from school triggers the most extensive process, whereas minor infractions may involve a brief give-and-take between school officials and students. Simply providing students the opportunity to be heard not only reduces mistakes, but also preserves trust in the school system.

OTHER DISCIPLINARY PRACTICES

As long as they are reasonable and align with federal, state, and local regulations, school authorities may implement additional disciplinary practices.

Educators have considerable latitude in controlling student behavior to maintain an appropriate educational environment and should not feel that the judiciary has curtailed their authority to discipline students. Despite this fact, students continue to challenge their discipline including transfers to alternative placements, corporal punishment, and academic sanctions.

Disciplinary Transfers to Alternative Educational Placements

Involuntary transfers of students to alternative educational placements for disciplinary reasons generally do not involve a denial of public education, but they may implicate protected liberty interests. Legal challenges to the use of disciplinary transfers have addressed primarily the adequacy of the procedures followed. Recognizing that students do not have an inherent right to attend a given school, some courts nonetheless have held that pupils facing involuntary reassignment are entitled to minimal due process if such transfers are the result of misbehavior[50] or if required by school board policy.[51]

A Pennsylvania federal district court ruled that transfers for disciplinary reasons affected liberty interests of sufficient magnitude to require procedural due process. Even

---

[48]Sughrue, Lewis & Alexander, *supra* note 44.

[49]*See, e.g.*, Barnett v. Baldwin Cty. Bd. of Educ., 60 F. Supp. 3d 1216 (S.D. Ala. 2014), *summary judgment granted*, 2015 WL 3614048 (S.D. Ala. June 9, 2015).

[50]*See, e.g.*, McCall v. Bossier Par. Sch. Bd., 785 So. 2d 57 (La. Ct. App. 2001).

[51]*See* Clodfelter v. Alexander Cty. Bd. of Educ., 2016 U.S. Dist. LEXIS 175014 (W.D.N.C. Dec. 19, 2016) (discussing that North Carolina law no longer entitles students transferred to alternative placements to a formal hearing before the school board as long as the placement will allow students to make adequate academic progress).

though such transfers involved comparable schools, the court reasoned that the transfer carried with it a stigma and thus implicated a protected liberty right. Noting that the transfer of a student "during a school year from a familiar school to a strange and possibly more distant school would be a terrifying experience," the court concluded that such transfers were more drastic punishments than suspensions, and thus necessitated due process.[52]

The Fifth Circuit, however, declined to find a federally protected property or liberty interest when a student arrested for aggravated assault was reassigned to an alternative education program. According to the court, the student was not even temporarily denied a public education. In dismissing the case, the court did note that to ensure fairness, the state and local school districts should provide students and parents an opportunity to explain why a disciplinary transfer may not be warranted; however, failure to do so does not infringe constitutional rights.[53]

Corporal Punishment

If not prohibited by law or school board policy, reasonable corporal punishment can be used as a disciplinary measure.[54] Many states have banned educators' use of corporal punishment either by law or state regulation. In 1971, only one state prohibited corporal punishment; as of 2017, twenty-eight states and D.C. proscribed its use.[55] Generally, when state law and school board policy permit corporal punishment, courts have upheld its reasonable administration. In evaluating whether corporal punishment was reasonable, courts have assessed the child's age, maturity, and past behavior; the nature of the offense; the instrument used; any evidence of lasting harm to the child; and the motivation of the person inflicting the punishment.

The Supreme Court held in *Ingraham v. Wright* that the use of corporal punishment in public schools does not violate either the Eighth Amendment's prohibition against the government's infliction of cruel and unusual punishment or the Fourteenth Amendment's procedural due process guarantees.[56] While recognizing that corporal punishment implicates students' constitutionally protected liberty interests, the Court

[52]Everett v. Marcase, 436 F. Supp. 397, 400 (E.D. Pa. 1977).

[53]Nevares v. San Marcos Consol. Indep. Sch. Dist., 111 F.3d 25 (5th Cir. 1997); *see also* Robinson v. St. Tammany Par. Pub. Sch. Sys., 569 F. App'x 303 (5th Cir. 2014) (affirming that a student who was transferred to another school for alleged sexual misconduct was not entitled to a list of the accusers, their allegations, nor a review by the school board); Harris v. Pontotoc Cty. Sch. Dist., 635 F.3d 685 (5th Cir. 2011) (concluding that an assignment to an alternative school does not involve a denial of education requiring procedural protection).

[54]Corporal punishment is physical punishment inflicted on a minor by an adult. This may include a variety of examples of physical touching including restraint or paddling.

[55]Of the twenty-two other states, fifteen state laws expressly permit corporal punishment and five states do not prohibit its use. Jess Clark, *Where Corporal Punishment Is Still Used in Schools, Its Roots Run Deep*, NPR (Apr. 12, 2017), http://www.npr.org/sections/ed/2017/04/12/521944429/where-corporal-punishment-is-still-used-its-roots-go-deep. The American Academy of Pediatrics has recommended that corporal punishment be abolished in all states because of its detrimental effect on students' self-image and achievement as well as possible contribution to disruptive and violent behavior. Am. Acad. of Pediatrics, *Corporal Punishment in Schools*, 106 PEDIATRICS 343 (2000) (reaffirming 2000 statement, 118 PEDIATRICS 1266 (2006)).

[56]430 U.S. 651 (1977).

emphasized that state remedies are available, such as assault and battery suits, if students are excessively or arbitrarily punished by school personnel.[57] In essence, the Court majority concluded that state courts, under provisions of state laws, should handle cases dealing with corporal punishment. The majority distinguished corporal punishment from a suspension from school by noting that the denial of school attendance is a more severe penalty, depriving students of a property right and thus necessitating procedural safeguards.

The Supreme Court's ruling in *Ingraham*, however, did not foreclose successful constitutional challenges to the use of *unreasonable* corporal punishment. Most federal appellate courts have held that students' substantive due process right to be free of brutal and egregious threats to bodily security might be impaired by the use of shockingly excessive corporal punishment.[58] For example, the Fourth Circuit concluded that excessive or cruel corporal punishment may violate students' substantive due process rights, which protect individuals from arbitrary and unreasonable governmental action.[59] Clearly, student challenges to the reasonable use of ordinary corporal punishment are precluded by this standard.

When students have claimed that schools' corporal punishment has violated their substantive due process rights, courts have maintained a high threshold for recovery. Minor pain, embarrassment, and hurt feelings do not rise to this level; actions must literally be 'shocking to the conscience.' Disciplinary actions that have *not risen* to this level include requiring a ten-year-old boy to clean out a stopped-up toilet with his bare hands;[60] physically and abusively restraining a student with disabilities in multiple incidents;[61] shoving a student's head into a trash can;[62] and shaking, screaming, and spitting on football players.[63] In contrast, substantive due process rights were implicated when conscience-shocking behavior involved a coach knocking a student's eye out of the socket with a metal weight lock;[64] a substitute teacher slamming an elementary student's head into a chalkboard, throwing her to the floor, and choking her;[65] and a teacher maliciously slamming the head

---

[57]*See also* Clayton *ex rel.* Hamilton v. Tate Cty. Sch. Dist., 560 F. App'x 293 (5th Cir. 2014).

[58]*See, e.g.*, Johnson v. Newburgh Enlarged Sch. Dist., 239 F.3d 246 (2d Cir. 2001); Neal v. Fulton Cty. Bd. of Educ., 229 F.3d 1069 (11th Cir. 2000). Two appellate courts, however, have held that constitutional claims cannot be raised if states prohibit unreasonable student discipline and provide adequate post-punishment civil or criminal remedies for abuse. Moore v. Willis Indep. Sch. Dist., 233 F.3d 871 (5th Cir. 2000); Wallace v. Batavia Sch. Dist. 101, 68 F.3d 1010 (7th Cir. 1995).

[59]Hall v. Tawney, 621 F.2d 607, 613 (4th Cir. 1980) (analyzing "whether the force applied caused injury so severe, was so disproportionate to the need presented, and was so inspired by malice or sadism rather than a merely careless or unwise excess of zeal that it amounted to a brutal and inhumane abuse of official power literally shocking to the conscience").

[60]Harris v. Robinson, 273 F.3d 927 (10th Cir. 2001).

[61]T.W. v. Sch. Bd. of Seminole Cty., 610 F.3d 588 (11th Cir. 2010); *see also* Muskrat v. Deer Creek Pub. Sch., 715 F.3d 775 (10th Cir. 2013) (holding that a student with developmental disabilities was not deprived substantive due process after employees physically battered the student and the principal forcefully placed him in a time-out room).

[62]Mahone v. Ben Hill Cty. Sch. Sys., 377 F. App'x 913 (11th Cir. 2010).

[63]Votta *ex rel.* R.V. v. Castellani, 600 F. App'x 16 (2d Cir. 2015); *see also* Faccio v. Eggleston, 2011 WL 3666588 (N.D.N.Y. Aug. 22, 2011) (determining no due process violation after a teacher spit on a student).

[64]Neal v. Fulton Cty. Bd. of Educ., 229 F.3d 1069 (11th Cir. 2000).

[65]Ellis *ex rel.* Pendergrass v. Cleveland Mun. Sch. Dist., 455 F.3d 690 (6th Cir. 2006).

of a student with severe physical and intellectual disabilities into a locker because he was not walking fast enough.[66]

If a state or district prohibits the use of corporal punishment, teachers can be disciplined or discharged for violating these provisions. For example, a Michigan teacher was dismissed because he violated board policy by using corporal punishment after having been warned repeatedly to cease.[67] In Illinois, a tenured teacher was dismissed on this ground for using a cattle prod in punishing students.[68] A Nebraska teacher who "tapped" a student on the head was suspended without pay for thirty days under a state law that prohibits the use of corporal punishment.[69] Beyond statutory or board restrictions, school employees can be charged with criminal assault and battery, which might result in fines and/or imprisonment. Civil assault and battery suits for monetary damages also can be initiated against school personnel.[70] If corporal punishment is used, school employees should keep a record of incidents and adhere to minimum procedural safeguards, such as notifying students of behavior that will result in a paddling, asking another staff member to witness the act, and providing parents written explanation for the punishment.

Academic Sanctions

School authorities have the right to use academic sanctions for poor academic performance. Courts have consistently upheld educators' decisions to assign failing grades, denial of credit, academic probation, and grade retention as legitimate means of dealing with poor academic performance. But less agreement exists regarding the use of grade reductions or academic sanctions as punishments for student absences and misbehavior. **When schools impose academic sanctions for nonacademic reasons, the sanctions should be reasonable; related to performance, absences, or other academic concerns; and serve a legitimate school purpose.** Furthermore, students must be informed of these consequences.

Many school boards impose academic sanctions for absences and justify this sanction as reasonable because it is rationally related to a valid educational purpose. Since students must attend class to benefit from the educational program, most courts have found that academic penalties for absenteeism serve a valid educational goal. In an illustrative case, the Supreme Court of Connecticut drew a sharp distinction between academic and disciplinary sanctions, noting that the school board's policy of reducing grades for unapproved absences was academic, rather than disciplinary, in intent and effect. Specifically, the court found that

---

[66]Williams v. Fulton Cty. Sch. Dist., 181 F. Supp. 3d 1089 (N.D. Ga. 2016); *see also* Hatfield v. O'Neill, 534 F. App'x 838 (11th Cir. 2013) (holding that forceful feeding and forcing the student's thumb down her throat did not shock the conscience; but, striking the student with disabilities on her head, where she had a soft spot resulting from surgery, was obviously excessive).

[67]Tomczik v. State Tenure Comm'n, 438 N.W.2d 642 (Mich. Ct. App. 1989).

[68]Rolando v. Sch. Dirs., 358 N.E.2d 945 (Ill. App. Ct. 1976).

[69]Daily v. Bd. of Educ., 588 N.W.2d 813 (Neb. 1999).

[70]*See, e.g.,* *Ex parte* Monroe Cty. Bd. of Educ., 48 So. 3d 621 (Ala. 2010) (ruling that a teacher was not entitled to state-agent immunity in a tort suit when she did not follow the school board's policy for administering corporal punishment); *see also* Chapter 2.

a board's determination that grades should reflect more than examinations and papers "constitutes an academic judgment about academic requirements."[71]

Some courts have upheld the imposition of academic penalties even though policies do not differentiate between excused and unexcused absences. For example, a New York appellate court found that a policy denying course credit for excessive absences was rational; students were permitted and encouraged to make up the classes before they exceeded the limit.[72]

Academic sanctions imposed for student misconduct also have been challenged. It is generally accepted that students can be denied credit for work missed while suspended from school. For example, the Supreme Court of Indiana upheld the denial of course credit for a high school junior expelled three days before the end of a semester. The court noted that state law did not mandate loss of credit, but the board could impose such a penalty.[73] In contrast, a Pennsylvania court found grade reductions for suspensions to be beyond a school board's authority in misrepresenting the students' scholastic achievement.[74] Overall, however, courts have ruled that schools may not deny students' academic course credit or high school diplomas for disciplinary reasons. For example, a Pennsylvania court held that a student who completed all coursework and final exams while expulsion proceedings were pending could not be denied a diploma, because state law specifies that a diploma must be issued once all requirements are met.[75] On the other hand, a student suspended at the end of the semester may be denied *participation* in the graduation ceremony.[76]

■ ■ ■ ■ ■

SEARCH AND SEIZURE

School personnel can search students' lockers or personal belongings based on reasonable suspicion that the students possess contraband that is either illegal or in violation of school policy.

The majority of search and seizure cases in schools involve the confiscation of either illegal drugs or weapons. Students have asserted that warrantless searches conducted by school officials impair their rights under the Fourth Amendment of the U.S. Constitution. Through an extensive line of decisions, the Supreme Court has affirmed that the basic purpose of the Fourth Amendment is to "safeguard the privacy and security of individuals against arbitrary invasions by governmental officials."[77] This amendment protects individuals against

[71]Campbell v. Bd. of Educ., 475 A.2d 289, 294 (Conn. 1984).

[72]Bitting v. Lee, 564 N.Y.S.3d 791 (App. Div. 1990).

[73]S. Gibson Sch. Bd. v. Sollman, 768 N.E.2d 437 (Ind. 2002).

[74]Katzman v. Cumberland Valley Sch. Dist., 479 A.2d 671 (Pa. Commw. Ct. 1984); *see also In re* T.H., III, 681 So. 2d 110 (Miss. 1996) (finding that under state law, a school board cannot count suspension days as unexcused absences for grading purposes as long as the student attends an alternative school during the suspension).

[75]Ream v. Centennial Sch. Dist., 765 A.2d 1195 (Pa. Commw. Ct. 2001).

[76]Walters v. Dobbins, 370 S.W.3d 209 (Ark. 2010); *see also* Khan v. Fort Bend Indep. Sch. Dist., 561 F. Supp. 2d 760 (S.D. Tex. 2008) (finding that a suspended student had no property right to attend the graduation ceremony or to deliver the valedictorian address).

[77]Camara v. Mun. Court, 387 U.S. 523, 528 (1967).

FIGURE 8.3 Comparison of Probable Cause and Reasonable Suspicion Standards

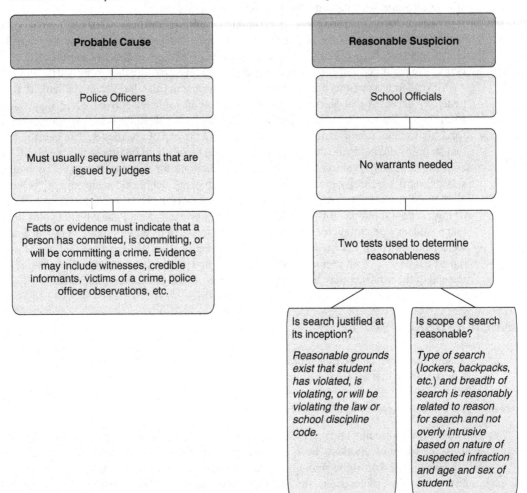

unreasonable searches by requiring state agents—who are typically police and other law enforcement officers—to obtain a warrant based on probable cause prior to conducting a search.[78] Under the *probable cause standard*, a governmental official must have reasonable grounds of suspicion, supported by sufficient evidence, to cause a cautious person to believe that the suspected individual is guilty of the alleged offense and that the search will produce evidence of the crime committed (see Figure 8.3). Governmental officials violating Fourth Amendment rights may be subject to criminal or civil liability, but the most important remedy for the aggrieved individual is the *exclusionary rule*, which renders evidence of an illegal search inadmissible in criminal prosecutions.

[78]This chapter uses the term "police officers" to refer to all law enforcement officers.

Application of the Fourth Amendment to Students

Because Fourth Amendment protections apply only to searches conducted by agents of the state, a fundamental issue in education cases is whether school authorities function as private individuals or as state agents. In 1985, the Supreme Court ruled in *New Jersey v. T.L.O.* that **public school officials are state agents, and all governmental actions—not merely those of police officers—come within the constraints of the Fourth Amendment.**[79]

Even though the Fourth Amendment is applicable, the Court in *T.L.O.* concluded that educators' substantial interest in maintaining discipline required "easing" the warrant and probable cause requirements imposed on police officers. The Court reasoned that requiring educators to obtain a warrant before searching students suspected of violating school rules or criminal laws would interfere with the administration of prompt and informal disciplinary procedures needed to maintain order. In modifying the level of suspicion required to conduct a search, the Court found the public interest was best served in the school setting with a standard less than probable cause. **Accordingly, the Court held that the legality of a search should depend "simply on the reasonableness, under all the circumstances, of the search."**[80] The standard for school officials remains *reasonable suspicion*; however, the increase of security guards, police officers, and school resource officers (SROs) in school settings has drawn into question who exactly is afforded this relaxed standard.[81]

In *T.L.O.*, a teacher had reported a student for smoking in the restroom.[82] Upon questioning by the assistant principal, the student denied smoking and, in fact, denied that she even smoked. The assistant principal, opening the student's purse seeking evidence to substantiate that she did smoke, found marijuana as well as other evidence implicating her in drug dealing. Using the reasonable suspicion test, the Supreme Court held that the search in *T.L.O.* was reasonable. The school official had a basis for suspecting that the student had cigarettes in her purse. Although possession was not a violation of a school rule, it was not irrelevant; discovery of cigarettes provided evidence to corroborate that she had been smoking and challenged her credibility. Characterizing this as a "common sense" conclusion, the Court noted that "the requirement of reasonable suspicion is not a requirement of absolute certainty: 'sufficient probability, not certainty, is the touchstone of reasonableness under the Fourth Amendment.'"[83]

As shown in Figure 8.3, the Court in *T.L.O.* advanced two tests for determining reasonableness. First, is the search justified at its inception? That is, reasonable grounds exist to suspect the search will yield evidence that the student has violated a school rule or the law.[84] Second, is the scope of the search reasonable? This means the type of search is related to the objective of the search and not excessively intrusive in light of the age and sex of the student and the nature of the infraction.[85]

---

[79]469 U.S. 325 (1985).

[80]*Id.* at 341.

[81]*See infra* text accompanying note 142 for cases discussing the standard applying to law enforcement officers in school settings.

[82]469 U.S. at 325 (1985).

[83]*Id.* at 346 (quoting Hill v. California, 401 U.S. 797, 804 (1971)).

[84]469 U.S. at 342.

[85]*Id.*

The "reasonableness" standard allows courts substantial latitude in interpreting Fourth Amendment rights. Among factors courts have considered in assessing reasonable grounds for a search are the:

- child's age, history, and school record;
- prevalence and seriousness of the problem in the school to which the search is directed (e.g., pervasive drug use);
- exigency to make the search without delay and further investigation;
- probative value and reliability of the information used as a justification for the search;
- school officials' experience with the student and with the type of problem to which the search is directed (e.g., past disciplinary issues); and
- type of search.

Clearly, reasonable suspicion requires more than a hunch, good intentions, or good faith. The Supreme Court, in upholding an exception to the warrant requirement for a "stop and frisk" search for weapons by police officers, concluded that to justify the intrusion the police officer must be able to point to "specific and articulable facts."[86] In recognizing an exception for school searches, it appears that, at a minimum, the judiciary will require searches of students to be supported by objective facts.

Informants often play an important role in establishing the "specific and articulable facts" necessary to justify a search. Reliability of informants can be assumed unless school officials have reason to doubt the motives of the reporting student, teacher, parent, or anonymous caller. The amount of detail given by an informant adds to the veracity of the report—that is, identifying a specific student by name, what the student is wearing, and the specific contraband and where it is located will support a decision to search.[87] Additionally, even with limited information, the level of danger presented by an informant's tip may require an immediate response (e.g., whether informant discusses weapons versus alcohol).

Another aspect of reasonableness is individualized suspicion. The Supreme Court in *T.L.O.* did not address individualized suspicion, but the Court did state that "exceptions to the requirement of individualized suspicion are generally appropriate only where the privacy interests implicated by a search are minimal and where 'other safeguards' are available 'to assure that the individual's reasonable expectation of privacy is not subject to the discretion of the official in the field.'"[88] **Courts have been reluctant to support personal searches lacking individualized suspicion (e.g., blanket searches) unless the safety of the students necessitates an immediate search.**

In assessing the constitutionality of searches in public schools, two questions are central: (1) What constitutes a search? (2) What types of searches are reasonable? According to the Supreme Court's rulings, essential considerations in determining whether an

[86]Terry v. Ohio, 392 U.S. 1, 21 (1968).

[87]*See* People v. Perreault, 781 N.W.2d 796 (Mich. 2010) (holding that an anonymous tip providing names of students, grade levels, vehicle types, and drugs being sold established reasonable suspicion to search a student's vehicle).

[88]*T.L.O.*, 469 U.S. at 342 n.8 (citing Delaware v. Prouse, 440 U.S. 648, 654–55 (1979)).

action qualifies as a search are an individual's reasonable expectation of privacy (reasonable in the sense that society is prepared to recognize the privacy)[89] and the extent to which the government intrudes upon that expectation of privacy.[90] The reasonableness of a specific type of search must be evaluated in terms of all of the circumstances surrounding the search. This would include variables such as who initiated the search, who conducted the search, the need for the search, the purpose of the search, information or factors prompting the search, what or who was searched, and use of the evidence.

An individual may waive entitlement to Fourth Amendment protection by consenting to a search or volunteering requested evidence. The consent, however, is valid only if voluntarily given in the absence of coercion. Serious questions arise as to whether a student's consent is actually voluntary. Did the student have a free choice? Was the student aware of his or her Fourth Amendment rights? The very nature of the school setting diminishes the presumption of consent. Students are accustomed to receiving and following instructions of school officials. A threat to call students' parents and the police if they do not cooperate can further substantiate a coercive atmosphere. The Sixth Circuit stated that there is "a presumption against the waiver of constitutional rights," placing the burden on school officials to show that students knowingly and intelligently waived their Fourth Amendment rights.[91] **Although some courts have found student consent valid, the inherent pitfalls of pursuing such a search in the absence of reasonable suspicion must be duly considered.** Additionally, it is good practice for the authorized person conducting a search to have another staff member present who can verify the procedures used in the search.

In the next sections, various types of school searches are examined as to their reasonableness. As can be seen in Figure 8.4, the degree of suspicion required to search rises as the invasiveness of the search increases.

Lockers and Other School-Owned Property

Courts have singled out school lockers as generating a *lower* expectation of privacy, frequently distinguishing locker searches on the basis that a locker is school property, and students do not retain exclusive possession. This is particularly likely when they have signed a form acknowledging that the locker is school property and subject to inspection. **Under the view of joint control, school officials have been allowed to inspect lockers or even to consent to locker searches by law enforcement officers.** For example, a California appellate court held a warrantless search of a student's locker was justified.[92] After an SRO received a tip about a student possibly possessing a weapon, a police officer assisted two SROs in searching multiple school lockers. During this search, they found a sawed-off shotgun belonging to a student who was not the student about whom the original tip was

---

[89]469 U.S. at 338 (quoting Hudson v. Palmer, 468 U.S. 517, 526 (1984)).

[90]United States v. Chadwick, 433 U.S. 1, 7 (1977), *overruled on other grounds sub nom.* California v. Acevedo, 500 U.S. 565 (1991).

[91]*In re* S.C., 583 So. 2d 188 (Miss. 1991) (quoting *T.L.O.*, 469 U.S. at 339).

[92]*In re* J.D., 170 Cal. Rptr. 3d 464 (Ct. App. 2014); *see infra* text accompanying note 142 for cases addressing law enforcement personnel.

FIGURE 8.4   Degree of Suspicion Required to Conduct Student Searches

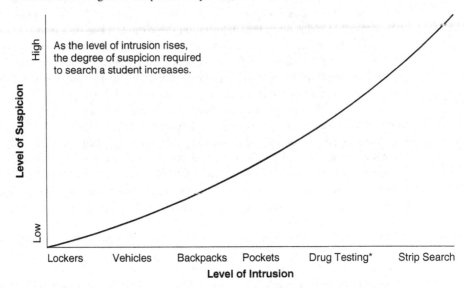

*Under school district drug-testing policies, athletes and students participating in extracurricular activities can be subjected to drug tests without individualized suspicion.

given. The court reasoned the search was justified in light of the special need to ensure campus safety.

Most student conduct codes and some state laws specify guidelines for locker searches. These codes or laws may establish that reasonable suspicion is required prior to conducting a search. In a Pennsylvania case, the student code specified that school authorities would notify students before searching lockers except for when school officials had reasonable suspicion that the locker contained materials that could harm students' health and safety.[93] The state supreme court held that students possessed a reasonable expectation of privacy in their lockers; yet, in balancing students' privacy interests and school officials' concerns, the court found a school-wide blanket search reasonable based on the heightened awareness of drug activity that permeated the entire school.

Some states have enacted broad laws eliminating any presumption of privacy in school lockers. For example, a Michigan law states: "A pupil who uses a locker that is the property of a school district . . . is presumed to have no expectation of privacy in that locker or that locker's content."[94] Furthermore, Michigan school officials can search the lockers at any time and can request the assistance of law enforcement officers.

School districts may also have policies relating to the searching and monitoring of school-issued computers, files stored on school servers, and even student-owned devices

[93]Commonwealth v. Cass, 709 A.2d 350, 353 (Pa. 1998); *see also In re* S.M.C., 338 S.W.3d 161 (Tex. Ct. App. 2011) (concluding that a student informant's tip indicating another student was "high" on drugs justified the search of a student and his locker).

[94]MICH. COMP. LAWS ANN. § 380.1306(1) (2018).

that are used at school. For example, a Connecticut district enacted an acceptable use policy with guidelines for all technology equipment that is owned or leased by the district, as well as equipment that is connected to the district's network. The policy reduces students' expectations of privacy by stating that files stored on the district's equipment are "the property of the District and, as such, may be inspected at any time and should not be considered private."[95] Therefore, the policy advises all users that they should have no any expectation of privacy in using electronic devices and digital storage.[96]

Search of Personal Possessions: Backpacks, Cell Phones, Cars, and Other Property

Students have a greater expectation of privacy in their personal property or effects than in their school lockers. **Most courts have noted that searches of students' personal possessions—such as cell phones, wallets, purses, and backpacks—violate students' subjective expectations of privacy and, as such, require individualized suspicion that a violation of a law or school rule has occurred.** The Eighth Circuit found that a Little Rock school district policy permitting school officials to conduct full-scale, random, periodic inspections of students' book bags and other personal possessions without any individualized suspicion constituted a major invasion of students' expectation of privacy.[97] The court held that school officials could not argue that students waived their privacy rights when they brought their possessions onto school property. However, in a more recent Eighth Circuit case upholding a drug dog sniffing backpacks in an empty classroom, the court found the five-minute sniffing differed from inspecting personal possessions because it was minimally intrusive.[98]

Additionally, the Supreme Court of Ohio upheld the search of an unattended backpack.[99] The school had an unwritten protocol to search unattended bags to identify their owners and ensure their contents were not dangerous. After a bag was found on a school bus, a school official completed a cursory search and was able to identify the owner. However, the bag was then brought to the principal who emptied its contents and found bullets. This discovery led to the arrest of a student for concealing a handgun. The court reasoned that the second search was reasonable because there was still a need to determine whether the bag's contents were dangerous. Similarly, the New York high court concluded that a

[95]*Fairfield Public Schools Information and Communication Technologies Acceptable Use Guidelines and Agreement* (Mar. 18, 2013), http://cdn.fairfieldschools.org/parent-resources/registration/AUP-District-02_02_2017.pdf.

[96]*Id.* at 2; *see also* Rochelle Valverde, *Lawrence School District to Monitor Student iPads; List of Rules Under Review*, LJ WORLD (July 11, 2016), http://www2.ljworld.com/news/2016/jul/11/lawrence-school-district-montior-student-ipads-lis/.

[97]Doe v. Little Rock Sch. Dist., 380 F.3d 349 (8th Cir. 2004). *But see* H.Y. *ex rel.* K.Y. v. Russell Cty. Bd. of Educ., 490 F. Supp. 2d 1174 (M.D. Ala. 2007) (holding that the classroom search of students' book bags and personal possessions for missing money was justified to promote order and discipline even though individualized suspicion did not exist).

[98]Burlison v. Springfield Pub. Sch., 708 F.3d 1034 (8th Cir. 2013).

[99]Ohio v. Polk, 78 N.E.3d 834 (Ohio 2017).

security officer's investigation of a student's book bag was reasonable based on hearing an "unusual metallic thud" when the student tossed the bag on a metal shelf. Following the sound, the security officer ran his fingers over the outside of the book bag and detected the outline of a gun. The court noted that the sound alone was insufficient to justify searching the bag, but the discovery of the presence of a gun-like shape established reasonable suspicion for him to open the bag.[100] In a California case, the court found the search of a student's pockets and backpack reasonable under the school district's established policy that all students who leave campus during the school day and return are subjected to a search.[101] Students and parents were informed of the policy, and it was deemed necessary to maintain a safe school environment.

Like other personal items, reasonable suspicion is needed to search students' cell phones.[102] In a Pennsylvania case, school officials seized a student's cell phone when it fell from his pocket; his action violated the school policy against displaying or using a cell phone during the school day.[103] School officials, attempting to determine if other students were violating the policy, used the student's seized phone to call classmates in the phone's directory, check the messages, and engage in instant messaging without identifying themselves. The court found school officials justified in taking the cell phone; however, the scope of the search was unreasonable. According to the court, the officials "had no reason to suspect at the outset that such a search would reveal that [the student] was violating another school policy; rather, they hoped to utilize his phone as a tool to catch other students' violations."[104] A Mississippi federal district court, however, held that school officials did not violate a middle school student's rights when they opened his phone and saw personal photographs of the student. Unlike the Pennsylvania case, the court noted that the cell phone was contraband, with the student having diminished expectations of privacy because he could not possess or use a cell phone at school.[105]

A student's car, like other personal possessions, may be searched if reasonable suspicion can be established. The Supreme Court of New Jersey rejected a student's claim that a greater expectation of privacy existed for his automobile parked on school grounds;

---

[100]*In re* Gregory M., 627 N.E.2d 500 (N.Y. 1993).

[101]*In re* Sean A., 120 Cal. Rptr. 3d 72 (Ct. App. 2010).

[102]*But see* Riley v. California, 134 S. Ct. 2473 (2014) (holding that law enforcement officers must have warrants to search digital information on cell phones and other personal electronic devices from arrested persons, unless an emergency exists).

[103]Klump v. Nazareth Area Sch. Dist., 425 F. Supp. 2d 622 (E.D. Pa. 2006); *see also* G.C. v Owensboro Pub. Schs., 711 F.3d 623 (6th Cir. 2013) (ruling that school officials' search of a student's text messages was unjustified; texting in class violated a school rule but did not establish reasonable grounds to suspect that the student was involved in any improper activity).

[104]*Klump*, 425 F. Supp. 2d at 640.

[105]J.W. v. Desoto Cty. Sch. Dist., 2010 U.S. Dist. LEXIS 116328 (N.D. Miss. Nov. 1, 2010); *see also* Koch v. Adams, 361 S.W.3d 817 (Ark. 2010) (rejecting student's claim that state law did not permit school authorities to seize his cell phone; the state law specified types of penalties for violating school discipline codes but did not limit school authorities in using others, such as seizure of a cell phone); *In re* Rafael C., 200 Cal. Rptr. 305 (Ct. App. 2016), *remanded on other grounds* (ruling that school officials search of cell phone data was reasonable due in part to the gravity of the situation that gave rise to the search, i.e., suspected firearm on campus).

thus, probable cause was not necessary to search his car.[106] Noting school officials' responsibilities to maintain safety and order, the state high court held that only reasonable suspicion was required. A report from a classmate who appeared to be intoxicated from a pill purchased from the student, as well as items found in his locker, established the necessary reasonable suspicion. Similarly, reasonable suspicion was found in an Idaho case when a school official searched a student's car because he smelled tobacco smoke on him.[107] A school policy banned the possession of tobacco products on campus; individualized suspicion existed that the student was in violation of this school rule. In contrast, the Supreme Court of Nebraska ruled that an assistant principal's search of a student's truck that was parked on a street across from the school was unlawful.[108] The assistant principal initially searched the student's belongings, which did not reveal any wrongdoing. Thus, the court ruled the student's suspension for possessing drug paraphernalia be removed from his school record, reasoning that the continued off-campus search of the student's truck was unreasonable.

Personal Search of Students

Warrantless searches of a student's person raise significant legal questions. The Fifth Circuit noted: "The Fourth Amendment applies with its fullest vigor against any intrusion on the human body."[109] **Students have a legitimate expectation of privacy in the contents of their pockets and their person, with reasonableness of the search assessed in terms of the specific circumstances of each case.**

Metal Detectors. Because metal detectors are used in airports and many public buildings, individuals have become accustomed to going through metal detectors. Even though their use does constitute a search for Fourth Amendment purposes, courts have ruled that schools may use metal detectors. **General scanning of students with metal detectors is only minimally intrusive on students' expectation of privacy when weighed against school officials' interest in providing a safe school environment.**

When metal detectors became more commonplace in schools in the 1990s, their constitutionality was challenged; however, courts clarified that individualized suspicion was not required. For example, the Pennsylvania high court upheld a general, uniform search of all students for weapons as they entered the high school building; each student's personal belongings were searched, and then a security officer scanned each student with a metal detector.[110] The court concluded that the search involved a greater invasion on students' privacy interests than the search of a locker, but with the nonintrusive nature of the search, it remained a minimal intrusion. Similarly, the Eighth Circuit found a search of all male students from grades six to twelve for dangerous weapons to be minimally intrusive based

[106]New Jersey v. Best, 987 A.2d 605 (N.J. 2010).

[107]Idaho v. Voss, 267 P.3d 735 (Idaho Ct. App. 2011).

[108]J.P. *ex rel.* A.P. v. Millard Pub. Schs., 830 N.W.2d 453 (Neb. 2013).

[109]Horton v. Goose Creek Indep. Sch. Dist., 690 F.2d 470, 478 (5th Cir. 1982).

[110]*In re* F.B., 726 A.2d 361 (Pa. 1999).

on reasonable suspicion that weapons had been brought to school that day.[111] Students were scanned with a metal detector after they removed their shoes and the contents of their pockets. If the metal detector sounded, a subsequent "pat down" search was conducted.

Search of Students' Clothing.   In applying the *T.L.O.* standard, a New Mexico appellate court found the search of a student's pockets reasonable.[112] After noticing a student's evasive behavior, the smell of marijuana, and a large bulge in his pocket, a police officer asked the student to empty his pockets. When the student refused, the officer reached into the student's pocket and pulled out a handgun. The court held that the search was justified and that the scope of the search was not excessive. Similarly, the Fourth Circuit determined that a teacher who reached into a student's pocket and retrieved marijuana conducted a reasonable search because the teacher had witnessed a hand-to-hand transaction between this student and a student who was known to have issues with marijuana.[113]

However, the Washington appellate court declined to support the search of a student's pockets based on his presence in the school parking lot during the school day—a violation of the closed campus policy. The court emphasized that "there must be a nexus between the item sought and the infraction under investigation."[114] In the absence of other suspicious factors about the student, violation of the school's closed campus rule did not justify the search that led to the discovery of marijuana. In a Louisiana case, a high school student was searched after being caught smoking cigarettes in the restroom. As part of the search, the student was required to remove his shoes, whereby narcotics were found. A state appellate court affirmed a lower court's ruling suppressing the evidence because the search of the shoes was "excessive and unwarranted."[115] While reasonable grounds existed to search the student, no reasonable grounds existed to search the shoes since it would not be possible to conceal cigarettes in shoes and still smoke them.

Strip Searches.   Early court decisions emphasized the legal issues that arise when school officials strip search students. The Second Circuit noted that "as the intrusiveness of the search intensifies, the standard of Fourth Amendment 'reasonableness' approaches probable cause, even in the school context."[116] The Seventh Circuit, in a strongly worded statement, proclaimed: "It does not require a constitutional scholar to conclude that a nude search of a thirteen-year-old child is an invasion of constitutional rights of some magnitude. More than that: it is a violation of any known principle of human decency."[117]

[111]Thompson v. Carthage Sch. Dist., 87 F.3d 979 (8th Cir. 1996); *see also* People v. Pruitt, 662 N.E.2d 540 (Ill. App. Ct. 1996) (reasoning that Chicago schools had a special need because the metal detectors resulted in an 85 percent reduction of the number of weapons confiscated).

[112]*In re* Josue T., 989 P.2d 431 (N.M. Ct. App. 1999); *see also In re* B.A.H., 263 P.3d 1046 (Or. Ct. App. 2011) (ruling under the Oregon Constitution that the search of a student's clothing was reasonable based on reliable information that he possessed illegal drugs).

[113]Louisiana v. K.L. (*In re* K.L.), 217 So. 3d 628 (4th Cir. 2017).

[114]Washington v. B.A.S., 13 P.3d 244, 246 (Wash. Ct. App. 2000).

[115]Louisiana v. Taylor, 50 So. 3d 922, 924 (La. Ct. App. 2010).

[116]M.M. v. Anker, 607 F.2d 588, 589 (2d Cir. 1979).

[117]Doe v. Renfrow, 631 F.2d 91, 92–93 (7th Cir. 1980).

The U.S. Supreme Court in *Safford Unified School District v. Redding* provided guidance regarding students' constitutional rights related to strip searches.[118] In this 2009 case, the assistant principal took an eighth-grade girl to his office based on another student's report that the girl had given her prescription-strength and over-the-counter pain medication. After searching the girl's backpack and finding no pills, a female assistant and the school nurse then searched the girl's jacket, socks, and shoes and told her to remove her pants and T-shirt. The girl also was told to pull her bra away from her body and shake it as well as to pull out the elastic of her underpants. No contraband was found.

The Supreme Court applied the reasonableness standard articulated in *T.L.O.*, finding sufficient evidence existed related to pill distribution to justify searching the girl's backpack and outer clothing. The further strip search, however, was found to be unreasonable. The Court noted that requiring the girl to expose her breasts and pelvic area violated "societal expectations of personal privacy," thereby "requiring distinct elements of justification on the part of school authorities for going beyond a search of outer clothing and belongings."[119] In this case, the level of suspicion fell far too short for the degree of intrusion. The painkillers, which violated school rules, posed only a limited threat to the school, and, furthermore, no evidence pointed to the girl hiding the pills in her underwear. Thus, the Court stated that there must be a reasonable suspicion of danger or that the search of underwear will produce evidence of wrongdoing before the "quantum leap from outer clothes and backpacks to exposure of intimate parts."[120]

In *Redding*, the Supreme Court concluded that school officials could not be held liable for the unreasonable search because the law was not well established regarding strip searches. However, several courts have denied school officials qualified immunity for similar actions. For example, the Sixth Circuit ruled that school officials were not entitled to qualified immunity when they subjected nursing students in a vocational school to a highly intrusive search for a missing credit card and some cash.[121] The students in this instance were required to unhook and shake their bras under their tops and lower their pants halfway down their thighs. The Eleventh Circuit also denied an assistant principal's motion for qualified immunity after conducting a strip search.[122] The court found that the inception of the search was reasonable because the assistant principal had been told the student was hiding marijuana in the waistband of his underpants. Yet, when the assistant principal forced the student to strip naked in front of his peers, the search was unnecessarily excessive in scope.

---

[118]557 U.S. 364 (2009).

[119]*Id.* at 374.

[120]*Id.* at 377. *But see* Lindsey *ex rel.* Lindsey v. Caddo Par. Sch. Bd., 954 So. 2d 272 (2d Cir. 2007) (rejecting mother's argument that an SRO's search where he asked student to fold down his waistband was unreasonable).

[121]Knisley v. Pike Cty. Joint Vocational Sch. Dist., 604 F.3d 977 (6th Cir. 2010); *see also* Brannum v. Overton Cty. Sch. Bd., 516 F.3d 489, 499 (6th Cir. 2008) (denying qualified immunity to school officials who installed security cameras in girls' and boys' locker rooms; the right to personal privacy was "clearly established"). *But see* Hearring v. Sliwowski, 712 F.3d 275 (6th Cir. 2013) (finding that a nurse was entitled to qualified immunity when she checked a six-year-old girl's vaginal area for a possible urinary infection without parental consent or a medical emergency; the nurse was not searching for contraband but attempting to check the student's medical condition).

[122]D.H. *ex rel.* Dawson v. Clayton Cty. Sch. Dist., 830 F.3d 1306 (11th Cir. 2016).

A Minnesota federal district court also concluded that school officials violated the Fourth Amendment rights of students after the students—who had disabilities—were subjected to daily searches of their backpacks and purses, as well as being asked to "remove their shoes and socks, turn down the waistband of their pants, empty their pockets, and (at least sometimes) submit to a patdown."[123] In another case, the New Mexico federal district court noted a substantial likelihood that students attending the high school prom would be successful in showing an intrusive pat down search of all students was in violation of the Fourth Amendment.[124] According to female students, the searches included cupping and shaking their breasts and lifting up their dresses to pat down their thighs. The court concluded that while this type of intrusive, suspicionless search was most likely unreasonable under the Fourth Amendment, a less intrusive search, such as a wand search, would probably be constitutional to serve the valid purpose in ensuring a safe environment.

The Supreme Court has not prohibited strip searches of students, but enough caveats exist to alert school officials of the inherent risks of such intrusive personal searches. Before conducting such a search, school officials must have individualized suspicion that a student is involved in wrongdoing that poses a threat to the health and safety of the school. Furthermore, the scope must not be more intrusive than demanded in the circumstances; a more dangerous item would justify a more intrusive search.

Drug Testing

In an effort to control drug use among students, some districts have considered school-wide drug-testing programs. Such programs raise serious questions about students' privacy rights. In 1989, the Supreme Court held that urinalysis, the most frequently used means for drug testing, is a search under the Fourth Amendment.[125]

The Supreme Court has rendered two decisions regarding the drug testing of students. **In 1995, the Court in *Vernonia School District v. Acton* upheld a school district's drug policy authorizing random urinalysis drug testing of students participating in athletic programs.**[126] Emphasizing the district's "custodial and tutelary" responsibility for children, the Court recognized that school personnel could exercise a degree of supervision and control over children that would not be permitted over adults. This relationship was held to be pivotal in assessing the reasonableness of the district's drug policy.[127] Addressing students'

[123]Hough v. Shakopee Pub. Schs., 608 F. Supp. 2d 1087, 1103 (D. Minn. 2009) (finding the searches to be extraordinarily intrusive).

[124]Herrera v. Santa Fe Pub. Schs., 792 F. Supp. 3d 1174 (D.N.M. 2011); *see also* Herrera v. Santa Fe Pub. Schs., 41 F. Supp. 3d 1188 (D.N.M. 2014) (denying school board's motion for summary judgment in part because questions remained about the district's supervision and training of security officers).

[125]Skinner v. Ry. Labor Execs. Ass'n, 489 U.S. 602 (1989); Nat'l Treasury Emps. Union v. Von Raab, 489 U.S. 656 (1989). The Court upheld the testing of government employees for drug use in two decisions, but the holdings were narrowly drawn and based on compelling governmental interests in ensuring public safety and national security.

[126]515 U.S. 646 (1995).

[127]*Id.* at 665. *But see* York v. Wahkiakum Sch. Dist., 178 P.3d 995 (Wash. 2008) (holding that a school district's policy allowing for random and suspicionless drug testing of student athletes violated a provision of the Washington Constitution).

legitimate privacy expectations, the court noted that the lower privacy expectations within the school environment are reduced even further when a student elects to participate in sports.

In 2002, the Supreme Court in *Board of Education v. Earls* again reviewed a drug-testing policy, but one that applied to students in all extracurricular activities, including athletics.[128] The policy required students to take a drug test prior to participation, to submit to random drug testing while involved in the activity, and to agree to be tested at any time when reasonable suspicion existed. In sustaining the drug-testing policy in *Earls*, the Court reasoned that the collection procedures were minimally intrusive, information was kept in confidential files with limited access, and test results were not given to law enforcement authorities. Based on these factors, the Court concluded that the drug-testing policy was not a significant invasion of students' privacy rights.

It is clear that specific subgroups of students, such as athletes and participants in extracurricular activities, can be subjected to drug testing; however, courts have not permitted blanket testing of *all* students. A Texas federal district court did not find exigent circumstances or other demonstrated compelling interests to justify a mandatory testing program of *all* students in grades six through twelve.[129] Accordingly, the federal court held the program unreasonable and unconstitutional under the Fourth Amendment.

Despite the fact that blanket or random drug testing of *all* students is not likely to withstand judicial challenge, **many schools subject students to urinalysis and breathalyzer testing based on individualized suspicion, and courts have upheld such practices**. Any drug-testing program, however, must be carefully constructed to avoid impairing students' Fourth Amendment privacy rights.[130] The policy must be clearly developed, specifically identifying reasons for testing. Data collection procedures must be precise and well defined.[131] Students and parents should be informed of the policy, and it is advisable to request students' consent prior to testing. If the test indicates drug use, the student must be given an opportunity to explain the results. Providing for the rehabilitation of the student rather than punishment strengthens the policy.

A charter school policy came under scrutiny after a student claimed he was forced to submit to a urinalysis or face expulsion. The policy allowed the school to demand a drug test (at the parent's expense), and the school could expel the student if he refused to submit to the test.[132] The school claimed that the student and his mother consented to the drug test; yet the Ohio federal district court disagreed, reasoning that the consent was not voluntary given the threat of expulsion. Ultimately the court found that the search was unreasonable at its inception. In contrast, the Eleventh Circuit ruled that school officials had reasonable

---

[128]536 U.S. 822 (2002); *see also* Hageman v. Goshen Cty. Sch. Dist., 256 P.3d 487 (Wyo. 2011) (ruling that blanket testing of all students participating in extracurricular activity did not violate the Wyoming Constitution).

[129]Tannahill *ex rel*. Tannahill v. Lockney Indep. Sch. Dist., 133 F. Supp. 2d 919 (N.D. Tex. 2001).

[130]*See* Gruenke v. Seip, 225 F.3d 290 (3d Cir. 2000) (concluding under the *Vernonia* standard that compelling a student athlete to submit to a pregnancy test, absent a legitimate health concern, was an unreasonable search).

[131]*See, e.g.*, Long v. Turner, 664 F. Supp. 2d 930 (S.D. Ind. 2009) (denying summary judgment to the school district because the manner in which the urinalysis test was administered violated the student's Fourth Amendment rights; he was required to provide a sample while facing two male school administrators).

[132]Cummerlander v. Patriot Prep. Acad., Inc., 86 F. Supp. 3d 808 (S.D. Ohio 2015).

suspicion to conduct a breathalyzer test on a group of students before allowing them to enter the prom.[133] After reasonably suspecting that the students had consumed alcohol on their "party bus," school officials instructed them to wait in a room to be breathalyzed. District policy prohibited alcohol at school functions and notified students of potential breathalyzer testing. All of the students passed the breathalyzer test, but the process took so long that they missed their prom. Nonetheless, the court reasoned the scope of the search was reasonable.

Seizure of Students

Courts have examined claims that detentions of students by school officials constitute an unlawful seizure. A seizure occurs when individuals feel they are not free to leave, such as when students are detained by school administrators for questioning. The Tenth Circuit, however, noted: "To qualify as a seizure in the school context, the limitation on the student's freedom of movement must significantly exceed that inherent in every day, compulsory attendance."[134]

As in the cases involving searches, courts examine school officials' actions to determine if a seizure or detainment of a student is reasonable—that is, justified at its inception and not excessively intrusive in light of the student's age and sex and the specific infraction. The Third Circuit found the "seizure" of a student for approximately four hours while school officials investigated a claim of sexual harassment to be reasonable in light of the serious nature of the accusation against the student.[135] Also, a California district court concluded that the detention of an eighth-grade student in the principal's office for three hours was justified in order to prevent classroom disruptions, discipline the student, and prevent her from using drugs or giving them to others.[136]

Emphasizing that students cannot leave the school premises during the school day, the Ninth Circuit held that detaining a classroom of students for five to ten minutes in a snack bar area while school officials conducted an "unquestionably legitimate dog sniff" was not an impermissible seizure under the Fourth Amendment.[137] Similarly, a federal district court found that a New Hampshire school district's removal of students from their classrooms to the football field for ninety minutes while multiple police dogs sniffed the classrooms did not constitute a seizure.[138] A teacher's momentary physical restraint of students has typically not been considered a "seizure" under the Fourth Amendment. Citing

[133]Ziegler v. Martin Cty. Sch. Dist., 831 F.3d 1309 (11th Cir. 2016) (finding that the SRO obtained consent from the bus driver to search the vehicle and found cups and an empty champagne bottle, making the search of the bus reasonable).

[134]Couture v. Bd. of Educ., 535 F.3d 1243, 1251 (10th Cir. 2008) (holding that repeated and lengthy time-outs were not unreasonable when related to the school's efforts to modify the student's behavior problems).

[135]Shuman ex rel. Shertzer v. Penn Manor Sch. Dist., 422 F.3d 141 (3d Cir. 2005). But see Jones v. Hunt, 410 F.3d 1221 (10th Cir. 2005) (finding that detaining a student in a high school for several hours by a social worker and police officer constituted a seizure and was not justified at its inception); Pacheco v. Hopmeier, 770 F. Supp. 2d 1174 (D.N.M. 2011) (holding that an unreasonable seizure occurred when a school principal permitted police officers to take a student, who was a potential witness to a crime, to the police station against his will).

[136]Bravo ex rel. Ramirez v. Hsu, 404 F. Supp. 2d 1195 (C.D. Cal. 2005).

[137]B.C. v. Plumas Unified Sch. Dist., 192 F.3d 1260, 1269 (9th Cir. 1999).

[138]Doran v. Contoocook Valley Sch. Dist., 616 F. Supp. 2d 184 (D.N.H. 2009).

the special nature of the school environment, courts have ruled that physical restraint in disciplinary situations in the school environment (e.g., physically escorting a student from a room) does not involve the deprivation of liberty that the Fourth Amendment prohibits.

In contrast, the Delaware Supreme Court found that an SRO's seizure of an eight-year-old student to elicit a classmate's confession was unreasonable.[139] Although the SRO was virtually certain that he already knew who had stolen a dollar from another child, the SRO nonetheless interrogated this innocent child, telling the boy that he could arrest him and send him to a detention center where "people are mean and children are treated like criminals."[140] The court explained that the seizure of the child to intentionally frighten him in order to teach another student a lesson violated the Fourth Amendment. In another example, the Ohio federal court denied the school's pretrial motion because it was plausible that the alleged behavior was so conscious-shocking that it denied a student substantive due process due to unlawful seizure. The pleadings claimed that a teacher had abused five children with disabilities in a self-contained special education class; one child was taped to a chair and placed in isolation on multiple occasions without any pedagogical purpose.[141]

Police, School Resource Officers, and Security Officers

Although the reasonable suspicion standard is used to assess the legality of school searches, a higher standard generally is required when police officers are involved. The nature and extent of such involvement are important considerations in determining whether a search is reasonable. **If the police role is one of finding evidence of a crime, a warrant based on probable cause would be required**.[142] Whereas early decisions generally supported police participation in searches initiated and conducted by school officials, more recently, courts have tended to draw a distinction between searches with and without police assistance.[143] The North Dakota Supreme Court enumerated a few factors to consider when determining whether the reasonable suspicion or probable cause standard should apply such as "whether the officer was in uniform. . . . who conducted the search, [and] whether other school officials were involved."[144]

---

[139]Hunt v. Delaware, 69 A.3d 360 (Del. 2013); *see infra* text accompanying note 147 discussing additional seizures by law enforcement officers in school settings.

[140]*Id.* at 364.

[141]H.M. v. Bd. of Educ. of the Kings Local Sch. Dist., 2015 WL 4624629 (S.D. Ohio Aug. 3, 2015).

[142]*Compare* Picha v. Wielgos, 410 F. Supp. 1214 (N.D. Ill. 1976) (holding probable cause was needed to conduct a search because police had been called to assist with the investigation), *with* Martens *ex rel.* Martins v. Dist., 620 F. Supp. 29 (N.D. Ill. 1985) (applying the reasonable suspicion standard to a case where police officer's involvement was limited and evidence was not used for criminal prosecution).

[143]However, searches by trained police officers employed by or assigned to a school district generally are governed by the *T.L.O.* reasonable suspicion standard rather than the probable cause standard. *See, e.g.*, North Dakota v. Alaniz, 815 N.W.2d 234 (N.D. 2012). *But see* Washington v. Meneese, 282 P.3d 83 (Wash. 2012) (finding that an SRO's search of a student's backpack required a warrant because the SRO was seeking evidence of a crime, not enforcing school discipline).

[144]*Alaniz*, 815 N.W.2d at 238; *see also* People *ex parte* T.S., 2015 WL 4505955 (V.I. Super. July 22, 2015) (analyzing the *Alaniz* factors to determine that police involvement was minimal and, thus, the reasonable suspicion standard should apply).

Since the 1990s, the regular presence of law enforcement officers in school environments has increased.[145] SROs are typically employed by an outside agency such as a police department; however, they serve a unique function. Unlike police officers, their role is to be a constant presence in schools.[146] SROs can also be distinguished from school security guards who typically monitor school entrances. Courts have applied a variety of standards when analyzing whether police, SROs, and security guards have violated the Fourth Amendment.

Handcuffing Students.   Recently, more attention has been given to law enforcement officers' handcuffing of students—especially in light of the national focus on the school-to-prison pipeline.[147] In a case involving the handcuffing of an eleven-year-old student with disabilities, the Ninth Circuit applied a reasonableness standard and concluded that the student was unlawfully handcuffed.[148] The police officers received a call about an unruly minor, but when they arrived, they found a quiet, unresponsive child. Because the officers handcuffed the child and placed him in a locked police car for thirty minutes, the court determined their response was excessively intrusive. In another case involving two elementary students with disabilities, a Kentucky federal district court ruled that the SRO's handcuffing of the students was an unconstitutional seizure.[149] The small children were not posing any immediate danger and their seizure was not objectively reasonable in consideration of the totality of circumstances. The court determined that the SRO's actions were unconstitutional and held the county that supervised the SRO liable for its failure to properly train the SROs.

In another case involving a student with a disability, however, the New York federal district court did not find it unreasonable for an SRO to handcuff an eleven-year-old child.[150] The court determined that the SRO's handcuffing for five minutes was reasonable because the SRO witnessed school personnel attempting to restrain the child as he attempted to head-butt and bite them.[151] The Washington federal court also ruled in favor of an SRO who had handcuffed a student after pushing his mother; yet, the court applied the probable cause standard.[152]

Claims of Excessive Force.   Law enforcement officers have also been accused of using excessive force. After a boy was arrested for disruptive horseplay in school, his mother

---

[145]Nathan James & Gail McCallion, Cong. Research Serv., R43126, *School Resource Officers: Law Enforcement Officers in Schools* (June 26, 2013) (noting that there were approximately 12,000 full-time SRO positions in schools in 1997 and 19,000 in 2007).

[146]Elizabeth Shaver & Janet Decker, *Handcuffing a Third Grader with ADHD? The Interactions Between School Resource Officers and Students with Disabilities*, 2017 Utah L. Rev. 229 (2017).

[147]*See infra* text accompanying note 48 that discusses the school-to-prison pipeline.

[148]C.B. v. City of Sonora, 769 F.3d 1005 (9th Cir. 2014).

[149]S.R. v. Kenton Cty. Sheriff's Office, 2017 WL 4545231 (E.D. Ky. Oct. 11, 2017).

[150]E.C. v. Cty. of Suffolk, 882 F. Supp. 2d 323 (E.D.N.Y. 2012); *see also* J.W. v. Corporal Carrier, 645 F. App'x 263 (4th Cir. 2016) (holding that an SRO acted reasonable when he lifted a student's arm to further immobilize the student who was already handcuffed after he threatened to harm himself).

[151]*See* Shaver & Decker, *infra* note 146, for discussion of cases involving students with disabilities and SROs.

[152]Hofschneider v. City of Vancouver, 182 F. Supp. 3d 1145 (W.D. Wash. 2016).

claimed the SRO's reaction violated her son's right to be free from excessive force.[153] The Tenth Circuit held that the SRO was entitled to qualified immunity, explaining that the boy was not injured and the officer could have reasonably assumed that arresting the student for violating a New Mexico law prohibiting disruption in schools was reasonable. In another case, the Seventh Circuit affirmed the verdict of a jury that found an SRO's use of force was reasonable because a student struck the officer in the face.[154] After the student refused to comply with the SRO's directive to remove his baseball cap, a physical altercation ensued between the SRO and the student.

Conversely, an Alabama federal district court refused to grant immunity to an SRO who was accused of using excessive force.[155] A student was sent to the principal's office after becoming upset in in-school suspension. As she walked down the school hallway, the SRO slapped her backpack. After the student responded, "leave me alone," the SRO shoved her "face first into a file cabinet and handcuffed her."[156] The student vomited in the police car and suffered arm injuries. The court denied the SRO's motion to dismiss reasoning that it was unreasonable for the officer to use that level of force in light of the circumstances.

Student Interrogations. Depending on a child's age and the nature of the questioning, the Supreme Court has held SROs or other police officers involved in *custodial interrogations* (i.e., where student's freedom of movement is restrained) must provide *Miranda* warnings—informing the student of the right to remain silent, that any statements may be used as evidence, and that he or she has the right to an attorney.[157] The Court specifically noted that determining whether an officer's conversation with a student is a custodial interrogation would be "nonsensical absent some consideration of the suspect's age."[158] According to the Court, to ascertain whether a custodial interrogation has occurred, the critical question is whether a reasonable juvenile of the child's age under the circumstances understood that he or she did not have to answer the police officer's questions and was free to leave at any time. Custodial interrogation is an issue only when law enforcement officers are involved in the questioning of students; school officials remain free to meet with students and inquire into their actions.[159] If a school leader interrogates a student about a

---

[153]A.M. v. Holmes, 830 F.3d 1123 (10th Cir. 2016).

[154]Griffin v. Bell, 694 F.3d 817 (7th Cir. 2012); *see also* Hawker v. Sandy City Corp., 591 F. App'x 669 (10th Cir. 2014) (holding that a police officer had not used excessive force when he employed a twist-lock to arrest a nine-year-old student).

[155]Avery v. City of Hoover, 2015 WL 4411765 (N.D. Ala. July 17, 2015).

[156]*Id.* at *2 (quoting the Plaintiff's Complaint).

[157]J.D.B. v. North Carolina, 564 U.S. 261 (2011). *See* Miranda v. Arizona, 384 U.S. 436 (1966) (holding that persons subjected to custodial interrogation must be advised of their right to remain silent, that any statement made may be used against them, and that they have the right to legal counsel).

[158]*J.D.B.*, 564 U.S. 261 at 275.

[159]Legal issues have arisen when school administrators question students with law enforcement officers. *See* J.D.B. v. North Carolina, 564 U.S. 261 (2011) (holding that a child's age is relevant in determining whether he has been taken into custody for police interrogation and was aware of his rights; a thirteen-year-old was questioned at school by police without being informed of his right to remain silent); *In re* T.A.G., 663 S.E.2d 392 (Ga. Ct. App. 2008) (affirming trial court's suppression of a student's statements when he was interviewed by an assistant principal and an armed police officer).

potential crime in the presence of an SRO, however, evidence could be suppressed if *Miranda* warnings were not given.[160]

Drug-Detecting Canines. Law enforcement officers at schools sometimes use drug-detecting dogs which raises several controversial questions regarding Fourth Amendment rights. Does the presence of a dog sniffing students constitute a search? Must reasonable suspicion exist to justify the use of dogs? Does the alert of a dog establish reasonable suspicion? A few courts have addressed these issues.

The Fifth Circuit confronted the question of whether sniffing by a dog is a search in terms of an individual's reasonable expectation of privacy.[161] The appellate court noted that most courts, including the U.S. Supreme Court, have held that law enforcement use of canines for sniffing objects does not constitute a search. Specifically, the appellate court referenced cases involving checked luggage, public lockers, and cars on public streets.[162] According to the court, a reasonable expectation of privacy does not extend to the airspace surrounding these objects. The court maintained that what has evolved is a doctrine of "public smell," equivalent to the "plain view" theory (that is, an object in plain view can be seized under certain circumstances).

Accordingly, the Fifth Circuit concluded that sniffing of student lockers and cars in public view was not a search, and therefore the Fourth Amendment did not apply. Even though permitting the use of dogs to detect drugs, the court held that reasonable suspicion is required for a further search by school officials of a locker or car.[163] The court additionally noted that reasonable suspicion could be established only on a showing that a dog is reliable in detecting the actual presence of contraband. However, the Supreme Court in 2013 ruled that police officers were not required to produce evidence of a dog's reliable performance to substantiate probable cause to search a vehicle.[164] The Court emphasized that the legality of a search must be assessed by whether all of the facts surrounding the dog's alert would lead a reasonable person to suspect that a search would turn up illegal drugs.

In most instances, judicial support for the use of dogs has been limited to the sniffing of objects. The Seventh Circuit, however, concluded that the presence of dogs in a classroom was not a search.[165] In this case, school officials with the assistance of police officers conducted a school-wide inspection for drugs in which trained dogs were brought

---

[160]*See, e.g.*, N.C. v. Kentucky, 396 S.W.3d 852 (Ky. 2013).

[161]Horton v. Goose Creek Indep. Sch. Dist., 690 F.2d 470 (5th Cir. 1982); *see also* Sims v. Bracken Cty. Sch. Dist., 2010 WL 4103167 (E.D. Ky. Oct. 18, 2010) (noting in a motion to dismiss that an alert from a drug-sniffing dog establishes reasonable suspicion to search a student's car).

[162]*But see* Florida v. Jardines, 569 U.S. 1 (2013) (finding a police officer's use of a drug-sniffing dog constituted a search when the dog was brought to the front porch of an individual's home because individuals have an expectation of privacy in their home and the immediate surrounding area).

[163]*See also* Idaho v. Doe, 2014 WL 1713796 (Idaho Ct. App. Apr. 29, 2014) (holding that when the drug-sniffing dog alerted the SRO to the driver's side door and not to the trunk that it was nonetheless reasonable for the SRO to search the entire vehicle including the trunk where a marijuana pipe was found).

[164]Florida v. Harris, 568 U.S. 237 (2013).

[165]Doe v. Renfrow, 631 F.2d 91 (7th Cir. 1980).

into each classroom. When a dog alerted beside a student, school officials requested that the student empty his or her pockets or purse; a continued alert by the dog resulted in a strip search. The appellate court concluded that the dog-sniffing did not constitute a search; the officials had reasonable suspicion to search the pockets and purses due to the dog's alert. Yet, the court found the strip search unconstitutional.

In contrast to the reasoning of the Seventh Circuit, the Fifth Circuit ruled that sniffing of students by dogs significantly intrudes on an individual's privacy, thereby constituting a search.[166] Although recognizing that the sniffing of a person is a search, the court did not prohibit such searches, and instead held that their intrusiveness must be weighed against the school's need to conduct the search. The court concluded that even with a significant need to search, individualized suspicion is required prior to the use of dogs because of the degree of intrusion on personal dignity and security. The Ninth Circuit concurred, noting that the significant intrusion on a student's expectation of privacy posed by dogs requires individualized suspicion.[167] Overall, school districts may prevent legal issues if they allow dogs to sniff only property or objects and not the students.[168]

REMEDIES FOR UNLAWFUL DISCIPLINARY ACTIONS

If students are unlawfully punished, they are entitled to be restored (without penalty) to their status prior to the punishment and to have their records expunged of any reference to the illegal punishment.

Several remedies are available to students who are unlawfully disciplined by school authorities. If students are physically or emotionally injured, they can seek damages through intentional tort suits.[169] For unwarranted suspensions or expulsions, students are entitled to reinstatement without penalty to grades and to have any reference to the illegal discipline removed from their school records. Remedies for violation of procedural due process rights may include reversal of a school board's decision. If academic penalties are unlawfully imposed, grades must be restored and transcripts altered accordingly. For unconstitutional searches, illegally seized evidence may be suppressed, school records may be expunged, and damages may be awarded if the unlawful search results in substantial injury to the student. Courts also may award court costs when students successfully challenge disciplinary actions.[170]

---

[166]*Horton*, 690 F.2d 470.

[167]B.C. v. Plumas Unified Sch. Dist., 192 F.3d 1260 (9th Cir. 1999).

[168]*See* Todd DeMitchell, *Canine Drug Searches: A Law and Policy Discussion*, 269 Educ. L. Rep. 435 (2011).

[169]*See* Chapter 2 for discussion of intentional torts. Students could also seek criminal prosecution if a crime was committed in connection with discipline (e.g., child abuse).

[170]On the other hand, students may have to pay school districts restitution for damages they have caused. *See, e.g.*, Wisconsin v. Vanbeek, 765 N.W.2d 834 (Wis. Ct. App. 2009) (ordering a student who made a bomb threat to pay $18,026.01 to a school district for losses incurred including salaries and benefits of the school staff for the time when school was evacuated).

The Supreme Court has held that school officials can be sued for monetary damages in state courts as well as in federal courts under Section 1983 of the Civil Rights Act of 1871 if they arbitrarily violate students' federally protected rights in disciplinary proceedings.[171] In *Wood v. Strickland*, the Court declared that ignorance of the law is not a valid defense to shield school officials from liability if they should have known that their actions would impair students' clearly established federal rights.[172] Other courts have reiterated school officials' potential liability in connection, but to date, students have not been as successful as teachers in obtaining monetary awards for constitutional violations.

In fact, the Supreme Court has placed restrictions on the amount of damages that could be awarded to students in instances involving the impairment of procedural due process rights. **In *Carey v. Piphus*, the Court declared that students who were suspended without a hearing, but were not otherwise injured, could recover only nominal damages (not to exceed one dollar).**[173] The Court also explained that students might be entitled to substantial damages if suspensions are proven to be unwarranted.[174] Students could obtain attorneys' fees; however, a student who pursues meritless litigation may be responsible for the school district's attorneys' fees.[175]

CONCLUSION

In 1969, Justice Black noted: "School discipline, like parental discipline, is an integral and important part of training our children to be good citizens—to be better citizens."[176] Accordingly, school personnel have been empowered with the authority and duty to regulate pupil behavior in order to protect the interests of the student body and the school. Reasonable sanctions can be imposed if students do not adhere to legitimate conduct regulations. Courts, however, will intervene if disciplinary procedures are arbitrary or impair students' protected rights. Because school personnel cannot be faulted for providing too much due process, but can be assessed damages for procedural and substantive due process violations, educators should take every precaution to afford fair and impartial treatment to students.

The following generalizations reflect the current status of the law on the topics covered in this chapter.

[171]Howlett v. Rose, 496 U.S. 356 (1990).

[172]420 U.S. 308 (1975).

[173]435 U.S. 247 (1978); *see also* Zamecnik v. Indian Prairie Sch. Dist., 636 F.3d 874 (7th Cir. 2011) (affirming damages in the amount of $25 when two students' free speech rights were violated).

[174]*See* Kennedy v. Dexter Consol. Schs., 10 P.3d 115 (N.M. 2000) (affirming award of substantial compensatory and punitive damages to two high school students subjected to an unconstitutional strip search).

[175]Workman v. Dist. 13 Tanque Verde Unified Sch., 402 F. App'x 292 (9th Cir. 2010).

[176]Tinker v. Des Moines Indep. Cmty. Sch. Dist., 393 U.S. 503, 524 (1969) (Black, J., dissenting).

1. When creating and implementing student codes of conduct, school authorities should ensure rules and consequences are written clearly and enforced in a nondiscriminatory fashion.

2. Every punishment should be paired with procedural due process (notice of violation and punishment, an opportunity to refute charges before an impartial decision maker, and explanation of decision based on evidence).

3. The extent of due process provided should increase as the punishments become more severe.

4. If a student is expelled, then the school must provide a number of procedural protections (e.g., a full and fair hearing before an impartial adjudicator, with the opportunity to confront and cross-examine witnesses).

5. Corporal punishment has not been found to be unconstitutional, but it may be prohibited by state law or local district policy.

6. A student's substantive due process rights are violated if the administration of discipline rises to the level of shocking the conscience.

7. Academic sanctions for nonacademic reasons should be reasonable; related to performance, absences, or other academic concerns; and serve a legitimate school purpose.

8. Students possess Fourth Amendment rights against unreasonable searches; however, school employees need only reasonable suspicion that a student is violating a school rule or the law to search a student.

9. The level of suspicion required increases with the intrusiveness of the search: searches that are highly intrusive must be supported by a greater degree of suspicion.

10. A search of a student must be reasonable at its inception and reasonable in scope.

11. Student athletes and those involved in extra-curricular activities can be drug tested without reasonable suspicion.

12. School personnel should refrain from conducting strip searches or blanket searches of groups of students.

13. Questions have been raised about the involvement of law enforcement officers, including SROs, in school settings if they use excessive force and problematic interrogation procedures.

CHAPTER NINE

CONDITIONS OF EMPLOYMENT AND COLLECTIVE BARGAINING

Can teachers' salaries be based on evaluation ratings? Before reporting child abuse and neglect, must school personnel have evidence? Are teachers allowed to strike? This chapter presents an overview of specific state requirements pertaining to licensure, contracts, tenure, collective bargaining, and other related aspects of employment. Employment issues concerning constitutional rights or antidiscrimination mandates are addressed in subsequent chapters.

Readers of this chapter should be able to:

- Describe the requirements to obtain and retain a teaching or administrative license.
- Recognize the authority of local school boards to hire, fire, assign, and transfer school employees.
- Define the elements of an employment contract and the types of school contracts (term, tenure, and supplemental).
- Discuss issues that have led to litigation surrounding personnel evaluations.
- Explain how to maintain personnel records in accordance with federal and state mandates.
- Detail the process for reporting child abuse and neglect.
- Distinguish between the collective bargaining processes for a teachers' union and the grievance procedures for individual school employees.

STATE OVERSIGHT OF EMPLOYMENT

States regulate employment in public schools, including granting and revoking licensure of teachers and administrators.

State legislatures are responsible for maintaining a uniform system of public schools and thus govern public school employment as well as some aspects of private school employment. The legislature enacts laws to establish the boundaries within which educational systems operate; however, the actual administration of school systems is delegated to state boards of education, state departments of education, and local school boards. These agencies enact rules and regulations pursuant to state law in order to oversee the operation of public schools.

State law cannot contradict federal law. State statutes and regulations play a prominent role in defining school personnel's employment rights, but they must be viewed as part of the larger system of state and federal constitutional provisions and civil rights laws. Additionally, the negotiated agreements between school boards and teachers' unions—referred to as collective bargaining agreements or master contracts—also outline employment matters. These agreements and federal law may restrict or modify options available under state employment law. For example, the authority to transfer teachers may be vested in the school board, but the board cannot use this power to retaliate against teachers for exercising their constitutional rights. The board's discretion may be further limited if it has agreed in the collective bargaining agreement to follow certain procedures prior to transferring an employee.

Among the areas affected by state statutory and regulatory provisions are the terms and conditions of educators' employment. As discussed in Chapter 4, most states have adopted the Common Core State Standards.[1] These efforts have had an impact not only on the curriculum and operation of schools but also on expectations for educators. Additionally, federal law can impact employment requirements.[2] Thus, local school boards must carefully attend to the ever-evolving employee requirements under state and federal law.

Licensure

To qualify for a teaching or leadership position in public schools, prospective teachers and administrators must acquire a valid license or certificate from their state.[3] Licenses are issued according to each state's statutory provisions.[4] States have not only the right but also the duty to establish minimum qualifications and to ensure that teachers and school leaders meet these standards. Minimum qualifications for licensure may include successful completion of a state-accredited preparation program as well as other prerequisites. Some states have adopted reciprocity policies where the state might accept a license from another state.[5] Although the responsibility for licensing resides with state legislatures, administration of the process has been delegated to state boards of education and departments of education.

---

[1]U.S. Dep't of Educ., *College-and Career-Ready Standards* (n.d.), https://www.ed.gov/k-12reforms/standards.

[2]For example, the No Child Left Behind Act (NCLB) demanded that students be taught only by highly qualified educators in core subjects, and then the Every Student Succeeds Act (ESSA) eliminated this requirement. ESSA did, however, keep the Title I equity provision from NCLB that requires low-income, minority students to be taught by effective and experienced teachers, 20 U.S.C. § 6312 (2018).

[3]The words *licensure* and *certification* are used interchangeably in this chapter.

[4]Courts have upheld legislative efforts to alter licensure standards by imposing new or additional requirements as prerequisites to renew a license. *See, e.g.*, Texas v. Project Principle, 724 S.W.2d 387 (Tex. 1987).

[5]Nat'l Ass'n of State Dirs. of Teacher Educ. & Certification, *Interstate Agreement* (n.d.), http://www.nasdtec.net/?page=interstate.

Teaching Certification.   Licenses are granted primarily on the basis of professional preparation. In most states, educational requirements include a college degree, with minimum credit hours or courses in various curricular areas. In response to teacher shortages in under-resourced schools or subject areas (e.g., special education), states have allowed for alternative certification that permits prospective teachers to forego completion of a traditional teacher preparation program. Some examples of alternative routes to becoming a teacher include transition-to-teaching and Teach for America programs that allow candidates to complete reduced coursework because they already have a bachelor's degree.[6] In addition to alternative certification, some states have begun to offer teacher leader licenses to certify that these teachers are prepared to assume leadership responsibilities in their schools.[7]

Prerequisites for earning a traditional teaching license may include being a certain minimum age, having U.S. citizenship, signing a loyalty oath, and passing a licensure examination. Additionally, an applicant for certification may be required to have "good moral character." The definition of what constitutes good character often is elusive, with several factors entering into the determination.[8]

Licensure of teachers by examination was common prior to the expansion of teacher education programs in colleges and universities. With the emphasis on improving the quality of teachers and the strong movement toward standards-based licensure, most states now require some type of standardized test or performance-based assessment for initial license, and/or license renewal.[9] **If a state establishes a test or assessment process as an essential eligibility requirement, it can deny a license to individuals who do not pass.** The U.S. Supreme Court has upheld the use of tests even though some have been shown to disproportionately disqualify applicants of color.[10]

Signing a loyalty oath may be a condition of obtaining a teaching license, but such oaths cannot be used to restrict association rights guaranteed under the U.S. Constitution. The Supreme Court has invalidated oaths that require teacher applicants to swear that they

---

[6]Teach For Am., *About Us* (n.d.), https://www.teachforamerica.org/about-us; *see also* Diane Rado, *State Allows Educators to Bypass Some Exams, Courses for Teacher Licensing*, Chic. Trib. (Sept. 29, 2017), http://www .chicagotribune.com/news/local/breaking/ct-teacher-certification-illinois-met-20170924-story.html.

[7]*See, e.g.*, Teacher Standards & Practices Comm'n, *Teacher Leader Licensure* (n.d.), http://www.oregon.gov/ tspc/Pages/Licensing/Teacher_Leader_License.aspx. Teacher leader licensure is also called teacher leader endorsement, certificate, license, or specialization.

[8]*See* Gonzaga Univ. v. Doe, 536 U.S. 273 (2002) (discussing a student who needed a good moral character affidavit to become certified to teach); Landers v. Ark. Dep't of Educ., 374 S.W.3d 795 (Ark. 2010) (upholding the denial of an applicant's teaching license because of her single felony theft conviction that had been expunged from her record); Wright v. Kan. State Bd. of Educ., 268 P.3d 1231 (Kan. Ct. App. 2012) (upholding the state board's denial of a disbarred attorney's application for a teaching license because of his prior conviction for felony theft). Courts generally will not rule on the wisdom of a certifying agency's assessment of character; they will intervene only if statutory or constitutional rights are abridged.

[9]Almost half the states have set up professional standards boards to govern and regulate standards-based criteria and assessment for licenses. The primary purpose of these boards, whose membership is composed mostly of teachers, is to address issues of educator preparation, licensure, and relicensure.

[10]United States v. South Carolina, 445 F. Supp. 1094 (D.S.C. 1977), *aff'd sub nom.* Nat'l Educ. Ass'n v. South Carolina, 434 U.S. 1026 (1978). *See* Chapter 11 for a discussion about discrimination challenges to teacher testing.

are not members of subversive organizations;[11] yet teachers can be required to sign an oath pledging faithful performance of duties and support for the U.S. Constitution and their state's constitution.[12] According to the Supreme Court, these oaths must be narrowly limited to affirmation of support for the government and a pledge not to act forcibly to overthrow the government.[13]

Licenses are issued for designated periods of time under various classifications such as emergency, temporary, provisional, professional, and permanent. Renewing or upgrading a license may require additional university coursework, continuing education activities, or passage of an examination. Licenses also specify professional position (e.g., teacher, administrator, librarian), subject areas (e.g., history, math), and grade levels (e.g., elementary, secondary). Where licensure subject areas have been established, a teacher must possess a valid license to teach a specific subject. A school district's failure to employ licensed teachers may result in the loss of state accreditation and financial support. In addition to state licensure, many teachers seek national certification, which involves an intensive assessment of teaching knowledge and skills by the National Board for Professional Teaching Standards. States and school districts may provide financial support for teachers seeking this national board certification.[14]

A license indicates only that a teacher has satisfied minimum state requirements; no absolute right exists to acquire a position. It does not entitle an individual to employment, nor does it prevent a local school board from attaching additional prerequisites to employment. For example, a California appellate court ruled that it was within a school board's authority to terminate a teacher who refused to obtain a certificate to teach English Learners.[15] Also, under most state laws, teachers must file their licenses with the school district where they are employed. Failure to renew a license prior to expiration or to meet educational requirements necessary to maintain or acquire a higher-grade license can result in loss of employment. Without proper licensure, a teaching contract is unenforceable.

License Revocation

The state is empowered not only to license educators but also to suspend or revoke licensure. Although a local board may initiate charges against school personnel, only the state can alter the status of their licenses. Revocation is a harsh penalty, generally foreclosing future employment as a teacher. As such, it must be based on statutory causes, such as immorality or incompetency with full procedural rights provided to the teacher.[16] Examples of actions justifying revocation include misrepresenting experience and credentials in a job application and altering the license to misrepresent areas of licensure

[11]Keyishian v. Bd. of Regents, 385 U.S. 589 (1967).

[12]Ohlson v. Phillips, 397 U.S. 317 (1970).

[13]Cole v. Richardson, 405 U.S. 676 (1972); Connell v. Higginbotham, 403 U.S. 207 (1971).

[14]For information regarding each state, *see* Nat'l Bd. for Prof'l Teaching Standards, *In Your State* (n.d.), http://www.nbpts.org/state-local-information.

[15]Governing Bd. v. Comm'n on Prof'l Conduct, 99 Cal. Rptr. 3d 903 (Ct. App. 2009).

[16]*See also* Chapter 12 for discussion of procedural due process.

(immorality);[17] theft of drugs and money (conduct unbecoming a teacher);[18] abusive comments to students and threats made in a letter of resignation (unprofessional conduct);[19] and assault on a minor (lack of good moral character).[20]

When revocation or suspension of a license is being considered, employees' actions outside the school setting that impair teaching effectiveness may be examined. A California appellate court upheld the suspension of a teacher's license because she had three drunk-driving convictions.[21] In a Texas case, an appellate court upheld the license revocation of a teacher who had exposed his penis in public and engaged in other indecent exposure incidents, finding the conduct rendered him unworthy to instruct.[22] Courts will not overturn the judgment of a state board regarding an educator's fitness to teach unless evidence clearly establishes that the decision is unreasonable, unlawful, or not specifically related to job duties. For example, an Oregon teacher's license was not renewed after she left her son in the school parking lot during school hours. The licensing body found this conduct to be a gross neglect of her professional duties; however, a state appellate court overturned the decision because there was not a strong enough connection between the teacher's job duties and the underlying conduct.[23]

EMPLOYMENT BY LOCAL SCHOOL BOARDS

School boards are vested with the power to hire teachers and administrators, as well as to establish professional and academic employment standards above the state minimums.

Although such powers are broad, school board actions may neither be arbitrary nor capricious, nor may they violate an individual's statutory or constitutional rights (i.e., decisions must be neutral as to race, religion, national origin, and sex).[24] Furthermore, boards must comply with mandated statutory procedures as well as locally adopted procedures. Unless protected individual rights are abridged, courts will defer to the school board's judgment in employment decisions made in good faith.

The responsibility for hiring teachers and administrators is vested in the school board as a collective body and cannot be delegated to the superintendent or board members individually. In most states, binding employment agreements between a teacher

---

[17]Nanko v. Dep't of Educ., 663 A.2d 312 (Pa. Commw. Ct. 1995).

[18]Crumpler v. State Bd. of Educ., 594 N.E.2d 1071 (Ohio Ct. App. 1991).

[19]Knight v. Winn, 910 So. 2d 310 (Fla. Dist. Ct. App. 2005).

[20]*In re* Morrill, 765 A.2d 699 (N.H. 2001).

[21]Broney v. Cal. Comm'n on Teacher Credentialing, 108 Cal. Rptr. 3d 832 (Ct. App. 2010).

[22]Gomez v. Tex. Educ. Agency, 354 S.W.3d 905 (Tex. Ct. App. 2011).

[23]Eicks v. Teacher Standards & Practices Comm'n, 349 P.3d 591 (Or. Ct. App. 2015).

[24]*See* Chapter 10 for a discussion of teachers' constitutional rights and Chapter 11 for a discussion of discriminatory employment practices. Under limited circumstances, sex may be a bona fide occupational qualification (e.g., supervision of the girls' locker room).

or an administrator and the school board must be approved at legally scheduled board meetings. Most state laws specify that the superintendent must make employment recommendations to the board; however, the board is not compelled to follow these recommendations unless mandated to do so by law. In fact, school boards have broad authority to establish job requirements and conditions of employment for school personnel. The following sections examine the school board's power to impose specific conditions on employment and to assign personnel.

Employment Requirements

The state's establishment of minimum licensure standards for educators does not preclude the local school board from requiring higher standards so long as they are applied in a uniform and nondiscriminatory manner. For example, school boards often establish continuing education requirements for teachers, and a board's right to dismiss teachers for failing to satisfy such requirements has been endorsed by the Supreme Court.[25] The Court concluded that school officials merely had to establish that the requirement was rationally related to a legitimate state objective, which in this case was to provide competent, well-trained teachers.

School boards can adopt reasonable health and physical requirements for school personnel. Courts have recognized that such standards are necessary to safeguard the health and welfare of students and other employees. For example, the First Circuit held that a school board could compel an administrator to submit to a psychiatric examination as a condition of continued employment because a reasonable basis existed for board members to believe that the administrator might jeopardize the safety of students.[26] Similarly, the Sixth Circuit ruled that a school board could justifiably order a teacher to submit to mental and physical examinations when his aberrant behavior affected his job performance.[27] Standards for physical fitness must be rationally related to the ability to perform teaching duties, and regulations must not contravene various laws designed to protect the rights of persons with disabilities.[28]

Under state laws, most school boards are required to conduct a criminal background check of all prospective employees.[29] The screening process may require individuals to consent to fingerprinting. Concern for students' safety also has led some school districts to

---

[25]Harrah Indep. Sch. Dist. v. Martin, 440 U.S. 194 (1979) (upholding a policy requiring teachers to earn an additional five semester hours of college credit every three years while employed).

[26]Daury v. Smith, 842 F.2d 9 (1st Cir. 1988); *see also* Down v. Ann Arbor Pub. Schs., 29 F. Supp. 3d 1030 (E.D. Mich. 2014) (denying a teacher's motion for preliminary injunction against the district because the district had good reason to ask the teacher to undergo an exam with a psychologist).

[27]Sullivan v. River Valley Sch. Dist., 197 F.3d 804 (6th Cir. 1999); *see also* Gardner v. Niskayuna Cent. Sch. Dist., 839 N.Y.S.2d 317 (App. Div. 2007) (finding that a school board is charged with determining that teachers are fit to teach; thereby, teachers may be required to submit to physical or mental exams).

[28]*See* Chapter 11 for a discussion of discrimination based on disabilities.

[29]*See* Denuis v. Dunlap, 209 F.3d 944 (7th Cir. 2000) (holding that a teacher was not required to relinquish constitutional privacy rights regarding medical or financial records for an employment background check).

require teacher applicants—and any employees applying for safety sensitive positions such as bus drivers—to submit to drug testing. To date, the Sixth Circuit is the only federal appellate court that has upheld such testing, noting that teachers occupy safety-sensitive positions in a highly regulated environment with diminished privacy expectations.[30] Multiple lower courts have also addressed this issue. For example, a Florida court in 2017 held that a school board had demonstrated that protecting students was a compelling governmental interest that outweighed the privacy interests of a substitute teacher who argued that a pre-employment drug test violated her Fourth Amendment rights.[31] In contrast, a West Virginia court prohibited a district from suspicionless drug testing of its employees because it was not justified based on a special need.[32]

Unless prohibited by law, school boards may require school personnel to live within the school district as a condition of employment. Typically, residency requirements have been imposed on urban communities and encompass all city employees, including educators. The Supreme Court upheld a municipal regulation requiring all employees hired after a specified date in Philadelphia to be residents of the city, finding no impairment of Fourteenth Amendment equal protection rights or interference with interstate and intrastate travel.[33] Lower courts have applied similar reasoning in upholding residency requirements for public educators; yet, some states by law do not permit residency requirements.[34]

Unlike residency requirements, school board policies requiring employees to send their children to public schools have been declared unconstitutional. Parents have a constitutionally protected right to direct the upbringing of their children, which cannot be restricted without a compelling state interest. The Eleventh Circuit held that a school board policy requiring employees to enroll their children in public schools could not be justified to promote an integrated public school system and good relationships among teachers when weighed against the right of parents to direct the education of their children.[35]

[30]Knox Cty. Educ. Ass'n v. Knox Cty. Bd. of Educ., 158 F.3d 361 (6th Cir. 1998); *see also* Aubrey v. Sch. Bd. of Lafayette Par., 148 F.3d 559 (5th Cir. 1998) (upholding the constitutionality of a Louisiana law requiring a school custodian to be drug tested because he interacted with students and operated potentially dangerous equipment). *See* Chapter 10 for discussion of Fourth Amendment rights of employees.

[31]Friedenberg v. Sch. Bd. of Palm Beach Cty., 257 F. Supp. 3d 1295 (S.D. Fla. 2017).

[32]Am Fed'n of Teachers v. Kanawha Cty. Bd. of Educ., 592 F. Supp. 2d 883 (S.D. W. Va. 2009); *see also* Smith Cty. Educ. Ass'n v. Smith Cty. Bd. of Educ., 2012 U.S. Dist. LEXIS 3020 (M.D. Tenn. Jan. 10, 2012) (holding drug policy unconstitutional by distinguishing this case from the Sixth Circuit decision upholding a drug-testing policy that specifically targeted only those applying for teaching positions or those seeking promotion within the district).

[33]McCarthy v. Phila. Civil Serv. Comm'n, 424 U.S. 645 (1976); *see also In re* Beck-Nichols v. Bianco, 964 N.Y.S.2d 456 (App. Div. 2013) (finding that the teacher had violated the city's residency requirement).

[34]*See, e.g.,* Providence Teachers' Union Local 958 v. City Council, 888 A.2d 948 (R.I. 2005); IND. CODE ANN. § 20-28-10-13 (2018); MASS. GEN. LAWS ch. 71, § 38 (2018).

[35]Stough v. Crenshaw Cty. Bd. of Educ., 744 F.2d 1479 (11th Cir. 1984).

Assignment of Personnel and Duties

The authority to assign teachers to schools within a district resides with the local school board; however, these decisions must not be arbitrary or made in bad faith or in retaliation for the exercise of protected rights. Within the limits of a license, a teacher can be assigned to teach in any school, at any grade level. Assignments designated in the teacher's contract, however, cannot be changed during a contractual period without the teacher's consent. That is, a board cannot reassign a teacher to a first-grade class if the contract specifies a fifth-grade assignment. If the contract designates only a teaching assignment within the district, the assignment still must be in the teacher's licensure area. Also, objective, nondiscriminatory standards must be used. School districts that have not eliminated the effects of school segregation may make assignments based on race as long as the racial classification is temporary and necessary to eradicate the effects of prior discrimination.[36]

Teacher reassignments and transfers often are challenged as demotions. Depending on state law, factors considered in determining whether a reassignment is a demotion may include reduction in salary, responsibility, and stature of position. A transfer from one grade level to another is not usually considered a demotion. As long as the assignments do not conflict with state law, federal rights, or the collective bargaining agreement, courts typically defer to superintendents and school boards.[37]

To illustrate, a South Carolina appellate court concluded that the reassignment of an assistant superintendent to a principal position was within the school board's discretion when it did not involve a reduction in salary or violate the district's regulations.[38] Similarly, the Seventh Circuit found that the reassignment of a principal to a central office position did not involve an economic loss requiring an opportunity for a hearing.[39] Moreover, reassignment from an administrative to a teaching position because of financial constraints or good faith reorganization is not a demotion requiring due process unless procedural protections are specified in state law.

Noninstructional duties such as lesson planning and parent conferences are often defined in a teacher's contract or in the collective bargaining agreement negotiated between the school board and the teachers' union. In the absence of such specification, school officials can make reasonable and appropriate assignments, such as activities that are an integral part of the school program and related to the employee's teaching responsibilities.[40] Reasonableness of an assignment is typically evaluated in terms of time involvement, teachers' interests and abilities, benefits to students, and the professional nature of the duty. Refusal to accept reasonable assigned duties can result in dismissal.

---

[36]*See, e.g.,* Straughter v. Vicksburg Warren Sch. Dist., 152 F. App'x 407 (5th Cir. 2005); *see also* text accompanying note 39, Chapter 11.

[37]*See, e.g.,* Kodl v. Bd. of Educ., 490 F.3d 558 (7th Cir. 2007) (finding that a middle school teacher's transfer to an elementary school did not violate any federal rights).

[38]Barr v. Bd. of Trs., 462 S.E.2d 316 (S.C. Ct. App. 1995).

[39]Bordelon v. Chi. Sch. Reform Bd. of Trs., 233 F.3d 524 (7th Cir. 2000).

[40]*See* Warwick Sch. Dep't v. R.I. State Labor Relations Bd., 2017 R.I. Super. LEXIS 30 (Super. Ct. Feb. 2, 2017) (arguing that duty assignments for homeroom teachers were unfair).

CONTRACTS

Teacher contracts must satisfy the general principles of contract law as well as conform to any additional specifications contained in state law or the collective bargaining agreement.

The employment contract defines the rights and responsibilities of the teacher and the school board in the employment relationship. Teachers should be aware of two contracts: (1) an individual contract that outlines the teacher's specific employment and (2) the collective bargaining agreement that outlines the employment for all the teachers in the district. State and district policy may also be considered part of the terms and conditions of the contract. Basic elements required in all legal contracts must be included in the individual teaching contract (see Figure 9.1)[41]

The authority to contract with teachers is an exclusive right of the board. The school board's *offer* of a position to a teacher—including (1) designated salary, (2) specified period of time, and (3) identified duties and responsibilities—creates a binding contract when *accepted* by the teacher. In most states, only the board can make an offer, and this action must be approved by a majority of the board members. In a Washington case, the coordinator of special services extended an offer of employment to a teacher at the beginning of the school year, pending responses from past employers to a reference check. The input from past employers was negative, and the teacher was not recommended to the board, even though she had been teaching for several weeks. A state appellate court held that no enforceable contract existed because the hiring authority resided with the board.[42]

Contracts also can be invalidated because of lack of *competent parties*. To form a valid, binding contract, both parties must have the legal capacity to enter into an agreement. A teacher who lacks a license or is under the statutorily required age for licensure is not considered a competent party for contractual purposes. Consequently, a contract made with such an individual is not enforceable.

Consideration is another essential element of a valid contract. Consideration is something of value that one party pays in return for the other party's performance. Teachers' monetary compensation and benefits are established in the salary schedule that is often negotiated between the school board and the teachers' association.[43] The contract also must involve a *legal subject matter* and follow the *proper form* required by law. Most states

[41]For a discussion of contract elements, *see* KERN ALEXANDER & M. DAVID ALEXANDER, AMERICAN PUBLIC SCHOOL LAW (8th ed. 2012).

[42]McCormick v. Lake Wash. Sch. Dist., 992 P.2d 511 (Wash. Ct. App. 2000). *But see* Trahan v. Lafayette Par. Sch. Bd., 978 So. 2d 1105 (La. Ct. App. 2008) (upholding employment contract executed by superintendent on behalf of board); KY. REV. STAT. ANN. § 160.370 (2018) (stating that superintendent has the power regarding employment contract decisions).

[43]*See* Davis v. Greenwood Sch. Dist., 620 S.E.2d 65 (S.C. 2005) (holding that an annual incentive payment for acquiring national board certification did not violate the teachers' contracts and was within the board's discretion to manage the district's finances).

[44]*See* Sexton v. KIPP Reach Acad. Charter Sch., 260 P.3d 435 (Okla. Civ. App. 2011) (finding an implied contract may have been created when a teacher was given a faculty-only cell phone, provided a letter of intent, and enrolled in a teachers' conference).

FIGURE 9.1   Contract Elements

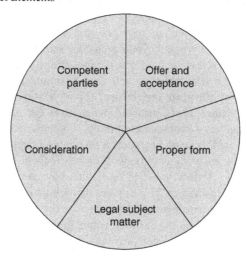

require a teacher's contract to be in writing to be enforceable,[44] but if there is no statutory specification, an oral agreement is legally binding on both parties. If a school district is found to have breached a teacher's contract, damages and attorneys' fees might be available. For example, an art teacher at a charter school alleged that school officials breached her employment contract after she was terminated mid-year when the school needed to use her salary to hire a new math teacher. Denying the school's motion for a directed verdict, the South Carolina Supreme Court found that there was evidence to support a finding that school officials had breached her contract and awarded damages and attorneys' fees to the teacher.[45]

Term and Tenure Contracts

Two basic types of employment contracts are issued to teachers: term contracts and tenure contracts. *Term contracts* are valid for a fixed period of time (e.g., one year). At the end of the contract period, renewal is at the discretion of the school board; nonrenewal requires no explanation unless mandated by statute. Generally, a school board is required only to provide notice prior to the expiration of the contract that employment will not be renewed. *Tenure contracts*, created through state law, ensure teachers that employment will be terminated only for adequate cause and that procedural due process will be provided. **After the award of tenure or *within* a term contract, school boards cannot unilaterally abrogate teachers' contracts. At a minimum, the teacher must be provided procedural protections consisting of notice of the dismissal charges and a hearing.**[46]

Because tenure contracts are regulated through state law, specific procedures and protections vary among the states. Most tenure statutes specify requirements and procedures for obtaining tenure and identify causes and procedures for dismissing a tenured teacher. In interpreting tenure laws, courts have attempted to protect teachers' rights while simultaneously preserving school officials' flexibility in personnel management.

[45]McNaughton v. Charleston Charter Sch. for Math & Sci., 768 S.E.2d 389 (S.C. 2015).

[46]*See* Chapter 12 for discussion of procedural due process requirements.

Prior to a school board awarding a tenure contract to a teacher, most states require a probationary period of approximately three years to assess a teacher's ability and competence. During this probationary period, teachers receive term contracts, and there is no guarantee of employment beyond each contract. Tenure statutes generally require regular and continuous service to complete the probationary period.

Although the school board confers tenure, it cannot alter the tenure terms established by the state legislature; the legislature determines the basis for tenure, eligibility requirements, and the procedures for acquiring tenure status. Thus, if a state law requires a probationary period, this term of service must be completed prior to the school board's awarding tenure. A board may be compelled to award tenure if a teacher completes the statutory requirements and the school board does not take action to grant or deny tenure. Unless specified by statute, however, tenure is not transferable from one school district to another. This ensures that school officials are provided an opportunity to evaluate teachers before granting tenure.

States often limit the award of tenure to teaching positions, thereby excluding administrative, supervisory, and staff positions. Where tenure is available for administrative positions, probationary service and other specified statutory terms must be met. Tenure as a teacher usually does not imply tenure as an administrator, yet most courts have concluded that continued service as a certified professional employee, albeit as an administrator, does not alter tenure rights that administrators already acquired as teachers.

Some state legislatures have begun to repeal teacher tenure laws.[47] In these instances, a teacher who has acquired tenure might find that under the new law, tenure can be threatened. In an illustrative case from North Carolina, teachers alleged that a repeal of the Career Status Law unlawfully infringed upon the contract rights of those teachers who had already achieved career status, which violated the U.S. Constitution's Obligation of Contracts Clause. The state supreme court agreed, finding the new state tenure law to be unconstitutional because teachers had relied on the promise of continued employment under the former law.[48]

In *Vergara v. State*, nine California public school students alleged that state laws—including the one granting teachers tenure—had resulted in the hiring and retaining of "grossly ineffective teachers" and that these teachers caused them harm.[49] The students also claimed that the grossly ineffective teachers were more likely to be assigned to low-income, Black, and Latino students. The trial court found that the state statutes violated the equal protection clause of the state constitution, but the California appellate court reversed this decision. According to the appellate court, there was no showing that the state laws caused the students to be provided with an education that was not equivalent to higher-income, White students.[49]

---

[47]As of 2017, three states (Florida, North Dakota, and Kansas) did not offer tenure for teachers. *See* FLA. STAT. § 1012.33 (2018) (allowing teachers with continuing contracts to retain such contracts); KAN. STAT. ANN. § 76-11a05 (2018) (explaining that teachers must receive notice of termination or nonrenewal); N.D. CENT. CODE § 15.1-15-05 (2018) (discussing that nonrenewal of teachers must not be "frivolous or arbitrary").

[48]N.C. Ass'n of Educators v. North Carolina, 786 S.E.2d 255 (N.C. 2016).

[49]Vergara v. California, 209 Cal. Rptr. 3d 532, 539 (Ct. App. 2016). Similar challenges in other states will likely continue. *See School Equity Lawsuits Face Setbacks: Have Judges Closed the Courthouse Door to Students?* THE74, (n.d.) https://www.the74million.org/article/school-equity-lawsuits-face-setbacks-have-judges-closed-the-courthouse-door-to-students/.

Supplemental Contracts

School boards can enter into supplemental contracts with teachers for duties beyond the regular teaching assignments. Generally, these are limited contracts specifying the additional duties, compensation, and time period. Extra duties often relate to coaching, chairing a department, supervising student activities or clubs, and other special assignments.

Supplemental contracts are usually considered outside the scope of tenure protections. Coaches, in particular, have asserted that supplemental contracts are an integral part of the teaching position and thereby must be afforded the procedural and substantive protections of state tenure laws. Generally, tenure rights apply only to employment in licensure areas, and the lack of licensure requirements for coaches in a state often negates tenure claims for such positions.

Some courts also have distinguished coaching and various extra duties from teaching responsibilities based on the extracurricular nature of the assignment and supplemental compensation. In denying the claim of a ten-year veteran baseball coach who was fired from his coaching position but not from teaching, the Ninth Circuit held that the coach did not have a protected interest in his coaching position since California law specified that extra-duty assignments could be terminated by the school board at any time.[50] When both classroom teaching and extra-duty assignments are covered in the same contract, however, protected property interests may be created. Accordingly, the teacher would be entitled to due process prior to the termination of the extra-duty assignment.

Because coaching assignments typically require execution of a supplemental contract, a teacher can resign from a coaching position and maintain the primary teaching position. School boards having difficulty filling coaching positions may tender an offer to teach on the condition that an individual assume certain coaching responsibilities.[51]

If teaching and coaching positions are combined, a qualified teaching applicant who cannot assume the coaching duties may be rejected. This practice, however, may be vulnerable to legal challenge if certain classes of applicants, such as women, are excluded from consideration. In an Arizona case, female plaintiffs successfully established that a school district was liable for sex discrimination by coupling a high school biology teaching position with a football coaching position. The school board was unable to demonstrate a business necessity for the practice that resulted in the elimination of all female applicants from the applicant pool.[52]

Domestic Partner Benefits

A domestic partnership exists where two people in a relationship reside together but are not married. State law and school district policies vary about whether domestic partners are

[50]Lagos v. Modesto City Sch. Dist., 843 F.2d 347 (9th Cir. 1988); *see also* Bd. of Educ. v. Code, 57 S.W.3d 820 (Ky. 2001) (ruling that the basketball coach was not entitled to a formal evaluation prior to nonrenewal of his contract).

[51]If a single teaching and coaching contract is found to be indivisible, a teacher may not be able to resign from the coaching duties without also relinquishing the teaching position. Individual state laws must be consulted to determine the status of such contracts. *See, e.g.*, Smith v. Petal Sch. Dist., 956 So. 2d 273 (Miss. Ct. App. 2006).

[52]Civil Rights Div. v. Amphitheater Unified Sch. Dist., 706 P.2d 745 (Ariz. Ct. App. 1985).

entitled to health, retirement, and other benefits comparable to spousal benefits. For years, LGBTQ couples fought to secure benefits for domestic partners. As a result, many states recognized civil unions, which created a legal relationship between same-sex couples and entitled them to domestic partner benefits (but did not provide federal benefits).

In the 2013 decision, *United States v. Windsor*, the Supreme Court struck down a federal law enacted in 1996 (the Defense of Marriage Act, DOMA), which had denied employment benefits to married same-sex couples. The *Windsor* Court observed that DOMA "violates basic due process and equal protection principles applicable to the Federal Government."[53] This decision guaranteed employment benefits to married same-sex couples. Then, in 2015, the Supreme Court held in *Obergefell v. Hodges* that it is unconstitutional to deny same-sex couples the right to marry.[54] This landmark decision affects school district employment policies.[55] The marriage equality opinion has many implications for schools, including "employee benefits, parental rights of access, and the . . . school atmosphere for gay youths."[56] For example, same-sex couples who marry must now receive the same benefits as opposite-sex partners under federal and state law. Employees who are unmarried—regardless of whether they are in a same-sex or opposite-sex relationship—may be entitled to domestic partner benefits dependent on state law and district policy.

Leaves of Absence

Contracts may specify various types of leaves of absence, such as sick leave, personal leave, pregnancy or childcare leave, sabbatical leave, disability leave, family leave, and military leave. Within the parameters of state and federal law, school boards have discretion in establishing requirements for these leaves. A school board may place restrictions on when teachers can take personal leave—for example, barring leaves on the day before or after a holiday or allowing no more than two consecutive days of personal leave.[57] This topic often is the subject of collective bargaining, with leave provisions specified in bargained agreements. **School boards, however, cannot negotiate leave policies that impair rights guaranteed by the U.S. Constitution and various federal and state laws.**[58]

[53]133 S. Ct. 2675, 2693 (2013).

[54]135 S. Ct. 2584 (2015).

[55]Nat'l Sch. Bds. Ass'n, *Same-Sex Marriage: What the* Obergefell *Decision Means for School Districts* (July 2015), https://cdn-files.nsba.org/s3fs-public/reports/NSBA_Same_Sex_Marriage%20Guide-Obergefell-Decision.pdf?mJ338QTbdxKd4F1VUR6SQaLi7C8sSwZg.

[56]Mark Walsh, *In Case Watched by Educators, Supreme Court Backs Right to Same-Sex Marriage*, EDUC. WK. (June 26, 2015), http://blogs.edweek.org/edweek/school_law/2015/06/supreme_court_backs_right_to_s.html.

[57]*See, e.g.*, Amaral-Whittenberg v. Alanis, 123 S.W.3d 714 (Tex. Ct. App. 2003).

[58]*See* Chapter 11 for a discussion about discrimination claims in connection with leave policies pertaining to family and pregnancy-related absences and the observance of religious holidays. State laws pertaining to leaves of absence usually specify eligibility for benefits, minimum days the employer must provide, whether leave must be granted with or without pay, and restrictions that may be imposed by local school boards. If an employee meets all statutory and procedural requirements for a specific leave, a school board cannot deny the request.

PERSONNEL EVALUATIONS

State and federal laws have increased regulations surrounding teacher and administrator evaluations in recent years.

A school board's extensive authority to determine teacher performance standards may be restricted by state-imposed evaluation requirements. Recently, ESSA introduced a teacher and school leader innovation program that offers grant money to school districts that link performance pay to teacher quality indicators.[59] Beyond the purposes of faculty improvement and remediation, the results of evaluations may be used in a variety of employment decisions, including retention, tenure, dismissal, promotion, salary, reassignment, and reduction-in-force. When employees are dismissed, demoted, or disciplined due to negative evaluations, legal concerns of procedural fairness arise. Were established state and local procedures followed? Did school officials employ equitable standards? Was sufficient evidence collected to support the staffing decision? Were evaluations conducted in a uniform and consistent manner?

Historically, school systems have had broad discretionary powers to establish teacher performance criteria, but more recently, state statutes impose specific evaluation requirements. In 2009, only fifteen states required that objective measures of student achievement be included in teacher evaluations. But as of 2017, forty-three states required that such measures be considered.[60] Content and requirements vary substantially across states, with some states merely mandating the establishment of an appraisal system and others specifying procedures and criteria to be used. For example, Indiana requires that the objective measure of student achievement inform the evaluation.[61] Maine enacted legislation that permits school districts to use student assessments as part of the teacher evaluations.[62]

The recent changes to the evaluation of teachers have led to litigation.[63] To illustrate, some teachers have alleged that the state's evaluation system violates their federal due process and equal protection rights. In Florida, a group of teachers and their union posited that the state's system evaluated some teachers based on test scores of students that the teachers taught in other subjects or did not teach at all. The Eleventh Circuit affirmed summary judgment for the school district, finding that the evaluation system, even though in some cases problematic, passed rational basis review and that the program advanced a legitimate

---

[59]81 Fed. Reg. 229 (Nov. 29, 2016).

[60]Kathryn Doherty & Sandi Jacobs, *State of the States: Evaluating Teaching, Leading & Learning*, Nat'l Council on Tchr. Quality (Nov. 2015), http://www.nctq.org/dmsView/StateofStates2015.

[61]IND. CODE ANN. § 20-28-11.5-4(c)(2) (2018).

[62]ME. REV. STAT. tit. 20A (2018).

[63]*See* Stephen Sawchuk, *Teacher Evaluation Heads to Court*, EDUC. WK. (Oct. 6, 2015), http://www.edweek.org/ew/section/multimedia/teacher-evaluation-heads-to-the-courts.html.

governmental interest.[64] Teachers in several states continue to challenge these evaluation systems with mixed outcomes.[65]

Courts generally require strict compliance with evaluation requirements and procedures as identified in statutes, board policies, or employment contracts. Where school boards have been attentive to these requirements, courts have upheld challenged employment decisions. Courts are reluctant to interject their judgment into the teacher evaluation process. Judicial review generally is limited to the procedural issues of fairness and reasonableness. Several principles emerge from case law to guide educators in developing equitable systems:

- standards for evaluating teaching adequacy must be defined and communicated to teachers;
- assessment criteria must be applied uniformly and consistently;
- an opportunity and direction for improvement must be provided to teachers; and
- procedures specified in state laws and school board policies must be followed.

PERSONNEL RECORDS

Maintenance, access, and dissemination of personnel information must conform to state and federal laws and contractual agreements.

Because multiple statutes in each state as well as employment contracts govern school records, it is difficult to generalize about the specific nature of teachers' privacy rights regarding personnel files. State privacy laws that place restrictions on maintenance and access to school records typically do so to protect personnel information. Among other provisions, these laws usually require school boards to:

- maintain only necessary and relevant information;
- provide individual employees access to their own files;
- inform employees of the various uses of the files; and
- establish a procedure for challenging the accuracy of information.

Collective bargaining agreements may impose additional and more stringent requirements regarding access and dissemination of personnel information.

A central issue in the confidentiality of personnel files is whether the information constitutes a public record that must be reasonably accessible to the general public. Public record,

---

[64]Cook v. Bennett, 792 F.3d 1294 (11th Cir. 2015); *see also* Trout v. Knox Cty. Bd. of Educ., 163 F. Supp. 3d 492 (E.D. Tenn. 2016) (granting school district's motion to dismiss teachers' claim that considering student assessment scores violated their due process rights).

[65]*See, e.g.*, Leff v. Clark Cty. Sch. Dist., 210 F. Supp. 3d 1242 (D. Nev. 2016) (granting in part and denying in part the school district's motion to dismiss teachers' due process claims); Hous. Fed'n of Teachers v. Hous. Indep. Sch. Dist., 251 F. Supp. 3d 1168 (S.D. Tex. 2017) (denying school district's motion for summary judgment with respect to teachers' due process claim); New Mexico v. Skandera, 346 P.3d.1191 (N.M. Ct. App. 2015) (rejecting teachers' challenge of regulations that tied teacher competency to student performance scores).

freedom of information, right-to-know laws that grant broad access to school records may directly conflict with privacy laws, requiring courts to balance the interests of the teacher, the school officials, and the public. The specific provisions of state laws determine the level of confidentiality granted to personnel records.[66] The federal Freedom of Information Act (FOIA),[67] which serves as a model for many state FOIAs, often is used by courts in interpreting state provisions. Unlike the federal law, however, many states do not exempt personnel records.

In the absence of a specific exemption, most courts have concluded that **any doubt concerning the appropriateness of disclosure should be decided in favor of public disclosure**. The Supreme Court of Michigan held that teachers' personnel files are open to the public because they are not specifically exempt by law.[68] The Supreme Court of Washington noted that the Public Records Act mandated disclosure of information that is of legitimate public concern.[69] As such, the state superintendent of public instruction was required to provide a newspaper publisher records specifying the reasons for teacher certificate revocations. However, the Supreme Court of Washington held in another case that the public had no legitimate interest in obtaining the identities of teachers accused of an unsubstantiated allegation of sexual misconduct.[70] The Supreme Court of Connecticut interpreted the state FOIA exemption, prohibiting the release of information that would constitute an invasion of personal privacy, to include employees' evaluations[71] but not their sick leave records.[72] In the termination of a teacher for conducting pornographic Internet searches on his work computer, the Supreme Court of Wisconsin held that materials created as part of a forensic analysis of the teacher's computer were "records" subject to release under the state's Open Records Law after the school district completed its investigation.[73] **In general, information that must be maintained by law is a public record (e.g., personal directory information, salary information, employment contracts, leave records, and teaching license) and must be released**. At least one state has volunteered to post teachers' past disciplinary records on a public website absent a public records request; however, a teachers' union has filed suit citing privacy concerns.[74]

---

[66]*See* Wakefield Teachers Ass'n v. Sch. Comm., 731 N.E.2d 63 (Mass. 2000) (concluding that a disciplinary report is personnel information that is exempt under the state's public records law); Bangor Area Educ. Ass'n v. Angle, 720 A.2d 198 (Pa. Commw. Ct. 1998) (confirming that teachers' personnel files are not public records); Abbott v. N.E. Indep. Sch. Dist., 212 S.W.3d 364, 367 (Tex. Ct. App. 2006) (concluding that a principal's memorandum to a teacher that notified her of complaints and provided her guidance for improvement was "a document evaluating the performance of a teacher" and thus exempt from release under the state's public information act).

[67]5 U.S.C. § 552 (2018).

[68]Bradley v. Bd. of Educ., 565 N.W.2d 650 (Mich. 1997).

[69]Brouillet v. Cowles Publ'g Co., 791 P.2d 526 (Wash. 1990).

[70]Bellevue John Does 1–11 v. Bellevue Sch. Dist., 189 P.3d 139 (Wash. 2008).

[71]Chairman v. Freedom of Info. Comm'n, 585 A.2d 96 (Conn. 1991).

[72]Perkins v. Freedom of Info. Comm'n, 635 A.2d 783 (Conn. 1993).

[73]Zellner v. Cedarburg Sch. Dist., 731 N.W.2d 240 (Wis. 2007); *see also* Navarre v. S. Wash. Cty. Schs., 652 N.W.2d 9 (Minn. 2002) (finding that the release of information about a disciplinary matter before *final* disposition violated the counselor's rights under state law protecting private personnel data).

[74]*See* Benjamin Wood, *Union Sues to Block Online Access to Past Utah Teacher Discipline Cases*, SALT LAKE TRIB. (July 13, 2017), http://www.sltrib.com/news/education/2017/07/13/union-sues-to-block-online-access-to-past-utah-teacher-discipline-cases/.

Educators have not been successful in asserting that privacy interests in personnel records are protected under either the Family Educational Rights and Privacy Act (FERPA) or the U.S. Constitution. As described in Chapter 4, FERPA applies only to students and their educational records, not to employees' personnel records. Similarly, employees' claims that their constitutional privacy rights bar disclosure of their personnel records have been unsuccessful. In a case in which a teacher's college transcript was sought by a third party under the Texas Open Records Act, the Fifth Circuit ruled that even if a teacher had a recognizable privacy interest in her transcript, that interest "is significantly outweighed by the public's interest in evaluating the competence of its school teachers."[75]

Access to personnel files also has been controversial in situations involving allegations of employment discrimination. Personnel files must be relinquished if subpoenaed by a court. The Equal Employment Opportunity Commission (EEOC) also is authorized to subpoena relevant personnel files to thoroughly investigate allegations that a particular individual has been the victim of discriminatory treatment.[76] Personnel files include emails and other digital communications created in the school system; thus, these types of documents must be preserved similar to other documents.

With respect to the maintenance of records, information clearly cannot be placed in personnel files in retaliation for the exercise of constitutional rights. Courts have ordered letters of reprimand expunged from files when they have been predicated on protected speech and association activities.[77] Reprimands, although not a direct prohibition on protected activities, may present a constitutional violation because of their potentially chilling effect on the exercise of constitutional rights.

REPORTING SUSPECTED CHILD ABUSE AND NEGLECT

Educators have a legal obligation to report suspected child abuse and neglect.

Child abuse and neglect are recognized as national problems, with 3.4 million referrals made to child protective agencies in 2015.[78] Because the majority of these children are school age, educators are in a unique position to detect signs of potential abuse and neglect. States, recognizing the daily contact teachers have with students, have imposed certain

[75]Klein Indep. Sch. Dist. v. Mattox, 830 F.2d 576, 580 (5th Cir. 1987).

[76]Univ. of Pa. v. EEOC, 493 U.S. 182, 193 (1990) (holding that confidential peer review materials used in university promotion and tenure decisions were not protected from disclosure to the EEOC). The Court ruled that under Title VII of the Civil Rights Act of 1964, the EEOC must only show relevance—not special reasons or justifications—in demanding specific records. The Federal Procedural Rules, effective Dec. 1, 2006, require employers to be more aware about the storage of electronic information.

[77]See Aebisher v. Ryan, 622 F.2d 651 (2d Cir. 1980) (concluding that a letter of reprimand for speaking to the press about violence in the school implicated protected speech); Columbus Educ. Ass'n v. Columbus City Sch. Dist., 623 F.2d 1155 (6th Cir. 1980) (holding that a letter of reprimand issued to a teacher who was also a union representative for zealous advocacy of a fellow teacher violated the First Amendment).

[78]Nat'l Children's All., *National Statistics on Child Abuse* (n.d.), http://www.nationalchildrensalliance.org/media-room/media-kit/national-statistics-child-abuse.

duties for reporting suspected abuse and neglect. Details about reporting requirements are found in state laws.

Several common elements are found in state child abuse and neglect statutes (see Figure 9.2). The laws mandate that certain professionals, such as doctors and educators, report suspected abuse and neglect. **Statutes do not require that reporters have absolute knowledge, but rather "reasonable cause to believe" or "reason to believe" that a child has been abused or neglected**. Once abuse or neglect is suspected, the report must be made immediately to the designated child protection agency, department of welfare, or law enforcement unit as specified in state law. All states grant immunity from civil and criminal liability to individuals if reports are made in good faith. Additionally, many states prohibit disclosure of the reporter's identity to the alleged perpetrator of the abuse or neglect.

Reporting may involve two steps. First, school districts often establish reporting procedures that require teachers to report suspected abuse to the principal, school counselor, or school social worker. Second, teachers may be required to follow up to ensure the suspected abuse was reported to the proper agency or to law enforcement. Some state laws, however, instruct teachers to immediately report abuse through a hotline and do not mandate that teachers follow up if someone else has already reported or will be reporting the incident. **Nonetheless, it is prudent for teachers to understand the requirements of their particular state and ensure that suspected abuse and neglect is reported**.

Most state laws impose criminal liability for failure to report suspected abuse and neglect. Penalties may include fines ranging from $500 to $5,000, prison terms up to one year, and/or community service. Civil suits also may be initiated against teachers for negligence in failing to make such reports.[79] In addition, school systems may impose disciplinary measures against a teacher who does not follow the mandates of the law. The Seventh Circuit upheld the suspension and demotion of a teacher-psychologist for not promptly reporting suspected abuse.[80] The court rejected the teacher's claim to a federal right of

FIGURE 9.2   Policies Governing Child Abuse and Neglect

Federal Law
■ provides guidance and funds to identify, treat, and prevent abuse
State Law
■ lists teachers and other school employees as mandatory reporters
■ defines physical, sexual, and emotional abuse, as well as neglect
■ may include penalties for failure to report
■ grants immunity for reports made in good faith
School District Policy
■ outlines procedures for reporting
■ may include a two-step process: (1) report, then (2) follow up

[79]*See* Chapter 2 for a discussion of the elements of negligence.

[80]Pesce v. J. Sterling Morton High Sch. Dist., 830 F.2d 789 (7th Cir. 1987).

confidentiality, noting the state's compelling interest to protect children from mistreatment. Other courts have addressed the need to quickly report suspected abuse to the appropriate authorities. In an illustrative case, an Indiana high school principal was convicted for violating the state's mandatory law to report child abuse because it took him more than four hours to report a rape that occurred in the school. Indiana law requires that abuse be reported "immediately." The Indiana Supreme Court affirmed the principal's conviction of a Class B misdemeanor and his sentence of 120 days in jail (which was suspended to probation), 100 hours of community service, a $100 fine, and court costs. This opinion emphasizes how important it is for educators to have a clear understanding of the exact requirements of their state laws governing reporting requirements.[81]

As mandatory reporters, educators must understand what qualifies as child abuse and neglect. Each state's code defines physical, sexual, and emotional abuse, as well as neglect, which may include educational and medical neglect.[82] Although specific aspects of the laws may vary from one state to another, definitions of abuse and neglect often are based on the federal Child Abuse Prevention and Treatment Act of 2010 (CAPTA), which provides funds to identify, treat, and prevent abuse. CAPTA identifies child abuse and neglect as "any recent act or failure to act on the part of a parent or caretaker, which results in death, serious physical or emotional harm, sexual abuse or exploitation, or an act or failure to act which presents an imminent risk of serious harm."[83]

State laws are explicit on reporting requirements for suspected child abuse, but it is difficult to prove that an educator had sufficient knowledge of abuse to trigger legal liability for failure to report. Therefore, it is desirable for school officials to establish policies and procedures that encourage effective reporting. The pervasiveness of the problem and concern about the lack of reporting by teachers also indicate a need for professional development to assist educators in recognizing signs of abused and neglected children. Such programs could also describe what occurs after a report is made. For example, many reports do not result in court intervention and may initiate a process that helps families receive support from social service agencies (e.g., drug rehabilitation).

COLLECTIVE BARGAINING

Collective bargaining is the process that entails bilateral decision making in which the teachers' representative and the school board attempt to reach mutual agreement on matters affecting teacher employment.

The U.S. Constitution has been interpreted as protecting public employees' rights to organize, but the right to form and join a union does not ensure the right to bargain collectively with a public employer; individual state statutes and constitutions govern such bargaining

[81]Smith v. Indiana, 8 N.E.3d 668 (Ind. 2014); *see also* Struble v. Blytheville Sch. Dist., 516 S.W.3d 269 (Ark. Ct. App. 2017) (upholding termination of a principal for failure to report suspected child abuse).

[82]*See e.g.*, IND. CODE §§ 31-34-1-1 to -5 and 31-34-1-8 to -11 (2018) (defining neglect, including medical and educational neglect, and abuse, including physical and sexual abuse).

[83]42 U.S.C. § 5101 (2018).

rights. During negotiations, a member of the teachers' union typically speaks on behalf of the collective interests of the teachers in a school district. There are two main teachers' unions in the United States: the National Education Association (NEA) and the American Federation of Teachers AFL-CIO (AFT). These national unions have statewide affiliates and district-level affiliates. The purpose of teachers' unions is to advocate for their members and share resources as a collective group. Through the strength and influence of their numbers, they believe they will have more success negotiating with their employer as a unified group rather than as individual teachers. Specific bargaining rights are conferred through state statutes and judicial interpretations of state constitutions, thus creating wide divergence in teachers' bargaining rights across states.

Several basic differences distinguish bargaining in the public and private sectors. First, in the public school environment, professionals are bargaining against other professionals, while in the private sector, the labor force is bargaining against management. Second, the removal of decision-making authority from public officials through bargaining has been viewed as an infringement on the government's sovereign power, which has resulted in the enactment of state labor laws strongly favoring public employers. Public employees' rights have been further eroded by prohibitions of work stoppages. Employees' ability to strike is considered *essential* to the effective operation of collective decision making in the private sector, but this view has been rejected in the public sector because of the nature and structure of governmental services (i.e., a teacher strike could cause a public school to shut down, resulting in the suspension of the education of students). Additionally, restrictions have been placed on fair share agreements, which allow unions to collect service fees from employees who are not members of the union.

Although there are basic differences in employment between the public and private sectors, collective bargaining laws (specifically, the National Labor Relations Act[84] and the Taft-Hartley Act[85]) that apply only to the private sector have been significant in shaping statutory and judicial regulation of public negotiations. Similarities between the two sectors can be noted in many areas, such as unfair labor practices, union representation, and impasse procedures.

Context of Bargaining Rights

Public employees historically had been deprived of the right to organize and bargain collectively. It was not until the late 1960s that public employees' constitutional right to join a union was firmly established. A large number of public employees actively participated in collective bargaining, but statutes and regulations in some states prohibited union membership. These restrictions against union membership were challenged as impairing association freedoms protected by the First Amendment. Although it did not address union membership, **the Supreme Court held in 1967 that public employment cannot be conditioned on the relinquishment of the right to freedom of association.**[86]

---

[84]The Act states that "employees shall have the right to self-organization, to form, join, or assist labor organizations, to bargain collectively through representatives of their own choosing, and to engage in concerted activities for the purpose of collective bargaining or other mutual aid or protection," 29 U.S.C. § 157 (2018).

[85]29 U.S.C. § 141 (2018).

[86]Keyishian v. Bd. of Regents, 385 U.S. 589 (1967).

Recently, unprecedented attacks on public employees' bargaining rights have occurred, resulting in radical changes to the public employee bargaining laws in some states—states that are experiencing financial crises. Governors in these states have used their financial predicaments to argue that public employers need to have greater flexibility in controlling their budgets. The most publicized of these situations occurred in Wisconsin, which, in 1959, was the first state to recognize public employees' right to bargain. Under the 2011 Wisconsin law for general public employees (but not public safety employees like police officers), the scope of bargaining was restricted as follows: base pay rates could not exceed the rate of inflation (unless submitted to a referendum for approval); checkoff—which enables union dues to be paid through payroll deduction—was prohibited; and fair share agreements—where nonmember employees pay a fee to the union—were impermissible.[87] This law severely restricted the rights of unions representing public employees to collectively bargain. The law was challenged, but the Seventh Circuit upheld it.[88]

Other states have taken similar approaches.[89] For example, the Ohio governor signed into law radical changes to the state's public employee bargaining law. However, through a public referendum, the new Ohio law was rejected in 2011 by 62 percent of the voters. Some states have introduced anti-union laws that attempt to limit the scope of bargaining, eliminate payroll deductions, prohibit arbitration over contract grievances, and increase pension contributions.

Diversity in labor laws and bargaining practices among the states makes it difficult to generalize about collective bargaining and teachers' labor rights. State labor laws, state employment relations board rulings, and court decisions must be consulted to determine specific rights because there is no federal labor law covering public school employees. Over two-thirds of the states have enacted bargaining laws, ranging from very comprehensive laws controlling most aspects of negotiations to laws granting the minimal right to meet and confer. Still other states, in the absence of legislation, rely on judicial rulings to define the basic rights of public employees in the labor relations arena.

Because of the variations in labor laws, as well as the lack of such laws in some states, substantial differences exist in bargaining rights and practices. Thus, the litigation in this area is often state specific.[90] A few states, such as New York, have a detailed, comprehensive collective bargaining statute that delineates specific bargaining rights. In contrast, negotiated contracts between teachers' organizations and school boards are prohibited in North Carolina. Under North Carolina law, all contracts between public employers and employee associations are invalid.[91]

---

[87]In addition, unions must be certified each year by a majority of the union members (not a majority of members voting), 2011 WIS. ACT 10 (2018).

[88]Wis. Educ. Ass'n Council v. Walker, 705 F.3d 640 (7th Cir. 2013).

[89]*See* Steven Greenhouse, *Wisconsin's Legacy for Unions*, N.Y. TIMES (Feb. 22, 2014), https://www.nytimes.com/2014/02/23/business/wisconsins-legacy-for-unions.html.

[90]*See, e.g.*, United Teachers of L.A. v. L.A. Unified Sch. Dist., 278 P.3d 1204 (Cal. 2012) (ruling that under the state code, an arbitrator has no authority to deny or revoke a school charter); Jay Classroom Teachers Ass'n v. Jay Sch. Corp., 55 N.E.3d 813 (Ind. 2016) (finding no evidence that the union's decision to adopt the school board's last best offer was invalid under state law); Phila. Fed'n of Teachers v. Sch. Dist., 144 A.3d 1281 (Pa. 2016) (observing that the powers afforded to a school reform commission under state law were lawful).

[91]N.C. GEN. STAT. § 95-98 (2018).

In contrast to North Carolina, other states without legislation have permitted negotiated agreements. The Kentucky Supreme Court ruled that a public employer may recognize an employee organization for the purpose of collective bargaining, even though state law is silent on the issue of public employee bargaining rights.[92] The decision does not impose a duty on local school boards to bargain, but merely allows a board the discretion to negotiate. This ruling is consistent with several other judicial decisions permitting negotiated contracts in the absence of specific legislation.

Teachers' Statutory Bargaining Rights

In states with laws governing teachers' bargaining rights, school boards must negotiate with teachers in accordance with the statutorily prescribed process. Generally, public employee bargaining laws address employer and employee rights, bargaining units, scope of bargaining, impasse resolution, grievance procedures, unfair labor practices, and penalties for prohibited practices. Many states have established labor relations boards to monitor bargaining under their statutes. Although the specific functions of these boards vary widely, their general purpose is to resolve questions arising from the implementation of state law.[93] Usually, judicial review cannot be pursued until administrative review (before labor boards) is exhausted. Thus, decisions of labor boards are an important source of labor law because many of the issues addressed by labor boards are never appealed to courts. When the labor boards' decisions are challenged in court, substantial deference is given to their findings and determinations.[94]

Like the National Labor Relations Act (NLRA) in the private sector, state statutes require that the parties bargain "in good faith." ***Good faith bargaining* has been interpreted as requiring the parties to meet at reasonable times and attempt to reach mutual agreement without compulsion on either side to agree**. Many states have followed the federal law in stipulating that this "does not compel either party to agree to a proposal or to require the making of a concession."[95] Failure of the school board or teachers' unions to bargain in good faith can result in the imposition of penalties.

Statutes impose certain restrictions or obligations on both the school board and the employee organization. Violation of the law by either party can result in an unfair labor

[92]Bd. of Trs. v. Pub. Emps. Council, 571 S.W.2d 616 (Ky. 1978); *see also* Indep.-Nat'l Educ. Ass'n v. Indep. Sch. Dist., 223 S.W.3d 131 (Mo. 2007) (holding that the state constitutional provision guaranteeing "employees" the right to organize and bargain collectively includes both public and private employees).

[93]Functions assigned to such boards include determination of membership in bargaining units, resolution of union recognition claims, investigation of unfair labor practices, and interpretation of the general intent of statutory bargaining clauses.

[94]*See, e.g., In re* Kennedy, 27 A.3d 844 (N.H. 2011); Dodgeland Educ. Ass'n v. Wis. Emp't Relations Comm'n, 639 N.W. 2d 733 (Wis. 2002). As collective bargaining has matured in the public sector, decisions of state labor relations boards have become a substantial source of legal precedent for each state, with courts rendering fewer decisions in the labor arena. In fact, courts defer to the boards' findings unless they are clearly contrary to law. Although specific rulings of labor boards are not included in this chapter, educators are encouraged to examine that extensive body of law if a labor board governs negotiations in their state.

[95]29 U.S.C. § 158(d) (2018); *see also* Bd. of Educ. v. Sered, 850 N.E.2d 821 (Ill. App. Ct. 2006) (finding that a tentative oral agreement made by the board's representatives was valid; the board could not disregard or modify the terms of the agreement).

practice claim. Allegations of unfair labor practices are brought before the state public employee relations board for a hearing and judgment. The most common prohibited labor practice is an employer or union interfering with, restraining, or coercing public employees in exercising their rights under the labor law.[96] Among other prohibited *employer* practices are:

- interference with union operations;
- discrimination against employees because of union membership;
- refusal to bargain collectively with the exclusive representative; and
- failure to bargain in good faith.

Unions may not:

- cause an employer to discriminate against employees on the basis of union membership;
- refuse to bargain or fail to bargain in good faith;
- fail to represent all employees in the bargaining unit;[97] and
- engage in unlawful activities identified in the bargaining law, such as strikes or boycotts.

Upon completion of the negotiation process, the members of the bargaining unit and the school board ratify the written agreement—referred to as the *collective bargaining agreement* or *master contract*. These agreements often contain similar standard contract language and clauses, beginning with recognition of the exclusive bargaining representative and union security issues (i.e., fair share fees). Collective bargaining agreements not only include issues of salary and benefits but also may address grievance procedures, employee evaluations, preparation time, length of workday, class size, employee discipline, transfers, layoff and recall procedures, assignment of duties, and processes for filling vacancies.

Scope of Negotiations

Should the teachers' organization have input into class size? Who will determine the length of the school day? How will extra-duty assignments be determined? Will reductions-in-force necessitated by declining enrollment be based on seniority or merit? These questions and others are raised in determining the scope of negotiations. *Scope* refers to the range of issues or subjects that are negotiable; determining scope is one of the most difficult tasks in public-sector bargaining.

---

[96]*See* Cal. Teachers Ass'n v. Pub. Emp't Relations Bd., 87 Cal. Rptr. 3d 530 (Ct. App. 2009) (holding that the act of organizing teachers through signing a letter was a protected act); Fort Frye Teachers Ass'n v. SERB, 809 N.E.2d 1130 (Ohio 2004) (ruling the nonrenewal of a teacher's contract for union activities constitutes an unfair labor practice).

[97]*See* United Teachers v. Sch. Dist., 68 So. 3d 1003 (Fla. Dist. Ct. App. 2011) (finding that the bargained agreement denied nonunion teachers the right of representation at performance review proceedings; the union committed an unfair labor practice when it entered into the agreement); S. Sioux City Educ. Ass'n v. Dakota Cty. Sch. Dist., 772 N.W.2d 564 (Neb. 2009) (ruling that the school board committed a prohibited labor practice when it classified a certificated teacher as a long-term substitute rather than a probationary teacher, resulting in compensation less than bargained for in the contract).

Proposed subjects for negotiation can be classified as mandatory, permissive, or prohibited. *Mandatory* items must be negotiated.[98] Failure of the school board to meet and confer about such items is evidence of lack of good faith bargaining. *Permissive* items can be negotiated if both parties agree; however, there is no legal duty to consider the items. Furthermore, in most states, permissive items cannot be pursued to the point of negotiation impasse, and an employer cannot unilaterally change these items if no agreement is reached. *Prohibited* subjects are those that may not be bargained because the power might already be reserved to the school board for a particular item.[99]

State laws specify that public employers cannot be required to negotiate governmental policy matters, and courts have held that it is impermissible for a school board to bargain away certain rights and responsibilities in the public policy area.[100] Generally, educational policy matters are defined through provisions in collective bargaining statutes, such as "management rights" and "scope of bargaining" clauses. Policy issues—like class size, teacher evaluation criteria, and the award of tenure—are excluded as negotiable items in a few states; however, most states stipulate only that employers are not *required* to bargain such policy rights.[101] If the board does negotiate a policy item, it is bound by the agreement in the same way as if the issue were a mandatory item.

Restrictions on the scope of bargaining vary considerably from state to state. Negotiable items in labor laws may include broad guidelines or detailed enumeration of specific issues. Consequently, to determine negotiable items in a particular state, the state's collective bargaining law, other statutes, and litigation interpreting these laws must be examined.[102] **As noted, many states have modeled their bargaining statutes after the NLRA, which stipulates that representatives of the employer and employees must meet and confer "with respect to wages, hours, and other terms and conditions of employment."**[103] A few states identify each item that must be negotiated; other states

[98]Wages definitely fall within the mandatory category. A wage-related area that has received attention is the payment of "signing bonuses" to attract teachers for difficult-to-fill positions. Failure to bargain these payments may constitute an unfair labor practice. *See, e.g.*, Ekalaka Unified Bd. of Trs. v. Ekalaka Teachers' Ass'n, 149 P.3d 902 (Mont. 2006).

[99]Nancy J. Hungerford & Mark Blom, Nat'l Sch. Bds. Ass'n, *Collective Bargaining & the Negotiation Process: A Primer for School Board Negotiators* (Apr. 2014), https://www.nsba.org/sites/default/files/reports/Collective%20Bargaining%20and%20the%20Negotiation%20Process.pdf.

[100]*See* City Univ. of N.Y. v. Prof'l Staff Cong., 837 N.Y.S.2d 121 (App. Div. 2007) (holding that the employer could not bargain away its right to inspect teacher personnel files; the agreement was against public policy to investigate discrimination complaints).

[101]Courts agree that school boards cannot be *required* to negotiate inherent managerial rights pertaining to policy matters, but some states view these rights as *permissive* subjects of bargaining. That is, the board may agree to negotiate a particular "right" in the absence of statutory or judicial prohibitions.

[102]*See* Bedford Pub. Schs. v. Bedford Educ. Ass'n, 853 N.W.2d 452 (Mich. Ct. App. 2015) (finding that the plain language of the state statute prohibited a public employer from paying any wage increase when there was no collective bargaining agreement in place).

[103]29 U.S.C. § 158(d) (2018).

specify prohibited subjects of bargaining (e.g., the school calendar).[104] Generally, statutory mandates cannot be preempted by collective bargaining agreements;[105] however, in a few states, the negotiated agreement prevails over conflicting laws.[106] A Pennsylvania court held that a school board could not deny a female teacher's request to return to work early after a pregnancy under a policy in the negotiated agreement permitting the return.[107] The board had argued that the agreement violated public policy against sex discrimination because no provision was made for males to request an early return from leave.

Judicial decisions interpreting negotiability illustrate the range of bargainable matters. In many states, the interpretation of what is negotiable resides with the labor relations board. Often, these boards, as well as courts, employ a balancing test, beginning with an inquiry into whether a particular matter involves wages, hours, and terms and conditions of employment. If so, then the labor board or court must determine if the matter also is one of managerial policy. If not, the matter is a mandatory subject of bargaining. However, if the issue also pertains to educational policy, the benefits of bargaining on the decision-making process must be balanced against the burden on the employer's authority. Accordingly, this process entails a fact-specific analysis. The Supreme Court of New Jersey narrowly interpreted *conditions of employment* to mean wages, benefits, and work schedules, thereby removing governmental policy items such as teacher transfers, course offerings, and evaluations.[108] Other courts have construed the phrase in broader terms. For example, the Nevada Supreme Court ruled that items *significantly* related to wages, hours, and working conditions are negotiable.[109] Distinguishing between educational policy and matters relating to teachers' employment is difficult because most school board decisions affect teachers either directly or indirectly. One court noted: "Virtually every managerial decision in some way relates to 'salaries, wages, hours, and other working conditions,' and is therefore arguably negotiable. At the same time, virtually every such decision also involves educational policy considerations and is therefore arguably nonnegotiable."[110]

---

[104]For example, Michigan's prohibited subjects include decisions related to the establishment of the starting date for the school year, composition of site-based decision-making bodies, interdistrict and intradistrict open enrollment opportunities, authorization of public school academies, and establishment and staffing of experimental programs, MICH. COMP. LAWS ANN. § 423.215(3)(4) (2018).

[105]Furthermore, collective bargaining agreements cannot deprive individuals of rights guaranteed by federal laws. *See, e.g.*, Abrahamson v. Bd. of Educ., 374 F.3d 66 (2d Cir. 2004) (finding that the teachers proved their case of age discrimination by demonstrating that they were excluded from early retirement provisions under new collective bargaining agreement).

[106]*See, e.g.*, Hickey v. N.Y.C. Dep't of Educ., 952 N.E.2d 993 (N.Y. 2011) (holding that the collective bargaining agreement waived procedures available under state law regarding placement of letters of reprimand in teachers' personnel files).

[107]W. Allegheny Sch. Dist. v. W. Allegheny Educ. Ass'n, 997 A.2d 411 (Pa. Commw. Ct. 2010).

[108]Ridgefield Park Educ. Ass'n v. Ridgefield Park Bd. of Educ., 393 A.2d 278 (N.J. 1978); *see also* Polk Cty. Bd. of Educ. v. Polk Cty. Educ. Ass'n, 139 S.W.3d 304 (Tenn. Ct. App. 2004) (ruling that a dress code policy constituted a "working condition," not a managerial prerogative).

[109]Clark Cty. Sch. Dist. v. Local Gov't Employee-Mgmt. Relations Bd., 530 P.2d 114 (Nev. 1974); *see also* Governing Bd. v. Comm'n on Prof'l Conduct, 99 Cal. Rptr. 3d 903 (Ct. App. 2009) (finding that the negotiated agreement requiring all teachers to acquire English Learner certification was "reasonably related" to hours, wages, and conditions of employment).

[110]Montgomery Cty. Educ. Ass'n v. Bd. of Educ., 534 A.2d 980, 986 (Md. 1987).

Union Security Provisions

To ensure their strength and viability, unions attempt to obtain various security provisions in the collective bargaining agreement. For example, unions seek to gain provisions that require all employees either to join the association or to pay fees for its services. Because a union must represent all individuals in the bargaining unit, it is argued that such provisions are necessary to eliminate "free riders" (i.e., the individuals who receive the benefits of the union's work without paying the dues for membership). The nature and extent of security provisions will depend on state laws and constitutional limitations.

Union security provisions take several forms. The *closed shop*, requiring employers to hire only union members, does not exist in the public sector and is unlawful in the private sector. The *union shop* agreement requires employees to join the union within a designated time period after being hired in order to retain a position; however, *union shop* agreements are not authorized by most public-sector laws and are limited in some states under "right-to-work" laws.[111] The security provisions most frequently found in the public sector are *agency shop* and *fair share* agreements—terms that often are used interchangeably. An agency shop provision requires employees to pay union dues but does not mandate membership, whereas a fair share arrangement requires nonmembers simply to pay a service fee to cover the cost of bargaining activities. Twenty-three states have laws requiring teachers to pay for collective bargaining activities, but teachers can choose to opt out of paying for the political activities associated with these fees.[112]

Nonunion teachers have challenged mandatory fees as a violation of their First Amendment speech and association rights. The Supreme Court, however, in *Abood v. Detroit Board of Education* upheld the payment of fair share fees by public employees.[113] The Court rejected the nonunion members' First Amendment claims, noting the importance of ensuring labor peace and eliminating "free riders." Yet, the Court concluded that **employees cannot be compelled to contribute to the support of ideological causes they oppose as a condition of maintaining employment as public school teachers**.

In 2016, a group of teachers in California sought to overturn the *Abood* decision. The teachers argued that the agency shop arrangement that required them to pay union dues violated their First Amendment rights. The federal district court upheld the practices of the teachers' union, and the Ninth Circuit affirmed.[114] Upon appeal, the U.S. Supreme Court divided evenly.[115] Thus, the Ninth Circuit's opinion stands as the final judgment. A similar

[111]In 2017, Missouri and Kentucky became the twenty-eighth and twenty-ninth states to sign "right-to-work" laws specifically declaring that an individual's employment cannot be conditioned on joining a union or paying fees to a union. A strong movement fueled by anti-union sentiment can be seen with right-to-work legislation being actively pursued across the country. *See* Nat'l Conference of State Legislatures, *Right-to-Work Resources* (2017), http://www.ncsl.org/research/labor-and-employment/right-to-work-laws-and-bills.aspx.

[112]Ctr. for Individual Rights, *Supreme Court Agrees to Hear Compelled Dues Case* (Oct. 3, 2017), https://www.cir-usa.org/2017/10/supreme-court-agrees-to-hear-compelled-dues-case/.

[113]431 U.S. 209 (1977).

[114]Friedrichs v. Cal. Teachers Ass'n, 2014 U.S. App. LEXIS 24935 (9th Cir. Nov. 18, 2014).

[115]Friedrichs v. Cal. Teachers Ass'n, 136 S. Ct. 1083 (2016) (resulting in a four-to-four split decision because of the vacancy left after Justice Scalia's death).

lawsuit against the California Teachers' Union was filed in 2017, and the U.S. Supreme Court has agreed to review this case.[116]

Although the Supreme Court has upheld fair share arrangements, they may not be permitted under some state laws. The Maine high court held that forced payment of dues was "tantamount to coercion toward membership."[117] The Maine statute ensures employees the right to join a union *voluntarily*, and the court interpreted this provision as including the right to *refrain* from joining. Similarly, the Vermont Supreme Court held that fees were prohibited under the state law that specified that teachers have the right to join or not to join, assist, or participate in a labor organization.[118] The U.S. Supreme Court addressed this issue as well when it examined Idaho's right-to-work law, which prohibits payroll deductions for political activities. After a labor union challenged Idaho's law prohibiting mandatory payroll reductions for union activities,[119] the Court held in favor of the state.[120] Accordingly, nonmember Idaho teachers cannot be forced to contribute to a union's political activities; fees must reflect only the costs of bargaining and contract administration.[121]

Exclusive Privileges

Sometimes, multiple unions exist within a school district and compete against each other. In attempts to strengthen its membership, one union often negotiates exclusive rights or privileges for its members, such as dues checkoff, the use of the school mail systems, and access to school facilities. Although exclusive arrangements strengthen the majority union and may make it difficult for minority unions to survive, courts often support such arrangements as a means of promoting labor peace and ensuring efficient operation of the school system.

Dues Checkoff.   The exclusive privilege most often included in collective bargaining agreements is dues checkoff, a provision that authorizes employers to deduct union dues and other fees when authorized by employees. Over half of the states with public employee bargaining laws specify dues checkoff as a mandatory subject for bargaining. The Supreme

[116]Janus v. Am. Fed'n, 851 F.3d 746 (7th Cir. 2017) (affirming the lower court's dismissal of the plaintiffs' complaint under the Abood precedent), *cert. granted*, 138 S. Ct. 54 (2017).

[117]Churchill v. Sch. Adm'r Dist. No. 49 Teachers Ass'n, 380 A.2d 186, 192 (Me. 1977).

[118]Weissenstein v. Burlington Bd. of Sch. Comm'rs, 543 A.2d 691 (Vt. 1988). *But see* Nashua Teachers Union v. Nashua Sch. Dist., 707 A.2d 448, 451 (N.H. 1998) (interpreting a state law that permits negotiation of "other conditions of employment" as authorizing agency fees to promote labor peace).

[119]IDAHO CODE §§ 44-2601–2605, 44-2004 (2018). Political activities are defined as "electoral activities, independent expenditures, or expenditures made to any candidate, political party, political action committee, or political issues committee or in support of or against any ballot initiative," § 44-2602(1)(e).

[120]Ysursa v. Pocatello Educ. Ass'n, 555 U.S. 353 (2009).

[121]The Supreme Court ruled in 2007 that a state law requiring unions to obtain affirmative authorization from nonmembers prior to spending agency fees for election-related purposes is constitutional. The state gave the unions the right to collect the fees and could also place limitations on their use. Davenport v. Wash. Educ. Ass'n, 551 U.S. 177 (2007); *see also* Knox v. Serv. Emps. Int'l Union, 567 U.S. 298 (2012) (finding that the union infringed on nonmembers' First Amendment rights by imposing an additional mandatory special fee for political purposes without informing the employees; such an assessment requires notice to the employees and affirmative consent from nonmembers).

Court, however, has held that **employee unions have no constitutional right to payroll deductions**.[122] Nonetheless, checkoff rights can be reserved for the exclusive bargaining unit and denied to rival unions if permitted under state law.

Use of School Mail Facilities.   Often, unions negotiate for *exclusive* access to the internal school mail system; if they are successful, rival unions are denied access. The Supreme Court clarified the constitutionality of exclusive use in an Indiana case where the negotiated agreement between the bargaining representative and a school board denied all rival unions access to the interschool mail system and teacher mailboxes.[123] One union challenged the agreement as a violation of the First and Fourteenth Amendments. The Supreme Court upheld the arrangement, reasoning that the First Amendment does not require "equivalent access to all parts of a school building in which some form of communicative activity occurs."[124] **The Court concluded that the school mail facility was not a public forum for communication, and thereby its use could be restricted to official school business.** The fact that several community groups (e.g., Boy Scouts, civic organizations) used the school mail system did not create a public forum.

Exclusive Recognition.   In most states, school boards negotiate only with the designated bargaining representative. Under this exclusive recognition, other unions and teacher groups can be denied the right to engage in official exchanges with an employer. The Supreme Court has held that nonmembers of a bargaining unit or members who disagree with the views of the representative have no constitutional right "to force the government to listen to their views."[125] The Court concluded that a Minnesota statute requiring employers to "meet and confer" only with the designated bargaining representative did not violate other employees' speech or associational rights as public employees or as citizens, because these sessions were not a public forum.

However, in a public forum, such as a school board meeting, **a nonunion teacher has a constitutional right to address the public employer, even concerning a subject of negotiation.** The Supreme Court concluded that a Wisconsin nonunion teacher had the right to express concerns to the school board.[126] In this case, the board and the union had reached a deadlock in their negotiations on the issue of an agency shop provision. A nonunion teacher, representing a small group of teachers, addressed the board at a regular public meeting and requested postponement of a decision until further study of the

---

[122]City of Charlotte v. Local 660, Int'l Ass'n of Firefighters, 426 U.S. 283 (1976); *see also* S.C. Educ. Ass'n v. Campbell, 883 F.2d 1251 (4th Cir. 1989) (ruling that state legislation permitting payroll deductions for charitable organizations, but not for labor unions, was not an infringement of the First Amendment; the law did not deny the union members the right to associate, speak, publish, recruit members, or express their views).

[123]Perry Educ. Ass'n v. Perry Local Educators' Ass'n, 460 U.S. 37 (1983); *see also* San Leandro Teachers Ass'n v. Governing Bd., 209 P.3d 73 (Cal. 2009) (ruling that state law prohibits unions from using school mailboxes to distribute political endorsement information; the contested law does not violate the state and federal constitutions).

[124]Perry Educ. Ass'n, 460 U.S. at 44.

[125]Minn. State Bd. for Cmty. Colls. v. Knight, 465 U.S. 271, 283 (1984) (noting that "the Constitution does not grant to members of the public generally a right to be heard by public bodies making decisions of policy").

[126]City of Madison v. Wis. Emp't Relations Comm'n, 429 U.S. 167 (1976).

proposal. The Court reasoned that the teacher was not attempting to negotiate but merely was speaking on an important issue before the board—a right every U.S. citizen possesses.

Grievances

Individual union members may undergo grievance arbitration when they believe an individual employment right has been violated (e.g., if they believe they were not allocated the number of sick days listed in the collective bargaining agreement). Disputes are resolved through the grievance procedures, which generally must be exhausted before pursuing review by state labor relations boards or courts. The exhaustion requirement ensures the integrity of the collective bargaining process, encouraging orderly and efficient dispute resolution at the local level. Grievance procedures usually provide for a neutral third party, generally an arbitrator, to conduct a hearing and render a decision. ***Grievance* arbitration, which addresses enforcement of contractual rights, differs from *interest* arbitration, which may take place in resolving an impasse between parties in the bargaining process**.

Depending on state law and the negotiated contract, grievance arbitration decisions may be advisory or binding, but legislative bodies have favored binding arbitration to settle labor disputes. About half of the states have enacted laws permitting school boards to negotiate grievance procedures with binding arbitration, and several states require binding arbitration as the final step in the grievance procedure.[127] With the widespread acceptance of grievance arbitration, it has become one of the most contested areas in collective bargaining. Suits have challenged the arbitrator's authority to render decisions in specific disputes as well as the authority to provide certain remedies.[128]

Negotiation Impasse

An impasse occurs in bargaining when an agreement cannot be reached and neither party will compromise. If negotiations reach such a stalemate, several options are available for resolution: mediation, fact-finding, and arbitration. As discussed below, the most effective means for resolving negotiation impasse—the strike—is not legally available to many public employees.[129] Most state statutes address impasse procedures, with provisions ranging from allowing impasse procedures to be negotiated to mandating detailed steps that must be followed.

Mediation is often the first step to reopening negotiations. A neutral third party assists both sides in working toward an agreement. The mediator serves as a facilitator rather than a decision maker, thus enabling the school board's representative and the teachers'

---

[127]Among the few states requiring binding grievance arbitration are Alaska, Florida, Illinois, Minnesota, and Pennsylvania. *See In re* Silverstein, 37 A.3d 382 (N.H. 2012) (finding that the state labor board had no authority to review a grievance under a bargaining contract that contained a final and binding grievance process within the district).

[128]*See, e.g.,* United Teachers of L.A. v. L.A. Unified Sch. Dist., 278 P.3d 1204 (Cal. 2012) (charter school petition); Bd. of Educ. v. Ill. Educ. Labor Relations Bd., 14 N.E.3d 1092 (Ill. App. Ct. 2014) (probationary teacher appointments); Kalispell Educ. Ass'n v. Bd. of Trs., 255 P.3d 199 (Mont. 2011) (teacher contract); *In re* Haessig & Oswego City Sch. Dist., 936 N.Y.S.2d 442 (App. Div. 2011) (teacher class loads).

[129]*See* DEL. CODE ANN. tit.14, § 4016 (2018); WIS. STAT. § 1189 (2018). *But see* OR. REV. STAT. § 243.726 (2018).

association jointly to reach an agreement. Mediation may be optional or required by law; the mediator is selected by the negotiation teams or, upon request, appointed by a public employee relations board.

Failure to reach an agreement through mediation frequently results in *fact-finding* (often called advisory arbitration). The process may be mandated by law or may be entered into by mutual agreement of both parties. This process involves a third party investigating the causes of the dispute, collecting facts and testimony to clarify the dispute, and formulating a judgment. Because of the advisory nature of the process, proposed solutions are not binding on either party. However, since fact-finding reports are made available to the public, they provide an impetus to settle that is not present in mediation. In a number of states, fact-finding constitutes the final step in impasse procedures, which may leave both parties without a satisfactory solution. However, a few states permit a third alternative—*binding interest arbitration*. This process is similar to fact-finding except that the decision of the arbitrator is binding on both parties.[130]

Although it is argued that there can be no true collective bargaining without the right to withhold services, which characterizes the bargaining process in the private sector, **state statutes often prohibit public school teachers from striking**. In those states that grant public employees a limited right to strike, certain conditions, specified by statute, must be met prior to the initiation of a work stoppage.[131] Designated conditions vary, but usually include (1) the exhaustion of statutory mediation and fact-finding steps, (2) expiration of the contract, (3) a required waiting period before commencing the strike, (4) written notice of the union's intent to strike, and (5) evidence that the strike will not constitute a danger to public health or safety. In contrast to the few states permitting strikes, most states with public employee collective bargaining statutes have specific "no-strike" provisions, and courts have generally denied the right to strike unless affirmatively granted by the state.

A strike is more than simply a work stoppage; states define the term broadly to include a range of concerted activities such as work slowdowns, massive absences for "sick" days, and refusal to perform certain duties. For example, the Massachusetts high court found that refusing to perform customary activities, such as grading papers and preparing lesson plans after the end of the school day, constituted a strike.[132] A Missouri appellate court upheld the right of the St. Louis school superintendent to request documentation from 1,190 teachers that a "sick" day was not related to a labor dispute surrounding the negotiation of a new contract.[133] Without documentation from the teachers, the school district could deny payment for the day.

---

[130]States that permit binding arbitration often place restrictions on its use. For example, Ohio and Rhode Island permit binding arbitration on matters of mutual consent, OHIO REV. CODE ANN. § 4117(C) (2018); R.I. GEN. LAWS § 28-9.3-9 (2018). Maine allows binding arbitration on all items except salaries, pensions, and insurance, ME. REV. STAT. tit. 26, § 979.D(4) (2018).

[131]A statutorily limited right to strike exists for public employees in Alaska, Colorado, Hawaii, Illinois, Minnesota, Montana, Ohio, Oregon, Pennsylvania, and Vermont. Alaska's law has been interpreted as prohibiting teachers from striking even though most other public employees are permitted to strike. Anchorage Educ. Ass'n v. Anchorage Sch. Dist., 648 P.2d 993 (Alaska 1982).

[132]Lenox Educ. Ass'n v. Labor Relations Comm'n, 471 N.E.2d 81 (Mass. 1984).

[133]Franklin v. St. Louis Bd. of Educ., 904 S.W.2d 433 (Mo. Ct. App. 1995).

Despite statutory prohibitions on strikes, some teachers participate in work stoppages. Public employers can seek a court injunction against teachers who threaten to strike or initiate such action. Most courts have granted injunctions, concluding, as did the Supreme Court of Alaska, that the "illegality of the strike is a sufficient harm to justify injunctive relief."[134] Failure of teachers and unions to comply with such a restraining order can result in contempt-of-court charges and resulting fines and/or imprisonment. For example, in one school district, the union's refusal to comply with an injunction resulted in a contempt-of-court charge and fines totaling $200,000 against two unions.[135] Teachers illegally participating in a strike are subject to court-imposed penalties and, in most states, to statutory penalties. Refusal of teachers to return to the classroom can result in dismissal.

CONCLUSION

Individual state laws, school board regulations, and collective bargaining agreements must be consulted to determine the specific terms and conditions of teachers' employment. Except for certain limitations imposed by constitutional provisions and federal civil rights laws, state statutes govern public educators' employment. The state prescribes general requirements for licensure, contracts, evaluations, personnel records, reporting child abuse and neglect, and collective bargaining. The following generalizations reflect the current status of the law on the topics covered in this chapter.

1. The terms and conditions of school employment are primarily regulated by state law, but state and federal constitutional provisions, civil rights laws, local school board directives, and collective bargaining agreements also govern school personnel.

2. States grant teacher and administrative licenses and can revoke them for causes such as immorality and unprofessional conduct.

3. School boards have the authority to hire and dismiss school employees; boards can also assign additional conditions of employment such as residency requirements.

4. The board assigns teachers to their positions in the district and can impose additional non-instructional duties.

5. Contracts are either term, tenure, or supplemental.

6. Contracts must include the following elements: (1) offer and acceptance, (2) competent parties, (3) consideration, (4) legal subject matter, and (5) proper form.

7. State and federal laws have increased regulations surrounding teacher and administrator evaluations which has led to litigation.

8. Personnel information that must be maintained by law is a public record (e.g., personal directory information, salary information, employment contracts, leave records, and teaching license) and must be released to the public when requested.

9. Teachers are legally required to report suspected abuse and neglect in a timely manner.

---

[134]Anchorage Educ. Ass'n, 648 P.2d at 998.

[135]Nat'l Educ. Ass'n-S. Bend v. S. Bend Cmty. Sch. Corp., 655 N.E.2d 516 (Ind. Ct. App. 1995).

10. The U.S. Constitution protects association rights; however, the right to collectively bargain is governed by state laws and constitutions.

11. The scope of teachers' collective bargaining rights has been restricted in some states in recent years.

12. Although the Supreme Court has upheld fair share arrangements, they may not be permitted under some state laws.

13. An individual union member who is dissatisfied may undergo grievance arbitration; whereas the entire union membership may undergo mediation, fact-finding, and arbitration if there is an impasse during collective bargaining.

14. Strikes for public school employees are prohibited in most states.

CHAPTER TEN

EMPLOYEES' SUBSTANTIVE CONSTITUTIONAL RIGHTS

Can school employees be disciplined for what they post on social media? What should teachers do when students ask them about their political affiliation? May schools dismiss teachers for their behavior outside of school? While the U.S. Supreme Court stated that both students *and teachers* do not leave their constitutional rights at the schoolhouse gate,[1] limitations may be placed on these rights because of the special context of the school environment. For public school employees, it becomes difficult to navigate through what is protected and what can be restricted.[2] This chapter presents an overview of the scope of public employees' constitutional rights as defined by the judiciary in connection with free expression, academic freedom, freedom of association, freedom of choice in appearance, and privacy rights. Some of the cases do not involve school settings, but the legal principles apply to all public employees.

Readers of this chapter should be able to:

- Describe the primary U.S. Supreme Court decisions relating to public employee expression.

- Distinguish between teachers' rights in dictating course content versus instructional strategies.

- Discuss when schools may violate employees' freedom of association rights.

- Identify what are reasonable restrictions that schools may place on employee appearance.

- Delineate the legal standard surrounding searching and drug testing employees, as well as the legal standard needed to discipline an employee for out-of-school conduct.

---

[1]Tinker v. Des Moines Indep. Cmty. Sch. Dist., 393 U.S. 503 (1969).

[2]This chapter discusses the law only as it relates to public school employees.

FREEDOM OF EXPRESSION

Public employees' comments on matters of public concern are protected expression if they are made as a citizen and not pursuant to official job duties.

Until the mid-twentieth century, it was generally accepted that public school teachers could be dismissed or disciplined for expressing views considered objectionable by the school board.[3] Since the late 1960s, however, the U.S. Supreme Court has recognized the free expression rights of public school employees, while also weighing their rights against the school district's interest in maintaining effective and efficient schools. This section reviews the evolution of legal principles and their application to specific school situations. It describes court decisions since the 1960s that carved out numerous exceptions to educators' free expression protections—including the Supreme Court's most recent restriction on employee speech if it is connected to employment duties or responsibilities.[4]

Legal Principles

Similar to student free speech cases, an initial determination must be made regarding whether the public employee's claim involves expression *at all*. An action constitutes expression for First Amendment purposes only if it attempts "to convey a particularized message" that will likely be understood by those receiving the message.[5] For example, a teacher's action in scheduling a student's therapy sessions and attending those sessions did not involve intent to convey any message deserving First Amendment protection.[6]

The U.S. Supreme Court has addressed the First Amendment within the public employment context on several occasions. The most significant cases are explained below to provide the general legal principles that relate to school employee expression. **In the landmark 1968 decision, *Pickering v. Board of Education*, the Supreme Court recognized that teachers have a First Amendment right to air their views on matters of public concern.**[7] A teacher wrote a letter to a local newspaper, criticizing the school board's fiscal policies, especially the allocation of funds between the education and athletic programs. The school board dismissed the teacher because of the letter, which included false statements allegedly damaging the reputations of school board members and district administrators, and the Illinois courts upheld his dismissal.

[3]*See* John Rumel, *Beyond Nexus: A Framework for Evaluating K–12 Teacher Off-Duty Conduct and Speech in Adverse Employment and Licensure Proceedings*, 83 U. Cɪɴ. L. Rᴇᴠ. 685, 689 (2015) (stating "by the mid-twentieth century, virtually all states granted power to state boards of education to suspend or revoke a teacher's certificate based on immoral conduct, moral turpitude, or conduct unbecoming of a teacher").

[4]Garcetti v. Ceballos, 547 U.S. 410 (2006).

[5]Texas v. Johnson, 491 U.S. 397, 404 (1989). Conduct that does not possess sufficient communicative elements is not shielded by the First Amendment.

[6]Montanye v. Wissahickon Sch. Dist., 218 F. App'x 126 (3d Cir. 2007).

[7]391 U.S. 563 (1968); *see also* Givhan v. W. Line Consol. Sch. Dist., 439 U.S. 410 (1979) (concluding that so long as the expression pertains to matters of public concern, rather than personal grievances, statements made in private or through a public medium are constitutionally protected; the forum where the expression occurs does not determine whether the speech is of public or private concern).

Reversing the state courts, the U.S. Supreme Court first identified expression pertaining to matters of public concern as constitutionally protected and reasoned that the funding and allocation issues raised by the teacher were clearly questions of public concern requiring free and open debate. Matters of public concern include comments relating to political, social, philosophical, or other issues of importance to the community. **The *Pickering* Court applied a balancing test, weighing the teacher's interest in expressing his views on public issues against the school board's interest in providing efficient educational services.**[8] The Court recognized that the school board would prevail if the teacher's exercise of protected expression jeopardized his (1) classroom performance, (2) relationships with his immediate supervisor or coworkers, or (3) school operations. Courts often refer to weighing these factors as the "*Pickering* balancing test."[9] Concluding that the teacher's letter did not have a detrimental effect in any of these areas, the Court found no justification for limiting his contribution to public debate. Indeed, the Court noted that a teacher's role provides a special vantage point from which to formulate an informed opinion on the allocation of school district funds, thus making it essential for teachers to be able to speak about public issues without fear of reprisal, unless false statements are intentionally or recklessly made.[10]

In 1977, the Supreme Court in *Mt. Healthy City School District v. Doyle* established the principle that a public educator can be disciplined or dismissed if sufficient cause exists *independent* of the exercise of protected speech. In this case, a nontenured teacher claimed he was not renewed in retaliation for speaking on a radio show about a proposed school policy. However, the teacher had been involved in multiple previous incidents including making obscene gestures to several female students.[11] The Supreme Court held that the **burden of proof is on the employee to show that the speech was constitutionally protected and was a substantial or motivating factor in the school board's adverse action.** The Court reasoned that the teacher's protected expression (his speech on the radio show) should not place him in a better or worse position with regard to continued employment. Because the board had established that there were sufficient grounds outside of the teacher's speech on the radio show to justify the board's decision, the Court upheld the teacher's nonrenewal.[12]

In a significant 1983 decision, *Connick v. Myers*, the Supreme Court narrowed the circumstances under which public employees can prevail in free expression cases—the speech must address a matter of public concern as opposed to a private grievance.[13] The case involved an assistant district attorney, dissatisfied with her proposed transfer, who

---

[8]Pickering, 391 U.S. at 568.

[9]*See, e.g.*, Bd. of Cty. Comm'rs v. Umbehr, 518 U.S. 688 (1996) (applying the Pickering balancing test to weigh the interests of independent contractors against the government's interests).

[10]Pickering, 391 U.S. 563.

[11]429 U.S. 274 (1977).

[12]Doyle v. Mt. Healthy City Sch. Dist. Bd. of Educ., 670 F.2d 59 (6th Cir. 1982).

[13]461 U.S. 138 (1983); *see also* Waters v. Churchill, 511 U.S. 661 (1994) (concluding that the government employer can reach its factual conclusions without being held to the evidentiary rules followed by courts; as long as the employer conducts an investigation and acts in good faith, it can discharge an employee for remarks *reasonably believed* to have been made); Rankin v. McPherson, 483 U.S. 378 (1987) (assessing the context, form, and content of a public employee's pejorative statement to a coworker following the assassination attempt on President Reagan and finding no basis for dismissal in the absence of interference with work relationships or performance).

circulated among coworkers a questionnaire concerning office operations and morale and was subsequently terminated. The Court ruled that the questionnaire related primarily to a personal employment grievance, which is not protected by the First Amendment, rather than to matters of public concern. Of particular importance was the Court's conclusion that **the *form* and *context*, as well as the *content*, of the expression should be considered in assessing whether it relates to public matters**.

In 2006, the Supreme Court decided *Garcetti v. Ceballos*, adding another threshold question in assessing constitutional protection of public employees' expression and making it even more difficult for public employees to prevail on claims that their expression rights have been abridged.[14] The Court established a bright-line rule that expression pursuant to official job responsibilities is not protected. **Thus, under *Garcetti*, whether the employee is speaking as a private citizen or as an employee is the first consideration, and if speaking as an employee, there is no further constitutional assessment; the First Amendment does not prohibit employers from disciplining employees for their speech in this situation**. However, if the employee is speaking as a private citizen on a matter of public concern, then the question becomes whether the public employer had an "adequate justification for treating the employee differently from any other member of the general public" and the expression is further analyzed under *Connick*, *Mt. Healthy*, and *Pickering*.[15]

In *Garcetti*, the Supreme Court ruled that the district attorney's office did not impair the free speech rights of Ceballos, an assistant district attorney, by allegedly denying him a promotion and retaliating against him in other ways for writing a memorandum indicating that a sheriff may have lied in the search warrant affidavit in a criminal case. The Supreme Court reasoned that Ceballos was speaking about a task he was paid to perform and concluded that "when public employees make statements pursuant to their official duties . . . the Constitution does not insulate their communications from employer discipline."[16] The majority reiterated that the forum where the comments were made was not the central consideration, but rather the controlling factor was whether the expression occurred as part of official responsibilities.[17]

In general, courts also have upheld reasonable time, place, and manner regulations on educators' expression. Such restrictions must not be based on the content of the speech, and they must serve significant governmental interests and leave alternative communication channels open.[18] Therefore, prior restraints on educators' expression are legally vulnerable, but reasonable time, place, and manner restrictions may be upheld if justified to prevent a disruption of the educational environment and if other avenues are available for employees to express their views.

---

[14]547 U.S. 410 (2006).

[15]*Id.* at 418.

[16]*Id.* at 421.

[17]*Id.* at 421–22. But the Court specifically left open whether its analysis would apply to speech related to instruction. *Id.* at 425; *see also* Lane v. Franks, 134 S. Ct. 2369, 2378 (2014) (referring to the unprotected speech in Garcetti as being "in the course of his ordinary job responsibilities"). *See infra* text accompanying note 30, discussing whistleblower cases post–Garcetti.

[18]*See* Educ. Minn. Lakeville v. Indep. Sch. Dist., 341 F. Supp. 2d 1070 (D. Minn. 2004) (rejecting union's argument that the school district's policy prohibiting the use of internal communication channels to distribute literature endorsing political candidates violated the First Amendment).

Expression outside the Classroom

In the majority of expression cases, educators have challenged reprisals for their speech out-side the classroom including their Internet speech. During the 1970s and early 1980s, courts relied on the *Pickering* guidelines in striking down a variety of restrictions on teachers' rights to express views on matters of public concern.[19] Since the early 1980s, however, courts have seemed increasingly inclined to view teachers' and other public employees' expression as relating to *private* employment disputes rather than to matters of public concern.

Many courts relied on *Connick*[20] in broadly interpreting what falls under the category of unprotected private grievances. To illustrate, courts considered the following types of expres-sion to be unprotected: discussing salaries during a break;[21] filing a grievance about being assigned a job-sharing teaching position;[22] accusing the superintendent of inciting student disturbances;[23] sending sarcastic, critical memoranda to school officials;[24] protesting unfavor-able performance evaluations;[25] and commenting about class size and lack of discipline.[26]

Yet, when courts have applied the *Pickering* balancing test, they often distin-guished whether disruption to school operations was truly caused by the employee's speech versus the impermissible heckler's veto—that is, courts have analyzed whether the disruption was caused by outsiders attempting to silence the speech instead of the speech itself.[27] A New York school district terminated a teacher for actively participating in a group supporting consensual sexual activity between men and boys. Although the teacher argued that the disruption was the result of the heckler's veto, the Second Circuit disagreed. It reasoned that the complaining parents were not outsiders seeking to heckle the teacher into silence. Instead, the disruption was internal and the teacher's speech and asso-ciation with a highly controversial group was likely to impair his teaching effectiveness.[28] Multiple courts have considered parent and student reactions when determining whether the response to a school employee's speech has negatively affected the efficiency of school operations (e.g. parents requesting their children be removed from the teacher's class).[29]

The *Garcetti* decision has added another initial consideration in deciding whether a public employee's expression will evoke the *Pickering* balancing test (see Figure 10.1).

[19]*See, e.g.*, Gieringer v. Ctr. Sch. Dist., 477 F.2d 1164 (8th Cir. 1973) (holding that a teacher's report that the school district could raise teachers' salaries was a protected matter of public concern, rendering the teacher's dismissal unconstitutional).

[20]461 U.S. 138 (1983).

[21]Bouma v. Trent, 2010 U.S. Dist. LEXIS 37565 (D. Ariz. Apr. 14, 2010) (holding that a complaint about a sal-ary schedule was not a matter of public concern); *see also* Koehn v. Indian Hills Cmty. Coll., 371 F.3d 394 (8th Cir. 2004) (reasoning that a salary discussion could address a matter of public concern; however, the plaintiff was speaking as an employee rather than a concerned taxpayer).

[22]Renfroe v. Kirkpatrick, 722 F.2d 714 (11th Cir. 1984).

[23]Stevenson v. Lower Marion Cty. Sch. Dist., 327 S.E.2d 656 (S.C. 1985).

[24]Hesse v. Bd. of Educ., 848 F.2d 748 (7th Cir. 1988).

[25]Day v. S. Park Indep. Sch. Dist., 768 F.2d 696 (5th Cir. 1985).

[26]Cliff v. Bd. of Sch. Comm'rs, 42 F.3d 403 (7th Cir. 1995).

[27]*See* text accompanying note 62, Chapter 5.

[28]Melzer v. Bd. of Educ., 336 F.3d 185, 194 (2d Cir. 2003) (noting that the activity "was not a specific instance of speech, or a particular disruptive statement, but an associational activity of which speech was an essential component").

[29]*See e.g.*, Munroe v. Cent. Bucks Sch. Dist., 805 F.3d 454 (3d Cir. 2015).

FIGURE 10.1   Analyzing Public Educators' Expression Rights

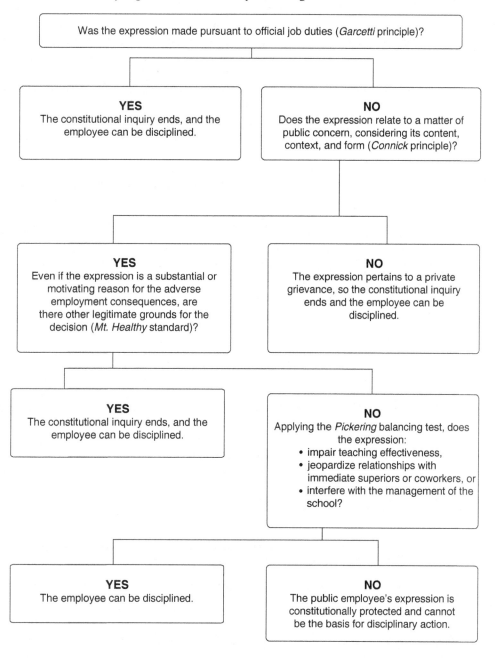

If the expression is made pursuant to official job responsibilities, it is not protected, and it is thus unnecessary to establish that the expression pertains to a private grievance or has a disruptive impact on school operations. Prior to the *Garcetti* ruling, the content of the expression appeared to be the crucial consideration, but post–*Garcetti*, the role of the speaker seems to trump the content. The broad protection once given to public educators' expression under *Pickering* currently is available only if the expression (1) does not occur pursuant to official duties (*Garcetti*), (2) relates to a public concern—considering its context and form as well as its content (*Connick*), and (3) is the motivating factor in the adverse employment action (*Mt. Healthy*). *Pickering* has not been overturned, but far fewer circumstances trigger its balancing test.

Whistleblowers.   When deciding *Garcetti*, the Court noted that legal protections already existed for whistleblowers (i.e., employees who exposed employment-related misconduct). For example, federal protection exists under the Whistleblower Protection Act of 1989.[30] Further, some federal statutes such as Title VI of the Civil Rights Act (Title VI) have anti-retaliation provisions incorporated into the statutory text. Title VI states: "No recipient or other person shall intimidate, threaten, coerce, or discriminate against any individual . . . because he has made a complaint, testified, assisted, or participated in any manner in an investigation, proceeding or hearing."[31] Plus, state laws typically protect whistleblowers.[32] Nonetheless, these federal and state whistleblowing protections do not always apply to school employees' unique circumstances.[33] Therefore, when employees claim retaliation for whistleblowing, courts apply the *Garcetti* standard (i.e., expression that is pursuant to official job responsibilities is unprotected) and often discover that the expression at issue *was* related to the employee's job.

As a result, whistleblowers have not been as successful in securing legal redress for retaliation as they were prior to *Garcetti*. For example, the Fifth Circuit held that an athletic director who wrote a letter to the school's office manager about appropriations for athletic activities was speaking pursuant to his official duties and could not claim retaliation for being removed from the athletic director position and for his contract not being renewed.[34] The Eleventh Circuit similarly found that a teacher's questions about the fairness of cheerleading tryouts pertained to her duties as a cheerleading sponsor and were not protected

[30]5 U.S.C. § 1213 (2018).

[31]34 CFR 100.7(e); *see also* Houlihan v. Sussex Tech. Sch. Dist., 461 F. Supp. 2d 252 (D. Del. 2006) (holding a school psychologist's complaints about the school's noncompliance with the Individuals with Disabilities Education Act were not protected by the First Amendment, but finding a valid cause of action for retaliation under the federal Rehabilitation Act); U.S. Equal Emp't Opportunity Comm'n *EEOC Enforcement Guidance on Retaliation and Related Issues* (Aug. 25, 2016), https://www.eeoc.gov/laws/guidance/retaliation-guidance.cfm; U.S. Dep't of Educ., *Retaliation Discrimination* (Oct. 15, 2015), https://www2.ed.gov/policy/rights/guid/ocr/retaliationoverview.html.

[32]*See* Nat'l Conference of State Legislatures, *State Whistleblower Laws* (Nov. 19, 2010), http://www.ncsl.org/research/labor-and-employment/state-whistleblower-laws.aspx.

[33]Garcetti v. Ceballos, 547 U.S. 410 (2006) (Souter, J., dissenting) (highlighting the limits of the existing whistleblower legislation).

[34]Williams v. Dallas Indep. Sch. Dist., 480 F.3d 689 (5th Cir. 2007).

expression relating to educational quality issues, as she claimed.[35] The Tenth Circuit also ruled that a superintendent's comments about the Head Start program and possible violations of federal law were not protected as they were made in the course of her job duties.[36] The Ninth Circuit held that a special education teacher's concerns about her school's special education program were not protected speech because they were made pursuant to her duties as an employee, even though some of her speech touched upon matters of public concern.[37] The teacher had been dismissed after voicing allegations that the district was not mainstreaming some students with disabilities due to financial reasons. In another case, the District of Columbia Circuit ruled a special education teacher's email to the chancellor of the school district accusing his principal of falsifying student test scores was also unprotected speech.[38]

In contrast, some whistleblowers have prevailed post–*Garcetti*. In 2014, the U.S. Supreme Court clarified the *Garcetti* standard to some extent. In *Lane v. Franks*, the Court emphasized that "citizens do not surrender their First Amendment rights by accepting public employment."[39] The Court held in favor of a public employee who had been fired after testifying about a former colleague's misconduct. Specifically, the Court clarified that the employee's speech was not made "in the course of his ordinary job responsibilities" (i.e., the speech was made while testifying), so it was considered citizen speech, and because it was also about a matter of public concern, the speech was protected by the First Amendment.[40] **Thus, the *Lane* Court distinguished speech based on information acquired on the job—which may be protected if it is about a matter of public concern—from speech made pursuant to *ordinary* job duties—which is unprotected.**

[35]Gilder-Lucas v. Elmore Cty. Bd. of Educ., 186 F. App'x 885 (11th Cir. 2006); *see also* Nagle v. Marron, 663 F.3d 100 (2d Cir. 2011) (holding that a teacher's complaint about an assistant principal forging her signature on a teaching evaluation form was not protected because it was not a matter of public concern; however, the teacher's complaints about the abuse of students was about a matter of public concern and was thus protected); Weintraub v. Bd. of Educ., 593 F.3d 196, 198 (2d Cir. 2010) (finding that a teacher's union grievance alleging that an administrator had failed to discipline a student who threw books at her was not protected speech because it related to the teacher's "core duties" of "maintaining class discipline").

[36]Casey v. W. Las Vegas Indep. Sch. Dist., 473 F.3d 1323 (10th Cir. 2007) (holding, however, that her reported concerns about the school board's failure to comply with New Mexico Open Meetings Act were outside the scope of her job, so her claim of retaliation for those comments was legally viable).

[37]Coomes v. Edmonds Sch. Dist., 816 F.3d 1255 (9th Cir. 2016); *see also* Fox v. Traverse City Area Pub. Schs. Bd. of Educ., 605 F.3d 345 (6th Cir. 2010) (finding the teacher's complaint to her supervisors that her special education caseload violated the law was unprotected because it was made pursuant to her official job duties).

[38]Mpoy v. Rhee, 758 F.3d 285 (2014); *see also* Williams v. Bd. of Educ., 2012 U.S. Dist. LEXIS 36936 (W.D.N.Y. Mar. 15, 2012) (holding an office assistant's complaints to a supervisor about another school official who had encouraged her to misappropriate federal funds were made pursuant to her official job duties and, thus, were unprotected speech).

[39]134 S. Ct. 2369, 2374 (2014).

[40]*Id.* at 2378; *see also* Mpoy, 758 F.3d at 294–95 (noting that regardless of its ultimate decision, the speech was unprotected; "the court's use of the adjective 'ordinary' nine times could signal a narrowing of the realm of employee speech left unprotected by Garcetti").

The Third Circuit clarified that the holding in *Lane* applied to speech beyond compelled testimony.[41] A Philadelphia school business officer was fired after revealing to newspaper reporters and government officials that the superintendent had engaged in unethical behavior. The court held that the school employee's speech concerned his employment duties, but was not made in the scope of his ordinary duties. The court lauded the employee's whistleblowing as "the archetype of speech deserving the highest rung of First Amendment protection."[42] Thus, when analyzing the speech using the *Pickering* balancing test, the court determined the disruption to the school operations caused by the employee's leaks to the press did not outweigh the "substantial public interest in exposing governmental misconduct."[43] Four years before *Lane* was decided, the Tenth Circuit ruled in favor of a speech-language pathologist who alleged First Amendment retaliation when adverse action was taken against her for advocating for students with disabilities in the school.[44] The court identified two factors to help determine that the employee is speaking as a private citizen: (1) the employee's job duties do not relate to the reporting of any wrongdoing, and (2) the employee went outside the chain of command.

Other Cases.   In post–*Garcetti* expression cases where whistleblowing has not been at issue, school personnel often have not prevailed. To illustrate, the Eleventh Circuit rejected a principal's claim that a Florida school board violated his First Amendment rights.[45] He claimed that he was unconstitutionally terminated in retaliation for urging his teachers to support conversion of their school to a charter school. Noting that *Garcetti* shifted the threshold question from whether the employee is speaking on a matter of public concern to whether the employee's speech relates to job duties, the Eleventh Circuit concluded that the principal was speaking in his professional role in seeking charter school status. Thus, his expression was not protected and could be the basis for dismissal. Likewise, the Tenth Circuit held that a principal's public opposition to the plans to close down her school was

---

[41]Dougherty v. Sch. Dist. of Phila., 772 F.3d 979 (3d Cir. 2014).

[42]*Id.* at 991.

[43]*Id.* at 992; *see also* Keeton v. Bd. of Educ., 2016 WL 5938699 (D. Del. Oct. 12, 2016) (reasoning that a school employee who was terminated after complaining to his principal that she was in violation of copyright law was speaking outside the scope of his ordinary job duties about a matter of public concern); McShea v. Sch. Bd., 58 F. Supp. 3d 1325 (M.D. Fla. 2014) (ruling that a reading coach was speaking as a citizen about a public concern when she revealed that her building administrators were misusing federal funds and improperly administering standardized tests).

[44]Reinhardt v. Albuquerque Pub. Schs. Bd. of Educ., 595 F.3d 1126 (10th Cir. 2010); *see also* Goudeau v. E. Baton Rouge Sch. Bd., 540 F. App'x 429 (5th Cir. 2013) (finding that a teacher's official complaint about principal's instruction to illegally inflate grades was protected speech relating to a matter of public concern). *But see* Holub v. Gdowski, 802 F.3d 1149 (10th Cir. 2015) (holding that whistleblowing speech about fraudulent budgeting practices made by an internal auditor for the school district was not protected because it was made within the scope of the auditor's ordinary job duties).

[45]D'Angelo v. Sch. Bd., 497 F.3d 1203 (11th Cir. 2007); *see also* Fernandez v. Sch. Bd., 2017 WL 2537281 (S.D. Fla. June 12, 2017) (applying Lane to three employees who claimed retaliation for attempting to convert their school to a charter school; the two administrators' speech was deemed unprotected, but the third employee's speech was outside the scope of her ordinary duties and thus, protected).

not protected speech.[46] It reasoned that because the principal was part of the management team, she had a professional duty to publicly support the policies of the superintendent and school board.

Employees other than school leaders have also not prevailed in their free speech claims. A football coach claimed that his prayer after games in view of students and spectators did not relate to his duties as a coach, but the Ninth Circuit found the speech at a school-sponsored event was within the scope of his duties.[47] The court noted that if the speech "owes its existence" to the school employee's position, then the employee is speaking as a public employee and thus, the speech is not protected.[48]

Some employees, however, have succeeded in their expression claims in post–*Garcetti* cases. For example, the Sixth Circuit ruled in favor of a superintendent who asserted that he was not named Director of Schools—which was a new position to replace his superintendent position—because he accepted an invitation to speak before a predominantly LGBTQ church congregation. The court reasoned that board members were not entitled to qualified immunity because the superintendent's expression was to occur during his personal time and did not relate to his work in the school district. Instead, the speech touched on matters of public concern. Even if the speech interfered with school operations because the board did not "condone homosexuality," the court reasoned that retaliating against the superintendent for this reason would be equivalent to retaliating against him for his beliefs which "would contravene the intent of the First Amendment."[49] A Tennessee federal court also found a teacher's speech was made in her role as a private citizen.[50] She complained to her principal that one of her students was making detailed threats about committing a mass shooting at school. Eventually, the teacher missed work because she was physically and emotionally upset about the continued threats. The court found that the district illegally retaliated against the teacher for her speech that was a matter of public concern.

In cases where both protected and unprotected speech is involved, courts have relied on *Mt. Healthy* to uphold terminations or transfers where other legitimate reasons justify the personnel actions. In an illustrative case, a principal who gave a speech at a public hearing expressing opposition to closing a school was demoted to a teaching position. He claimed retaliation for his protected expression, but a Kentucky federal court found insufficient evidence that the speech was the motivating factor in the demotion.[51] The Seventh Circuit also rejected a teacher's challenge to disciplinary action for her critical comments pertaining to the need for additional textbooks at her school. The court ruled that the teacher failed to prove that her speech was a substantial or motivating factor in the disciplinary action, given the well-documented incidents of the teacher's misconduct or insubordination.[52] The Tenth Circuit similarly found that a director of bilingual education could not establish that speaking about the program's noncompliance with state guidelines and writing a letter to the

---

[46]Rock v. Levinski, 791 F.3d 1215 (10th Cir. 2015) (applying a five-part test that is similar to Figure 10.1).

[47]Kennedy v. Bremerton Sch. Dist., 869 F.3d 813 (9th Cir. 2017). *See* text accompanying note 56, Chapter 3.

[48]*Id.*

[49]Scarbrough v. Morgan Cty. Bd. of Educ., 470 F.3d 250, 258 (6th Cir. 2006).

[50]Ellison v. Knox Cty., 157 F. Supp. 3d 718 (E.D. Tenn. 2016).

[51]Painter v. Campbell Cty. Bd. of Educ., 417 F. Supp. 2d 854 (E.D. Ky. 2006).

[52]Smith v. Dunn, 368 F.3d 705 (7th Cir. 2004).

editor of the local newspaper were the motivating factors in her termination and held instead that poor job performance justified the action.[53]

School authorities cannot rely on *Mt. Healthy* to justify termination or other disci plinary action if the school officials' stated reasons for personnel decisions are merely a pretext to restrict protected expression. For example, a federal district court denied a school district's motion for summary judgment because an administrator, who was allegedly fired for not complying with the district's school improvement plan, may have actually been fired in retaliation for complaining to the superintendent that many of the elementary school classrooms were racially segregated.[54]

Once determined that expression is protected, the employee then has the burden of demonstrating that it was a key factor in the dismissal or disciplinary decision. **Even if the employee can establish that expression on matters of public concern was the sole basis for the adverse action, the public employer still may prevail under the *Pickering* balancing test by showing that its interests in protecting the public agency outweigh the individual's free speech rights.**[55]

Internet and Other Electronic Speech

Educators' speech on social networking sites, as well as in email and text messages, has been the subject of recent litigation and numerous media accounts.[56] In some cases, courts have relied on *Garcetti* if the teacher wrote something that was pursuant to his or her job responsibilities. For speech outside the scope of one's job duties, *Pickering* and *Connick* have also been used. Typically, educators have not prevailed when challenging discipline or dismissal due to their social media posts.

Cases Involving Students.   Unsurprisingly, courts have upheld the dismissals and criminal convictions of teachers who have attempted to form sexual relationships with students over the Internet.[57] Courts have also upheld the discipline of teachers who have communicated with or about students in an unprofessional manner.[58] The Third Circuit ruled that a

---

[53]Deschenie v. Bd. of Educ., 473 F.3d 1271 (10th Cir. 2007) (holding that the time between the expression and termination was too attenuated to show a causal connection).

[54]Howell v. Marion Sch. Dist., 2009 U.S. Dist. LEXIS 22723 (D.S.C. Mar. 19, 2009).

[55]*See* Fales v. Garst, 235 F.3d 1122 (8th Cir. 2001) (finding the teachers' interests in speaking about incidents with special education students was outweighed by the school district's interest in efficiently administering the middle school, given the upheaval caused by the expression).

[56]*See* Ian Shapira, *When Young Teachers Go Wild on the Web*, WASH. POST (Apr. 28, 2008), http://www .washingtonpost.com/wp-dyn/content/article/2008/04/27/AR2008042702213.html; Nancy Solomon, *Friendly Advice for Teachers: Beware of Facebook*, NPR (Dec. 7, 2011), http://www.npr.org/2011/12/07/143264921/ friendly-advice-for-teachers-beware-of-facebook.

[57]*See, e.g.*, Brown v. Indiana, 67 N.E.3d 1127 (Ind. Ct. App. 2017) (finding a school band director guilty of child seduction after he communicated with students over social media).

[58]*See, e.g.*, Wax v. Horne, 844 So. 2d 797 (Fla. Dist. Ct. App. 2003) (affirming the permanent revocation of an educator's teaching certificate after she emailed students sexually suggestive jokes laced with profanity); *In re* Tenure Hearing of O'Brien, 2013 WL 132508, at *2 (N.J. Super. Ct. App. Div. Jan. 11, 2013) (upholding the dismissal of a teacher after posting "I'm not a teacher—I'm a warden for future criminals!"). *But see* Rubino v. City of N.Y., 965 N.Y.S.2d 47 (App. Div. 2013) (finding that a teacher's inappropriate post was unprotected speech, but the district's dismissal was excessively harsh).

teacher's personal blog was not protected expression.[59] On her blog that had only nine followers, the teacher described her students as "devil's spawn," "frightfully dim," "whiny," "lazy," and "rat-like."[60] After students learned of the blog and parents requested that their children not be placed in the teacher's classes, the district gave the teacher negative evaluations and ultimately terminated her. The teacher claimed the administration harassed her in retaliation for her blog. In analyzing the teacher's claim, the court reluctantly assumed that some of the blog touched upon matters of public concern and applied the *Pickering* balancing test. The court ruled that because the teacher's speech disrupted the operations of the school, her dismissal was legal.

In another case, a teacher alleged that school officials violated his First Amendment rights when his contract was not renewed as a result of comments he had posted on his social media page. Specifically, the teacher had interacted like a peer with the students and had included pictures of naked men on his profile. Although finding his dismissal justified on other grounds, the court reasoned that dismissal could have been based on the posts, which were likely to disrupt school activities.[61] Teachers have not been the only school employees gaining notoriety for their online posts. A high school administrator resigned after the superintendent discovered her posts referencing students as "germ bags" and their parents as "snobby."[62] Similarly, a superintendent was forced to resign after he discussed a confidential personnel issue on Facebook.[63]

Other Cases. School employees have also been disciplined for speech that does not directly involve their students, but relates to their school employment. For example, the Ninth Circuit found that a curriculum specialist's job reassignment did not violate her First Amendment rights. The court assumed that the specialist's postings on her personal blog, which included inappropriate comments about colleagues, were of public concern. Nonetheless, the court dismissed the case using the *Pickering* balancing test because the specialist's comments interfered with her relationships at school.[64] In another case, a teacher was dismissed for his website post calling the superintendent and treasurer "cockroaches" and "common thieves of public money."[65] The West Virginia Supreme Court held that the teacher had no First Amendment right at stake because his statements both on and off the website would not be considered matters of public concern. The court further noted that the teacher's comments could have destroyed feelings of loyalty and confidence among his colleagues.

---

[59]Munroe v. Cent. Bucks Sch. Dist., 805 F.3d 454 (3rd Cir. 2015).

[60]*Id.* at 459–60.

[61]Spanierman v. Hughes, 576 F. Supp. 2d 292 (D. Conn. 2008).

[62]Nancy White, *Cohasett School Official Resigns over 'Snobby and Arrogant' Comments on Facebook*, PATRIOT LEDGER (Aug. 18, 2010), http://www.patriotledger.com/topstories/x1104157578/Cohasset-school-administrator-resigns-over-snobby-and-arrogant-comments-on-Facebook.

[63]Allison Manning, *Educators Advised to Use Common Sense on Facebook*, EDUC. WEEK. (Sept. 28, 2010), https://www.edweek.org/ew/articles/2010/09/29/05facebook.h30.html.

[64]Richerson v. Beckon, 337 F. App'x 637 (9th Cir. 2009).

[65]Alderman v. Pocahontas Cty. Bd. of Educ., 675 S.E.2d 907, 912 (W.Va. 2009). *But see* Meagher v. Andover Sch. Comm., 94 F. Supp. 3d 21 (D. Mass. 2015) (finding that a dismissed teacher was retaliated against for protected speech when she wrote an email on her personal computer, distributed it using a personal email account, and sent it to colleagues' personal email accounts, despite the fact that the content of the teacher's email was about union negotiations with the school board).

Student teachers should also be cautious when using social networking sites. In a Pennsylvania case, a federal district court denied a student teacher injunctive relief in a case involving her postings on social media.[66] The student teacher was not awarded her teacher certification after she received unsatisfactory ratings during student teaching as a result of her unprofessionalism involving her social media posts that her students had viewed. One picture showed the student teacher holding an alcoholic drink with a caption that read, "drunken pirate."[67] The court determined that her postings related only to personal matters and did not touch upon matters of public concern.

Despite courts' likelihood of offering more protection to speech if it relates to matters of public concern, school employees should be cautious when sharing their political beliefs online. After controversial political posts attracted public scrutiny, districts have disciplined educators. For example, a substitute teacher settled a lawsuit against a district after claiming that he was fired for criticizing a police officer in a Facebook post.[68]

Policies Restricting Employees' Electronic Expression and Access.   Problems with teachers posting controversial or inappropriate commentary on their Facebook pages has led some states to consider laws to regulate employees' Internet speech, as well as their freedom to communicate with students over electronic modes (e.g., text and instant messaging). Such laws have created a backlash with employees arguing that the laws abridge First Amendment rights. Missouri passed a law prohibiting teachers and students from being friends on Facebook, but the law was later repealed as a result of First Amendment concerns.[69] On the other hand, a Louisiana law that requires districts to develop policies prohibiting teacher-student electronic communication occurring on unapproved networks still stands.[70] Many states and districts have also issued guidance and model policies restricting school employees' use of electronic communication.[71]

Most districts provide employees with written expectations for appropriate use of technology through the district's acceptable use policy. But even without written policies in place, courts have generally supported school districts' disciplinary actions for employees' inappropriate emails and improper use of school computers. For example, the

---

[66]Snyder v. Millersville Univ., 2008 WL 5093140 (E.D. Pa. Dec. 3, 2008).

[67]*Id.* at *6.

[68]Sarah Elms, *Sylvania Schools, ACLU Reach Settlement on Fired Teacher*, BLADE (Jan. 20, 2017), http://www .toledoblade.com/Education/2017/01/20/Sylvania-Schools-ACLU-reach-settlement-on-fired-teacher.html.

[69]Amy Hestir Student Protection Act, 2011 Mo. LAWS 1162 (stating "no teacher shall establish, maintain, or use a nonwork-related Internet site which allows exclusive access with a current or former student"), *repealed by* Act of Oct. 21, 2011, S.B. 1, 96th Gen. Assemb., 1st Extra Sess. § 162.069 (Mo. 2011).

[70]LA. REV. STAT. ANN. § 17.81(Q)(2)(a)–(j) (2018) (requiring district policies that forbid school employees from communicating with students through electronic means other than through school-provided structures, such as school email and school-sponsored websites, unless they have been granted permission from the principal or his designee).

[71]*See, e.g.*, Associated Press, *Wisconsin School District Changes Staff Social Media Policy*, STARTRIBUNE (July 23, 2017), http://www.startribune.com/wisconsin-school-district-changes-staff-social-media-policy/436154253/; Jessica Farrish, *Teacher, Student Texting Banned by BOE*, REGISTER-HERALD (Oct. 9, 2013), http://www .register-herald.com/news/local_news/teacher-student-texting-banned-by-boe/article_c81f4867-bf67-5ddf-aea4-c166f3f5aef1.html.

Fourth Circuit held that public employees do not have a free speech right to use state computers for purposes not related to the agency's business and upheld restrictions on state employees using such equipment to access sexually explicit Internet materials.[72] Also, the Seventh Circuit upheld the dismissal of a teacher who had accessed pornography on school computers.[73] A Connecticut court endorsed the termination of a computer ethics teacher who had written sexual emails to his supervising principal from his school email account.[74] A New Jersey appellate court upheld the dismissal of a tenured media specialist who claimed she was surfing pornographic websites to test a problem with the school's Internet filter.[75]

Classroom Expression

Courts have long-recognized restrictions placed on teachers' expression when interacting with students. **Because classrooms are a nonpublic forum where teachers have a captive student audience, courts have traditionally upheld restrictions on classroom expression.**[76] Since 1988, many courts have applied *Hazelwood v. Kuhlmeier* to assess the constitutionality of teachers' classroom expression of personal opinions,[77] holding that such expression could be curtailed for legitimate pedagogical reasons, an easy standard for school districts to satisfy. For example, the First Circuit held that a teacher's discussion of aborting fetuses with Down syndrome could be censored, noting that the school board may limit a teacher's classroom expression in the interest of promoting educational goals.[78] The Tenth Circuit relied on *Hazelwood* in upholding disciplinary action against a teacher who made comments during class about rumors that two students had engaged in sexual intercourse on the school tennis court during lunch hour, reasoning that the ninth-grade government class was not a public forum.[79] Also, a Missouri federal district court upheld the termination of a teacher for making disparaging classroom comments about interracial relationships, finding no protected expression and noting that the teacher was aware of the district's anti-harassment policy.[80]

In several cases, public school teachers have not prevailed in their efforts to express their views via materials posted in their classrooms or on the adjacent hall walls. To illustrate, the Ninth Circuit agreed with the decision of school authorities to censor material a teacher had posted outside his classroom that denounced being gay and extolled traditional family values to offset the school district's materials recognizing Gay and Lesbian

[72]Urofsky v. Gilmore, 216 F.3d 401 (4th Cir. 2000).

[73]Zellner v. Herrick, 639 F.3d 371 (7th Cir. 2011).

[74]Arlington Pub. Schs. v. Coughlin, 26 Mass. L. Rptr. 472 (Super. Ct. 2010).

[75]*In re* Tenure Hearing of Donahue, 2008 WL 553029 (N.J. Super. Ct. App. Div. Mar. 3, 2008).

[76]Busch v. Marple Newtown Sch. Dist., 567 F.3d 89 (3d Cir. 2009).

[77]484 U.S. 260 (1988).

[78]Ward v. Hickey, 996 F.2d 448 (1st Cir. 1993). *But see* Cockrel v. Shelby Cty. Sch. Dist., 270 F.3d 1036 (6th Cir. 2001) (holding that a teacher's controversial speech about the benefits of hemp related to political and social concerns in the community; therefore, her classroom speech was protected and her termination was improper).

[79]Miles v. Denver Pub. Schs., 944 F.2d 773 (10th Cir. 1991).

[80]Loeffelman v. Bd. of Educ., 134 S.W.3d 637 (Mo. Ct. App. 2004).

Awareness Month.[81] Reasoning that the teacher was speaking for the school, the court concluded that teachers are not entitled to express views in the classroom that are counter to the adopted curriculum. The Ninth Circuit held also that a math teacher had no First Amendment right to display religious banners in his classroom, observing that a public school teacher may not present his personal views of the role of God.[82]

In the years immediately after *Garcetti*, some courts were uncertain whether *Hazelwood* or *Garcetti* should be applied.[83] Indeed, the *Garcetti* majority emphasized that "we need not, and for that reason do not, decide whether the analysis we conduct today would apply in the same manner to a case involving speech related to scholarship or teaching."[84] However, all federal appellate courts, except for the Fourth Circuit, appear to be relying on *Garcetti* in assessing teachers' expression pursuant to their instructional duties.

In a recent Seventh Circuit case, a middle school teacher caught students passing a note in class that contained the offensive N-word.[85] The teacher considered it a teachable moment and explained why such words are harmful; however, the teacher was disciplined based on a policy forbidding the use of racial epithets. The teacher claimed that *Garcetti* did not apply because his speech was related to teaching; yet, the court dismissed this argument, noting that the Seventh, Third, Sixth, and Ninth circuits have applied *Garcetti* to teachers' instructional speech. In another Seventh Circuit case, the court ruled that classroom expression clearly is part of public educators' official duties and can be censored to protect the captive student audience.[86] Accordingly, the court ruled that the teacher's expression of negative views about the war in Iraq during a current events session was not constitutionally protected. The court reasoned that *Garcetti* directly applied in this case because the teacher's current events lesson was an assigned classroom task.

Also, federal district courts have addressed classroom expression issues. For example, a teacher in Michigan alleged that he was retaliated against after he wore a T-shirt to school that contained a printed message about the teachers' union not being under contract. The federal district court held that the T-shirt worn in his classes caused or had the potential to cause disharmony in the workplace. Although recognizing that the issue of labor negotiations touches on a matter of public concern, the court found the school district's interest in ensuring a professional workplace outweighed the teacher's rights in this

[81]Downs v. L.A. Unified Sch. Dist., 228 F.3d 1003 (9th Cir. 2000); *see also* Newton v. Slye, 116 F. Supp. 2d 677 (W.D. Va. 2000) (ruling that a teacher likely did not have a First Amendment right to post outside his classroom door the American Library Association's pamphlet listing banned books, which the principal and superintendent felt potentially compromised the school's family life education program and other initiatives).

[82]Johnson v. Poway Unified Sch. Dist., 658 F.3d 954 (9th Cir. 2011). *See* Lee v. York Cty. Sch. Div., 484 F.3d 687 (4th Cir. 2007) (finding a school district did not violate a teacher's rights when it ordered him to remove religious material from his classroom's bulletin board).

[83]*See, e.g.*, Sheldon v. Dhillon, 2009 U.S. Dist. LEXIS 110275 (N.D. Cal. Nov. 25, 2009) (noting that the Ninth Circuit has applied Hazelwood to classroom speech); Kramer v. N.Y.C. Bd. of Educ., 715 F. Supp. 2d 335 (E.D.N.Y. 2010) (applying both Hazelwood and Garcetti after noting the disagreement amongst federal courts of appeal regarding which case to apply). *But see* Evans-Marshall v. Bd. of Educ., 624 F.3d 332 (6th Cir. 2010) (finding that Garcetti does extend to a teacher's classroom speech).

[84]Garcetti v. Ceballos, 547 U.S. 410, 425 (2006).

[85]Brown v. Chi. Bd. of Educ., 824 F.3d 713 (7th Cir. 2016).

[86]Mayer v. Monroe Cty. Cmty. Sch. Corp., 474 F.3d 477 (7th Cir. 2007).

instance. The court noted that under *Garcetti*, "government employers, like private employers, need a significant degree of control over their employees' words and actions; without it, there would be little chance for the efficient provision of public services."[87]

Litigation over teachers' classroom comments seems likely to continue. Whether courts apply *Garcetti* or *Hazelwood* may have little practical significance because teachers' classroom expression has always been subject to restrictions to protect students from proselytization.[88] **In sum, when faced with a question of whether a school employee's speech is protected under the First Amendment, a good first step is to determine whether the employee was speaking as a private citizen or public employee**. If the speech was pursuant to the employee's ordinary job duties, then school districts have broad latitude in disciplining the employee.

ACADEMIC FREEDOM

Teachers lack legal authority to control the curriculum, but they do have the academic freedom to choose relevant instructional strategies.

The concept of academic freedom historically was applied to postsecondary education and embodied the principle that faculty members should be free from government controls in conducting research and imparting knowledge to students. **Public school teachers have asserted a similar right to academic freedom, but courts have not extended the protections found in higher education to public elementary and secondary schools.**[89] Courts have typically resolved controversies about the academic freedom of K–12 educators on a case-by-case basis where they have balanced teachers' interests in academic freedom against school boards' interests in ensuring an appropriate instructional program and efficient school operations.

Course Content

Public school teachers do not have a right to determine the content of the instructional program. Recognizing that the state, as employer, controls the curriculum, the Ninth Circuit rejected a vagueness challenge to California legislation holding teachers personally liable for actual damages if they willfully refuse to teach predominantly in English.[90] The court concluded that in the vast majority of instances, teachers would clearly know when they were dispensing instruction that would be subject to the language restriction.

[87]Montle v. Westwood Heights Sch. Dist., 437 F. Supp. 2d 652, 654 (E.D. Mich. 2006).

[88]*See, e.g.,* People *ex rel.* McCollum v. Bd. of Educ., 333 U.S. 203, 236 (1948) (Jackson, J., concurring) (noting that the Court "can forbid forthright proselyting in the schools"). For a discussion of proselytization based on religion, *see* text accompanying note 45, Chapter 3.

[89]*See* Brown v. Chic. Bd. of Educ., 824 F.3d at 716 (distinguishing that academic freedom differs between a public school and university setting).

[90]Cal. Teachers Ass'n v. State Bd. of Educ., 271 F.3d 1141 (9th Cir. 2001). *See* text accompanying note 71, Chapter 6, discussing California legislation that eliminates this requirement.

Despite the state's legal authority to impose such curricular restrictions, state law often delegates to local school boards considerable authority to make instructional decisions. Several courts have declared that school boards are not legally obligated to accept teachers' curricular recommendations in the absence of a board policy to that effect. To illustrate, the Fifth Circuit held that teachers cannot assert a First Amendment right to substitute their own supplemental reading list for the officially adopted list without securing administrative approval.[91] And the Fourth Circuit ruled that a high school teacher did not have complete discretion to select the plays performed by her acting class students, recognizing school officials' legitimate pedagogical interests in regulating the curriculum.[92] In a New York case, a federal district court granted the school district's motion to dismiss because an English teacher was not due First Amendment protection. The teacher disregarded her principal's instruction to not teach a lesson to her ninth grade class centered around the Central Park Five in which five Black teenagers were wrongly convicted of raping a White woman.[93]

Teachers are not permitted to ignore or omit prescribed course content under the guise of academic freedom. To exemplify, the Seventh Circuit upheld a school board's dismissal of a kindergarten teacher who, for religious reasons, refused to teach patriotic topics.[94] Similarly, the Supreme Court of Ohio upheld the dismissal of a teacher after he taught creationism and intelligent design in contradiction to proscribed curriculum.[95] The court explained that teacher did not have a free exercise right to refuse to follow directives to stop proselytizing to his students. Also, the Third Circuit held that a teacher could not assert a First Amendment right to disregard school board instructions and continue to allow students the responsibility for establishing class rules and grading procedures.[96]

Educators are not legally vulnerable when they are teaching the prescribed curriculum, even though their superiors instruct them not to do so.[97] For example, the Sixth Circuit ruled in favor of a teacher who was teaching a life science course in compliance with the school board's directives, finding that community protests did not justify school authorities placing restrictions on his course content that was consistent with the

---

[91]Kirkland v. Northside Indep. Sch. Dist., 890 F.2d 794 (5th Cir. 1989).

[92]Boring v. Buncombe Cty. Bd. of Educ., 136 F.3d 364 (4th Cir. 1998).

[93]Lee-Walker v. N.Y.C. Dep't of Educ., 220 F. Supp. 3d 484 (S.D.N.Y. 2016); *see also* Kramer v. N.Y.C. Bd. of Educ., 715 F. Supp. 2d 335 (E.D.N.Y. 2010) (finding transfer of the teacher to noninstructional duties was warranted after the teacher had students identify slang words for body parts).

[94]Palmer v. Bd. of Educ., 603 F.2d 1271 (7th Cir. 1979).

[95]Freshwater v. Mount Vernon Cty. Sch. Dist., 1 N.E.3d 335 (Ohio Sup. 2013). *See* text accompanying note 129, Chapter 3.

[96]Murray v. Pittsburgh Bd. of Educ., 141 F.3d 1154 (3d Cir. 1998); *see also* Bd. of Educ. v. Wilder, 960 P.2d 695 (Colo. 1998) (upholding the termination of a teacher for showing his high school class portions of a movie that included nudity, profanity, and graphic violence in disregard of a policy requiring administrative review of controversial materials); *infra* text accompanying note 101.

[97]It should also be noted that school counselors may discuss controversial issues in confidence with counselees and provide information as well as referrals. For example, counselors can provide factual information on the legal status of abortions, but they cannot urge or coerce students to have an abortion. *See* Arnold v. Bd. of Educ., 880 F.2d 305 (11th Cir. 1989).

course objectives.[98] After a Maine teacher received several complaints about his curriculum from members of a Christian church, the school board ordered the teacher to refrain from teaching certain social science subjects pertaining to prehistoric times and Greek, Roman, and Asian history. The teacher challenged the board's action, and the district court denied the board's request for summary judgment, reasoning that the teacher was threatened with termination for teaching "non-Christian" ancient history. The court emphasized that classrooms cannot be used to promote Christian ideology.[99] In contrast, a New York federal district court upheld a school district's decision to not renew a probationary teacher's contract after she used an icebreaker exercise in a human reproduction lesson where she asked the students to sketch the male reproductive system. The court reasoned that the teacher could have explained the reproductive system in a more appropriate way.[100]

Teaching Strategies

State laws and school board policies establish the basic contours of the curriculum, but teachers retain some discretion in choosing *relevant strategies* to convey prescribed content. In reviewing school board restrictions on teachers' classroom activities, the judiciary considers several factors, such as:

- whether teachers have been provided adequate notice that use of specific teaching methodologies or materials will result in disciplinary action;
- relevance of the method to the course of study and age and maturity of the students;
- support of the method by the profession;
- threat of disruption posed by the method; and
- impact of the strategy on community norms.

A primary consideration in reviewing the legitimacy of classroom activities is whether instructional strategies are related to course objectives. Relevancy applies also to the age and maturity of the students; a controversial topic appropriate for high school students would not necessarily be suitable for elementary and middle school students. Relevance has been found lacking in several cases in which teachers have shown R-rated movies to public school students.[101] Also, the Eighth Circuit upheld termination of a teacher who willfully violated board policy by permitting her students to use profanity in their creative writing assignments.[102]

---

[98]Stachura v. Truszkowski, 763 F.2d 211 (6th Cir. 1985), *rev'd and remanded on other grounds* (compensatory damages) *sub nom.* Memphis Cmty. Sch. Dist. v. Stachura, 477 U.S. 299 (1986).

[99]Cole v. Me. Sch. Admin. Dist., 350 F. Supp. 2d 143 (D. Me. 2004).

[100]Kirby v. Yonkers Sch. Dist., 767 F. Supp. 2d 452 (S.D.N.Y. 2011).

[101]*See, e.g.,* Fowler v. Bd. of Educ., 819 F.2d 657 (6th Cir. 1987); Borger v. Bisciglia, 888 F. Supp. 97 (E.D. Wis. 1995); Bd. of Educ. v. Wilder, 960 P.2d 695 (Colo. 1998).

[102]Lacks v. Ferguson Reorganized Sch. Dist., 147 F.3d 718 (8th Cir. 1998); *see also* Oleske v. Hilliard City Sch. Dist. Bd. of Educ., 764 N.E.2d 1110 (Ohio Ct. App. 2001) (upholding dismissal of a teacher who told dirty jokes to middle school students and referred to another teacher by a derogatory name).

Among the factors courts examine in assessing restrictions on classroom instruction is whether a teacher's action poses a threat of disruption to the operation of the school. To illustrate, an Oregon federal district court found a school board's policy banning all political speakers from the high school unreasonable on several grounds, including the fact that no disruption had occurred or could be anticipated from political discussions.[103] However, an Illinois federal district court recognized that a school board does not necessarily have to show that instructional materials actually caused a disruption to justify nonrenewal of a teacher's contract. Materials may be considered inappropriate for classroom use (e.g., an R-rated film with vulgarity and sexually explicit scenes), despite the fact that students "quietly acquiesce" to their use.[104]

Courts have been protective of school boards' authority to design the curriculum to reflect community values. A New York appeals court held that a teacher, who defied warnings that use of certain materials and sexual words in classroom discussions offended community mores, had no First Amendment grounds to challenge his reprimand.[105] **Teachers, however, cannot be forced to discontinue instructionally relevant activities solely because of parental displeasure**. The Fifth Circuit ruled that a teacher's use of a simulation to teach about post–Civil War U.S. history was related to legitimate educational objectives, and therefore dismissal for refusing to stop using the simulation impaired the teacher's academic rights.[106] If a particular strategy is instructionally relevant and supported by the profession, it likely will survive judicial review even though it might disturb some school patrons.

FREEDOM OF ASSOCIATION

A public educator's participation in political activities outside the classroom cannot be the basis for adverse employment decisions unless the employee has policy-making responsibilities or such activities negatively affect job performance.

Although freedom of association is not specifically addressed in the First Amendment, the Supreme Court has recognized that associational rights are "implicit in the freedoms of speech, assembly, and petition."[107] The Court has consistently declared that infringements on the right to associate for expressive purposes can be justified only by a compelling government interest, unrelated to suppressing ideas, which cannot be achieved through less restrictive means.[108] Accordingly, public educators cannot be disciplined for forming or joining political, labor, religious, or social organizations.

[103]Wilson v. Chancellor, 418 F. Supp. 1358 (D. Or. 1976).

[104]Krizek v. Bd. of Educ., 713 F. Supp. 1131, 1141 (N.D. Ill. 1989); *see also* Solmitz v. Me. Sch. Admin. Dist., 495 A.2d 812 (Me. 1985) (upholding a school board's cancellation of a Tolerance Day program for legitimate safety concerns over bomb threats received).

[105]*In re* Arbitration Between Bernstein & Norwich City Sch. Dist., 726 N.Y.S. 2d 474 (App. Div. 2001).

[106]Kingsville Indep. Sch. Dist. v. Cooper, 611 F.2d 1109 (5th Cir. 1980).

[107]Healy v. James, 408 U.S. 169, 181 (1972).

[108]*See, e.g.,* Roberts v. U.S. Jaycees, 468 U.S. 609 (1984).

Associational activities can be limited, however, if they disrupt school operations or interfere with teachers' professional duties. This section presents an overview of teachers' association rights in connection with political affiliations and activities. Public educators' rights to intimate association are discussed in this chapter's section on privacy rights, and union issues are addressed in Chapter 9.

Political Affiliations and Activity

Conditioning public employment on partisan political affiliation has been controversial.[109] In some instances, public educators have asserted that employment decisions have been based on their party affiliation. In such cases, the employee has the burden of substantiating that protected political affiliation was the motivating factor in the board's employment decision.[110] If an employee satisfies this burden, then the board must demonstrate by a preponderance of evidence that it would have reached the same decision in the absence of the political association.

Campaigning and Other Activities. Teachers, like all citizens, are guaranteed the right to participate in the political process through their First Amendment association and free speech rights. For example, the Sixth Circuit held that the coordinator of gifted education, which was not a policy-making position, could not be reassigned for the exercise of constitutionally protected political expression and association in actively supporting an unsuccessful superintendent candidate.[111] However, a North Carolina federal court was not convinced by a teacher's claim that the school board and principal retaliated against him for his past role as a political consultant for a state legislator.[112] The court highlighted the teacher's inappropriate behavior with students, reasoning that the teacher failed to prove his past political activity was the motivating factor for his termination. Similarly, an Oregon federal court sided with a school district that terminated a teacher. The teacher claimed he was retaliated against because of his affiliation with an anti-abortion group and his vocal opposition of Planned Parenthood. Again, the court reasoned there was ample evidence of the teacher's unprofessional and harassing behavior that warranted his termination.[113]

Political activity that would cause divisiveness within the school district can be restricted. A federal district court upheld a regulation that prohibits teachers from wear-

---

[109]*See* Elrod v. Burns, 427 U.S. 347 (1976) (holding public employees who lost their jobs solely because of their partisan affiliation had stated a valid claim of constitutional deprivation); Rutan v. Republican Party, 497 U.S. 62 (1990) (stating that employment decisions based on political affiliation is unconstitutional).

[110]*See* Piazza v. Aponte Roque, 873 F.2d 432 (1st Cir. 1989) (finding that nonrenewal of teachers' aides because of their political party affiliation impaired associational rights).

[111]Hager v. Pike Cty. Bd. of Educ., 286 F.3d 366 (6th Cir. 2002); *see also* Beattie v. Madison Cty. Sch. Dist., 254 F.3d 595 (5th Cir. 2001) (finding an insufficient causal link between employee's termination and her support for the nonincumbent candidate for school superintendent).

[112]Penley v. McDowell Cty. Bd. of Educ., 2015 WL 7721244 (W.D.N.C. Aug. 19, 2016).

[113]Diss v. Portland Pub. Schs., 2016 WL 6901360 (D. Ore. Nov. 22, 2016).

ing political campaign buttons in school buildings because of legitimate pedagogical concerns related to entanglement of public education with partisan politics.[114] The court observed that the board's regulation of the campaign buttons was based on good faith professional judgment. Since 2016, the discipline of school employees for their political expression has garnered national attention. For example, a California teacher was placed on administrative leave for kneeling during the national anthem at a school event while holding a Black Lives Matter sign;[115] a Georgia teacher was disciplined for telling students that wearing President Trump campaign shirts were similar to wearing swastikas;[116] and a New Jersey teacher was placed on administrative leave for editing a picture of a student in the Yearbook by removing the Trump campaign message on the student's shirt.[117] **Teachers cannot take advantage of their position of authority with an impressionable captive audience to impose their political views.**[118] However, if campaign issues are related to the class topic, a teacher can present election issues and candidates in a nonpartisan manner.

Holding Public Office.   Certain categories of public employees have been prevented from running for political office. In 1973, the Supreme Court upheld a federal law (the Hatch Act) that prevents *federal* employees from holding formal positions in political parties, playing substantial roles in partisan campaigns, and running for partisan office.[119] The Court recognized that legitimate reasons exist for restricting political activities of public employees, such as the need to ensure impartial and effective government, to remove employees from political pressure, and to prevent employee selection based on political factors. Conversely, the Supreme Court struck down a school board policy requiring any school employee who became a candidate for public office to take a leave of absence.[120] Laws or policies prohibiting *all* public employees from running for *any* political office have been struck down as overly broad.[121]

---

[114]Weingarten v. Bd. of Educ., 680 F. Supp. 2d 595 (S.D.N.Y. 2010); *see also* Turlock Joint Elementary Sch. Dist. v. Pub. Emp't Relations Bd., 5 Cal. Rptr. 3d 308 (Ct. App. 2003) (concluding that teachers could be prohibited from wearing union buttons while delivering instruction).

[115]Benjy Egel & Diana Lambert, *Teacher Was Removed From Class for Kneeling During National Anthem. She Returned Tuesday*, SACRAMENTO BEE (OCT. 17, 2017), http://www.sacbee.com/news/local/education/article179408436.html.

[116]Ellen Eldridge, *Teacher Who Compared Trump Slogan to Swastika No Longer in Classroom*, ATLANTA J.-CONST. (SEPT. 12, 2017), http://www.ajc.com/news/local/teacher-who-compared-trump-slogan-swastika-longer-classroom/k5THgySGliORr20JH9zhNN/.

[117]*Teacher Suspended After Removing 'Trump' From Yearbook*, BBC NEWS (June 13, 2017), http://www.bbc.com/news/world-us-canada-40263647.

[118]*See* Mayer v. Monroe Cty. Cmty. Sch. Corp., 474 F.3d 477 (7th Cir. 2007).

[119]U.S. Civil Serv. Comm'n v. Nat'l Ass'n of Letter Carriers, 413 U.S. 548 (1973); 5 U.S.C. § 7324 (2018).

[120]*See* Dougherty Cty. Bd. of Educ. v. White, 439 U.S. 32 (1978).

[121]*See, e.g.,* Cranston Teachers All. v. Miele, 495 A.2d 233, 236 (R.I. 1985); *see also* Jenkins v. Bishop, 589 P.2d 770 (Utah 1978) (holding that Utah teachers and administrators could serve in state legislature).

PERSONAL APPEARANCE

School officials can place constraints on educators' personal appearance if there is a rational basis for such restrictions.

Historically, school boards often imposed rigid grooming restrictions on teachers. In the 1970s, such attempts to regulate teachers' appearance generated considerable litigation, as did grooming standards for students.[122] Controversies have subsided for the most part, but a few constraints on school employees' appearance continue to be challenged.[123] School boards have defended their efforts to regulate teacher appearance on the perceived need to provide appropriate role models, set a proper tone in the classroom, and enforce similar appearance and dress codes for students. Teachers have contested these requirements as abridgments of their constitutionally protected privacy, liberty, and free expression rights.

Most courts since the mid-1970s have supported school officials in imposing reasonable grooming and dress restrictions on teachers as long as they do not conflict with employees' practice of sincerely held religious beliefs.[124] For example, the Second Circuit upheld a Connecticut school board's requirement that all male teachers wear ties as a rational means to promote respect for authority, traditional values, and classroom discipline.[125] Because of the uniquely influential role of teachers, the court noted that they may be subjected to restrictions in their professional lives that otherwise would not be acceptable. Applying similar reasoning, the First Circuit upheld a school board's dismissal of a teacher for wearing short skirts.[126]

Restrictions will not be upheld, however, if found to be arbitrary, discriminatory, or unrelated to a legitimate governmental concern. To illustrate, the Seventh Circuit overturned a school bus driver's suspension after he violated a regulation prohibiting bus drivers from wearing mustaches.[127] The court found no valid purpose for the policy. Additionally, a school police officer settled his lawsuit with a school district after alleging discrimination in its grooming policy requiring beards to be no longer than one quarter inch.[128] The officer claimed that the district had not accommodated his religious faith that

[122]*See, e.g.*, 350 F. Supp. 713 (N.D. Miss. 1972).

[123]*See* Polk Cty. Bd. of Educ. v. Polk Cty. Educ. Ass'n, 139 S.W.3d 304 (Tenn. Ct. App. 2004) (noting that the adoption of an employee dress code may be a management prerogative, but its enforcement must be bargained with the teachers' association).

[124]*See, e.g.*, Kelley v. Johnson, 425 U.S. 238 (1976) (upholding a hair grooming regulation for police officers).

[125]E. Hartford Educ. Ass'n v. Bd. of Educ., 562 F.2d 838 (2d Cir. 1977).

[126]*See* Tardif v. Quinn, 545 F.2d 761 (1st Cir. 1976).

[127]Pence v. Rosenquist, 573 F.2d 395 (7th Cir. 1978); *see also* Nichol v. Arin Intermediate Unit 28, 268 F. Supp. 2d 536 (W.D. Pa. 2003) (upholding an instructional assistant's right to wear a small cross and reasoning that the state's religious garb statute was overtly adverse to religion because it singled out and punished only religious, and not secular, symbolic expression).

[128]David Chang, *Philly School District, Department of Justice Reach Settlement in Beard-Length Lawsuit*, NBC10 (Sep. 9, 2014), http://www.nbcphiladelphia.com/news/local/Philly-School-District-Department-of-Justice-Reach-Settlement-in-Beard-Length-Lawsuit-274411951.html.

prevented him from cutting his beard. In 2015, the U.S. Supreme Court also held that a Muslim prisoner had a constitutional right to grow a beard[129] and a clothing store applicant prevailed in her employment discrimination claim arguing that she was not hired because she wore a headscarf.[130] Thus, schools should be careful to provide reasonable religious accommodations to grooming and dress policies.

▪ ▪ ▪ ▪ ▪ ▬▬▬

CONSTITUTIONAL PRIVACY RIGHTS

School employees have privacy rights; however, school districts can discipline teachers when their out-of-school conduct negatively impairs their job performance.

Public employees have asserted the right to be free from unwarranted governmental intrusions into their personal activities.[131] The U.S. Constitution does not explicitly enumerate personal privacy rights, but the Supreme Court has recognized that certain *implied* fundamental rights warrant constitutional protection because of their close relationship to explicit constitutional guarantees. For example, protected privacy rights have been interpreted as encompassing personal choices in matters such as marriage, contraception, sexual relations, procreation, family relationships, and child rearing.[132] Employment decisions cannot be based on relinquishing such rights without a compelling justification. **Litigation covered in this section focuses on constitutional privacy claims initiated under the Fourth Amendment (protection against unreasonable searches and seizures), the Ninth Amendment (personal privacy as an unenumerated right reserved to the people), and the Fourteenth Amendment (equal protection rights and protection against state action impairing personal liberties without due process of law).**

In some instances, public employees have asserted that governmental action has impaired their privacy right to intimate association related to creating and maintaining a family. To assess such claims, courts must weigh the employee's rights against the government's interests in promoting efficient public services. To illustrate, educators cannot be deprived of their jobs because of the politics or other activities of their partners or spouses. Recognizing a classified employee's First Amendment right to associate with her husband who disagreed with policies of the school system, the Sixth Circuit found an inference that the superintendent's nonrenewal recommendation was impermissibly based on the employee's marital relationship.[133] However, educators have little likelihood to succeed when

---

[129]Holt v. Holmes, 135 S. Ct. 853 (2015); *see also* Chapter 11, discussing religious discrimination in employment.

[130]Equal Emp't Opportunity Comm'n v. Abercrombie & Fitch Stores, Inc., 135 S. Ct. 2028 (2015).

[131]Most states have laws giving employees access to their personnel files and safeguarding the confidentiality of the records. *See, e.g.*, CAL. GOV'T CODE § 6254(c) (2018); LA. STAT. ANN. § 44:11 (2018).

[132]*See* Lawrence v. Texas, 539 U.S. 558 (2003); Roe v. Wade, 410 U.S. 113 (1973); Loving v. Virginia, 388 U.S. 1 (1967); Griswold v. Connecticut, 381 U.S. 479 (1965); Skinner v. Oklahoma *ex rel.* Williamson, 316 U.S. 535 (1942); Pierce v. Soc'y of Sisters, 268 U.S. 510 (1925).

[133]Adkins v. Bd. of Educ., 982 F.2d 952 (6th Cir. 1993) (finding that the plaintiff made a prima facie case of a violation and remanding for further proceedings).

arguing that anti-nepotism policies prohibiting teachers from reporting to their spouses or working in the same building as their spouses violate their associational and privacy rights.[134]

The Fifth Circuit recognized that a teacher's interest in breast-feeding her child at school during noninstructional time was sufficiently close to fundamental rights regarding family relationships and child rearing to trigger constitutional protection.[135] The court acknowledged, however, that trial courts must determine whether school boards' interests in avoiding disruption of the educational process, ensuring that teachers perform their duties without distraction, and avoiding liability for potential injuries are sufficiently compelling reasons to justify restrictions imposed on teachers' fundamental privacy interests. Accordingly, courts in some cases have concluded that governmental interests in ensuring the welfare of students override teachers' privacy interests.[136]

Search and Seizure

Public educators, like all citizens, are shielded by the Fourth Amendment against unreasonable governmental invasions of their person and property. This amendment requires law enforcement officers to secure a search warrant (based on probable cause that evidence of a crime will be found) before conducting personal searches. The Supreme Court has not addressed teachers' rights in connection with searches initiated by public school authorities, but it has upheld warrantless personal searches of students based on *reasonable suspicion* that contraband detrimental to the educational process is concealed.[137]

While technology has eased communication in the workplace, it has also presented privacy issues for employees. In 2010, the Supreme Court held that a police department's search of an officer's employer-provided pager was reasonable under the Fourth Amendment. The police department searched the pager because the officer went over his allotted monthly amount on the pager plan, and the employer was interested in learning whether the texting plan needed to be increased. During the search of the officer's pager, the police department found sexually explicit text messages. The officer had signed a policy stating that pager users have no expectation of privacy.[138]

[134]*See* Parks v. Warner Robins, 43 F.3d 609, 616 (11th Cir. 1995) (holding that the anti-nepotism policy did not violate the plaintiff's right of association because it did not "directly and substantially" interfere with the right to marry).

[135]Dike v. Sch. Bd., 650 F.2d 783 (5th Cir. 1981), *overruled on other grounds sub nom.* Shahar v. Bowers, 114 F.3d 1097 (11th Cir. 1997).

[136]*See, e.g.*, Flaskamp v. Dearborn Pub. Schs., 385 F.3d 935 (6th Cir. 2004) (upholding suspension and denial of tenure to a teacher who had an intimate relationship with a former student; the school board could prohibit such activity within a year or two of graduation, given the importance of deterring student/teacher sexual relationships); Strong v. Bd. of Educ., 902 F.2d 208 (2d Cir. 1990) (ruling that a teacher's rights were not violated when the school board required her to submit medical records after an extended medical absence); Daury v. Smith, 842 F.2d 9 (1st Cir. 1988) (requiring a principal to undergo psychiatric examination before returning to work because there was reason to believe that the welfare of students was at stake).

[137]New Jersey v. T.L.O., 469 U.S. 325 (1985). *See* text accompanying note 79, Chapter 8, for a discussion of the reasonable suspicion standard.

[138]City of Ontario v. Quon, 560 U.S. 746 (2010); *see also* O'Connor v. Ortega, 480 U.S. 709 (1987) (finding that public employees have a reasonable expectation of privacy in their desks and files, but that a warrant was not required for work-related searches that are necessary to carry out the business of the public agency).

The judiciary has recognized that the reasonableness of a job-related search or seizure by a supervisor in public schools rests on whether educational interests outweigh the individual employee's expectation of privacy.[139] For example, a federal district court held that a teacher had a reasonable expectation of privacy with her password-protected email account even though school officials had warned that emails may be discoverable.[140] The court reasoned that the district's acceptable use policy stated that teachers had a limited expectation of privacy, and it was not common practice to monitor the email accounts of employees. It is important to note that when school districts have policies that clearly indicate employees' Internet activities may be monitored, the employees' expectation of privacy will be much lower.

In some cases, employers have attempted to gain access to employees' Facebook pages.[141] It is not surprising that requests by employers for job applicants' Facebook passwords have been criticized. In California and Maryland, for example, lawmakers made the practice of employers asking applicants for Facebook passwords illegal.[142] The Fourth Amendment prohibits *arbitrary* invasions of teachers' personal effects by school officials, but in some situations, the school's interests are overriding.[143]

Public school employees' Fourth Amendment rights also have been asserted in connection with post-employment drug-screening policies.[144] Teachers in a Tennessee school district secured an injunction prohibiting the school board from requiring all teachers to submit to random, suspicionless drug testing.[145] Likewise, a North Carolina appellate court found a school board's policy requiring all employees to submit to random, suspicionless drug and alcohol testing violated the guarantee against unreasonable searches.[146] The court observed that there was no reason for the employees to have a reduced expectation of privacy because they worked in a school and that there was no evidence of any drug problems among the school employees. A Georgia federal district court in an earlier case also struck down a statewide drug-testing law that would have required all new state employees and veteran employees transferring to another school district or state agency to submit to urinalysis

---

[139]*See, e.g.*, Gillard v. Schmidt, 579 F.2d 825 (3d Cir. 1978) (invalidating search of school counselor's desk by a school board member because the search violated the counselor's reasonable expectation of privacy and the school board member was acting under the color of state law).

[140]Brown-Criscuolo v. Wolfe, 601 F. Supp. 2d 441 (D. Conn. 2009).

[141]*See* Palmieri v. United States, 72 F. Supp. 3d 191 (D.D.C. 2014) (discussing how the government accessed an employee's Facebook page through the employee's Facebook "friend").

[142]*See, e.g.*, CAL. LAB. CODE § 980(b)(1) (2018); MD. CODE ANN., EDUC. § 26-401 (2018).

[143]*See, e.g.*, Alinovi v. Worcester Sch. Comm., 777 F.2d 776 (1st Cir. 1985) (finding that a teacher had no expectation of privacy in withholding from the school administration a paper she had written for a graduate course—and shared with others—about a student with disabilities in her class).

[144]For discussion of pre-employment drug testing, *see* text accompanying note 30, Chapter 9.

[145]Smith Cty. Educ. Ass'n v. Smith Cty. Bd. of Educ., 781 F. Supp. 2d 604 (M.D. Tenn. 2011) (explaining that the drug-testing policy was unconstitutional because it was for *all* teachers instead of only teachers applying for teaching positions or those seeking promotion within the district); *see also* Am. Fed'n of Teachers–W. Va. v. Kanawha Cty. Bd. of Educ., 592 F. Supp. 2d 883 (S.D.W. Va. 2009) (prohibiting school district from suspicionless drug testing of employees).

[146]Jones v. Graham Cty. Bd. of Educ., 677 S.E.2d 171 (N.C. Ct. App. 2009).

screening.[147] The court reasoned that the general interest in maintaining a drug-free workplace was not a compelling governmental interest to justify testing *all* job applicants.

In contrast to *blanket* testing, support for *limited* drug testing of public employees can be found in two Supreme Court decisions.[148] Although these cases did not involve school employees, the Court found that the safety and security interests served by the programs outweighed employees' privacy concerns. The Fifth Circuit also let stand drug testing of school employees in safety-sensitive positions, including the school custodian, who interacted with students and operated potentially dangerous equipment.[149]

What constitutes safety-sensitive roles in the school context, however, remains unclear. Some courts now seem more inclined than they were in the past to interpret expansively the positions in this category. The Tenth Circuit considered employees at a juvenile detention center working with at-risk minors to be in a safety-sensitive role that necessitated all employees to be randomly screened for drug use.[150] A Kentucky federal district court also upheld random, suspicionless drug testing of a school district's employees in safety-sensitive roles, including teachers, as justified to further the policy goals of the Drug-Free Workplace Act of 1988.[151] But the Fifth Circuit struck down policies in two Louisiana school districts that required employees injured in the course of employment to submit to urinalysis, finding an insufficient nexus between such injuries and drug use.[152]

Of course, employees, like students, can be subjected to alcohol and drug testing where there is reasonable suspicion that the individual is under the influence of those substances. For example, a Texas federal district court found that because two witnesses raised concerns about a teacher being under the influence of some substance, there was sufficient reason to justify drug testing the teacher.[153] Employees can be discharged for refusing to submit to such a test,[154] but in some instances, such dismissals may be overturned when

---

[147]Ga. Ass'n of Educators v. Harris, 749 F. Supp. 1110 (N.D. Ga. 1990); *see also* Chandler v. Miller, 520 U.S. 305 (1997) (striking down a Georgia law requiring candidates for state office to pass a drug test; finding no special need based on public safety that could override the candidate's privacy interests).

[148]Skinner v. Ry. Labor Execs.' Ass'n, 489 U.S. 602 (1989) (upholding mandatory drug and alcohol testing of all railroad employees involved in accidents). *See also* Nat'l Treasury Emps. Union v. Von Raab, 489 U.S. 656 (1989) (upholding mandatory drug testing of customs employees who carry guns or are involved in the interdiction of illegal drugs).

[149]Aubrey v. Sch. Bd., 148 F.3d 559 (5th Cir. 1998); *see also* English v. Talladega Cty. Bd. of Educ., 938 F. Supp. 775 (N.D. Ala. 1996) (upholding random drug testing of school bus mechanics).

[150]Washington v. Unified. Gov't, 847 F.3d 1192 (10th Cir. 2017); *see also* Down v. Ann Arbor Pub. Schs., 29 F. Supp. 3d (E.D. Mich. 2014) (rejecting the teacher's argument that a compulsory psychological exam was an unconstitutional search because the teacher was in a safety-sensitive position).

[151]Crager v. Bd. of Educ., 313 F. Supp. 2d 690, 703 (E.D. Ky. 2004) (citing 41 U.S.C. § 8103 (2018), formerly 41 U.S.C. § 702 (2011)). This law stipulates that federal grant and contract recipients cannot receive federal funds unless they implement policies to ensure that workplaces are free from the illegal use, possession, and distribution of controlled substances, § 8103(a).

[152]United Teachers v. Orleans Par. Sch. Bd., 142 F.3d 853 (5th Cir. 1998).

[153]Catlett v. Duncanville Indep. Sch. Dist., 2010 U.S. Dist. LEXIS 91931 (N.D. Tex. Sept. 2, 2010).

[154]*See, e.g.*, Hearn v. Bd. of Pub. Educ., 191 F.3d 1329 (11th Cir. 1999) (upholding the termination of a teacher who refused to undergo urinalysis after a drug-detecting dog identified marijuana in her car).

reasonable suspicion is not established to justify targeting particular individuals.[155] The law is still evolving regarding what constitutes individualized suspicion of drug use and the circumstances under which certain public employees can be subjected to urinalysis without such suspicion.

Also, as more states legalize marijuana, there will likely be increased attention on educators' use of this drug. At least eight states have laws permitting recreational use, and thirty states have laws permitting the medical use of marijuana. In these states, educators should understand that school officials may still be able to discipline this type of out-of-school conduct, even if marijuana use is legal in the state. Many state laws do not explicitly discuss the use of marijuana and employment, but there are some laws that specifically defer to the decisions of the employer.[156]

Out-of-School Conduct

The Supreme Court has acknowledged that a "teacher serves as a role model for . . . students, exerting a subtle but important influence over their perceptions and values."[157] Recognizing that teachers are held to a higher standard of conduct than general citizens, the judiciary has upheld dismissals for immoral or unbecoming behavior, even if it takes place during the summer break.[158]

In recent years, teachers frequently have challenged school officials' authority to place restrictions on their out-of-school conduct. Although the right to such personal freedom is not an enumerated constitutional guarantee, it is a right implied in the concept of personal liberty embodied in the Fourteenth Amendment. Constitutional protection afforded to teachers' privacy rights is determined not only by the *location* of the conduct but also by the *nature* of the activity. The judiciary has attempted to balance teachers' privacy rights against the school board's legitimate interests in safeguarding the welfare of students and the effective management of the school. Sanctions cannot be imposed solely because school officials disapprove of teachers' private conduct, but districts can discipline off-duty conduct that is detrimental to job performance. Educators can be terminated based on evidence that would not be sufficient to support criminal charges,[159] but they cannot be dismissed for unsubstantiated rumors.[160] **Some courts have based termination decisions**

[155]*See, e.g.*, Warren v. Bd. of Educ., 200 F. Supp. 2d 1053 (E.D. Mo. 2001) (finding genuine issues as to whether the teacher's behavior suggested drug use and whether she consented to the drug test).

[156]*See* Francesca Liquori, *The Effects of Marijuana Legalization and Employment Law*, NAGTRI J. (Feb. 2016), http://www.naag.org/publications/nagtri-journal/volume-1-number-2/the-effects-of-marijuana-legalization-on-employment-law.php.

[157]Ambach v. Norwick, 441 U.S. 68, 78–79 (1979).

[158]*See, e.g.*, Bd. of Educ. v. Wood, 717 S.W.2d 837 (Ky. 1986).

[159]*See, e.g.*, Montefusco v. Nassau Cty., 39 F. Supp. 2d 231 (E.D.N.Y. 1999) (holding that although the criminal investigation surrounding the teacher's possession of candid pictures of teenagers taken at his home did not result in criminal charges, the school board could suspend the teacher with pay and remove him from extracurricular assignments).

[160]*See, e.g.*, Peaster Indep. Sch. Dist. v. Glodfelty, 63 S.W.3d 1 (Tex. Ct. App. 2001) (noting that widespread gossip triggered by unproven allegations of sexual misconduct could not be the basis for not renewing teachers' contracts).

on whether teachers' out-of-school conduct had a negative impact on their teaching effectiveness.[161]

The precise contours of public educators' constitutional privacy rights have not been clearly delineated; constitutional claims involving pregnancies out of wedlock, unconventional living arrangements, sexual improprieties, and being LGBTQ usually have been decided on a case-by-case basis. Because many of these cases also are discussed in Chapter 12 in connection with dismissals based on charges of immorality, the following discussion is confined to an overview of the constitutional issues.

Recognizing that decisions pertaining to marriage and parenthood involve constitutionally protected privacy rights, courts have been reluctant to support dismissal actions based on teachers' unwed, pregnant status in the absence of evidence that the condition impairs fitness to teach.[162] Compelled leaves of absence for pregnant, unmarried employees similarly have been invalidated as violating constitutional privacy rights.[163]

Most courts have reasoned that public employees, including educators, have a protected privacy right to engage in consenting sexual relationships out of wedlock and that such relationships cannot be the basis for dismissal unless teaching effectiveness is impaired.[164] Some courts, however, have upheld dismissals or other disciplinary actions based on employees' conduct that involve adulterous or other unconventional sexual relationships or activities that allegedly impaired job performance. To illustrate, the U.S. Supreme Court upheld the dismissal of a police officer for selling videotapes of himself stripping off a police uniform and masturbating.[165] The Court rejected the officer's assertion that his off-duty conduct was constitutionally protected expression unrelated to his employment.

In a case involving privacy issues and the Internet, a teacher was forced to resign over pictures posted on Facebook that showed her drinking alcohol. Despite the teacher's restricted privacy settings, school officials learned about the pictures. The teacher claimed that she was pressured into resigning and then sued the district when it refused to reinstate her. A Georgia trial court judge ruled that the school district was not required to hold a reinstatement hearing for the teacher.[166] Had the teacher been dismissed as a result of the

---

[161]*See, e.g.,* Land v. L'Anse Creuse Pub. Sch. Bd. of Educ., 2010 Mich. App. LEXIS 999 (Ct. App. May 27, 2010) (reinstating a teacher who was terminated after pictures were posted on the Internet of her simulating the act of fellatio on a male mannequin at a bachelorette party because her ability to teach effectively was not adversely impacted enough to justify the dismissal); Teacher Standards & Practices Comm'n v. Bergerson, 153 P.3d 84 (Or. 2007) (reinstating a teacher who took large quantities of prescription drugs and ran her car into her estranged husband's truck because there was no clear nexus between her misconduct and her ability to teach effectively).

[162]*See, e.g.,* Andrews v. Drew Mun. Separate Sch. Dist., 507 F.2d 611 (5th Cir. 1975) (equating birth of an illegitimate child with immoral conduct impairs equal protection and due process rights).

[163]*See* Ponton v. Newport News Sch. Bd., 632 F. Supp. 1056 (E.D. Va. 1986).

[164]*See, e.g.,* Littlejohn v. Rose, 768 F.2d 765 (6th Cir. 1985) (holding that a nonrenewal of a nontenured teacher's contract because of her involvement in a divorce would abridge her constitutional privacy rights); Sherburne v. Sch. Bd., 455 So. 2d 1057 (Fla. Dist. Ct. App. 1984) (overturning school board's termination of an unmarried teacher for lacking good moral character because she spent the night with an unmarried man).

[165]City of San Diego v. Roe, 543 U.S. 77 (2004) (finding no protected expression involved).

[166]Merritt Melancon, *Barrow Teacher Presses Forward with Facebook Lawsuit*, ATHENS BANNER-HERALD (Oct. 11, 2011), http://onlineathens.com/local-news/2011-10-11/barrow-teacher-denied-her-old-job-presses-forward-lawsuit.

Facebook pictures instead of resigning, it seems unlikely that the school district would have prevailed in this case.

Whether employment decisions can be based on a teacher's sexual orientation has been controversial, and the scope of constitutional protections afforded to LGBTQ educators continues to evolve. Among factors courts consider are the nature of the conduct, the notoriety it generates, and its impact on teaching effectiveness.[167] In 2003, the Supreme Court delivered a significant decision, *Lawrence v. Texas*, in which it recognized a privacy right for consenting adults of the same sex to have sexual relations in the privacy of their homes by striking down a Texas law imposing criminal penalties for such conduct.[168] This ruling overturned a 1986 Supreme Court decision in which the Court upheld a Georgia law attaching criminal penalties to public *or private* consensual sodomy.[169] The Court in *Lawrence* emphasized that private, consensual sexual behavior in one's home is constitutionally protected and cannot be the basis for criminal action.

In addition to asserting protected privacy rights, some LGBTQ employees have claimed discrimination under the Equal Protection Clause of the Fourteenth Amendment. Discrimination in employment is discussed in detail in Chapter 11, so equal protection claims pertaining to LGBTQ educators are reviewed only briefly here. To substantiate an Equal Protection Clause violation, a teacher must prove that sexual orientation was the motivating factor in the adverse employment action and that there was no rational basis for the differential treatment.[170]

Judicial interpretations of the legality of terminating educators based solely on sexual orientation have also changed over time. From the 1960s through the early 1990s, a few federal circuit courts permitted school districts to dismiss LGBTQ teachers or reassign them to nonteaching roles, even when there was no link to teaching effectiveness.[171] **Litigation since the late 1990s, however, has required school districts to provide evidence that one's sexual orientation has a negative impact on teaching effectiveness before**

---

[167]*See* Nat'l Gay Task Force v. Bd. of Educ., 729 F.2d 1270 (10th Cir. 1984), *aff'd by an equally divided court*, 470 U.S. 903 (1985).

[168]539 U.S. 558 (2003).

[169]Bowers v. Hardwick, 478 U.S. 186 (1986).

[170]*See* Romer v. Evans, 517 U.S. 620 (1996) (invalidating an amendment to the Colorado Constitution that prohibited all legislative, executive, or judicial action designed to protect gay individuals).

[171]*See, e.g.*, Jantz v. Muci, 976 F.2d 623 (10th Cir. 1992) (granting immunity to a principal who refused to hire a gay teacher); Rowland v. Mad River Local Sch. Dist., 730 F.2d 444 (6th Cir. 1984) (upholding the nonrenewal of a guidance counselor after she revealed that she was a lesbian to colleagues and two students); Burton v. Cascade Sch. Dist. Union High Sch., 512 F.2d 850 (9th Cir. 1975) (refusing to reinstate a nontenured teacher who was dismissed for being gay); Snyder v. Jefferson Cty. Sch. Dist., 842 P.2d 624 (Colo. 1992) (upholding termination of a teacher who let his teaching certificate expire while on leave to have sex-reassignment surgery). But during the same time, some courts required evidence of impaired teaching effectiveness to discharge teachers for being gay. *See, e.g.*, Gaylord v. Tacoma Sch. Dist., 559 P.2d 1340, 1347 (Wash. 1977) (stating "we do not deal here with homosexuality which does not impair or cannot reasonably be said to impair his ability to perform the duties of an occupation in which the homosexual engages and which does not impair the effectiveness of the institution which employs him"). *See also* Soraya Nadia McDonald, *Teacher Fired for Being Gay Gets an Apology– 42 Years Later*, WASH POST (July 15, 2014), https://www.washingtonpost.com/news/morning-mix/wp/2014/07/15/teacher-fired-for-being-gay-gets-an-apology-42-years-later/?utm_term=.7e9acb3ad188.

disciplinary action can be imposed. To illustrate, a Utah federal court overturned the school district's removal of a girls' volleyball coach, finding no job-related reason for the coach's removal, which was based solely on the community's negative response to her sexual orientation. The court also noted that the school district could not instruct the coach to avoid mentioning her sexual orientation and ordered the school district to reinstate her and pay damages.[172] An Ohio federal district court similarly awarded a teacher reinstatement, back pay, and damages after finding that his contract was not renewed because of his sexual orientation rather than for his teaching deficiencies as the school board had asserted.[173]

A New Jersey teacher prevailed on his claim that he was harassed by teachers and students because he was gay and that his resulting anxiety attacks forced him to take a leave of absence, after which his contract was not renewed.[174] A New York federal district court also held that a teacher had stated a valid claim, precluding summary judgment, that a school district violated her Fourteenth Amendment equal protection rights when it failed to discipline students who harassed the teacher because she was a lesbian and treated her differently from other similarly situated non-LGBTQ teachers.[175] However, the Seventh Circuit held that a school had not violated a teacher's equal protection rights in connection with parental and student harassment of the teacher based on sexual orientation, because school officials took some action to respond to the teacher's complaints of harassment and treated the allegations as they would treat harassment complaints filed by other teachers.[176]

After the Supreme Court upheld marriage equality in 2015,[177] LGBTQ educators may mistakenly believe that they will now be free from discriminatory practices in their schools.[178] Yet, there are no specific federal protections for employees who have been discriminated against based on their sexual orientation,[179] and eighteen states have no protections in place for public employees.[180] Some school districts and municipalities, however,

---

[172]Weaver v. Nebo Sch. Dist., 29 F. Supp. 2d 1279 (D. Utah 1998).

[173]Glover v. Williamsburg Local Sch. Dist., 20 F. Supp. 2d 1160 (S.D. Ohio 1998).

[174]Curcio v. Collingswood Bd. of Educ., 2006 U.S. Dist. LEXIS 46648 (D.N.J. June 28, 2006); *see also* Murray v. Oceanside Unified Sch. Dist., 95 Cal. Rptr. 2d 28 (Ct. App. 2000) (ruling in favor of an award-winning biology teacher who used the California nondiscrimination law to challenge years of sexual orientation harassment by her colleagues).

[175]Lovell v. Comsewogue Sch. Dist., 214 F. Supp. 2d 319 (E.D.N.Y. 2002).

[176]Schroeder v. Hamilton Sch. Dist., 282 F.3d 946 (7th Cir. 2002).

[177]Obergefell v. Hodges, 135 S. Ct. 2584 (2015). *See* text accompanying note 46, Chapter 11.

[178]Amanda Machado, *The Plight of Being a Gay Teacher*, ATLANTIC (Dec. 16, 2014), http://www.theatlantic .com/education/archive/2014/12/the-plight-of-being-a-lgbt-teacher/383619/ (discussing the lack of federal protection for teachers who are discriminated against based on sexual orientation).

[179]*See* Chris Riotta, *Trump Administration Says Employers Can Fire People for Being Gay*, NEWSWEEK (Sept. 28, 2017), http://www.newsweek.com/trump-doj-fired-being-gay-lgbt-issues-jeff-sessions-673398 (noting that the Justice Department has argued that the Civil Rights Act of 1964 provides no protections for employees who are fired based on their sexual orientation). *But see* Hively v. Ivy Tech Cmty. Coll., 853 F.3d 339 (7th Cir. 2017) (ruling that discrimination based on sexual orientation is sex discrimination under Title VII); *see also* text accompanying note 46, Chapter 11.

[180]Human Rights Campaign, *State Maps of Laws & Policies: Employment* (Apr. 25, 2017), http://www.hrc.org/ state-maps/employment.

offer specific protections from discrimination, and despite the lack of protections under federal and some state laws, it is unlikely that a dismissal would survive an equal protection challenge. There is no rational reason to treat LGBTQ teachers differently from other employees.

CONCLUSION

The U.S. Constitution places constraints on government, not private, action. Thus, public employees, but not usually those working in the private sector, can challenge employment decisions as violating their constitutional rights. If public employees can show that they have suffered adverse employment consequences because of the exercise of protected expression, association, or privacy rights, then the burden shifts to the employer to justify the restriction on protected rights as necessary to carry out the work of the government agency. In the school context, this means that the employee's action has impaired teaching effectiveness, relations with superiors, or school operations. The public employer also can prevail by showing that there are legitimate reasons for the personnel action aside from the exercise of protected expression or other constitutional rights. In short, under certain circumstances, restrictions on constitutional freedoms can be justified by overriding government interests.

The following generalizations reflect the current status of the law on the topics covered in this chapter.

1. Public employees' expression pursuant to official job responsibilities is not protected by the First Amendment.

2. A school can discipline a teacher for expression perceived as school-sponsored, including classroom expression, if it raises legitimate pedagogical concerns or is pursuant to official job duties.

3. If public educators make personal grievances about work, their speech is not constitutionally protected.

4. Known as the *Pickering* balancing test, a school can discipline an educator for speech that is a matter of public concern if it (1) impairs teaching effectiveness; (2) interferes with relationships with superiors/coworkers; or (3) jeopardizes the management of the school.

5. A public employee's protected speech will not invalidate a dismissal action if the school board can show by a preponderance of evidence that it would have dismissed the employee had the protected speech not occurred.

6. Reasonable time, place, and manner restrictions can be imposed on educators' expression, but arbitrary prior restraints on the content and channel of communication violate the First Amendment.

7. Teachers lack legal authority to dictate the curriculum, but they do retain some discretion when choosing relevant instructional strategies.

8. School employees' participation in political activities outside of the classroom cannot be the basis for adverse employment decisions, unless the employee has policy-making responsibilities and such participation would jeopardize relationships at work.

9. School officials can impose reasonable restrictions on employees' personal appearance as long as it does not offend or interfere with the practice of employees' sincerely held religious beliefs.

10. Educators' desks, files, and computers at school can be searched based on reasonable suspicion that the search is necessary for educational reasons.

11. If reasonable suspicion of drug use exists, any public educator could be subjected to a drug test; however, reasonable suspicion is not needed to drug test employees in safety-sensitve roles.

12. Teachers have privacy rights, but they can be disciplined if their out-of-school conduct has a negative effect on job performance.

CHAPTER ELEVEN

DISCRIMINATION IN EMPLOYMENT

Can a teacher be dismissed because she is a lesbian or has epilepsy? Can a teacher wear his yarmulke in class or be replaced by a younger, less expensive teacher? All persons and groups are potential victims of discrimination in employment. People of color and women may claim discrimination in traditionally segregated job categories, whereas some White and male employees assert that affirmative action has denied them the right to compete on equal grounds. The young could argue that the old already hold the good jobs and that entry is nearly impossible, and older employees may contend that they often are let go when "downsizing" occurs. Religious minorities might not be allowed to dress the way they please or may be denied leave for religious observances, and some religious majorities (particularly in private schools) have concerns about governmental intrusion into their homogeneous work environments. Persons with disabilities often complain that they are not given the opportunity to show what they can do, whereas employers may argue that the costs of accommodating those with disabilities can be significant and never-ending. Given these diverse factors, it is not surprising that literally thousands of employment discrimination suits are filed each year. This chapter explores school employees' allegations of discrimination based on race, national origin, sex, religion, age, and disability.

Readers of this chapter should be able to:

- Describe the differences among the federal laws and constitutional provisions that are most relied upon in employment discrimination cases.
- Apply relevant court decisions related to discriminatory practices against teachers and school leaders to scenarios that may arise in schools.
- Examine current developments in the law that focus on discriminatory practices involving race, sex, sexual orientation, religion, age, and disability.

LEGAL CONTEXT

Extending constitutional protections, numerous federal laws prohibit discrimination in public and private employment.

Most, but not all, forms of employment discrimination violate either federal or state law. Foremost among these legal protections are the Fourteenth Amendment to the U.S. Constitution and Title VII of the Civil Rights Act of 1964; both are discussed here, given their broad application. Other more narrowly tailored statutes are reviewed in the respective sections addressing discrimination based on various characteristics (see Figure 11.1).[1]

Fourteenth Amendment

The Fourteenth Amendment to the U.S. Constitution mandates that no state shall deny any person within its jurisdiction equal protection of the laws. As noted in Chapter 6, the Equal Protection Clause of the Fourteenth Amendment requires the application of strict scrutiny in cases involving discrimination based on race, national origin, or alienage. Intermediate scrutiny is applied in cases in which sex discrimination is at issue. The lowest level of scrutiny, rational basis, is applied in sexual orientation and disability cases (see Figure 6.1, Chapter 6). The Equal Protection Clause has been interpreted as prohibiting intentional discrimination and applies to subdivisions of the state, including public school districts. Districts may be found guilty of facial discrimination (e.g., if the policy, on its face, is discriminatory, such as when an administrative position is reserved for a female applicant), or facially neutral discrimination (e.g., a school district's employment criteria results in hiring a disproportionately larger share of men than women from a qualified pool with equal numbers of men and women).

Title VII

Title VII is enforced by the Equal Employment Opportunity Commission (EEOC) and prohibits discrimination on the basis of race, color, religion, sex, or national origin, and covers hiring, promotion, and compensation practices as well as fringe benefits and other terms and conditions of employment.[2] However, protection against discriminatory employment practices is not absolute for individuals within these classifications because both Congress and the courts have identified exceptions. For example, employers might not accommodate a Jewish basketball coach's request to be excused from every Friday and Saturday night basketball game so that he may observe the Jewish Sabbath from sundown on Friday until sundown on Saturday **if the accommodation creates an undue hardship on the school district**. Before an educator can file a legal complaint against a school district under Title VII, a charge with the EEOC must first be filed. If the EEOC agrees that the claim has merit, the EEOC might sue on the educator's behalf or may issue a "right to sue" letter to allow the educator to begin the litigation process.

---

[1]*See* Chapter 1 for a discussion about the Fourteenth Amendment and other constitutional amendments that appear in educational litigation.

[2]42 U.S.C. § 2000e (2018).

FIGURE 11.1 Selected Federal Laws Prohibiting Employment Discrimination

FEDERAL LAW	PUBLIC SCHOOLS	PRIVATE SCHOOLS	RECIPIENTS OF FEDERAL FINANCIAL ASSISTANCE	NUMBER OF EMPLOYEES NECESSARY FOR LAW TO APPLY	RACE	NATIONAL ORIGIN, ALIENAGE	SEX	AGE	RELIGION	DISABILITY
Fourteenth Amendment to the U.S. Constitution	X				X	X	X	X	X	X
42 U.S.C. § 1983	X				X	X	X	X	X	X
42 U.S.C. § 1981	X	X			X				X	
Title VII of Civil Rights Act of 1964	X	X		15	X	X	X		X	
Equal Pay Act of 1963	X	X		20			X			
Section 504 of Rehabilitation Act of 1973			X							X
Americans with Disabilities Act	X	X		15						X
Age Discrimination in Employment Act	X	X		20				X		

Title VII applies to public and private schools and other employers with fifteen or more employees, each of whom works twenty or more weeks during the calendar year. In *Walters v. Metropolitan Educational Enterprises*,[3] the Supreme Court adopted the "payroll method" to assess whether an individual is an actual employee. All that is necessary under this approach is to determine if the person is on the employer's payroll.[4]

Disparate Treatment and Impact.   Courts have developed two legal theories to evaluate Title VII claims: disparate treatment and disparate impact. ***Disparate treatment* applies when an individual claims less favorable treatment as compared to other applicants or employees**. ***Disparate impact* is applicable when an employer's ostensibly neutral practice has a discriminatory impact on the class to which the claimant belongs**.

In proving disparate treatment, plaintiffs may use direct or circumstantial evidence to prove their employer's discriminatory intent. Plaintiffs usually do not have direct evidence of discrimination (e.g., "you are fired for being too religious"[5]). Thus, they often rely on circumstantial evidence to substantiate that they received less favorable treatment and that such conduct, if otherwise unexplained, is "more likely than not based on the consideration of impermissible factors."[6] To support a circumstantial claim, the plaintiff must show that he or she:

- was a member of a protected class;
- applied for and was qualified for the job; and
- was denied the position, while the employer continued to seek applicants with the plaintiff's qualifications.

These criteria were articulated by the Supreme Court in 1973 in *McDonnell Douglas Corporation v. Green*[7] and, with some modification,[8] are applied beyond claims of hiring discrimination to alleged disparate treatment in areas such as promotion, termination, and tenure.

If the claim is supported, the burden shifts to the employer to state a "legitimate nondiscriminatory" reason for its action that does not violate Title VII. Such a reason may be either objective (e.g., a higher-level academic degree), subjective (e.g., stronger interpersonal skills), or a combination. Given the ease of presenting a nondiscriminatory reason, employers in nearly every instance provide a response. After the employer provides a rebuttal, the employee then has the additional burden of proving by a preponderance of the evidence not only that the proffered reason was false, but also that it served as a pretext for prohibited intentional discrimination. In most instances of alleged discrimination, the

---

[3]519 U.S. 202 (1997).

[4]Although Walters is a Title VII retaliation case, the definition established by the Supreme Court has been applied to cases under the Americans with Disabilities Act (ADA), given the similarity of the two statutes. *See, e.g.,* Owens v. S. Dev. Council, 59 F. Supp. 2d 1210 (M.D. Ala. 1999).

[5]Dixon v. Hallmark Cos., 627 F.3d 849, 853 (11th Cir. 2010).

[6]Furnco Constr. Corp. v. Waters, 438 U.S. 567, 577 (1978).

[7]411 U.S. 792 (1973).

[8]Tex. Dep't of Cmty. Affairs v. Burdine, 450 U.S. 248 (1981).

plaintiff is unable to show that the employer's purported nondiscriminatory basis was pretextual. Because most qualifications for initial employment in educational settings (e.g., degree, licensure) are required to perform jobs satisfactorily and to meet state standards and accountability mandates, disparate impact claims are difficult to win. However, a few plaintiffs have been able to show that no legitimate grounds supported the employer's decision and that the selection may have been based on impermissible factors.[9]

In contrast to disparate treatment claims, to prove disparate impact, the plaintiff is not initially required to show discriminatory intent, but must establish that an employer's facially neutral practice had a disproportionate impact on the plaintiff's protected class. This generally is accomplished through the use of statistics. Once this type of prima facie case is established, the employer then must show that the challenged policies or practices are job related and justified by a business necessity.

The Supreme Court has recognized, however, that mere awareness of a policy's adverse impact on a protected class does not constitute proof of unlawful motive; a discriminatory purpose suggests that the decision maker "selected or reaffirmed a particular course of action at least in part 'because of,' not merely 'in spite of,' its adverse effects upon an identifiable group."[10] Nonetheless, foreseeably discriminatory consequences can be considered by courts in assessing intent, although more will be needed to substantiate unlawful motive. Furthermore, the employee may prevail if it is shown that the employer refused to adopt an alternative policy identified by the employee that realistically would have met the employer's business needs without resulting in disparate impact.

Retaliation.   By the time a complaint is filed with the EEOC or a state or federal court, the working relationship between the employer and the employee is strained, sometimes beyond repair. In response to filing, an employee may not be terminated, demoted, or harassed, but less extreme acts such as rudeness or "the cold shoulder" by the employer will not typically violate Title VII.[11] Where actionable behavior occurs, the employee may file a second claim alleging retaliation.[12] To support this type of case, the employee is required to show that:

- he or she participated in statutorily protected activity (i.e., the filing of a complaint or suit);
- an adverse employment action was taken by the employer; and
- a causal connection existed between the protected activity and the adverse action.

Although these three requirements were enunciated by the U.S. Supreme Court in a retaliation case under Title VII, they have since been applied by a number of courts to other retaliation provisions, including those under the Americans with Disabilities Act (ADA)

---

[9]*See, e.g.*, Stern v. Trs. of Columbia Univ., 131 F.3d 305 (2d Cir. 1997).

[10]Personnel Adm'r of Mass. v. Feeney, 442 U.S. 256, 279 (1979).

[11]DAVID WALSH, EMPLOYMENT LAW FOR HUMAN RESOURCE PRACTICE (5th ed. 2015).

[12]*See* Thompson v. N. Am. Stainless, L.P., 562 U.S. 170 (2011) (finding that Title VII protected a worker who was fired in retaliation for a complaint made by his fiancé who was also an employee).

and the Age Discrimination in Employment Act (ADEA).[13] If the employee can show that filing the complaint was the basis for the adverse employment decision, even when the original complaint of discrimination fails, the court will provide appropriate relief.[14]

Relief.   If it is proven that the employee was a victim of prohibited discrimination, courts have the authority to require a *make-whole remedy* where the person is placed in the same position he or she otherwise would have been, absent discriminatory activity. In meeting this objective, courts may:

- provide injunctive and declaratory relief;
- require that a person be reinstated, hired, tenured, or promoted;
- direct the payment of back pay, interest on back pay, or front pay;[15]
- assign retroactive seniority;
- provide attorneys' fees and court costs; and
- provide compensatory and punitive damages in cases in which intentional discrimination is proven.

RACE AND NATIONAL ORIGIN DISCRIMINATION

Without a proven history of prior discrimination, an employer may not use race as a factor in making employment decisions.

The history of racial discrimination within the school employment context is long and complex.[16] And, despite 140 years of protective statutes and constitutional amendments, race and national origin discrimination in employment continue.[17] Lawsuits are filed under the Fourteenth Amendment, Title VII, and Section 1981. Section 1981 applies when either race or ethnicity discrimination is alleged in making, performing, modifying, and terminating

[13]Laura Schnell & Peter Basso, *Proving Retaliation Under Federal Non-Discrimination Statutes*, A.B.A. (n.d.), https://www.americanbar.org/content/dam/aba/administrative/labor_law/meetings/2011/ac2011/041.authcheck-dam.pdf.

[14]*See* Jackson v. Birmingham Bd. of Educ., 544 U.S. 167 (2005) (holding that retaliation against a girls' basketball coach who had complained of discrimination could support a sex-discrimination suit under Title IX, even though the coach's initial complaints of sex discrimination were unfounded).

[15]For example, if a teacher is denied a principalship because of race, the court may direct the district to hire the teacher for the next available position. And the court could require that the difference in salary be awarded to the teacher up to the time of promotion to a principalship. That portion of the salary paid in the future is termed "front pay," while the portion due for the period between the failure to hire and the court's ruling is termed "back pay."

[16]JENNIFER HOCHSCHILD, THE NEW AMERICAN DILEMMA: LIBERAL DEMOCRACY AND SCHOOL DESEGREGATION (1984) (observing that shortly after the Brown v. Bd. of Educ. decision in 1954, Black teachers were often disproportionately fired when schools were restructured or merged with White schools).

[17]*See* T. Rees Shapiro & Moriah Balingit, *Study of Fairfax County Schools Finds Discrimination Against Black Teacher Applicants,* WASH. POST (May 4, 2017), https://www.washingtonpost.com/local/education/black-teacher-applicants-face-discrimination-in-a-wealthy-school-district-study-finds/2017/05/04/ea192b50-2a90-11e7-a616-d7c8a68c1a66_story.html?utm_term=.f2b3ac850c91 (finding that Black teacher applicants were far less likely than White applicants to receive a job offer).

contracts, as well as in the enjoyment of all benefits, privileges, terms, and conditions of the contractual relationship. Employment discrimination challenges often arise when an employee claims that an employment related decision was based on the employee's protected status rather than on actual qualifications. Such decisions might relate to recruiting, hiring, evaluating, promoting, firing, or requesting information on the job application. Discrimination in these types of employment-related decisions is prohibited.

Hiring and Promotion

Unless a school district is under a narrowly tailored court order to correct prior proven acts of race discrimination, it may not advantage or disadvantage an applicant or employee because of that individual's race. **When unsuccessful candidates believe that race played a role in the decision-making process, they will generally allege disparate treatment, requiring the heightened proof of discriminatory intent.** In attempting to support such a claim, many plaintiffs have difficulty overcoming employers' purported nondiscriminatory reasons for their decisions. For example, in a Fifth Circuit case, a substitute teacher alleged race discrimination and other claims under Title VII against a school district when she was not hired for three full-time history teaching positions. Instead of choosing the substitute teacher, the district hired one Black male, one White female, and one White male for the three different positions. Finding in favor of the school district, the court held that the teacher failed to demonstrate pretext for discrimination or that her qualifications were more impressive than those of the three candidates who were hired.[18] Likewise, a Black teacher who was not promoted to various positions in her school district, claimed the district engaged in race discrimination under Title VII. The teacher had obtained her administrator's license, was pursuing her doctorate, and was chosen as teacher of the year in 2010. However, when she had applied for twelve different assistant principalships in the district over an eight-year period, the positions were filled with other White and Black applicants. The Seventh Circuit affirmed the district court's decision, finding that she could not demonstrate that the district promoted someone outside her protected class in violation of Title VII.[19]

In other cases, the employee has been able to establish a viable claim for race discrimination. To illustrate, a former employee with the professional development team claimed that her school district engaged in racial discrimination in violation of Title VII. The plaintiff, who is Black, and another woman who is White, had worked in the same department but had both been laid off during a large-scale district layoff. When the district began to rehire, the White woman was chosen over the Black plaintiff, even though the plaintiff had a more impressive teaching background and had earned two master's degrees. The Seventh Circuit reversed the district court's decision, finding that a reasonable jury could conclude that the plaintiff was better qualified for the job than the other

---

[18]Godfrey v. Katy Indep. Sch. Dist., 395 F. App'x 88 (5th Cir. 2010); *see also* Flowers v. Troup Cty., 308 F.3d 1327 (11th Cir. 2015) (affirming school district's motion for summary judgment because no pretext for race discrimination was found when school officials investigated coach for recruitment violations); Brown v. Unified Sch. Dist., 459 F. App'x 705 (10th Cir. 2012) (finding no showing of pretext in teacher's race discrimination claim when teacher was not rehired for three positions).

[19]Riley v. Elkhart Cmty. Schs., 829 F.3d 886 (7th Cir. 2016).

applicant and that race may have been a decisive factor in the hiring process.[20] It should be noted that Title VII also prohibits discrimination against Whites on the same terms as racial discrimination against non-Whites.[21] The Tenth Circuit observed that in these "reverse discrimination" cases, the protected-class requirement for a prima facie case under *McDonnell Douglas* is substituted for the requirement that the plaintiff demonstrate facts to support an inference that "the defendant is one of those unusual employers who discriminates against the majority."[22]

A Fourth Circuit case focused on national origin discrimination; the teacher was of Russian descent and was not hired for a teaching position. Even though she had superior teaching credentials, the school district deviated from its hiring procedures and hired someone else. After the teacher complained that the district had not followed hiring protocol by not interviewing the most qualified applicant, she was told that the district would not hire a Russian. Reversing the district court's dismissal of the complaint, the appellate court remanded the case because the applicant sufficiently stated a claim that she was the most qualified for the position.[23]

Testing

Among the more controversial objective measures used in hiring and promotion (e.g., academic degree level, a specified number of years' experience) is the use of standardized test scores. In *United States v. South Carolina*, the Supreme Court affirmed a lower court's conclusion that South Carolina's use of the National Teachers Examination (NTE) for teacher certification and salary purposes satisfied the Equal Protection Clause.[24] The federal district court had held that the test was valid since it measured knowledge of course content in teacher preparation courses, and that it was not administered with an intent to discriminate against minority applicants for teacher certification. Despite the Supreme Court guidance, the topic of teacher testing remains controversial. For example, recent reports suggest that as states increase test score requirements for teachers on statewide exams, questions arise about the tests' relevance and the passage rates of teachers of color.[25] In 2015, a federal judge in New York determined that the state teacher exam was racially discriminatory and violated Title VII because the test failed to measure those skills that were necessary to become a teacher.[26]

Tests may not be discriminatorily administered, nor may their results be discriminatorily used. Moreover, employers may not use different cutoff scores for different racial groups

---

[20]Hutchens v. Chi. Bd. of Educ., 781 F.3d 366 (7th Cir. 2015)

[21]McDonald v. Santa Fe. Trail Transp. Co., 427 U.S. 273 (1976).

[22]Notari v. Denver Water Dep't., 971 F.2d 585, 589 (10th Cir. 1992); *see also* Lacava v. Pittsburgh Pub. Schs., 2014 U.S. Dist. LEXIS 103319 (W.D. Pa. July 29, 2014) (establishing a prima facie case under Title VII for racial discrimination after a White teacher received an unsatisfactory rating on her job performance).

[23]Dolgaleva v. Va. Beach City Pub. Schs., 364 F. App'x 820 (4th Cir. 2010).

[24]445 F. Supp. 1094 (D.S.C. 1977), *aff'd sub nom.* Nat'l Educ. Ass'n v. South Carolina, 434 U.S. 1026 (1978).

[25]Elizabeth Harris, *Tough Tests for Teachers, with Questions of Bias*, N.Y. TIMES (June 17, 2015), https://www.nytimes.com/2015/06/18/nyregion/with-tougher-teacher-licensing-exams-a-question-of-racial-discrimination.html.

[26]Gulino v. Bd. of Educ., 113 F. Supp. 3d 663 (S.D.N.Y. 2015).

or adjust scores based on race.[27] The EEOC requires employers to conduct validity studies for tests used in making employment decisions if they result in an adverse impact on a protected class. For tests with a disparate impact to be used, they must be reliable and valid, and they must qualify as a business necessity.[28] Also, tests may be administered to applicants for positions other than those for which the tests have been validated, but only if there are no significant differences in the skills, knowledge, and abilities required by the jobs.[29]

It is likely that states, districts, and teacher-training institutions will continue to use tests as a requirement for admission to teacher education training programs; a prerequisite to licensure; and a basis for graduation, hiring, and promotion. To avoid discriminatory actions, test performance should not be the sole criterion for making personnel decisions.

Dismissal and Nonrenewal

Employers cannot dismiss, decline to renew, or demote employees on the basis of race or national origin. In an illustrative case, a nontenured teacher established a Title VII claim for discrimination by submitting evidence that the principal made derogatory remarks about her Polish national origin, which could be linked to the teacher's contract not being renewed at the end of the year.[30] Reversing the district court's decision, the Seventh Circuit remanded the national origin claim because it was a question for the jury to decide regarding whether there was a connection between the principal's discriminatory statements and the nonrenewal of the teacher's contract.

In some cases, plaintiffs have difficulty showing that the conduct of their employers qualifies as adverse actions (e.g., change of school, grade level, teaching assignment). An Indian teacher, for example, failed to show that her dismissal was based on national origin discrimination.[31] The teacher taught third grade in the district and was reassigned to seventh grade as a result of budget cuts. She was later terminated because of her poor teaching evaluations. Her national origin discrimination claim failed when the Seventh Circuit ruled that being moved from third to seventh grade should not be considered an adverse employment action. Also, the principal's alleged statement that the teacher should try to find a job on "the North side where most of the Indians go" was not related to her discharge.[32]

As discussed, Title VII prohibits employers from engaging in retaliatory conduct against employees and others who engage in protected activity to enforce Title VII's prohibitions on discrimination based on race, gender, religion, or other protected characteristics. In an illustrative case, a school district did not renew a Black public school teacher's employment contract after he had engaged in protected activity by complaining internally

[27]See Ricci v. DeStefano, 557 U.S. 557 (2009) (holding that the city fire department's choice to ignore test results for promotions because no Black firefighter scored high enough to be considered for promotion violated Title VII).

[28]Griggs v. Duke Power Co., 401 U.S. 424 (1971). In Griggs, the Supreme Court held that a private company's use of both a high school diploma requirement and a test of general intelligence as prerequisites to initial employment and a condition of transfer violated Title VII; neither requirement was shown to be related to successful job performance, and both operated to disqualify applicants of color at a higher rate than those who were White.

[29]Albemarle Paper Co. v. Moody, 422 U.S. 405 (1975).

[30]Darchak v. Chi. Bd. of Educ., 580 F.3d 622 (7th Cir. 2009).

[31]Dass v. Chi. Bd. of Educ., 675 F.3d 1060 (7th Cir. 2012).

[32]Id. at 1071.

to his supervisors about being subject to race discrimination by one of his co-employees. The Fifth Circuit held that there were genuine issues of fact on the causation aspect of his retaliation claim that entitled him to a jury trial.[33]

Affirmative Action

Within the context of employment, affirmative action has been defined as "steps taken to remedy the grossly disparate staffing and recruitment patterns that are the present consequences of past discrimination and to prevent the occurrence of employment discrimination in the future."[34] Correcting such imbalances requires the employer to engage in activities such as:

- expanding its training programs;
- becoming actively involved in recruiting underrepresented groups;
- eliminating invalid selection criteria that result in disparate impact; and
- modifying collective bargaining agreements that impermissibly restrict the promotion and retention of minorities.

Courts will uphold most strategies that the EEOC identifies as affirmative action under both Title VII (for which the EEOC has regulatory authority) and the Fourteenth Amendment (for which the EEOC does not have regulatory authority). However, courts will prohibit the use of affirmative action plans that provide a discriminatory "preference" rather than an "equal opportunity."[35]

In 1989, the Supreme Court began to question a variety of public-sector practices that allowed racial preferences.[36] In the aggregate, these cases applied strict scrutiny to race-based affirmative action programs operated by federal, state, and local levels of government; discredited societal discrimination as a justification for such programs; required showing specific discriminatory action to impose a race-based remedy; and allowed only narrowly tailored plans that would further a compelling interest. Given these precedents, existing public-sector affirmative action plans that provide racial preferences without a proven history of discrimination or are based only on underrepresentation are likely to be found unconstitutional and in violation of Title VII. To illustrate, the Eighth Circuit held that a White teacher presented sufficient evidence of unlawful discrimination and demonstrated that genuine issues of material fact remained about whether the school district's affirmative action policy was valid. The teacher claimed that she was not promoted to an assistant principal position because the district's affirmative action policy unlawfully required that at least one assistant principal at each school be a different race than the school's principal.[37]

---

[33]Jackson v. Frisco Indep. Sch. Dist., 789 F.3d 589 (5th Cir. 2015).

[34]U.S. Comm'n on Civil Rights, *Statement on Affirmative Action for Equal Employment Opportunities* 16 (1973).

[35]*See* Perrea v. Cincinnati Pub. Schs., 709 F. Supp. 2d 629 (S.D. Ohio 2010) (finding a district's policy of racially balancing its teaching staff to be unconstitutional).

[36]*See, e.g.,* Adarand Constructors v. Pena, 515 U.S. 200 (1995); Ne. Fla. Chapter of Associated Gen. Contractors of Am. v. City of Jacksonville, 508 U.S. 656 (1993); Martin v. Wilks, 490 U.S. 755 (1989).

[37]Humphries v. Pulaski Cty. Special Sch. Dist., 580 F.3d 688 (8th Cir. 2009); *see also* Taxman v. Bd. of Educ., 91 F.3d 1547 (3d Cir. 1996) (concluding that an affirmative action plan preferring minority teachers over equally qualified nonminority teachers violated Title VII).

In addition to affirmative action in hiring and promotion, efforts have been made to protect the diversity gained through court order and voluntary affirmative action by providing a preference in organization downsizing. When a reduction in school staff is necessary due to financial exigency, declining enrollment, or a change in education priorities, it generally is based, at least in part, on tenure and seniority within teaching areas.[38] School policies have been challenged if they consider race as a preference on such lists. The Supreme Court in *Wygant v. Jackson Board of Education* addressed a voluntary affirmative action plan that included a layoff quota.[39] In this 1986 case, the Court struck down a school district's collective bargaining agreement that protected minority teachers from layoffs in order to preserve the percentage of minority personnel employed prior to the reduction-in-force (RIF). The Court reasoned that the quota system, which resulted in the release of some White teachers with greater seniority than some of the minority teachers who were retained, violated the Equal Protection Clause. Societal discrimination alone was not sufficient to justify the class preference. Recognizing that racial classifications in employment must be justified by a compelling governmental interest and that means must be narrowly tailored to accomplish that purpose, the Court concluded that the layoff provision did not satisfy either of these conditions. The Court further rejected the lower courts' reliance on the "role model" theory.[40]

SEX DISCRIMINATION

Sex generally may not be used as a basis in determining whom to hire, what salary to provide, or any other term or condition of employment.

Prior to 1963, there were no federal statutes prohibiting discrimination based on sex. Women were commonly denied employment when qualified male applicants were in the pool, were offered less money for the same or similar job, or were expected to do work that would not have been asked of a man. Today, most forms of sex discrimination are prohibited, including those associated with hiring, promotion, and virtually all terms and conditions of employment. The Fourteenth Amendment, Title VII of the Civil Rights Act of 1964, and other federal and state laws have played significant roles in allowing victims of sex discrimination to attempt to vindicate their rights in court. **However, not all sex-based distinctions are prohibited, as Title VII explicitly allows for a bona fide occupational qualification (BFOQ) exception.** For a BFOQ to be upheld, it needs to be narrowly defined and applied only when necessary to achieve the employer's objectives. There have been few school-based BFOQ cases, since the vast majority of jobs in education can be performed by either males or females. The only readily identifiable BFOQ in education would be the hiring of a female to supervise the girls' locker room and the hiring of a male to supervise the boys' locker room.

[38]*See, e.g.*, Franks v. Bowman Trans. Co., 424 U.S. 747 (1976).

[39]476 U.S. 267 (1986).

[40]*Id.* at 275–76. *See* Figure 6.1, Chapter 6.

Hiring and Promotion

Sex discrimination occurs when an employer openly seeks a person of a particular sex (e.g., the posting of a position for a female guidance counselor) and where being male or female is unrelated to meeting job requirements (e.g., hiring only males as basketball coaches).[41] This is known as facial discrimination. At other times, employment practices are facially neutral (e.g., requiring head coaching experience in football in order to qualify as the athletic director), but nevertheless result in nearly the same level of exclusion as when the discrimination is facial. If this occurs, an action will be upheld only if found to qualify as a business necessity, and other less discriminatory options do not meet the needs of the organization.

If applicants or employees have been treated unfairly solely because of their sex, a plaintiff typically files a Title VII suit alleging disparate treatment. The standards for a sex-based prima facie case are similar to those used for race. Also, assuming that a claim is supported, the employer then must identify a basis other than sex for its decision, such as showing that the successful applicant was equally or better qualified or that the plaintiff was unqualified.[42] Where a nondiscriminatory basis has been identified, applicants still may obtain relief if the reasons are shown to be pretextual.[43] For example, rejected applicants could likely prevail where employers base their decisions on stereotypic attitudes about the capabilities of the applicant's sex; job advertisements include phrases, "prefer male" or "prefer female"; or job descriptions are specifically drafted to exclude qualified applicants of a particular sex.

In 1981, the Supreme Court rendered a significant decision involving sex-based discrimination in promotion, *Texas Department of Community Affairs v. Burdine*.[44] In this case, a female accounting clerk was denied promotion and later was terminated along with two other employees, although two males were retained. In response to the female's prima facie case, the public employer claimed that the three terminated employees did not work well together and that the male who was promoted to the position sought by the female employee was subjectively better qualified, although he had been her subordinate prior to the promotion. In rendering its decision, the Court emphasized that Title VII does not require the hiring or promotion of equally qualified women or the restructuring of employment practices to maximize the number of underrepresented employees. Instead, the employer has the discretion to choose among *equally qualified* candidates so long as the decision is not based on unlawful criteria. In this case, the female employee failed to show pretext, resulting in a decision for the employer.

For many years, courts have grappled with whether Title VII provides protections for discrimination based on sexual orientation. In 2017, the Seventh Circuit held that discrimination based on sexual orientation is sex discrimination under Title VII.[45]

---

[41]*See, e.g.*, Fuhr v. Sch. Dist., 364 F.3d 753 (6th Cir. 2004) (upholding jury award because the school board failed to appoint a female to coach boys' basketball team, and evidence suggested the decision not to appoint her was motivated by sex).

[42]*See, e.g.*, Straughter v. Vicksburg Warren Sch. Dist., 152 F. App'x 407 (5th Cir. 2005).

[43]*See, e.g.*, Goodwin v. Bd. of Trs., 442 F.3d 611 (7th Cir. 2006).

[44]450 U.S. 248 (1981).

[45]Hively v. Ivy Tech Cmty. Coll., 853 F.3d 339 (7th Cir. 2017); *see also* Zarda v. Altitude Express, 2018 U.S. App. LEXIS 4608 (2d Cir. Feb. 26, 2018) (finding Title VII covers sexual orientation discrimination).

This opinion is particularly significant because it was the first time a federal circuit court interpreted Title VII as covering discrimination based on sexual orientation. In this case, an adjunct faculty member who is a lesbian filed a lawsuit under Title VII alleging that school officials neither renewed her contract nor hired her when she applied multiple times for full-time positions because of her sexual orientation. The majority wrote that if she had been dating a man, she would not have experienced this type of discrimination. Accordingly, the court explained she encountered discrimination only because she is a woman dating another woman. The EEOC has also viewed "sex" broadly under Title VII as covering sexual orientation[46] and gender identity.[47] Opinions from the EEOC are not legally binding, however.

Twenty-nine states along with a variety of cities prohibit discrimination based on sexual orientation and gender identity under state and local laws. An additional five states only provide protections based on sexual orientation; these laws do not include gender identity.[48] For example, if a public educator does not live within the jurisdiction of the Seventh Circuit or within one of the thirty-four states with protections, there may not be protections for sexual orientation discrimination available. **An employee who experiences sexual orientation discrimination could also rely on the Equal Protection Clause of the Fourteenth Amendment as a viable legal avenue, but school officials would only need to have a rational basis to treat LGBTQ teachers differently than other teachers.**[49]

Compensation Practices

Claims of sex-based compensation discrimination involving comparative entry salaries, raises, supplemental or overtime opportunities, or other perquisites and benefits are not uncommon within business and industry and even sometimes occur in higher education. The U.S. Supreme Court in *Ledbetter v. Goodyear Tire and Rubber Company*. held that the statute of limitations for alleging an equal pay lawsuit begins when the employer makes the initial discriminatory wage decision.[50] As a result of the public outcry related to this decision concerning the statute of limitations, Congress passed the Lilly Ledbetter Fair Pay Act of 2009, which addresses the time for filing a claim under Title VII for sex discrimination in employment.[51] These amendments to the Civil Rights Act of 1964 changed the 180-day statute of limitations for filing an equal pay lawsuit. Under the amended law, notice of pay discrimination resets with the issuance of each new discriminatory paycheck. This Act allows plaintiffs who allege compensation discrimination a much longer window to file their claims. Although the Act would apply to the public school context, most PK–12 salary decisions are based on objective criteria such as seniority and degree level.

[46]Baldwin v. Foxx, 2015 WL 4397641 (EEOC July 16, 2015).

[47]Macy v. Holder, 2012 WL 1435995 (EEOC Apr. 20, 2012).

[48]Movement Advancement Project, *Non-Discrimination Laws* (2017), http://www.lgbtmap.org/equality-maps/non_discrimination_laws.

[49]*See* Figure 6.1, Chapter 6.

[50]550 U.S. 618 (2007).

[51]42 U.S.C. § 2000e-5(e) (2018).

The Fourteenth Amendment, Title VII, and the Equal Pay Act (EPA) of 1963 may be used where plaintiffs claim that their salaries are based in whole or in part on their sex. The EPA applies only when the dispute involves sex-based wage discrimination claims of unequal pay for equal work.[52] As a result, the Act does not apply when race-based or age-based salary differences are challenged or when the work is unequal.[53] The plaintiff need not prove that the employer intended to discriminate, as with Title VII disputes; proof that the compensation is different and not based on factors other than sex will suffice. Furthermore, the law prohibits the lowering of the salaries for the higher paid group and therefore requires the salaries for the lower paid group to be raised.[54] In one case, a principal asserted that the district discriminated against her by paying male principals more in violation of the EPA. The female principal argued that five male principals at other similarly situated high schools had higher salaries, bonuses, and other financial incentives. Holding in favor of the school district, the federal district court ruled that the female principal failed to produce any evidence that the male principals had comparable job duties.[55]

Because the EPA is limited to controversies dealing with equal work, its application is restricted to those circumstances where there are male and female employees performing substantially the same work but for different pay. Accordingly, if there are no male administrative assistants for a salary comparison, there can be no EPA violation, regardless of how abysmal the salaries of female administrative assistants may be.[56]

Dismissal and Nonrenewal

In Title VII disparate treatment cases based on sex discrimination, the employee is required to prove that the employer elected to terminate or not renew the employee's contract due to sex rather than job performance, inappropriate conduct, interpersonal relationships, financial exigency, or other just cause. As in most cases where proof of intent is required, employees alleging sex discrimination often have difficulty supporting their claims, even if true. Occasionally, however, corroborating evidence will be inadvertently provided by officials responsible for making personnel decisions.

In a Tenth Circuit case, a female former principal was "bumped" by an associate superintendent who assumed her position as well as his own. The district initially proposed

---

[52]29 U.S.C. § 206(d) (2018).

[53]See, e.g., Vasquez v. El Paso Cty. Cmty. Coll., 177 F. App'x 422 (5th Cir. 2006). In the 1980s, the comparable worth doctrine had been used as an attempt to remedy pay inequity that resulted from a history of sex segregation in employment. For example, if working in child care (historically a profession dominated by females) is as important and difficult as working as a butcher (historically a profession dominated by males), then child-care workers and butchers should receive similar pay. Although courts have been skeptical of this doctrine, its merits continue to be debated.

[54]It is important to note that relief under the EPA is not barred by Eleventh Amendment immunity. See text accompanying note 136, Chapter 12.

[55]Musgrove v. District of Columbia, 775 F. Supp. 2d 158 (D.D.C. 2011), aff'd, 458 F. App'x 1 (D.C. Cir. 2012).

[56]With regard to sex discrimination in retirement benefits, in 1978, the Supreme Court rejected the use of sex-segregated actuarial tables in retirement benefits programs. The Court invalidated a retirement program requiring women to make a higher contribution to receive equal benefits on retirement, noting that sex was the only factor considered in predicting life expectancy. City of L.A. Dep't of Water & Power v. Manhart, 435 U.S. 702 (1978).

that the RIF was necessary due to financial exigency but later claimed that the female principal had continuing difficulty with her faculty, which allegedly was the basis for her contract not being renewed. The appeals court found the evidence to be contradictory, including the superintendent's annual evaluation of the principal in which she received high marks for establishing and maintaining staff cooperation and creating an environment conducive to learning. Given such discrepancies, the appeals court reversed the lower court's grant of summary judgment for the school district.[57] Plaintiffs have also been successful in their sex discrimination claims under the Equal Protection Clause. The Eleventh Circuit granted a government employee's motion for summary judgment after she was fired because of her gender identity.[58]

Where facial discrimination does not exist, most plaintiffs will attempt to show that persons of the opposite sex were treated differently (e.g., required to meet different standards or assessed differently in meeting the same standards). With this approach, however, it often is difficult to identify a comparable party or to challenge subjective judgments regarding performance or potential.

Sexual Harassment

Sexual harassment generally refers to repeated and unwelcome sexual advances, sexually suggestive comments, or sexually demeaning gestures or acts. Both men and women have been victims of sexual harassment from persons of the opposite or same sex.[59] The harasser may be a supervisor, an agent of the employer, a coworker, a nonemployee, or even a student. Critical to a successful claim is proof that the harassment is indeed based on sex. **There are two types of harassment cognizable under Title VII:[60] quid pro quo and hostile work environment**. Each is reviewed briefly here.

Quid pro quo literally means "this for that" or, in this context, giving something for something. To establish a prima facie case of quid pro quo harassment against an employer, the employee must show that:

- he or she was subjected to unwelcome sexual harassment in the form of sexual advances or requests for sexual favors;
- the harassment was based on the person's sex; and
- submission to the unwelcome advances was an express or implied condition for either favorable actions or avoidance of adverse actions by the employer.

[57]Cole v. Ruidoso Mun. Schs., 43 F.3d 1373 (10th Cir. 1994). *But see* Atkinson v. LaFayette Coll., 460 F.3d 447 (3d Cir. 2006) (determining that the university administration provided sufficient documentation showing that the plaintiff had alienated others in her leadership role and that her ineffective interpersonal skills created poor relations and low morale within her unit).

[58]Glenn v. Brumby, 663 F.3d 1312 (11th Cir. 2011).

[59]*See, e.g.,* Oncale v. Sundowner Offshore Servs., 523 U.S. 75 (1998).

[60]In addition to filing a Title VII claim, plaintiffs may file charges under state employment law or state tort law. Tort claims may include intentional infliction of emotional distress, assault and battery, invasion of privacy, and defamation. *See* Chapter 2 for a discussion of tort law.

Although only a preponderance of evidence is required in such cases, acquiring the necessary 51 percent can be difficult, particularly given that the violator is unlikely to provide corroborating testimony. If the employee succeeds, however, the law imposes strict liability on the employer because of the harasser's authority to alter the terms and conditions of employment.

Under the theory of a hostile work environment, the plaintiff must show that the environment in fact was hostile. **The harassment needs to be severe or pervasive, unreasonably interfere with an individual's work performance (actual physical or psychological injury is not required),[61] and be either threatening or humiliating**. A single offensive utterance generally will be insufficient.[62] If the victims are able to substantiate their claims, the employer may be vicariously liable for the acts of its supervisors who have immediate authority over an alleged victim.[63] However, the employer may raise an affirmative defense to liability if the employee suffered no tangible employment loss. Such a defense requires that the employer exercise reasonable care to prevent or promptly correct harassing behavior *and* that the employee failed to take advantage of preventive and corrective opportunities provided by the employer. Accordingly, to guard against liability, school districts should:

- prepare and disseminate sexual harassment policies;
- provide appropriate in-service training;
- establish appropriate grievance procedures, including at least two avenues for reporting in case one avenue is blocked by the harasser or supportive colleague;
- consider claims seriously and investigate promptly;
- take corrective action in a timely manner; and
- maintain thorough records of all claims and activities.

Furthermore, investigators should have no stake in the outcome of the proceedings, and both male and female investigators should be available.

Employer liability in hostile environment claims is more difficult to establish than in quid pro quo claims, but it may be easier to substantiate in light of *Burlington Industries v. Ellerth*[64] and *Faragher v. City of Boca Raton*.[65] In these cases, the Supreme Court proclaimed that an employer is subject to vicarious liability for the acts of its supervisors with immediate authority over an alleged victim. However, the employer may raise an affirmative defense to liability if the employee suffered no tangible employment loss. Such a defense requires that the employer be able to show that it exercised reasonable care to prevent or promptly correct harassing behavior *and* that the employee failed to take advantage of the preventive and corrective opportunities provided by the employer.[66] While most of

---

[61]Meritor Savs. Bank v. Vinson, 477 U.S. 57 (1986).

[62]Harris v. Forklift Sys., 510 U.S. 17 (1993).

[63]Faragher v. City of Boca Raton, 524 U.S. 775 (1998).

[64]524 U.S. 742 (1998).

[65]Faragher, 524 U.S. at 775.

[66]*See* Pa. State Police v. Suders, 542 U.S. 129 (2004) (holding that although the employee did not avail herself of her employer's anti-harassment procedures, a question of triable fact remained regarding the adequacy of those procedures). The employer is expected to ensure that the reasons for any tangible loss, such as dismissal, are legitimate; thus, an affirmative defense cannot be asserted in those cases.

this discussion has focused on employers harassing employees, there have been some cases where teachers have alleged under Title VII that they were harassed by students.[67]

Pregnancy Discrimination

Under the Pregnancy Discrimination Act (PDA),[68] an amendment to Title VII enacted in 1978, employers may not discriminate based on pregnancy, childbirth, or related medical conditions.[69] As such, pregnancy may not be used as a basis for refusing to hire an otherwise qualified applicant; denying disability, medical, or other benefits; or terminating or nonrenewal of employment. To succeed, the employee must show that the employer knew she was pregnant prior to the adverse action and that the pregnancy, rather than some other factor, was the basis of an adverse decision.[70]

If an employer requires a doctor's statement for other conditions, it also may require one for pregnancy prior to granting leave or paying benefits.[71] And, when employees are unable to perform their jobs due to pregnancy, the employer is required to treat them the same as any other temporarily disabled person.[72] **Possible forms of accommodation may include modified tasks, alternate assignments, or disability leave (with or without pay).** If a pregnant employee takes a leave of absence, her position must be held open the same length of time that it would be if she were sick or disabled. Moreover, maternity leave cannot be considered an interruption in employment for the purposes of accumulating credit toward tenure or seniority if employees retain seniority rights when on leave for other disabilities.[73]

A teacher was successful in her PDA claim when school officials chose not to renew her contract after she requested leave related to her pregnancy. The district had alleged that there was no pretext for discrimination and that there had been concerns with the teacher's effectiveness. According to the court, the district was not able to support such claims because the teacher had received only positive reviews from her administrators. The court also examined evidence revealing that only the three non-tenured teachers who requested pregnancy-related leave were considered for nonrenewal whereas the other sixteen nontenured teachers were not affected. Denying the school district's motion for summary judgment, the court found that the

[67]*See* Lucero v. Nettle Creek Sch. Corp., 566 F.3d 720 (7th Cir. 2009) (rejecting a teacher's claim that she had been harassed by students because students had been disciplined by school officials); Mongelli v. Clay Consol. Sch. Dist., 491 F. Supp. 2d 467 (D. Del. 2007) (finding harassment of a teacher by a special education student was actionable under Title VII).

[68]42 U.S.C. § 2000e(k) (2018).

[69]The PDA was passed in response to two Supreme Court decisions in which the denial of benefits for pregnancy-related conditions was found not to violate either Title VII or the Fourteenth Amendment. *See* Gen. Elec. Co. v. Gilbert, 429 U.S. 125 (1976); Geduldig v. Aiello, 417 U.S. 484 (1974).

[70]*See, e.g.*, Silverman v. Bd. of Educ., 637 F.3d 729 (7th Cir. 2011) (holding that a principal's decision not to renew a teacher's contract was not pregnancy discrimination because the principal's decision was based on the need to eliminate a teaching position).

[71]EEOC v. Elgin Teachers Ass'n, 27 F.3d 292, 295 (N.D. Ill. 1994) (validating the association's maternity leave procedures, which conditioned the teacher's pay on a showing of "actual inability to work" during the six-week period).

[72]29 C.F.R. § 1604 app. (2018).

[73]Nashville Gas Co. v. Satty, 434 U.S. 136 (1977).

teacher had composed "a convincing mosaic of circumstantial evidence that would allow a jury to infer intentional discrimination."[74]

Mandatory pregnancy leave policies requiring teachers to take a leave of absence prior to the birth of their children and specifying a return date also violate the Due Process Clause by creating an *irrebuttable presumption* that all pregnant teachers are physically incompetent as of a specified date.[75] School boards, however, may establish maternity leave policies that are justified by a business necessity, such as the requirement that the employee notify the administration of her intended departure and return dates, assuming this is required for other forms of extended personal leave. The business necessity of such a policy is to allow for planning and staffing in the employee's absence.

Finally, school personnel are also relying on the Family and Medical Leave Act (FMLA) for pregnancy-related claims.[76] Under the FMLA, employees are entitled to twelve workweeks of unpaid leave for a year for the birth of a child and to care for that child.[77] There are typically two types of claims that arise under this law: 1) interference claims where an employer limits the employee's right to take the leave, and 2) retaliation claims where an employer retaliates against an employee who requests or takes such leave.

DISCRIMINATION BASED ON RELIGION

When discrimination based on religion occurs, or an employer fails to provide reasonable accommodations, First and Fourteenth Amendment claims have been filed, as well as claims under Title VII.

The United States is now more culturally and religiously diverse than at any time in its history. As a result, courts have been asked to address several employment-related religious discrimination cases. The first issue in this type of litigation is whether the discrimination is based on sincerely held religious beliefs. Where the employee suffers an adverse employment outcome due to religion, the employer then must show either that an accommodation was offered, but not taken, or that no reasonable accommodation existed that would not result in hardship for the employer. If an employee claims an Equal Protection Clause violation due to religious-based facial discrimination by the government, either strict scrutiny or rational basis scrutiny could apply, depending on the form of the discrimination. When the government infringes upon the employee's First Amendment right to exercise religious

[74]Maples v. City of Madison Bd. of Educ., 2016 U.S. Dist. LEXIS 138790, at *63 (N.D. Ala. Oct. 6, 2016) (quoting Smith v. Lockheed-Martin Corp., 644 F.3d 1321, 1328 (11th Cir. 2011)).

[75]Cleveland Bd. of Educ. v. LaFleur, 414 U.S. 632 (1974).

[76]Maples, 2016 U.S. Dist. LEXIS 138790.

[77]29 U.S.C. § 2612(a)(1) (2018). The FMLA applies also to adoption, placement of a child in foster care, family or personal illness, and military leave. In order to qualify for this unpaid leave, an employee must have worked at the school for at least twelve months. For more information on the FMLA, *see* U.S. Dep't of Labor, *Wage and Hour Division* (n.d.), https://www.dol.gov/whd/fmla/.

beliefs (a fundamental right), strict scrutiny is applied. On the other hand, if the employee is a victim of discrimination based on religion, rational basis scrutiny is applied. Intent must be proved in cases involving facially neutral discrimination.

Hiring, Promotion, and Dismissal

At times, employees have claimed religious discrimination when they have been transferred, demoted, not renewed, terminated, or denied tenure.[78] As with other claims of employment discrimination, the burden is on the employee to prove that the adverse action was motivated by an impermissible reason—specifically, the employee's religious beliefs, practices, or affiliation. Employees experience difficulty in winning such cases because employers typically can identify one or more legitimate bases for the adverse action (e.g., lack of commitment,[79] excessive absenteeism[80]). Of course, an employee's religion may not be the basis for negative employment decisions.

It is important to note that private religious organizations are exempt from First and Fourteenth Amendment claims and in large part from the religious restrictions imposed by Title VII.[81] In a significant case involving a private school, *Hosanna-Tabor Evangelical Lutheran Church v. EEOC*, the U.S. Supreme Court recognized a "ministerial exception" to Title VII and other employment discrimination laws.[82] A teacher who developed narcolepsy and was terminated from her parochial school position, filed a complaint with the EEOC, claiming that her firing violated the ADA. The EEOC eventually sued the religious institution, and the Supreme Court recognized the ministerial exception, which bars lawsuits filed on behalf of ministers by their churches. The teacher's role in the school was considered ministerial because she completed religious training and taught religion courses at the school. This decision's broad interpretation of the ministerial exception affects religious school employees in Title VII and other discrimination claims.

Additionally, private schools are not generally prohibited from establishing religion as a BFOQ. For example, a Methodist theological seminary can require that its instructors be Methodists. In contrast, **religion will never qualify as a BFOQ in public education, and public employers may not inquire as to an applicant's religious beliefs, use the interview process as an opportunity to indoctrinate, or require prospective employees to profess a belief in a particular faith or in God**.[83] A person's religious affiliation or practice, if any, should not be considered in making an employment decision.

[78]Hunt v. Cent. Consol. Sch. Dist., 951 F. Supp. 2d 1136 (D.N.M. 2013) (denying school district's motion to dismiss a Title VII disparate treatment claim that involved two school employees who plausibly stated that the school district demoted them because of their Mormon religion).

[79]*See, e.g.*, Lee v. Wise Cty. Sch. Bd., 1998 U.S. App. LEXIS 367 (4th Cir. Jan. 12, 1998).

[80]*See, e.g.*, Rosenbaum v. Bd. of Trs., 1999 U.S. App. LEXIS 4744 (4th Cir. Mar. 19, 1999).

[81]42 U.S.C. § 2000e-1(a) (2018).

[82]565 U.S. 171 (2012).

[83]Torcaso v. Watkins, 367 U.S. 488 (1961).

Accommodation

Recommended forms of religious accommodation include activities such as accepting voluntary substitutions and assignment exchanges, using a flexible schedule, and modifying job assignments. If requested accommodations would compromise the constitutional, statutory, or contractual rights of others (e.g., interfere with a bona fide seniority system), or result in undue hardship, Title VII does not require the employer to make the accommodation.[84] **Undue hardship results when extensive changes are required in business practices or when the costs of religious accommodations are more than minimal.** Some of the more frequently litigated controversies regarding religious accommodation in public education involve dress codes, personal leave, and job assignments. For example, a Louisiana school district was not required to hire a substitute teacher every week so that the teacher requesting the religious accommodation could observe the Sabbath.[85] Likewise, school officials did not violate employment requirements when they forgot to reimburse a teacher for his kosher meal at a school meeting.[86]

Attire Restrictions

As a general rule, public school district restrictions on the wearing of religious apparel, even if also purportedly cultural, will be upheld where young and impressionable students would perceive the garment as religious. In an illustrative case, the Third Circuit held that a district's refusal to accommodate a Muslim substitute teacher who sought to wear religious attire in the public school classroom did not violate Title VII.[87] The district's action was pursuant to a state statute that regarded the wearing of religious clothing as a significant threat to the maintenance of a religiously neutral public school system. A similar decision was reached by a federal court in Mississippi when it upheld the termination of a teacher's aide who refused to comply with the school's dress code proscribing religious attire.[88] In a more recent nonschool case, the Supreme Court ruled that a retail store violated Title VII when it would not hire a sales clerk who wore a hijab because it conflicted with the company's dress code.[89] Educators also have challenged state laws that prohibit religious garb in the classroom on First Amendment grounds. For example,

---

[84]Harrell v. Donahue, 638 F.3d 975 (8th Cir. 2011) (determining that it would be an undue hardship and a violation of the collective bargaining agreement to accommodate a postal employee who is a Seventh Day Adventist by not scheduling him to work on Saturdays).

[85]Slocum v. Denezin, 948 F. Supp. 2d 661 (E.D. La. 2013).

[86]Weber v. City of N.Y., 973 F. Supp. 2d 227 (E.D.N.Y. 2013).

[87]United States v. Bd. of Educ., 911 F.2d 882 (3d Cir. 1990). *But see* Brown v. F.L. Roberts & Co., 896 N.E.2d 1279 (Mass. 2008) (overturning summary judgment for the employer and holding that a Rastafarian service technician may have had a legitimate religious discrimination claim under state law after the employer required him to have short hair and to shave).

[88]McGlothin v. Jackson Mun. Separate Sch. Dist., 829 F. Supp. 853 (S.D. Miss. 1992).

[89]EEOC v. Abercrombie & Fitch Stores, 135 S. Ct. 2028 (2015); *see also* Holt v. Hobbs, 135 S. Ct. 853 (2015) (holding that prisoner must be allowed to grow a beard in accordance with his religion; public institutions may not impose any unjustified burden on the free exercise of religion).

an elementary school teacher was successful in her lawsuit against the district when it did not permit her to wear a cross necklace in class.[90]

Personal Leave

Although most public school calendars allow time off for Christmas and Easter to coincide with semester and spring breaks, holy days of religions other than Christianity are not routinely accommodated. But when a school district serves a significant number of students or employs a large number of teachers or staff of another religion, it is not uncommon for schools to be closed on several of the more significant days of worship for that religion as well. The "secular purpose" of such an act is the need to operate the school efficiently.

Modest requests for religious absences are typically accommodated, but others may result in hardship both for the district as well as for students.[91] **The Supreme Court has held that an employer could satisfy Title VII by offering a reasonable accommodation, which may or may not be the one the employee preferred.** Where leave has been provided, some employees have been satisfied when allowed to have the day off without pay; others have requested that leave be accompanied with full or partial pay. In *Ansonia Board of Education v. Philbrook*, a teacher asserted that the negotiated agreement violated Title VII by permitting employees to use only three days of paid leave for religious purposes, whereas three additional days of paid personal business leave could be used for specified secular activities.[92] The teacher proposed either permitting the use of the paid personal business leave days for religious observances or allowing employees to receive full pay and cover the costs of substitute teachers for each additional day missed for religious reasons. The Supreme Court, in upholding the agreement, held that the employer was not required to show that each of the plaintiff's proposed alternatives would result in undue hardship, and noted that the employer could satisfy Title VII by offering a reasonable accommodation, even though not the employee's preference.

It is important to note that religious leave need not be paid unless compensation is provided for other forms of leave. In a Tenth Circuit case, the court rejected a teacher's claim that the school district's leave policy violated Title VII and burdened his free exercise of religion because he occasionally had to take unpaid leave to observe Jewish holidays.[93] The policy allowed teachers two days of paid leave that could be used for religious purposes. The court concluded that the availability of unpaid leave for additional religious observances constituted a reasonable accommodation under Title VII and did not place a substantial burden on free exercise rights. In another case, a Muslim teacher sued the school district for religious discrimination when she was denied an unpaid three-week leave of absence so she could make a pilgrimage to Mecca, Saudi Arabia. The once-in-a-

---

[90]Nichol v. Arin Intermediate Unit, 268 F. Supp. 2d 536 (W.D. Pa. 2003); Isaacs v. Bd. of Educ., 40 F. Supp. 2d 335 (D. Md. 1999) (finding the teacher had no First Amendment right to wear an African headwrap to celebrate her cultural heritage).

[91]*See* Trans World Airlines v. Hardison, 432 U.S. 63 (1977) (finding no Title VII violation involving an employee who, for religious reasons, could not work on Saturdays; the employer was not required to bear more than minimal costs in making religious accommodations).

[92]479 U.S. 60 (1986).

[93]Pinsker v. Joint Dist., 735 F.2d 388 (10th Cir. 1984).

lifetime pilgrimage, or Hajj, is considered one of the most important religious requirements for the Muslim faith. The U.S. Department of Justice reached a settlement with the school district, which accommodated the teacher with unpaid leave.[94]

AGE DISCRIMINATION

Under the Age Discrimination in Employment Act, persons age forty and over may claim age discrimination when the criteria used to make the adverse decision are correlated with age (e.g., seniority, vesting in retirement).

Unlike other characteristics that generate charges of discrimination, age is unique in that everyone is subject to the aging process and eventually will fall within the age-protected category. Age discrimination employment claims may be filed under the Age Discrimination Act (any age),[95] Equal Protection Clause (any age),[96] the Age Discrimination in Employment Act (ADEA) (over age forty),[97] and state statutes. The EEOA is responsible for the enforcement of the ADEA.

The purpose of the ADEA is to promote the employment of older persons based on their ability, to prohibit arbitrary age discrimination in employment, and to find ways of addressing problems arising from the impact of age on employment. The ADEA specifically stipulates that "it shall be unlawful for an employer . . . to fail or refuse to hire or to discharge any individual or otherwise discriminate . . . with respect to his compensation, terms, conditions, or privileges of employment, because of such individual's age."[98] However, if the employment decision is based on any reasonable factor other than age, even though correlated with or associated with age, there is no violation of the ADEA. This standard requires less than is mandated under Title VII (i.e., intent in disparate treatment cases; proof that the practice, policy, or requirement was job related and justified by a business necessity in disparate impact cases). Moreover, if a reasonable factor is identified, the employer avoids liability even if other factors with less discriminatory impact are available and not used. Also, for a violation to be substantiated, age must play a role in the decision-making process *and* have a determinative influence on the outcome.[99]

[94]Matthew Mooney, *Between a Stone and a Hard Place: How the Hajj Can Restore the Spirit of Reasonable Accommodation to Title VII*, 62 DUKE. L.J. 1029 (2013).

[95]Age Discrimination Act of 1975, 42 U.S.C. §§ 6101-6107 (2018) (prohibiting age discrimination in programs and activities receiving federal funding and applying to *all* ages).

[96]Facially discriminatory procedures and practices that classify individuals on the basis of age can satisfy the Equal Protection Clause if they are rationally related to a legitimate governmental objective, whereas facially neutral criteria may be successfully challenged only with proof of a discriminatory intent.

[97]29 U.S.C. § 621 (2018).

[98]29 U.S.C. § 623(a)(1) (2018).

[99]*See, e.g.*, Hazen Paper Co. v. Biggins, 507 U.S. 604 (1993). Future application of the ADEA in public school cases will be limited at times, however, because the Supreme Court in Kimel v. Florida Bd. of Regents, 528 U.S. 62 (2000), held that Eleventh Amendment immunity may be claimed as a defense where money damages to be paid out of the state treasury are sought in federal court. Accordingly, immunity will apply when state laws consider school districts to be "arms of the state" rather than political subdivisions. But even when the Eleventh Amendment is used as a defense, plaintiffs can sue under comparable state statutes to vindicate their rights.

Hiring and Promotion

As indicated, under the ADEA, except in those circumstances where age qualifies as a BFOQ, selection among applicants for hiring or promotion may be based on any factor other than age. Although a BFOQ defense in an educational setting is unlikely in cases involving staff, teachers, or administrators, claims could conceivably be made for school bus drivers and pilots. **Where a BFOQ is applied, the employer carries the burden of persuasion to demonstrate that there is reasonable cause to believe that all, or substantially all, applicants beyond a certain age would be unable to perform a job safely and efficiently.** With Title VII cases, most employers who are alleged to have engaged in age discrimination simply respond that a better qualified applicant was hired, irrespective of age. In the effort to show pretext, an employee need not discredit each and every proffered reason for the rejection, but must cast substantial doubt on many, if not most, of the purported bases so that a fact finder could rationally disbelieve the remaining reasons.

In an illustrative Second Circuit case, a less experienced, unqualified, younger teacher was selected over the plaintiff.[100] The school district purported that the selected applicant performed better during the interview and was chosen largely on that basis. In ruling that pretext had been shown, the court noted that the successful candidate did not possess the specified degree and had submitted an incomplete file; that the employer had made misleading statements and destroyed relevant evidence; and that the plaintiff possessed superior credentials, except perhaps as to the interview. The fact that the previously selected applicant also was over the age of forty was irrelevant; what mattered was that she was substantially younger (i.e., forty-two) than the plaintiff (sixty-four).[101]

In contrast, a sixty-three-year-old tenured principal alleged that the school board decided not to renew his contract due to his age in violation of the ADEA. The principal claimed that one of the school district's administrators was given a list of five or six principals who should be fired and replaced with "younger and brighter" school leaders. Before the principal's contract was not renewed, this supervisor had put him on notice for insubordination for a variety of reasons (e.g., failing to respond to parent issues), and he was placed on academic probation as a result of the school's low academic achievement levels. The district court did not find that the principal provided convincing circumstantial evidence to demonstrate that the board engaged in any discrimination. The principal also failed to show that his supervisor harbored discriminatory animus against him. The Seventh Circuit affirmed the district court's decision to grant summary judgment to the board.[102]

---

[100]Byrnie v. Town of Cromwell, 243 F.3d 93 (2d Cir. 2001).

[101]*See also* Brennan v. Metro. Opera Ass'n, 192 F.3d 310 (2d Cir. 1999) (noting that the fact that the replacement is substantially younger than the plaintiff is a more valuable indicator of age discrimination than whether the replacement was over age forty).

[102]Bordelon v. Bd. of Educ., 811 F.3d 984 (7th Cir. 2016). *But see* Papagolos v. Lafayette Cty. Sch. Dist., 972 F. Supp. 2d 912 (N.D. Miss. 2013) (denying a school district's motion to dismiss an ADEA claim that was initiated by a high school coach who alleged that he was replaced by a younger inexperienced coach).

Retirement

Given that the mandatory retirement of school employees has been eliminated, school districts have attempted to entice older employees to retire through attractive retirement benefits packages. **Under the ADEA, employers can follow the terms of a bona fide retirement plan so long as the plan is not a subterfuge to evade the purposes of the Act.**[103] Also, employers may not reduce annual benefits or cease the accrual of benefits after employees attain a certain age as an inducement for them to retire.[104]

In a 1993 Supreme Court decision, *Hazen Paper Company v. Biggins*, the plaintiff was fired at age sixty-two, only a few weeks before completing ten years of service and being vested in his pension plan.[105] Two issues before the Supreme Court were whether the employer's interference with the vesting of pension benefits violated the ADEA *and* whether the standard for liquidated damages[106] applied to informal age-based decisions by employers in addition to those that were based on formal policies that facially discriminate based on age. In a unanimous opinion, the Court vacated and remanded the lower court decision for a determination of whether the jury had sufficient evidence to find an ADEA violation.

Although it is difficult to prevail in an age-discrimination claim, expect the number of cases to remain high as the "baby boomers" become sexagenarians and septuagenarians over the next decade. Some will be denied employment, promotion, or vesting, whereas others may be disappointed in their retirement packages. Plaintiffs will allege age discrimination, but in most instances, those claims will be successfully rebutted by employers.

DISABILITY DISCRIMINATION

Federal disability law protects only those individuals who can show that they qualify as having a disability and are otherwise qualified for the job.

Some of the most frequent legal issues involving the disability discrimination in schools include determining disability and qualification status, providing reasonable accommodations, and addressing and avoiding retaliation. Prior to 1973, federal claims regarding disability discrimination in employment were filed under the Equal Protection Clause.[107] The Fourteenth Amendment is now less often used due to the applicability of two federal statutes: **the Rehabilitation Act of 1973 (particularly Section 504**[108]**), which applies to recipients of federal financial assistance, and the ADA,**[109] **which applies to most**

---

[103]*See, e.g.*, United Air Lines v. McMann, 434 U.S. 192 (1977).

[104]29 U.S.C. § 623(i)(1) (2018).

[105]507 U.S. 604 (1993).

[106]For a discussion of liquidated damages, *see* Trans World Airlines v. Thurston, 469 U.S. 111 (1985).

[107]The Fourteenth Amendment requires the application of rational basis scrutiny in cases where disability discrimination is facial and proof of intent where the alleged discrimination is facially neutral.

[108]29 U.S.C. § 794 (2018). The Supreme Court has held that a state employer is immune from paying damages in an ADA case. *See* Bd. of Trs. v. Garrett, 531 U.S. 356 (2001).

[109]42 U.S.C. § 12101 (2018). *See* Figure 6.1, Chapter 6 and text accompanying note 118, Chapter 7.

employers with fifteen or more employees. These statutes require nondiscrimination against employees with disabilities involving any term, condition, or privilege of employment. Section 504 complaints are submitted to the Office for Civil Rights within the Department of Education.[110] In comparison, the EEOC, the Department of Justice, and private litigants have enforcement rights under the ADA. The ADA is most often at issue in employment cases because of its broader application, and it forbids employers from discriminating against qualified individuals because of their disabilities. A plaintiff may show discrimination in either of two ways: by presenting evidence of disparate treatment or by showing a failure to accommodate a disability. To show disparate treatment under the ADA, a plaintiff may proceed under either the direct or the indirect method. Under the direct method, plaintiffs must show: (1) that they are disabled within the meaning of the ADA; (2) that they are qualified to perform the essential functions of the job with or without accommodation; and (3) that they have suffered an adverse employment action because of their disability.[111] The elements of an ADA failure to accommodate claim are: "(1) the plaintiff must be a qualified individual with a disability; (2) the employer must be aware of the plaintiff's disability; and (3) the employer must have failed to reasonably accommodate the disability."[112]

Qualifying as Disabled

When cases are filed, courts often are asked to resolve questions regarding whether the plaintiff is in fact disabled and, if so, what accommodations are required. A person qualifies as disabled under Section 504 and the ADA if he or she:

- has a physical or mental impairment that substantially limits one or more major life activities;
- has a record of impairment;[113] or
- is regarded as having an impairment.[114]

However, more is required than simple knowledge of a condition that is physically or mentally limiting for the employee to establish that the employer regarded the employee as having an impairment. To illustrate, the Eighth Circuit granted the school district's motion for summary judgment because a teacher with multiple sclerosis did not demonstrate that she had an impairment that substantially limited a major life activity, had a record of impairment,

---

[110]Complaint forms must be filed in a timely manner and signed by the employee. *See* Fry v. Muscogee Cty. Sch. Dist., 150 F. App'x 980 (11th Cir. 2005) (concluding that an employee with morbid obesity failed to sign and thereby verify her ADA complaint—her attorney had signed it for her, but later failed to acquire her signature or properly amend the claim).

[111]42 U.S.C.S. § 12101 (2018).

[112]Brumfield v. City of Chic., 735 F.3d 619, 631 (7th Cir. 2013).

[113]For example, when employees are discriminatorily treated because of having a history of hospitalization due to tuberculosis, alcoholism, or drug addiction, they would qualify for protection as they are viewed as having a record of impairment.

[114]To illustrate, when a person is discriminatorily treated because of being HIV positive, but does not have AIDS or any type of current physical impairment limiting a major life activity, the person would qualify for protection as regarded as having an impairment.

or was regarded as having an impairment. The court reasoned that the school district's knowledge of the teacher's physical impairments did not establish that school officials regarded her as disabled, nor did the accommodations that were provided establish such.[115]

Although federal regulations define physical or mental impairment broadly,[116] persons who currently are involved in the use of illegal drugs,[117] are unable to perform the duties of the job due to alcohol use, have a contagious disease,[118] or otherwise represent a direct threat to the safety or health of themselves or others do not qualify as disabled. If the individual is disqualified because of health issues, the decision must be based on current medical evidence and not on stereotypes or fears. Likewise, persons claiming discrimination due to pedophilia, exhibitionism, voyeurism, sexual behavior disorders, compulsive gambling, kleptomania, pyromania, and psychoactive substance use disorders resulting from current illegal drug use are not protected by either the ADA or Section 504.

Qualifying as disabled requires a two-step process: identifying a physical or mental impairment *and* determining whether the impairment substantially limits a major life activity. The EEOC identifies several major life activities (i.e., walking, seeing, hearing, speaking, breathing, learning, and working) in its guidelines for the ADA[119] and others in related manuals (i.e., caring for oneself, sitting, standing, lifting, concentrating, thinking, and interacting with others),[120] while the Supreme Court has expanded the list also to include both reproduction and performing manual tasks.[121] It is important to note that in 2008, the ADA was amended to clarify that mitigating measures should not be considered when determining whether someone has a disability under the ADA. In other words, even individuals who are able to control their disabilities with medication would still be considered disabled.[122] The amendment broadened the circumstances under which an individual will be considered disabled. Thus, a court assumed that a teacher was disabled where she could not go outdoors because of allergies; could not bend, lift, or use stairs due to having been in an automobile accident; and had taken an extended leave to recover from hepatitis.[123] In contrast, another court ruled that a teacher's sprained ankle was a temporary injury that did not substantially limit a major activity so as to constitute a disability under the ADA.[124]

---

[115]Nyrop v. Indep. Sch. Dist., 616 F.3d 728 (8th Cir. 2010).

[116]34 C.F.R. § 104.3(j)(2)(i) (2018).

[117]*See, e.g.*, McKissick v. Cty. of York, 2011 U.S. Dist. LEXIS 123158, at *30 (M.D. Pa. Oct. 25, 2011) (noting that drug addiction can constitute a physical or mental impairment under the ADA, but the term "qualified individual with a disability" does not include individuals currently using illegal drugs).

[118]*But see* P.R. v. Metro. Sch. Dist. of Wash. Twp., 2010 U.S. Dist. LEXIS 116223 (S.D. Ind. Nov. 1, 2010) (finding HIV infection is a physical impairment that substantially limits a major life activity).

[119]29 C.F.R. §1630.2(i) (2018).

[120]EEOC, *A Technical Assistance Manual on the Employment Provisions (Title I) of the Americans with Disabilities Act*, at II-3 (Jan. 1992), http://archive.org/details/technicalassista00unse; *EEOC Enforcement Guidance on the Americans with Disabilities Act and Psychiatric Disabilities*, 1997 WL 33159166, at *6–7 (EEOC Marc. 25, 1997).

[121]Bragdon v. Abbott, 524 U.S. 624 (1998) (reproduction); Toyota Motor Mfg. v. Williams, 534 U.S. 184 (2002) (manual tasks).

[122]ADA Amendments Act of 2008, 42 U.S.C. § 12101 (2018).

[123]Weatherby v. Fulton Cty. Sch. Sys., 2013 U.S. Dist. LEXIS 13548 (N.D. Ga. Sept. 23, 2013).

[124]Mazur v. N.Y.C. Dep't. of Educ., 53 F. Supp. 3d 618 (S.D.N.Y. 2014).

Performance is substantially limited when an employee is unable to perform, or is significantly restricted in performing, a major life activity that can be accomplished by the average person in the general population. The nature, severity, duration, and long-term impact of the impairment are considered when determining whether a condition is substantially limiting.[125] Also, an impairment that is substantially limiting for one person may not be for another. To qualify, it must prevent or restrict an individual from performing tasks that are of central importance to most people's daily lives. If the life activity claimed is working, impairments are not substantially limiting unless they restrict the ability to perform a broad range of jobs and not just a single or specialized job.[126] In such cases, courts will consider the geographic area to which the plaintiff has reasonable access and the nature of the job from which the individual was disqualified, as well as other jobs that require similar training, knowledge, ability, or skill.[127] When contagious disease is involved, the employer should consider how the disease is transmitted, how long the employee is infectious, the potential harm to others, and the probability of transmission.

Otherwise Qualified

If a person qualifies as disabled, it then must be determined whether he or she is "otherwise qualified." **To be an otherwise qualified individual with a disability, the applicant or employee must be able to perform the essential functions of the job in spite of the disability, although reasonable accommodation at times may be necessary.** Generally, employers should not impose a blanket exclusion of persons with particular disabilities, but rather should provide individual review of each person. Only in rare instances will a particular disability disqualify an applicant (e.g., where federal or state law establishes health or ability requirements for particular types of employment).

In identifying the essential functions of the job, courts will give consideration to what the employer perceives to be essential. So long as each identified requirement for employment is either training related (for initial employment) or job related, the employer should not have difficulty in substantiating its claim of business necessity. For example, being on time to work and being at work on a regular daily basis can qualify as a business necessity for most positions in education as well as elsewhere. Employees often have claimed that their respective disabilities were the basis for their lateness or nonarrival. Although this may have been true, courts generally have not found such employees to be otherwise qualified.

However, in *School Board of Nassau County, Florida v. Arline*, a teacher had three relapses of tuberculosis over a two-year period for which leave was given, and she was terminated prior to returning to work following the third leave.[128] The Supreme Court held that the teacher qualified as disabled under Section 504 due to her record of physical

---

[125]29 C.F.R. § 1630.2(j)(1), (2) (2018).

[126]*See, e.g.*, Samuels v. Kan. City Mo. Sch. Dist., 437 F.3d 797 (8th Cir. 2006).

[127]29 C.F.R. § 1630.2(j)(2)(3) (2018).

[128]480 U.S. 273 (1987), *on remand*, 692 F. Supp. 1286 (M.D. Fla. 1988).

impairment and hospitalization, but remanded the case for the district court to determine whether risks of infection to others precluded her from being otherwise qualified and whether her condition could be reasonably accommodated without an undue burden on the district. Following remand, the teacher was found to be otherwise qualified since she posed little risk of infecting others, and was ordered reinstated with back pay.

Reasonable Accommodation

Persons with disabilities must be able to perform all of the essential functions of the position, either with or without accommodation. Employers are responsible for providing reasonable accommodations, such as making necessary facilities accessible and usable, restructuring work schedules, acquiring or modifying equipment, and providing readers or interpreters.[129] In an illustrative case, a Florida school district argued that a former teacher with diabetes could not perform the essential functions of the job. When the district accommodated the teacher by giving him the gifted and talented class, he still could not perform the essential job function of disciplining students. Affirming the district court's decision, the Eleventh Circuit did not find that the teacher was a "qualified individual" under the ADA because he was not able perform an essential function of the job with or without accommodations.[130] Likewise, a Wisconsin teacher with severe arthritis was unsuccessful in her ADA claim against the district. The Seventh Circuit ruled that she failed to meet her obligation under the ADA to participate in identifying reasonable accommodations. The teacher had suggested five different positions, but the school district pointed out that four of these positions involved working with unruly students, which her doctor forbid. The fifth position she identified was a promotion, which under the ADA, the district is not required to offer.[131]

Also, when not restricted by bargaining rights or other entitlements, transfer within the organization may qualify as a reasonable accommodation.[132] However, federal law does not require the employer to bump a current employee to allow a person with a disability to fill the position, to fill a vacant position it did not intend to fill, to violate seniority rights, to refrain from disciplining an employee for misconduct, to eliminate essential functions of the job, or to create a new unnecessary position. Moreover, an employer need not transfer the employee to a better position, or select a less-qualified or unqualified applicant solely because of disability.[133] Such forms of accommodation may be theoretically possible but would result in undue hardship to the employer and discriminate against other employees.

Courts determine whether undue hardship results after a review of the size of the program and its budget, the number of employees, the type of facilities and operation, and

---

[129]*See* Lowe v. Indep. Sch. Dist., 363 F. App'x 548 (10th Cir. 2010) (holding that the school district failed to identify an appropriate accommodation for a teacher with a post-polio condition who resigned after being reassigned to a small and crowded classroom); Ekstrand v. Sch. Dist., 683 F.3d 826 (7th Cir. 2012) (finding that a jury could determine that the school district was required under the ADA to provide a classroom with natural light for a teacher who suffered from seasonal affective disorder).

[130]Siudock v. Volusia Cty. Sch. Bd., 568 F. App'x 659 (11th Cir. 2014).

[131]Brown v. Milwaukee Bd. of Sch. Dirs., 855 F.3d 818 (7th Cir. 2017).

[132]*See, e.g.*, Smith v. Midland Brake, 180 F.3d 1154 (10th Cir. 1999) (en banc).

[133]*See, e.g.*, Lors v. Dean, 595 F.3d 831 (8th Cir. 2010) (finding that the ADA is not an affirmative action statute).

the nature and cost of accommodation. Because there is no fixed formula for calculations, courts have differed markedly in identifying what they consider reasonable.

Finally, the ADA prohibits retaliation by an employer in response to an employee engaging in protected activity seeking to enforce rights granted by the ADA. Many courts have concluded that teachers have engaged in protected activity—and may not be subjected to retaliation for doing so—where they requested accommodation for themselves from a school district and lodged a complaint with a school board when the accommodation was not granted.[134]

CONCLUSION

Federal law requires that employment decisions be based on qualifications, performance, merit, seniority, and the like, rather than factors such as race, national origin, sex, religion, age, or disability. Statutes vary considerably, however, about what they require. Moreover, federal regulations are extensive, complex, and at times confounding. As a result, courts differ in applying the law.

When preparing a policy related to personnel, it will be important to consider (1) whether it facially discriminates only in legal and appropriate ways and (2) whether it adversely affects a protected class, even though the policy may be facially neutral. Treating all persons the same may not accommodate individual needs and may inadvertently result in subtle forms of discrimination. In the alternative, treating persons differently may advantage some over others. Given the different types of discrimination that can be present in the workplace and the complexities of the law, there is no simple solution. Even though many questions remain, the following generalizations reflect the current status of the law.

1. The U.S. Constitution and various civil rights laws protect employees from discrimination in employment based on race, national origin, sex, sexual orientation, religion, age, and disability.

2. For Fourteenth Amendment facial discrimination cases, race, and national origin discrimination claims, courts apply strict scrutiny; sex and illegitimacy discrimination receive intermediate scrutiny; and all other employment classifications need to be justified by any rational basis.

3. For Fourteenth Amendment facially neutral cases, regardless of the type of classification involved, the employee is required to show that the employer intended to discriminate.

4. Race may never qualify as a bona fide occupational qualification, although sex, religion, national origin, and age may be used under narrowly tailored conditions.

5. A reliable and valid standardized test can be used to screen job applicants, even though it has a disproportionate impact on a protected class, so long as the test is used to advance legitimate job objectives.

6. In Title VII disparate treatment cases, plaintiffs argue that they are receiving less favorable treatment than other employees; they must prove that the employer had discriminatory intent.

[134]Ortega v. Chic. Pub. Schs., 2015 U.S. Dist. LEXIS 115806 (N.D. Ill. Sept. 1, 2015).

7. Public employers may not engage in affirmative action plans involving preferences in hiring and promotion unless a court has determined that the institution has been involved in specific prior acts of discrimination and the affirmative action plan is narrowly tailored to attain a workforce reflecting the qualified relevant labor market.

8. Under narrowly tailored circumstances, courts may order hiring and promotion preferences to remedy prior acts of intentional employment discrimination but may not impose layoff quotas.

9. Employees can gain relief under Title VII for unfair treatment in hiring, promotion, and compensation, as well as for sexual harassment that results in the loss of tangible benefits or creates a hostile working environment.

10. Persons who are victims of sexual orientation discrimination may file suit under the Fourteenth Amendment or Title VII in some jurisdictions.

11. School boards can establish bona fide retirement benefits programs, but the ADEA precludes mandatory retirement based on age.

12. For a violation to be substantiated under the ADEA, age must play a role in the decision-making process *and* have a determinative influence on the outcome.

13. Employers must make reasonable accommodations to enable employees to practice their religious beliefs; however, Title VII does not require accommodations that result in undue hardship to the employer.

14. An otherwise qualified individual cannot be excluded from employment solely on the basis of a disability, and employers are required to provide reasonable accommodations for employees with disabilities.

CHAPTER TWELVE

TERMINATION OF EMPLOYMENT

If teachers get arrested for driving under the influence of alcohol are they automatically fired? What is the difference between nonrenewal and dismissal? What can employees do if they believe they have been wrongfully discharged? School boards have the authority to terminate employees, a role they are granted through state law. Generally, these state laws specify the causes for which a teacher may be terminated and the procedures that must be followed. This chapter addresses the entitlements, protections, and procedures for probationary (nontenured) and tenured public school employees.

Readers of this chapter should be able to:

- Define key terms including tenure, dismissal, nonrenewal, as well as property and liberty interests.
- Distinguish what due process protections are required for teachers who are not renewed versus dismissed.
- Describe the common causes for dismissal found in state statutes.
- Discuss what remedies are available for employees who believe they were wrongfully terminated.

OVERVIEW OF EMPLOYEES' DUE PROCESS RIGHTS

School employees are entitled to procedural due process if termination of employment impairs a property or liberty interest.

Individuals' due process rights derive from the U.S. Constitution. Basic due process rights are embodied in the Fourteenth Amendment, which guarantees that no state shall "deprive any person of life, liberty, or property without due process of law."[1] Due process safeguards apply not only in judicial proceedings (e.g., the right to be represented by an attorney in criminal cases), but also to acts of governmental agencies including school boards. As discussed in Chapter 1, constitutional due process entails *substantive* protections against

[1] As noted in Chapter 1, the Fourteenth Amendment restricts state, in contrast to private, action.

arbitrary governmental action and *procedural* protections when the government threatens an individual's life, liberty, or property interests. Most school employee termination cases have focused on procedural due process requirements.

The individual and governmental interests at stake and applicable state laws influence the nature of procedural due process required. **Courts have established that school employees' interest in public employment may entail significant "property" and "liberty" rights necessitating due process prior to employment termination**. A *property interest* is a legitimate claim of entitlement to continued employment that is created by state law.[2] The granting of tenure conveys such a right to a teacher. Also, a contract establishes a property right to employment within its stated terms. A property interest in continued employment, however, does not mean that an individual cannot be terminated; it simply means that an employer must follow the requirements of due process and substantiate cause.

The judiciary has recognized that Fourteenth Amendment *liberty rights* encompass fundamental constitutional guarantees, such as freedom of speech. Procedural due process is always required when a termination implicates such fundamental liberties. A liberty interest also is involved when termination creates a stigma or damages an individual's reputation in a manner that forecloses future employment opportunities. If protected liberty or property interests are implicated, the Fourteenth Amendment entitles the school employee at least to notice of the reasons for the school board's action and an opportunity for a hearing. When teachers are released, the terminations are classified as either dismissals or nonrenewals. The distinction between the two has significant implications for teachers' procedural rights.

Dismissal

Dismissal refers to the termination for cause of any tenured employee or of a probationary employee within the contract period. Both tenure statutes and employment contracts establish a property interest entitling employees to full procedural protection. Beyond the basic constitutional requirements of appropriate notice and an opportunity to be heard, state laws and school board policies often contain detailed procedures that must be followed. Failure to provide these additional procedures, however, results in a violation of state law, rather than constitutional law. Statutory procedures vary as to specificity, with some states enumerating detailed steps and others identifying only broad parameters. In addition to complying with state law, a school district must abide by its own procedures, even if they exceed state law. For example, if school board policy provides for a preliminary notice of teaching inadequacies and an opportunity to correct remediable deficiencies prior to dismissal, the board must follow these steps.

A critical element in dismissal actions is a showing of justifiable cause for termination of employment. If causes are identified in state law, a school board must base dismissal on those grounds. Failure to relate the charges to statutory grounds can invalidate the termination decision. Because statutes typically list broad causes—such as incompetency, insubordination, immorality, unprofessional conduct, and neglect of duty—notice

[2]*See* Bd. of Regents v. Roth, 408 U.S. 564 (1972).

of discharge must indicate specific conduct substantiating the legal charges. Procedural safeguards ensure not only that an employee is informed of the specific reasons and grounds for dismissal, but also that the school board bases its decision on evidence related to those grounds. Detailed aspects of procedural due process requirements and dismissal for cause are addressed in subsequent sections of this chapter.

Nonrenewal

In those states that offer tenure status, teachers and other eligible school employees are considered probationary until they have met the criteria listed in state law to become tenured.[3] In some states, probationary or nontenured employees must receive satisfactory evaluations as defined by state law before they can achieve tenure status.[4] Unless specified in state law, procedural protections are not afforded to the probationary employee when the employment contract is not renewed. At the end of the contract period, employment can be terminated for any or no reason, so long as the reason is not constitutionally impermissible (e.g., denial of protected speech).[5]

The most common statutory requirement is notification of nonrenewal on or before a specified date prior to the expiration of the contract. The timeliness of nonrenewal notices is strictly construed. The fact that the school board has set in motion notification (e.g., mailed the notice) generally does not satisfy the statutory requirement; the employee's actual receipt of the notice is critical. An employee, however, cannot avoid or deliberately thwart delivery of notice and then claim insufficiency of notice.[6] **Failure of school officials to observe the notice deadline may result in an employee's reinstatement for an additional year or even the granting of tenure in some jurisdictions**.

In the nonrenewal of employees' contracts, some districts may afford additional due process protections for teachers through their collective bargaining agreements. Moreover, some state laws require a written statement of reasons and may even provide an opportunity for a hearing at the employee's request.[7] Unlike evidentiary hearings for dismissal of an employee, the school board is not required to show cause for nonrenewal; an employee is simply provided the reasons underlying the nonrenewal and an opportunity to address the school board. In the states where the school board is required to provide reasons, broad general statements such as "the school district's interest would be best served," or "the

[3]Educ. Comm'n of the States, *50 State Comparison: Teacher Tenure-Requirements for Earning Nonprobationary Status* (May 2014), http://ecs.force.com/mbdata/mbquestRTL?rep=TT01. *See infra* text accompanying note 54 for a discussion of at-will employees and administrator contracts.

[4]Some state laws stipulate that tenured teachers will be returned to probationary status based on unsatisfactory evaluations. *See* Stephen Sawchuk, *Report: More States Linking Evaluations to Tenure*, EDUC. WK. (May 22, 2014), http://blogs.edweek.org/edweek/teacherbeat/2014/05/report_more_states_linking_eva.html.

[5]*See, e.g.,* Barbee v. Union City Bd. of Educ., 559 F. App'x 450 (6th Cir. 2014); Grossman v. S. Shore Pub. Sch. Dist., 507 F.3d 1097 (7th Cir. 2007); Back v. Hastings, 365 F.3d 107 (2d Cir. 2004); Flaskamp v. Dearborn Pub. Schs., 385 F.3d 935 (6th Cir. 2004); *see also* Chapter 10 for a discussion of employees' constitutional rights.

[6]*See* Sullivan v. Centinela Valley Union High Sch. Dist., 122 Cal. Rptr. 3d 871 (Ct. App. 2011) (finding notice adequate when a teacher avoided timely notification by not attending work and leaving his home for the day).

[7]*See, e.g.,* 70 OKLA. STAT. § 6-101.22-25 (2018) (listing the grounds that a school board must use when providing written notice that it is not renewing a probationary teacher's contract).

term contract has expired" will not suffice; the employee must be given specific information about deficiencies, such as lack of classroom control or ineffective classroom instruction. Of course, if school officials communicate stigmatizing reasons for nonrenewal, they may be required to hold a name-clearing hearing.

Additionally, when state law establishes specific requirements and procedures for nonrenewal, failure to abide by these provisions may invalidate a school board's decision. A coach claimed that his nonrenewal was in violation of a Minnesota law, stating that the existence of parental complaints could not be the sole reason for nonrenewal of a coaching contract. The Eighth Circuit disagreed, holding that the school board's nonrenewal adhered to the state law stipulating that the board had "considerable discretion" as to whether to renew a coaching contract.[8]

Importantly, a school board must also comply substantially with its own nonrenewal procedures and state law. Even when local and state procedures do not offer specific procedural protections, an employee's interest in continued public employment may be constitutionally protected if a liberty or property right guaranteed by the Fourteenth Amendment has been abridged. Infringement of these interests entitles a probationary employee to due process rights similar to the rights of tenured employees.

Establishing Protected Property and Liberty Interests

The U.S. Supreme Court addressed the scope of protected interests encompassed by the Fourteenth Amendment in two significant decisions: *Board of Regents v. Roth*[9] and *Perry v. Sindermann*.[10] These decisions addressed whether the infringement of a liberty or property interest entitles a probationary employee to due process rights similar to the rights of tenured employees. The cases involved faculty members at the postsecondary level, but the rulings are applicable to public elementary and secondary school employees.

In *Roth*, the question before the Court was whether a nontenured teacher had a constitutional right to a statement of reasons and a hearing prior to nonreappointment. Roth had been hired on a one-year contract, and the university elected not to rehire him for a second year. Because Roth did not have tenure, there was no entitlement under Wisconsin law to an explanation of charges or a hearing. Roth challenged the nonrenewal, alleging that failure to provide notice of reasons and an opportunity for a hearing impaired his due process rights.

The Supreme Court held that nonrenewal does not require procedural protections unless impairment of a protected liberty or property interest can be shown. **To establish infringement of a liberty interest, the Court held that the teacher must show that the employer's action (1) resulted in damage to his or her reputation and standing in the community or (2) imposed a stigma that foreclosed other employment opportunities**. The evidence presented by Roth indicated that there was no such damage to his reputation or future employment.[11] In rejecting Roth's claim that he had a property interest in continued

---

[8]McGuire v. Indep. Sch. Dist., 863 F.3d 1030, 1035 (8th Cir. 2017).

[9]408 U.S. 564 (1972).

[10]408 U.S. 593 (1972).

[11]Roth, 408 U.S. 564.

employment, the Court held that **in order to establish a valid property right, an individual must have more than an "abstract need or desire" for a position; there must be a "legitimate claim of entitlement" grounded in state laws or employment contracts**.[12]

On the same day it rendered the *Roth* decision, the Supreme Court in the *Sindermann* case explained the circumstances that might create a legitimate expectation of reemployment for a nontenured teacher.[13] Sindermann was a nontenured faculty member in his fourth year of teaching when he was notified, without a statement of reasons or an opportunity for a hearing, that his contract would not be renewed. He challenged the lack of procedural due process, alleging that nonrenewal deprived him of a property interest protected by the Fourteenth Amendment and violated his First Amendment right to freedom of speech.

In advancing a protected property right, Sindermann claimed that the college, which lacked a formal tenure system, had created an informal, or de facto, tenure system through various practices and policies. Specifically, Sindermann cited a provision in the faculty guide stating: "The College wishes the faculty member to feel that he has permanent tenure so long as his teaching services are satisfactory."[14] The Supreme Court found that Sindermann's claim, unlike Roth's, might have been based on a legitimate expectation of reemployment promulgated by the college. According to the Court, the lack of a formal tenure system did not foreclose the possibility of an institution fostering entitlement to a position through its personnel policies. In assessing Sindermann's free speech claim that he was retaliated against for publicly criticizing college policies, **the Supreme Court confirmed that a teacher's lack of tenure does not void a claim that nonrenewal was based on the exercise of constitutionally protected conduct**. Procedural due process must be afforded when a substantive constitutional right is violated.

The *Roth* and *Sindermann* cases are the legal precedents for assessing the procedural rights of nontenured teachers (see Figure 12.1). Because the Supreme Court has held that impairment of an employee's property or liberty interests triggers procedural protections, the question arises as to what constitutes a violation of these interests. Courts have purposely avoided precisely defining the concepts of liberty and property, preferring to allow experience and time to shape their meanings.

Property Interest.   In general, a nontenured employee does not have a property claim to reappointment unless state or local governmental action has clearly established such a right. For example, a teacher challenged his nonrenewal claiming the district violated his property interest.[15] The Seventh Circuit disagreed explaining that teacher could not base a legitimate expectation of continued employment on his principal's mid-year positive evaluation. The nonrenewal was because the teacher demonstrated a lack of professionalism in handling several incidents with students after the principal's evaluation of him. In contrast, the Supreme Court affirmed the Seventh Circuit's holding that a school board's promise of

---

[12]*Id.* at 577; *see also* Lautermilch v. Findlay City Sch., 314 F.3d 271 (6th Cir. 2002) (finding that a substitute teacher without a contract did not have a protected property interest in continued employment); Meyers v. Kishimoto, 217 F. Supp. 3d 563 (D. Conn. 2016) (holding that a previously tenured teacher no longer had property rights under state statute because he failed to meet a recertification requirement).

[13]408 U.S. 593 (1972).

[14]*Id.* at 600.

[15]Halfhill v. Ne. Sch. Corp., 472 F.3d 496 (7th Cir. 2006).

FIGURE 12.1 Procedural Due Process for Nonrenewed Employees

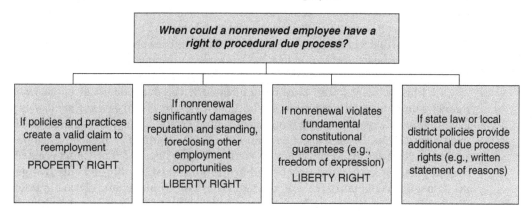

two years of employment to a coach/athletic director established a legitimate expectation of continued employment for that time period.[16]

Protected property interests are not created by mere longevity in employment. Both the Fourth and Tenth Circuits found that issuing an employee a series of annual contracts did not constitute a valid claim to continued employment in the absence of a guarantee in state law, local policy, or an employment contract.[17] Similarly, a statute or collective bargaining agreement providing an employee, upon request, a hearing and statement of reasons for nonrenewal does not confer a property interest in employment requiring legally sufficient cause for termination. Such a provision simply gives the employee an opportunity to present reasons that the contract should be renewed.

Although a contract establishes a property interest within the contract terms, due process generally is not required in transferring or reassigning an employee unless an economic impact can be shown. For example, a principal who was reassigned to the central office was not entitled to a hearing because he would continue to receive his regular salary and benefits; deprivations related to professional satisfaction and reputation did not constitute actionable injuries.[18] In contrast, the Sixth Circuit reasoned that a collective bargaining agreement specifying that teachers may not be transferred except for "good cause" and "extenuating circumstances" established a property interest in a particular position in a specific school.[19]

---

[16]Vail v. Bd. of Educ., 466 U.S. 377 (1984).

[17]Martin v. Unified Sch. Dist., 728 F.2d 453 (10th Cir. 1984); Robertson v. Rogers, 679 F.2d 1090 (4th Cir. 1982); *see also* Crosby v. Univ. of Ky., 863 F.3d 545 (6th Cir. 2017) (determining that university policy did not create a de facto contract; therefore, tenured professor lacked a property interest in his position as departmental chair); Ray v. Nash, 438 F. App'x 332 (5th Cir. 2011) (holding that a teacher's expectancy of reemployment because she had been successful in her teaching did not create a protected property interest).

[18]Bordelon v. Chi. Sch. Reform Bd. of Trs., 233 F.3d 524 (7th Cir. 2000); *see also* Roybal v. Toppenish Sch. Dist., 871 F.3d 927 (9th Cir. 2017) (agreeing that the principal had a property interest claim after his salary was reduced from $92,000 to $56,500; however, the principal's procedural rights were not violated).

[19]Leary v. Daeschner, 228 F.3d 729 (6th Cir. 2000).

Liberty Interest.   As noted previously, liberty interests encompass fundamental constitutional guarantees such as freedom of expression and privacy rights. If governmental action in the nonrenewal of employment threatens the exercise of these fundamental liberties, procedural due process must be afforded.[20] Most nonrenewals, however, do not overtly implicate fundamental rights, and thus the burden is on the aggrieved employee to prove that the proffered reason is pretextual to mask impermissible grounds.

A liberty interest also may be implicated if the nonrenewal of employment damages an individual's reputation. The Supreme Court established in *Roth* that damage to a teacher's reputation and future employability could infringe Fourteenth Amendment liberty rights. In subsequent decisions, the Court identified prerequisite conditions for establishing that an unconstitutional stigma has been imposed. **The Court created a stigma-plus test that states: procedural protections must be afforded only if stigma or damaging statements (1) are related to loss of employment, (2) are publicly disclosed, (3) are alleged to be false, and (4) virtually foreclose opportunities for future employment.**[21]

Under this stigma-plus test, governmental action damaging an employee's reputation, standing alone, is insufficient to invoke the Fourteenth Amendment's procedural safeguards.[22] While many employment actions may stigmatize and affect an employee's reputation, they do not constitute a deprivation of liberty in the absence of loss of employment.[23] As the Ninth Circuit noted, "nearly any reason assigned for dismissal is likely to be to some extent a negative reflection on an individual's ability, temperament, or character," but circumstances giving rise to a liberty interest are narrow.[24] Charges must be serious implications against character, such as immorality and dishonesty, to create a stigma of constitutional magnitude that virtually forecloses other employment.[25] According to the Fifth Circuit, a charge must give rise to "a 'badge of infamy,' public scorn, or the like."[26]

Among accusations that courts have found to necessitate a hearing are a serious drinking problem, emotional instability, mental illness, dishonesty, immoral conduct, child

---

[20]Violations of teachers' fundamental constitutional rights are discussed in Chapter 10; this section focuses on the violations of liberty rights where a teacher's reputation is damaged in the process of nonrenewal.

[21]Codd v. Velger, 429 U.S. 624 (1977); *see also* O'Connor v. Pierson, 426 F.3d 187 (2d Cir. 2005); Bordelon v. Chi. Sch. Reform Bd. of Trs., 233 F.3d 524 (7th Cir. 2000).

[22]State constitutions, however, may provide greater protection of due process rights encompassing damage to reputation.

[23]*See, e.g.,* Brown v. Simmons, 478 F.3d 922 (8th Cir. 2007); Ulichny v. Merton Cmty. Sch. Dist., 249 F.3d 686 (7th Cir. 2001). *But see* Winegar v. Des Moines Indep. Cmty. Sch. Dist., 20 F.3d 895 (8th Cir. 1994) (holding that a teacher's disciplinary transfer to another school because of the physical abuse of a student involved a significant liberty interest necessitating an opportunity to be heard).

[24]Gray v. Union Cty. Intermediate Educ. Dist., 520 F.2d 803, 806 (9th Cir. 1975).

[25]*But see* Stodgill v. Wellston Sch. Dist., 512 F.3d 472 (8th Cir. 2008) (ruling that an employee's statements about cheating occurring under the superintendent's watch were not allegations of his dishonesty and therefore not stigmatizing enough to violate the superintendent's liberty interests); Stead v. Unified Sch. Dist., 92 F. Supp. 3d 1088 (D. Kan. 2015) (determining that a principal accused of testing violations had waived her rights under a state law—including the right to a name-clearing hearing—that would allow her to sustain a liberty interest claim).

[26]Ball v. Bd. of Trs., 584 F.2d 684, 685 (5th Cir. 1978).

sexual abuse, and extensive professional inadequacies.[27] Reasons held to pose no threat to a liberty interest include job-related comments, personality differences, difficulty in working with others, hostility toward authority, incompetence, aggressive behavior, ineffective leadership, and poor performance.[28] For example, an Illinois federal district court did not find a violation of a teacher's liberty interest.[29] The teacher was not renewed after the teacher's roommate had sex with a student; the district was concerned that the teacher had prior knowledge of her roommate's illegal behavior. The court reasoned that the teacher had failed to establish that the stigma of her nonrenewal precluded her from future employment because, within one year of her nonrenewal, she was able to secure a job in another district. **Charges relating to job performance may have an impact on future employment but do not create a stigma of constitutional magnitude.**

Liberty interests are not implicated unless damaging reasons are publicly communicated in the process of denying employment.[30] The primary purpose of a hearing is to enable individuals to clear their names. A protected liberty interest generally is affected only if the school board (rather than an individual, the media, or another source) publicizes the stigmatizing reasons. Accordingly, statements that are disclosed in a public meeting requested by the teacher or made by the teacher to the media or others do not require a name-clearing hearing. Likewise, rumors or hearsay remarks surfacing as a result of nonrenewal do not impair liberty interests.

PROCEDURAL REQUIREMENTS IN DISCHARGE PROCEEDINGS

When a liberty or property interest is implicated, the Fourteenth Amendment requires that an employee be notified of the charges and provided with an opportunity for a hearing that usually includes representation by counsel, examination and cross-examination of witnesses, and a record of the proceedings.

Because termination of a tenured or a nontenured employee during the contract period requires procedural due process, the central question becomes, what process is due? Courts have noted that no fixed set of procedures apply under all circumstances. Rather, due

[27]Donato v. Plainview-Old Bethpage Cent. Sch. Dist., 96 F.3d 623 (2d Cir. 1996) (extensive professional inadequacies); Vanelli v. Reynolds Sch. Dist., 667 F.2d 773 (9th Cir. 1982) (immoral conduct); Carroll v. Robinson, 874 P.2d 1010 (Ariz. Ct. App. 1994) (child sexual abuse); Knox v. N.Y.C. Dep't of Educ., 924 N.Y.S.2d 389 (App. Div. 2011) (dishonesty).

[28]Gilder-Lucas v. Elmore Cty. Bd. of Educ., 186 F. App'x 885 (11th Cir. 2006); Lybrook v. Members of Farmington Mun. Schs. Bd., 232 F.3d 1334 (10th Cir. 2000); Hayes v. Phx.-Talent Sch. Dist., 893 F.2d 235 (9th Cir. 1990).

[29]Wood v. Peoria Sch. Dist., 162 F. Supp. 3d 786 (C.D. Ill. 2016).

[30]*See, e.g.*, Vega v. Miller, 273 F.3d 460 (2d Cir. 2001); Vandine v. Greece Cent. Sch. Dist., 905 N.Y.S.2d 428 (App. Div. 2010); *see also* Segal v. City of N.Y., 459 F.3d 207 (2d Cir. 2006) (holding that placement of damaging statements in a teacher's personnel file can meet the public disclosure aspect of a stigma-plus claim; future employers may have access to the file).

process entails a balancing of the individual and governmental interests affected in each situation. Minimally, the Fourteenth Amendment requires that dismissal proceedings be based on established rules or standards. Actual procedures will depend on state law, school board regulations, and collective bargaining agreements, but they cannot drop below constitutional minimums. For example, a statute requiring tenured teachers to pay half the cost of a hearing that the school board must provide was found to impair federal rights.[31]

In assessing the adequacy of procedural safeguards, the judiciary looks for the provision of certain basic elements to meet constitutional guarantees.[32] **Courts generally have held that teachers facing a severe loss such as termination must be afforded full procedural due process** (see Figure 12.2).[33] Beyond the constitutional considerations, courts also strictly enforce any additional procedural protections conferred by state laws and local policies. Examples of such requirements might be providing detailed performance evaluations prior to termination, notifying teachers of weaknesses, and allowing an opportunity

FIGURE 12.2   Procedural Due Process in Termination Proceedings

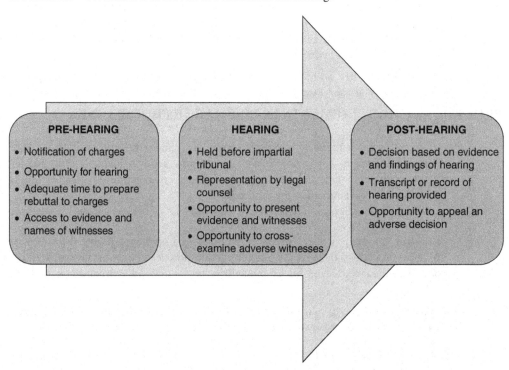

PRE-HEARING
- Notification of charges
- Opportunity for hearing
- Adequate time to prepare rebuttal to charges
- Access to evidence and names of witnesses

HEARING
- Held before impartial tribunal
- Representation by legal counsel
- Opportunity to present evidence and witnesses
- Opportunity to cross-examine adverse witnesses

POST-HEARING
- Decision based on evidence and findings of hearing
- Transcript or record of hearing provided
- Opportunity to appeal an adverse decision

[31]Rankin v. Indep. Sch. Dist., 876 F.2d 838 (10th Cir. 1989).

[32]At the same time, courts will not find a deprivation of procedural due process rights if educators do not avail themselves of the offered safeguards. *See, e.g.,* Segal, 459 F.3d 207; Christensen v. Kingston Sch. Comm., 360 F. Supp. 2d 212 (D. Mass. 2005).

[33]This chapter focuses on procedural protections required in teacher terminations. It should be noted, however, that other school board decisions (e.g., transfers, demotions, or mandatory leaves) may impose similar constraints on decision making.

for improvement before dismissal. Although failure to comply with these stipulations may invalidate the school board's action under state law, federal due process rights per se are not violated if minimal constitutional procedures are provided. Except in limited circumstances, individuals are required to exhaust administrative procedures or the grievance procedures specified in the collective bargaining agreement prior to seeking judicial review. Pursuing an administrative hearing promotes resolution of a controversy at the agency level. Exhaustion is not required before initiating a lawsuit, however, if administrative review would be futile or inadequate.

Discharged employees may allege that due process proceedings were insufficient. Questions arise regarding issues such as the appropriateness of notice, impartiality of the board members, and placement of the burden of proof. The aspects of procedural due process that courts frequently scrutinize in assessing the fundamental fairness of school board actions are examined next.

Notice of Charges

In general, a constitutionally adequate notice is timely, informs the employee of specific charges, and allows the employee sufficient time to prepare a response. Beyond the constitutional guarantees, state laws and regulations as well as school board policies usually impose very specific requirements relating to form, timeliness, and content of notice.[34] In legal challenges, the adequacy of notice is assessed in terms of whether it meets constitutional and other requirements. Failure to comply substantially with mandated requisites will void school board action.

The form or substance of notice is usually stipulated in state statutes. In determining appropriateness of notice, courts generally have held that substantial compliance with form requirements (as opposed to strict compliance required for notice deadlines) is sufficient. Under this standard, the decisive factor is whether the notice adequately informs the teacher of the pending action. For example, if a statute requires notification by certified mail and the notice is mailed by registered mail or is personally delivered, it substantially complies with the state requirement. Yet, oral notification will not suffice if the law requires written notification; similarly, emailed notice may also not be sufficient.[35] If the form of the notice is not specified by statute, any timely notice that informs a teacher is adequate.

For notice to comply with constitutional due process guarantees, reasonable efforts must be made for the employee to receive the notice. In a New York case, the board of education mailed the notice of intent to terminate a teacher's employment by certified and regular mail to an outdated address.[36] The regular mail copy was not returned, but the certified copy was returned as unclaimed. Consequently, the teacher argued he did not receive

---

[34]*See* Sajko v. Jefferson Cty. Bd. of Educ., 314 S.W.3d 290 (Ky. 2010) (interpreting a state law that requires a teacher challenging a dismissal to notify school officials within ten days of the receipt of termination notice to mean *actual* receipt—*not* postmarked within ten days).

[35]Angstadt v. Red Clay Consol. Sch. Dist., 4 A.3d 382 (Del. 2010).

[36]Norgrove v. Bd. of Educ., 881 N.Y.S.2d 802 (Sup. Ct. 2009); *see also* Taylor v. Huntsville Cty. Bd. of Educ., 143 So. 3d 219 (Ala. Civ. App. 2014) (reversing the lower court's assumption that certified mail was sufficient when the teacher was able to overcome the rebuttable presumption that the letter arrived).

the notice and could not request a hearing. The court held that the notice did not meet statutory requirements because the board of education was aware that the notice was returned as unclaimed and did not make additional efforts, such as hand delivery of the notice to the teacher in his classroom.

Although form and timeliness are important concerns in issuing notice, the primary consideration is the statement of reasons for an action. **With termination of a teacher's contract, school boards must bring specific charges against the teacher, including the factual basis for the charges**. State laws may impose further specifications, such as requirements that reasons for termination in the notice must be based on issues raised in prior written evaluations.[37] If the state law identifies grounds for dismissal, charges also must be based on the statutory causes. But a teacher cannot be forced to defend against vague and indefinite charges that simply restate the statutory categories, such as incompetency or neglect of duty. Notice must include specific accusations to enable the teacher to prepare a proper defense. The Arkansas Supreme Court interpreted its state Teacher Fair Dismissal Act as requiring sufficient notice "such that *a reasonable teacher* could defend against the reasons given."[38] Furthermore, only charges identified in the notice can form the basis for dismissal.

Hearing

In addition to notice, some type of hearing is required *before* **an employer makes the initial termination decision;** post-termination hearings do not satisfy federal constitutional due process requirements.[39] Courts have not prescribed in detail the procedures to be followed in administrative hearings. Basically, the fundamental constitutional requirement is fair play—that is, an opportunity to be heard at a meaningful time and in a meaningful manner. Beyond this general requirement, the specific aspects of a hearing are influenced by the circumstances of the case, with the potential for grievous losses necessitating more extensive safeguards. According to the Missouri Supreme Court, a hearing generally should include a meaningful opportunity to be heard, to state one's position, to present witnesses, and to cross-examine witnesses; the accused also has the right to counsel and access to written reports in advance of the hearing.[40] Implicit in these rudimentary requirements are the assumptions that the hearing will be conducted by an impartial decision maker and will result in a decision based

---

[37]*See, e.g.*, Hoffner v. Bismarck Pub. Sch. Dist., 589 N.W.2d 195 (N.D. 1999).

[38]Russell v. Watson Chapel Sch. Dist., 313 S.W.3d 1 (Ark. 2009).

[39]Cleveland Bd. of Educ. v. Loudermill, 470 U.S. 532 (1985); *see also* Curtis v. Montgomery Cty. Pub. Schs., 242 F. App'x 109 (4th Cir. 2007) (concluding that the predismissal process provided to a teacher, including notice that he was being investigated regarding serious allegations and placed on suspension, satisfied pre-termination rights).

[40]Valter v. Orchard Farm Sch. Dist., 541 S.W.2d 550 (Mo. 1976); *see also* McClure v. Indep. Sch. Dist., 228 F.3d 1205 (10th Cir. 2000) (holding that a teacher was deprived of due process rights when she was not allowed to cross-examine witnesses who provided testimony by affidavit at her termination hearing); Kimble v. State Bd. of Educ., 16 N.E.3d 169 (Ill. App. Ct. 2014) (ruling that a teacher accused of choking a student was denied due process when she was not able to cross-examine the student).

on the evidence presented. This section examines issues that may arise in adversarial hearings before the school board.

As noted, due process rights afford an individual the opportunity to be heard at a meaningful time. This implies sufficient time between notice of the hearing and the scheduled meeting. Unless state law designates a time period, the school board can establish a reasonable date for the hearing, taking into consideration the specific facts and circumstances. In a termination action, the school board would be expected to provide ample time for the teacher to prepare a defense, but the teacher bears the burden of requesting additional time if the length of notice is insufficient to prepare an adequate response.[41]

Although a hearing is an essential element of due process, a teacher can waive this right by failing to request a hearing, refusing to attend, or walking out of the hearing.[42] **Voluntary resignation of a position also waives an individual's entitlement to a hearing**. In some states, a hearing before the school board may be waived if an employee elects an alternative hearing procedure, such as a grievance mechanism or an impartial referee. For example, the Third Circuit held that an employee's choice of *either* a hearing before the school board *or* arbitration under the collective bargaining agreement met the constitutional requirements of due process; the school board was not required to provide the individual a hearing in addition to the arbitration proceeding.[43]

A central question raised regarding hearings is the school board's impartiality as a hearing body; however, the U.S. Supreme Court firmly established that **the school board is a proper review body to conduct dismissal hearings**.[44] This question of impartiality has arisen because school boards often perform multiple functions in a hearing; they may investigate the allegations against an employee, initiate the proceedings, and render the final judgment. Employees have contended that such expansive involvement violates their right to an unbiased decision maker. Rejecting the idea that combining the adjudicative and investigative functions violates due process rights, courts generally have determined that prior knowledge of the facts does not disqualify school board members.[45] In addition, the fact that the board makes the initial decision to terminate employment does not render its subsequent review impermissibly biased. Boards have also been permitted to conduct a preliminary inquiry to determine if there is a basis for terminating an employee. Because hearings are costly and time consuming, such a preliminary investigation may save time.

---

[41]Birdwell v. Hazelwood Sch. Dist., 491 F.2d 490 (8th Cir. 1974) (finding that a one-day notice was constitutionally sufficient when the teacher did not attend the meeting to raise objections).

[42]*See, e.g.*, Jefferson v. Sch. Bd., 452 F. App'x 356 (4th Cir. 2011); Miller v. Clark Cty. Sch. Dist., 378 F. App'x 623 (9th Cir. 2010).

[43]Pederson v. S. Williamsport Area Sch. Dist., 677 F.2d 312 (3d Cir. 1982).

[44]Hortonville Joint Sch. Dist. v. Hortonville Educ. Ass'n, 426 U.S. 482 (1976) (noting that the state legislature authorized school boards with decision making power and presumed boards will act with honesty and integrity); *see also* James v. Indep. Sch. Dist., 448 F. App'x 792 (10th Cir. 2011) (ruling that board members' previous criticisms of administrators' performance did not render them biased when they eliminated positions due to urgent financial conditions).

[45]*See, e.g.*, Withrow v. Larkin, 421 U.S. 35 (1975).

Although the school board is the proper hearing body, bias on the part of the board or its members is constitutionally unacceptable. An employee challenging the impartiality of the board has the burden of proving actual, not merely potential, bias.[46] This requires the employee to show more than board members' predecision involvement or prior knowledge of the issues.[47] A high probability of bias, however, can be shown if a board member has a personal interest in the outcome of the hearing or has suffered personal abuse or criticism from a teacher.[48]

Evidence.   Under tenure laws, the burden of proof is on the school board to show cause for dismissal. The standard of proof generally applied to administrative bodies is to produce a *preponderance of evidence*. Administrative hearings are not held to the more stringent standards applied in criminal proceedings (i.e., clear and convincing evidence beyond a reasonable doubt). Proof by a preponderance of evidence simply indicates that the majority of the evidence supports the board's decision or, as the New York high court stated, is "such relevant proof as a reasonable mind may accept as adequate to support a conclusion."[49] If the board fails to meet this burden of proof, the judiciary will not uphold the termination decision. For example, the Illinois appellate court, in overturning the board's dismissal decision, concluded that terminating a tenured teacher for immorality was against the manifest weight of evidence.[50]

Only relevant, well-documented evidence presented at the hearing can be the basis for the board's decision. Unlike formal judicial proceedings, hearsay evidence may be admissible in administrative hearings.[51] Courts have held that such evidence provides the background necessary for understanding the situation. Comments and complaints of parents have been considered relevant, but hearsay statements of students generally have been

---

[46]Seiden v. Adams, 150 So. 3d 1215 (Fla. Ct. App. 2014) (finding board's review was proper despite the fact that members had children with disabilities and the teacher's termination involved improper conduct toward students with disabilities).

[47]*See, e.g.*, Say v. Umatilla Sch. Dist. 6, 364 F. App'x 385 (9th Cir. 2010); Beischel v. Stone Bank Sch. Dist., 362 F.3d 430 (7th Cir. 2004).

[48]*See, e.g.*, McKee v. Peoria Unified Sch. Dist., 963 F. Supp. 2d 911 (D. Ariz. 2013) (refusing to dismiss a teacher's claim that the board was biased in part because it had a pecuniary interest in the outcome and was retaliating against the teacher for reporting safety issues after a student drowned); *Ex parte* Greenberg v. Ala. State Tenure Comm'n, 395 So. 2d 1000 (Ala. 1981) (invalidating a teacher's termination for intolerably high bias created by a board member's son testifying against the teacher).

[49]Altsheler v. Bd. of Educ., 464 N.E.2d 979, 979–80 (N.Y. 1984).

[50]Jackson v. Bd. of Educ., 53 N.E.3d 381 (Ill. App. Ct. 2016) (finding evidence of a teacher's falsification of employment application and failure to report cheating were insufficient grounds for termination); *see also* Schulz v. Bd. of Educ., 315 N.W.2d 633 (Neb. 1982) (holding dissatisfaction of parents was not sufficient evidence to substantiate incompetency charges against a teacher with above-average evaluations).

[51]*See, e.g.*, Colon v. City of N.Y. Dep't of Educ., 941 N.Y.S.2d 628 (App. Div. 2012); Drummond v. Todd Cty. Bd. of Educ., 349 S.W.3d 316 (Ky. Ct. App. 2011); *see also* Waisanen v. Clatskanie Sch. Dist., 215 P.3d 882 (Or. Ct. App. 2009) (holding that a student's polygraph exam results were admissible, particularly since the student was subject to cross-examination).

given little weight.[52] At the conclusion of the hearing, the board must make specific findings of fact; these written findings describe the rationale for the board's decision.[53]

DISMISSAL FOR CAUSE

Causes for dismissal vary widely among the states, but usually include such grounds as incompetency, immorality, insubordination, unprofessional conduct, neglect of duty, and other good and just cause.

The proper procedures for the termination of a school employee depends on the type of employee. Most public school employees can be classified as at-will, probationary, or tenured employees. At-will employees (e.g., bus drivers, cafeteria workers, paraprofessionals, temporary and substitute teachers) can be discharged at any time.[54] If policies such as the collective bargaining agreement do not require certain procedures to be followed, at-will employees can be dismissed for any legal reason but not for discriminatory or other unlawful grounds.[55] Probationary and tenured employees (e.g., teachers) are under contracts that specify a specific duration of their employment.

The employment rights of administrators (e.g., superintendents, principals, special education directors) and other school employees (e.g., nurses, social workers, school counselors) vary based on state law. For example, a principal challenged his dismissal claiming that he was not afforded proper due process according to the statutes pertaining to teacher termination.[56] The Indiana Supreme Court disagreed, reasoning that the principal's reliance on teacher termination statutes was improper because state law specifically addressed principal termination. Further, the school board provided sufficient due process because the procedures were substantially less in dismissing principals compared to teachers.

---

[52]*See, e.g.*, Daily v. Bd. of Educ., 588 N.W.2d 813 (Neb. 1999) (rejecting the lower court's decision that the school board had erroneously relied upon hearsay evidence); Gongora v. N.Y.C. Dep't of Educ., 930 N.Y.S.2d 757, 773 (Sup. Ct. 2010) (holding that a student's hearsay evidence of "uncertain reliability" was not a consideration in determining a preponderance of evidence; the student did not appear at the hearing, so the credibility of her statements could not be assessed).

[53]If an independent panel or hearing officer conducts the hearing, the board is bound by the panel's findings of fact but can accept or reject the panel's conclusions and recommendations. *See, e.g.*, Raitzik v. Bd. of Educ., 826 N.E.2d 568 (Ill. App. Ct. 2005).

[54]*See, e.g.*, W.Va. Bd. of Educ. v. Marple, 783 S.E.2d 75 (W. Va. 2015) (finding that a superintendent did not have a property interest in her employment, derivable from her employment contract, because she was an at-will employee). Private school employees and most charter school employees are at-will.

[55]*See* Alexander v. Lafayette Par. Sch. Bd., 7 So. 3d 135 (3d Cir. 2009) (holding that the school board had followed district policy in terminating nonprofessional employees and that teacher's assistant was not entitled to further procedural due process); *see also* Chapter 11 for discussion of employment discrimination claims that are available to at-will school employees.

[56]Hewitt v. Westfield Wash. Sch. Corp., 46 N.E.3d 425 (Ind. 2015).

Moreover, superintendents may also find that state statutes provide them with considerably fewer due process protections than teachers.[57] Administrators have been successful in challenging their terminations, however, when the school board has failed to follow state law (e.g., providing proper notice).[58]

Tenure laws are designed to assure competent teachers continued employment so long as their performance is satisfactory. **With the protection of tenure, a teacher can be dismissed only for cause and only in accordance with the procedures specified by law.** Tenure rights accrue under state laws and therefore must be interpreted in light of each state's provisions.[59] When grounds for dismissal of a permanent teacher are identified by statute, a school board cannot base dismissal on reasons other than those specified.[60] To cover unexpected matters, statutes often include a catchall phrase such as "other good and just cause." Causes included in statutes vary considerably among states and range from an extensive listing of individual grounds to a simple statement that dismissal must be based on cause. The most frequently cited causes are incompetency, immorality, and insubordination.

Since grounds for dismissal are determined by statute, it is difficult to provide generalizations that apply to all teachers. The causes are broad in scope and application; in fact, individual causes often have been attacked for impermissible vagueness. It is not unusual to find dismissal cases with similar factual situations based on different grounds. In addition, several grounds often are introduced and supported in a single termination case. Illustrative case law is examined here in relation to the more frequently cited grounds for dismissal.

Incompetency

The U.S. Supreme Court has defined incompetency as the "lack of ability, legal qualifications, or fitness to discharge the required duty."[61] Although incompetency has been challenged as unconstitutionally vague, courts have found the word sufficiently precise to give fair warning of prohibited conduct. These cases often involve issues relating to teaching methods, grading procedures, classroom management, and professional relationships.

[57]Poteat v. Harrisburg Sch. Dist., 3 F. Supp. 2d 384 (M.D. Penn. 1999) (granting school board's motion for summary judgment because the terminated superintendent did not have protected liberty or property interests at stake). Administrators have also been unsuccessful in their claims under federal law. *See* Royster v. Bd. of Trs., 774 F.2d 618 (4th Cir. 1985) (ruling that the terminated superintendent did not have a constitutional right to a pre-termination hearing because his contract was satisfied when he was fully compensated after his dismissal).

[58]Boss v. Fillmore Cty. Sch. Dist., 251 Neb. 669 (Neb. 1997) (holding that the superintendent's termination was improper in part because, under state law, he was to be provided periodic evaluations).

[59]*See* Educ. Comm'n of the States, *50-State Comparison: Teacher Tenure-Reasons for Dismissal* (May 2014), http://ecs.force.com/mbdata/mbquestRTL?rep=TT05; *see also* PBSNewshour, *Teacher Tenure Rules Are in State of Flux Across the Nation* (Nov. 29, 2014), http://www.pbs.org/newshour/updates/teacher-tenure-rules-state-flux/.

[60]Recent litigation has challenged the practice of providing teachers with tenure. *See, e.g.*, Vergara v. California, 209 Cal. Rptr. 3d 532 (Ct. App. 2016). State legislatures have also enacted legislation that reduces teacher tenure protections. *See* Derek Black, *The Constitutional Challenge to Teacher Tenure*, 104 CAL. L. REV. 75 (2016)*; see also* text accompanying note 48, Chapter 9.

[61]Beilan v. Bd. of Pub. Educ., 357 U.S. 399, 407 (1958).

Some states measure incompetency through results of teaching evaluations.[62] **Dismissals for incompetency are generally based on several factors or a pattern of behavior rather than isolated incidents**. Indicators of incompetency might include poor rapport with students, inappropriate use of class time, irrational grading of students, lack of student progress, and deficiencies in judgment and attitude. However, the Massachusetts Supreme Court determined that failure to meet an English fluency requirement did not justify one teacher's termination because the results of the teacher's fluency tests were unreliable.[63] Termination for incompetency usually requires school officials systematically to document a teacher's performance. Providing opportunities and support for a teacher to achieve expected performance standards can be an important component in substantiating that a teacher had adequate notice of deficiencies.

Immorality

Immorality, one common cause for dismissal, is typically not defined in state laws.[64] Although societal perceptions of what is considered immoral changes over time,[65] the judiciary has tended to interpret immorality broadly as unacceptable conduct that affects a teacher's fitness to teach.[66] **Teachers and school leaders are viewed as role models whose conduct is influential in shaping the lives of young students, so educators are held to a higher standard than required for the general public.**

Sexually related conduct per se between a teacher and student has consistently been held to constitute immoral conduct justifying termination of employment. The Supreme Court of Colorado stated that when a teacher engages in sexually provocative or exploitative conduct with students, "a strong presumption of unfitness arises against the teacher."[67] Similarly, a Washington appellate court found that a teacher's sexual relationship with a student justified dismissal and the board did not need to show an adverse effect on fitness to teach.[68]

---

[62]See, e.g., IND. CODE § 20-28-7.5-1(b)(3) (defining incompetency as being deemed "ineffective" on two consecutive performance evaluations or earning performance ratings of "ineffective or "improvement necessary" in three years of any five-year period); see also, Raitzik v. Bd. of Educ., 826 N.E.2d 568 (Ill. App. Ct. 2005) (affirming teacher's dismissal after she failed to complete a remediation plan that was prescribed after her negative evaluations).

[63]Sch. Comm. of Lowell v. Robishaw, 925 N.E.2d 803 (Mass. 2010).

[64]Expectations for teachers' morality may also be found in state professional code of ethics, which may carry the force of law. See Regina Umpstead et al., *Educator Ethics: A Comparison of Teacher Professional Responsibility Laws in Four States*, 42 J.L. & EDUC. 183 (2013).

[65]See John Rumel, *Beyond Nexus: A Framework for Evaluating K–12 Teacher Off-Duty Conduct and Speech in Adverse Employment and Licensure Proceedings*, 83 U. CIN. L. REV. 685 (2015) (discussing past teacher dismissals based on drinking alcohol, gambling, out-of-wedlock pregnancies, and cohabitation).

[66]See, e.g., McFerren v. Farrell Area Sch. Dist., 993 A.2d 344, 353–54 (Pa. Commw. Ct. 2010) (explaining that immoral behavior is more serious than unprofessional conduct and "moral standards of the community will not be presumed; they must be proved by substantial evidence").

[67]Weissman v. Bd. of Educ., 547 P.2d 1267, 1273 (Colo. 1976).

[68]Denton v. S. Kitsap Sch. Dist., 516 P.2d 1080 (Wash. Ct. App. 1973); see also Gongora v. N.Y.C. Dep't of Educ., 951 N.Y.S.2d 137 (App. Div. 2012) (finding that calling a student's home, asking the student out on a date, and urging the student not to report the call constituted sexual misconduct justifying the termination of a teacher).

Rather, the court concluded that when a teacher has an inappropriate relationship with a student, the conduct is unquestionably harmful to the school district. In upholding the termination of a teacher involved in a sexual relationship with a minor, the Supreme Court of Delaware declared that such sexual contact directly relates to a teacher's fitness to teach and affects the community.[69]

In addition to sexual improprieties with students, which are automatic grounds for dismissal, other conduct that sets a bad example for students may be considered immoral under the role model standard.[70] **Courts, however, generally have required school officials to show that an employee's misconduct—including out-of-school behavior—has had an adverse impact on fitness to teach**. They have recognized that allowing dismissal merely based on a showing of immoral behavior without consideration of the nexus between the conduct and fitness to teach would be an unwarranted intrusion on a teacher's right to privacy.

A California appellate court examined whether a teacher's immoral conduct rendered him unfit to teach.[71] In this case, the teacher, also a dean of students in a middle school, posted a sexually explicit ad with pornographic images of himself on Craigslist in the "men seeking men" category. An anonymous report to the local police led to the police notifying local school officials and the subsequent termination of the teacher. Although the teacher argued that no connection existed between his behavior and his teaching effectiveness, the appellate court disagreed, noting that at least one parent and several school officials had seen the ad. In upholding the termination, the court noted: "There are certain professions which impose upon persons . . . responsibilities and limitations on freedom of action which do not exist in regard to other callings."[72] The court also noted that judges, police officers, and teachers are in this category.[73]

In the past, LGBTQ teachers were sometimes dismissed under immorality statutes, but courts have been reluctant to support the dismissal of an LGBTQ educator simply because the school board does not approve of the teacher's sexual orientation. For example, an Ohio federal court concluded that the nonrenewal of a teacher because he was gay did not bear a rational relationship to a legitimate government purpose, thereby violating the Equal Protection Clause.[74]

---

[69]Lehto v. Bd. of Educ., 962 A.2d 222 (Del. 2008); *see also* Kansas v. Edwards, 288 P.3d 494 (Kan. Ct. App. 2012) (upholding the constitutionality of a statute that makes a sexual relationship between a teacher and a student a crime).

[70]Ambach v. Norwick, 441 U.S. 68, 77–78 (1979) (stating "a teacher serves as a role model for his students, exerting a subtle but important influence over their perceptions and values"); *see also* text accompanying note 157, Chapter 10.

[71]San Diego Unified Sch. Dist. v. Comm'n on Prof'l Competence, 124 Cal. Rptr. 3d 320 (Ct. App. 2011).

[72]*Id.* at 327.

[73]The California court cited a U.S. Supreme Court decision holding that a police officer could be terminated for selling sexually explicit videos of himself on eBay, establishing that termination for public distribution or posting of such material does not violate constitutional rights of public employees. *See* City of San Diego v. Roe, 543 U.S. 77 (2004).

[74]Glover v. Williamsburg Local Sch. Dist. Bd. of Educ., 20 F. Supp. 2d 1160 (S.D. Ohio 1998); *see also* text accompanying note 173, Chapter 10, and text accompanying note 46, Chapter 11.

In attempts to define immoral conduct, one court noted that it covers conduct "hostile to the welfare of the school community."[75] Such hostile conduct has included, among other things, dishonest acts, criminal behavior, and drug-related conduct. Specific actions substantiating charges of immorality have included misrepresenting absences from school as illness,[76] being involved in the sale of illegal drugs,[77] pleading guilty to grand larceny,[78] altering student transcripts,[79] reporting to school under the influence of marijuana,[80] fighting with a student,[81] and pressuring a student to give up her eleven-month-old child for adoption.[82] In addition to teachers, administrators have had their teaching certificates revoked on immorality grounds. For example, the Georgia appellate court upheld revocation of a principal's teaching credentials after she was fired for cheating on standardized tests.[83]

Employees have successfully challenged some dismissals based on immorality grounds. For example, a California appellate court found insufficient evidence to support a finding that a teacher's behavior was so immoral that it rendered him unfit to teach; a student had said that she felt "weird" when he touched her lower back, but there was no other evidence that anything immoral or inappropriate had occurred.[84] Another teacher was reinstated with back pay after a New York appellate court reasoned that her misconduct of engaging in sexual conduct with an adult colleague in an empty classroom after hours did not warrant termination.[85]

Although immorality is an abstract concept that can encompass broad-ranging behavior, it is understood to refer to actions that violate moral standards and render an educator unfit to teach. To justify termination for immorality, school officials must link the challenged conduct to impairment of the teacher's effectiveness in the classroom.

[75]Jarvella v. Willoughby-Eastlake City Sch. Dist., 233 N.E.2d 143, 145 (Ohio Com. Pl. 1967).

[76]Riverview Sch. Dist. v. Riverview Educ. Ass'n, 639 A.2d 974 (Pa. Commw. Ct. 1994).

[77]Woo v. Putnam Cty. Bd. of Educ., 504 S.E.2d 644 (W. Va. 1998); *see also* Westmoreland Intermediate Unit #7 v. Westmoreland Intermediate Unit #7 Classroom Assistants Educ. Support Pers. Ass'n, 72 A.3d 755 (Pa. Commw. Ct. 2013) (vacating an arbitrator's reinstatement of a classroom assistant who was recovering from a drug addiction, reasoning that elementary children should not be exposed to illegal drugs or those under the influence of drugs).

[78]Green v. N.Y.C. Dep't of Educ., 793 N.Y.S.2d 405 (App. Div. 2005); *see also* Patterson v. City of N.Y., 946 N.Y.S.2d 472 (App. Div. 2012) (finding misconduct justifying dismissal when a teacher provided an Albany address to avoid paying New York City income taxes).

[79]Hill v. Indep. Sch. Dist., 57 P.3d 882 (Okla. Civ. App. 2002); *see also* Gootee v. Sch. Bd., 201 So. 3d 115 (Fla. Dist. Ct. App. 2015) (rejecting teachers' claims that they should not have been dismissed for falsifying school records because their supervisor instructed them to do so).

[80]Younge v. Bd. of Educ., 788 N.E.2d 1153 (Ill. App. Ct. 2003).

[81]Watkins v. McDowell Cty. Bd. of Educ., 729 S.E.2d 822 (W. Va. 2012).

[82]Homa v. Carthage R-IX Sch. Dist., 345 S.W.3d 266 (Mo. Ct. App. 2011).

[83]Dukes-Walton v. Atlanta Indep. Sch. Sys., 784 S.E.2d 37 (Ga. Ct. App. 2016); *see also* Kinavey v. W. Jefferson Hills Sch. Dist., 2016 WL 3266301 (Pa. Commw. Ct. 2016) (upholding board's dismissal of a superintendent for dishonesty, plagiarism, and acting deceptively in an employment matter).

[84]San Diego Unified Sch. Dist. v. Comm'n on Prof'l Competence, 154 Cal. Rptr. 3d 751 (Ct. App. 2013).

[85]Mauro v. Walcott, 982 N.Y.S.2d 109 (App. Div. 2014).

Insubordination

Insubordination is generally defined as the willful disregard of or refusal to obey school regulations and official orders. Teachers can be dismissed for violation of administrative regulations and policies even though classroom performance is satisfactory; school officials are not required to establish a relationship between the insubordinate conduct and fitness to teach.

With the plethora of regulations enacted by school districts, wide diversity is found in the types of behavior adjudicated as insubordination. Dismissals based on insubordination have been upheld in cases involving refusal to abide by specific school directives, unwillingness to cooperate with superiors, unauthorized absences, and numerous other actions. Because conduct is measured against the existence of a rule or policy, a school board may more readily document insubordination than most other legal causes for dismissal.

Teachers cannot persistently ignore reasonable directives and policies of administrators or school boards. Many state laws and court decisions require that acts be "willful and persistent" to be considered insubordinate. A Florida teacher's continued refusal to provide lesson plans during school absences resulted in termination for insubordination. A Florida appellate court, affirming the dismissal, noted that insubordination under state law is "constant or continuing intentional refusal to obey a direct order, reasonable in nature, and given by and with proper authority."[86] A California appellate court upheld the termination of a tenured teacher for repeatedly refusing to pursue certification to teach English Learners required for all teachers.[87] The court ruled that it was within the school board's authority to impose this additional requirement.

A key determinant generally is whether the teacher has persisted in disobeying a *reasonable* school policy or directive. For example, if the school board has prohibited corporal punishment, teachers must strictly adhere to board requirements. In upholding the termination of a Colorado teacher, the state supreme court ruled that tapping a student on the head with a three-foot pointer supported termination when the teacher had been warned and disciplined previously for using physical force in violation of district policy.[88] The Eleventh Circuit found that insubordination was established when a teacher refused to undergo a drug test within two hours of the discovery of marijuana in her car in the school parking lot as required by school policy.[89] The Eighth Circuit upheld the dismissal

[86]Dolega v. Sch. Bd., 840 So. 2d 445, 446 (Fla. Dist. Ct. App. 2003); *see also* Miller v. Clark Cty. Sch. Dist., 378 F. App'x 623 (9th Cir. 2010) (holding that evidence showing prior warnings, admonitions, and suspensions established grounds to dismiss a teacher for insubordination); Chattooga Cty. Bd. of Educ. v. Searels, 691 S.E.2d 629 (Ga. Ct. App. 2010) (finding termination was justified when a teacher continued to make inappropriate statements about students after repeated warnings from her principal).

[87]Governing Bd. v. Comm'n on Prof'l Conduct, 99 Cal. Rptr. 3d 903 (Ct. App. 2009); *see also* Overton v. Bd. of Educ., 900 N.Y.S.2d 338, 339 (App. Div. 2010) (ruling that both misconduct and insubordination were established by the teacher's "pattern of poor work performance and disruptive behavior").

[88]Bd. of Educ. v. Flaming, 938 P.2d 151 (Colo. 1997). *But see* Principe v. N.Y.C. Dep't of Educ., 941 N.Y.S.2d 574 (App. Div. 2012) (finding the termination of a middle school dean of students for violating the policy against corporal punishment excessive when he physically restrained students in two separate incidents; the action was found not to be premeditated and was taken in his role as disciplinarian).

[89]Hearn v. Bd. of Pub. Educ., 191 F.3d 1329 (11th Cir. 1999), text accompanying note 154, Chapter 10.

of a teacher for violating a school board policy that prohibited students' use of profanity in the classroom; students had used profanity in various creative writing assignments such as plays and poems.[90]

The Supreme Court of New Hampshire, on the other hand, failed to find a school counselor insubordinate for violating policy and not following directives.[91] The counselor disagreed with the principal on the appropriate protocol for notifying the parents of a student seeking an abortion. The counselor was not renewed because she did not "go up the chain of command" by discussing the matter with superiors before seeking outside legal counsel. The court, however, reinstated the counselor, reasoning that the principal had not instructed the counselor to cease her efforts on behalf of the student and no clear policy instructed the counselor to contact the superintendent before an outside attorney. Similarly, a South Carolina appellate court did not determine that a teacher's disobedience of her supervisors' directives constituted a pattern of insubordination.[92] The teacher disregarded her principal's instructions by contacting the superintendent about a personnel matter, as well as communicating with a board member about another issue. The court did not believe these two acts coupled with past unprofessional conduct were "willful and persistent" enough to warrant dismissal.

Unprofessional Conduct

Some states identify either unprofessional conduct or conduct unbecoming a teacher as cause for dismissal. A teacher's activities both inside and outside of school can be used to substantiate this charge when it interferes with teaching effectiveness. Dismissals for unprofessional conduct, neglect of duty, and unfitness to teach often are based on quite similar facts. Facts that establish unprofessional conduct in one state may be deemed neglect of duty in another state. **Most courts have defined unprofessional conduct as actions directly related to the fitness of educators to perform in their professional capacity**.[93] The Supreme Court of Nebraska defined unprofessional conduct as breaching the rules or ethical code of a profession or "unbecoming a member in good standing of a profession." Under this definition, the court reasoned that a teacher had engaged in unprofessional conduct when he "smacked" a student on the head hard enough to make the student cry, thereby violating the state prohibition against corporal punishment.[94]

Courts have upheld dismissals for unprofessional conduct based on several grounds, such as taking photos of a female student nude above the waist,[95] engaging in sexual harassment of female students,[96] wrapping a student in an electrical cord and verbally humiliating

---

[90]Lacks v. Ferguson Reorganized Sch. Dist. R-2, 147 F.3d 718 (8th Cir. 1998); *see also* Haji v. Columbus City Schs., 621 F. App'x 309 (6th Cir. 2015) (upholding teacher's dismissal based on his repeated violations of attendance policy; he left school early to participate in services at a mosque without signing out).

[91]Appeal of Farmington Sch. Dist., 138 A.3d 496 (N.H. 2016).

[92]Toney v. Lee Cty. Sch. Dist., 797 S.E.2d 55 (S.C. Ct. App. 2017).

[93]*See, e.g.*, Fed. Way Sch. Dist. v. Vinson, 261 P.3d 145 (Wash. 2011).

[94]Daily v. Bd. of Educ., 588 N.W.2d 813, 824 (Neb. 1999) (affirming school board's decision to suspend teacher for thirty days).

[95]Dixon v. Clem, 492 F.3d 665 (6th Cir. 2007).

[96]Conward v. Cambridge Sch. Comm., 171 F.3d 12 (1st Cir. 1999).

him in front of other students,[97] losing complete control of the classroom,[98] engaging in inappropriate touching of students,[99] and showing a sexually explicit film to students without previewing it.[100]

As with dismissals based on incompetency, courts often require prior warning that the behavior may result in dismissal. In a case where an employee prevailed, a tenured teacher who had taught for twenty-seven years and had a reputation as a "great teacher" was dismissed based on one negative evaluation.[101] The district provided the teacher with an improvement plan, but it was not individualized to her needs as required by board policy.

Neglect of Duty

Neglect of duty arises when an educator fails to carry out assigned duties. This may involve an intentional omission or may result from ineffectual performance. The U.S. Supreme Court upheld the dismissal of an Oklahoma teacher for "neglect of duty" in failing to comply with the school board's continuing education requirement.[102] The Court reasoned that the dismissal was rationally related to the board's objective of improving its teaching force. In a Colorado case, neglect of duty was found when a teacher failed to discipline students consistent with school policy.[103] Similarly, the Louisiana high court ruled that a teacher repeatedly sending unescorted students to the principal's office in violation of school policy substantiated neglect of duty.[104]

Some court decisions involve employees who have engaged in a heightened level of willful disregard for the teaching profession. For example, a West Virginia teacher "willfully" neglected her duties by colluding with students to spray Axe Body cologne all over the classroom despite the fact that her co-teacher was sensitive to perfumes and had asked students to refrain from wearing them. The event became known as "Axe the Teacher Day," and one student testified that the purpose of the plan was to put the co-teacher back in the hospital so she could not teach anymore.[105]

[97]Johanson v. Bd. of Educ., 589 N.W.2d 815 (Neb. 1999).

[98]Walker v. Highlands Cty. Sch. Bd., 752 So. 2d 127 (Fla. Dist. Ct. App. 2000).

[99]*In re* Watt, 925 N.Y.S.2d 681 (App. Div. 2011).

[100]Fowler v. Bd. of Educ., 819 F.2d 657 (6th Cir. 1987).

[101]Harrison v. Shelby Cty. Bd. of Educ., 2016 WL 1250782 (Tenn. Ct. App. Mar. 30, 2016).

[102]Harrah Indep. Sch. Dist. v. Martin, 440 U.S. 194 (1979).

[103]Bd. of Educ. v. Flaming, 938 P.2d 151 (Colo. 1997); *see also* Flickinger v. Lebanon Sch. Dist., 898 A.2d 62 (Pa. Commw. Ct. 2006) (concluding that the principal's failure to respond immediately to a report of a gun in the middle school established willful neglect of duty; school procedures specified that such a crisis situation must be handled without delay).

[104]Wise v. Bossier Par. Sch. Bd., 851 So. 2d 1090 (La. 2003); *see also* Bellairs v. Beaverton Sch. Dist., 136 P.3d 93 (Or. Ct. App. 2006) (holding a teacher's failure to maintain a professional working relationship with students, parents, staff, and other teachers constituted neglect of duty).

[105]Smith v. Berkeley Cty. Bd. of Educ., 2015 WL 7628692, at *1 (W. Va. Nov. 20, 2015); *see also* Ragland v. Nash–Rocky Mount Bd. of Educ., 787 S.E.2d 422 (N.C. Ct. App. 2016) (upholding a teacher's dismissal after the teacher took off his shirt in anticipation of fighting an unruly student and then, on the next day, flirted with a female student about his muscles while stroking her hair).

A Louisiana appellate court agreed that a school board had ample evidence that a tenured teacher had neglected her duties. When the principal conducted an observation of the teacher, her classroom was unorganized, she was only grading her students based on participation (meaning that every student had an A+ in the course), and the students' behavior was "atrocious." [106] The teacher failed to report for work on parent-teacher conference day, violated testing protocols, failed to provide adequate lesson plans after being placed into an intensive assistance plan, and left pills unsecured on her desk.

The Nebraska high court, however, held that a superintendent's failure to file a funding form did not constitute neglect of duty to support the termination of his contract.[107] Likewise, a Louisiana appellate court held that a teacher's showing of an R-rated film did not warrant dismissal for neglect of duty.[108] In another case, the Louisiana Supreme Court concluded that a teacher bringing a loaded gun to school in his car did not substantiate willful neglect of duty to support termination.[109] The court commented that his action was certainly a mistake and possibly endangered students, but it did not involve a failure to follow orders or an identifiable school policy that required dismissal under state law.

Teachers can be discharged for neglect of duty when their performance does not meet expected professional standards. Often charges relate to a failure to perform but also can be brought for ineffective performance. Again, as with other efforts to terminate employment, documentation must substantiate that performance was unacceptable. One way school leaders can do this is by identifying known problems in improvement plans for employees and documenting the employees' efforts to remedy those issues.

Other Good and Just Cause

Not unexpectedly, "other good and just cause" as grounds for dismissal has frequently been challenged as vague and overbroad. Courts have been faced with the task of determining whether the phrase's meaning is limited to the specific grounds enumerated in the statute or whether it is a separate, expanded cause. An Indiana appellate court interpreted it as permitting termination for reasons other than those specified in the tenure law if evidence indicated that the board's decision was based on "good cause."[110] As such, dismissal of a teacher convicted of a misdemeanor was upheld even though the teacher had no prior

---

[106]Nickerson v. Webster Par. Sch. Bd., 152 So. 3d 247, 254 (La. Ct. App. 2014).

[107]Boss v. Fillmore Cty. Sch. Dist., 559 N.W.2d 448 (Neb. 1997). *But see* Smith v. Bullock Cty. Bd. of Educ., 906 So. 2d 938 (Ala. Civ. App. 2004) (ruling that a principal's failure to establish procedures to prevent the theft of about $25,000 of athletic funds was neglect of duty).

[108]Jones v. Rapides Par. Sch. Bd., 634 So. 2d 1197 (La. Ct. App. 1993); *see also* Beggs v. Bd. of Educ., 72 N.E.3d 288 (Ill. 2016) (invalidating dismissal of a teacher for arriving late for work and failing to submit lesson plans while she was taking care of her dying mother).

[109]Howard v. W. Baton Rouge Par. Sch. Bd., 793 So. 2d 153 (La. 2001) (identifying, in the dissenting opinion, the legislation mandating gun-free school zones). *But see* Sias v. Iberia Par. Sch. Bd., 74 So. 3d 800 (La. Ct. App. 2011) (ruling that the school board had sufficient evidence to substantiate willful neglect of duties when a principal was arrested for possession of various drugs, weapons, and counterfeit money in his house).

[110]Gary Teachers Union v. Sch. City of Gary, 332 N.E.2d 256, 263 (Ind. Ct. App. 1975); *see also* Hierlmeier v. N. Judson San Pierre Bd. of Sch. Trs., 730 N.E.2d 821 (Ind. Ct. App. 2000) (ruling that sexual harassment of female students and other inappropriate conduct toward students substantiated good and just cause for termination).

indication that such conduct was sufficient cause. A Connecticut court found good cause to be any ground put forward in good faith that is not "arbitrary, irrational, unreasonable, or irrelevant to the committee's task of building up and maintaining an efficient school system."[111] Terminating a teacher for altering students' responses on state mandatory proficiency tests was held to be relevant to that task.

The Supreme Court of Iowa relied on "just cause" to support the termination of a teacher for shoplifting.[112] Although she claimed that her compulsion to shoplift was related to a mental illness, the court found substantial evidence to dismiss the teacher's employment, weighing her position as a role model, the character of the illness, and the school board's needs. In a subsequent case, the Iowa high court ruled "just cause" existed to terminate a teacher who had knowledge of her son and his high school friends drinking at a campsite on her property. She failed to monitor their activities, and four students who left to buy more beer died in a car crash. The court agreed with the school board that the teacher's effectiveness as a role model was significantly diminished.[113] A principal's ability to lead was similarly compromised when he had a consensual sexual relationship with a subordinate teacher.[114] The Indiana Supreme Court held that the board's decision to discharge him was based on just cause.

Reduction-in-Force

In addition to dismissal for causes related to teacher performance and fitness, legislation generally permits the release of teachers for reasons related to declining enrollment, financial exigency, and school district consolidation. Whereas most state statutes provide for such terminations, some states have adopted legislation that specifies the basis for selection of released teachers, procedures to be followed, and provisions for reinstatement. These terminations, characterized as reduction-in-force (RIF), also may be governed by board policies and negotiated collective bargaining agreements.

Unlike other termination cases, the employee challenging a RIF decision shoulders the burden of proof. There is a presumption that the board has acted in good faith with permissible motives. Legal controversies in this area usually involve questions related to the necessity for the reductions, board compliance with mandated procedures, and possible subterfuge for impermissible termination (such as denial of constitutional rights, subversion of tenure rights, or discrimination). For example, an Alabama trial court reversed a hearing officer's decision to reinstate an employee who was terminated under a RIF plan.[115] The hearing officer reinstated the employee reasoning that the board failed to provide specific evidence that firing the employee would yield significant savings for the district; however, the trial court explained that the board only needed to show the district had a general financial need and that there was not an improper motive behind the employee's termination.

---

[111]Hanes v. Bd. of Educ., 783 A.2d 1, 6 (Conn. App. Ct. 2001) (referencing Rinaldo v. Sch. Comm. of Revere, 1 N.E.3d 37 (Mass. 1936)).

[112]Bd. of Dirs. v. Davies, 489 N.W.2d 19 (Iowa 1992).

[113]Walthart v. Bd. of Dirs., 694 N.W.2d 740 (Iowa 2005).

[114]Hewitt v. Westfield Wash. Sch. Corp., 46 N.E.3d 425 (Ind. 2015).

[115]Huntsville City Bd. of Educ. v. Johnson, 140 So. 3d 469 (Ala. Civ. App. 2014).

If statutory or contractual restrictions exist for teacher layoffs, there must be substantial compliance with the provisions. Often policies dictate a method for selecting which teachers will be laid off. **Traditionally, reductions were based on seniority, and a tenured teacher, rather than a nontenured teacher, was retained if both were qualified to fill the same position; but some districts are now using teachers' evaluation ratings in RIF determinations.** Therefore, some state statutes clarify that not only seniority, but also evaluation ratings may be included in the determination of reductions. To illustrate, a tenured teacher challenged her dismissal that was part of a RIF plan arguing that she had a right to be recalled before the nontenured teachers who were also part of the RIF. She also claimed that she had a right to be recalled before a new teacher was hired to fill her former position. An Illinois appellate court upheld the tenured teacher's dismissal reasoning that her recent unsatisfactory performance rating was a legitimate reason for the district to choose not to recall her (despite her tenured status).[116]

Both the Montana and Nebraska high courts concluded that school boards have broad discretion in deciding what factors to use in their RIF policies and how to weigh those factors.[117] Guidelines or criteria established by state or local education agencies, however, must be applied in a uniform and nondiscriminatory manner. For example, in a New Mexico case, the school board was required to determine that no alternative positions existed for teachers targeted for release.[118]

The Fourteenth Amendment requires procedural protections in dismissals for cause, but courts have not clearly defined the due process requirements for RIFs. The Eighth Circuit noted that tenured teachers possess a property interest in continued employment and thereby must be provided notice and an opportunity to be heard.[119] The Eighth Circuit emphasized that the law protected the released teacher, who, subject to qualifications, was entitled to the next vacancy. Similarly, a Pennsylvania commonwealth court held that a hearing must be provided to assure the teacher (1) that termination was for reasons specified by law and (2) that the board followed the correct statutory procedures in selecting the teacher for discharge.[120]

State law or other policies may give employment preference to teachers who are released because of a RIF. Typically, under such requirements, a school board cannot hire a nonemployee until each qualified teacher on the preferred recall list is reemployed.[121] Although statutes often require that teachers be appointed to the first vacancy for which

[116]Segobiano-Morris v. Grayslake Cmty. Consol. Sch. Dist., 34 N.E.3d 584 (Ill. App. Ct. 2015).

[117]Scobey Sch. Dist. v. Radakovich, 135 P.3d 778 (Mont. 2006); Nickel v. Saline Cty. Sch. Dist., 559 N.W.2d 480 (Neb. 1997).

[118]Aguilera v. Bd. of Educ., 132 P.3d 587 (N.M. 2006).

[119]Boner v. Eminence R-1 Sch. Dist., 55 F.3d 1339 (8th Cir. 1995).

[120]Fatscher v. Bd. of Sch. Dirs., 367 A.2d 1130 (Pa. Commw. Ct. 1977).

[121]*See* Davis v. Chester Upland Sch. Dist., 786 A.2d 186 (Pa. 2001) (ruling that teachers who challenged the school district's failure to recall them must exhaust collective bargaining grievance procedures before filing for judicial review). *But see* Chi. Teachers Union v. Bd. of Educ., 476 F. App'x 83 (7th Cir. 2012) (vacating an injunction after the Supreme Court of Illinois ruled that teachers had no recall rights under the state law; such rights would exist only if specified in the negotiated agreement).

they are licensed and qualified, courts have held that reappointment is still at the board's discretion. In addition, a board is generally not obligated to realign or rearrange teaching assignments to create a position for a released teacher.

REMEDIES FOR VIOLATIONS OF PROTECTED RIGHTS

Wrongfully terminated employees may be entitled to compensatory and punitive damages, reinstatement with back pay, and attorneys' fees for the violation of their constitutional rights.

When it can be established that school districts or officials have violated an employee's rights that are protected by law, several remedies are available to the aggrieved individual. In some situations, the employee may seek a court *injunction* ordering the unlawful action to cease (e.g., when the district has unconstitutionally restrained teacher's expression). Where terminations, transfers, or other adverse employment consequences have been unconstitutionally imposed, courts will order school districts to return the employees to their original status with back pay. Educators also can bring damages suits for actions that violate their federally protected rights under Section 1983 of the Civil Rights Act of 1871 (Section 1983).

Liability of School Officials

In Section 1983 claims, public school employees acting under color of state law can be held personally liable for actions that violate students' or teachers' federal constitutional or statutory rights (e.g., racial discrimination).[122] Suits seeking damages under Section 1983 can be initiated in federal or state courts, and exhaustion of state administrative remedies is not required before initiating a federal suit.[123]

School officials, however, cannot be held liable under Section 1983 for the actions of their subordinates, thus rejecting the doctrine of respondeat superior, even when school officials have general supervisory authority over the activities of the wrongdoers. In order to be found liable, the officials must have personally participated in or had personal knowledge of the unlawful acts or promulgated official policy under which the acts were taken.[124]

[122]Maine v. Thiboutot, 448 U.S. 1 (1980).

[123]When a federal law requires a nondamages remedy, however, a § 1983 suit is precluded. *See, e.g.,* Gonzaga Univ. v. Doe, 536 U.S. 273 (2002). The Supreme Court, however, has ruled that damages can be sought under § 1983 for Fourteenth Amendment equal protection violations if a federal statute lacks an expressed private remedy. Specifically, the Court held that Title IX of the Education Amendments of 1972 does not preclude individuals from also pursuing a § 1983 damages claim for unconstitutional sex discrimination under the Equal Protection Clause, Fitzgerald v. Barnstable Sch. Comm., 555 U.S. 246 (2009).

[124]*See* Ashcroft v. Iqbal, 556 U.S. 662 (2009); Am. Mfrs. Mut. Ins. Co. v. Sullivan, 526 U.S. 40 (1999); Rizzo v. Goode, 423 U.S. 362 (1976).

Furthermore, school officials are absolutely immune from suit under Section 1983 for their legislative activities.[125] These actions involve discretionary policy-making decisions and enactment of regulations. Subsequently, courts have clarified that employment decisions related to individual employees (such as hiring, dismissal, or demotion) are administrative, not legislative, in nature.[126]

In some circumstances, school officials can claim qualified immunity to avoid personal liability.[127] In 2002, the Supreme Court emphasized that the overriding issue regarding qualified immunity was whether the law at the time an individual acted gave "clear and fair warning" that rights were established.[128] The "clear and fair warning" standard, however, has resulted in a range of interpretations by lower courts.[129] Additionally, school officials have been denied qualified immunity when they have disregarded well-established legal principles in areas such as due process, protected expression, and privacy.[130] Public officials are not expected to predict the future course of constitutional law, but they are expected to adhere to principles of law that were *clearly established* at the time of the violation.

Liability of School Districts

In 1978, the Supreme Court ruled that local governments are considered "persons" under Section 1983.[131] **In essence, school districts can be assessed damages when action taken pursuant to official policy violates federally protected rights**. To prevail against a school district, an individual must present evidence that the district acted with deliberate indifference in establishing and maintaining a policy, practice, or custom that directly deprived an individual of his or her constitutionally protected rights.

The school district (like the school official) cannot be held liable under the respondeat superior doctrine for the wrongful acts committed solely by its employees. Liability against the school can be imposed when an individual with final authority follows a district

---

[125]Bogan v. Scott-Harris, 523 U.S. 44 (1998).

[126]*See, e.g.*, Canary v. Osborn, 211 F.3d 324 (6th Cir. 2000); Harhay v. Town of Ellington Bd. of Educ., 323 F.3d 206 (2d Cir. 2003).

[127]Harlow v. Fitzgerald, 457 U.S. 800, 818 (1982) (ruling that "government officials performing discretionary functions generally are shielded from liability for civil damages insofar as their conduct does not violate clearly established statutory or constitutional rights of which a reasonable person would have known"); *see also* Filarsky v. Delia, 566 U.S. 377 (2012) (unanimously ruling that a private individual employed by the government to perform a job can claim qualified immunity from suit under § 1983).

[128]Hope v. Pelzer, 536 U.S. 730 (2002); *see also* Ashcroft v. al-Kidd, 563 U.S. 731, 743 (2011) (holding that qualified immunity gives officials "breathing room to make reasonable but mistaken judgments about open legal questions"; if properly applied, "it protects 'all but the plainly incompetent or those who knowingly violate the law'" (quoting Malley v. Briggs, 475 U.S. 335, 341 (1986))).

[129]*See* Safford Unified Sch. Dist. v. Redding, 557 U.S. 364, 378 (2009) (granting immunity to school officials who had strip searched a student because of the divergent lower court rulings about searching students); *see also* Pearson v. Callahan, 555 U.S. 223 (2009) (granting lower courts discretion to consider whether immunity exists prior to considering the alleged constitutional violation).

[130]*See, e.g.*, Evans-Marshall v. Bd. of Educ., 428 F.3d 223 (6th Cir. 2005); Baird v. Bd. of Educ., 389 F.3d 685 (7th Cir. 2004).

[131]Monell v. Dep't of Soc. Servs., 436 U.S. 658 (1978).

policy that impairs a federally protected right.[132] School districts also cannot claim qualified immunity based on good faith actions of their officials.[133] To avoid liability for constitutional violations, school districts have introduced claims of Eleventh Amendment immunity; under this amendment, citizens of one state are prohibited from suing another state without its consent.[134] School districts have asserted Eleventh Amendment protection based on the fact that they perform a state function. Admittedly, education is a state function, but it does not necessarily follow that courts will grant school districts Eleventh Amendment immunity. For the Eleventh Amendment to be invoked in a suit against a school district, the state must be the "real party in interest."[135]

Remedies

When districts violate employees' rights, courts order remedies depending on employment status (e.g., tenure), court discretion, and federal and state law. Statutes often identify the type and limitation of the damages that may be recovered. Unless these provisions restrict specific remedies, courts have broad discretionary power to formulate equitable settlements.

Damages.   If a school official or school district is found liable for violating protected rights, damages are assessed to compensate the employee for the injury. **Actual injury, however, must be shown for the employee to recover damages; without evidence of monetary or psychological injury, the plaintiff is entitled only to nominal damages (not to exceed one dollar), even though an impairment of protected rights is established.**[136] Significant monetary damages may be awarded if an employee is able to

---

[132]*See, e.g.*, Collins v. City of Harker Heights, 503 U.S. 115 (1992); Seamons v. Snow, 206 F.3d 1021 (10th Cir. 2000).

[133]Owen v. City of Independence, 445 U.S. 622 (1980) (acknowledging that under certain circumstances, sovereign immunity can shield districts from tort suits, but concluding that § 1983 abrogated governmental immunity in situations involving the impairment of federally protected rights). *See* text accompanying note 43, Chapter 2, for a discussion of governmental immunity under tort law.

[134]*See* Hans v. Louisiana, 134 U.S. 1 (1890); *see also* Will v. Mich. Dep't of State Police, 491 U.S. 58 (1989) (holding that § 1983 does not permit a suit against a state; Congress did not intend the word "person" to include states). A state can waive this immunity by specifically consenting to be sued, and Congress can abrogate state immunity through legislation if the federal legislation explicitly states this.

[135]Mt. Healthy City Sch. Dist. v. Doyle, 429 U.S. 274 (1977) (determining that districts are more like counties or cities than extensions of the state and thus, Eleventh Amendment immunity does not shield them from liability); *see also* Adams v. Recovery Sch. Dist., 463 F. App'x 297 (5th Cir. 2012). *But see* Belanger v. Madera Unified Sch. Dist., 963 F.2d 248 (9th Cir. 1992) (holding that California school boards are indivisible agencies of the state and thus entitled to Eleventh Amendment immunity).

[136]*See* Farrar v. Hobby, 506 U.S. 103 (1992) (concluding that an award of nominal damages is mandatory when a procedural due process violation is established but no actual injury is shown); Carey v. Piphus, 435 U.S. 247 (1978) (holding that pupils who were denied procedural due process in a disciplinary proceeding would be entitled only to nominal damages unless it was established that lack of proper procedures resulted in actual injury to the students).

demonstrate substantial losses. At the same time, individuals must make an effort to mitigate damages by seeking appropriate employment.[137] In illustrative cases, an Illinois teacher received $750,000 in compensatory damages for her wrongful termination based on an out-of-wedlock pregnancy,[138] and a North Carolina teacher received $78,000 in damages based on mental distress following procedural violations in his termination.[139]

In some instances, employees have sought punitive as well as compensatory damages.[140] School officials can be liable for punitive damages (to punish the wrongdoer) if a jury concludes that the individual's conduct is willful or in reckless and callous disregard of federally protected rights.[141] **Section 1983 only authorizes the award of punitive damages against individual wrongdoers and not a municipality.**[142] Therefore, school officials, but not school districts, can be sued for punitive damages.

Reinstatement. When a tenured teacher is unjustly dismissed, the property interest gives rise to an expectation of reemployment; reinstatement in such instances is usually the appropriate remedy. A nontenured teacher, wrongfully dismissed during the contract period, however, is normally entitled only to damages, not reinstatement unless the termination involves the violation of a constitutionally protected right.

A valid property or liberty claim entitles a teacher to procedural due process, but the teacher can still be dismissed for cause after proper procedures have been followed. If a nontenured teacher who has been nonrenewed can prove that the actual reason for nonrenewal is retaliation for the exercise of constitutional rights (e.g., protected speech), reinstatement would be warranted, although substantiation of such a claim is difficult.[143] Additionally, districts' failure to comply with statutory requirements in nonrenewals and dismissals may result in reinstatement. For example, a Pennsylvania teacher was terminated for cursing and discussing sexual topics with students; yet, due to the district's failure to follow required procedures—such as holding a termination hearing—he was entitled to

---

[137]*See* Hecht v. Nat'l Heritage Acads., Inc., 886 N.W.2d 135 (Mich. 2016) (vacating a jury's award of future damages because the trial court erred in admitting evidence on an employer's discloser of the employee's unprofessional conduct to a prospective employer).

[138]Eckmann v. Bd. of Educ., 636 F. Supp. 1214 (N.D. Ill. 1986).

[139]Crump v. Bd. of Educ., 392 S.E.2d 579 (N.C. 1990).

[140]Compensatory damages may include back pay for wages lost due to wrongful termination. *See* Everhart v. Bd. of Educ., 660 F. App'x 228 (D. Md. 2016) (awarding teacher $198,170 as back pay after teacher was wrongfully discharged for complaining about racial harassment).

[141]*See* Smith v. Wade, 461 U.S. 30 (1983)*; see also* Pac. Mut. Life Ins. Co. v. Haslip, 499 U.S. 1 (1991) (refusing to limit the amount of punitive damages that properly instructed juries may award in common law suits, unless unacceptable under the Due Process Clause of the Fourteenth Amendment); Ciccarelli v. Sch. Dep't, 877 N.E.2d 609 (Mass. App. Ct. 2007) (upholding a $50,000 punitive damages award to a provisional teacher who was not rehired after her name appeared on a witness list for another teacher who had filed a sex discrimination complaint).

[142]City of Newport v. Fact Concerts, 453 U.S. 247 (1981) (reasoning that punitive damages are intended to deter individuals from similar conduct and not to punish taxpayers).

[143]*But see* Capece v. Schultz, 986 N.Y.S.2d 533 (App. Div. 2014) (holding that a probationary teacher, who was also a union leader, was entitled to reinstatement and back pay after her principal retaliated against her).

reinstatement.[144] If a state statute lists the deadline when districts must provide teachers notice of nonrenewal, failure to comply strictly with the deadline provides grounds for reinstatement of the teacher. In contrast to the remedy for lack of proper notice, the remedy for failure to provide an appropriate hearing is generally a remand for a hearing, not reinstatement.[145]

Attorneys' Fees.   Attorneys' fees are not automatically granted to the teacher who prevails in a lawsuit, but are dependent on statutory authorization.[146] In congressional debate concerning attorneys' fees, it was stated: "Private citizens must be given not only the rights to go to court but also the legal resources. If the citizen does not have the resources, his day in court is denied him."[147]

To receive attorneys' fees, the teacher must be the prevailing party; that is, damages or some form of equitable relief must be granted to the teacher. A prevailing party is one who is successful in achieving some benefit on any significant issue in the case, but not necessarily the primary issue.[148] If a plaintiff achieves only partial success, the fees requested may be reduced. A plaintiff who prevails in a civil rights suit may, at the court's discretion, be entitled to attorneys' fees, but the same standard is not applied to defendants. Such fees cannot be imposed on a plaintiff unless the claim was "frivolous, unreasonable, or groundless."[149] Although uncommon for defendants to be awarded damages, awards have been made to deter plaintiffs from filing groundless lawsuits.

CONCLUSION

Through state laws and the U.S. Constitution, extensive safeguards protect educators' job security. Most states have adopted tenure laws that precisely delineate teachers' employment rights in termination and disciplinary proceedings. Furthermore, in the absence of specific state guarantees, the Fourteenth Amendment ensures that teachers will be afforded procedural due process when property or liberty interests are implicated. At a minimum, the

[144]Sch. Dist. of Phila. v. Jones, 139 A.3d 358 (Pa. Commw. Ct. 2016); *see also* McDaniel v. Princeton City Sch. Dist., 45 F. App'x 354 (6th Cir. 2002) (awarding reinstatement, back wages, and attorneys' fees for a total award of $172,675 after wrongful termination).

[145]*See* Snowden v. Adams, 814 F. Supp. 2d 854 (C.D. Ill. 2011) (noting that an inadequate name-clearing hearing may entitle an individual to compensatory damages when remand for another hearing would be too late to remedy the damage to reputation).

[146]The Civil Rights Attorneys' Fees Award Act gives federal courts discretion to award fees in federal civil rights suits, 42 U.S.C. § 1988(b) (2018).

[147]122 CONG. REC. 33,313 (1976).

[148]Tex. State Teachers Ass'n v. Garland Indep. Sch. Dist., 489 U.S. 782 (1989).

[149]Christiansburg Garment Co. v. EEOC, 434 U.S. 412, 422 (1978); *see also* Jefferson v. Jefferson Cty. Pub. Sch. Sys., 360 F.3d 583 (6th Cir. 2004); Potlatch Educ. Ass'n v. Potlatch Sch. Dist., 226 P.3d 1277 (Idaho 2010).

employee is entitled to notice of the charges and an opportunity to be heard. The following generalizations reflect the current status of the law on the topics covered in this chapter.

1. Tenure status, defined by state law, confers upon teachers a property interest in continued employment; tenured teachers can be dismissed only for cause specified in state law.

2. Probationary employment generally does not involve a property interest, except within the contract period.

3. If nonrenewal implicates a constitutional right, imposes a significant stigma, or forecloses opportunities for future employment, then a probationary employee may establish a liberty interest in receiving procedural due process.

4. Once a property or liberty interest has been implicated, employees must be provided procedural due process (i.e., notification of charges, hearing, representation by counsel, examination and cross-examination of witnesses, and record of proceedings); however, formal trial procedures are not required.

5. School boards are considered impartial hearing tribunals unless bias of its members can be clearly established.

6. In a dismissal hearing, the board bears the burden of proof to introduce sufficient evidence to support the employee's dismissal.

7. Causes for dismissal vary widely among the states, but usually include such grounds as incompetency, neglect of duty, immorality, insubordination, unprofessional conduct, and other good and just cause.

8. Incompetency is generally defined in relation to classroom performance—including, classroom management, teaching methods, grading, student/teacher relationships, and general attitude.

9. Immorality includes dishonesty, sexual misconduct, criminal acts, and other improprieties that have a negative impact on teaching effectiveness.

10. Dismissal for insubordination is based on an employee's refusal to follow school policies and the supervisor's directives.

11. Reduction-in-force is permissible with declining enrollment and financial exigencies.

12. Wrongfully terminated employees can seek the following remedies: reinstatement with back pay, compensatory and punitive damages, and attorneys' fees.

13. Punitive damages to punish the wrongdoer are available against individual school officials, but not against districts.

CHAPTER THIRTEEN

ALTERNATIVES TO INCREASE EDUCATIONAL CHOICE

Are charter schools public schools? Do parents have to satisfy state standards if they want to educate their children at home? Can parents send their children to private schools at public expense? These and related questions are being raised due to an increased focus on offering educational options for families—a movement commonly referred to as *school choice*. While some alternatives to traditional public schools, such as charter schools, are being provided under the public education umbrella,[1] other options use public funds for students to pursue private education.[2] This chapter addresses charter schools, home schooling, and various strategies to expand private educational choices for families in our nation.

Readers of this chapter should be able to:

- Explain the rationale for establishing charter schools and controversial issues involving these schools.

- Describe how states regulate home schooling.

- Discuss vouchers, tax-credit scholarships, and education savings account programs that allow public funds to flow to private education.

- Analyze federal and state challenges to state efforts to increase family access to private education.

---

[1]Other strategies to increase options *within* public education include intra-district open enrollment plans, under which students can attend any school within the district; inter-district open enrollment, allowing students to cross district lines; magnet schools that offer specialized curricula not available in the neighborhood schools, such as a math/science magnet; career and technical schools; alternative schools for students exhibiting particular risk factors; and schools designed for students with specific disabilities, such as hearing loss.

[2]Of the 98,176 public schools in 2014–2015, there were an estimated 89,386 regular public, 6,747 charter, 5,449 alternative, 1,954 special education, and 1,387 career and technical schools. That same year, there were an additional 33,619 nonpublic (private) schools in operation. Nat'l Ctr. for Educ. Statistics, *Table 216.20: Number and Enrollment of Public Elementary and Secondary Schools, by School Level, Type, and Charter and Magnet Status: Selected Years, 1990–91 through 2014–15*, U.S. Dep't of Educ. (Oct. 2016); Nat'l Ctr. for Educ. Statistics, *Number of Private Schools, Students, and Teachers (Headcount), by School Membership in Private School Associations: United States, 2013–14*, U.S. Dep't of Educ. (n.d.).

CHARTER SCHOOLS

> Although charter schools are considered public schools, they share some features with private schools.

Charter schools are given additional flexibility to innovate while at the same time being held accountable for student achievement. Charter schools are exempt from many of the regulations and statutes that apply to other public schools. A significant difference is that the charter is a performance contract, which establishes the school's mission and goals. If the charter school does not meet the requirements specified in its charter, it could be closed by the school's authorizer or sponsor.

Charter schools first emerged in the early 1990s following a call from Al Shanker, President of the American Federation of Teachers, for more innovative schooling models.[3] Since 2000, charter schools have grown both in number and their impact on education in our nation. In 2016–2017, there were 6,900 charter schools serving over 3.1 million students in forty-four states.[4] **States vary as to what entities, such as school districts, mayors, and universities, can authorize charter schools, and they differ regarding the number allowed (commonly referred to as charter school caps[5]).** Additionally, states reflect a range as to who may submit charter applications and what state regulations apply to charter schools. Charter schools can stand alone, be part of a local school district, or be part of a charter school network. Increasingly, charter management organizations are overseeing networks of charter schools that reflect particular philosophies and instructional approaches, but many single-school charters exist. Most charter school teachers and administrators are considered at-will employees, which means that they can be dismissed at any time without reason. Some charter school teachers have begun to unionize, which provides greater employee protections.[6]

A body of law is starting to emerge in which charter schools are asserting specific rights, while others are contesting charter school practices.[7] State charter school laws require that the schools be free and open to all students. Many state charter school laws allow schools to give preference using selection criteria such as sibling attendance, prox-

---

[3]Richard Kahlenberg & Halley Potter, *The Original Charter School Vision*, N.Y. TIMES (Aug. 30, 2014), https://www.nytimes.com/2014/08/31/opinion/sunday/albert-shanker-the-original-charter-school-visionary.html?mcubz=1.

[4]Nat'l All. for Pub. Charter Schs., *Estimated Charter Public School Enrollment 2016–2017* (Feb. 1, 2017), http://www.publiccharters.org/wp-content/uploads/2017/01/EER_Report_V5.pdf.

[5]For a state-by-state comparison of laws regarding charter school caps, *see* Nat'l All. of Pub. Charter Schs., *No Caps* (2017), http://www.publiccharters.org/law-database/caps/.

[6]*See* Emmanuel Felton, *Unionization of Charter Schools: Where the Movement Stands Now*, EDUC. WK. (Apr. 21, 2017), http://blogs.edweek.org/edweek/teacherbeat/2017/04/where_the_charter_school_union.html.

[7]Suzanne Eckes & Regina Umpstead, *Charter Schools and Legal Issues*, *in* THE WILEY HANDBOOK OF SCHOOL CHOICE (Fox & Buchanan, eds., 2017).

imity to school, and/or parents who helped develop the school or are working at it. They also typically require a random selection process or lottery for admission to charter schools that are oversubscribed.

However, due to the increased flexibility that charter schools have to experiment within public education, charter school personnel have more freedom than traditional public school authorities to recruit a certain population of students. This additional leeway has led to the creation of some charter schools designed to attract specific populations related to culture, language, religion, ability level, or other characteristics. Thus, it is not surprising that there have been legal challenges related to racial and ethnic aspects of charter schools,[8] student ability,[9] and religious issues in charter schools.[10]

Additionally, even though charter schools are considered public schools, there has been litigation that raises questions about whether they are actually public. For example, an Arizona teacher's contract was not renewed after there were some concerns about suspicious phone contacts he had with a female student. The teacher sued the charter school and alleged that his liberty interests in being able to find and obtain work were violated under Section 1983 of the Civil Rights Act of 1871, which allows lawsuits for damages for the violation of federally protected rights.[11] Like many charter schools throughout the United States, a private, non-profit management company ran this particular charter school. At issue in this case was whether the charter school was a state actor under Section 1983. Upholding the district court's dismissal of the case, the Ninth Circuit found that although a private entity might be considered a state actor for some purposes, it is still possible to function as a private actor in other ways.[12] This decision left many people wondering if charter schools are truly public schools.

Other legal challenges have addressed similar issues about whether charter schools are indeed state actors. To illustrate, a California state appellate court reasoned that charter schools are exempt from many laws that govern school districts. In this case, a student brought a knife to school and was dismissed from the charter school. The student

---

[8]Beaufort Cty. Bd. of Educ. v. Lighthouse Charter Sch. Comm., 576 S.E.2d 180 (S.C. 2003) (discussing the requirement that racial demographics of charter school should mirror that of the community); *see also* Arianna Prothero, *Diversity in Charter Schools: Another Look at the Data and the Debate*, EDUC. Wk. (Dec. 4, 2017), http://blogs.edweek.org/edweek/charterschoice/2017/12/diversity_in_charter_schools_another_look_at_the_data_and_the_debate.html (discussing high levels of racial segregation in many charter schools).

[9]Cent. Dauphin Sch. Dist. v. Founding Coal. of the Infinity Charter Sch., 847 A.2d 195 (Pa. 2004) (finding that a charter school enrolling high numbers of gifted students did not violate state law); Sch. Dist. v. Provident Charter Sch. for Children with Dyslexia, 134 A.3d 128 (Pa. Commw. Ct. 2016) (holding that a charter school designed for children with dyslexia did not have a discriminatory admissions policy).

[10]ACLU v. Tarek Ibn Ziyad Acad., 2009 U.S. Dist. LEXIS 62567 (D. Minn. July 21, 2009) (rejecting charter school's motion to dismiss a suit because Establishment Clause claims were raised in connection with a prayer posted on a school wall and teacher-led Friday afternoon prayers); *see also* Robert Fox et al., *The Line Between Cultural Education and Religious Education: Do Ethnocentric Niche Charter Schools Have a Prayer?* 36 REV. RES. IN EDUC. 282–83 (2012) (noting that some charter schools have been accused of creating ethnic and religious enclaves).

[11]Caviness v. Horizon Cmty. Learning Ctr., Inc., 590 F.3d 806 (9th Cir. 2010).

[12]*Id.*

argued that he was entitled to due process, but the court found that charter schools are exempt from the state law that addresses student disciplinary matters.[13] Likewise, in 2013 the National Labor Relations Board (NLRB) sided with a Chicago charter school and found it to be a private institution.[14] As a result, teachers at the school are required to organize under private-sector labor laws rather than as public-sector employees. In 2016, the NLRB again decided in two separate cases that charter schools in New York and Pennsylvania are private corporations and not public schools.[15] Some scholars have criticized charter schools for not having to play by the same rules as traditional public schools.[16]

Although a few courts and the NLRB did not find charter schools to be state actors, many other courts have taken a different approach. A Texas appellate court reasoned that a charter school could be sued by a teacher for wrongful termination under the Texas Whistleblower Protection Act.[17] Despite the charter school's contention that holding charter schools to this act would "open a Pandora's Box with respect to what other laws these (and other) private corporations may be subject to," the court denied a request to dismiss the case.[18] Further, the court reasoned it would be problematic if charter schools were given more immunity than traditional public school districts and other purely governmental entities. Similarly, the Supreme Court of South Carolina held that a charter school was considered a state entity in a case involving a charter school teacher's breach of contract claim.[19] Several other courts also have found charter schools to be state actors or governmental bodies.[20] Because the majority of courts have found that charter schools are state actors, the case outcomes are often similar to those of traditional public schools.

[13]Scott B. v. Bd. of Trs., 58 Cal. Rptr. 3d 173 (Ct. App. 2013). However, charter schools in some school districts are required to follow state law in terms of student due process procedures. For example, charter schools in the Los Angeles Unified School District (LAUSD) must "provide due process for all students, including adequate and timely notice to parents/guardians and students of the grounds for all suspension and expulsion recommendations and decisions and their due process rights . . ., including rights of appeal" in conformance with state law. LAUSD, *District Required Language for Independent Charter School Petitions (New and Renewal) and Material Revisions* 17 (Aug. 11, 2017).

[14]Valerie Strauss, *Charter School Ruled Private Entity for Labor Relations*, WASH. POST (Jan. 4, 2013), https://www.washingtonpost.com/news/answer-sheet/wp/2013/01/04/charter-school-ruled-private-entity-for-labor-relations/?utm_term=.13f5d4e834ce.

[15]Nat'l Labor Relations Bd., *Summary of NLRB Decisions* (Aug. 2016), https://www.nlrb.gov/cases-decisions/weekly-summaries-decisions/summary-nlrb-decisions-week-august-22-26-2016.

[16]*See* Preston Green, Bruce Baker & Joseph Oluwole, *Having it Both Ways: How Charter Schools Try to Obtain Funding of Public Schools and the Autonomy of Private Schools*, 63 EMORY L.J. 2 (2014).

[17]Pegasus Sch. of Liberal Arts & Scis. v. Ball-Lowder, 2013 WL 6063834 (Tex. App. Nov. 18, 2013).

[18]*Id.* at *7.

[19]McNaughton v. Charleston Charter Sch. for Math and Sci., 768 S.E.2d 389 (S.C. 2014).

[20]Scaggs v. N.Y. State Dep't of Educ., 2007 U.S. Dist. LEXIS 35860 (E.D.N.Y. May 16, 2007); Irene B. v. Phila. Acad. Charter Sch., 2003 U.S Dist. LEXIS 3020 (E.D. Pa. Jan. 29, 2003); Riester v. Riverside Cmty. Sch., 257 F. Supp. 2d 968 (S.D. Ohio 2002); Daughtery v. Vanguard Charter Sch. Acad., 116 F. Supp. 2d 897 (W.D. Mich. 2000); Jones v. SABIS Educ. Sys., 52 F. Supp. 2d 868 (N.D. Ill. 1999).

Nevertheless, there are many other unique legal issues that have arisen within the context of charter schools related to accountability,[21] caps on enrollment,[22] facilities,[23] charter revocation,[24] denial of charter applications,[25] extra-curricular activities,[26] and issues surrounding cyber charters.[27] Given the growth in the number of charter schools, legal challenges are likely to continue. Figure 13.1 provides the number of students participating in charter schools and other schooling options in the United States in 2016–2017.

FIGURE 13.1   Estimated Number of U.S. Students Participating in Various Schooling Options[28]

Charter School Students	3,100,000
Home Schooled Students	2,300,000
Voucher Recipients	178,624
Tax-Credit Scholarship Recipients	257,661
Education Savings Account Recipients	11,482
Traditional Public School Students	50,300,000

[21]El Centro de la Raza v. Washington, No. 16-2-18527-4 SEA (Wash. Sup. Ct. Feb. 17, 2017) (ruling that state's charter school program is constitutional; plaintiffs had alleged that public funds were used for schools that were not accountable to the public).

[22]Richard Allen Preparatory Charter Sch. v. Sch. Dist., 123 A.3d 1101 (Pa. Commw. Ct. 2015) (holding school district did not have the authority to impose enrollment caps on the charter schools).

[23]Doe v. Elmbrook Sch. Dist., 687 F.3d 840 (7th Cir. 2012) (finding that a charter school holding graduation and other school-related events in a church raised Establishment Clause concerns); *see also* N.Y.C. Parents Union v. Bd. of Educ., 1 N.Y.S.3d 76 (App. Div. 2015) (dismissing lawsuit challenging the city's policy of co-locating charter schools in district schools).

[24]Graystone Acad. Charter Sch. v. Coatesville Area Sch. Dist., 99 A.3d 125 (Pa. Commw. Ct. 2014) (upholding decision to revoke the school's charter for failing to meet student achievement goals).

[25]Insight PA Cyber Charter Sch. v. Dep't of Educ., 162 A.3d 591 (Pa. Commw. Ct. 2017) (overturning charter school board's decision to deny applicant's charter request).

[26]Parents of charter school students have also argued that their children have the right to participate in the traditional public school's extracurricular activities. *See* Harpswell Coastal Acad. v. Me. Sch. Admin. Dist., 2015 U.S. Dist. LEXIS 154278 (D. Me. Nov. 16, 2015) (dismissing charter school parents' complaint that their children should have the right to enroll in the public school's extracurricular activities).

[27]*See, e.g.*, Slippery Rock Area Sch. Dist. v. Pa. Cyber Charter Sch., 612 Pa. 486 (Pa. 2011) (finding that the public school district was not obligated to fund a cyber-charter school's program for a four-year-old student; the district had exercised its discretion in *not* providing services for this age group). Although there are few recent legal challenges involving cyber-charter schools, given the popularity of online programs, legal challenges are likely to increase. News reports suggest widespread concern. *See* Arianna Prothero, *Fight Over One of the Largest Virtual Charters Heads to Ohio's High Court*, EDUC. WK. (Sept. 13, 2017), http://blogs.edweek.org/edweek/charterschoice/2017/09/fight_over_largest_virtual_charter_school_heads_to_ohio_supreme_court.html; Maya Riser-Kositsky, Benjamin Herold & Arianna Prothero, *Map: Cyber Charters Have a New Champion in Betsy DeVos, But Struggles Continue*, EDUC. WK. (Dec. 14, 2017), http://www.edweek.org/ew/section/multimedia/cyber-charters-widespread-reports-of-trouble.html.

[28]*See* EdChoice, *Fast Facts* (2017), https://www.edchoice.org/resource-hub/fast-facts/; Nat'l All. for Pub. Charter Schs., *Estimated Charter Public School Enrollment 2016–2017* (2017); Nat'l Ctr. for Educ. Stats., *Elementary and Secondary Enrollment* (May 2017), https://nces.ed.gov/programs/coe/pdf/coe_cga.pdf; Brian Ray, *Research Facts on Homeschooling*, Nat'l Home Educ. Res. Inst. (Mar. 23, 2016), https://www.nheri.org/research/research-facts-on-homeschooling.html.

HOME SCHOOLING

Parental rights to direct the upbringing of their children include the right to educate them at home.

Not until the 1990s did all states authorize home education, and since then, many states have reduced restrictions on home schooling; no state has strengthened such regulations. Eleven states have few to no requirements; sixteen states have minimal, eighteen have moderate, and only five states have extensive regulations for home education.[29] More than 3 percent of American students (2.3 million) are educated at home.[30]

The most common reason given by parents for home schooling is their dissatisfaction with the environment in schools, which is closely followed by religious concerns.[31] Recent court decisions regarding home schooling have involved a variety of issues, including compulsory attendance and child-custody issues. For example, parents were convicted for violating the state's compulsory attendance law when they did not send their children to school from September to November while they were seeking approval from the state to educate their children at home, which they received in November. The Nebraska Supreme Court overturned the conviction, finding that parents who home school are not required to enroll their children in formal schooling until they receive such approval.[32]

Other cases have addressed various family-related matters. In an illustrative decision involving a special education student, the Eighth Circuit held that a school district could not override a parent's objection to an evaluation for his child who was home schooled.[33] Also, when awarding child support in a divorce case, the Louisiana Supreme Court found the fact that the mother home schooled the children was a legitimate factor to be considered in determining spousal support.[34] In a custody case in Delaware, a family court granted a father's request to make educational decisions for his six children who were being educated at home by their mother. Independent testing demonstrated that the children were substantially behind academically, and the mother was reluctant to seek outside educational support.[35]

Another controversial issue is whether private school students and those who are home schooled are entitled to take selected courses and participate in extracurricular activities in public schools. A few states authorize such participation by law, but statutes in most states are silent on this issue.[36] In the absence of a state law, the Tenth Circuit upheld an

[29]Home Sch. Legal Def. Ass'n, *Homeschool Laws in Your State* (n.d.), https:www.hslda.org/laws/#.

[30]Ray, *supra* note 28.

[31]Nat'l Ctr. for Educ. Statistics, *1.5 Million Homeschooled Students in the United States in 2007*, U.S. Dep't of Educ. (Dec. 2008), https://nces.ed.gov/pubs2009/2009030.pdf.

[32]Nebraska v. Thacker, 834 N.W.2d 597 (Neb. 2013).

[33]Fitzgerald v. Camdenton R-III Sch. Dist., 439 F.3d 773 (8th Cir. 2006).

[34]Rhymes v. Rhymes, 125 So.3d 377 (La. 2013).

[35]L.S.W. v. M.S.W., 2013 WL 9600758 (Del. Fam. Ct. Sept. 27, 2013).

[36]*See* Joshua Roberts, *Dispelling the Rational Basis for Homeschooler Exclusion from High School Interscholastic Athletics*, 38 J. L. & EDUC. 195 (2009).

Oklahoma school district's prohibition on part-time enrollment except for fifth-year seniors and special education students.[37] The school district justified its policy because it could not receive state aid for part-time students, and the court found no burden on the religious liberties or parental rights of families who educate their children at home. An Indiana appeals court also vacated the Indiana State Board of Education's order for a school district to enroll two home-schooled students on a part-time basis, reasoning that state law authorized local districts to deny such part-time enrollment.[38] This issue and others will continue to attract attention even though the number of students who are home schooled may have reached a plateau. There is some sentiment that home education is no longer growing because other options, such as virtual charter schools and state funds for private school tuition, increasingly are available.[39] But if school choice plans provide public funds for parents to educate their children at home, this could provide an impetus for the growth of home schooling.

PUBLIC SUPPORT OF PRIVATE CHOICE OPTIONS

A major component of current school reform efforts across states entails strategies to increase parents' ability to select private education for their children.

The term "school choice" often is used to refer to strategies that increase private school enrollment. It was established in 1925 that parents can satisfy compulsory school attendance mandates by sending their children to nonpublic schools. The Supreme Court in *Pierce v. Society of Sisters* declared that "the fundamental theory of liberty upon which all governments in this Union repose excludes any general power of the state to standardize its children by forcing them to accept instruction from public teachers only."[40] **In essence, parents do not have the right to determine *whether* their children are educated, but they do have some control over *where* and *how* such education takes place**. Many of the current legal controversies focus on using public funds to support nonpublic educational options.

How do voucher and tax-credit scholarship programs differ? What are the most popular approaches to increase educational choice beyond public education? Does school

---

[37]Swanson v. Guthrie Indep. Sch. Dist., 135 F.3d 694 (10th Cir. 1998); *see also* Goulart v. Meadows, 345 F.3d 239 (4th Cir. 2003) (upholding county's policy prohibiting the use of its community centers for private educational activities that resulted in denial of home-school parents' request to use community centers for their classes and meetings).

[38]Ind. State Bd. of Educ. v. Brownsburg Cmty. Sch. Corp., 865 N.E.2d 660 (Ind. Ct. App. 2007); *see also* Hassberger v. Bd. of Educ., 345 F. Supp. 3d 239 (N.D. Ill. 2003) (upholding school district's denial of a request for a private school student to enroll in a public school algebra course).

[39]*See* Arianna Prothero, *Why Have Homeschooling Numbers Flattened Out After a Decade of Growth*, EDUC. WK. (Oct. 2, 2017), http://blogs.edweek.org/edweek/charterschoice/2017/10/why_have_homeschooling_numbers_flattened_out_after_a_decade_of_growth.html.

[40]268 U.S. 510, 535 (1925); *see also* Troxel v. Granville, 530 U.S. 57, 66 (2000) (recognizing extensive precedent leaving little doubt "that the Due Process Clause of the Fourteenth Amendment protects the fundamental right of parents to make decisions concerning the care, custody, and control of their children" in holding that a state's overbroad child visitation law as applied to grandparent visitations violated a mother's fundamental right to direct the upbringing of her child).

privatization have implications for funding public education? With encouragement from the U.S. Department of Education, states are considering and adopting various methods to use public funds for private educational services.[41] And unlike charter schools, there is no assertion that these private schools are operating under the auspices of public education. This section begins by briefly describing school privatization approaches and then discusses the federal and state litigation addressing these strategies.

Private School Choice Approaches

Initially, state legislative efforts to increase school choice beyond public school options focused on voucher programs under which a set amount of public funds would be available for parents to use for their children to attend private schools.[42] These original *voucher programs* were targeted toward specific populations, usually low-income families and/or children with disabilities or other special needs.[43] **More recent voucher programs, such as Indiana's, have broadened eligibility to middle class families**. Usually, the amount for each voucher is based on a portion of the per-pupil allotment available for public school students, with the specific portion varying across voucher plans. Although in theory the voucher goes to the parent who then uses it at a participating private school, the money typically is transferred directly from the state to the school selected. As of 2017, fourteen states and Washington, D.C. had adopted some type of voucher program under which parents can use public funds to send their children to private schools, and several states have more than one voucher program.[44]

Recent national attention has focused on private, religious schools that accept vouchers and then engage in discriminatory practices. To illustrate, a recent study found that no states have voucher laws that provide explicit anti-discrimination provisions for all marginalized populations based on religion, race, national origin/ethnicity, disability, sex, and sexual orientation, and most states were found to have provided specific protections for only race and ethnicity.[45] **This research suggests that few safeguards exist in state laws to ensure that vouchers are offered in a nondiscriminatory fashion.**[46] Similarly, a 2017 report demonstrated that many private, religious schools that accept vouchers have clear

---

[41]School choice strategies that support private school options at public expense have been discussed since Milton Friedman wrote his classic book, CAPITALISM AND FREEDOM, in 1962. However, the adoption of such strategies across states did not become popular until the past two decades.

[42]Although voucher plans are most often adopted in state law, a school district in Colorado adopted a voucher program that was recently rescinded; *see infra* text accompanying notes 98, 101.

[43]In 1990, Milwaukee established the first continuing voucher program, the Milwaukee Parental Choice Program, targeting students from low-income families.

[44]*See* Nat'l Conference of State Legislatures, *Interactive Guide to School Choice* (June 15, 2017), http://www .ncsl.org/research/education/interactive-guide-to-school-choice.aspx.

[45]Suzanne Eckes, Julie Mead & Jessica Ulm, *Dollars to Discriminate: The (Un)intended Consequences of School Vouchers*, 91 PEABODY J. EDUC. 537 (2016).

[46]Some vouchers schools have been criticized for using public money to teach religion, racism, and sexism within the adopted curriculum. *See* Cory Turner, Eric Weddle & Peter Balonon-Rosen, *The Promise and Peril of School Vouchers*, NPR (May 12, 2017), https://www.npr.org/sections/ed/2017/05/12/520111511/the-promise-and-peril-of-school-vouchers.

policies against enrolling LGBTQ students.[47] As noted in Chapter 6, private schools that do not admit Black students based on school officials' religious beliefs risk losing their tax-exempt status because such discriminatory practices are contrary to U.S. public policy.[48] It will be interesting to observe whether voucher schools that discriminate against gay students will also lose their tax-exempt status or be challenged on other grounds.[49]

A second approach to increase access to private school options entails *tax-credit scholarship programs* **that allow parents and/or corporations to take a credit on their state income taxes that is applied toward scholarships for children to attend a private school.** In most of these programs, the state creates an entity to collect the credits and distribute the scholarships, and parents apply to these organizations to receive scholarships for their children. Usually these organizations can restrict the scholarships to schools of a particular religious faith. And under some programs, taxpayers can earmark their credits for nondependent students such as neighbors or grandchildren, even though they cannot fund their own children's private education with their credits. These tax-credit scholarship programs differ from vouchers in that the tax credits never are technically in the state coffers, whereas vouchers are usually distributed to private schools from the state treasury.[50]

Tax-credit scholarship programs to date have been the most popular school strategy to increase access to private education. In 2017, Illinois became the eighteenth state to adopt some type of private-school-scholarship program funded by individual and/or corporate tax credits.[51] Unlike vouchers, the tax credits are collected and the scholarships distributed by private entities the state establishes.

Currently, *education savings accounts* (ESAs) are gaining popularity and may soon become the dominant school choice approach. **These ESAs change the paradigm from providing vouchers or scholarships for private school tuition to empowering parents to customize the education of their children by purchasing a range of educational services.**[52] As of 2017, ESAs had been adopted in six states and were being considered in seventeen others.[53] Usually, an ESA provides parents of eligible children a bank account of

---

[47]Julie Donheiser, *Choice for Most: In Nation's Largest Voucher Program, $16 Million Went to Schools with Anti-LGBT Policies*, CHALKBEAT (Aug. 10, 2017), https://www.chalkbeat.org/posts/us/2017/08/10/choice-for-most-in-nations-largest-voucher-program-16-million-went-to-schools-with-anti-lgbt-policies/.

[48]Runyon v. McCrary, 427 U.S. 160 (1976). *See* text accompanying note 37, Chapter 6.

[49]Questions also have been raised about discrimination in admitting children with disabilities in schools receiving vouchers. *See* Complaint, ACLU Found. Racial Justice Program v. Wisconsin, U.S. Dep't of Justice (June 7, 2011), https://www.aclu.org/files/assets/complaint_to_doj_re_milwaukee_voucher_program_final.pdf.

[50]It creates some confusion in distinguishing the types of privatization approaches, since some voucher legislation also refers to these plans as "scholarship programs." The central difference is whether the state directly funds the vouchers in contrast to using tax credits or deductions to fund the programs.

[51]*See* Madeline Will, *After Fierce Fight, Illinois Enacts Tax-Credit Scholarship Program*, EDUC. WK. (Sept. 1, 2017), https://www.edweek.org/ew/articles/2017/08/31/after-fierce-fight-illinois-enacts-tax-credit-scholarship.html. Four states also allow parents to take deductions for educational expenses prior to calculating their state taxes, but credits subtracted from the amount of taxes owed are by far more popular currently.

[52]*See* Lindsey Burke & Greg Lawson, *Education Savings Accounts: Expanding Education Options for Ohio*, Buckeye Inst. (May 31, 2017).

[53]*See* EdChoice, *Fast Facts, supra* note 28.

a designated amount, accessed by a debit card, which can be used for private school tuition, online programs, tutoring, and therapeutic services for their children.[54] Money not spent in one year can be carried over to the next year or even saved for students' college expenses. In programs currently operating, parents are saving almost one-third of the money to use for their children's higher education.[55]

To date, ESAs are targeted toward children with disabilities or other special student populations, but the Arizona program is slated to increase by targeted grade levels until 2022, when it will be available to all the state's children.[56] Also, Nevada's program (which is not yet implemented) would make ESAs available to all school-age children after they spend a short time in a public school.[57] ESAs are touted as making all schools more efficient and competitive because parents will comparison shop so they can use the money they save at a later date.[58] Advocates also assert that ESAs and related strategies will provide school choices for low-income families that only the wealthy have previously enjoyed.

Critics, however, fear that parents may slight their children's K–12 education to save for their college expenses or that parents will educate their children at home for economic reasons rather than the educational welfare of their children.[59] Opponents note that all of these choice strategies focus on individual advancement rather than the collective good. If parents select schools where the families look and think like they do, schools could become more homogeneous internally with more diversity across schools. Such developments could have implications for how future generations embrace diversity and the attainment of social justice goals in our nation.[60]

U.S. Supreme Court Decisions: Private School Choice

The first Supreme Court decision addressing a tax benefit that parents could use for private school tuition actually occurred during the height of the Supreme Court applying the stringent *Lemon* test.[61] In 1973, the Court in *Committee for Public Education and Religious*

---

[54]*See* Matthew Ladner, *The Way of the Future: Education Savings Accounts for Every American Family*, Friedman Found. for Educ. Choice (Oct. 2012).

[55]EdChoice, *What Is an Education Savings Account?* (2017), https://www.edchoice.org/school-choice/types-of-school-choice/education-savings-account/.

[56]Opponents were successful in blocking implementation of Arizona's law until it is submitted to a referendum in 2018, but supporters of the law have filed a suit to invalidate the referendum. *See Ariz. Petitioners Get Go-Ahead to Take Universal Voucher Issue to Voters*, EDUC. WK. (Sept. 12, 2017), at 4.

[57]*See infra* text accompanying note 105.

[58]*See* Burke & Lawson, *supra* note 52.

[59]For a discussion of criticisms of various privatization approaches, *see* M. David Alexander, *Should Education Be Considered a Commodity? Global Privatization of Education*, *in* WILEY HANDBOOK OF EDUCATION POLICY (Rosemary Papa & S.W.J. Armfield, eds. 2018).

[60]*See id.*; Dana Thompson Dorsey & Jonathan Plucker, *Deregulation and the American Education Marketplace*, 91 PEABODY J. EDUC. 424 (2016); James Harvey, *Privatization: A Drain on Public Schools*, 69 EDUC. LEADERSHIP 48 (2012).

[61]Lemon v. Kurtzman, 403 U.S. 612 (1971); *see also* the discussion of this case in text accompanying note 3, Chapter 3.

Liberty v. Nyquist struck down the New York program that allowed tax deductions only for parents sending their children to private schools, finding that the program was designed to aid religious schools in violation of the Establishment Clause.[62]

By the time the Supreme Court rendered its next decision in 1983, the Court was starting to become more accommodationist in terms of allowing public funds to flow to religious schools. In *Mueller v. Allen*, the Court upheld a Minnesota tax-deduction program permitting parents of public or private school students to claim a limited state income tax deduction for tuition, transportation, and secular textbook expenses incurred for each elementary or secondary school dependent. **The Court majority declared that Minnesota law was "vitally different" from the New York program, which clearly benefitted only families of private school students.**[63] The majority reasoned that Minnesota's "decision to defray the cost of educational expenses incurred by parents—regardless of the type of schools their children attend—displays a "secular and understandable" purpose.[64]

Almost two decades later, the Supreme Court rendered its only decision to date addressing a voucher program, *Zelman v. Simmons-Harris.*[65] In this five-to-four decision, the Court upheld the program giving private-school choices to economically disadvantaged families in the Cleveland City School District. Despite almost all of the participating schools being religiously affiliated, the Court majority did not find an Establishment Clause violation. **The majority emphasized that parents, rather than the government, made the decision for the funds to flow to private schools.** Thus, the Court considered the program to be religiously neutral—a program of "true private choice" among public and private schools.[66]

In 2011, the Supreme Court rendered *Arizona School Christian Tuition Organization v. Winn*—its most recent ruling on a school privatization initiative.[67] In a divided decision, the Court rejected a challenge to the Arizona tax-credit scholarship program. This program allows taxpayers to receive tax credits for contributions to student tuition organizations (STOs) that distribute scholarships for students to attend private schools. The STOs can limit their scholarships to schools of particular faiths, and the three largest STOs provide scholarships for Catholic and Evangelical Christian schools. A student can receive scholarships from more than one STO,[68] and while parents cannot earmark contributions for their own children, they can target their credits for nondependents.

---

[62]413 U.S. 756 (1973). The Court in this case also struck down direct tuition reimbursement for parents of private school students and aid for the maintenance and repair of private school facilities.

[63]463 U.S. 388, 398 (1983) (contrasting Nyquist, 413 U.S. 756).

[64]*Id.* at 395.

[65]536 U.S. 639 (2002).

[66]*Id.* at 640. The *Zelman* dissenters criticized the majority for its reliance on the fact that the money passed through parents' hands, recognizing that the end result was the same as if the state had distributed the money directly to religious schools. *See id.* at 684 (Stevens, J., dissenting); *id.* at 686 (Souter, J., dissenting, joined by Stevens, Ginsburg, & Breyer, JJ.); *id.* at 717 (Breyer, J., dissenting, joined by Stevens & Souter, JJ.).

[67]563 U.S. 125 (2011).

[68]Alia Beard Rau, *Controversial Arizona Tax-Credit Scholarship Program Grants $1B to Students*, Az CENT. (Aug. 20, 2017), http://www.azcentral.com/story/news/politics/arizona-education/2017/08/18/controversial-arizona-education-tax-credit-scholarship-program-gives-students-1-billion/554058001/.

The Ninth Circuit in *Winn* had ruled that the program was not intended to expand parental choice but instead to aid religious education,[69] but the Supreme Court disagreed. The Court majority avoided the substantive issue by concluding that taxpayers did not have standing to initiate an Establishment Clause challenge to the tax-credit scholarship program. **The majority reasoned that since the money had *not* already been placed in the state treasury, it could not be considered state funds and, thus, taxpayers could not challenge its use**. This rationale did not appear in *Zelman* or in prior decisions in which taxpayers contested the use of public funds in private schools, despite the fact that parents made the decisions regarding their children's schools in the earlier cases.[70] But in the *Winn* ruling, the Supreme Court concluded that state money is not involved in the tax-credit scholarship program, even though taxpayers cannot keep the funds if they do not contribute to an STO.[71]

Two other Supreme Court decisions are pertinent to school choice, although they did not focus directly on using government funds to support parents selecting private education for their children. **The Supreme Court in *Locke v. Davey* upheld states' discretion to adopt more stringent antiestablishment provisions than demanded by the First Amendment**.[72] In this 2004 case, students in the state of Washington could receive state scholarships to attend public or private institutions of higher education, but they could not use such government funds to pursue a pastoral degree. The Supreme Court held that the Washington constitutional provision was intended to keep schools free from sectarian control, rejecting the contention that it emanated from religious bigotry as a so-called Blaine Amendment.[73]

The second more recent ruling, *Trinity Lutheran Church v. Comer*, was rendered by the Supreme Court in 2017.[74] As discussed in Chapter 3, this case involved a religious daycare center's request to be considered in a competitive grant program for playground resurfacing, but its proposal was refused on religious grounds since the state constitution bars using public funds for religious purposes. Reversing the courts below, for the first

---

[69]Winn v. Ariz. Christian Sch. Tuition Org., 562 F.3d 1002 (9th Cir. 2009).

[70]For illustrative Supreme Court cases where taxpayer standing was not questioned, *see* Zelman v. Simmons-Harris, 536 U.S. 639 (2002), *supra* text accompanying note 65; Mueller v. Allen, 463 U.S. 388 (1983), *supra* text accompanying note 63; Comm. for Pub. Educ. & Relig. Liberty v. Nyquist, 413 U.S. 756 (1973), *supra* text accompanying note 62. Additionally, the "lack of standing" rationale was not used in a previous case challenging the Arizona tax credit program, Hibbs v. Winn, 542 U.S. 88, 100–12 (2004) (holding that the Tax Injunction Act, barring federal courts from curbing state tax collection in a controversy resolvable in state court, was not applicable as no restriction on the state's ability to collect taxes was alleged; noting that taxpayers had shown standing to challenge tax schemes based on the Establishment Clause in numerous other cases).

[71]The *Winn* dissenters claimed that the majority's opinion pillaged the Supreme Court's ruling in Flast v Cohen, 392 U.S. 83 (1968) (holding that to demonstrate standing, plaintiffs need to show that the state has used its taxing and spending power to violate the Establishment Clause). Winn, 563 U.S. at 147 (Kagan, J., dissenting, joined by Ginsberg, Breyer, & Sotomayor, JJ.).

[72]540 U.S. 712 (2004).

[73]*Id.* at 724 n.7 (finding that Washington's constitutional prohibition on the use of public funds for religious worship, exercise, or instruction was *not* modeled on a failed constitutional amendment proposed by former House Speaker James Blaine in 1875, which allegedly reflected anti-Catholic sentiment).

[74]137 S. Ct. 2012 (2017).

time the Supreme Court found federal Free Exercise Clause rights at stake in a case involving public support flowing to a religious institution. **Applying strict scrutiny, the Court declared that under a generally available public-aid program, the funds could not be denied to an institution solely on the basis of religion.** The Court's rationale will likely be significant in future efforts to use public funds for private education including strategies to increase school choice. If state courts follow the Supreme Court's lead, most state anti-establishment barriers to governmental support of school privatization initiatives, which are more stringent that the federal Establishment Clause, will be overridden by First Amendment free exercise rights.

State Cases Pertaining to Private School Choice Strategies

Given the *Zelman* and *Winn* Supreme Court rulings, the federal Establishment Clause does not appear to pose a barrier to states' adoptions of voucher, tax-credit scholarship, or ESA programs. And states increasingly are considering and enacting such programs to provide public funds for private, mainly religious, education.

Most states have constitutional provisions barring the use of public funds by religious institutions and prohibiting the government from compelling citizens to support religion, and all states have provisions placing an obligation on the legislature to provide for a system of free public education. Even though state religion clauses often are more restrictive than the federal Establishment Clause,[75] the Supreme Court's *Trinity Lutheran* decision[76] may call into question the continued vitality of these provisions if religious schools successfully assert a free exercise entitlement to participate in government funding programs. **Thus, state education clauses appear to be more viable than state religion clauses as grounds upon which to challenge various school choice strategies that involve private schools.** State decisions focusing on these school choice initiatives are addressed in the next two sections. These cases are a moving target, as legal challenges are mounted as soon as new programs are adopted, and often state high courts overturn the courts below.[77]

Courts Upholding Private School Choice Programs. Presented chronologically, two of the earliest state decisions voicing approval of voucher plans were rendered by the Wisconsin and Ohio Supreme Courts. These state high courts rejected challenges to voucher programs under the federal Establishment Clause and their respective state religion clauses.[78] Both courts concluded that the public funds flow to religious institutions only because of decisions made by parents, constituting permissible *indirect* state aid to religious institutions.

---

[75]*See* Locke v. Davey, 540 U.S. 712 (2004), *supra* text accompanying note 72.

[76]137 S. Ct. 2012, *supra* text accompanying note 74, *infra* text accompanying note 100.

[77]*See, e.g.*, Magee v. Boyd, 175 So. 3d 79 (Ala. 2015), *infra* note 91; Duncan v. New Hampshire, 102 A.3d 913 (N.H. 2014), *infra* note 86; Hart v. North Carolina, 774 S.E.2d 281 (N.C. 2015), *infra* note 92; Oliver v. Hofmeister, 368 P.3d 1270 (Okla. 2016), *infra* note 93.

[78]Simmons-Harris v. Goff, 711 N.E.2d 203 (Ohio 1999); Jackson v. Benson, 578 N.W.2d 602 (Wis. 1998); Davis v. Grover, 480 N.W.2d 460 (Wis. 1992).

The Arizona Supreme Court subsequently dismissed a *facial* challenge to tax credits for donations to STOs that provide scholarships for children to attend private schools. This court reasoned that this program should not be treated differently from tax deductions for educational expenses upheld by the Supreme Court in *Mueller*.[79] And as discussed previously, the U.S. Supreme Court in 2011 rejected an Establishment Clause challenge to its *implementation* based on the rationale that the taxpayers lacked standing to challenge this state-established program.[80]

In a more recent decision, the Arizona Supreme Court declined to review an appellate ruling upholding empowerment scholarships, which were the original ESAs.[81] These ESAs were available for children with disabilities and other special student populations to attend private schools. The court cited its prior reasoning in concluding that the parents, rather than the state, control how the money is used; thus, there was no violation of the state constitution's religion clauses. While this specific program applied to a relatively small number of students, eligibility was subsequently extended to siblings of current or previous scholarship students, students in failing public schools (rated D or F), those in foster care, adoptees, Native Americans living on reservations, and several other targeted student populations.[82]

As noted previously, the Arizona legislature in 2016 enacted a law under which ***all*** **students in the state may be eligible for ESAs by 2022.**[83] Arizona's ESAs are funded at 90 percent of the amount that would normally go to the recipient's public school district and at 100 percent for the lowest income families, with a supplement for students with special needs. The funds can be used by families for private school tuition and fees, textbooks, tutoring, and related educational services. Allocated funds not used can be saved for the student's college expenses.

Despite significant differences in the federal and state constitutions in terms of the provision of education, several courts have followed the Supreme Court's lead in its 2011 *Winn* decision by using various grounds to deny taxpayer standing.[84] **When rejecting standing to challenge voucher and tax-credit scholarship programs, these courts have avoided the substantive claims under state religion and education clauses**. For example, in 2012, the Oklahoma Supreme Court found that a school district lacked standing to challenge the state's voucher program for children with disabilities.[85] The Oklahoma high court reasoned that the party must have a sufficient interest in the case outcome to establish standing, noting that the funds were from the state and not from county revenues in local

[79]Kotterman v. Killian, 972 P.2d 606, 611 (Ariz. 1999) (*citing* Mueller v. Allen, 463 U.S. 388 (1983)).

[80]Ariz. Christian Sch. Tuition Org. v. Winn, 563 U.S. 125 (2011); *supra* text accompanying note 67.

[81]Niehaus v. Huppenthal, 310 P.3d 983 (Ariz. Ct. App. 2013).

[82]ARIZ. REV. STAT. § 15-2401(7) (2018).

[83]Ariz. S.B. 1279, 52nd Leg., 2d Reg. Sess. (Ariz. 2016); *see also* Bob Christie, Associated Press, *Arizona Senate Votes for Vouchers for All School Students*, RAYCOM (Feb. 23, 2016), http://raycomgroup.worldnow.com/story/31297468/arizona-senate-votes-for-vouchers-for-all-school-students. But there have been recent efforts to halt implementation of this law, *see supra* note 56.

[84]563 U.S. 125 (2011); *supra* text accompanying note 67.

[85]Indep. Sch. Dist. v. Spry, 292 P.3d 19 (Okla. 2012); *see also* McCall v. Scott, 199 So. 3d 359 (Fla. Cir. Ct. App.1st 2016) (finding no standing for taxpayers to challenge Florida's tax-credit scholarship program), *infra* note 92.

school districts. Also, the New Hampshire Supreme Court overturned the lower court and ruled in 2014 that taxpayers did not have standing to challenge a tax-credit scholarship program as they did not demonstrate personal injury.[86] This court further invalidated a 2012 state law that attempted to give taxpayers such standing. Denying standing is easier for courts than addressing the substantive issues, so this may become a popular strategy for courts inclined to reject challenges to voucher, tax-credit scholarship, and other school choice initiatives that allow public funds to flow to private education.

The Indiana Supreme Court in 2013 upheld a comprehensive voucher program making vouchers available to more than half of the students in the state.[87] The court found no violation of the state constitution's two religion clauses, equating the benefit to religious schools with fire and police protection.[88] Also finding no abridgment of the state's education clause, the court reasoned that this clause contains two separate duties involving the encouragement and improvement of schools and the provision of a general and uniform system of public schools; the first is not a condition of the second.[89] In essence, the state can encourage education through a voucher system as long as the legislature also makes provisions for a system of public schools. And the voucher program did not run afoul of the state's requirement for the legislature to provide a uniform system of education, even if more than half of the student population would, as projected, take advantage of the vouchers to attend private schools.[90]

In 2015, two state high courts upheld strategies to expand parents' options to send their children to private schools at public expense. The Alabama Supreme Court rejected a challenge to a tax-credit scholarship program, overturning a lower court ruling that had struck down the Alabama Accountability Act, which contains the contested initiative.[91] The state high court reasoned that private individuals decide how the scholarship funds are used and that the indirect aid to religious schools does not abridge the U.S. Constitution or the state constitution's religion or education clauses. Because the money going to private schools has not yet been deposited in the state treasury, the court also found no illegal appropriation of state funds.

Also, the North Carolina Supreme Court in 2015 overturned the lower court and upheld the state's Opportunity Scholarship Program.[92] This program provides scholarships for K–12 students from low-income families and is referred to as a voucher program. The state high court ruled that the scholarship program satisfies the state constitution's uniformity mandate, reasoning that this provision applies only to public schools and not to initiatives funded beyond public education. The court further held that the program satisfies the

---

[86]Duncan v. New Hampshire, 102 A.3d 913 (N.H. 2014).

[87]Meredith v. Pence, 984 N.E.2d 1213 (Ind. 2013).

[88]*Id.* at 1225–30.

[89]*Id.* at 1221–23.

[90]*Id.* at 1223.

[91]Magee v. Boyd, 175 So. 3d 79 (Ala. 2015).

[92]Hart v. North Carolina, 774 S.E.2d 281 (N.C. 2015); *see also* McCall v. Scott, 199 So. 3d 359 (Fla. Cir. Ct. App. 2016) (allowing corporate tax funds that otherwise would be paid to the state treasury to be redirected to intermediate entities, which transmit the money for scholarships to participating private schools).

constitutional "public purpose" requirement because it benefits the public generally, and the money is not taken from funds earmarked for public education.

In 2016, the Oklahoma Supreme Court again addressed a challenge to the state's voucher program for children with disabilities, but unlike its 2012 ruling, this time the court addressed the merits of the case. The state high court reversed the court below and upheld the state-funded voucher program to offset tuition costs for students with disabilities to enroll in participating private schools. Reasoning that the parents make the decisions as to where their children enroll, the court ruled that even though public funds flow to religious schools, the program does not violate the state's constitutional provision barring the use of public money or property to benefit religious institutions.[93] Most of the recent state high court decisions endorsing voucher or tax-credit scholarship programs have overturned the rulings of courts below, reflecting the continued volatility of these challenges.

Courts Invalidating Private School Choice Programs.   Some state high courts have struck down voucher programs as violating state law, although no state supreme court to date has struck down a tax-credit scholarship program. The earliest litigation in this regard took place in Vermont and Maine and involved tuition-reimbursement programs rather than traditional voucher plans. Under these reimbursement programs (called tuitioning plans), small school districts that do not operate high schools provide tuition up to a cap for students living within their boundaries to attend secular private schools or neighboring public schools. The Vermont Supreme Court upheld the exclusion of religious schools from the state's tuitioning program, relying on the state constitutional provision that prohibits compelling taxpayers to support religious worship.[94] In Maine, the exclusion of religious schools in its tuitioning program was upheld by both state and federal courts to comply with the federal Establishment Clause,[95] despite the lack of prohibitions on state aid to or compelled support of religious institutions in the Maine Constitution. Whether the Supreme Court's rationale in its 2017 *Trinity Lutheran* decision[96] would strengthen plaintiffs' challenges to the exclusion of religious schools from such tuition-reimbursement programs remains to be tested.

The Colorado Supreme Court has struck down voucher programs in two rulings that relied on different grounds. In 2004, the state high court used the local control provision in the state constitution to invalidate a pilot voucher program that took control away from local school districts.[97] Since Colorado is one of only six states with a constitutional provision that gives local school districts authority to control the expenditure of funds raised locally for instruction, this rationale is not likely to appear in many other decisions.

[93]Oliver v. Hofmeister, 368 P.3d 1270 (Okla. 2016).

[94]Chittenden Town Sch. Dist. v. Vt. Dep't of Educ., 738 A.2d 539 (Vt. 1999).

[95]Eulitt v. Me. Dep't of Educ., 386 F.3d 344 (1st Cir. 2004); *Strout* v. Albanese, 178 F.3d 57 (1st Cir. 1999); Anderson v. Durham, 895 A.2d 944 (Me. 2006); Bagley v. Raymond Sch. Dep't, 728 A.2d 127 (Me. 1999).

[96]Trinity Lutheran Church v. Comer, 137 S. Ct. 2012 (2017), *supra* text accompanying note 74.

[97]Owens v. Colo. Cong. of Parents, Teachers, & Students, 92 P.3d 933 (Colo. 2004).

In 2015, the full Colorado Supreme Court held that a school district's voucher program violated the state constitution's anti-establishment provision that is more stringent than the federal Establishment Clause.[98] The court recognized the Colorado Constitution's explicit prohibition on using public funds to support religious schools. Finding a clear violation of the state Constitution, the court declared that the invalidated program awarded "public money to students who may then use that money to pay for a religious education."[99]

However, the U.S. Supreme Court in 2017 vacated this ruling and sent the case back for the Colorado high court to reconsider in light of its *Trinity Lutheran* decision, in which the Court ruled that an institution could not be barred from participating in a generally available public funding program on the sole basis of religion.[100] If the Colorado Supreme Court and other state courts conclude that religious schools have a Free Exercise Clause entitlement to state monies in school choice programs,[101] there will be no legal constraint to the implementation of such initiatives under state religion clauses.

As noted, **it has appeared recently that the most promising grounds to strike down these choice strategies that allow government funds to flow to private schools may be state education clauses (requiring the legislature to provide for a uniform, thorough and efficient, or adequate system of education) or other state requirements that are not based on religion clauses in state constitutions**. The leading decision in this regard was rendered by the Florida Supreme Court in 2006.[102] The court relied specifically on the state's education clause in striking down a voucher program, the Opportunity Scholarship Program, which allowed children attending public schools performing poorly to transfer to private schools. Florida's high court held that the state's paramount duty to provide an adequate education in a uniform and high-quality system of public schools was violated by the voucher program that diverted funds away from the public schools.[103] The court further concluded that the voucher program abridged the constitutional uniformity requirement because less stringent standards were applied to the private school curriculum and its teachers.

The Louisiana Supreme Court also invalidated a Louisiana voucher program based on nonreligious grounds, but the court did not rely on the state's education clause.[104]

---

[98]Taxpayers for Pub. Educ. v. Douglas Cty. Sch. Dist., 351 P.3d 461 (Colo. 2015) (en banc).

[99]*Id.* at 471.

[100]Douglas Cty. Sch. Dist. v. Taxpayers for Pub. Educ., 137 S. Ct. 2325 (2017) (granting *cert.*, vacating judgment, and remanding to the Supreme Court of Colorado for reconsideration in light of Trinity Lutheran, 137 S. Ct. 2012); *see also* Moses v. Skandera, 367 P.3d 838 (N.M. 2015) (barring the state's use of public funds to loan textbooks to private schools under the state constitution's prohibition on appropriating funds to support private and religious schools), *vacated sub nom.* N.M. Ass'n of Nonpublic Schs. v. Moses, 137 S. Ct. 2325 (Mem.) (2017) (granting *cert.*, vacating judgment, and remanding to the Supreme Court of New Mexico for reconsideration in light of Trinity Lutheran); *see* text accompanying note 160, Chapter 3.

[101]Even though the Douglas County school board passed a resolution on Dec. 5, 2017 to rescind the district's voucher program, the litigation is expected to proceed. *See* Douglas Cty. Sch. Dist., *Choice Scholarship Program* (n.d.), https://www.dcsdk12.org/legal-counsel/choice-scholarship-program.

[102]Bush v. Holmes, 919 So. 2d 392 (Fla. 2006).

[103]*Id.* at 409.

[104]La. Fed'n of Teachers v. Louisiana, 118 So. 3d 1033 (La. 2013).

The state high court ruled that the contested program violated the state constitutional requirement for the legislature to develop a funding formula for the cost of a minimum foundation program for public education and to equitably distribute funds accordingly. The court held that the state could not divert funds into private education that must be allocated to public schools.

Nevada adopted the most expansive school privatization program to date in 2015, but it has not yet been implemented. This initiative allows families to receive ESAs worth slightly less than the amount spent on public school students in the state. These ESAs can be used on private schooling, online programs, and other educational services. Under this program, almost all of the state's students would be eligible to receive state money to attend a private school after spending 100 days in a public school. This program was immediately challenged, and two lower courts reached opposite conclusions on the constitutionality of the program. On appeal, the Nevada Supreme Court upheld the program's constitutionality but not its funding through the state's distributive school account that must be used for public education.[105] The court required the legislature to find alternative funding, so the initiative's fate is unknown.

It seems assured that increasingly expansive private school choice programs will be considered and enacted across states. And these programs will elicit legal challenges resulting in a growing body of state litigation. The case outcomes may be similar to the range reflected in school finance cases, which also must be resolved on the basis of state law.[106]

CONCLUSION

Alternatives to traditional public schooling are a central component of school reform efforts nationally. It remains unclear what the implications of these initiatives will be. Charter schools are expanding rapidly, and regulation of home education continues to be lax in many states. The private school choice movement is gaining momentum, and the Supreme Court has not been receptive to challenges to voucher and tax-credit scholarship programs that allow public funds to flow to private education. The state judicial scoreboard is mixed, with state high courts often overturning the courts below, making judicial developments difficult to follow. Voucher, tax-credit scholarship, and/or ESA programs have been introduced in all states, and a majority of the states have adopted one or more of these initiatives. Many questions remain regarding the academic progress of students, potential discrimina-

---

[105]*See* Schwartz v. Lopez, 382 P.3d 886 (Nev. 2016); Jason Bedrick, *Nevada Supreme Court: Education Savings Accounts Are Constitutional, Funding Mechanism Isn't*, CATO Inst. (Sept. 29, 2016), https://www.cato.org/blog/nevada-supreme-court-education-savings-accounts-are-constitutional-funding-mechanism-isnt. Since the legislature does not meet again until 2019 and has shifted from a Republican to a Democratic majority, implementation of the program is in limbo.

[106]As a result of the Supreme Court's decision in San Antonio Indep. Sch. Dist. v. Rodriguez, 411 U.S. 1 (1973) (rejecting a Fourteenth Amendment challenge to inequities in the Texas school funding system), the legality of public school finance plans must be decided by state courts and varies across states. *See* Spencer Weiler, Luke Cornelius & Edward Brooks, *Examining Adequacy Trends in School Finance Litigation*, 345 Educ. L. Rep. 1 (2017).

tion against certain groups of students, socialization of students in terms of understanding those who look and think differently, and many other issues. The following generalizations depict topics covered in this chapter.

1. Proposals for state legislatures to adopt alternatives to traditional public schooling at public expense are increasing in the United States.

2. Charter schools, operating in forty-four states, are considered public schools but have more flexibility in staffing and programmatic decisions.

3. Even though charter schools are public schools, a few courts have ruled that they are not state actors in terms of applying constitutional guarantees.

4. Some charter schools have focused their curriculum on a specific language, culture, or ability level, which has raised legal concerns.

5. There has been a trend for more than three decades of states deregulating home schooling; eleven states have little to no regulations in place.

6. The recent rise in virtual schooling and interest in funding education through education savings accounts may affect the number of students educated at home.

7. Tax-credit scholarship programs that allow individual and/or corporate tax credits for private school scholarships are the most popular private school choice strategy currently, although some states still have voucher programs that allow government funds to flow to private, primarily religious, schools.

8. Voucher laws typically do not include the same civil rights protections that are required for public schools, and some voucher programs have been accused of discriminating against LGBTQ students and students with disabilities.

9. Under tax-credit scholarship programs, states establish entities to collect the tax credits and distribute the scholarships; these entities can restrict scholarships to schools of a specific faith.

10. Education savings accounts for parents are receiving the most current attention as a way for parents to customize the educational experiences for their children and possibly save money for college expenses.

11. The U.S. Supreme Court has rejected challenges to state initiatives to increase parental choice by providing public funds for students to attend private schools.

12. No state high court has struck down a tax-credit scholarship program, but a few voucher programs have not withstood challenges under state law, primarily on the basis of state education clauses or other nonreligious grounds.

13. Religious schools may have a Free Exercise Clause right to participate in choice initiatives that are open to secular private schools, despite state restrictions on using public funds for religious purposes.

CHAPTER FOURTEEN

SUMMARY OF
LEGAL GENERALIZATIONS

In the preceding chapters, principles of law have been presented as they relate to specific aspects of school leaders', teachers', and students' rights and responsibilities. Constitutional and statutory provisions, in conjunction with judicial decisions, have been analyzed in an effort to portray the current status of the law. Many diverse topics have been explored, some with clearly established legal precedents and others where the law is still evolving.

The most difficult situations confronting school personnel are those without specific legislative or judicial guidance. In such circumstances, educators must make judgments based on their professional training and general knowledge of the law as it applies to education. For example, the U.S. Supreme Court has not addressed whether Title VII of the Civil Rights Act of 1964 bars employment discrimination based on sexual orientation and gender identity, and lower courts have rendered different opinions in this regard. So school authorities in many jurisdictions are left to decide how to handle controversies involving LGBTQ discrimination. The following broad generalizations, synthesized from the preceding chapters, are presented to assist educators in making such determinations where the status of the law may not be clear.

GENERALIZATIONS

The Legal Control of Public Education Resides with the State.   In attempting to comply with the law, school personnel must keep in mind the scope of the state's authority to regulate educational activities. Courts consistently have held that state legislatures possess plenary power in establishing and operating public schools; this power is restricted only by federal and state constitutions and civil rights laws. Where the federal judiciary has interpreted the U.S. Constitution as prohibiting a given practice in public education, such as racial discrimination, the state or its agents cannot enact laws or policies that conflict with the constitutional mandate.

In contrast, if the Federal Constitution and civil rights laws have been interpreted as permitting a certain activity, such as the use of corporal punishment in public schools, states retain discretion in either restricting or expanding the practice. Under such circumstances, standards vary across states, and legislation becomes more important in specifying the scope of protected rights. For example, the U.S. Supreme Court has rejected the claim that probationary teachers have an inherent federal right to due process prior to contract nonrenewal, but state legislatures have the authority to create such a right under state law. Similarly, the Supreme Court has found no Fourth Amendment violation in blanket or random drug testing of public school students who participate in extracurricular activities; however, state law may place restrictions on school authorities in conducting such searches. Also, the Supreme Court has found no Establishment Clause violation in providing tax credits for private school tuition and the participation of sectarian schools in state-supported voucher programs to fund education, but these programs might run afoul of state constitutional provisions that obligate state legislatures to provide for a uniform system of free public education for all citizens.

Unless constitutional rights are at stake, courts defer to the will of legislative bodies in determining educational matters. State legislatures have the authority to create and redesign school districts; collect and distribute educational funds; and determine teacher qualifications, curricular offerings, and minimum student performance standards. With the pervasive control vested in the states, a thorough understanding of the operation of a specific educational system can be acquired only by examining an individual state's statutes, administrative regulations, and judicial decisions that interpret these provisions.

Certain prerequisites to public school employment are defined through statutes and state board of education regulations. For example, all states stipulate that a public school teacher must possess a valid teaching license based on satisfying specified requirements. State laws also regulate the dismissal procedures for tenured and nontenured teachers, and the extent to which teachers can engage in collective bargaining.

State laws similarly govern conditions of school attendance. Every state has enacted a compulsory attendance statute to ensure an educated citizenry. These laws are applicable to all children, with only a few legally recognized exceptions, but parents have options in satisfying such compulsory education requirements. In addition to mandating school attendance, states have the authority to prescribe courses of study and instructional materials in public schools. Courts will not invalidate these decisions unless constitutional rights are abridged. Private schools and charter schools have more instructional flexibility, but state legislatures retain the authority to regulate such alternatives to traditional public schooling.

Courts also apply comparable reasoning in upholding the state's power to establish academic standards and graduation requirements to determine whether students and school districts are progressing in a manner consistent with state and federal expectations. Student assessments determine the level and type of instruction provided, whether the student should be promoted from grade to grade or is eligible for graduation, and if the local school district has achieved required outcomes. Many states and local districts have policies that base the evaluation of school personnel in part on their students' standardized test scores.

It is a widely held perception that local school boards control public education, but local boards hold only those discretionary powers conferred by the state. Depending on the state, a local board's discretionary authority may be quite broad, narrowly defined by statutory guidelines, or somewhere in between. School board regulations enacted pursuant to statutory authority are legally binding on employees and students. For example, school boards can place conditions on employment (e.g., continuing education requirements, residency requirements) beyond state minimums, if not prohibited by law.

Courts will not overturn decisions made by local school boards unless clearly arbitrary, discriminatory, or beyond their scope of authority. School board discretion, however, may be limited by collective bargaining agreements with teachers' unions. These bargained agreements may affect terms and conditions of employment in areas such as teacher evaluation, work calendar, teaching loads, extra-duty assignments, and grievance procedures. Negotiated agreements in some states can take precedence over state laws under certain circumstances so long as protected rights are not impaired. It is imperative for educators to become familiar with all of these sources of legal rights and responsibilities and how they vary depending on the state and the nature of their assignments.

All Public School Policies and Practices that Impinge on Protected Personal Freedoms Must Be Substantiated as Necessary to Advance the School's Educational Mission. The state and its agents have broad authority to regulate public schools, but policies that impair federal constitutional rights must be justified by an overriding public interest. Although courts do not enact laws as legislative bodies do, they significantly influence educational policies and practices by interpreting constitutional and statutory provisions. Both school attendance and public employment traditionally were considered privileges bestowed at the will of the state, but the Supreme Court has recognized that teachers and students do not lose their constitutional rights when they enter public schools. The state controls education, but this power must be exercised in conformance with the Federal Constitution.

It is important to keep in mind that the Bill of Rights places restrictions on governmental, not private, action that interferes with personal freedoms. To illustrate, public schools may have to tolerate private student expression under certain circumstances, but expression representing the school can be censored for educational reasons. Similarly, the Establishment Clause prohibits public school employees from directing or condoning devotional activities in public education, whereas student-initiated religious groups in secondary schools must be treated like other student groups during noninstructional time. Furthermore, community religious groups, even those involved in religious instruction targeting elementary school children, must be granted school access during nonschool hours the same as other community groups. Private schools that do not have sufficient government involvement to constitute state action are not subject to federal constitutional provisions.

In balancing public and individual interests, courts weigh the importance of the protected personal right against the governmental need to restrict its exercise. For example, courts have reasoned that there is no overriding public interest to justify compelling students to salute the American flag if such an observance conflicts with religious or philosophical beliefs. In contrast, mandatory vaccination against communicable diseases has been upheld as a prerequisite to school attendance, even if opposition to immunization is based on religious grounds. Courts have reasoned that the overriding public interest in safeguarding the health of all students justifies such a requirement.

Restrictions can be placed on students' activities under certain conditions. The judiciary has recognized that students' constitutional rights must be assessed in light of the special circumstances of the school. Consequently, school authorities can impose dress codes, and even student uniforms, if shown to advance legitimate school goals, such as reducing disciplinary problems and gang influences, and the requirement is not intended to stifle expression. As noted, student expression that gives the appearance of representing the school also can be censored to ensure its consistency with educational objectives. Additionally, vulgar speech or expression promoting illegal activity that might be protected by the First Amendment for adults can be curtailed among public school students to further the school's legitimate interest in maintaining standards of decency. And even private student expression of ideological views, including electronic expression initiated off school grounds, can be restricted if linked to a disruption of the educational process and possibly if it collides with the rights of others. Moreover, although school authorities are considered state officials, they can conduct warrantless searches of students based on reasonable suspicion that contraband posing a threat to the school environment is concealed.

Similarly, constraints can be placed on school employees if justified by valid school objectives. Prerequisites to employment, such as examinations and residency requirements, can be imposed if necessary to advance legitimate governmental interests. Furthermore, restrictions on teachers' rights to govern their appearance and out-of-school conduct can be warranted when their behavior impinges on their effectiveness in the classroom. Although teachers enjoy a First Amendment right to express views on matters of public concern, expression pursuant to ordinary job responsibilities is not protected by the First Amendment. Even if educators are speaking as private citizens, expression relating to private employment grievances, rather than a matter of public concern, can be the basis for disciplinary action. And teachers' expression on public issues can be curtailed if it impedes the management of the school, work relationships, or teaching effectiveness. Also, educators' expression on school-owned computers and other equipment can be monitored for educational reasons.

Every regulation that impairs individual rights must be based on valid educational considerations and be necessary to carry out the school's mission. Such regulations also should be clearly stated and well publicized so that all individuals understand the basis for the rules and the penalties for infractions.

School Policies and Practices Must Not Disadvantage Specific Individuals or Groups.   The inherent personal right to remain free from governmental discrimination has been emphasized throughout this book. Strict judicial scrutiny has been applied in evaluating state action that creates a suspect classification, such as race. In school desegregation cases, courts have charged school officials with an affirmative duty to take necessary steps to overcome the lingering effects of past discrimination. Similarly, intentional racial discrimination associated with testing methods, suspension procedures, employee hiring, and promotion practices has been prohibited. Whether voluntary race-based school or program assignments that further the goal of diversity will be upheld in de facto segregated school districts will depend on the ability of school officials to devise narrowly tailored means to achieve a compelling governmental interest.

In contrast, neutral policies, uniformly applied, are not necessarily unconstitutional, even though they may have a disparate impact on people of color. For example, prerequisites to employment, such as tests that disqualify a disproportionate number of minority applicants, have been upheld so long as their use is justified by legitimate employment objectives and not accompanied by discriminatory intent. Also, the placement of a disproportionate number of minority students in lower instructional tracks is permissible if such assignments are based on legitimate educational criteria that are applied in the best interests of students. Likewise, school segregation that is not the result of intentional state action does not implicate constitutional rights.

In addition to racial classifications, other bases for distinguishing among employees and students have been invalidated if they disadvantage individuals. Federal civil rights laws, in conjunction with state statutes, have reinforced constitutional protections afforded to various segments of society that traditionally have suffered discrimination. Indeed, the judiciary has recognized that legislative bodies are empowered to go beyond constitutional minimums in protecting citizens from discriminatory practices. Accordingly, laws have been enacted that place specific responsibilities on employers to ensure that employees are not disadvantaged on the basis of race, sex, age, religion, national origin, sexual orientation, pregnancy, or disability. If an inference of discrimination is established, employers must produce legitimate nondiscriminatory reasons to justify their actions. Educators should ensure that all school policies are applied in a nondiscriminatory manner, and school authorities can be held liable for damages if it is substantiated that benefits have been withheld from certain individuals because of their inherent characteristics.

Courts will scrutinize grouping practices to ensure that they do not impede students' rights to equal educational opportunities. Nondiscrimination, however, does not require identical treatment. Students can be classified according to their unique needs, but any differential treatment must be justified in terms of providing more appropriate services. Indeed, judicial rulings and federal and state laws have placed an obligation on school districts to provide appropriate programs and services to meet the needs of students with disabilities and to eliminate the language barriers for English Learners. Litigation involving the rights of students with disabilities is the most prevalent among school law topics, and most of the cases involve interpretations of entitlements for these children under the Individuals with Disabilities Education Act.

Due Process is a Basic Tenet of the U.S. Justice System—The Foundation of Fundamental Fairness. The notion of due process, embodied in the Fifth and Fourteenth Amendments, has been an underlying theme throughout the discussion of teachers' and students' rights. The judiciary has recognized that due process guarantees protect individuals against arbitrary governmental action impairing life, liberty, or property interests, and ensure that procedural safeguards accompany any governmental interference with these interests.

In the absence of greater statutory specificity, courts have held that the U.S. Constitution requires, at a minimum, notice of the charges and a hearing before an impartial decision maker when personnel actions impair public educators' property or liberty rights. A property claim to due process can be established by tenure status, contractual agreement, or school board action that creates a valid expectation of reemployment. A liberty claim to due process can be asserted if the employer's action implicates constitutionally protected rights or damages the teacher's reputation by imposing such a stigma that the opportunity to obtain other employment is foreclosed.

Many state legislatures have specified procedures beyond constitutional minimums that also must be followed before public schools can dismiss tenured teachers. The provision of federal and state due process procedures does not imply that a teacher will not be dismissed or that sanctions will not be imposed. But it does mean that the teacher must be given the opportunity to refute the charges and that the decision shall be made fairly and be supported by evidence.

Students, as well as teachers, have due process rights. Students have a state-created property right to attend school that cannot be denied without procedural requisites. The nature of the proceedings depends on the deprivation involved, with more serious impairments necessitating more formal proceedings. If punishments are arbitrary or excessive, students' substantive due process rights may be implicated. Students with disabilities have due process rights in placement decisions as well as in disciplinary matters. Since school authorities are never faulted for providing too much due process, at least minimum procedural safeguards are advisable when making any nonroutine change in a student's status.

Inherent in the notion of due process is the assumption that all individuals have a right to a hearing if state action intrudes on protected rights. Such a hearing need not be elaborate in every situation; an informal conversation can suffice under some circumstances, such as brief student suspensions from school. Moreover, such an informal hearing can serve to clarify issues and facilitate agreement, thus eliminating the need for more formal proceedings. The crucial element is for all affected parties to have an opportunity to air their views and present evidence that might alter the decision.

Educators Are Expected to Follow the Law, to Act Reasonably, and to Anticipate Potentially Adverse Consequences of Their Actions.   Public school personnel are presumed to be knowledgeable of federal and state constitutional and statutory provisions as well as school board policies affecting their roles. The Supreme Court has emphasized that ignorance of the law is no defense for violating clearly established legal principles. For example, being unaware of the Supreme Court's interpretation of Title IX restrictions under the Education Amendments of 1972 would not shield a school district from liability for school authorities' failure to respond to student complaints of sexual harassment.

Educators hold themselves out as having certain knowledge and skills by the nature of their special training and certification. Accordingly, they are expected to exercise sound professional judgment in the performance of their duties. To illustrate, in administering pupil punishments, teachers are expected to consider the student's age, mental condition, and past behavior as well as the specific circumstances surrounding the rule infraction. Failure to exercise reasonable judgment can result in dismissal or possibly financial liability for impairing students' rights.

Moreover, teachers are expected to make reasonable decisions pertaining to academic programs. Materials and methodology should be appropriate for the students' age and educational objectives. If students are grouped for instructional purposes, teachers are expected to base such decisions on legitimate educational considerations. In addition, educators are accountable for acting reasonably in supervising students, providing appropriate instructions, maintaining equipment in proper repair, and warning students of any known dangers. Teachers must exercise a standard of care commensurate with their duty to protect students from unreasonable risks of harm. Personal liability can be assessed for negligence if a school employee should have foreseen that an event could result in injury to a student.

Educators also are expected to exercise sound judgment in personal activities that affect their professional roles. Teachers do not relinquish their privacy rights as a condition of public employment, but private behavior that impairs teaching effectiveness or disrupts the school can be the basis for adverse personnel action. As role models for students, teachers and other school personnel are held to a higher level of discretion in their private lives than expected of the general public.

Alternatives to Traditional Public Schools Increasingly Are Being Provided across States. Charter schools, although technically public schools, operate more like private schools in some states. Often charter schools are exempt from specific state regulations applied to other public schools in order to foster innovative practices. Also, state tenure laws and collective bargaining agreements usually do not govern charter school employees. Where charter school personnel are considered at-will employees, they are not entitled to the procedural protections prior to dismissal that are afforded to other public school employees.

Proposals to establish voucher, tax-credit scholarship, and education savings account programs, under which public funds can be used to support private, primarily religious, education, are being considered or adopted across states. Private school employees are governed primarily by the provisions of their contracts (or employment agreements). Federal constitutional rights do not apply to private school employees unless their schools have sufficient state involvement to trigger constitutional guarantees, which is rare. Similarly, private school students do not usually enjoy the same constitutional protections applied in public schools. Many civil rights laws, however, apply to both public and private institutions and provide grounds to challenge racial and other types of discrimination in private education. Religious schools are exempt from complying with some civil rights provisions that interfere with their religious practices.

School privatization initiatives potentially may change the focus of education in the United States from an emphasis on the general welfare and common good to individual choice and advancement. By giving parents options to customize their children's educational experiences, the state's role in regulating education is being questioned. The common school movement in the 1800s focused on making schooling available to all on equal terms, and although this goal has never been fully achieved, it has guided school policies especially since the 1960s. The school privatization movement has a very different goal— that of empowering parents to determine the education of their children. Whether school privatization will have a negative impact on the equalization of educational opportunities, the socialization of students to embrace diversity, and the future of public schooling in our nation remains to be seen.

CONCLUSION

One objective of this book has been to alleviate educators' fears that the scales of justice have been tipped against them. It is hoped that this objective has been achieved. In most instances, courts and legislatures have not imposed on school personnel any requirements that fair-minded educators would not impose on themselves. Courts have consistently upheld reasonable policies and practices based on legitimate educational objectives. If anything, legislative and judicial mandates have clarified and supported the authority as well as the duty of school personnel to make and enforce regulations that are necessary to maintain an effective and efficient educational environment.

The federal judiciary in the late 1960s and early 1970s expanded constitutional protection of individual liberties against governmental interference. Since the 1980s, however, federal courts have exhibited more restraint and reinforced the authority of state and local education agencies to make decisions necessary to advance the school's educational mission, even if such decisions impinge on protected personal freedoms. Of course, courts will continue to invalidate school practices and policies if they are arbitrary, unrelated to educational objectives, or impair protected individual rights without an overriding justification.

Because reform is usually easier to implement when designed from within than when externally imposed, educators should become more assertive in identifying and altering those practices that have the potential to generate legal intervention. Internet censorship, peer sexual harassment, bullying, hazing, and other intimidating behaviors are a few issues now requiring educators' attention. Furthermore, school personnel should stay abreast of legal developments since new laws are enacted each year, and courts are continually interpreting constitutional and statutory provisions.

In addition to understanding basic legal rights and responsibilities, educators are expected to transmit this knowledge to students. Pupils also need to understand their constitutional and statutory rights, the balancing of interests that takes place in legislative and judicial forums, and the rationale for legal enactments, including school regulations. One high school civics course is not sufficient; students from an early age need to learn about our legal system and understand the law governing citizenship in our nation. Only with increased awareness of fundamental legal principles can all individuals involved in the educational process develop a greater respect for the law and for the responsibilities that accompany legal rights.

absolute privilege   protection from liability for communication made in the performance of public service or the administration of justice. *(p. 47)*

***amicus* brief**   a brief provided by nonparties to inform or perhaps persuade the court (also termed "amicus curiae" briefs or "friend-of-the-court" briefs).

appeal   a petition to a higher court to alter the decision of a lower court. *(p. 18)*

appellant   an individual who appeals a court decision because of losing in the lower court. The appellant may be called the petitioner in some jurisdictions.

appellate court   a tribunal having jurisdiction to review decisions on appeal from lower courts. *(p. 18)*

appellee   an individual who won in the lower court but now must defend that decision because the lower court case has been appealed. The appellee may be called the respondent in some jurisdictions.

arbitration (binding)   a process whereby an impartial third party, chosen by both parties in a dispute, makes a final determination regarding a contested issue. *(p. 260)*

assault   the placing of another in fear of bodily harm. *(p. 28, 30, 40)*

at-will employment   where an employee can be dismissed by an employer for any reason and without any warning; no cause is necessary.

battery   the unlawful touching of another with intent to harm. *(p. 28, 31, 40)*

certiorari   a writ of review whereby an action is removed from a lower court to an appellate court for additional proceedings. *(p. 22)*

circuit split   when two or more circuit courts of appeal provide conflicting decisions on the same legal issue. *(p. 22)*

civil action   a judicial proceeding to redress an infringement of individual civil rights, in contrast to a criminal action, which is brought by the state to redress public wrongs.

civil right   a personal right that accompanies citizenship and is protected by the Constitution (e.g., freedom of speech, freedom from discrimination). *(p. 3)*

class-action suit   a judicial proceeding brought on behalf of a number of persons similarly situated. *(p. 18)*

common law/case law   a body of rules and principles derived from usage or from judicial decisions enforcing such usage. *(p. 8, 29, 94)*

compensatory damages   a monetary award to compensate an individual for injury sustained (e.g., financial losses, emotional pain, inconvenience) and restore the injured party to the position held prior to the injury (also termed "money damages"). *(p. 48)*

concurring opinion   a statement by a judge or judges, separate from the majority opinion, that endorses the result of the majority decision but offers its own reasons for reaching that decision.

consent decree   an agreement, sanctioned by a court, that is binding on the consenting parties.

consideration   something of value given or promised for the purpose of forming a contract. *(p. 18, 35)*

contract   an agreement between two or more competent parties that creates, alters, or dissolves a legal relationship. *(p. 1, 5, 7)*

criminal action   a judicial proceeding brought by the state against a person charged with a public offense. *(p. 292)*

damages   an award made to an individual because of a legal wrong. *(p. 14, 18)*

declaratory relief   a judicial declaration of the rights of the plaintiff without an assessment of damages against the defendant. *(p. 18)*

de facto segregation   separation of the races that exists but does not result from action of the state or its agents. *(p. 139)*

de jure segregation   separation of the races by law or by action of the state or its agents. *(p. 139)*

de minimis   something that is insignificant, not worthy of judicial review. *(p. 168)*

de novo   a new review.

defamation   a false and intentional communication that injures a person's character or reputation; slander is spoken and libel is written communication. *(p. 27, 28, 44)*

defendant   the party against whom a court action is brought. *(p. 16)*

dictum   a statement made by a judge in delivering an opinion that does not relate directly to the issue being decided and does not embody the sentiment of the court.

directed verdict   the verdict provided when a plaintiff fails to support a prima facie case for jury consideration or when the defendant fails to present a necessary defense. *(p. 241)*

discretionary power   authority that involves the exercise of judgment. *(p. 245)*

dissenting opinion   a statement by a judge or judges who disagree with the decision of the majority of the justices in a case. *(p. 347)*

en banc   the full bench; refers to a session where the court's full membership participates in the decision rather than the usual quorum of the court. *(p. 21)*

fact-finding   a process whereby a third party investigates an impasse in the negotiation process to determine the facts, identify the issues, and make a recommendation for settlement. *(p. 260)*

fraudulent conveyance   a transfer of property intended to defraud or hinder a creditor or to put such property beyond the creditor's reach.

friend-of-the-court briefs   briefs provided by nonparties to inform or perhaps persuade the court (also termed "amicus curiae" briefs). *(p. 137)*

governmental function   activity performed in discharging official duties of a federal, state, or municipal agency. *(p. 38)*

governmental immunity   the common law doctrine that governmental agencies cannot be held liable for the negligent acts of their officers, agents, or employees. *(p. 28, 37)*

impasse   a deadlock in the negotiation process in which parties are unable to resolve an issue without the assistance of a third party. *(p. 251, 260)*

injunction   a writ issued by a court prohibiting a defendant from acting in a prescribed manner. *(p. 18)*

in loco parentis   in place of parent; charged with rights and duties of a parent. *(p. 198)*

jurisdiction   the authority of a legal body (e.g., court) to administer justice within a defined area (e.g., geographic area or subject matter). *(p. 3, 9, 19)*

liquidated damages   contractual amounts representing a reasonable estimation of the damages owed to one of the parties for a breach of the agreement by the other. *(p. 319)*

mediation   the process by which a neutral third party serving as an intermediary attempts to persuade disagreeing parties to settle their dispute. *(p. 98, 184, 260)*

ministerial duty   an act that does not involve discretion and must be carried out in a manner specified by legal authority.

motion to dismiss   usually a defendant's request for the court to dismiss the case because the plaintiff cannot prove its case based on the evidence presented. *(p. 17)*

negligence   the failure to exercise the degree of care that a reasonably prudent person would exercise under similar conditions; conduct that falls below the standard established by law for the protection of others against unreasonable risk of harm. *(p. 19, 28)*

per curiam   a court's brief disposition of a case that is not accompanied by a written opinion. *(p. 127)*

plaintiff   the party initiating a judicial action. *(p. 16)*

plenary power   full, complete, absolute power. *(p. 375)*

plurality opinion   when no single opinion was supported by a majority of the justices, but this opinion received the most votes. *(p. 78, 141)*

precedent   a judicial decision serving as authority for subsequent cases involving similar questions of law. *(p. 11, 17)*

preliminary injunction   a temporary order from the court that stops one party from pursuing an activity until a trial on the merits occurs. *(p. 18)*

preponderance of evidence   a standard that requires more evidence to support than refute a claim; it also is termed the 51 percent rule. *(p. 283, 338)*

prima facie on its face presumed to be true unless disproven by contrary evidence. *(p. 148, 300)*

probable cause reasonable grounds, supported by sufficient evidence, to warrant a cautious person to believe that the individual is guilty of the offense charged. *(p. 9, 212)*

procedural due process the fundamental right to notice of charges and an opportunity to rebut the charges before a fair tribunal if life, liberty, or property rights are at stake. *(p. 11)*

proprietary function an activity (often for profit) performed by a state or municipal agency that could as easily be performed by a private corporation. *(p. 38)*

punitive damages a monetary punishment where the defendant is found to have acted with either malice or reckless indifference. *(p. 14, 18, 48)*

qualified immunity an affirmative defense that shields public officials performing discretionary functions from civil damages if their conduct does not violate clearly established statutory or constitutional rights. *(p. 67, 351)*

qualified privilege protection from liability for communication made in good faith, for proper reasons, and to appropriate parties. *(p. 47)*

reasonable suspicion specific and articulable facts, which, taken together with rational inferences from the facts, justify a warrantless search. *(p. 211, 212, 213)*

regulation a rule made by administrative agencies (e.g., departments of education) that has the force of law. *(p. 1, 4)*

remand to send a case back to the original court for additional proceedings. *(p. 18)*

respondeat superior a legal doctrine whereby the master is responsible for acts of the servant; a governmental unit is liable for acts of its employees. *(p. 31)*

save harmless an agreement whereby one party agrees to indemnify and hold harmless another party for suits that may be brought against that party. *(p. 48)*

stare decisis the doctrine of abiding by decided cases; adhering to precedent. *(p. 17)*

statute a written law passed by the legislative branch of government. *(p. 1, 3, 8, 12)*

substantive due process requirements embodied in the Fifth and Fourteenth Amendments that legislation must be fair and reasonable in content as well as application; protection against arbitrary, capricious, or unreasonable governmental action. *(p. 11)*

summary judgment disposition of a controversy without a trial when there is no genuine dispute over factual issues. *(p. 18)*

tenure a statutory right that confers permanent employment on teachers, protecting them from dismissal except for adequate cause. *(p. 11, 24)*

tort a civil wrong, independent of contract, for which a remedy in damages is sought. *(p. 27)*

ultra vires beyond the scope of authority to act on the subject. *(p. 5)*

vacate to set aside; to render a judgment void. *(p. 55)*

verdict a decision of a jury on questions submitted for trial. *(p. 18)*

SELECTED SUPREME COURT CASES

INDEX